Great Pianists of the Golden Age

Great Pianists

of the

Golden Age

by

Marguerite and Terry Broadbent

The North West Player Piano Association
Wilmslow, Cheshire

By the same authors:

AN EDWARDIAN QUINTET

THE MELODY LINGERS ON

LEGINSKA - FORGOTTEN GENIUS OF MUSIC

Published by The North West Player Piano Association
Research Section: 49, Grange Park Avenue,
Wilmslow,
Cheshire, SK9 4AL.

Copyright © 1996 by Marguerite and Terry Broadbent

No part of this book may be reproduced, stored in a retrieval system, or transmitted in any form, or by any means electronic, mechanical, photocopying, recording or otherwise, without the prior permission of the copyright holders.

ISBN 0 9525101 0 3

Printed and bound by Danilo Printing Ltd.,
Unit 8,
Indescon Court,
Millharbour,
London, E14 9TN.

Contents

Foreword by Vladimir Ashkenazy	v
Co-author's note	vi
Authors' preface	viii
Acknowledgments	xiv
Picture credits	xv
1. Camille Saint-Saëns	1
2. Vladimir de Pachmann	11
3. Teresa Carreño	23
4. Ignace Paderewski	41
5. Moriz Rosenthal	59
6. Ferruccio Busoni	73
7. Leopold Godowsky	85
8. Sergei Rachmaninov	97
9. Harold Bauer	113
10. Josef Lhevinne	125
11. Josef Hofmann	143
12. Alfred Cortot	157
13. Ossip Gabrilowitsch	171
14. Mark Hambourg	187
15. Wanda Landowska	203
16. Artur Schnabel	215
17. Percy Grainger	229
18. Wilhelm Backhaus	243
19. Ethel Leginska	257
20. Artur Rubinstein	273
21. Benno Moiseiwitsch	287
22. Myra Hess	301
23. Walter Gieseking	315
24. Vladimir Horowitz	327
25. Dinu Lipatti	341
Bibliography	352
Appendices	
1. Discography (Gramophone discs)	359
2. Rollography (Piano rolls)	373
3. Player Piano Associations	400
Index	401

The musicians are presented in chronological order of their birthdates but the chapters are self-contained and may be read in any order.

Great Pianists of the Golden Age

Foreword

The piano's "magical" appeal to composers and music-lovers alike is probably not too hard to explain in practical terms. First of all, its range of registers and colours, or in other words its "completeness" and self-sufficiency, accounts for the fact that it has a larger repertoire than any other instrument. And on the more mundane plane its relatively "easy" sound production for the beginner could be the reason that there is such a tremendous number of would-be pianists of all ages.

Whatever the reasons, the piano is still called by many "The King of Instruments"; although the attitude to music and interpretation has changed dramatically in the last few decades we nevertheless owe a great debt to our forerunners who were the great pianists of their day. No matter what the future holds for the instrument there is no shortage of present-day aficionados of the piano who will not abandon their devotion to the piano at any price. Those people will find this book of *Great Pianists of the Golden Age* particularly fascinating. It has been thoroughly and sympathetically researched with care and love, and it gives an insight into the lives of the artists of former days. I have enjoyed reading it, and commend it to other lovers of the piano.

Vladimir Ashkenazy

Co-author's Note

Between 1979 and 1994 Marguerite and I completed 37 biographical articles on musicians for the Journal of the North West Player Piano Association and three more were outlined in draft form. They were nearly all on musicians of the player piano era and more than half of them were concerned with the great pianists of that period. In the late 1980s we proposed to publish the articles on pianists in book form. A draft book including an Authors' Preface was prepared. It was entitled *Great Pianists of the Golden Age* and the eminent pianist and conductor Mr Vladimir Ashkenazy kindly wrote a Foreword for us. The book was accepted for publication by a London publisher but his subsequent market research indicated that because of the economic recession then taking hold, combined with the limited public interest in former musicians, he would probably only sell one or two thousand copies and he would need to sell several thousands to recoup the outlay and make an adequate profit. He therefore reluctantly withdrew his offer of publication. At that time Marguerite was not very well and we decided to put the project on one side until such time as her health improved. However, in view of our hope that the book would be published one day, we revised and updated the material from time to time in order to correct errors and to accommodate new information that had come to light.

Unfortunately Marguerite's health did not improve. After her sad, sudden and totally unexpected death in April 1994 it seemed appropriate to me that the book should be published as soon as possible as a tribute to Marguerite. It also seemed fitting to invite The North West Player Piano Association to be the publisher, if it so wished, as the book's chapters were all

Co-Author's Note

based on articles originally written for the Association. The Association gladly agreed to do so, for which I express my thanks.

As companion volumes, our articles on ten popular musicians have been collected together, revised and published as *The Melody Lingers On,* and the remaining five articles have been published as *An Edwardian Quintet.* In both books appropriate appendices have been added to supplement the information in the chapters. Our fourth and final book is a biography entitled *Leginska - Forgotten Genius of Music.* Marguerite and I spent a lot of time in the 1980s delving into the life of this talented and charismatic musician.

Marguerite and I never laid claim to great literary expertise but we always researched our subjects thoroughly and have tried to write accurately and interestingly about these great musicians of the past. I believe this book is the only one available, now or previously, which gives a comprehensive account of the lives of the leading pianists of the first half of the present century. Much of the material exists elsewhere but is very difficult to find, being scattered thoughout many books, mainly biographies of or articles about individual musicians, and entries in other reference works. These sources are often very old, obscure, long out of print and available only overseas and through inter-library loan schemes. Our aim in putting together this book was to search for and find the relevant material, assemble it, and to summarise the lives of these pianists in one volume in what is hoped is an interesting and readable manner. I hope we have succeeded.

Terry Broadbent

April 1996

Authors' Preface

The Golden Age! What a treasure-house of delights that phrase evokes. But we must be precise, and if the story of the pianists of the Golden Age is to be told, the period which this term is intended to portray must be defined.

Generally we are speaking of the years 1900 to 1950, which represented a Golden Age in so many spheres. That was the period in which our modern way of living developed. The motor car was a curiosity at the beginning of the era but by 1950 we had motoring for the masses. Air travel, unknown in 1900, became a standard mode of transport. Above all, leaders in many fields of endeavour graced our lives, whilst legendary figures, giants in their time, plied their various skills. Rutherford split the atom in Manchester, Hobbs and Hutton played cricket for England, a host of literary figures enriched our heritage, and Melba and Gigli delighted their audiences. Everywhere there was talent and achievement.

We have to admit that the Golden Age was scarred by two of the most terrible wars in the history of mankind. But that apart, in many ways life was pleasanter and more peaceful than is our hectic existence today. It was possible to walk down the road with little fear of being robbed. There was a greater sense of national purpose, and people of different outlooks were less prone to the constant bickering and acrimony that seem to be prevalant today. Every age has its dark side and in the period we are considering there was poverty, war, cruelty and need. But it is the other side, the positive side, that we are looking at in defining our Golden Age. It is the good and memorable things that we wish to consider. All around there were great men and women, not least in the world of music. They were the outstanding figures of their day, shaped by the standards and norms of their age.

Amongst the gifted men and women of that era there were a number of outstanding pianists and it is those people, or at any rate some of them, who are the subject of this book. The pianists featured here have two things in common. Firstly, they were all immensely talented and were regarded in their day as leaders in their profession. Secondly, they were all active and at their peak at some stage in the period 1900 to 1950. Some, those born around the middle of the nineteenth century or earlier, were approaching the end of their careers in our Golden Age and indeed died during the years in question. In the case of others, their careers spanned the whole of the period and even went on beyond. Most of them learned their skills in the 'romantic era' which coincided with the second half of the nineteenth century. If you take any year between 1900 and 1950 and look through the concert

Authors' Preface

announcements in *The Times* or any other quality newspaper, the names of the pianists you will see will be some of those who form the subject of this book. Many led extraordinarily interesting, colourful and in some cases adventurous lives to complement their musical skills.

Why did we write this book? The answer is, we felt these great pianists of the Golden Age should not be forgotten. Their style of playing, especially of the earlier ones, is a reminder of an age long gone, yet these pianists were in their day regarded as the finest of their era. Without doubt they all possessed tremendous musical skill. We have heard them all play on gramophone records or on reproducing piano rolls. We were fortunate enough to hear a few of them in person. In particular, we recall hearing Artur Rubinstein play at his last appearance in Manchester. The recital, given at the Free Trade Hall, was memorable. As the appointed time for the recital drew near we all sat in eager anticipation looking at the platform, empty but for the enormous black grand piano with the word STEINWAY emblazoned down the side. At 8 p.m. a little silver-haired old man padded onto the stage. Rubinstein, the great pianist, pupil of Joachim, had arrived. He looked frail; too frail still to be able to give a performance worthy of his name. He seated himself at the piano and we waited expectantly for him to begin. As the first chords of Schubert's Sonata in B flat major rang out we knew that Rubinstein was still the great pianist of old. His vitality was phenomenal. And he was 86 years old! The evening was unforgettable. It was moments like that which prompted us to find out more about these great pianists and to tell their story.

The pianists whose lives form the subject of this book were all brilliant exponents of their art. In the years when they were performing, contemporary critics often referred to their 'technique', and adjectives were used to describe it; there were reports of Busoni's phenomenal technique, Godowsky's brilliant technique, and so on. If the word is to mean anything it must be defined, having regard to the way it was used in the Golden Age. 'Technique' in this context referred to the purely mechanical part of a pianist's armoury.* It was concerned entirely with the ability to play rapidly

---

* The subject of technique is dealt with in *Famous Pianists and Their Technique* by R. Gerig (see Bibliography of this book for the reference), a perusal of which indicates that the word means different things to different pianists. A good definition is that given by Ivan Galamian. "Technique is the ability to direct mentally and to execute physically all of the necessary playing movements of left and right hands, arms and fingers. A complete technique means the development of all the elements of skill to the highest level. In short, it is the complete mastery over all the potentialities of the instrument. It implies the ability to do justice, with unfailing reliability and control, to each and every demand of the most refined musical imagination. It enables the performer, when he has formed an ideal concept of how any work should sound, to live up to this concept in actual performance."

and accurately; it had nothing to do with the quality of a pianist's interpretation, or the ability to produce a singing tone, or with 'touch', an attribute that enabled Pachmann, for example, to excel in the creation of 'ethereal pianissimos'. In the parlance used in ice-skating championships, 'technique' referred to 'technical merit' as opposed to 'artistic impression' and other qualities. Thus, when the great piano teacher Leschetizky first heard the 24-year old Paderewski and told him, "It's too late - you have no technique", he was not criticising Paderewski's musicianship which he had immediately recognised; he was simply saying that he did not have the manual dexterity required of a first-class pianist. Under Leschetizky's direction Paderewski worked sixteen hours a day to attain it. Rachmaninov possessed excellent technique at an earlier stage and needed to practise only four hours a day to maintain it.

In the early Victorian era technique was regarded as of paramount importance. Liszt defined the three requirements of a great pianist as "Technique, technique and technique." Others obeyed this maxim so that technique became the master of the pianist's art rather than its servant, and a pianist who was able to interpret slower music well but was unable or unwilling to display pyrotechnics was not thought to be worthy of serious consideration. Therefore, in Victorian times, the music of the classical masters was not often played in public because it did not provide the opportunity for the pianist to dazzle by technique, and when it was played, it was deemed legitimate to change the bass notes in, say, a Beethoven sonata into trills or tremolos to display the pianist's dexterity.

This philosophy persisted into the beginning of the Golden Age and it was only then that musical feeling, or 'interpretation', began to be really important. It is therefore not surprising that pianists of the Golden Age, whose musical skill was measured by how many notes could be played accurately in a given time, were superb technicians, for the development of brilliant fingerwork was encouraged; indeed, it was obligatory. We have heard piano roll performances of pianists of long ago in which showers of notes are played so rapidly that someone has been prompted to remark, "He couldn't possibly have played like that, it's physically impossible. The roll must have been doctored." The short answer is, they *were* able to play like that; their training demanded it. They *had* to be able to play like that to survive in a competitive world.

It is easy to judge the work of, for example, an author, for long after his or her death it is possible to read what has been written and to form our own opinion of its worth. Similarly, the standing of a composer can be assessed by listening to the music. With pianists it is not so easy to judge, as once a

Authors' Preface

concert or recital has taken place it disappears into history or memory. We therefore have to rely partly on contemporary accounts and judgments. If a pianist was considered by his peers and the musical critics over a long period of time to be a giant of his age then he was. Times and fashions change, and a man or woman can be judged only by the standards of the day. In the case of pianists these judgments may be supplemented by the recordings they left behind. Ignoring the early and primitive cylinder recordings there remain the gramophone disc and the piano roll. It is worth briefly considering these in turn.

Gramophone discs manufactured prior to the mid 1920s are in the main unsatisfactory. Made by the acoustic method, the process was incapable of responding to dynamic nuances, as the pianist had to play at more or less fortissimo level into a large horn placed near the piano. Thus all light and shade were lost. Furthermore, the discs could accommodate only about four minutes of playing time. This meant that a pianist was often called upon to play a piece at breakneck pace in order to finish in time. Consequently many of these early recordings offered little more than a travesty of the pianist's skills. With the passing of the years the acoustic process improved, but not dramatically so, and it was only with the coming of the electrical recording process in the mid 1920s that a tolerable musical standard could be achieved, and even then the records were scratchy and not entirely satisfactory.

Very few original records of the pianists whose story is told in these pages are commercially available today, except those of the artists who recorded after the Second World War. Most of the recordings of the earlier pianists were long since deleted from the catalogues, though some are now available as 'historic' recordings on compact disc. Many an hour's fun can be had in rooting through old 78s in second-hand shops, at jumble sales and so on. It is surprising how often one can still come across original 78rpm recordings of Paderewski, Cortot and their contemporaries. Modern transfers onto compact disc of 'historic' pianists come and go from the catalogues with alarming rapidity but it is always worth glancing at the 'historic' section in record shops. Some companies (e.g. Pavilion Records; see Appendix 1) specialise in the re-issue of the recordings of vintage artists.

Attention has been drawn to the shortcomings of the gramophone disc, especially in the first half of the Golden Age (i.e. 1900 - 1925) when recording was accomplished by the acoustic process. Fortunately, the piano had a rival, the player piano. Based on the 'pianola', in which a piano was fitted with a special 'action' mechanism which enabled the instrument to play music from perforated paper rolls, the 'reproducing piano', as it was called, was able to reproduce to a high degree of accuracy the actual performance of the pianist who 'recorded' the work. The recording was achieved by means of a special recording piano played by the celebrity pianist. The performance was faithfully recorded onto a master roll which encapsulated not only the notes played but also all the nuances of tempo, phrasing, dynamics and pedalling. From the master rolls, paper rolls were manufactured for purchase by the owners of the special reproducing pianos designed for use with these rolls. Thus, in effect, the leading pianists of the day could be heard playing one's own piano in one's own home, a fact much publicised by the companies who manufactured the instruments. All the leading pianists of the day recorded on piano rolls, and all of them publicly endorsed the veracity and accuracy of their recordings.

The most popular systems were manufactured by the Aeolian Company (which produced Duo-Art rolls), the American Piano Company (Ampico rolls), the Welte Company (Welte rolls), the Hupfeld Company (Animatic and Triphonola rolls) and the Wilcox and White Company (Artrio-Angelus rolls). There were several other smaller companies. Many reproducing pianos still exist in pristine working condition, and so enable us to listen to the performances of such masters of the keyboard as Busoni, Pachmann, Paderewski and Rachmaninov. The player piano rose to prominence in the early 1900s and declined in popularity after 1930 when the gramophone became capable of delivering results of acceptable quality and when radio was beginning to make its mark. But for a period from about 1905 to 1926 it is to the reproducing piano that we should first turn if we wish to listen to and judge the art of the earlier pianists in this book. Its peak of popularity coincided with the middle of the Golden Age.

There are in Britain two flourishing groups which promote the player piano. They are The Player Piano Group founded in London in 1959 and The North West Player Piano Association founded in Manchester in 1972. Members of both groups lovingly restore instruments, and at their meetings, held in the homes of members, the performances (on piano roll) of the pianists of the Golden Age can be heard. There are similar groups in the USA and in other parts of the world. It is also a happy fact that in these modern days the art of the gramophone recording engineer has combined with that of the reproducing piano enthusiast, and classic piano roll performances of many of the world's great pianists of former days are now available on compact disc (see Appendix 1).

A gentle word of warning must be given before the performances of some of these pianists are listened to for the first time, whether the recording be a gramophone record or a reproducing piano roll. Fashions in music

Authors' Preface

change and the musical conventions and interpretations that were considered normal in the Golden Age differ from those of today. In those far-away days pianists (and orchestras too) were more liberal in their interpretations of the music. The earlier pianists, notably those of the Pachmann and Paderewski era, used *tempo rubato* freely and even altered the notes if it suited them. The total concept of how a piece should be played could be, and often was, quite different from the ideas of the present generation of pianists. It must be remembered that in the days when these pianists learned their music you could not switch on the radio or play a gramophone record to hear an 'accepted' performance of a musical composition. The only way to hear anyone else's interpretation was to go to hear them in person, wrong notes and all. This encouraged top-class pianists to create their own interpretation, rather than to conform to a generally accepted standard. For this reason there was more individuality in the Golden Age, especially in the earlier part of it, than at present, and that resulted in more freedom of expression.

The musical interpretations of the pianists of bygone days can, on first hearing, therefore sound strange, and even wrong, to present-day listeners. But this is the way music was played in those days, and when heard again one can move into the era of those pianists and derive pleasure from their performances. It is not that the present day pianists are right in their interpretations and those of the past were wrong, or vice versa. It is just that ideas are different nowadays. One cannot compare an Ashkenazy with a Paderewski, or a Barenboim with a Busoni. Times change, and with them, outlooks.

This, then, is the background to the book. Its purpose is to tell the story of some of the great pianists of the Golden Age. Our choice is a personal one and many fine pianists have had to be omitted. But our 'top twentyfive' are arguably the best of the Golden Age; the book tells something of their music and a lot about their lives. They all contributed to the musical heritage that is ours today, and their work and influence deserve to be remembered.

Marguerite and Terry Broadbent

Wilmslow, Cheshire.

Acknowledgments

The authors wish to thank many organisations and individuals for their assistance in locating source material relating to the pianists featured in this book, especially the following:

Britain: John Rylands University of Manchester Library; Henry Watson Music Library, Manchester; Royal Northern College of Music, Manchester; British Library, London and Boston Spa; EMI Archives Department, Hayes, Middlesex; Members of the North West Player Piano Association and of the Player Piano Group, especially Messrs Francis Bowdery, Michael Broadway, Brian Chesters, Raymond Ince, Keith Shipley, Nicholas Simons and Gerald Stonehill; the staff of the Piano Museum, Brentford; Mrs Gertrude M. Attwood and Mr Norman Staveley, both of Hull; Miss Judith Broadbent, London; Mr Arthur Walker, formerly of the University of Manchester Music Department; The Superintendent Registrar of Births, Deaths and Marriages, Hull.

U.S.A: Public Libraries of Boston, Los Angeles and New York; The Musicians' Union, Los Angeles; The New York Times; Registrar of Births, Deaths and Marriages, Los Angeles; Professor Marilyn Neeley, University of Baltimore; Mrs Marguerite Baum-Heller, Mr Tom Curtis, Mr Joseph Enos and Mr Daniel Pollack, all of Los Angeles; and Miss Beverly Carmen, New Mexico.

Thanks are also due to Eric Dalton of London for editorial advice in the early stages of the preparation of the book, to Judith Broadbent, Susan Clews and Raymond Ince for patiently checking the proofs, and to Nigel Clews for advice on word-processing software.

Finally, the authors wish to express their thanks to Mr Vladimir Ashkenazy for finding time, in the midst of a busy concert schedule, to write the Foreword.

Picture Credits

The photographs of Saint-Saëns, Pachmann, Carreño, Paderewski, Busoni, Godowsky, Rachmaninov, Cortot, Hambourg, Landowska, Schnabel, Grainger, Backhaus (front cover and page 242), Rubinstein, Moiseiwitsch, Hess, Gieseking and Horowitz were all supplied by The Hulton Deutsch Collection Ltd. which holds the copyright. Their help in locating and supplying these photographs is acknowledged.

The photograph of Lipatti is reproduced by permission of EMI Ltd.

The other photographs, all of them publicity pictures dating from the latter part of the last century or the early years of the present one, are acknowledged as follows:
- Rosenthal: The London Stereoscopic Co. Ltd.;
- Lhevinne: Photograph by George Maillard Kesslare;
- Bauer and Leginska: The Ampico Corporation;
- Hofmann: The Aeolian Co.;
- Gabrilowitsch: Photographer unknown - a picture dating from 1899 when Gabrilowitsch was 21.

Although appropriate enquiries have been made it has proved impossible to ascertain whether copyright still exists on these six very old photographs. The co-author (Terry Broadbent) apologises for any unwitting infringement.

Cover picture: A youthful Wilhelm Backhaus, soon after the start of his international career.   *Picture by courtesy of The Hulton Deutsch Collection Ltd.*

Great Pianists of the Golden Age

Camille Saint-Saëns

Facing Page 1

1. Camille Saint-Saëns

One of the most remarkable facts about the French pianist, organist and composer, Camille Saint-Saëns, was the long period of time in which he was active as a musician. He composed his first piece when he was three years old and gave his first recital as a talented infant of four and a half. Chopin, Liszt, Mendelssohn and Schumann were then young men rapidly climbing to the top of the musical ladder, and the deaths of Beethoven and Schubert were events of recent memory. More than eighty years later, and within the lifetime of many people who are fit and active today, the old musician was still composing, conducting and giving piano and organ recitals throughout Europe. The life of this interesting musician thus takes us from the classical era, through the romantic and impressionist periods, on to the age when Schoenberg and Stravinsky had turned the image of music upside down, and modernists like Stockhausen were looming on the horizon.

Charles Camille Saint-Saëns (he was called Camille from birth) was born on 9th October, 1835. The surname was said to derive from Sanctus Sidonius, Sidonius being an Irishman in charge of a Normandy monastery about AD 700. The family's ancestors came from Dieppe and Camille's father worked in a Government office. The baby Camille had an unpropitious start in life for he was only two months old when his father died of the dreaded disease rife at the time - consumption. Camille's tiny body already showed signs of the disease and he was taken to the country in the hope that the fresh air would bring about an improvement. He spent two years there and returned to Paris at the age of two and a half, apparently restored to health. In spite of the longevity already noted he was to have recurrences of chest trouble throughout his life. The Paris of that time was still basically a medieval city of narrow streets - the Paris of Balzac; the wide thoroughfares were still in the future, and it was in Paris that Saint-Saëns was based for the rest of his life.

Following his father's untimely death he was brought up by his mother and his great-aunt, both formidable ladies. The family owned an old upright piano that had not been played for years; young Camille showed interest in it so was allowed to tinker, and immediately demonstrated his outstanding talent. He possessed the gift of perfect pitch and at two and a half years the tiny infant could, from an adjoining room, name any note struck on the piano keyboard, and could tell if other pianos he heard were tuned below standard pitch. His great-aunt gave him piano lessons which were so successful that at four years and seven months he played the piano part of a Beethoven violin sonata from memory, a feat noted in the press. He also started to compose and from his first piece had progressed to his first sonata by the age of seven.

The precocious child's abilities continued to blossom and from seven years of age he was taught by a professional teacher. At eight he played a Mozart concerto in a semi-private performance well received by all the musicians present and on 6th May 1845, at the age of 9, he made his official debut, playing a Mozart and a Beethoven concerto at an immensely successful concert. As an encore he offered to play from memory any of Beethoven's 32 sonatas. At that tender age his style of playing was the same as it remained throughout his life; unpretentious, clinically accurate, with no show of emotion. He walked to the piano, sat down and played with no fuss, no drooping over the keyboard, and at the end walked unobtrusively away. At this age young Camille was already a vastly accomplished musician. When his mother was asked after his debut concert, "If he plays like this now, what sort of music will he be playing at 20?" she replied quietly, "He will be playing his own."

About this time Camille started to take organ lessons in the nearby church of St. Germain and soon became as able an organist as a pianist. His fame was already spreading and, inevitably, he was talked of as the "French Mozart". When he was 10 he met Gounod, 17 years his senior, and was on friendly terms with him for the remainder of Gounod's life. At 13 he entered the Paris Conservatory whose Principal at the time was the operatic composer Daniel Auber, who in his youth had been a pupil of Cherubini. Camille studied piano, organ and composition and at 15 was awarded first prize for the organ. He was composing prolifically and his *Ode à St. Cécile*, composed at 16, was widely acclaimed. At 17 he heard Liszt play in the drawing room of François Seghers, a Belgian violinist whose Paris home was a well-known meeting place for musicians. Camille was astonished at the Master's technique and immediately became his disciple. Soon Liszt, in turn, discovered that the young Saint-Saëns was himself an outstanding pianist and promising composer and took the boy under his wing. A friendship and mutual respect for each other's music developed which continued until Liszt's death.

At 17 Camille was appointed organist at the church of St. Merry in Paris. The post provided him with a small income which gave him plenty of opportunity to compose, and Symphony No. 1 in E flat was soon produced. Gounod and Berlioz were both enthusiastic about the work and hailed Saint-Saëns as a first-rate musician. By the age of 20 Camille's life had fallen into the pattern it was to follow for the next 60 years; writing music and travelling around as a virtuoso pianist and organist. He was already an established figure in the mid-19th century musical world of Paris and he knew all the leading French musicians of the day; Berlioz, Bizet, Delibes, Franck (French by naturalisation), Gounod, Lalo and Massenet, as well as foreign ones such as Wagner and also Rossini who lived in wealthy retirement in Paris.

In appearance and manner Saint-Saëns was small and dapper, with a rather sallow complexion. He walked with a bird-like springy gait and this, coupled with his beaky nose and pince-nez in front of myopic eyes gave him a characteristic parrot-like appearance which was easy for the cartoonists of the day to caricature. He had a loud booming voice which did not match his diminutive figure.

After he had been at St. Merry for a few months a magnificent new organ was installed there by Aristide Cavaillé-Coll, one of the 19th century's most distinguished organ builders who had constructed several in Britain. Saint-Saëns struck up a friendship with him and at Cavaillé-Coll's request often gave recitals for him in later years to inaugurate new organs.

On 7th December 1857, when Saint-Saëns was 22, he was appointed organist at the church of St. Madeleine, the most fashionable in Paris. This provided him with a stipend of 3000 francs a year and a great measure of prestige, for the church was frequented by most of the influential people in Paris. Liszt heard his own *St. Francis of Assisi Preaching To the Birds* played by Saint-Saëns on the Madeleine organ and immediately pronounced Saint-Saëns to be the greatest organist in the world. Saint-Saëns stayed in his post at the St. Madeleine church for 19 years and this period was the happiest in his life. He always composed at great speed and with apparent facility - "As a tree produces apples" was how he put it. Though he was turning out compositions at a vast rate he still found time for other interests, such as archaeology and astronomy. He earned himself 500 francs to buy a telescope by writing *Six Duos for Harmonium*, the music being commissioned to help promote sales of the instrument.

For a few years in his 20s Saint-Saëns held a part-time teaching post at the Niedermeyer School of Music in Paris. He was not much older than most of his pupils and he was very popular with them. He often played for them, and taught by example. Two of his pupils were Messager and Fauré, the latter becoming a lifelong friend. By his early 30s Saint-Saëns was on good terms with the Russian pianist Anton Rubinstein, then considered the only pianist approaching Liszt in ability. Rubinstein was to conduct a concert in Paris in May 1868 and asked Saint-Saëns to compose a work for it. The result was his Piano Concerto No. 2, still popular today, written down by Saint-Saëns in 17 days from ideas already in his mind. Rubinstein conducted and Saint-Saëns played the piano part at the concert. From 1870 the company which published Saint-Saëns' compositions undertook to publish everything he submitted to them. He had already written symphonies, violin concertos, piano concertos, operas and many other works. His home had become a meeting place for musicians, as was Seghers', and all the leading musicians of the day were regular visitors.

Saint-Saëns always practised for at least two hours a day to keep his fingers supple. The actual mechanics of playing the right notes presented no problem and visitors to his home often found him at practice, rattling off one of Liszt's more frenzied offerings whilst reading a newspaper propped on top of the piano. In public performances his playing was very precise and accurate though some felt it lacked feeling and was 'too' correct - "arid" was how one critic put it.

When the Franco-Prussian war of 1870-71 was clearly imminent Saint-Saëns enrolled for military service. He was put on sentry duty and when war came amused himself by noting the pitch of the noise made by the shells as they whistled overhead. When hostilities ceased he returned to civilian life and soon afterwards, in collaboration with the music teacher Romain Bussine, founded the Société Nationale de Musique, an organisation dedicated to promoting the works of French composers. He thereby assisted numerous young French musicians whose work would otherwise have remained unpublished and unheard. At the same time Saint-Saëns resumed his career as a travelling virtuoso and by the mid 1870s, when he was nearly 40, was well known throughout Europe as both performer and composer. He played at the inauguration concert of the new organ at the Royal Albert Hall in London in 1871 and was very impressed by the instrument, the bellows of which were driven by a steam engine far below. Many other visits to Britain followed and in 1874 he made the first of numerous trips to Algiers, on this occasion to recuperate following a spell of ill health.

On 3rd February 1875 the 39 year old musician married. His 19 year old bride, Marie Truffot, was the sister of one of his pupils and the proposal seems to have come out of the blue - there was little if any previous romance. On 6th November 1875 a son, André, was born. Meanwhile Saint-Saëns' journeyings continued. He visited Russia in 1875 and met Tchaikovsky. In April 1877 Saint-Saëns resigned his post at St. Madeleine; he was well off and no longer needed the stipend. A second son, Jean, was born on 13th December 1877 shortly after the family had moved to a larger, fourth floor, flat. Life was going well, but on 28th May 1878 an appalling tragedy occurred. At about 3pm little André, then two and a half, was playing near an open window in his home, with no-one else in the room, when he was attracted by voices from outside, and fell from the window to his death on the cobblestones four stories below. The parents were devastated and more tragedy was to follow, for their baby son, Jean, always a sickly child, died six weeks later on 7th July. From then on a measure of bitterness entered Saint-Saëns' personality. In July 1881, when he and his wife were on holiday, he left her, and later confirmed by letter his intention of not returning, though there was no legal separation. Saint-Saëns evidently felt that the death of their sons was partly her fault. Moreover the dominating presence of Saint-Saëns' mother who lived nearby and was known to disapprove of the marriage could well have contributed to its breakdown. Saint-Saëns' wife returned to her family and never saw her husband again, though she was present at his state funeral many years later. She died aged 94 years in Bordeaux on 30th January 1950.

Following his sons' death and the failure of his marriage Saint-Saëns threw all his energies into his work, and a stream of compositions followed. This high rate of production continued virtually throughout his life and his total output of musical compositions was immense. It included a concerto for cello and orchestra, others for violin and orchestra (he wrote three but only two of them achieved any success), several symphonies, much chamber music, and five piano concertos. Two of these piano concertos (numbers 2 and 4) have withstood the test of time and are as popular today as in Saint-Saëns' lifetime.

The one field in which Saint-Saëns suffered continued disappointment was opera. His only real success was *Samson et Delila* which was as much an oratorio as an opera and indeed was presented as an oratorio in Victorian Britain which considered religious subjects inappropriate for stage presentation. One reason for his failure was that Parisian audiences expected their operatic composers to be specialists in that field, and Saint-Saëns was very much an all-rounder. Another reason was his refusal to include a ballet in his operas, a practice popular at the time but in Saint-Saëns' view pointless. More importantly, Saint-Saëns' music was basically classical and formal in structure and he probably did not have the dramatic flair which is required in opera. Some great composers, like Mozart, had it, and others equally great, like Beethoven, did not. The success of his arch-rival, Massenet, in opera was a constant source of irritation to Saint-Saëns. Massenet was the one contemporary whom Saint-Saëns hated and the rivalry between the two was intense.

As is the case with many composers, the works by which Saint-Saëns is best remembered are not the ones he would have chosen to be remembered by. As an example, he composed the popular *Carnival of the Animals* as a private joke and thought, probably rightly, that if published during his lifetime it would detract from his status as a serious composer. In accordance with his wishes it was not published until after his death, 36 years after it was composed. The only piece from it which he allowed to be published whilst he was alive was *The Swan*, one of his most popular compositions. *Danse Macabre*, a weird and non-typical piece, has also achieved lasting popularity.

In 1880 Saint-Saëns played the piano and organ for Queen Victoria at Windsor, an honour repeated on later occasions. Following the death of his 79 year old mother in 1888 he grew more lonely and lived only for his music. In 1893 he received an honorary doctorate from Cambridge University at a ceremony in which degrees were also conferred on Bruch, Grieg and Tchaikovsky. Soon afterwards Oxford, not to be out-done, conferred one on him. By his early sixties he was becoming a patriarchal figure. He played a Mozart concerto at a concert celebrating the 50th anniversary of his official debut (the same concerto he had played as a child) and in the early years of the present century the elderly musician's life became a succession of festivals, anniversaries and the receipt of honours.

By this relatively late stage of his life Saint-Saëns had become rather irritable, bad-tempered and tactless. He lived alone except for his elderly man-servant, his dog and his memories. Most of his old friends and adversaries had gone but he derived much pleasure from his friendship with the Fauré family and became a sort of benevolent uncle to the Fauré children. In 1912 he had the satisfaction of writing Massenet's obituary for the *Echo de Paris*. Following Massenet's death Saint-Saëns was awarded the 'Grande Croix de la Légion d'Honneur', the greatest accolade in French music. Whilst Massenet and Saint-Saëns were both alive the authorities had not dared award it to one without offending the other, for their animosity towards each other was well known. Saint-Saëns also derived great and rather childish delight from the fact that a full-length statue of him had been erected in Dieppe, where a Saint-Saëns Museum had been established, whereas Massenet was commemorated only by a modest head-and-shoulders near the Monte Carlo Opera House.

Towards the end of his life Saint-Saëns' musical image became a little tarnished, especially in the eyes of the younger generation, because his musical inclinations were firmly rooted in the past. For most of his life he had shown an intelligent regard for the work of others, but as he grew older his pronouncements were regarded by many as illogical, for he allowed himself to be dominated by patriotic and sometimes irrational sentiments.

Debussy resisted the influence of Wagner because he thought his music was detrimental to French art. Saint-Saëns, on the other hand, resisted Wagner because he was a German, and his emotive language on the subject did him much harm in the minds of the musical public, even more than did his virulent attacks against modern music.

French impressionist music was the last straw as far as Saint-Saëns was concerned. Perhaps this is not surprising, for he was over 60 when it began to take hold; he had been composing in the classical tradition since childhood and most of his work was behind him. In particular, he made no attempt to hide his dislike of the 'new' music of Debussy, a much younger composer whom he nevertheless outlived. This is a pity, because Saint-Saëns had, in his day, been a very good composer, and a more gracious approach to the work of his young successors would have done him credit. Perhaps his own compositions were too numerous; his facility for invention was apt sometimes to produce quantity at the expense of quality. His best compositions were fine pieces but many of his others, most of which are now rarely performed, lack the beauty and the emotional evocative imagery of Debussy, Ravel and others of the younger school. If we are looking for sensuous, sensitive art in the music of Saint-Saëns we will seek in vain. If on the other hand we are looking for classical purity, founded more often than not on a good tune, it is there in Saint-Saëns' music.

Nowadays Saint-Saëns is remembered mainly as a composer, for it is over 70 years since his death and at that distance his skills as a pianist are impossible to assess by present-day standards. But, applying the criterion of how he was received in his own day, there is no doubt that he was one of the leading keyboard virtuosi of his era, both as a pianist and as an organist. Moreover, he was a brilliant improviser on either instrument. Henry Wood recalled that when Saint-Saëns was in London for the Queen's Hall Concerts of 1902 he (Saint-Saëns) would come round to the hall at 8.30 am to enjoy an hour of improvisation on the magnificent organ there before rehearsals began. Wood used to sit and listen, unseen, at the back of the hall, enjoying Saint-Saëns' "unique extemporisation". Other contemporary critics were unanimous in extolling the brilliance of Saint-Saëns as a pianist, though, in the same way that his compositions were noted for their constructional correctness rather than their beauty, his playing was characterised by technical clarity, brilliance and accuracy rather than emotional feeling.

For a pianist who died when the present century was only 20 years old it would be too much to hope that his gramophone recordings would give more than a hint at his ability as a pianist. On 26th June 1904 he recorded five of his own compositions on 12" single-sided discs in France. They were an improved cadenza from *Africa*, Op. 89; *Valse Mignonne*, Op. 104; *Valse Nonchalante*, Op. 110; extracts from the G Minor Piano Concerto; and *Rhapsodie d'Auvergne*, Op. 73. On the same day he recorded four 10" single-sided discs as accompanist for the Belgian soprano Meyriane Héglon (who at the time was one of the stars of the Paris Opéra) in four of his songs; they were *Air* from the opera *Ascanio*; *Rêverie*; *Printemps qui Commence* from *Samson et Delila*; and *La Solitaire*, probably Op. 26, No. 3. As disc recording, or indeed any form of gramophone recording, was then primitive in the extreme the records tell us little about the quality of Saint-Saëns' playing. More reliable, perhaps, are four records made in France in 1919, again of his own compositions. They were his *Rêverie à Blidah* from the *Suite Algérienne*, Op. 60; *Marche Militaire Française* from the same suite; *Prelude* from the Oratorio *La Deluge*; and *Élégie*, Op. 143; the last two items accompanying a violinist, Gabriel Willaume. Though recording techniques had advanced considerably since the 1904 recordings, the discs were still produced by the acoustic process and therefore lacked authentic quality. Furthermore, Saint-Saëns was by then 84 years old and can hardly have possessed the skills of his earlier years. The above discs comprise the sum total of his gramophone recordings.

Saint-Saëns' scanty output for the gramophone was supplemented by about 40 piano roll recordings dating from the early years of this century. For the Aeolian Company's Duo-Art system he recorded six rolls, all of his own music except for Chopin's Impromptu, Op. 36 in F sharp. He recorded about 13 rolls for the German Welte system, eight of which were of his own compositions. The other three were of music by Beethoven (Sonata, Op. 31, No. 1, second movement); Chopin (Nocturne, Op. 15, No. 2) and Schumann (*Waldszenen*, Op. 82, No. 9). One of the Welte rolls (part of his own *Samson et Delila*) was re-mastered and issued in the USA by the Artecho Company. For Hupfeld (another German company), he recorded at least 15 compositions, all of which were of his own music. Two of them (Finale to Act 1 of *Samson et Delila*, and *Valse Langoureuse*, Op. 120) were adapted for the American Ampico system and appeared in that company's catalogues for many years. Finally, he recorded eight rolls, all of his own compositions, for the Philipps Company of Germany. The piano rolls quoted above probably provide a better indication of Saint-Saëns' style as a pianist than his gramophone records, but for someone who was a noted pianist for nearly 80 years the total recorded output on disc and roll is disappointingly small.

One of Saint-Saëns' minor claims to fame in his later years was that he wrote the music to accompany a moving picture, and was the first major composer to do so. It was *The Assassination of the Duc de Guise*, a 15-

minute silent film released in 1908. The film was an influential one in the early history of the cinema.

Saint-Saëns was still touring in his late seventies, playing the piano and organ with indefatigable energy. His last appearance in Britain was in 1914 when he played a Mozart concerto conducted by Sir Thomas Beecham, with whom he had some irritable exchanges during rehearsal. He would probably have come again but for the outbreak of war. English audiences always felt at home with the small, neatly-dressed figure, far removed from the Bohemian extravagances they associated with some foreign musicians. His personality when he was on tour was one of contrasts. Amongst his friends, like Henry Wood, he could be boisterously jovial, whereas with others he was often irritable and tetchy. He rarely, if ever, signed autographs and Henry Wood recalled how, when confronted by a pile of autograph books in the artist's room, Saint-Saëns pushed them onto the floor.

In 1915, at the age of 80, Saint-Saëns made his first visit to the USA as his country's official representative to the San Francisco Exhibition. He was not the world's best diplomat. When asked by reporters what he thought of American composers he replied "I've never heard of any." In 1916 he went on to South America. On his return to France he gave charity concerts for war wounded.

By the end of the First World War Saint-Saëns had achieved the status of a sort of national monument, an establishment figure respected by many, despised as out-of-date by some, but a musician whose stature over an immense period of time no one could deny. The old, but still active, living legend continued to compose and give recitals. Late in 1921 he went on one of his routine visits to Algiers. On 16th December he did his normal two hours of practice, arranged some manuscripts, wrote a few letters, and quietly and unexpectedly died in the late evening. He was 86. Someone once said that Saint-Saëns was the greatest musician who was not also a genius. They were probably right.

Vladimir de Pachmann

2. Vladimir de Pachmann

Pachmann was not just a pianist, he was a colourful personality. Though his musical talents were remarkable, it was as a unique individual that he endeared himself to his audiences in a way that no other concert pianist has since been able to do. His confidential asides to the audience, his impromptu lectures and his friendly smiles annoyed some, but they pleased a great number of people. Whether they were the conscious tricks of a shrewd actor or the naïve outbursts of a genius is difficult to say, but by the strength of his personality Pachmann could hold the attention of a crowded gathering.

Vladimir de Pachmann came from the most impeccable of musical backgrounds, for his father was a celebrated amateur musician in Vienna in the early part of the 19th century, when the great classical tradition there was at its height. Pachmann senior, a violinist, came into contact with Beethoven, Weber and the other great musicians of that time. He later took a teaching post at the University of Odessa in the Ukraine, and it was there that Vladimir was born, on 27th July 1848. He did not begin to learn the piano until he was 10, but from then on his exceptional musical talent was apparent. For many years Vladimir's tuition was provided by his father, under whose capable direction his talents prospered, but at the age of 18 he was sent to the Vienna Conservatory where he studied for two years under Joseph Dachs, a famous piano teacher.

At the conclusion of his period of study in Vienna in 1868 he won a gold medal for piano playing before returning home to Russia in 1869, and in the same year he made his official debut, giving a series of concerts in his home town of Odessa. They were very successful, and many a lesser pianist would have regarded these triumphs as an 'open sesame' to a career as a concert artist. But Vladimir's standards were high; he was dissatisfied with his own performances and retired to concentrate on further study. This lasted no less than eight years, after which he emerged to give successful concerts at a number of cities including Berlin and Leipzig. But again Pachmann was his own most severe critic, and after giving a further series of public performances he retired once more, this time for two years, to devote himself to hard study. After this long period of apprenticeship, Pachmann was at last satisfied and re-emerged as a fully-fledged artist, giving three concerts in Vienna and three in Paris, all of which were highly successful.

One of the leading figures on the London musical scene of those days was Wilhelm Ganz, the German-born conductor of the New Philharmonic Society, who presented numerous concerts. After 1880 the orchestra's performances were billed as "Mr. Ganz's orchestral concerts". On 20th May 1882 Pachmann, then 33, appeared in one of Ganz's concerts, playing Chopin's F minor Concerto, and achieved a brilliant reception. From then on until his death half a century later his career was uniformly prosperous, though the nature of his performances was always controversial, as we shall see.

At the outset of his career, when his reputation was being established, Pachmann's behaviour was relatively conventional. It had to be, for no one would have taken him seriously otherwise. But once he had set himself up in the forefront of the pianists of his time by a series of masterly performances, particularly in the works of Chopin, in whose music he excelled, Pachmann's exuberant and extrovert personality began to manifest itself during his recitals in a variety of ways. So began the happenings which made Pachmann a legendary figure in the world of music. Before he was 35 he had developed the habit of chatting to his audiences not only before and after his recitals but also during them, conduct which exasperated the critics but was the delight of the ordinary concert-goer.

In the midst of establishing this reputation as the 'enfant terrible' of the concert platform he married Marguerite Oakey, a talented Australian pianist, who had been having lessons with Pachmann and had also given some recitals. Further recitals were arranged for her on Pachmann's first tour of the USA in 1891, and during her performances Pachmann would sit himself in the audience and applaud vigorously, going through contortions of delight, and shouting "Bravo, Charmante, Magnifique!" and so on. But the marriage was not successful and in 1892 the couple were divorced. Marguerite Oakey later married Fernand Labori, a brilliant French lawyer, one of whose claims to fame was that he defended Captain Dreyfus in the famous trial of 1899. Pachmann married again, more than once, in later years. He kept his personal life a closely guarded secret and the number of his marriages is in dispute.

When Pachmann gave a recital there was always plenty to see as well as to hear, and his performances were not just a musical experience, they were an entertainment. For most of his active life, from early middle age to old age, they followed a standard pattern. To begin with, his recitals never started punctually. At last, when the audience was starting to get impatient, the dapper little figure with its shock of greyish hair would amble gently onto the platform. He would survey the piano with the delight of a child presented with an expensive new toy, and then followed a good deal of by-play with the music stool, whose height and distance from the piano had to be most minutely adjusted. Sometimes he would rush to the wings and come back with a large book, whose pages were then ripped out and placed on the seat until its height was exactly right. Next the keys had to be dusted with a silk handkerchief. After all this had been completed to his satisfaction he would sit down, smile angelically at the audience, and begin to play.

These preliminaries were not the only manifestation of Pachmann's idiosyncrasies. In the middle of playing he would sigh, talk, gesticulate, and wink at the audience, and would address sundry remarks to it, generally of a self-congratulatory nature. During an exquisite passage he would turn to those seated nearby and would seek to heighten the effect of the music by a series of ecstatic exclamations, perfectly sincere, if somewhat disconcerting. Sometimes he would place his hand on his heart and shake his head sorrowfully. Pachmann did not pose at the piano, gazing abstractedly forward in complete absorption, as many pianists do. It was his custom to turn his face to the assembled company, and he would fix his gaze on a member of the audience as he played. If any such recipient of his stare should seem to be resenting it, he took no notice; his dark, heavy eyes would still linger on that face, and he would give the impression he was playing for that individual alone.

Pachmann's personality was magnetic, and as he fixed his audience with his glowing black eyes he held his listeners in complete control. If he heard so much as a whisper whilst he was playing he would promptly call the offender to order. Sometimes he would stop in the middle of a piece and ask the audience what it thought of his performance. There would be applause and cheers, whereupon Pachmann would inform the assembled company that they were all deaf, that he was playing terribly, but that now he would play as only Pachmann could. If he received more applause than he thought he deserved, his gesticulations with hands and arms would indicate that there had been more than enough acclaim. If the audience insisted on more encores than he wanted to give he would not yield unconditionally, but would first consult his watch to see if there were time. Sometimes he would take as many as a dozen recalls at the conclusion of a performance, and would eventually draw from his pocket an immaculate handkerchief, and wave it as a last farewell. If anyone else did it, it would have been ridiculous. Done by Pachmann, it was most graceful.

Some pianists get flustered and embarrassed if they have a lapse of memory during a recital, or perpetrate a rash of wrong notes. Not so Pachmann; indeed, Shaw once wrote, "M. de Pachmann passes off mishaps so effectively that he has been suspected by evil-minded persons of bringing them about on purpose."

As might be expected from his style on the concert platform, Pachmann was something of a humorist. Once he saw an advertisement for piano lessons given by a lady at a fee of tenpence an hour. He answered the advertisement in person, and on being asked to give a demonstration of his abilities, sat down and bungled through a Chopin waltz. "That's shocking", said the lady. "You've been very badly taught." "Yes", replied Pachmann, "but I began so late!" Then he paid his fee, and left his card in the hands of the terrified instructress.

Fellow pianists trembled when, from the stage, they spotted Pachmann in the audience at one of their recitals, for they never knew what was going to happen. At a Godowsky concert he rushed onto the stage at one point. "No, no, Leopold", he cried, to the vast amusement of the audience and the crimson blush of Godowsky, "You must play it like *so!*" Pachmann then played it like so, and told the audience he wouldn't have given the demonstration for any old pianist. "But Godowsky", he said, "is ze zecond greatest liffing pianist." At a Busoni concert he rushed to the stage and kissed Busoni's coat-tails. "Busoni is ze greatest Bach player", he announced; "I am ze greatest Chopin player." On another occasion, during a recital in London, Pachmann crouched over the keyboard so that nobody could see his hands. "Vy I do zis?" he asked the audience. "I vill tell. I see in ze owdience mein alte freund Moriz Rosenthal, and I do not vish him to copy my fingering." Once, when playing in Portsmouth, Pachmann stopped in the middle of a piece, pointed to a man in the audience and said: "Zat man is not in sympathy with Chopin!" He would not continue until the unfortunate individual left the hall.

Pachmann was never one to hide his light under a bushel. When asked about his standing he would say "I am the king of pianists." Being once asked to name the first five living pianists in order of merit, he began: "Second, Godowsky; third, Rosenthal; fourth, Paderewski; fifth, Busoni!" As early in his career as his London debut of 1882, Pachmann's quick wit was able to produce an apt remark when required. After his triumphal concert an interviewer asked Pachmann, who was visiting the capital for the first time, what he thought of London. The little man drew himself up to his full height. "Zat is not ze qvestion. Ze qvestion is, vat do London zink of Pachmann?" When asked about Liszt, whom Pachmann had heard play many times, Pachmann replied: "Liszt? Ah yes, he play very, very well. But me, I play like a god."

From what has been written so far, the reader might form the impression that Pachmann was not to be taken seriously as a pianist. Undoubtedly the court jester of the pianistic circle, was he not just an entertainer, a kind of precursor of Liberace - a joker? The fact is that Pachmann *was* taken seriously, for one excellent reason; he was a very, very good pianist, provided he restricted himself to a repertoire that suited him. It is doubtful whether the purpose of his antics was to gain cheap applause - it is more likely that he was simply expressing his personality. He was happiest playing in an informal, relaxed manner, as someone might be at home entertaining a few friends, where asides and interpolations would be regarded as normal and acceptable. He did not like a stuffy, formal atmosphere.

When Pachmann was at the peak of his career a contemporary observer, J. Cuthbert Hadden, wrote of him in these terms:

"Why should the musician not seek to enter into personal relations with the audience, if it so happens to suit his fancy? Pachmann is all through the friend of the audience. Suppose he plays a scale. It is like a string of pearls. "Bon!" he says, delightedly. And he is quite right; it *is* beautiful. Or the charm of some passage strikes him anew, "The melody!" he exclaims enthusiastically, and he marks out the melody for a bar or two, so that the audience may be under no mistake. It is a recital and a lecture in one. "Preposterous!" some people say. But the listener who cannot profit by the remarks of Pachmann knows more than Pachmann, and that kind of listener is not usually present at his recitals! It is best to accept the strange pianist as he is, with all his foibles. He is undoubtedly a genius. And all this elaborate presentment of his personality is no mere pose, as many think; it is a thing natural to himself; a manner over which he has no control. Moreover, his behaviour, however unusual it may look, never upsets his superlative playing."

And so, what can we say of Pachmann's playing that earned the respect of his peers and allowed serious critics to overlook the eccentricity of his performances? It became evident to Pachmann at an early stage in his career that his technique had its limitations - it lacked the breadth, nobility and intellectuality necessary to do justice to the larger works, especially the concertos, of some of the great composers, for example Beethoven, Brahms and Schumann. But he possessed wonderful fingerwork and a beautiful tone quality - soft, sweet and caressing. Experts wrote of his "marvellous velvety tone", "ethereal pianissimo" and "superbly sensitive touch". These gifts inclined Pachmann towards the tonally beautiful miniatures, and it was in these that he excelled, particularly in the works of Chopin.

Pachmann became a Chopin specialist at an early stage of his career, and in later life he played little except the music of the Polish master. His interpretation of Chopin's music made his playing the envy of many colleagues and his reputation was based largely on his skill as an exponent of the music of that composer. Occasionally he would play a movement from Bach, Scarlatti, Mendelssohn or Henselt, but predominantly Pachmann was a Chopin man, *the* Chopin pianist in the minds of many knowledgeable musicians. It was this fact, coupled with the little man's eccentric behaviour, that earned him the nickname "The Chopinzee", an apt epithet coined by the American critic James Huneker. From his rise to eminence in the early 1880s, Pachmann enjoyed uninterrupted popularity in Europe, the USA and elsewhere, and was always in demand for recitals. Occasionally he appeared with an orchestra, generally in a performance of a Chopin concerto, but it was as a recitalist that his reputation was based. His skill as a pianist and the unique nature of his performances always ensured that a Pachmann recital was an occasion to remember.

Pachmann's career spanned the heyday of the player piano, in particular the reproducing piano, and he recorded several rolls for the Aeolian Company (Duo-Art rolls) and the Welte Company. Later in life he wore his hair long, like Liszt, and the small, silver-haired pianist looked the epitomy of the popular image of the concert pianist, a point not lost on the Welte advertising team who not only quoted his frequent pronouncements in their publicity material but also featured him prominently in their photographs. The music he recorded for both companies was the same as that with which he was associated on the concert platform. An examination of the 1932 Duo-Art catalogue reveals that 13 Pachmann rolls were on offer, 12 of which featured the compositions of Chopin (one ballade, one étude, one impromptu, one mazurka, four nocturnes, one polonaise, one prelude, one waltz, and one 'biographical' roll, comprising a selection of appropriate examples to illustrate aspects of Chopin's compositions). The 'odd roll out', as it were, was Mendelssohn's *Song Without Words*, No. 46, Op. 102, No. 4. For Welte he recorded nearly 40 rolls of which 20 were of Chopin's music. The others were distributed between Bach (3 rolls), Godowsky (1), Henselt (1), Liszt (1), Mendelssohn (2), Mozart (3; the three movements of Sonata No. 11 in A, K. 331), Pachmann (3), Raff (1), Schubert (1), Schumann (2) and Verdi (1). The three compositions of his own in this list were *Improvisation in the form of a Gondola Song; Improvisation on Thekla Badarczewska's 'A Maiden's Prayer'; and Sabouroff* (a Polka). In addition to his Duo-Art and Welte rolls which comprised the bulk of his piano-roll recording work, Pachmann also recorded seven rolls for Artecho; three were of music by Chopin and the other four were compositions by Liszt, Mendelssohn, Schubert and Schumann.

As befitted a major artist, Pachmann was also engaged to make gramophone records, though he came late onto the recording scene because recordings did not become technically acceptable until he was getting on in years. His recording career began in 1907 when he was 59, and between then and 1924 he made over 50 acoustic recordings of which some were for The Gramophone Company (HMV) in London, others for Columbia, also in London, and a few for the Victor Company in New Jersey. Needless to say, most of his recordings featured the works of Chopin, but a few other composers were also represented. When electric recording was introduced in the mid 1920s Pachmann was 77, but the HMV Company lost no time in getting a few new Pachmann recordings 'in the can' before it was too late, and between 1925 and 1928 about 17 Pachmann discs were recorded; all but one of them were compositions by Chopin. The non-Chopin recording was Mendelssohn's *Prelude in E minor*, Op. 35, No. 1, released in 1928. Pachmann's recordings were very popular and were issued in many countries under the labels of HMV's associated companies.

The HMV record catalogue for 1937-38 quoted 13 Pachmann records currently on offer, of which four were 10-inch and nine were 12-inch, featuring 20 works by Chopin (one ballade, four études (one with spoken comments by the pianist), one impromptu, seven mazurkas, one polonaise, two preludes and four waltzes) and six works by other composers. The latter pieces consisted of four by Mendelssohn (*Prelude, Spinning Song, Spring Song* and *Venetian Gondola Song*), one by Raff (*La Fileuse*) and one by Schumann (*Prophet Bird*).

Some of Pachmann's performances, whether on piano roll or gramophone record, sound very odd when judged by present-day standards. He applied the technique of *rubato* in what would now be considered an excessive manner, but was certainly acceptable in his day. Moreover the rhythms are sometimes unusual, but again musical fashions change as the years pass. Pachmann's gramophone and piano-roll recordings suffer from another disadvantage; he was at his best when *en rapport* with his audiences, and to get the best from a Pachmann recital it was necessary to be physically present. The recordings seem somewhat empty and fail to transmit the magnetism of his personality, but the beautiful soft tone is nevertheless apparent. Pachmann never worried too much about the need to remain faithful to the composer's wishes and always felt free to adapt or modify the music as he thought fit, a practice considered to be perfectly acceptable in Pachmann's time but frowned upon by the purists of the present day.

Unlike many of his fellow concert artists, Pachmann never looked upon the United States as the Mecca for his profession. Born in Russia but of Austrian descent, he remained a European in domicile and outlook for the whole of his life, though naturally his concert appearances took him round the world, including frequent tours of the USA. Once he had become established on the professional circuit he left his native Russia and went to live in Berlin, where he remained for a while, and later in life he lived in Italy.

Pachmann often appeared in Britain where his recitals, or lecture-recitals as we might call them, became legendary, and in 1916 he was awarded the Beethoven medal of the London Philharmonic Society as a mark of the esteem in which he was held in Britain. He played several times in the Queen's Hall in London, his last appearance there being in 1925. Robert Elkin, the Hall's historian, said of Pachmann:

"He was certainly the most eccentric personality that has ever appeared on the Queen's Hall platform. But in spite of his eccentricities (some of them strongly suggestive of Grock and the other great clowns of the music hall), Pachmann's playing, especially of Chopin, was supremely beautiful, and my own view is that his odd behaviour at the piano was not to be attributed to conceit or to a conspicuous desire to 'play to the gallery', but to a childlike and perfectly genuine delight in what he was doing."

During the 1920s, when Pachmann was in his 70s, his career still prospered, to the delight of his faithful audiences. It was then that the Aeolian Company made a short advertising film in order to promote sales of their piano rolls. It showed Pachmann playing the 'recording piano', then throwing up his hands in mock amazement as a technician appeared immediately afterwards trailing a length of master roll bearing the recorded music.

By this stage of his career Pachmann's performances were almost exclusively of the works of Chopin, and he promoted his image of being the 'Chopin King' by dressing himself whilst at home in an old dressing gown which he claimed had belonged to Chopin. He would be attired in it when receiving visitors, and when he was on holiday at a farm he would wear it as he pottered around the farmyard and milked cows, one of his favourite occupations. He said that it would never do to let his fingers stiffen, and claimed that milking cows was better finger exercise than any exercises devised by man.

Pachmann's views on health were expressed in an article written in 1925:

"The doctors say that nicotine is bad for you. Well, I smoke eight cigars every day. The doctors say you must have exercise, walk in the air or play with the ball. Well, I have never taken any exercise in my life, unless you count the four hours a day practice at the piano. I have a beautiful little summer house at Fabriano, in Italy, with a lovely garden, but I never walk in it. All the fresh air I want comes in through the window. So there is my life. And I am seventy-seven. But I do not expect everyone to follow my example, for after all I am Pachmann, the unique. I laugh at your doctors."

Pachmann was regularly in demand as a contributor to magazines, for the musings of the eccentric genius were always worth reading, and he was given columns in which he had a free hand to philosophise or give his opinions on musical issues. In one such article published in *The Strand Magazine* in 1921, Pachmann claimed to have developed a 'new method' of piano playing:

"I have been playing the piano ever since I was a boy of ten years old, and yet for sixty years I played without a knowledge of my present method. Then, three and a half years ago I happened upon it. To a man of my age it was the discovery of real gold, the elixir of life. During the past three and a half years in which I have used this new method I have expended about one fourth the energy demanded of me over a similar period. It was when I was playing in Rome that I accidentally alighted on the new method. I was looking through the *Gradus ad Parnassum* of Clementi, which was written when the piano was very young. I noticed that the composition was written for a very unusual style of playing: that instead of crossing the hands as is done for many of the big compositions - Scarlatti's sonatas, for instance - it provided for one hand completing the runs begun with the other, so that the hands came together in the centre of the keyboard, but never crossed. It gave me an idea. If, by moving the arms, I could do this and keep my hands horizontal and always in an almost straight line from my wrists, I might save myself considerable effort and wrist strain. I experimented and found that this could be done. Even when my hands were at either end of the keyboard, I found they could strike the notes without their being at an angle with the wrists.

"This new method may seem very simple, but the saving of effort is phenomenal. After many hours of practice, I tried my new method in public in Rome. At the end of a three hours' recital I felt more fresh than I had done for many years past. Until then it had been usual for me to finish a recital with my fingers tired and stiff. After using the new method my fingers are not even moist, my wrists work perfectly, and they never give that ominous click which they did after long hours of playing with the old method. And all because my hands are kept horizontal and the wrists are never forced. My doctor, who recently examined my hands, was surprised at their remarkably healthy and supple state. By the use of this new method I hope to continue my public appearances for another 20 years at least."

This extract gives an insight into the mind of Pachmann the technician. Famous for his velvety touch, he was still prepared, at an advanced age (he was 73 at the time) to experiment and to develop new ideas and methods. Interestingly also, he intended, or said that he intended, to continue his career into his 90s, as Artur Rubinstein was to do 50 years later.

In another magazine article of the same period Pachmann expresses his opinions about the music of Chopin, describing the composer as 'The Poet of the Piano'. It is worth noting Pachmann's thoughts, in view of his status as a Chopin exponent. In an opening paragraph of faultless logic, Pachmann states:

"Of all composers, not one is so generally popular or so widely appreciated as Chopin. Yet it is safe to say that the works of no other composer are so horribly murdered by the amateur and the mediocre pianist. This is primarily because Chopin is played more than any other composer by the amateur and mediocre pianist." Pachmann then makes the courageous observation: "It is not to be supposed that all the work of any great man could possibly be of the same high standard, and Chopin is no exception to the rule. About one-third of his compositions are comparatively poor, and are, in consequence, not played at concerts."

In the same article, Pachmann went on to assess particular compositions of Chopin, concentrating on the preludes, which he reviewed in detail. Naturally he preferred some to others, and, reviewing them in numerical order, reached the teens and announced, "The 15th is my favourite", from which we might conclude that that is the one he liked best. But in true mercurial Pachmann style he followed this up in the next sentence with "The 16th is my great favourite." Some are summarily dismissed: "I do not like the 13th Prelude." Pachmann concluded with some general remarks on the interpretation of Chopin:

"Perhaps more than any other composer Chopin requires deep thought and study, for his nature was such that he created, quite naturally, particular effects of tone and colour arrived at by none of his predecessors. These effects cannot be merely copied from the works of anyone else, so that Chopin-playing becomes a special study in itself, requiring special training and special methods of interpretation. A fine painter will light up each little beauty in his pictures until the smallest detail is attractive, it is only the mediocre whose work is characterised by sameness and lack of interest. There must be no mediocrity in the playing of Chopin."

Pachmann's hope that he would play until he was over ninety was not to be fulfilled, for he died in Rome on 7th January 1933, aged 84 years. It is unlikely that we shall ever see another Pachmann, for his unconventional conduct and his liberal and sometimes whimsical interpretations of the music would not be accepted in the more formal musical circles of today, where authenticity and conformity to the wishes of the composer are regarded as of paramount importance. But Pachmann was a child of his time, when freedom of interpretation was not frowned upon, when interplay with the audience was accepted as part of the musical entertainment. See Pachmann as you will: a jester, the clown prince of the concert platform, a showman, an entertainer. Yes, he was all these things. But he was not a

Vladimir de Pachmann

charlatan, for he remained throughout his life a fine musician, and it was his musicianship that demanded respect, that ranked him as one of the foremost pianists of his era. If you went to hear Pachmann play you might have been amused, surprised, or put off by his volatility, or you might have been moved by the beauty of his playing. But one thing is certain. You would never have been bored, for an evening's entertainment by Pachmann was never dull.

Great Pianists of the Golden Age

Teresa Carreño

3. Teresa Carreño

It was a cold, wet, winter's evening in New York, but in spite of the weather the concert hall was filling up rapidly. Manuel Carreño paced nervously up and down in the backstage dressing room whilst his wife made sure that little Teresa's simple white dress was tidy and uncreased. Teresa tried to remember her father's advice; "Walk to the piano, Teresita, don't run!" The big moment duly arrived. Partially forgetting what her father had told her, the tiny figure walked demurely towards the piano across the long stage but progressed into a charming accelerando as she neared the instrument. She gave a shy, appealing nod to the audience and climbed the piano stool. It had been mounted on a special platform with two metal rods running through it to actuate the pedals she was too small to reach. Safely in position, she gave her accompanying group an 'A' with the professional aplomb that amused and delighted her audience. They had heard child prodigies before. No doubt they would hear them again. The best that could be expected was a pleasant evening's entertainment, due allowance being made for the extreme youth of the main participant.

The orchestral players were ready; so was Teresa. The music began. Instantly all was transformed. Gone was the small eight year old child, disarming her audience with her naïvity. Instead here was the artist, the musician, talented far beyond her years. Her musicianship and technical skills were amazing. She made the music sound simple and crystal-clear. As the Rondo by Hummel finished, the audience erupted into tumultuous applause. Teresa, diffidently wondering what all the fuss was about, was showered with flowers, and an old man presented her with a large doll which she eagerly clutched as she ran from the stage. In her dressing room congratulations flowed in from all around. It was the same later in the programme when she played solo music by Thalberg and Gottschalk. Finally came an encore, *The Gottschalk Waltz*, a little piece she had composed herself in honour of her idol, Louis Moreau Gottschalk, who had himself given a recital on this very piano only a few days earlier.

The audience and the critics were astonished. How could she do at eight years of age the things that a competent musician could not hope to do after eight years of study? Where did she get her insight - her feeling for the music? A critic said: "How those hands can stretch an octave is a mystery, and yet her octave passages are clear and accurate. I don't understand it; I just don't understand it!" Overnight, the little marvel from Venezuela had become the talk of New York.

Let us see how this tiny musician came to be making her debut in a strange land, whose language neither she nor her parents could speak. The Carreño family were well-known in Caracas, the capital of Venezuela, in the most northern part of South America. The family had originated in the Carreño district of Spain. Early members of the family, adventurous by nature, had sailed the seas in search of fame and fortune. One helped to discover Bermuda and his son became governor of Havana. Around the turn of the 17th century a Carreño settled in Venezuela and originated a family whose descendants were to play a notable part in Venezuelan life, culture and music, for it became almost a tradition for the Carreños to take a leading part in organising the music at the Cathedral in Caracas. Manuel Antonio Carreño, who married a lady rejoicing in the name of Clorinda Garcia de Sena y Toro, was no exception to the family propensity for musical talent; but he did not see music as a remunerative profession and instead took up politics. A well-balanced and cultured man, his family had been associated with the Bolivars, famous in the history of Venezuela and other South American countries; his wife's family, also musical, were related to the Bolivars. By the middle of the 19th century Manuel had risen to the office of Minister of Finance in the Venezuelan government.

Emilia, the first-born of Manuel and Clorinda, was eight years old when Maria Teresa was born on 22nd December 1853. 'Maria' was a family name and it was as 'Teresita' that she was always known to her family and friends. To the outside world she was 'Teresa'. Her musical ability at an early age amused and amazed her family. At under a year old she could keep time to music with her head and hands; she listened in absorbed silence whilst music was played. She sang before she could walk, and as soon as she could walk, she danced. At two she sang an aria from Donizetti's *Lucia di Lammermoor* in what was described as a "sweet, true voice". There were two pianos in the family home; a grand, which she was not allowed to touch, and an upright, which she started to play when she could barely reach the keys from a standing position. This soon became her piano!

At five, Teresa taught herself to play dances and at six, lessons started in earnest. Her father taught her, and, methodical man that he was, he constructed a set of 500 exercises which covered all techniques and rhythms. She could soon play all of them in any key, and interspersed them, for variety, with Czerny's Studies, Bach's Inventions, and the like. Soon she could play Thalberg's *Norma* Fantasia. She was also a brilliant sight-reader. Manuel Carreño knew how Teresa's mind worked and he knew how to get the best out of her. He used to say, "Teresita, I know that you can play this study in the key of C; that is easy. But I don't believe you can play it in the key of B; that would be too difficult for a little girl!" Next day she played it not only in B but also through the other keys. Transposing her pieces became a favourite game and she also improvised with great skill.

Manuel Carreño was the most accomplished amateur musician in Caracas but he realised he was being out-distanced musically by his daughter, so a professional teacher was found, Julius Hohenus, who introduced Teresa to the work of composers such as Mendelssohn and Chopin. Her proficiency increased at an incredible pace. Away from music she was a normal child, happy and fun-loving. The Carreño home was a regular meeting place for the important personages of Caracus and on one occasion, whilst they were in conclave, Teresa noticed the long row of black hats arrayed on the family's hat stand. She took them away one by one and carefully arranged them on the branches of a tree in the garden so that they looked like a lot of black ravens perched there. She then awaited results. Fortunately the visitors also had a sense of humour! On another occasion, in collusion with the family's retainer who had secretly been asked by Teresa to prepare food, she invited all sorts of people to the Carreño household for an evening's entertainment, without telling her parents. As Teresa's parents settled down for a quiet evening, the first guests arrived, then others - and others! People of all sorts of political complexions who should not have mixed were there - but the evening was a great success.

When Teresa was eight years old a decision had to be made about her musical education, for it was clear that she had already absorbed all that Caracas had to offer. The family had fallen upon hard times to some extent, for there had been a political revolution, a different party had seized power, and Manuel was out of a job. He derived a small income from a book he had written, *Manual of Civility and Good Manners*, but this, coupled with the money he was able to derive from giving music lessons, was hardly enough. It seemed to Manuel and his wife, no doubt rightly, that Teresa's talent was so exceptional as to make her future of paramount importance.

After much thought it was decided that they should go to New York, a centre of musical excellence, to try their luck. Accordingly most of the Carreño family, with servants and relatives, a party numbering 14 travellers in all, departed from Puerto Cabello in July 1862. The youngest of the party was one year old and the oldest 75. Three weeks later they arrived in New York. Plans for their arrival had been made beforehand so they were not unexpected and accommodation was arranged through Venezuelan friends. Teresa's sister Emilia, now 16, had stayed in Caracas to marry, but Teresa was soon enrolled in a small private school in New York whilst Manuel set about the task of securing her future.

The idol of New York at that time was Louis Moreau Gottschalk, virtuoso pianist and composer, and he seemed to be the most influential person to approach. But, like many professional musicians, he was known to dislike prodigies. Nevertheless, through the good offices of a mutual acquaintance, a glowing report of Teresa's prowess was presented to Gottschalk, and he agreed to hear her play when he was next in New York. When he heard her, he too was astonished, for her performance justified all that had been said and written. It was Gottschalk who was responsible for her New York debut, already described. Indeed, he did more than that, for he paved the way for this official debut by arranging a private audition two and a half weeks before the recital, to which many prominent New York musicians were invited. Thus the musical establishment of New York was alerted to the forthcoming event.

Teresa's debut concert was such a triumph that from then onwards she could be regarded as a professional musician; indeed, for several years she was the chief breadwinner for the family. Mr. L.F. Harrison, manager of the Irving Hall where the recital took place, had astutely anticipated the likely success of the event by advertising a second concert on the programme of the first without reference to Teresa's father. This second concert was as successful as the first. Gottschalk wrote to Harrison from Cincinnati:

"Little Teresa seems according to what I see in the paper to be quite the furore now. I am very much pleased with it. She is not only a wonderful child but a real genius. As soon as I am in New York, settled down and at leisure, I intend to devote myself to her musical instruction. She must be something great, and shall be."

Teresa did receive lessons from Gottschalk and other concerts followed, five in three weeks, before Manuel Carreño decided the time had come to call a halt. The impresario, Harrison, thought otherwise and arranged a farewell 'benefit' concert to coincide with Teresa's 9th birthday on 22nd December 1862. The public thought they were contributing to Teresa's birthday funds; in fact Harrison pocketed the takings, apart from Teresa's modest fee. Nevertheless, the concerts had served their purpose, for her name was now well and truly known. Offers poured in from other parts of America and Teresa played in Boston (20 concerts) and in other cities such as Providence, Cambridge, New Haven and Salem. All the time she was adding to her repertoire, and she attended performances of other musicians and operatic productions to widen her musical knowledge. Once, after attending a performance of *Fidelio* she asked her father: "Do those who are married in operas stay married?" A highlight of Teresa's tour of the USA was an appearance with the Boston Philharmonic Orchestra when she played

Mendelssohn's *Capriccio Brillante* in B minor, Op. 22, a piece she had learned in three days. Boston took the Carreños to their hearts. It was said that in New York it was Teresa the novelty; in Boston it was Teresa the musician.

After Boston there was a visit to Cuba, again a huge success. Some of the family then went back to Venezuela whilst Teresa and her parents returned to New York. She learned English very quickly, paid attention to her schooling and gave concerts and recitals as occasion presented itself. She also had one of her compositions published, *The Gottschalk Waltz*, which she had played at her debut concert. It had a photograph of herself on the cover.

A highlight of this period came in the autumn of 1863 when Teresa, then nine, was invited to play for President Lincoln at the White House. She had by now become somewhat wilful and assertive; not surprising in view of the course her life had taken, and could not agree with her father about the programme she should play for the President. Her father favoured the classics; she wanted to play Gottschalk, Thalberg and the other popular, 'showy' composers of the day. Manuel insisted that she should do as he wanted. But after she had seated herself at the presidential piano she looked her father straight in the eye and plunged into Gottschalk's *Marche de Nuit*, modulating into *The Last Hope* and finishing with *The Dying Poet*. Fortunately the President's brow was rather near to the ground and he enjoyed every minute of it. Only her father's accustomed self-restraint saved him from apoplexy! As Manuel cringed in embarrassment, Teresa then complained that the piano was out of tune. (Even before she started, having run her hands over the keys, she had remarked that its action was hard and its keys squeaked!) But Lincoln gently asked her, "Teresita, do you know my favourite song, *Listen To the Mocking Bird*?" She nodded. "Would you play it for me?" She did so, adding a lengthy set of improvised variations. There were tears in the President's eyes. To Manuel Carreño it had been a fiasco. To the President, it had been a marvellously rewarding experience.

During the next two or three years Teresa added many of the standard but (to ordinary mortals) difficult works of the classical composers to her repertoire. On her 10th birthday Manuel bought her a large book into which he pasted clippings of all her concerts and recitals. For a while Teresa's performances were kept to a minimum, for Manuel was all too aware that his daughter was growing fast, was becoming disobedient, demanding and generally difficult. But eventually he decided to take her to Paris for the next phase of her musical education. The family set sail on the *City of Washington* in the spring of 1886 when Teresa was 12. The journey proved adventurous for the ship first hit a sandbank, then burst a boiler and finally lost its rudder, rendering it immobile in mid-ocean. After wallowing helplessly for some time, the passengers were hazardously transferred at sea to the *Propontis* which itself developed engine trouble and had to proceed by sail. Eventually they arrived in Liverpool and thence travelled through Britain and France to Paris, arriving on 3rd May 1866.

In Paris, Mme Érard, wife of the proprietor of the famous firm of piano manufacturers, took Teresa and her family under her wing and decided to do what she could to help the child. She sent a piano round to the family's apartment and arranged for two good pianists to hear Teresa. They were highly impressed and it was decided to present her in the annual concert to be given by Eugène Vivier, a respected musician, at the Salle Érard. But before the concert, and only a week after the family's arrival in Paris, another helpful meeting was to take place, for Teresa and her father were taken to meet the famous 74 year old composer Rossini in his Paris apartment. She played for the great musician and he was absolutely captivated. He urged that she should be presented in London and promised to help pave the way. He was as good as his word, acting as a sort of agent, commandeering one after another of his influential acquaintances to the service of his "little colleague" as he liked to call her.

Another stroke of luck followed. Liszt was visiting Paris and was persuaded by Mme Érard to come to the Érard showrooms on the morning of Teresa's evening concert (14th May) to hear her play. He did so, bringing with him three young musicians who turned out to be Saint-Saëns, Jaell and Planté. First Liszt played a piece by Beethoven for Teresa, then he asked her to play for him. She played music by Gottschalk, a composer he knew only by reputation. Liszt's reaction was the same as Rossini's had been. He put his hands on her head and said, "Little girl - God has given you the greatest of gifts - genius! Work - develop your talents." Liszt thereupon offered to teach Teresa in Rome, but Manuel Carreño decided not to avail himself of this offer.

Needless to say, Teresa's concert was yet another triumph. *L'Événement* reported:

"There has just arrived in Paris a little girl - if she reads this she will be furious - I wish to say, a very young person, who is a pure wonder. She is a pianist with a power that is really terrific, a Liszt in petticoats. I am told under oath that this little Spaniard is simply a star that is rising. Let me then record its first gleams."

Manuel Carreño took Rossini's advice and travelled with his daughter to London after she had been turned down by the Paris Conservatory on the grounds that she was already beyond their highest graduation standard. Later she returned to Paris and was taught privately by Georges Matthias (a former pupil of Chopin) and had private lessons in harmony and counterpoint from Emmanuel Bazin, who had been a pupil of Auber, and was currently a Professor at the Paris Conservatory. Sadly, Teresa's mother died in Paris of cholera in 1866 and for a time Teresa wore a black mourning dress at her recitals. Father and daughter were from then on more united than ever. In 1867 they returned to Paris after a tour of Spain, and Teresa widened her circle of musical friends further, to include Gounod, Auber (then 80), Berlioz, Ambroise Thomas and Adelina Patti. Her friendship with Patti and Rossini fired her ambition to add singing to her accomplishments for she possessed a pleasant mezzo-soprano voice. Accordingly she took singing lessons and these continued from time to time for several years. Another success was the publication by the local publishing firm, Hengel, of a number of her compositions. Prior to this the only one that had been published was *The Gottschalk Waltz*.

In 1868 in London Teresa met another highly influential figure, Anton Rubinstein, the great Russian pianist. This turned into a friendship of kindred spirits. At their first meeting Teresa played Schumann, Beethoven, Chopin, Mendelssohn and some of her own compositions. The master was captivated. He remarked on the similarity in the shape of their hands, and offered to teach her. Though 'lessons' were infrequent (he acted more as an adviser and mentor than a teacher), Rubinstein did for the teenage Teresa what Gottschalk had done for her as a child. He supplied the finishing touches, and under Rubinstein she became a mature artist. The two had similar temperaments. At her last 'lesson' with the great man, Rubinstein was declaiming on a certain point and Teresa had the temerity to disagree. Rubinstein bristled. He was not used to his view being queried. Teresa stuck to her guns on the point in question. Rubinstein too was adamant. "You must play this as I do!" commanded the Master. "Why must I?" asked Teresa. Rubinstein drew himself angrily to his full height, pointed to himself, and thundered "I am Rubinstein!" Teresa was not to be outdone. Jumping from her stool, she too stood to her full height, repeated his gesture and voice to the last detail, and retorted, "And I am Carreño!" For an instant the two vividly strong personalities confronted each other in indignation, then both dissolved into peals of laughter born of mutual understanding. He had to concede that she was worthy of equal right of self-expression. Little Teresa, the child prodigy, had gone. From that moment she would carve her own musical destiny. It was, for the next 50 years, to be "I am Carreño!"

Over the next few years Teresa's travellings took her between London and Paris many times and she became an established pianist on the concert circuit. In 1869, when still only 15, she appeared in Adelina Patti's 'Grand Concerts' in London, she toured Holland, Belgium and Switzerland, and in 1871, at 17, played in the London Promenade Concerts at the Covent Garden Theatre, conducted by Arthur Sullivan. She now had many concertos in her repertoire including Mendelssohn's G major and Beethoven's *Emperor*. She played at the Monday Popular Concerts organised by Chappell & Co. Ltd., the well-known firm of music publishers, concert agents, concert organisers and piano manufacturers. She was also associated with such celebrities as Hallé, Joachim, Richter and Clara Schumann.

Whilst appearing as piano soloist in a British concert tour of the provinces she made an unexpected professional debut as a singer. The touring party was in Edinburgh when the concert manager, Colonel Mapleston, appeared one day in a frantic state. The singer who was to play the Queen in Meyerbeer's *Les Huguenots* was ill. He knew Teresa could sing. Would she do it? "Indeed not!" said Teresa. The conversation went on in this vein for some time. By Teresa's side was Thérèse Tietjens, one of the operatic stars touring with the company. She understood Teresa's personality and had been biding her time. "Teresa is absolutely right!" she said. "It is much too difficult a thing to expect of her!" Teresa had her weaknesses, but modesty was not one of them. She bit her lip and muttered - "I'll consider it". True to her nature, Teresa duly stepped in and sang the role with credit. The *Atheneum* reported: "Mlle Carreño has not only taken a place in the front rank of lady pianists but she is also an accomplished vocalist." Teresa, cheerful and extrovert, was an ideal touring companion; her sunny, albeit at times hot-tempered, disposition contributed to the happy atmosphere.

In the summer of 1872 the 18 year old Teresa embarked on a tour of the USA with several other musicians including Émile Sauret, a violinist, later to achieve fame and distinction. Whilst in New York she visited Anton Rubinstein who was then appearing in the city. He had become quite attached to his young protegée and when she left he joked to a friend: "I have lost her! I have lost my sunshine!" It soon became clear, as the tour developed, that it was to be Émile Sauret who was to be the object of Teresa's sunshine. She took a maternal interest in looking after the slight, anaemic-looking young man, whilst he in turn accepted her solicitations with endearing helplessness. The tour visited Boston where Teresa had last played on her 10th birthday, and Teresa and Émile's joint performance in works such as Beethoven's *Kreutzer* sonata became notable musical events. Clearly a romance was developing, and in June 1873, against her father's advice, Émile and 19 year old Teresa were married. Afterwards she appeared as Mme Carreño-Sauret. On their return to Britain they took up residence in Maida Vale. So began Teresa's troubled and much publicised marital adventures. On 23rd March 1874 a daughter, Émilita, was born. But Teresa, still only 20, was not to be kept from the concert platform any longer than was absolutely necessary and she and Émile were appearing in joint recitals within three months of the birth.

In the eyes of Manuel Carreño, Teresa's marriage was a disaster. It seemed to him that his own life had no further meaning. For 15 years he had devoted himself to his daughter; he had taught her, managed her affairs, encouraged her and cared for her needs, and he had loved every minute of it. Now he felt redundant; supplanted. Furthermore, he was ill. With his purpose in life removed, his physical condition deteriorated. In August 1874 he died and was buried in Paris. As a new chapter in Teresa's life opened, an old one closed.

It was not long afterwards that Teresa and Émile set sail for the USA again on another tour, leaving the baby to be looked after by a friend, Mrs Bischoff. But the marriage, after a happy beginning, was not turning out well. Émile was a problem, not a support. Teresa's emotional barometer registered extreme ups and downs and quarrels became frequent. This culminated in an occasion when the pair were practising a sonata together. Teresa became irritated by the tapping of Sauret's foot as he marked the beat of the music. Words were spoken but the infuriating tapping continued. Eventually Teresa erupted in a rage. "I am enough of a musician to count without your assistance!" Sauret, equally livid, smashed his valuable violin to the ground, damaging it beyond repair. Next day they were not on speaking terms.

A truce was called, but the pair were not really suited. The quarrels became even more frequent and heated, and eventually, in 1875, Émile departed for good, dividing their money equally between them. Teresa was heavily pregnant at the time. The arguments and final parting were not conducive to an easy birth and the baby was stillborn. Meanwhile, Mrs Bischoff, who had been looking after Émilita, wrote to Teresa, asking if she could adopt the child. She presented powerful arguments which Teresa indignantly rejected out of hand. But after due consideration, knowing that she was destined to spend her days as an itinerant pianist and knowing that the baby's father had gone for good, she had second thoughts and duly signed the adoption papers, albeit with misgivings and much emotional turmoil.

Soon afterwards Teresa attempted to make a fresh start to her life in Boston, USA, and there she met and impressed Hans von Bülow. Again she embarked on a tour of the USA, this time as pianist with an opera company, and in 1876 she appeared in the major singing role of 'Zerlina' in Mozart's *Don Giovanni*. The 'Don' in this performance was the baritone Giovanni Tagliapietra, known to his friends, not surprisingly, as 'Tag', a handsome and dashing singer. Teresa sang her role in the opera creditably enough, but taking stock afterwards she realised that her talents as a pianist far exceeded those she possessed as a singer. She therefore pushed her singing into the background, though occasionally, to inject variety into her appearances, she would sing encores at the end of her piano recitals, a practice which always delighted her audiences.

At this period of her life Teresa was under contract to the Weber Piano Company. She sometimes played clad in a scarlet dress, and years later the famous American critic, Huneker, remarked, "Even her manner of playing, for me, has always been scarlet, as Rubinstein's was golden and Joseffy's silver." Also at this time the young Edward MacDowell (14) was brought to Teresa for lessons. He learned a lot from her musically in his formative years and later she helped him on the road to fame by including his compositions in her programmes.

Following Teresa's appearance as Zerlina, a romance developed between her and Tag. She was not yet divorced from Sauret, but she was something of a rebel against what she felt were the smothering conventions of the day. Accordingly she and Tag set up home in a small house which they rented in New York. Nowadays no-one would think twice about such a thing but in those days it was a bold step. Common-law marriages were at that time legal in New York State and the couple therefore considered themselves to be married. Teresa appeared as Teresa Carreño-Tagliapietra, her concerts continuing with unabated success, but they were interrupted for a short time in the spring of 1878 by the birth of a daughter, Lulu.

In 1881 tragedy struck, for Lulu died. Both Teresa and Tag were crushed. Moreover, the marriage was not working out any better than the previous one had done. Tag was somewhat jealous of his wife's outstanding professional success. Also, he was extravagant and carefree. Resenting the adulation and acclaim she received everywhere she went, far outstripping his own, he turned to gambling and drink. But the marriage struggled on and two further children were born, Teresita (December 1882) and Giovanni (January 1885). On each occasion Teresa's absence from the concert platform following her confinement was kept to an absolute minimum. In 1882 she composed the *Hymn To Bolivar* commissioned by the Venezuelan government to celebrate his centenary. This led to the oft-repeated but incorrect assertion that she had composed the Venezuelan National Anthem.

By the mid 1880s Teresa Carreño, now in her early 30s, had become more matronly in figure. Her favourite concert dress was of stiff black 'moire antique' with lace trimmings and sleeves and with a long train that trailed behind as she walked on to give a recital. It was an impressive sight. Once, as she swept onto the stage in London, one cockney stagehand said to another, "Cor, what do you think of that train?" The other replied succinctly, "It ain't the train, it's the engine wot's pullin' it that I'm lookin' at!"

In 1885 an invitation arrived from the Venezuelan government to visit the country and give a series of concerts. Teresa and her husband gladly accepted the invitation. She was accorded a tumultuous reception in Caracas in celebration of her first visit to her homeland for over 20 years. Civic receptions followed, distinctions were conferred daily, and she was given the Freedom of Caracas. Tag did not fit easily into this scheme of things. He resented playing the role of Prince Consort and was rude and arrogant on social occasions, much to the embarrassment of those present.

Soon afterwards Teresa was asked by the government of Venezuela to organise a season of opera and this she did, but the finance was poor, the artists unequal to the task, and the performances were not a success. This, coupled with the unfortunate behaviour of Tag whose drinking and gambling had worsened, soured the return to her native land. Moreover, although she had been received with honour by the civic authorities, there was much behind the scenes tongue-wagging from noted figures in Venezuelan society who disapproved of her 'marriage' with Tag, the circumstances of which were known to the staunchly-catholic citizens of Caracas. All in all, Teresa was glad to leave when the time came and she was never to set foot in her native land again. She returned to the United States; occasionally Tag was with her, but often he wasn't. The pair were rapidly drifting apart. In 1888 Teresa, now 34, toured the United States again, playing 150 concerts in the year. In ten years, the number of concerts she had given was estimated to be in the region of 1650, probably more than any other pianist at that time.

Teresa's friends eventually persuaded her to leave Tag and make a fresh start in Germany, a country of great musical opportunity but in which she was so far unknown except by reputation. Once again signing her name as Teresa Carreño, and accompanied by her two children, she sailed for Europe in June 1889 fortified by a loan of $5000 from a friend. On arrival in Germany a concert was arranged by her new manager, Hermann Wolff, who in his usual efficient way made sure it would be well publicised. Teresa practised for this concert more intensely than she had done for any other, knowing that on its success was likely to depend her future fortunes in Germany. Playing a Bechstein (a make of piano with which she was not until then familiar) her concert was given on 18th November 1889 with the Berlin Philharmonic Orchestra under Gustav Kogel, the then conductor and director of the orchestra. Her part of the programme consisted of the Grieg Piano Concerto, Schumann's twelve Symphonic Études, and the Weber-Liszt *Polonaise Brillante*.

Teresa had never played better than she did on this occasion and her performance in front of an audience used to the more restrained efforts of Clara Schumann was a revelation. The *Allgemeine Muzikzeitung* music critic wrote:

"It is a long time since I have heard a pianiste who has attracted me so strongly as Frau Carreño. Here at last comes an independent personality, standing out from so much mediocre talent which, neatly combed and brushed, pervades the wide avenues of prevailing pianism. With complete and blinding technical virtuosity, with strength sufficient for two pianists, and with an uncommonly and strongly sculptured sense of rhythm, Frau Carreño combines spiritual freedom and independence of interpretation, which lifts her far above mere pianism into the realms of true art." Another critic said: "She plays like Rubinstein on one of his good days!"

From the day of this concert Carreño's success in Germany was assured. Concert followed concert, each as successful as the last, and she soon repaid her loan. On the strength of her obvious popularity in Germany she decided to make her home in Berlin, with her children, and she remained there, except when touring, for the next 25 years.

One of the other artists managed by Wolff was Eugen d'Albert, the diminutive, gnome-like pianist who specialised in the interpretation of Beethoven. Though Scottish-born of French parents, he liked to consider himself a true German. It was inevitable that his path and Teresa's would cross sooner or later and in 1891, after Teresa had toured Germany, Holland, Belgium, Britain and Russia, they did. At first Teresa was not attracted to the insignificant-looking man, but when she heard him play Beethoven she was captivated. He in turn admired her fire and power. Although he was only 26 at the time and 11 years Teresa's junior, a romance developed. It is doubtful whether such would have been the case had they not both been internationally renowned pianists. He needed the lift her vitality gave him; she sought a deeper insight into a nature which revealed itself so marvellously in his playing. She called him her 'Liebchen', and after a holiday together, they moved into a house which d'Albert bought and Carreño ran.

Without doubt Teresa learned a lot musically from d'Albert. Up to that stage of her career her reputation as a top-class pianist was founded on her power, vitality and fire which earned her the nickname of "The Walküre of the Piano". After her association with d'Albert her taste developed. She discarded from her repertoire the flashy works of Vogrich, Gottschalk, Rubinstein, and even some of the music of MacDowell. Her playing acquired an inner unity and her tone took on subtle shades. As never before she studied to find deeper values in the music she played. She enlarged her repertoire appreciably and became as noted for her interpretation as she had been previously for her technical fire and brilliance. For the next twenty years she was regarded by many as the world's foremost woman pianist.

Eugen d'Albert had been married before and already had a son, Wolfgang. At the time he and Teresa set up their joint household he was not yet divorced, but when that matter was settled in July 1892 he and Teresa were married in London and she became Teresa d'Albert-Carreño. Two daughters were born; Eugenia (September 1892) and Hertha (September 1894). Naturally the marriage of two such great artists created a tremendous box-office draw and at many concerts Teresa played the d'Albert Second Piano Concerto which he had written with her in mind, whilst he conducted. The sight of the regal figure of Teresa sweeping onto the concert platform, whilst the diminutive d'Albert tripped along behind, became a regular feature of the European musical scene. Teresa's first performance of the d'Albert Concerto led to the following report by one critic:

"Last night Carreño played for the first time the second concerto of her third husband in the fourth Philharmonic concert of the season."

Plenty of concert engagements were forthcoming but before the couple had been married for long deep differences of opinion were becoming apparent. This marriage would fare no better than Teresa's previous ones. She had outbursts of temper; he had sarcastic digs. Mindful of the problems and wishing to re-establish a measure of independence, Teresa started to have herself billed as Carreño-d'Albert instead of d'Albert-Carreño. But what appears to have really killed the marriage was d'Albert's egocentric character. He couldn't bear to play second fiddle to anyone and was furious when Teresa stole his thunder. Particularly galling to him were the frequent occasions when, after Teresa had played his concerto, the critics lauded the performance whilst denigrating the composition. The presence of the children of their previous marriages at their home, an unusual state of affairs in those days, did not help. There is an apocryphal story that d'Albert once burst into the Carreño wing of their home shouting, "Teresa, come quickly! Your child and my child are quarrelling with <u>our</u> child!"

Things went from bad to worse. He expected Teresa to minister to his wants, accept his stinginess, and to shut her eyes to his philanderings.

Teresa wouldn't do this and reached the point of openly belittling him. Eventually he left home in a fit of temper. Sympathy in general was with Teresa for it was well known that d'Albert could be mean and objectionable. After much acrimony and legal correspondence Teresa was granted a divorce in 1895 on the grounds of d'Albert's desertion. A cynic remarked: "Here endeth the third lesson." A month later d'Albert married someone else. He was to marry six times in all.

After yet another marital failure Teresa immersed herself in her work, and even took up composition again. Now in her forties, the 'Lioness of the Keyboard' as she was sometimes known, had become imposing in manner and majestic in appearance. She had a rapier-like mind and a sharp wit. One night, after a busy evening of rehearsals, she stood on a bridge over the Elbe watching the sun set over the river. A young man, impressed by her appearance and possibly mistaking her profession, asked if he might accompany her. "Young man!" she replied haughtily, "I have just been accompanied by 70 gentlemen!" With that she strode away.

Her professional success continued without interruption and she appeared in a concert to mark Max Bruch's 60th birthday, playing Bruch's Fantasia for Two Pianos, Op. 11, with Josef Hofmann. She toured worldwide and was very reliable in her appearances, often playing when she was ill. Only the illness of one of her children would cause her to cancel a concert. She often played in Britain. Henry Wood said: "From the conductor's point of view it was an absolute inspiration to look down from the rostrum into those intensely beautiful Spanish eyes as she was seated at the piano, looking what she was - complete master of her instrument." She was practical and never afraid to do physical work. Once, returning from a tour of Australia, she was asked to give a concert in Fiji. There was no piano technician on the islands and only one piano, very out of tune. Teresa tuned it herself with the aid of a pair of pliers.

In 1900 Teresa embarked on a tour of the USA backed by the Steinway Company, and one of the people with whom she renewed acquaintance during the tour was Arturo Tagliapietra, younger brother of her second husband. A different personality completely from his brother, Arturo was not a musician. At the time he was working as a typewriter salesman. Poor, dapper, but neat, and a good organiser, Teresa suggested as a joke, just before she left the USA, that he should become her secretary. To her astonishment he duly arrived in Berlin some weeks later to take up his duties. Teresa, not one to go back on her word, set him up in a little office in her home. He ran errands and generally knew how to make himself useful. Furthermore, he was devoted to Teresa and knew how to soothe her nerves.

Teresa soon decided he was worthy of a higher status than that of secretary. To his amazement, she proposed to him. He accepted. When the marriage was announced it was regarded by the outside world as a joke. "The great artist, Teresa Carreño, marrying a poor little typewriter salesman!" As matters turned out, this was the only one of her four marriages that was happy. He understood Teresa. He was a shoulder to cry on; he was not a musician, he was not a rival. When she was acclaimed by the critics, he rejoiced as much as she did. With all her other husbands the reverse had been the case. Someone once said that at last a husband appeared who tamed Carreño. That is not true. She had found someone who truly loved her, and she knew it.

After her marriage to Arturo in June 1902, Teresa lived happily in his company to the end of her life 15 years later. To the end her recitals and journeyings continued. Yet, in spite of the fact that she earned vast amounts of money in fees, she never built up any financial reserves and she never managed to do much more than break even on a tour. There were two reasons. Firstly, she often travelled with a considerable entourage, all of whom had to be accommodated in hotels of a standard to which she was accustomed. Secondly, her many children regarded her as a fount of eternal wealth and were always asking for money, in particular Teresita (for whom Teresa had composed her most popular composition, the *Mi Teresita* waltz, many years earlier) and Giovanni, both children of her second husband. When her eldest daughter Émilita, who had been adopted as a toddler by Mrs Bischoff, reached the age of 31 she sought out Teresa, much to the latter's joy. But Teresa's rejoicing was soon quelled when she realised that the reason for the visit was purely financial. Émilita assumed that her mother could be regarded as a source of untold riches.

To a large extent Teresa had brought these troubles on herself. Her mother-love and generous nature encouraged her children to be dependent on her. Both Teresita and Giovanni were musical, to professional standards, Teresita as a pianist and Giovanni as a singer, but neither rivalled in the slightest degree their mother's outstanding ability, and they lacked her motivation and dedication to hard work. If they wanted to travel, Teresa provided the money. If they wanted lessons in the piano, singing or anything else, Teresa paid. When Giovanni took it upon himself to learn the violin, Teresa bought him an expensive instrument. All this when they were grown up. Teresa always saw them as children. When Giovanni was 30 Teresa still wrote in her letters: "My darling baby boy." One of Arturo's major managerial tasks was endeavouring to minimise the lump sums Teresa doled out to her various children.

Sadly, Teresa Carreño made no gramophone records at all. On the other hand, and fortunately for posterity, she recorded well over 60 piano rolls. The companies she recorded for were Aeolian (Duo-Art) (8 rolls), Welte (14), Hupfeld (12), Philipps (27), Artecho (3) and Recordo (2). Four of her Hupfeld rolls were adapted and issued by Ampico, and two other adaptations were released by Artrio. The composers represented in these recordings were Beethoven, Carreño, Chopin, Handel, Liszt, MacDowell, Poldini, Rubinstein, Schubert, Schumann, Smetena and Tchaikovsky. The recordings include two complete Beethoven sonatas; Op. 27, No. 2 (*Moonlight*) (on 3 Duo-Art rolls) and Op. 31, No. 3 (on 3 Philipps rolls). Two of her own compositions were issued on roll. She recorded *Teresita Waltz* (sometimes known as *Little Waltz*) for several of the companies named above, and her *Spanish Dance* was recorded for Hupfeld; an adaptatation of this roll was also issued by Ampico. Teresa's daughter, Teresita, recorded three rolls for Welte, one of which was her own composition, *Petite Berceuse*.

When war broke out in 1914, Teresa and her husband were still based in Berlin. She made a few appearances in Germany for charitable purposes before leaving with Arturo to tour Holland, Scandinavia, Spain and Rumania; she also devoted more of her time to teaching. It had been her custom for many years to spend the summer holiday months in the Alps teaching a group of pupils, and taking long walks with them all in the afternoons. She was a good teacher who based her tuition on three principles:

1. Master the fundamentals.
2. Know what to do.
3. Do it.

As a teacher she was very forthright and demanding. A young American girl, technically maladjusted, was one day initiated into Carreño's way of doing things, very unlike her own. "But Madame!" the girl pleaded, "You're not going to change my technique, are you?" "Don't worry, my dear!", Carreño reassured her. "I'm not going to change your technique. I'm going to give you some!"

In 1916 Teresa and Arturo decided to leave the apartment in Berlin that had been her home for 22 years and to avail themselves of an invitation for yet another concert tour of the USA. They arrived there in September 1916 after a mercifully uneventful Atlantic crossing. Carreño had always been a stickler for physical fitness but of recent years had suffered increasingly from rheumatism. More seriously, she had fallen victim to prolonged attacks of bronchitis, which were not helped by the fact that she was a lifelong heavy smoker. Nevertheless, in spite of the fact that she was not very well, the tour went ahead and in December 1916 she received the honour of being asked to play for President Woodrow Wilson at the White House, over 50 years after she had played there for Abraham Lincoln as a child. Part of the tour took her to Cuba where, in poor health, she gave what proved to be her final public performance on 21st March 1917. Her eyesight had been troubling her and three eminent New York physicians had diagnosed a condition known as diplopia. Old professional that she was, Carreño battled on through the concert in spite of seeing two keyboards. Her final encore was Handel's *Harmonious Blacksmith* variations played on the Steinway. With that completed, the great Teresa Carreño bowed out of public life. Weak with nervous prostration, she returned to New York and died there on 12th June 1917, aged 63.

Many famous musicians were present at the funeral two days later and the pall-bearers included Ignace Paderewski, Ernest Hutcheson, Walter Damrosch, Mischa Elman and Charles Steinway. Contemporary reports noted that the cremation afterwards was heralded by a crash of thunder!

Carreño had requested that her ashes be lain to rest in the country of her birth, Venezuela. This did not come about until 1938 when, with due ceremony, they were repatriated to her native land and placed in the Central Cemetery. In 1977 the Venezuelan government ordered that they be re-interred in the National Pantheon. There is a Teresa Carreño museum in Caracas, the mementos of which include the Weber piano which was specially built in New York for her Venezuelan tour of 1885.

Carreño was, after the decline of the ageing Clara Schumann, the greatest woman pianist of her era. In spite of giving birth to seven children she was rarely absent from the concert platform in her 54-year long professional career. Fluent in five languages, she was a woman of immense personality and talent. Regrettably, in the absence of any gramophone records it is left to a number of player piano rolls to give us a hint of the skills of this remarkable woman. That, and the contemporary accounts of those who heard her and were astonished by her brilliance. As Henry Wood said, "This great woman looked a queen among pianists - and *played* like a goddess."

Great Pianists of the Golden Age

Ignace Paderewski

4. Ignace Paderewski

If John Lill or any of his musical contemporaries were to become Prime Minister of Britain we should think it very remarkable, but Paderewski, the most famous pianist of his day, interrupted his career at a time of political turmoil to become Prime Minister of his country by popular acclaim. He re-established Poland as an independent nation before resuming his place as a celebrated concert pianist. His achievement in rising to the top in two spheres, music and statesmanship, is unique.

Ignace Jan Paderewski was born on 6th November 1860 in a village in Podolia, a province of the old Polish republic later annexed by Russia. His mother was musical and gave him his first piano lessons at the age of about three, but sadly she died soon after that, and Ignace's father, Jan Paderewski, who was an estate administrator, had to bring the child up single-handedly. Poland at that time was in a state of political upheaval and at odds with its gigantic neighbour, Russia, and Ignace's father suffered a spell in prison for alleged political deviations. His release from prison was achieved by a deputation from the people. The Paderewskis were not Jews but the local Jews often used to come to Jan with their problems instead of to their Rabbi, for he was a respected figure known for his fair and impartial advice.

Young Ignace's only playmate was his sister, two years his elder. He was a melancholy child; most of his companions were visitors to the house, elderly people born in the 18th century, who remembered the Napoleonic wars. After the death of his mother he used to play piano duets with his sister, Antonina, but at first they had no proper teacher. When he was about six a piano teacher was found, a local man named Peter Sowinski, who taught him 4-handed arrangements of operas but gave little formal piano instruction. Jan Paderewski employed a governess to provide the children's basic education and they soon became fluent in French and Russian as well as their native language. Ignace was also good at arithmetic and could multiply two four-figure numbers in his head. A visual memory enabled him to do this; similarly, he could remember pages of poetry. A private tutor replaced the governess and Ignace's studies flourished, but the piano tuition he was receiving was not very systematic and by the age of ten he had little correct knowledge of piano-playing technique. Though he could play numerous pieces he was virtually self-taught, and his method of playing, acquired by improvising, which he loved to do, had many imperfections.

Ignace's sister also had a talent for the piano and in 1872, when Ignace was 11, the two children played at a charity concert, with sweets as a reward.

Ignace wanted to play the piano well and was anxious to learn, but the continued absence of a good teacher hindered his progress. At about 12 he started to play at concerts without his sister, who was less ambitious. He used to do tricks as encores, such as playing the piano with a towel over the keyboard. With all his technical faults Ignace's inborn talent was obvious and after a short spell of tuition at Kiev (paid for by wealthy patrons) he was accepted at 13 without examination to enter the Warsaw Conservatory. It might have been expected that he would now receive suitable piano teaching, but his tutors thought he would never make the grade as a pianist as he had "no technique". They decided he would make a better composer than pianist, and consequently concentrated on developing that aspect of their pupil's talent.

At the Conservatory young Ignace enjoyed being with boys of his own age for the first time and earned a reputation for mischievousness. His friends called him "squirrel" because of his hair colour; the only squirrels in Poland at that time were of the red variety! Whilst at the Conservatory he learned to play several instruments and played the trombone in the Conservatory orchestra. He was a young man of principle and fell into dispute with the Director over a problem concerning rehearsals; the Director insisted that the students should rehearse for a concert the day before examinations, whilst Ignace believed that study for the examinations should take priority. Most of the staff were on Ignace's side but the Director nevertheless expelled him. Later he was re-admitted, only to be expelled again later over a similar issue and once more re-admitted, after which amicable relations prevailed.

At 16 Ignace made a short tour of the nearby regions of Russia with two companions, a cellist (22) and a violinist (18). The other two soon dropped out, leaving Ignace to soldier on alone in conditions of the utmost cold and poverty, having to borrow pianos from people's homes for his recitals, and living from hand to mouth. The tour was not a great success. Still 16, he finished his studies at the Conservatory and, notwithstanding his technical deficiencies, he played the Grieg Concerto with the college orchestra at the graduation ceremony. He then remained at the Conservatory as a teacher.

Early in 1880 Paderewski, then only 19, married Antonina Korsak, a music student at the Conservatory. The marriage soon ended tragically, for Antonina died on 10th October of the same year, nine days after giving birth to a son, Alfred. At the time Ignace was very hard up indeed; he and his wife had barely enough money to eat, and some said that his wife's tragic death might have been precipitated by Ignace's inability to provide her with proper nourishment and nursing, an allegation that must have hurt

Paderewski deeply and added to his sadness.

Desolate after the death of his wife, Paderewski felt there was no future for him in Moscow except as a teacher, so he decided to go to Berlin for further study. Not yet 21, he left his son, who was an ailing child from birth, with his wife's mother and set off for Berlin. There he enrolled as a private student with Friedrich Kiel, a well-known teacher, to study composition, a facet of music for which Paderewski possessed natural talent.

As part of his general musical studies Paderewski had to learn to play various musical instruments, including the violin and cello. He was sent to have lessons with teachers of those instruments, people who had no knowledge of his ability as a pianist, and this led to an amusing incident involving his violin teacher. The teacher in question gauged Paderewski's musical prowess purely on his skills as a violinist, which were almost non-existent. He was always scathing about Paderewski. "Why do you study the violin? You will never be a violinist - never. You are not a musician. You have not even a good ear for music, it seems to me. You have absolutely no talent for music. You should stop the lessons now. It is a waste of money." Paderewski, unruffled, plodded on to the end of his series of violin lessons and never said a word in protest. But after the last lesson, Paderewski took his teacher into the room where his piano was, and played, first one of his own compositions, then a Chopin mazurka. The violin teacher stood dumbfounded. "Oh, Stop! Stop!" he cried. "I have made a fool of myself. I said you had no talent for music and you can play like that!"

Paderewski studied under Kiel for only a few months, but it was a valuable period of his musical apprenticeship. Moreover, whilst in Berlin he met a number of the leading musicians of the day, many of them at the home of Hugo Bock, the publisher. They included Joachim, Sarasate and Richard Strauss. Paderewski and Strauss (Paderewski's junior by four years) became good friends and often played dance music together at lively evenings in Bock's home. Strauss was not a great pianist; he was of course to become famous as a composer, but his efforts at the piano were to be of value indirectly to Paderewski's progress as a pianist for an unusual reason. Paderewski noticed that when Strauss played, his performance was accompanied by grotesque facial contortions. Paderewski knew that he himself was guilty of similar mannerisms to a lesser degree, but had always thrust it to the back of his mind. But Strauss, an extreme example of the habit, brought home to Paderewski the importance of eliminating this particular problem from his own playing. Consequently he spent many hours practising in front of a mirror and gradually eliminated the facial distortions completely. At the end of this period of self discipline, he was able to play as calmly and with as much dignity as any pianist, a quality he always retained.

Another musical figure Paderewski met at Boch's home was Anton Rubinstein, the great Russian pianist. When Paderewski played for him, Rubinstein recognised at once that Paderewski had never been taught a proper technique, but said, "You have an inborn technique, and you could have, I am sure, a splendid pianistic career." These words overwhelmed Paderewski and spurred him on even further in his efforts to become a good pianist. Not only did Rubinstein inspire Paderewski to succeed as a pianist, he also encouraged him to compose. Further help was forthcoming from Moritz Moszkowski who liked some of Paderewski's pieces and helped to get several of them published.

After a year's hard work in Berlin Paderewski's funds had run low and he returned to his teaching at the Warsaw Conservatory. He had to teach students how to play correctly and this helped him to improve his own technique. He also composed more pieces and by his mid twenties about 30 had been published. It was a busy period in his life; he taught, he composed, and at the same time he studied, for he wished to become a well-educated man, and to achieve this objective he engaged private tutors in mathematics, Latin, literature and history. To add to all this, he was invited by a newspaper editor to write articles on musical criticism, which after initial reluctance, he did. All these activities combined meant that he usually worked into the small hours.

Profitable though this work was from the point of view of improving his general education, Paderewski knew that if he was to succeed as a pianist he must improve his knowledge of orchestration. With this in mind he returned to Berlin and embarked on a period of study with Professor Heinrich Urban, violinist, music critic, teacher and composer. This provided the necessary finishing touches to Paderewski's formal musical education. Whilst still a student with Urban he played in public whenever possible; he was determined to become a great pianist.

At about the time Paderewski was finishing his studies with Urban, he played at a concert in Cracow (Poland's equivalent of Oxford) and shortly afterwards went for a short holiday to the Tatra mountains. Whilst there he met Modjeska, a celebrated Polish actress whose real name was Helena Modrzejewska. She promised to finance further piano studies for Paderewski with Theodor Leschetizky, the greatest piano teacher of the day, in Vienna. It was to alter the course of his life dramatically.

Leschetizky knew of Paderewski through his compositions, which were starting to enjoy some success, before he arrived in Vienna, but the young pianist's first meeting with the great master was discouraging. After Paderewski had played to him, Leschetizky paced thoughtfully up and down saying "You *could* have become a great pianist - but it's too late - too late". But gradually Leschetizky decided that perhaps it wasn't too late, and started to work on Paderewski's technique, with profitable results. It was whilst he was a student with Leschetizky that Paderewski was taught the famous maxim, "If a man wishes to derive pleasure from the piano he must play. If he wishes other people to have pleasure from his playing he must work!"

Paderewski built up a small repertoire under Leschetizky's guidance including the Saint-Saëns Concerto No. 2, and whilst in Vienna he had the opportunity to play to Brahms. At this period of his life Paderewski was allowed by Leschetizky to play at an increasing number of minor concerts under primitive conditions. The pianos were often poor, having been housed in damp rooms, and Paderewski often had to work on the piano actions before recitals in order to unstick the hammers. The piano in one recital had hammers which still refused to free properly even after his best attentions and he had to have an assistant at the concert to flick them down after he had played the notes. The assistant's hands raced up and down the strings like those of a harpist as Paderewski played - a remarkable dual performance.

Paderewski only had about 30 lessons with Leschetizky altogether, spread over the period 1884 to 1887, but it was Leschetizky who diagnosed what Paderewski was doing wrong in his playing and showed him how to put it right. It was Leschetizky who instilled into Paderewski the need to practise in order to improve his technique, and to practise for hours on end. All that Leschetizky instructed, Paderewski did - and he gradually turned himself into a very good pianist. Paderewski, generous man that he was, ascribed all his success in later years to the teaching of Leschetizky, and retained a deep affection for him. Leschetizky, in turn, benefited from Paderewski's success.

In 1885 Leschetizky recommended Paderewski for a professorship of piano playing at the Strasbourg Conservatory. He accepted the post and it gave him increased opportunities to play in public. About this time he composed his famous Minuet in G which has remained his most popular piece. The story behind its composition is interesting. One of his friends was a lover of the music of Mozart, and whenever Paderewski visited him would say, "Play me some Mozart". Paderewski always did his best to oblige, but eventually, tiring of Mozart, he decided he would play a joke. He composed *Minuet in G* in what he considered to be the style of Mozart, and played it to his friend on his next visit, passing it off as the work of the great composer. "Marvellous!" said his friend. "Mozart is magnificent!" He was somewhat nonplussed when Paderewski owned up to his bit of harmless deception - but soon reconciled himself to being led up the garden path, and laughed as heartily as Paderewski. The piece became enormously popular and helped to make him famous. Indeed, the composition paved the way for Paderewski's early visits to Britain, for no-one then knew of his skill as a pianist; he was known only, at the time, as the composer of Minuet in G.

In 1887, whilst still receiving instruction from Leschetizky, Paderewski made his official Viennese debut. It was Leschetizky who secured the engagement for him. One of Leschetizky's friends, the singer Pauline Lucca, was giving a charity concert in Vienna and wanted a pianist to fill part of the programme. With her agreement Leschetizky invited his pupil, and it was arranged that Paderewski would play a few pieces by Beethoven and Chopin. He played to a full house under fashionable patronage and created a very good impression. The concert was an important landmark in his career.

In the following year, 1888, an even more notable concert took place when Paderewski, then 27, made his Paris debut at the Salle Érard before an audience that included Tchaikovsky, the eminent conductors Colonne and Lamoureux, and Mme Essipoff, the concert pianist who was Leschetizky's wife at that time. Amongst the pieces he played were Liszt's 6th Hungarian Rhapsody and the 32 Variations in C minor by Beethoven. Again the hall was crowded, and the audience was so enthusiastic that Paderewski had to play an hour of encores after the recital. At the close a milling throng of admirers descended on Paderewski, including Lamoureux and Colonne. Of these two Lamoureux arrived first and immediately engaged Paderewski to play a concerto with his orchestra. The minor composer and the little-known pianist had suddenly arrived!

Paderewski later referred to this recital as the success which came too soon, for there were few compositions he could play to concert standard at the time. A frantic period of learning followed, for Paderewski was in demand for other engagements, and in three weeks he learned enough pieces to give another concert with a completely different programme. This was in marked contrast to the eight months he had spent in preparing for the first recital.

In 1889 Paderewski made his Vienna debut as a solo pianist at the Bösendorfer Hall. He was then 28 and referred to the occasion as his 'real' debut, for he was now able to give a whole series of different programmes. Again the event was a brilliant success. He was also gaining a considerable reputation as a composer, for his list of published work was growing steadily and had extended in range to include a piano concerto. This received its first public performance in Vienna at about the same time as Paderewski's own solo debut there, although it was not played by Paderewski but by Mme Essipoff. Paderewski had naturally wanted to give the first performance of the concerto himself but Leschetizky thought it better for Mme Essipoff to play, as Paderewski was not yet well known. Paderewski generously conceded that she gave a fine performance of his concerto. Leschetizky always did all he could to promote the career of his young protegé. On one occasion he introduced Paderewski to a gathering of musicians and said, "Watch Paderewski's career, watch it well, for you will hear a great deal about this young man." His prophecy could not have been more accurate.

Following his successes in Paris and Vienna, Paderewski played in Brussels, Liège, Antwerp and various provincial Belgian towns. He also met Saint-Saëns; years later he played with Saint-Saëns at a concert performance of Saint-Saëns' Polonaise for Two Pianos at the composer's invitation. In Paris he met Mme Dubois, a piano teacher who had been present at his debut recital in Paris. She claimed to have been the last pupil of Chopin*. She told Paderewski how Chopin liked his music played; advice he never forgot. In 1890 he played before Queen Victoria for the first time and made 40 other recital appearances in London. He also toured Britain under the management of Daniel Mayer, and played under Charles Hallé in Manchester and Liverpool.

In 1891 Paderewski, the new lion of the concert platform, was invited to tour the USA; 80 concerts were proposed in a series sponsored by the Steinway Company at a fee guaranteed at $30,000. The tour started in the Carnegie Hall and Paderewski immediately became the idol of his American audiences. The tour was so successful that an extra 27 concerts were arranged, with an appropriate increase in fee. During the next few years he made several more tours of the USA, all brilliantly successful. No longer the little-known artist playing in minor halls, he had been miraculously transformed into the world's highest paid concert pianist. He had also become the pop-star of his day. His tours were like Royal processions; he travelled in style in a private train (with an Érard piano, for practice) and with numerous acolytes. He was met everywhere by stampeding crowds of enthusiasts. In particular, he was the recipient of more female adulation than any pianist since Liszt. Crowds would wait at railway crossings hoping for a glimpse of the hero as his train sped by.

---

* The claim of Mme Camille Dubois (née O'Meara) to be the last pupil of Chopin is substantiated by documentary evidence. She is mentioned in the last letter he ever wrote (to Auguste Franchomme) written on 17th September 1849, a month before his death. He refers to the fact that she had helped him to find new accommodation.

Paderewski did not seek all this publicity for he was a quiet and modest man. But it came to him nevertheless. All he wanted to do was to give the best possible performance on the concert platform. He was well aware of the deficiencies that still remained in his technique but he was a dedicated professional and practised many hours a day to iron them out. It was said that Liszt used to practise ten hours a day, Sauer eight, Anton Rubinstein little, once he had made his name. It was not uncommon for Paderewski to practise 15 or 16 hours a day; in fact he practised almost all the time, at any rate in his younger days, when he was not eating, sleeping or playing in concerts. To a large extent he had to do it to build up his technique and repertoire. He would even practise between courses at meals, or whilst dressing; in fact whenever a minute could be spared.

When presenting new programmes in New York Paderewski would practise through the night. Not wanting to disturb the other residents in his hotel he would go to the Steinway warehouse on the evening before a concert and would practise by gaslight from 10pm until 4am under the inscrutable gaze of his solitary audience, the night-watchman, lucky enough to be present at a private performance by the world's great superstar of the piano. Paderewski would then go back to his hotel and sleep for ten hours. He was then ready to give his evening recital. He took good care of his hands; he would get his valet to massage his fingers one by one, then the palms of his hands, and would soak his hands in very hot water just before a concert to make them warm and supple. His only real relaxation during a busy concert season was playing billiards, which he found particularly soothing both mentally and physically.

Acknowledged as the most famous pianist of his day, it is estimated that Paderewski earned more than $10 million during his career. But he was always generous and gave large sums of money away to deserving causes. Highly intelligent, he mastered five languages and even as a young man he established a reputation as a public speaker and as a wit. He was once to be guest of honour at a party at which another guest was a famous polo player. Paderewski was unavoidably delayed and the hostess prevailed upon the polo player, who could play the piano moderately well, to play whilst the guests were waiting for Paderewski to arrive. Paderewski slipped in unnoticed during the performance. When the man had finished playing, Paderewski made his presence known and praised his performance. "Ah!" said the young man modestly, "It is kind of you to congratulate me but no one is more painfully aware than I of the difference between us." "Not at all", said Paderewski, "the difference isn't so great at all. You are a dear soul who plays polo, while I am a poor Pole who plays solo!"

Paderewski was a phenomenon, the ordinary man's image of what a concert pianist should be. His appearance was striking, characterised by his romantic and noble bearing and his aureole of red-gold hair. His fans, mainly women, were always begging locks of his hair, and much of his mail consisted of such requests. He generally obliged. Someone once said to him, "You give away so much hair you'll soon be bald." Paderewski replied, "Not me - my dog!"

But it wasn't just his appearance that attracted such attention, it was his whole personality. His air of melancholy mystery was magnetic. When he played, his music was emotional but his face was like the Sphinx; white, placid, clear-cut, immobile. His eyes were often closed as he played. He hypnotised his audience by his indefinable personal appeal. And at the conclusion of his performance he gave his famous bows. It was said that no young girl fresh from a school of deportment bowed half so gracefully as Paderewski. If you had asked a man or woman in the street to name the world's greatest pianist they would have said "Paderewski".

In fact, he was not the greatest pianist in the world for there were others technically more gifted. His fellow musicians ranked several pianists higher than Paderewski in terms of technical ability although he was the most famous of them all. His performances could be glitteringly brilliant, but he was apt to slow down in difficult passages and would sometimes simplify the music to a level he could cope with adequately, a practice common at the time. When Moriz Rosenthal was asked after one of Paderewski's recitals what he thought of his playing he said, "He plays well, I suppose, but he's no Paderewski." This sums up Paderewski's status. He was the greatest name in concert pianists and to the ordinary concert-goer it mattered little whether or not he had the best technique. Audiences went to hear and see Paderewski the personality - the idol. Cynics said that whilst the critics counted his wrong notes, Paderewski counted the dollars.

In 1897, when Paderewski was 36 and at the height of his powers, Robert Newman took the bold step of engaging him at an enormous fee for an orchestral concert at the Queen's Hall in London. Newman's venture paid off, and he engaged the famous artist for a piano recital as well, for which Paderewski was paid a fee of 1000 guineas. Paderewski's drawing power was such that Newman still made a profit of £200 on the recital. Henry Wood, conductor at the Queen's Hall concert, recalled his meeting with Paderewski and described how he was struck by his magnetic personality and his quiet, forceful, but utterly dignified bearing. Wood contrasted Paderewski with Pachmann; Pachmann, on the concert platform, was always aware of people and things, especially of his audience, whereas

Paderewski's whole attention was fixed on the orchestra.

At Henry Wood's rehearsal of the Schumann Concerto with Paderewski, the pianist asked, in his usual courteous manner, "Mr. Wood, would you permit me to suggest that you move your first clarinet to a position where I can see him?" Wood made the requested adjustment, and in the performance Paderewski appeared to devote himself, according to Wood, to "accompanying" the flute, oboe and clarinet solos of the concerto. Wood said he did not think he had ever heard those sections of the work played in the same beautiful manner since, and remarked how gratifying it was to him as a conductor that Paderewski took such trouble to obtain a perfect ensemble. Paderewski never looked for glory.

Paderewski the solo pianist was a different man. Wood remarked that "The brilliance and force of his octave playing were electrifying; his almost overpowering tone in the left hand was something I shall never forget." In one of his encores at the Queen's Hall concert, an arrangement of *The Erl King*, Paderewski's left hand was "almost a miracle", according to Wood. In Schumann's *Warum?* the conductor noted Paderewski's "lovely singing tone". Paderewski was always able to tailor his playing to the demands of the particular music in his wide-ranging repertoire.

Henry Wood, in his autobiography, told a story which shed light on Paderewski's humility and magnanimity as a man. When Wood conducted for him at the Queen's Hall concert referred to above, Wood's father, then getting on in years, was present in the audience. He had told someone previously that he would like to meet Paderewski one day if it were possible and this had somehow reached the ears of the great pianist. After saying complimentary things to Wood about his conducting at the end of the concert, Paderewski said he had heard that Wood's father would like to meet him. So Mr Wood senior was brought. Paderewski shook his hand and said how honoured and pleased he was to have met him, and congratulated him on having such a son. Henry Wood's father was deeply moved by this and told a friend afterwards, "Of all the great artists appearing at Queen's Hall, possibly not one ever gave a thought or wondered whether Henry ever *had* a father - except Paderewski, the greatest of them all."

Paderewski impressed many leading musicians apart from Henry Wood. Saint-Saëns said of him, "He is a genius who plays the piano." Mark Hambourg said that, as a musician, Paderewski shone alone in his eyes. Edwin Fischer remarked that his real musical education began the day he first heard Paderewski play. Aldrich, the famous critic, told of "a beauty of line as well as of colour and atmosphere, a poignancy of phrase, a quality of tone, a lyrical accent such, so it seemed, as to make his playing something never till then divined."

In May 1899 Paderewski married for a second time. The marriage was to Mme Helena Gorska, Baroness de Rosen, recently divorced from her husband. He had known her for years; she was a friend not only of Paderewski himself but as a young woman (Helena de Rosen) she had been a friend of Antonina, his first wife. Indeed, legend has it that as Antonina lay dying she entrusted the upbringing of their new-born infant to Helena. Whether or not that is true, it is a fact that it was Mme Gorska who did in fact bring up Paderewski's son, Alfred. Not long after his marriage to Mme Gorska the tragic event that had been half expected for years occurred. Alfred Paderewski, who from his birth had never been well, died in 1901, aged 20, when Paderewski was away on a concert tour of Spain.

From the time of his first American tour Paderewski's fame was assured, but the many exhausting tours inevitably made heavy demands on his health and stamina. In one period of 117 days he played in 107 concerts and attended 86 dinner parties, all in an era when travel was slow and hazardous. In spite of all his endeavours to keep fit and fresh, the incessant travelling and the vast number of concerts eventually took their toll and the situation was made worse at one stage by an injury to the tendons in an arm and hand which threatened to put his career in jeopardy. For these reasons he grew weary of the life of the travelling virtuoso and in the years 1900 to 1910 he gradually cut down on his concert appearances. Instead he devoted himself more and more to teaching, and also to composition, which was his professed primary interest, as it was in the case of several brilliant pianists. Consequently he devoted less time to practice and his concert reviews became less complimentary than previously. By 1910 he had given up playing in public almost completely, at any rate for the time being. His distaste for the piano at that stage was so intense that he used to ask his pupil Ernest Schelling to deputise for him in recitals.

As a young man, Paderewski the pianist had been a brilliant success, possibly the most successful of all time - especially as far as the general public was concerned. What of Paderewski the composer? His Minuet in G, Op. 14, No. 1, composed when he was a young man of 25 was, and remains, his most famous piece. It is one of a set of Six Humoresques for Piano. The generally-accepted list of Paderewski's compositions runs from Opus 1 to Opus 21, with an un-numbered Impromptu in addition. His most important compositions are his Piano Concerto in A minor, Op. 17, his Polish Fantasy for piano and orchestra, and an opera in three acts, *Manru*, from a Polish text by Alfred Nossig. The story was based on the novel *A Hut Behind the Village* by Kraszewski, a famous Polish writer, and dealt with life of Tatra mountaineers. The opera received its debut performance in Dresden on 29th May 1901 where it was an immediate success, and on 14th February 1902 it was performed at the Metropolitan Opera House, New York. In the same season (1901-2) it was also presented in Philadelphia, Boston, Pittsburgh, Chicago and Baltimore. However, it gradually dropped out of the repertoire.

Paderewski's Piano Concerto is now heard only rarely; this contrasts with its popularity when he was a relatively young man, for at the turn of the century it was one of the most-played piano concertos in the western world. The remainder of Paderewski's compositions consist of miscellaneous pieces for piano, violin and piano, and a number of songs. It is a pity that from his list of tuneful compositions all that is ever performed nowadays or heard on radio, apart from the rare exception, is Minuet in G.

Most of Paderewski's life was devoted to music and he had little time for leisure, but one interest he developed whilst still a young man was livestock. This came about through his numerous purchases of estates and farms. He became quite an authority on cattle and pigs and would talk to farmers on the subject for hours. There is a story that he once bought some pigs in Ireland to be sent to his estate in Switzerland. The following week the Irish farmer took another batch of similar pigs to market and someone complained to him that they were too thin. "They must be good", said the farmer. "Only last week I sold some of the same lot to Mr Paderewski, the famous Polish pig-dealer."

Livestock was not the only 'outside interest' that Paderewski had. In the period 1900-1910 when he gradually, though temporarily, almost gave up his career as a concert pianist in favour of composition, his attention turned more and more towards politics, for he was a great patriot and Poland, harassed by its neighbours for generations, was in turmoil. In 1910 he gave the money for the creation of a monument at Grünwald (commemorating a great Polish victory over the Teuton knights in 1410) and supervised its design. At the unveiling of the monument he made an impassioned patriotic speech of great impact which marked him as a man of character, vision and stature and enhanced his reputation as a fine orator.

In the war years which followed, events confirmed Paderewski's patriotism to be of a tougher texture than that of the artist who idealises his country in music but does little else. He devoted himself to raising money for the Polish Victims' Relief Fund by his performances in America, and made more than 300 speeches for the cause of an independent Poland. It was largely due to his persistent and untiring efforts in placing his country's claims before the allies that Poland was re-created as an independent nation by the Treaty of Versailles. His arrival in Poland was followed by a triumphant reception in Warsaw. In 1919 he became Prime Minister (not President as is sometimes said) and Minister of Foreign Affairs of the first government of Independent Poland, the first internationally-known musician to become Prime Minister of his country. There is a story, probably apocryphal, that at the Versailles Treaty Conference in 1919 the veteran French statesman, Clemenceau, then Prime Minister of France, said to Paderewski, "You, a famous pianist - a Prime Minister! What a comedown!"

But Paderewski was not really a politician at heart; essentially he was a patriot who, because of his fame, eloquence and the ardour of his patriotism, had been diverted into affairs of state. With Poland re-created he had no need or wish to continue with the day-to-day affairs of running his country and in 1920, his political aims achieved, he retired from politics and devoted himself again, at the age of nearly 60, to his interrupted career of concert pianist, having apparently rediscovered his enthusiasm for playing in public. He had bought himself a home at Morges, Switzerland in 1896 and also one in Paso Robles, California in 1914. From these bases he toured Europe, the USA and many other countries of the world through the 1920s and 1930s. He continued to be as highly paid as any other artist but he gave away vast sums of money for the endowment of scholarships and other charitable causes, and consequently from 1918 onwards he was never as wealthy as he had been before the war. In 1932, for example, he played to an audience of 16,000 in Madison Square Gardens, New York, and raised $50,000 for unemployed musicians from that one recital alone. His composing dwindled as the years went by.

On one of Paderewski's Australian tours his wife bought a number of parrots which accompanied them on their tour. One became a particular favourite and lived at the Paderewski home in Switzerland for many years. It used to sit on his foot as he practised, bobbing up and down as he operated the sustaining pedal, crooning, "How beautiful - how beautiful!" It had its uses too, for when unwanted visitors knocked on the door it would shriek from the depths of the house, "Go away - Go away!" The perplexed visitors, not knowing of the parrot, would often slink away, thinking the voice was that of a member of the household.

Naturally Paderewski was in demand as a recording artist, though it was not until 1911, when he was 50, that the first Paderewski discs were cut. They were a set recorded acoustically in Morges for the Gramophone Company and featured music by Chopin (nocturnes, waltzes and a polonaise), Schubert/Liszt (*Hark! Hark! The Lark*) and Paderewski (Minuet in G, Op. 14, No. 1). In 1912 other discs were recorded in Paris and London for The Gramophone Company, and in 1914 and 1917 recordings were made in the United States for the Victor Company. Over the next few years Paderewski recorded more acoustic Victors. By the close of the acoustic recording era in 1924 about 70 titles had been issued of music played by Paderewski. With the introduction of electric recording in 1926 Paderewski's recording career continued for Victor (later RCA Victor) in the United States until 1931. There was then a six-year gap, following which, in 1937 and 1938, the ageing pianist made 16 recordings for HMV at their Abbey Road studios in London. When Paderewski made his last recording on 15th November 1938 he was nearly 79 years old and the number of his recordings made by the electrical process was about equal to the number recorded in earlier years by the acoustic method.

It is a pity that electric recording, which was able to produce such an immense improvement in sound quality as compared with the earlier acoustic process, did not become available until he was about 65 years old. It is a generally accepted fact that at this stage of his career his technique was less reliable than in former years. The authors' disc of Minuet in G which he recorded in 1938 is spattered with wrong notes; nevertheless it still provides a hint of the majestic quality of Paderewski's playing. Paderewski's records always sold well, for as far as the general public was concerned he was always the world's greatest concert pianist. His emergence during and after the First World War as a major political figure and statesman enhanced his aura of greatness still further, so inevitably the commercial success of his records was assured. In the 1937-38 HMV catalogue 19 Paderewski 78rpm discs were available for purchase - and this was before his final HMV records had been made. In 1953, 11 discs were still on offer in the HMV standard catalogue (all 78rpm) and even today many of his recordings, re-issued on CD, are available.

Running parallel with Paderewski's gramophone recording career was his recording work for various manufacturers of reproducing piano rolls. For the Aeolian Company's Duo-Art system he recorded over 30 rolls, featuring music by Beethoven, Chopin, Liszt, Mendelssohn, Schubert and six rolls of Paderewski's own compositions (Caprice, Op. 14, No. 3; *Chants du Voyageur*, Op. 8, No. 3; *Cracovienne Fantastique*, Op. 14, No. 6; *Légende*, Op. 16, No. 1; Minuet, Op. 14, No. 1 and Nocturne, Op. 16, No. 4). Four of these Duo-Art recordings (on five rolls) were adapted by Ampico and issued by that company. For the Welte Company he recorded about 15 rolls, of music by Beethoven, Chopin (7 rolls), Liszt, Paderewski himself (Minuet in G; and Nocturne, Op. 16, No. 4), and Schubert. He also recorded at least eight rolls for Artecho; Beethoven (1 roll), Chopin (4), Paderewski (Minuet in G; and Nocturne, Op. 16, No. 4) and Schubert's Impromptu, Op. 142, No. 3 (*Rosamunde*) which he also recorded for Duo-Art and Welte.

Paderewski's playing on these rolls is very characteristic of his general style. It may be criticised on the grounds of the liberties he took with the tempo, a characteristic common to many pianists of his era. Also, some critics used to say that Paderewski never put both hands down on the keys at the same time, the left hand generally preceding the right. But in spite of the occasional idiosyncrasy we find Paderewski's performances interesting and enjoyable; he does not carry eccentricity to contrived lengths which would spoil the music. He had a fine sense of style, and some of his personality seems to come through in the music. The fine legacy of music that Paderewski recorded on piano rolls is of course free from the crackle and hiss of early gramophone recordings. It is a reminder of a pianist who had personality, dignity and glamour. Amongst his many achievements he helped to bring about the immense popularity of the player piano through his roll recordings. The use of his famous name was perhaps the most valuable advertisement that the player piano industry could have had.

On his concert tours Paderewski used to travel with two pianos, a grand for the performances and an upright for practice, and the same tuner travelled with him for thirty years. He always played Steinways in the USA except for two years before the First World War when he had an argument with the Steinway firm and played Webers instead. In Europe he often used Érards.

Paderewski was such an eminent figure in the musical world that honours and distinctions were bestowed on him by many universities and institutions. His generosity in devoting the proceeds of his work in the Great War to war charities had been universally commended and after a series of recitals given for the British Legion in 1925 he was created Knight Commander of the British Empire. Paderewski's untiring work on behalf of Poland won him great esteem amongst his countrymen. A poor Polish workman once left the equivalent of $50 in his will to Paderewski, with a note saying "All I have I give to you" - a message which deeply moved Paderewski.

From the late 1920s onwards Paderewski's wife, Helena, was unwell, and from the early 1930s she became increasingly senile. Towards the end of her life she was no longer able to tour with him as she had done in the past, but when he was at home he would sit with her for hours, even though she had little idea of what was happening. She died in January 1934, aged 78, and Paderewski arranged for her body to be taken to Paris where it was buried next to that of his son, whom she had brought up as though he had been her own.

In 1936, when Paderewski was in his mid seventies, he starred in a film, *The Moonlight Sonata*, made at Denham Studios, Buckinghamshire. It was shown in the USA as well as in Britain. The idea came from Harold Bauer and others, who felt that, old and frail as Paderewski was, something of his magnetism and grandeur should be preserved on film for posterity. Appearing with him in the film were Marie Tempest and Eric Portman. The plot is somewhat contrived, for the story is essentially a vehicle to enable Paderewski to play the piano. Lengthy sections are devoted to uninterrupted passages of piano music, which include his own Minuet in G, a Chopin impromptu, and the first movement of Beethoven's *Moonlight* Sonata. When the film was completed Paderewski spent much of the period 1936 to 1938 supervising the preparation of a complete edition of Chopin's works, published by the Chopin Institute in Warsaw.

Paderewski's last tour of Britain was in 1938, and it was then that Fred Gaisberg of HMV persuaded him to make a few more records for his company, though Gaisberg was well aware he was no longer the pianist of his earlier years. Paderewski was now in his late seventies and walked, with difficulty, with the aid of a stick. But on the concert platform, though his performances were by now erratic, he could still move his audiences by the dignity of his playing. He retained the power to produce a performance more sensuously exciting and intellectually satisfying, than almost anyone else. His personality still shone through. His last tour of the USA began in 1939, but petered out after he suffered a mild heart attack in May of that year.

The outbreak of the Second World War in 1939 grieved and depressed him. After the invasion of Poland by Germany and Russia, the second time it had been invaded in his lifetime, he joined the Polish Government in Exile in Angers, France, and was appointed 'Speaker' of its parliament (equivalent to President) on 23rd January 1940. He immediately resumed his efforts on behalf not only of Poland but also Great Britain and Greece, making many inspiring speeches in spite of his advanced age.

But the famous musician was now weak and tired. The efforts he was making proved too much, and he died on 29th June 1941 at the Buckingham Hotel, New York, following an attack of pneumonia. He was 80. His body lay in state at the hotel and hundreds of people filed past his coffin. He was given a State Funeral at the Arlington National Cemetery on the orders of President Roosevelt who said he would lie there "until Poland is free". It is sad that Paderewski's last sight of the world was one in which tyranny appeared to have the upper hand and his beloved country, Poland was once again overrun.

Ignace Paderewski

With the collapse of the Soviet bloc in the late 1980s it was finally decided that Poland was a free country once again, and early in 1992 it was announced that Paderewski's body would at last be repatriated. The proposed exhumation was not to everyone's liking and there were protests at the Arlington Cemetery by demonstrators who felt that he should be left to lie in peace. However, the objections were to no avail; his body was taken to Poland and another State Funeral took place on Sunday, 5th July 1992 at St. John's Cathedral, Warsaw. This was the cathedral where Paderewski had married for the second time in May 1899. His re-burial in Poland was seen by many as a fitting finale for a great musician and statesman.

So ends the story of one of the most remarkable pianists of all time - and a remarkable personality. He beguiled his audiences by the charisma of his presence and the beauty and majesty of his interpretations. He spoke a new language in music, introducing, in his youth, a poetry and a romantic eloquence hitherto unknown. Above all, as a statesman and as a man, he was one of the great figures of his generation.

Great Pianists of the Golden Age

Moriz Rosenthal

5. Moriz Rosenthal

Two great pianists of the Golden Age earned the nickname of 'The Little Giant of the Keyboard'. One was Eugen d'Albert, the diminutive, tetchy, brilliant Beethoven specialist, the third husband of the formidable Teresa Carreño and sometime husband of five other women. The other was Moriz Rosenthal, short and stocky but of powerful build, moustached, possessing an amazing technique which, allied to his intellectual gifts, made him one of the foremost pianists of his era. Like so many of his generation he enjoyed an astonishingly long career - in his case more than sixty years. He began under the tutelage of Liszt when the 19th century still had over 20 years to run, and was still active after the Second World War ended. This gifted pianist truly spanned the whole period from the romantic to the modern age in music.

Like the great Chopin and the legendary Paderewski, Moriz Rosenthal was born in Poland. His parents were Jewish. His mother, Auguste, gave birth to the future pianist on 18th December 1862 in Lemberg (now called Lwow) where his father was a professor at the Academy. Young Moriz was soon allowed to try his hand at playing the family's piano. However, formal piano studies did not begin until he was eight years old when lessons were arranged with a local man named Golath. He was easy-going; his pupils were allowed to improvise, modulate and transpose as they wished. Little attention was paid to discipline and technique. Moriz was playing Beethoven before he learned the rudiments of correct fingering; some pedants would say his playing could have been ruined completely, but fortunately, due to his own inborn ability, it was not.

After nearly two years of lessons with Golath, 10-year old Moriz entered the Lemberg Conservatory and was taught by Karol Mikuli, the Director. Mikuli, a former pupil of Chopin, was so impressed by his new pupil that within a few months of his arrival at the Conservatory, Moriz and his teacher appeared in a joint public recital playing Chopin's Rondo in C for Two Pianos. Progress under Mikuli's direction continued apace and after a couple of years had elapsed it was obvious that the boy's talent was truly exceptional. In order to further his musical studies the family moved to Vienna in 1875 when Moriz was 13. There he became a pupil of the celebrated Hungarian pianist Rafael Joseffy, himself only 23, later to achieve fame and fortune in the USA. Joseffy had been a pupil of the brilliant pianist and composer Tausig, and of Liszt. In the early 1870s he was being hailed as the successor to Tausig, who had died of typhus in 1871 at the age of 30. A disciple of Tausig, Joseffy taught according to the 'Tausig method', which he instilled into the youthful Moriz Rosenthal.

Joseffy's efforts bore rich fruit, for Moriz's talents blossomed to such an extent that an official debut concert was arranged for him in Vienna in 1876 when he was not quite 14 years old. He played Beethoven's 32 Variations, Chopin's F minor Concerto, and some pieces by Liszt and Mendelssohn. Franz Liszt, king of 19th century pianists, was present and warmly praised Moriz's performance. "There is within you a great pianist who will surely work his way out", he said. Immediately after this concert a tour of Rumania was arranged, and in Bucharest this lad of 14 was appointed Court Pianist, a position of high-sounding status but carrying few duties, and in no way interfering with his education.

After this debut recital which had so impressed Liszt, Moriz Rosenthal was accepted into the much-envied ranks of Liszt's pupils as possibly the youngest of the great man's disciples. Rosenthal wrote later:

"His highly encouraging prognostication" [this was after the debut recital] "sounded to me like a magic word, which seemed to open wide for me the door of art and of the future; and I followed him, the great magician, to Weimar, Rome and Tivoli."

It might have seemed that Moriz was set for several years of uninterrupted study under the great master, Liszt. He did in fact study with him in Weimar and Rome from 1876 until 1878, in which year he made concert appearances (billed as Liszt's pupil) in Warsaw, Paris and St. Petersburg. But Moriz Rosenthal's remarkable talents were not just in the field of music. He was a person of sensitivity and intelligence, well-read even in his youth. He had always been very interested in literature; his favourite poet was Heine and it was said he could recite any of Heine's poems if given the first line. Wisely he resolved to withdraw temporarily from the concert platform in order to devote himself to aspects of his education other than music. After his successful concerts of 1878 he enrolled as a student of philosophy and aesthetics at the University of Vienna and was awarded a Master of Arts degree four years later. Although he was temporarily absent from the concert platform during this period he kept up his piano studies throughout and maintained contact with Liszt, who was to remain his adviser until 1886 when the great man died.

After graduation from Vienna University, Moriz Rosenthal diligently prepared himself for re-emergence as a concert pianist, knowing that now he was an adult much would be expected of him. His new debut following six years of absence was in 1884, and he caused amazement by his marvellous technique and seemingly endless physical endurance. His impact on the musical scene in Europe was immediate and devastating; he appeared in Vienna, Leipzig and other major cities in rapid succession and was recognised immediately as a musician of the first rank. One of his recitals in 1884 was attended by Eduard Hanslick (1825-1904), one of the first fully professional music critics, who contributed to the *Weimar Zeitung*. Hanslick wrote vividly of his impressions:

"In his unprepossessing outward appearance Moriz Rosenthal recalls Tausig. Nor is that the end of the similarity. He also resembles Tausig in the extraordinary brilliance of his playing. Through many years of acquaintance with modern piano virtuosity I have almost forgotten what it is to be astonished, but I found young Rosenthal's achievements indeed astonishing. His technique scorns the most incredible difficulties, his strength and endurance the most inordinate demands. I need recall only two offerings which, in respect of technical difficulties, represent the ultimate in the piano literature: Liszt's *Don Juan Fantasie* (which he played for the first time with the uncut ending) and Brahms's Variations on a Theme of Paganini, Opus 35. In this last piece, Brahms, not content with the obvious tests of dextral strength and velocity, has added latent (particularly rhythmic) difficulties hardly perceptible to the listener but enough to drive the player to despair."

"The Paganini Variations (on the last of the twenty-four Capriccios) suggest a bold campaign of discovery and conquest in the field of piano virtuosity, an experiment in the capacities and possibilities of the instrument. To report that Rosenthal mastered them faultlessly, and with utter security and freedom, is to rank him automatically among the first pianists of the time. Less satisfactory was his performance of Schumann's Novellette, No. 2. The element of virtuosity was intrusive, not only by way of fast tempi, but also by way of certain liberties (slighting of certain notes, separation of melodically related notes and phrases, etc.) which here and there gave a stilted effect to the melodious middle section. I was unfavourably impressed, also, by too frequent recourse to the pedals and by the unlovely violence with which the keys were pounded in fortissimo passages. And yet, these are details characteristic of all the youngsters of the Liszt-Tausig school. Such impetuosity may well subside with the years, as it did with Liszt and Tausig, and make way for more tenderness and warmth. Rosenthal's modest bearing and his quiet and unaffected manner at the piano merit special praise."

From those early days in 1884 when some critics pronounced that he was the greatest living pianist in the world in terms of technique, Rosenthal's standing as a first-class pianist was assured. His attributes were vitality, power, physical endurance and accuracy. There were still defects in his playing, as indicated by Hanslick, but they would be ironed out as he grew in experience. He continued to receive advice from Liszt as the old man's life drew to a close, but after his death Rosenthal was on his own and ready to begin his career in earnest.

Engagements were not long in coming. Rosenthal was soon snapped up for more tours of various European cities and in 1888 a tour of the USA was arranged in which Rosenthal was to play in numerous concerts. In some of them he was supported by the 13 year old Viennese violinist Fritz Kreisler whose fee was $50 for each performance. Rosenthal was accompanied on his tour by an orchestra conducted by the youthful Walter Damrosch, later to become the highly respected conductor of the New York Symphony Orchestra. Rosenthal was only 25, a year younger than Damrosch, when he made his American debut in Boston on 9th November 1888, a performance followed up four days later by his New York debut at Steinway Hall. The critics were immediately enthusiastic, reports referring to him as "a thunderbolt", "a giant of ability" and "the perfect pianist". The success of this and subsequent performances of Rosenthal on his tour of the USA in 1888-89 assured him of a place amongst the great international pianists of his day, and set the pattern of his life which was to continue into old age.

Rosenthal's success, achieved whilst he was still in his twenties, brought him rich financial rewards and acclaim in high places. The appointment of the teenage Rosenthal to be Court Musician to the royal family in Rumania has already been noted. Only a few years later, a similar accolade was bestowed when he became Concert Pianist to the venerable Emperor Franz Josef I of Austria, in whose country Rosenthal was spending much of his time.

The young Rosenthal always made a great impression on those hearing him for the first time. In 1889 Josef Hofmann, then a 13 year old boy prodigy, heard Rosenthal, who would then have been 26, in Berlin. "He was *terrific*", wrote Hofmann later, "and I started pounding the piano at our Berlin home for six hours daily, trying to imitate Rosenthal."

There must have been a musical gene in the Rosenthal family, for seven months after Moriz's birth his cousin, Fannie Blumenfeld, was born in Austria. Her parents emigrated with her to Chicago when she was five and took the name Bloomfield, but Fannie went back to Austria as a 15 year old to study with Leschetizky in Vienna (he called her "my little electric wonder") and became a brilliant pianist. At the age of 22, back home in America, she married a Chicago lawyer, Sigmund Zeisler, and thereafter, as Fannie Bloomfield Zeisler, started to achieve great success only a year or two after Moriz Rosenthal's early triumphs. She later enjoyed a distinguished career as a concert pianist and indeed, was recognised as one of the outstanding pianists of her time.

It would be pointless to catalogue Moriz Rosenthal's tours, for his life was spent in journeying through Europe, Britain, the USA and other parts of the world. Suffice it to say that his London debut was in 1895 under Hans Richter, after which he became a familiar and regular visitor to London and other British cities. After tours of the USA in 1888, 1896, 1898 and 1906 Rosenthal did not tour there again until 1923, a gap of 17 years. His visits to America then became more frequent and by 1938 he had made 12 major tours of the USA.

Rosenthal, along with the other famous pianists of his generation, was obliged to spend much of his time travelling, and recalled that in one tour of the United States he played in 126 concerts, and in the month of March of that year, 30 of the 31 nights in the month were spent in railway sleeping cars. Many pianists would have been burned out at an early age by such exploits but Rosenthal was blest by a constitution like an ox, and the short, stocky figure with the Kaiser Wilhelm moustache was able to take it all in his stride.

The life of the travelling virtuoso suited Rosenthal and it was not long before he had mastered a large repertoire, though his favourite composers were always Beethoven and Chopin. Much of his life was naturally spent in hotels and to enable him to practise without disturbing other residents he always took a practise keyboard with him on his travels. This was a rather thin, simple affair which he propped up between two chairs. It was hinged in the middle so as to fold up in order to be tucked away in a trunk or travelling case. It had no regulated action or "touch" and was silent except for the clatter of the keys. It had been specially made for Rosenthal according to his specification.

Henry Wood remarked that Rosenthal hated any kind of extraneous noise:

"Whenever he went to an hotel he would take stock of his surroundings with the greatest care. Perhaps he would see a pair of child's shoes outside the bedroom next to his. "That won't do!" he would say to himself. "I can't have children next to me!" Off he would go to the manager and demand that his room be changed forthwith. He has even been known to preserve asylum in this respect by taking four rooms beside his own. He was very smart in this because he made his own room the central one, taking those above, below and to either side. At one time he had a mania for taking his own supply of drinking water which he carried about in a huge leathern bag of sufficient size to take at least two gallons."

Rosenthal's claim to fame as a virtuoso pianist was his colossal technique, equal to that of any of his contemporaries. Anton Rubinstein, the great master pianist, once said, "I never knew what technique was until I heard Rosenthal." It is therefore worthwhile to consider the views of his contemporaries on his abilities. One observer wrote:

"Rosenthal possesses a stupendous technique equal to anything. His peculiar temperament, sometimes hard but never lean in its expression of musical truths, readily lends itself to the grandiloquent, the magnificent, the sonorous, the nobility in decoration, and all that is lofty and sublimated in pure thought."

An American critic detected defects in Rosenthal's playing:

"He misses, or rather neglects, the softer, serener side of art. There is no twilight in his playing, yet he controls every nuance of the piano palette. Pachmann and Rosenthal can draw from the instrument remarkably varied tonal qualities. Rosenthal's tone is the thunderbolt, Pachmann's like a rose leaf; yet Rosenthal, because of sheer power, can whisper quite as poetically as the Russian."

Those views were written early in the present century when Rosenthal's playing did indeed still suggest "thunderbolts", when it was noted for sheer power rather than finesse. But Hanslick was right to suggest that Rosenthal's playing would mellow as he grew older. It did precisely that; as he passed into middle age and beyond he thundered less, and progressed instead to developing beauty of tone and perfect phrasing. The result was a more balanced performance than that of his impetuous youth. In his later years contemporaries said that he developed a dynamic range from an exquisite pianissimo to a mezzoforte. So, from his early days as a brilliant, fiery virtuoso technician, Rosenthal underwent a metamorphosis that eventually transformed him into a masterful musician known for his sensitive tonal balance and sustained phrasing.

Rosenthal became one of the finest interpreters of Chopin's music. He excelled also in Beethoven, Schubert and certain modern composers, though he was choosy about which modern works he would play. Indeed, his views on modern music were definite and forthright. In an interview with Harriette Brower in the USA in the 1920s Rosenthal said:

"I am sometimes asked if I am in sympathy with modern music and if it finds a place on my programmes. If 'modern music' really means ultra-modern music, I answer emphatically in the negative. Much of this extremely modern so-called music is poor stuff indeed, lacking in form, shape, melody and harmony. It amazes me that such distortion and cacophony can be set down and performed in the name of music, and that people should ever consider it seriously. There are a few modern composers who have put forth some interesting music for the piano. I play some Scriabin, though not his later compositions. I also play some Albéniz and Debussy, though not a great deal of the latter. But there are worthy works that are unknown, simply for lack of public interest, or of the manager's either. To mention one composer whose work is little known as yet, is to speak of the Polish master, Xaver Scharwenka. He has written several concertos which are excellent, but they are seldom heard, and are quite unknown in America. I consider them finer than the Saint-Saëns concertos. I have proposed the Fourth Concerto by Scharwenka to orchestral leaders here, but they refuse to put it on their programmes. I suppose they don't want to take time to study a new work of that kind."

As a pianist noted for his remarkable technique, Rosenthal was often asked to advise young pianists on how they should study. His views are summarised in the same interview with Harriette Brower:

"First of all, I am not favourable to a great deal of time being given to finger exercises, so called. They can be interminably repeated, *ad nauseam*, without intelligence and without imagination. Such useless repetition is for many pupils as though they were in a boat, rowing aimlessly about, not knowing whither - having no destination. Young people often take up the study of music with no natural ability and no aim in view. It would be more profitable for such students to undertake some other branch of study, as with no innate ability they will only make a failure of music. It requires both intelligence and imagination to grasp technical principles and to work them out."

"A necessity for the pianist is a correct understanding of the legato touch. In reality we seldom find it understood by the general student. Legato does not mean holding one key tightly till the next is struck, although many players think it does. Artistic legato means that the keys are depressed in such a manner and with such a quality of tone that the sounds seem to be connected, even though there may be a very slight separation between them. Imagination here plays a large role in securing the result. In early stages, the pupil should naturally learn principles of touch and movements for arm, wrist and fingers, and how to apply them in trills, scales, chords, arpeggios and octaves."

Rosenthal then went on to detail the various books of studies he recommended for developing the many skills necessary for a concert pianist, in particular those of Czerny, Clementi, Moscheles, Chopin (the two books of Études) and Liszt. All had to be carefully and systematically mastered, in Rosenthal's view, as he when a youth had mastered them himself. His prowess as a mature artist had not come about by chance. Natural ability had been there in abundance but it was coupled with years of structured hard work.

Rosenthal married relatively late in life, for it was not until 1922 that he took this important step. He was then 59 and his bride, Hedwig (Kanner by a former marriage, Loewy by birth) was 13 years his junior. She had a son by her previous marriage. She was a fine pianist, a former pupil of Leschetizky in Vienna and of Rosenthal himself, and a noted piano teacher. After her marriage she taught as Mme Loewy-Rosenthal until her death.

Moriz Rosenthal, an intellectual man as well as a fine pianist, wrote widely on a variety of topics associated with music. His *Reminiscences of*

Liszt give an intimate insight into the character of that remarkable man. His general style of writing was crisp, acerbic and contentious. He often crossed swords with music critics and was forthright in his trenchant comments. He was also noted for his rather caustic wit and could be sarcastic and somewhat scathing about other people, especially musicians. Arthur Shattuck, the pianist, knew him for over 30 years and alleged that in all that time Rosenthal never said a kind word about any of his fellow artists. There are many 'Rosenthal stories', some apocryphal and others told in a variety of versions. Here are a few of them:

When he heard that Artur Schnabel had been rejected by the army on medical grounds Rosenthal said: "Well, what do you expect? No fingers!"

Another story relates to the pianist Bernhard Stavenhagen, a Liszt disciple who limited himself to playing a few works only, priding himself in the perfection of what he did perform rather than in an extensive selection. One evening in the artists' room after a concert in which Stavenhagen played and had had a rousing success, a lady came in and asked him admiringly to write a line or two of music in her autograph album. "Pray, master", she said, "Just write something short." Stavenhagen turned to Moriz Rosenthal who was standing nearby and said, "Well, Moriz, what shall I write that is short and complete?" Rosenthal answered smoothly, "Why not write your repertoire?"

Child prodigies were not spared from Rosenthal's dry wit. Once he was forced to listen to a prodigy and the conversation went thus:

"How old are you?"
"Seven, sir."
"And what would you like to play for me?"
"Please sir, the Tchaikovsky B flat minor Concerto, sir."
"You're too old!"

A few years later, Rosenthal met a former child prodigy, and asked: "Tell me, how old are you still?"

On another occasion Rosenthal was scathing in the condemnation of music of the ultra-modern variety. He remarked of certain contemporary composers, "They know nothing and capitalise on their ignorance."

Rosenthal could never resist a clever jibe, usually directed at his musical colleagues, but he was not a vindictive man and most of his jokes were 'tongue in cheek'. This must have been so, for he numbered several pianists amongst his close friends, including Anton Rubinstein and Mark Hambourg. Referring to Anton Rubinstein, Hambourg wrote of an occasion in his youth when he was invited to play to Rubinstein privately. "He was most encouraging to me, and after I had finished playing he introduced me to his friend Moriz Rosenthal as being "a new star arisen in the pianistic firmament." Hambourg wrote:

"My friendship with Rosenthal, which began then, has remained unimpaired ever since. Rosenthal, although a pupil of Liszt's, was a great admirer of Anton Rubinstein and modelled himself very much on that master's style. As a young man he travelled a good deal with Rubinstein on his concert tours, and he tells interesting stories of the great man's characteristics. I also like a story Rosenthal tells about himself on tour, in connection with Rubinstein. Rosenthal was engaged to play at some very insignificant little town, and someone said to him as he was proceeding to the concert hall, "I suppose you do not give yourself much trouble about how to play in a twopenny-halfpenny town like this one, as no-one in the audience is likely to know whether you are playing indifferently or superlatively." Rosenthal went on to the platform, looked at the small provincial audience assembled to hear him, and wondered if it really did matter how he played. Luckily he was in a good mood and gave of his best. When the concert was over, someone who had been in the audience sent in his card to congratulate the pianist. On the card was written 'Anton Rubinstein'. "So you see", said Rosenthal, "one never does know who may be at the concert, criticising one's performance, even in the most insignificant place." Rosenthal's immense technical powers created a sensation, and he is without doubt one of the outstanding representative pianists of the post-Lisztian era."

Again referring to his friendship with Rosenthal, Hambourg wrote:

"Amongst all the pianists I knew I had two dear friends, Moriz Rosenthal and Ferruccio Busoni. Moriz was erudite and an astonishing technician. He could simulate anything on the piano by the power of his brain. He genuinely loved the piano, it was his spiritual home, and he was never happy except when playing."

Hambourg also mentioned Rosenthal when writing about the strain of a concert pianist's life:

"Playing as much as 120 times a year as I have to do, with the accompanying travelling and anxiety, is wearing to the nerves, and there is no hard and fast axiom how to meet this strain. I can never eat anything before playing, but Moriz Rosenthal used to stuff himself up with a couple of steaks before a concert. He said that he could not play on an empty stomach."

There is a story that Rosenthal once went into a restaurant and ordered three helpings of steak. Growing restless when the order failed to arrive, he asked the waiter why it had not been served. "I'm waiting for your two guests to arrive, sir", he replied. "I have no guests!" thundered Rosenthal. "Those are for me!"

Moriz Rosenthal visited Britain many times and often played in the Henry Wood Promenade Concerts. Rosenthal impressed Wood in a variety of ways, as Wood recalled in his autobiography published in 1938. He observed:

"A pianist for whom I had the profoundest respect was Moriz Rosenthal who came to us in 1909 to play the Chopin E minor and the Liszt E flat major Concertos. He had an extraordinary technique and always fascinated me whenever I looked at his hands. He held them in such a position that even his clear octaves *looked* as though he were striking chords; and yet nothing except the octaves sounded, for his playing was crystal clear. I accompanied the same Chopin concerto for him at Huddersfield three years ago and again noticed the same characteristic."

"I always persuaded Rosenthal to play his arrangement of Johann Strauss's waltzes, which were really paraphrases but most masterly and ingenious. I admire their cleverness, for Rosenthal brings out the melody of one of them with his left hand somewhere in the tenor register and superimposes the melody of another up in the treble."

Like most first-rate pianists, Rosenthal devoted some of his considerable talent to composition, and a small array of interesting pieces of his adorns the music shelves. Some of them were in the 'salon' style but are of extreme technical difficulty. His *Papillons* is well-known, as are his arrangements of Johann Strauss's music in *Wiener Carnaval* (*Carnaval de Viènne*) and a paraphrase of *Blue Danube* which Wood referred to. His compositions also included Variations on a Single Theme, a Romance, and several études and preludes for the piano. He also wrote, jointly with Ludvig Schytte, a Danish pianist and composer, a treatise on the technique of playing the piano entitled *Schule des Höheren Klavierspiels*, a classic book which has been translated into several languages. Like other master technicians such as Godowsky, Rosenthal spent a lot of time analysing the problems of technique, and his mastery of the subject stood him in good stead as a teacher. When not on tour he had a large clientèle of pupils, some of whom, after his marriage, also had lessons with his wife.

Rosenthal made many gramophone records but pre-dating them all are a number of piano roll recordings he made for the Ampico Company when he was in his mid sixties. About a dozen titles were released including a Chopin Étude (Op. 25, No. 6 in G sharp minor); a Chopin Waltz (Op. 42 in A flat); and the same composer's *Chant Polonaise* (Op. 74, No. 5); two of Mendelssohn's Songs Without Words (Op. 19, No. 1 in E, and Op. 62, No. 30 (*Spring Song*)); and Anton Rubinstein's Valse Caprice in E flat. Also included are Handel's *Harmonious Blacksmith* Variations, and pieces by Bortkiewicz and Albéniz. Completing the recordings are some of Rosenthal's own compositions, namely *Carnaval de Viènne*, *Papillons*, and Prelude in F sharp minor. These piano rolls were made when Rosenthal was at his best as a pianist and can still be enjoyed today on reproducing pianos throughout the world. As an added bonus, several of these piano roll recordings were re-issued a few years ago on long-playing discs by L'Oiseau-Lyre as a tribute to the artistry of Rosenthal. Ampico was the only company for whom Rosenthal recorded piano rolls.

Outnumbering Rosenthal's fine Ampico recordings were those he made for the gramophone. He recorded about 60 tracks altogether, all of standard length, which in those days was about 3½ to 5 minutes. Rosenthal arrived late on the recording scene. It was not until 8th May 1928 that he cut his first disc, his own arrangement of Strauss's *Blue Danube* Waltz, which occupied both sides of a 12-inch Victor record. In one way it is fortunate that Rosenthal delayed his entry into the recording studio, for by 1928 electric recording had become standard and consequently the quality of recordings was then reasonably acceptable. On the other hand, Rosenthal was 65 years old at that time, and though still acknowledged as a fine pianist, the edge might have gone slightly from his playing as compared with, say, his performance at 50. Nevertheless, many of his discs are impressive.

Rosenthal recorded for five companies: Victor (which became RCA Victor in 1929); Edison; the Lindström Group (Parlophone/Odeon); Ultraphon and HMV. Although Victor and HMV were associated companies, the Victor recordings were American and the HMV ones British. Rosenthal recorded only six tracks for Victor. After his initial recording session for them in 1928, when he recorded his *Blue Danube* Paraphrase, he did not work again for the company until June 1939 when he recorded Handel's *Harmonious Blacksmith* Variations and Chopin's Sonata in B minor, Op. 58. Then, in March 1942, he recorded two Chopin compositions. The six tracks were therefore spread over a 14 year period.

For Edison, Rosenthal recorded four preludes and two études of Chopin in March 1929 for both the normal 'side to side' tracking system and for the company's 'hill and dale' system. He also recorded a Chopin Nocturne, Op. 9, No. 2 in E flat. His discs for the Lindström Group, which comprised his largest batch of work for the gramophone, were all made between May 1929 and March 1931 and comprise about 27 tracks of which 21 are of pieces by Chopin, three were of music by Rosenthal or Strauss/Rosenthal, and the others were of Albéniz, Debussy and Liadov. In 1930 three Liszt recordings were made for Ultraphon in Germany and he also recorded Chopin's Berceuse in D flat, Op. 57, for the same company.

Completing Rosenthal's recordings are a set of 19 tracks he made for HMV in London between November 1935 and October 1937, 13 of which are of music by Chopin (mazurkas, nocturnes, preludes and waltzes). These HMV recordings were re-issued in 1987 on LP by Archive Records. The Chopin F minor Prelude and his own Strauss paraphrases are particularly impressive, as is his disc of the Schubert-Liszt *Soirée de Vienne*, No. 6 in A minor. Some of his recordings of the waltzes and mazurkas of Chopin, dating from the 1930s, also testify to the unerring skill of the old pianist. Several of his recordings have been re-issued on compact disc.

Amongst Rosenthal's gramophone disc recordings there is only one piano concerto. It is the Chopin Concerto No. 1 in E minor, Op. 11, which was recorded for the Lindström Group during sessions in November 1930 and March 1931. At that time the practice of issuing truncated versions of major works in order to fit onto a small number of discs had largely ceased. This Chopin work lasts about 40 minutes and to accommodate it Rosenthal's recording was issued in the curious format of 3 ten-inch and two twelve-inch discs.

Rosenthal made all his recordings between the ages of 65 and 79. Compared with the tiny number of recordings made by some of the earlier pianists in this book, Rosenthal's recorded output of 60 tracks seems quite prolific. In reality very little of his time was spent in recording. His Victors were recorded on four separate days; the Edison records were made in two or possibly three days; the 27 Lindström tracks occupied about seven days; the Ultraphone one or two days; and the 19 HMV tracks were recorded on nine separate days. Thus, all his recordings were made in about 25 days. Clearly, recordings comprised an infinitesimally minute fraction of Rosenthal's life's work. And yet this is the only tangible evidence on disc by which his playing can now be judged! The same can be said of his piano roll recordings; they too will have involved only a handful of recording sessions. Similar considerations apply to the recorded work of most of the earlier pianists in this book. Modern pianists spend a significant fraction of their working lives in the recording studio and record a vast amount of music but it was not so for the pianists of Rosenthal's era.

Moriz Rosenthal and his wife resided in Austria for many years, but it was not a suitable or safe place for a Jewish pianist in the 1930s. As Hitler's machinations grew ever more menacing the Rosenthals decided to move to the United States, where Moriz had spent so much time on tour in the past, and they took up residence there in 1938. At the age of 75 Rosenthal could have been forgiven for receding quietly into the background, but that was not his way of doing things. Though old, he was a stickler for physical fitness and still visited his local gymnasium, where he used to skip and lift weights. The retired operatic bass Herman Devries reviewed a Rosenthal recital at that time and remarked: "The 75 year old musical Hercules is the wonder of the age, for the fountain of youth flows from fingers that know neither difficulties nor fatigue."

There was still plenty of life in the old musician. For the next few years, as the Second World War raged, he taught in Chicago and at the Curtis Institute in Philadelphia and still gave concerts occasionally, the last of Liszt's pupils still to be playing professionally. Meanwhile his wife continued in her well-established teaching practice. The couple lived in New York during the war and it was there, on 3rd September 1946, that Moriz Rosenthal's long and active life came to an end. He had not been in good health for two or three years but had been confined to bed for only a week when he died at his apartment in the Great Northern Hotel at the age of 83.

Thus ended the life of one of the world's legendary pianists, a man talented in literature as well as music, acknowledged as one of the most technically brilliant keyboard masters of his generation.

Rosenthal's wife, Hedwig, continued working as a piano teacher after her husband's death until she herself died in Asheville, North Carolina in 1959, also aged 83, whilst visiting her son by her former marriage; he was Dr Oscar Kanner, then Chief Pathologist at the Veterans' Administration Hospital in Oteem, North Carolina. Her obituary was printed in *The New York Times*. By a macabre quirk this was the second time it had been printed, for in 1956 a woman purporting to be her niece had submitted information regarding her 'death' to *The New York Times* which printed an obituary. To the time of her death she lived and taught at the Great Northern Hotel where her husband had died 13 years earlier.

Ferruccio Busoni

6. Ferruccio Busoni

If we had to decide who was the greatest pianist of all time, surely one of the chief contenders to the title would be Ferruccio Busoni. For nearly 20 years at the beginning of the present century he towered above almost all his contemporaries in terms of technique and many believed his powers exceeded those of his idol, Liszt. Associated with his unparalleled pianistic brilliance was a deep understanding of music. He was a giant of the keyboard whose extraordinary ability set new standards in piano playing.

Ferruccio Dante Michelangiolo Benvenuto Busoni was born on 1st April 1866 at Empoli, half way between Pisa and Florence, in Italy. Not surprisingly, he dropped all but the first of his Christian names later in life. His father, Ferdinando, was a talented virtuoso clarinetist but was volatile and wayward in his lifestyle. His mother, Anna (née Weiss) who was of German ancestry, was a very good pianist and was much in demand as a private teacher for young ladies. She included a Mozart and a Weber concerto in her repertoire. The couple had met when both appeared at the same concert in Trieste in May 1865, and were married soon afterwards. Following their marriage they toured together and Anna played in the presence of Liszt in Rome in March 1866; immediately afterwards Ferdinando rushed Anna home for her confinement and Ferruccio was born a week after the concert. After his marriage, Ferdinando called himself Weiss-Busoni for a time, believing that this would enhance the concert opportunities for both himself and his wife. Because of their touring commitments young Ferruccio was left in the care of relatives for much of the time and for several years received little formal schooling. Most of his earliest years were spent in Trieste with his grandfather Weiss who was a widower, and with an aunt. The Busoni grandparents had been dead for several years.

By 1868 the musical travels of Ferdinando and Anna had taken them to Paris, where they did well, and Ferruccio at last came to live with them. Whilst there he showed, even at the age of two, a propensity towards music. In January 1869 Anna wrote to a niece: "You should see Ferruccio at the pianoforte and how he puts those dear little hands on the keyboard. He tries to imitate me and plays scales and glissandos." When he was four Anna wrote:

"He sits at the pianoforte like an angel, and holds his violin as if he had been practising for three years. He has a little toy flute too, on which he accompanies my pieces, and it is astonishing how he feels the expression of the movement. He is all music, and when he hears a beautiful melody he dances and jumps for joy and is quite beside himself. How you would laugh if you saw him!"

No wonder the ladies of Paris admired the talented little boy with pink cheeks, blue eyes and golden curls.

When rumours grew of an impending war the Busonis left Paris and went to Trieste, but Ferruccio continued to spend much of his time with relatives. His parents often went separate ways, partly because of their different concert engagements and partly because of their somewhat incompatible temperaments. Nevertheless Ferdinando was shrewd enough to realise that Ferruccio's talent for music was quite exceptional and for a time took charge of the boy's tuition himself. It would perhaps have been better if his mother, a pianist, had done it. Ferruccio wrote years later:

"My father knew little about the pianoforte and was erratic in rhythm, so he made up for these shortcomings with an indescribable combination of energy, severity and pedantry. For four hours a day he would sit by me at the pianoforte with an eye on every note and every finger. There was no escape and no interruption except for his explosions of temper, which were violent in the extreme. A box on the ears would be followed by copious tears, accompanied by reproaches, threats and terrifying prophecies, after which the scene would end in a great display of paternal emotion, assurances that it was all for my good, and so on to a final reconciliation - the whole story beginning again the next day."

At seven and a half years of age Ferruccio made his public debut in Trieste, playing a movement from a Mozart sonata, Schumann's *Povero Orfanello* and a Clementi sonatina, amongst other pieces. He had already started to compose, and from those early years to the end of his life he maintained that composition was the truest form of self-expression.

Ferruccio had little settled home life; his parents were constantly coming and going, but from six years of age he went to school and a sound education was added to his musical proficiency, His travels had helped him to achieve an early mastery of the French and German languages in addition to his native Italian. One feature of his father's eccentric tuition which stood Ferruccio in good stead, as he generously pointed out later, was a rigorous study of Bach, and he was to become a world authority on Bach's music. At the age of nine he was playing the Mozart C minor Concerto in public (reports said "with much delicacy and precision") and in the autumn of 1875 Ferdinando took the boy to Vienna where they met Anton Rubinstein, premier pianist of the day, and heard Brahms play. Later Ferruccio wrote:

"He considered me mature enough to take me to Vienna as pianist, composer and improviser, shielded under the sonorous name of Ferruccio Benvenuto Weiss-Busoni; not forgetting to take his clarinet with him too, but otherwise with hardly enough means to make his way."

In the autumn of 1875 Ferruccio entered the Vienna Conservatory as a pupil. The intention was that he should study there for five years, but he soon concluded that his teachers were not interested in him and that he learned more from his father, with all his faults, than from them. His studies at the Conservatory were thus short-lived and he resumed his previous mode of life, in which his father's tuition was punctuated by regular public appearances as a child pianist. Under this regime he developed rapidly and he was further helped by the fact that in Vienna there was plenty of opportunity to attend operas and concerts.

Ferruccio bought and studied the musical scores of operas, and he composed perpetually. It had been suggested that he should return to the Vienna Conservatory to study counterpoint but his father thought him too young. As it happened, counterpoint seemed to come to him naturally. In a letter written when he was 10 he said:

"I am starting to arrange my Overture for Orchestra and it will soon be finished, I hope. We got a gentleman to come over who knows counterpoint and he said that all the parts were well fitted and well written. As soon as it is written I will send it to you for four hands and in score."

Following a recital in Vienna in 1876, at which he included some of his own compositions, the 10 year old boy wonder became ill and had to return to Trieste, but after a spell in the country near Salzburg he was able to return to Vienna late in 1876. In March 1877 Liszt came to Vienna for the commemoration of the 50th anniversary of Beethoven's death. Ferruccio heard Liszt (then 66) play the Beethoven E flat Concerto but the performance fell well short of the level of brilliance he had expected. Liszt had by then virtually retired as a concert pianist and appeared in public only on rare occasions, by special request. In addition, he had injured his left hand before the concert and played the concerto without using his left forefinger at all. Later someone arranged an introduction and young Busoni played before the Master at the rooms of Liszt's cousin, where the pianist was staying. Unfortunately no account of the meeting has survived.

Later in 1877 Ferruccio's progress was once again interrupted by illness. This time he contracted diphtheria and it took him a long time to recover. Eventually his health returned and during the next four or five years his prowess as a pianist and musician became increasingly evident. Indeed, he was being talked of as a second Mozart and in 1880, through the kindness of a wealthy patron, he was able to study composition for a year at Graz. The following year, when he was 15, he passed the examination which enabled the Academia Filarmonica of Bologna, founded in 1666, to confer upon him its diploma for composition and piano playing. No composer since Mozart, who had received this honour at the age of 14, had achieved it at so early an age. In the same year as this award, Ferruccio made a successful concert tour of Italy.

From Ferruccio's early childhood his father had assumed that the boy would be a 'comfort' to himself and his wife, in other words, that he would keep them financially. By 1881 Ferdinando's clarinet playing had deteriorated and it was generally expected from then on that Ferruccio's duty was to support his parents. Indeed to a large extent he did until 1909 when both parents died. But his talents and enforced lifestyle had deprived him of a normal childhood and adolescence. He had lived entirely in a world of music; there had been few contacts with other children and his life had been rather lonely. He was a voracious reader and a witty letter writer; even as a young child he had been able to give interesting written accounts of the situations in which he found himself. This ability stayed with him throughout his life.

By the age of 18 Busoni had matured into a brilliant pianist. He was well-known in Vienna and in other parts of Europe and was on good terms with Anton Rubinstein, Brahms, Richter, d'Albert and a host of other successful musicians of the day. At 20 he had established himself on his own in Vienna, without his father, and was in great demand. In addition, his composition was flourishing. When he was 20 he met Grieg, Mahler and Delius, who was his contemporary. But loneliness was still a problem. In 1886 he wrote from Leipzig where he was playing and studying:

"Here I have not made a single friend who is on my own level. There are two who learn from me, so I get nothing from them except the pleasure of watching their progress under my teaching. That is the worst of precocious talent - one cannot associate with people of one's own age, and older people do not wish to associate with me - hence complete isolation! If I had not the gift of being able to adapt myself for the moment to other people, which does no harm now and then, for after all man is here to be with other men - I might well spend the whole of my life in utter solitude!"

Busoni solved the problem by buying himself a dog, 'Lesko', a black Newfoundland bitch, of which he grew very fond. Much of the money he earned in concerts and recitals was sent to his father, who was always in debt. Ferdinando used to tot up his son's earnings and complained if he was apparently not sent enough. In addition, Ferdinando was often an embarrassment to his son in other ways; he had a very quick temper and made enemies wherever he went, which was not much help to a son seeking to establish himself in a musical career. In spite of these family problems Ferruccio's career as a concert pianist prospered and he often played in Vienna, Leipzig and other European cities.

Ferruccio Busoni

In 1888, when he was 22, Ferruccio received, and accepted, the offer of a post as a teacher of the pianoforte at Helsingfors in Finland. One of the students at the time was Sibelius, who was a few months older than Busoni. The Conservatory turned out to be of poor standard musically and Ferruccio was so disappointed that he left after a year, but the appointment had one very happy outcome. Whilst there he met Gerda Sjöstrand, the daughter of a Swedish sculptor who had settled in Helsingfors. It seems to have been a case of love almost at first sight, for the couple were engaged a few days after they met and were married the following year, despite disapproval from the Busoni parents who saw their son's first duty as being to them. The marriage was uncloudedly happy from the start and was to be blest with two sons, Benvenuto (Benni) born in 1892, and Raffaello (Lello) born in 1900. Ferruccio was devoted to his sons; they were a joy to him throughout his life. Both had a talent for art, as indeed had their father, and later became professional artists.

At the time of his appointment to the Helsingfors post Ferruccio was a pianist outstanding enough to be known throughout the musical circles of Europe. Two years later, in 1890, he won the Rubinstein Prize for Composition at its first adjudication. Many of the judges thought that he should also have won the Prize for Piano Playing, but Rubinstein had decreed that as it was the first time the prizes were to be awarded, one at least of them had to be given to a Russian. Consequently the pianoforte prize went to a pianist named Dubassov of whom little was heard later. Five years later the prizes were awarded for a second time with Busoni as a member of the jury. Vassily Safonoff, then Director of the Moscow Conservatory, made a speech describing the first award. At one stage he pointed to Busoni, saying, "Here stands the man who ought to have received both prizes."

After winning the Rubinstein Prize in 1890 Busoni took up an appointment at the Moscow Conservatory. But he was not happy there; some of the staff were jealous of him and disliked having a foreigner in their midst. Moreover, the Busonis' lodgings were poor and dirty and he felt cut off from western culture. So, when an offer came of a teaching post in the New England Conservatory in Boston, Massachusetts in 1891, he accepted gratefully and resigned his Moscow post. Added attractions were that his old friend Arthur Nikisch was the conductor of the Boston Symphony Orchestra and his stipend was to be three times what he had earned in Moscow - an important consideration, for Ferruccio's father was again in debt.

It was whilst the Busonis were in Boston that Benni was born, an event that brought them much happiness. But they did not stay long in Boston for he disliked the routine teaching chores demanded by the post. In 1892 they moved to New York so that Ferruccio could concentrate on playing and he gave 40 concerts in the USA and Canada. In 1894 Busoni and his family returned to Europe and settled in Berlin, which he considered to be a good centre for a concert pianist, as Teresa Carreño had done a few years earlier. Berlin remained his home for most of the rest of his life, though he made further visits to the USA in 1904, 1910, 1911 and 1915, and toured Europe frequently, including Britain. At the turn of the century, when he was still only 33, he was universally acclaimed as a supreme pianist with a technique unsurpassed by anyone else at that time.

By then Busoni's musical preferences had crystallised. Though capable of playing anything set before him (he could sight-read amazingly difficult compositions) and though he possessed a large and wide-ranging repertoire, his preferences were, and remained, the music of Bach, Liszt and the later compositions of his fellow-Italian, Verdi. He made a deep and scholarly study of the music of Bach and transcribed many of Bach's organ works for the piano. These transcriptions are extremely effective and faithful to the spirit of the music. He often played these Bach-Busoni transcriptions at his recitals and Gerda was sometimes teasingly referred to as Mrs Bach-Busoni. He promoted Liszt's music, much of it hitherto little-played, with missionary zeal. His devotion to the music of Liszt, which was constant throughout his career, was not merely the result of the admiration of one virtuoso pianist for another of an earlier age - it was a genuine respect for Liszt's compositions.

Surprisingly, Busoni disliked the music of Schumann, and respected only some of Chopin's compositions. He disliked the valses and mazurkas, which he felt to be trite and inconsequential, but liked some of the études and had a particular regard for the preludes. As he grew older he came to understand and love the music of Mozart, some of whose concertos became regular items in his concert programmes. He wrote his own cadenzas for several of the concertos, though their form is perhaps more akin to the style of Busoni than Mozart and in recent years they have fallen into musical disfavour for that reason.

In 1901 Busoni was invited to start Master Classes for young pianists of exceptional promise and these took place at Weimar in the Eastern part of Germany, thus carrying on the tradition of Liszt who had a long association with the town. In New England Busoni had soon become weary of the dreary routine of teaching in the Conservatory, but in Weimar it was different; there were many gifted students and he enjoyed the stimulus of teaching eager and enthusiastic musicians. Later he gave Master Classes in other European cities. They became an important feature of his musical life and many notable pianists of the future were numbered amongst his students at various times, including Alexander Brailowsky, Rudolf Ganz, Percy Grainger and Egon Petri.

Busoni's first concert visit to London was in 1897 and the city enthralled him at once. Many more visits to Britain followed in subsequent years and he regularly played in Manchester, Nottingham and Glasgow. On his frequent visits to Manchester he used to stay with his friend and former pupil Egon Petri, another famous concert pianist who was then Professor at the Royal Manchester College of Music. He had known the Petri family, all of whom were musicians, from his early days in Leipzig, and he had known Egon since he was five. At home in Berlin the Busoni house was always open to visiting musicians and to his own pupils. Gerda Busoni was a charming hostess and though Ferruccio himself did not like social events he was a genial host in his own home. The atmosphere was enhanced by the two Busoni boys who were full of life and popular with visitors. Busoni's extensive travellings, recitals and musical writing left him little time for other interests but he liked walking and, in common with some of the other pianists in this book, he enjoyed a game of billiards. When he was appearing in major cities he liked to walk through the back streets to observe the humbler aspects of city life. He had a good sense of humour and used to dissolve into peals of laughter at anything he thought was funny.

The first dozen years of the new century marked the high plateau of Busoni's career as pianist, composer, music scholar and conductor, a role in which he was becoming increasingly famous. Concert engagements continued worldwide and musical compositions poured out, whilst his two great works of musical scholarship, the annotated editions of the music of Bach and Liszt, were internationally respected. Life continued in this happy vein until 1913 when Busoni decided to return to his native Italy, accepting a post at the Liceo Rossini (a music college) in Bologna. Busoni by then regarded himself as the leader of Italian music, which indeed he was, and thought that his return home would be a symbolic act. But the archaic and fossilised atmosphere at the Liceo, with its cold, lofty halls and relics of the past, such as Rossini's wig in a glass case, did not suit him and he soon returned to Berlin.

Following the outbreak of war, Busoni sailed for the USA in January 1915 to begin his fifth tour there. America gave him its usual warm welcome and six famous pianists were present at his first concert; they were Harold Bauer, Carl Friedberg, Percy Grainger, Mark Hambourg, Joseph Hofmann and Rafael Joseffy. He did not stay long in the USA and soon set sail for Europe, leaving behind Benni, then aged 23, who had dual Italian/

United States nationality, having been born in Boston. Later Benni enlisted in the United States forces when that country entered the war. Busoni's short and unsatisfactory sojourn in Italy had provided him with as much as he wanted to see of his native land and he decided to live in Zurich, as did several other leading musicians at that time. He remained there until 1920, when he returned to Berlin to a position of honour and a hero's welcome.

In any survey of Busoni's life and musical career, his work as a composer cannot be ignored. It has already been noted that he had composed from childhood, and as he grew older his work in this field became increasingly important to him. Indeed, like many other famous pianists before and since, he regarded his composition as being as important as his piano playing, if not more so. As far as his compositions were concerned his career could be split into three phases. In the first, which lasted until about 1890 when he was 23, he composed a lot, though later he regarded his work of that period as belonging to his formative years and not always of high quality. From about 1890 to 1900 he composed very little, concentrating on his career as a pianist, and it was in those years that the full flower of his pianistic genius blossomed. Finally, from 1900 until the end of his life, he turned again to composition, but combined it with his concert career as a pianist and conductor, and with his literary output, for he wrote a vast number of scholarly articles, essays and treatises on musical subjects. It is from this third period that most of the compositions for which he is now remembered date. Amongst his musical offerings were a large number of pieces for solo piano, for two pianos, a piano concerto, a clarinet concerto, much chamber music, songs, and many arrangements of the works of other composers, in particular his famous transcriptions of the music of Bach, Beethoven and others.

The most important works in Busoni's long list of musical compositions were four operas, including *Doktor Faust*, on which he worked intermittently for about ten years, and which was uncompleted at his death. 'Faust' as a subject had of course attracted the attention of other composers previously and was a character who fascinated Busoni. He felt he had affinities with Faust and from about 1913 became obsessed with the project, working on it whenever he could spare time from his many other commitments. Work was frequently interrupted, often for long periods, and it sometimes seemed that he would abandon the opera completely. But its magic always reasserted its hold on Busoni and the opera is probably his most profound composition. Busoni wrote the libretto as well as the musical score. He regarded the work as his spiritual legacy. After his death it was completed by his friend and pupil, Philipp Jarnach.

Busoni, then, was a man of many talents; as composer, teacher, conductor and musical scholar. But though these were notable facets of his brilliant career, it was as a pianist that he achieved most distinction in his lifetime. It is instructive to read the many contemporary accounts of Busoni's playing and from them to discern the special gifts that made him a unique pianist. Busoni's musical colleagues were unanimous in their view that his talents were quite extraordinary. One of the features that distinguished his playing from that of his contemporaries was his ability to 'bring out' themes from complex music in which various tunes were occurring simultaneously - a skill which gave the music an orchestral quality and which founded a new school of piano playing. Moreover, his power and accuracy were phenomenal. Percy Grainger once said of him:

"I cannot recall ever seeing or hearing Busoni play a wrong note. He did not seem to 'feel' his way about the keyboard by touching adjacent notes - as most of us do - he smacked the keys right in the middle."

Other experts waxed lyrical in their praise of Busoni as a pianist. His attributes of literacy and scholarliness were reflected in his performances at the keyboard. From the turn of the century he was said by many to have the most powerful individuality and the greatest technical mastery since Liszt. But, great interpreter that he was, he never displayed his virtuosity for its own sake, but always made sure it remained subservient to his powerful intellect and cultured mind. His playing of complex music with multiple themes was astonishingly clear and bold, and this dazzling brilliance was complemented by a fascinating elegance and precision in his ornamental work. Coupled to all this, according to Henry Wood, was an amazing skill in the use of the sustaining pedal. This enabled him to create marvels of sound such as have never been heard before or since.

It is a pity that Busoni was born a little too early to have made much impact as a recording artist, at least as far as the gramophone is concerned. Most of his only known recordings are thought to have been made on the same day, 27th February 1922, when he recorded a number of pieces for the Columbia Company in London. Chopin was represented in four pieces: Étude in G flat, Op. 10, No. 5; Prelude in A, Op. 28, No. 7; Nocturne in F sharp, Op. 15, No. 2; and Étude in E minor, Op. 25, No. 5. The other compositions were Bach's Prelude and Fugue, No. 1, from *Well Tempered Clavier*, Book 1; Bach-Busoni, Organ Prelude, *Rejoice Beloved Christians*; Beethoven-Busoni, Écossaises; and finally, Liszt's Hungarian Rhapsody, No. 13 (abridged). A disc of the Liszt-Gounod *Faust* Waltz was also recorded, possibly at an earlier date, but is not thought to have survived. These recordings are quoted in full because of their importance as the sole recorded output on disc of such a great artist. Lucky indeed is the collector who happens to come across any of these in a second-hand shop!

Unfortunately Busoni's recordings, valuable as they are as collectors' items, fail to do justice to this marvellously gifted pianist. They are acoustic recordings, of 'tinny' quality and with a poor dynamic range. Nevertheless, they are better than nothing and we can be thankful that Busoni did leave something behind on disc for posterity. He hated making gramophone records and for good reason. Some idea of the deficiencies of the recording process at that time is indicated in a letter he wrote to his wife :

"My suffering over the toil of making gramophone records came to an end yesterday, after playing for three and a half hours! I feel rather battered today, but it is over . . . Here is an example of what happens. They wanted the *Faust* Waltz (which takes a good ten minutes), *but it was only to take four minutes.* This meant quickly cutting, patching and improvising, so that there should still be some sense left in it, watching the pedal (because it sounds bad); thinking of certain notes which had to be stronger or weaker to please this devilish machine; not letting one's self go for fear of inaccuracies; and being conscious the whole time that every note was going to be there for eternity; how can there be any question of inspiration, freedom, swing or poetry? Enough that yesterday for nine pieces all of four minutes each (half an hour in all) I worked for three and a half hours."

These observations by Busoni make it very obvious why he so hated recording for the gramophone, and may explain why his piano roll recordings outnumbered his gramophone discs. He recorded a total of well over 70 rolls, shared between five different companies. For Welte he recorded about 14 rolls, mainly of music by Beethoven, Chopin and Liszt but including (inevitably!) a Bach-Busoni transcription. He recorded 14 rolls for Hupfeld, which include five rolls of Liszt's music and four of Chopin. Four of these Hupfeld rolls were adapted and issued in the USA by Ampico; they were compositions by Chopin, Liszt (2 rolls) and Verdi-Liszt. About 16 rolls appeared under the Philipps label, including three Bach-Busoni transcriptions, three Beethoven-Busoni ones, and six rolls of Liszt's music. He also recorded eight 4-handed recordings for Philipps jointly with Michael Zadora. These include two compositions of Schubert and three of Schumann. For Artecho, Busoni recorded six rolls; three were of music by Chopin and the other three of Liszt.

But perhaps the most significant of Busoni's piano roll recordings are the 19 or so rolls he made for the Aeolian Company's Duo-Art system. They include a Bach Chaconne (transcribed by Busoni), four compositions of Liszt, and Busoni's most important contribution to the Duo-Art catalogue, his recording of all Chopin's 24 Preludes, issued on 14 rolls. This complete set of the Chopin Preludes gives a hint of the real Busoni. It provides the opportunity to hear him in a series of related compositions by the same composer in music which he was known to like.

A further point worthy of mention is that Busoni's piano roll recordings reflect his musical interests. All the roll companies were anxious to have the 'big names' record for them, and a pianist of Busoni's stature would have been allowed to record what he wanted on roll, rather than what he was told to record. Thus, it is not surprising that an inspection of his list of music recorded on piano roll contains a lot of Beethoven, Chopin and Liszt, as well as his own transcriptions of the music of Bach and others.

After the First World War Busoni continued to give concerts but they were less frequent and the years of travelling and neglect of himself had taken their toll of his health. By 1921, though only 55, he was much aged, and a young musician who saw him for the first time at the Free Trade Hall in Manchester that year said he looked "like a corpse". None of his skill had been lost, however, though he missed his favourite Bechstein piano. At that time Bechstein instruments were not allowed on concert platforms in Britain because of anti-German feeling. Over the next year or two his health continued to deteriorate and his concert performances became even fewer and further between. His last public concert appearance took place on 29th May 1922 in Berlin at which he played the Beethoven E flat Concerto (*The Emperor*). After this his health grew steadily worse and he died in Berlin on 27th July 1924, aged 58. Rumours were rife at the time that he had died as a result of drink and his biographer, Edward Dent, found it necessary to write two pages refuting this accusation, concluding that his death was due to heart and liver disease, probably accelerated by personal neglect.

Busoni's outstanding technical brilliance is legendary. As a pianist he was a transitional figure, brought up in the late Victorian era when pianists felt free to interpret as they pleased and even to change the music when it suited them, but he had the strength of character and the musicianship to move forward the art of piano playing. He was a reluctant virtuoso who always believed that virtuosity should remain subsidiary to interpretation. To all of this he added a wealth of scholarly literary material on the subject of music and a vast number of musical compositions including operas, instrumental and orchestral work, and transcriptions, many of which have received less attention than they probably deserve. He was a remarkable man, a pioneer of the modern technique of piano playing, whose contribution to music should never be forgotten.

Leopold Godowsky

7. Leopold Godowsky

Around the turn of the century, and for a few years afterwards, a small number of pianists travelled the world filling concert halls wherever they went. Paderewski was one, Busoni another, and the subject of this chapter, Leopold Godowsky, was a third. Whilst Paderewski was the shining star as far as the general public was concerned, Godowsky was very highly regarded by his fellow pianists who respected and admired his technique and prodigious skill. Godowsky was sometimes referred to as "the pianist's pianist" because of the awe in which he was held by the other giants of the concert platform. As a composer his music was noted for its extreme difficulty, and as a musical scholar he was amongst the masters of his day.

Leopold Godowsky was born in Wilna, Poland (now part of Russia) on 13th February 1870, the son of Jewish parents, Mathew and Anna Godowsky. Mathew Godowsky was a physician in Wilna and would have been able to provide Leopold with a stable and financially sound upbringing, but whilst Leopold was still a baby Mathew died, leaving Anna to bring up the family in far from prosperous circumstances. The infant Leopold soon started to play the piano at his uncle's piano shop, and in common with other famous pianists of his generation, showed an early talent, to such an extent that it was soon reckoned that he was destined for a career in music. One story tells that at three years of age he heard the local regimental band play a selection from Flotow's *Martha*; a year later he played it correctly on the piano, not having heard it again in the meantime, and not at that stage having had any instruction.

At the age of seven Leopold was composing industriously, and at nine he gave his first official recital in his native town. Its success was so emphatic that a tour of Germany and Poland was hurriedly arranged. Leopold was legally being looked after by a guardian, and it seemed that in his early teenage years his progress might be marred by the exploitation of his undoubted talent. But at 13 he was saved from this fate by the generosity of a Königsberg banker, Herr Feinberg, who recognised in Leopold a potential genius, and arranged to finance his studies at the Hochschule in Berlin.

Leopold was nearly 14 when he went to Berlin, and for the next few months he studied under various teachers including, according to some sources, the famous violinist Joseph Joachim. This tuition ended when another tour was arranged for him, this time to the United States; it was probably felt that this was an opportunity to gain experience that could not be refused. In America he toured with singers Clara Louise Kellogg and

Emma Thursby, both fine singers who were very well-known in their day. Leopold then made a tour of Canada with the celebrated Belgian violinist, Ovide Musin. At the conclusion of his Canadian tour Leopold returned to Europe.

Word of the young pianist's talent had by this time reached the ears of the famous French musician Camille Saint-Saëns, and for the next three years he took young Leopold under his wing in Paris. To be the protégé of such a distinguished man must have benefited Leopold, but later in life he tried to discount Saint-Saëns' contribution, perhaps being proud of his reputation of being virtually a self-made musician. In 1924 he told an interviewer, when recalling his early years:

"I went to Paris and played a good deal for Saint-Saëns, though he did not give me any lessons. When I played for him, even my own compositions, he would invariably say, "Mais, c'est charmant!", or "Admirable!", or "Épatant, mon cher!" or something of the same sort, and even though spoken from the heart, this hardly amounts to constructive criticism."

So Leopold had no important teachers, according to his own account, and the comments of Saint-Saëns in what could be considered to be individual 'Master Classes' were allegedly so uncritical that his claim to be self-taught was probably true. From the beginning young Leopold was a great student of the piano and its technique, and most of what he knew he had worked out for himself.

After the period with Saint-Saëns, which lasted from 1887 when he was 17 to 1890, Leopold was on his own. A very accomplished pianist at 20, he already had the talent and the technical knowledge to earn himself a good living as a pianist and teacher. America was the land of great opportunity for a young musician and after his departure from Paris he took a teaching post in New York. In 1891 he met and married an American called Frieda Saxe, and took American nationality. For the next ten years, and then again later in his life, the United States was to be his home. He stayed in New York until 1894 and then became Director of the Piano Department at the Broad Street Conservatory of Music in Philadelphia from 1894 to 1895 and then moved to the Chicago Conservatory of Music where he was Director of the Piano Department from 1895 to 1900. He was still only in his twenties but these teaching posts gave him the opportunity to continue with his concert tours. These were a great success and in consequence, as he travelled around giving concerts and recitals, his fame steadily grew.

In 1900 Godowsky returned to Europe and on 6th December of that year he made a spectacular debut in Berlin. The Berlin recital was sensational. In a letter written by Godowsky 18 days later he said:

"I was greatly astonished to find that I was well known among German pianists and teachers, though many of the musical public knew nothing of my existence ... The Beethoven Hall was crowded and all the Berlin pianists were at the concert ... I played the [Chopin] Study for the left hand alone. To describe the noise after this Study would be impossible. The tremendous ovation was overwhelming."

Referring to the response of the audience to other items on the programme, Godowsky wrote:

"The success was greater than anything I have ever witnessed, not excepting a Paderewski enthusiasm. I could have repeated everything, but I did not care to have the concert too long. To tell how many times I had to come out after the paraphrases would be impossible. I could not count them. Pianists like Pachmann, Josef Weiss, Hambourg and the entire audience actually went mad. They were screaming like wild beasts, waving handkerchiefs, etc ... The scene in the artist's room will never be forgotten by those who witnessed it. People almost suffocated in the mad rush to meet me. Mrs Godowsky and some friends could only reach me by going on stage and through the stage door. All criticisms are so wonderful that I am told nobody ever got such notices. My success is the most sensational within the recollection of all musicians."

So Godowsky paints a picture of a scene of triumph, and he was not exaggerating for the report was corroborated by contemporary accounts. Godowsky had conquered Berlin, and for the next few years he gave several recitals there each season. His big rival in Berlin was Busoni, the Italian who had settled there and strode like a colossus over the Berlin musical scene. He too gave recitals equal in number to those of Godowsky and for several seasons the two strove to outdo each other. Each had a prodigious technique and could play anything placed before them. Teresa Carreño, another wonderfully gifted pianist, was also living in Berlin, but men and women pianists tended not to be regarded as rivals; they were looked upon as being in different categories even if they possessed equal gifts.

Godowsky stayed in Berlin with his wife and family from the time of the Berlin recital triumph until 1909 when he was offered and accepted an appointment as the Director of the Imperial Royal Meisterschule for Piano at the Imperial Royal Academy of Music in Vienna. This appointment caused a few eyebrows to be raised, for it was unheard of for a Jew to be offered such a post in Vienna. He held the appointment with great distinction for he was an excellent teacher, and the prestige of his standing as a concert pianist added lustre to the post. Apart from Busoni, Poles such as Friedman, Paderewski, Hofmann and Rosenthal had dominated the concert scene for years, and now Godowsky was added to their number, enhancing the national tradition.

Godowsky remained in Vienna until the outbreak of war in 1914, whereupon he resigned his post and returned with his family to the United States where he was to be based for the rest of his life, though from the end of the war onwards he was to make regular concert tours to most parts of the world. The triumphant Berlin recital described earlier, with its Paderewski-style adulation, probably marked the peak of Godowsky's career as far as his concert appearances were concerned, though he remained in the top rank of artists for many years.

Godowsky always said that he played at his best on the concert platform, stimulated by his audiences. That might have been true in his youth, when he probably had the capacity and inclination to play to the gallery, but it seemed to many of his contemporaries that as time progressed he became less able to do himself justice on the concert platform, or even in the recording studio, though not because of any falling-away in ability. He became preoccupied with technical perfection and his concert performances were somewhat restrained as a result. It was as though he was so obsessed with perfection that he was determined to play well within himself in public recitals for fear of making a mistake. After a Godowsky recital in London, Bernard Shaw, in his role of music critic, referred to "a certain shyness" about Godowsky's performance, at the same time praising his undoubted technical brilliance. His colleagues who knew his real genius regretted this inhibition.

Those who knew Godowsky and had the knowledge to judge all agreed that none of his later public performances, or even the recordings that he made, were able to match the freedom and beauty of his playing in an intimate atmosphere, in the presence only of his friends and colleagues, many of whom were big names in the world of music. Inhibitions were then put aside and his playing was superlative. Josef Hofmann once said to the pianist Abram Chasins as they left Godowsky's home, "Never forget what you heard tonight, never lose the memory of that sound. There's nothing like it in this world. It is tragic that the public has never heard Popsy as only he can play."

Godowsky's friends were not all musicians by any means. He had the kind of personality that attracted attention wherever he went and it was said of him that no musician was more capable of gathering around him creative companions in so many fields of work.

As a student of the technique of playing the piano, Godowsky not only mastered existing principles but considerably advanced them, and it was this original contribution which merited for him a reputation as an innovator. He was scientific in outlook and developed his own method of 'weight and relaxation', applying it to his playing to become an outstanding performer and extending the potentialities of the instrument. He paid particular attention to the left hand, which he felt was the stronger and more elastic of the two, training it to do the work of both hands, thereby leaving the right hand free to do other work. This brought him the nickname of "The Apostle of the Left Hand". Another nickname he acquired was "The Brahma of the Keyboard", for he was short and plump and with his round face and inscrutable Slavic eyes he had something of the appearance of a Buddha.

All the time that Godowsky had been establishing his world-wide reputation as pianist, innovator and musical scholar he had been composing, and by the time he returned to the United States in 1914 his output was large. His works all have two things in common; firstly, with the exception of a very small number of short violin pieces, they were all written for the pianoforte; and secondly, they are all fearfully difficult to play - for they employ the principles he had developed and mastered himself, which enabled one pianist to play virtually as two. This was fine so far as Godowsky himself was concerned. He was a technical master and could play his pieces without difficulty. But such was not the case with other pianists, even good ones.

Perhaps the best known of Godowsky's compositions are his 53 Studies on the Chopin Études. Most pianists would regard Chopin's Études as difficult to play well, but to Godowsky they were far too simple and required elaboration. The Godowsky Studies are really original compositions, not merely transcriptions, and are full of technical merit, though they distort Chopin's originals by piling additional difficulties on them. They combine Chopin's various themes in ingenious counterpoint, a good example being No. 47, entitled *Badinage*, in which he combines the two G-flat Études (the *Black Key* and the *Butterfly*) so that they are played simultaneously in juxtaposition.

Naturally these 'arrangements' by Godowsky brought howls of protest from the purists when they were first published. Critics accused him of making an arrogant attempt to improve on the originals. Godowsky knew that these fantastic exercises pushed piano technique to heights undreamed of even by Liszt, and in one edition of the pieces he defended himself by saying:

"The 53 Studies based on 26 Études of Chopin have manifold purposes. Their aim is to develop the mechanical, technical and musical possibilities of piano playing, to expand the peculiarly adapted nature of the instrument to polyphonic, polyrhythmic and polydynamic work, and to widen its possibilities in tone coloring."

But Godowsky's protestations have fallen largely on deaf ears. For one thing, the present age regards tinkering with Chopin's work as sacrilegious. For another, the pieces are so horrendously difficult as to be self-defeating, if it was Godowsky's aim that they should be played. In Godowsky's own day the Chopin specialist Vladimir de Pachmann floundered when trying to play them, and in spite Pachmann's weirdness and eccentricity, we have to grant that he was a fine pianist. So if Pachmann couldn't play them, how many pianists could? Nowadays very few pianists ever attempt them.

The same kind of criticism applies to most of Godowsky's compositions. He had a talent for transcribing and elaborating the works of others, and such efforts form the main part of his output, 22 of them being for the left hand alone. Apart from the Studies based on the Chopin études his published work included several paraphrases of waltzes by Johann Strauss II, a transcription of Weber's *Invitation To the Dance* (for two pianos, with a part for a third as an optional extra!); *Renaissance* (24 transcriptions from pieces by early composers); *Triakontameron* (30 pieces, one for each day of the month, including the popular *Alt Wien*); *Java Suite* (12 pieces); 46 Miniatures for piano duet; transcriptions of 12 Schubert songs; and transcriptions for the piano of three Bach sonatas written for cello alone. There were numerous other compositions.

Most of Godowsky's music is so strewn with difficulties that it finds little favour with the present generation, which knows Godowsky, if at all, only through his rather sober gramophone records. All the same, many of his pieces, on the rare occasions when they are played, are pleasant to listen to. It has to be admitted that the Chopin transcriptions are clever and interesting. His *Java Suite* gives an evocative portrayal on the piano of chattering Javanese monkeys, and one of the *Renaissance Suite* pieces, a transcription of a gigue by John Baptiste Loeillet (1673-1728) is delightful.

During the 1920s, when he had made his home on the Pacific Coast of the United States, Godowsky gave regular Master Classes and had a very successful teaching practice. As a great student of technique, he was good at diagnosing and rectifying his students' faults. Many very good pianists were taught and he did not restrict himself to those destined for the concert platform. Thomas 'Fats' Waller and James P. Johnson, two famous names from the world of jazz, both came to him for lessons. 'Fats' Waller was Johnson's protégé and was the first of the pair to come to Godowsky for instruction in 'serious' music. He must have found the lessons useful because Johnson came soon afterwards. Godowsky's teaching was interspersed with lengthy concert tours which took him through the United States and to Europe, Canada, Mexico, Cuba, Japan, China, Java, the

Philippines, Hawaii, South America and many other places. His recording activity was also at its height during the 1920s, and in addition to all this, Godowsky somehow found time to write many scholarly articles on music. He also edited numerous editions of music. Some of his writings were concerned with technique (or 'technic' as it was sometimes called), which is not surprising in view of his acknowledged status as an expert on the subject. In an article written for the magazine *The Étude* in 1928 he remarked:

"The finger mechanism is to my mind only a small part of technic; for the word should embrace phrasing, touch, expression, nuance, rhythm and so forth."

In similar vein, he wrote in *The New York Evening World*:

"In playing, sensibility and feelings are of more worth than virtuosity."

Reference has been made to Godowsky's work as a recording artist, and in this sphere his output was prolific. About 120 of his recordings were issued, of which the first 55 (approximately) were made by the acoustic process. As already noted, many experts believe that, with rare exceptions, his records do not do him justice, though some of his discs were extremely successful commercially, especially the Chopin Sonata in B minor, Op. 35, and the Grieg Ballade, Op. 24. All his recordings date from the years of his prime as a pianist. The earliest set of his acoustic recordings were made in 1913 for the Columbia Company in the USA when he was 43. He recorded for Columbia again in 1916 and made records for Brunswick, also in the United States, in 1920, 1921, 1922 and 1924. A great range of composers was represented in these recordings. These acoustic discs were gradually withdrawn from the catalogues once electric recording was introduced, Godowsky's last acoustic recording disappearing from the lists in 1930.

When electric recording was introduced in the mid 1920s, Godowsky's services were again in great demand, and his 65 or so electric recordings all date from the years 1925 to 1930. About 25 of them were made for Brunswick in 1925 and 1926, whilst the rest of his recordings, which include some made for Columbia in London, date from 1928, 1929 and 1930. Some of his discs were issued in many countries under the labels of companies associated with Brunswick and Columbia. A curious fact is that he never recorded a concerto, though there were many in his repertoire and he wrote cadenzas for several.

Although Godowsky recorded so many compositions on disc, the player piano was not neglected and he was in fact as prolific in his recording for that instrument as he was for the gramophone. In all, a total of over 125 of Godowsky's recordings for the reproducing piano were issued, spread between six different company labels. In descending order of the number of rolls recorded, they were Hupfeld, Artrio, Recordo, Ampico, Artecho and

Duo-Art. For Hupfeld, the main recipient of his services, he recorded about 40 rolls, nearly half of which were of the music of Chopin. For the American company which produced rolls under the Artrio label he recorded at least 24 rolls, including five of Chopin's music and four pieces of his own from *Triakontameron*. He also made 24 rolls for Recordo; four were of Chopin's music, four of Godowsky's own compositions, and the remainder were shared between a number of composers. He recorded 21 rolls for Ampico, of which 11 were of music by Chopin, or in some cases adaptations of Chopin. Nine rolls were recorded for Artecho; five were of Chopin's music and the others were of Liszt, Mendelssohn, Ravel and Tchaikovsky (one each). Finally, eight rolls were recorded for the Duo-Art system; Chopin (3 rolls), Henselt (2), and Moszkowski, Rubinstein and Schumann (one each).

Some of Godowsky's Duo-Art rolls were adapted and issued in a cheaper 'hand-played' version, identical to the normal Duo-Art roll except that some of the extra perforations which the reproducing piano required in order to give a true reproduction of the pianist's performance were lacking. This meant that the rolls could be played on an ordinary player piano (a pianola) with the operator putting in the 'expression'. In the hands of a skilled practitioner a close approximation to Godowsky's performance could be obtained by this process. His 'hand-played' standard roll (non Duo-Art) of Chopin's Ballade, Op. 23 was a very popular issue and is a classic that is a favourite in many a collection.

Most pianists who recorded for the player piano would make their recording and then depart at the earliest opportunity, leaving everything else to the editor and the production team. But Godowsky, scientifically minded as he was and a perfectionist into the bargain, interested himself at Ampico (and probably also at the premises of the other companies for whom he recorded) in the details of the roll's production and was glad to assist the roll editor in producing the best possible result in the finished roll.

In the 1920s Godowsky signed an agreement with the Hallet & Davis Piano Company of New York for a series of instructional rolls to be marketed under the 'Angelus' label of their associated company, Wilcox & White. It was Wilcox & White who manufactured the 'Artrio' rolls discussed earlier. The full name of these rolls was the Artrio-Angelus, these being the 'reproducing' version of Wilcox & White's 'standard' Angelus rolls. These special instructional rolls were recorded about the same time as the conventional Artrio-Angelus reproducing rolls and were entitled The New Angelus 'Master and Pupil' rolls. The advertising literature reported in glowing terms:

Leopold Godowsky

"Leopold Godowsky, the master pianist who developed the new teaching method, says of it: 'This is my personal piano instruction system and I am glad to say that the Angelus reproduces my playing with absolute fidelity. It is not designed to wholly teach the pupil but rather to augment the work of the teacher.' 42 of these rolls are included in the complete set, the first issue of which has just been announced, all the compositions by Godowsky, bearing the title *Godowsky Miniatures*. Each is a full length Angelus roll, to be used in the Angelus reproducing piano. Each is arranged to give the pupil the personal instruction of the composer. Each roll will be accompanied by the appropriate sheet music, scored as it would be for any musician and each roll is personally recorded by the great pianist who perfected the system."

"The rolls are divided into three sections. Carefully following the music, the child plays the roll on the Angelus. In the first section, Godowsky plays the entire composition for the student, then (in the second section) the child who is following the instruction plays the treble to accompany the bass which is played by Godowsky. In the third section the situation is reversed, the instructor plays the treble while the child plays the bass. Thus the composition is played by the master's hands, the melody being interwoven as only Godowsky can interweave it, while the child observes, and the roll once played in this fashion the child is free to practise it, following the melody from the notes, observing how it was done by the master pianist. Timing, accent, every feature of playing are shown exactly and carefully by the master; the pupil is forced to improve. It is necessary to play well in the last two parts of the roll, to follow the playing of Godowsky, and having played well each half of the selection the pupil can hardly fail to combine them well, under the very eyes, as it were, of Godowsky himself."

Though the Angelus leaflet claims that the pupil "is forced to improve" the logic of this statement leaves a lot to be desired, and we can think of several reasons why the pupil should not necessarily improve. For one thing, he or she might have little talent or motivation. For another, the fact that the compositions used were Godowsky's own, albeit the easier ones, would seem to apply the kiss of death to the scheme. Something simpler should have been used. However, it was an enterprising experiment at a time of great competition between companies. It is doubtful, however, whether the company benefited much financially, or the terrified pupils musically.

Little has been said so far about Godowsky as a person. The piano seems to have been his life. A reflection of this is that practically all his published compositions, which amounted to over 400, were written for the piano. It must be unique for a composer with such a long list of works to his credit to write almost exclusively for one instrument. To him the piano was everything, and possibly his life was a rather lonely one because of it. He once said, "I love the piano and people who love the piano." In his chosen profession he left nothing to chance. A lady once asked him how he spent the day when he had a concert in the evening. "Madam!" exclaimed Godowsky in horror, "I wouldn't dream of playing in a concert unless I'd practised for eight to ten hours beforehand!" Artur Rubinstein said:

"I couldn't sit eight, ten hours a day at the piano. I lived for every second. Take Godowsky. I was awed. It would take me 500 years to get that kind of mechanism. But where did it get him? He was an unhappy, compulsive man, miserable away from the keyboard. Did he enjoy life? It made me think a bit."

Here we have the opinion of a man who knew Godowsky well, and who paints a picture of someone perhaps driven on relentlessly by his chosen vocation. Godowsky's reputation as a martyr to long hours of practice was corroborated by Mark Hambourg, who wrote:

"Leopold Godowsky (the "Great Little Lep", as we called him on account of his being so small) was a good friend. I used to admire the way he would go on imperturbably practising every day for at least eight hours, while his countless family ran in and out of his room all the time, appealing to him, talking incessantly, yet never seeming to disturb his equanimity, or stop his scales and exercises."

Some of Leopold Godowsky's talent seems to have been passed on to his children. His elder son, Leopold junior, was an accomplished violinist who inherited his father's scientific outlook, and whilst still a student became coinventor of the Technicolor process of cinema photography. He married Frances Gershwin, sister of George and Ira. Leopold senior's daughter Dagmar became a movie actress and appeared in films with Chaplin and Valentino. Another daughter, Vaneta, married the concert pianist David Saperton who was a good interpreter of Godowsky's music.

The 1920s ended in an unfortunate manner for Godowsky as he lost most of his large fortune in the Wall Street Crash of 1929. Nevertheless he was still at the height of his powers and would have been able to make good much of his loss in concert fees, but a tragic blow befell him in 1930 when he suffered a stroke in London whilst fulfilling an engagement to record the four scherzos and all the études of Chopin. He was 60 at the time. This event proved to be catastrophic for it paralysed his right hand and finished his career as a concert pianist. However, true to his nature as a dedicated professional, he determinedly concentrated on developing and improving his left hand technique. It is perhaps ironic that many years earlier he had emphasised the value of the left hand and had written special studies for it. More tragic events were to follow, for two years later his youngest son, Gutram, committed suicide, and shortly afterwards Leopold's wife died.

Although the last few years of his life were sad, he remained active except as a professional pianist. He continued to compose, he edited editions of music, and wrote about music. He died in New York on 21st November 1938, aged 68.

It is now many years since Godowsky died and his career can be viewed in a historical perspective, He was regarded in his day as one of the greatest living pianists. Like Busoni, he was a transcendent technician who worked things out for himself. Neither of them had an important teacher and both were fastidious perfectionists. Godowsky could slave away at the keyboard for hours on end, and after recitals would work through the night to rectify what he considered to be imperfections. Paderewski became the idol of his audiences through the magnetism of his personality rather than the brilliance of his technique. Godowsky did not have that kind of personality, but his fellow pianists considered him to be the supreme artist when he was playing for his friends, and they were the people best able to judge. Rachmaninov, no mean pianist himself, said, "We all sit at Godowsky's feet."

Great Pianists of the Golden Age

Sergei Rachmaninov

8. Sergei Rachmaninov

Sergei Rachmaninov was not the jolliest of musicians in appearance or demeanour. Gloomy and forbidding of countenance, his cold and austere aspect was enough to put off the most fervent of concert goers. But when he started to play all was forgiven. As a wealth of marvellous sounds unfolded his chilly manner was soon forgotten. His stature as a pianist is nowadays all too easily overlooked, for he is remembered mainly for his compositions. But in his day his mastery of the keyboard as a performing artist was legendary, and his playing of his own piano concertos has never been bettered by any other pianist.

Rachmaninov's ancestors came from wealthy, noble Russian families. His father, Vasily, was one of nine children of Arkady Rachmaninov, who was a keen amateur musician and capable pianist, a former pupil of John Field. His mother, Lyubov, was the daughter of Pyotr Butakov, a wealthy army general. Vasily Rachmaninov inherited some of his father's musical ability but none of his business acumen. He spent vast sums of money on personal pleasure and in consequence the family estates he had inherited dwindled year by year. Not surprisingly, this led to domestic arguments and upheavals between himself and Lyubov, for she had a practical temperament. Six children were born to the couple; in order of their birthdates they were Elena, Sofia, Vladimir, Sergei, Varvara (who died as a baby) and Arkady. By the time Sergei arrived most of his mother's dowry had been frittered away in paying his father's debts and it was on one of the last remaining family estates, Semyonova (not Oneg as stated in many reference books) that Sergei Vassilievitch Rachmaninov was born on 1st April 1873. Soon afterwards the family was reduced to a single estate, Oneg, set in beautiful countryside 20 miles from Novgorod, and it was there that Sergei spent his childhood.

It was Sergei's mother who first taught him to play the piano. Later she engaged a professional teacher, Anna Ornatskaya, from St. Petersburg and Sergei studied with her for several years. He also learned to play duets with his grandfather. By 1882 when Sergei was nine his father had succeeded in squandering all the family fortune and it became necessary for Oneg to be sold; the Rachmaninovs then moved into a small flat in St. Petersburg.

In Sergei's lifetime the surname was usually spelt 'Rachmaninoff' or 'Rachmaninof' in the West. Currently 'Rachmaninov' is in favour and is used in this book but some authorities have moved to 'Rakhmaninov'. Similarly, his first name is spelt variously as 'Sergei', 'Sergey' or 'Serge'.

Sergei's elder brother, Vladimir, entered a military academy, thereby easing the family's finances, whilst Sergei, whose musical talents were plain for all to see, was awarded a scholarship to the St. Petersburg Conservatory. There he studied piano with Vladimir Demyansky and later with Gustav Cross, head of the piano class.

Sergei's studies were beset by domestic problems. First the family was stricken with diphtheria. Vladimir, Sergei and Sofia all caught it and were gravely ill. The boys eventually pulled through but Sofia died. On top of this, relations between Sergei's parents had become increasingly strained, and eventually they agreed to separate. Sergei's mother was left to look after the four remaining children in St. Petersburg. Occasionally Sergei's maternal grandmother came over from Novgorod to visit the family. Sergei was her special favourite and, possibly with the talented boy in mind, she bought a small estate near the river Volkhov.

Throughout this period of family upheaval Sergei continued to study as a day pupil at the St. Petersburg Conservatory. His piano playing advanced rapidly and at the same time he studied harmony with Alexander Rubets and attended classes in languages, history, mathematics, Russian, and orthodox doctrine. His musical talent could not be denied, but he was lazy by nature, more interested in games than study, and in his end of term examinations in the spring of 1885 he failed all his general subjects. This was a major calamity, for the Conservatory hinted that musical excellence was not enough; his scholarship might be withdrawn. Sergei's mother realised drastic action was urgently needed if her son's natural musical talents were not to be wasted. Fortunately there was in the family a distinguished relative, one of Sergei's paternal cousins, who could be called upon for advice. He was Alexander Siloti, a former pupil of Liszt and an eminent pianist, who taught at the Moscow Conservatory. He suggested that the best solution was to place Sergei in the hands of his own former teacher, Nikolai Zverev, knowing that he would subject the boy to a regime of strict discipline and hard work. Sergei's chickens had come home to roost!

On Siloti's recommendation Sergei was accepted by Zverev as a pupil and lessons were arranged to begin at the Moscow Conservatory in the autumn of 1885. Sergei viewed the move with apprehension. The one bright aspect of the situation was that his sister Elena would be in Moscow and he would be able to visit her; she was an excellent contralto singer who had been auditioned for and accepted by the Bolshoi Theatre for the 1885-86 season. But fate cruelly intervened, for in the summer of 1885 Elena died of pernicious anaemia before she even moved to Moscow. Thus Sergei embarked on the new and rigorous phase of his life alone. His easy-going ways were in for an abrupt change. Life in Moscow was to be very different from anything he had experienced before.

It was the custom of Zverev and his sister Anna to provide accommodation for some of the Conservatory's pupils, and after a three-day stay at his aunt's home Sergei took up residence in the Zverev apartment. Zverev was an indefatigable worker, who began private lessons at 8 am, taught at the Conservatory from 9 am till 12 noon, and then took more pupils from 2 pm to 10 pm. The regime was equally hard for his pupils. Practice began at 6 am and after Zverev left for the Conservatory the pupils were supervised by Anna. This harsh system was just what Sergei needed. The errant child's technique improved rapidy and he gained a sound general musical knowledge by playing 4-handed arrangements of symphonies with his teachers. He also attended concerts and operas and heard the famous celebrities of the day, such as Anton Rubinstein, in action.

Sergei was fortunate in his musical contacts, for Rubinstein and other famous musicians often visited the Zverev home. On Sunday afternoons the place was an 'open house' for musicians, and visitors included Siloti, Arensky and Tchaikovsky. The pupils used to play for the distinguished guests on these occasions. Whilst living in Moscow with the Zverevs, Sergei was never allowed a holiday, but Zverev used to take all his pupils to his villa near Moscow, which was of course equipped with a piano to ensure that practice did not suffer. Rachmaninov started serious composition at about that time and at 14 he put together a scherzo in D in the style of Mendelssohn for orchestra, and two nocturnes. Other compositions followed but none of these early works was published in Rachmaninov's lifetime.

At the age of 15, in 1888, Rachmaninov moved into the senior class of Alexander Siloti at the Conservatory, though he continued to lodge at the Zverev home. He distinguished himself in his musical studies and at the end of session examinations gained the highest possible grades in theory and composition. He began to take part in student concerts, and continued to compose. Rachmaninov's desire to compose caused a rift with Zverev, because Sergei requested more privacy, away from the sound of practising, so that he could write music undisturbed. Zverev refused to accede, so Sergei went to live with his aunt Varvara at her secluded home near Moscow. There he was able to compose to his heart's content and a large number of compositions were produced at that time though there was nothing of enduring quality. In 1890 Sergei received his first commission, when he was invited to prepare a piano arrangement of Tchaikovsky's *Sleeping Beauty*.

Meanwhile a new Director had been appointed at the Conservatory and relations between him and Siloti were strained from the start. In May 1891

Siloti resigned and his pupils had to find other teachers. Sergei had only one more year of study left at the Conservatory before his finals. He was reluctant to take up study under a new teacher at that stage of his course and asked the new Director if he could take his piano finals a year early. He was putting himself at considerable risk in making this request, for the final examinations were due to take place in three weeks' time and he had obviously prepared nothing. Nevertheless permission was granted. He embarked on a course of intensive study of the set pieces which were Chopin's B flat minor Sonata and Beethoven's *Appassionata* Sonata. He passed the pianoforte examinations with flying colours in June 1891. At about the same time he finished writing his First Piano Concerto and a Prelude in F.

Life should have been rosy for Sergei but shortly afterwards he contracted typhoid and the illness dragged on for months. He gradually recovered, but suffered from depression for a long time afterwards. In the following year, 1892, he took his final examinations in composition at the Conservatory. It was a set test for which each student had to write an opera, *Aleko*, based on a poem by Pushkin. He wrote his opera very quickly at his father's flat in Moscow where he had taken up summer residence. The examiners were highly impressed by Sergei's work; he received maximum grades and was awarded the Great Gold Medal which had been awarded only twice previously. Afterwards Zverev, who had been a member of the adjudicating panel, congratulated Rachmaninov, and to heal the breach that had marred their relationship he presented the young musician with his own gold watch as a memento. After graduation in June 1892 the 19 year old composer and pianist was ready to embark on his career.

It was not long before Rachmaninov sold his opera, two cello pieces and six songs to Karl Gutheil who remained his publisher for many years, and another important success was soon to follow. The youthful composer wrote a set of preludes whilst studying at his aunt's flat in Moscow and one of these, the Prelude in C sharp minor (Op. 3, No. 2) achieved enormous popularity. Just as Rubinstein's Melody and Paderewski's Minuet dogged their creators for the rest of their lives, so did Rachmaninov's Prelude. Ernest Newman dubbed the piece "The" Prelude, or "It". Rachmaninov was required to perform "It" as an encore at virtually every recital he gave for the rest of his life and it was only on rare occasions that he dared summon up the resolve to refuse. There were no doubt many occasions over the years that he rued the day when he had committed the piece to paper, but in 1892, as a teenager, its success was highly welcome, for it sold all over Europe and put him on the road to success as a composer.

Sergei Rachmaninov

In 1893 the opera *Aleko* was performed in Moscow at the Bolshoi Theatre; quite an occasion for the newly-graduated young musician. It was well received and many eminent musicians were present at the premiere, including Tchaikovsky who leaned out of his box to applaud, knowing that this action would help the young composer. Tchaikovsky wanted to help Rachmaninov in his quest for recognition, but died later that year in mysterious circumstances. When Rachmaninov heard of Tchaikovsky's death he immediately began work on *Trio Elégiaque* in D minor which he dedicated to Tchaikovsky. In the two or three years that followed, Sergei often visited his maternal grandparents and composed whilst he was there, including a *Capriccio on Gypsy Themes*. He also improved his finances by teaching privately and at the Mariinsky Girls' Academy, where he assisted until 1901. Compositions continued to be produced meanwhile, including a Choral Fantasy, *The Rock*.

Rachmaninov embarked on a concert tour of Russia in 1895 with the Italian violinist Teresina Tua, and on 27th March 1897 his First Symphony received its premiere, with Glazunov conducting. The performance was a disaster, due in no small part, according to contemporary accounts, to bad conducting. The work was never again performed in Rachmaninov's lifetime and the complete manuscript has never been found, though the piece has subsequently been reconstructed from the orchestral parts. Shattered by this failure, Rachmaninov composed little for two years. In his own eyes he was a failure at 24. But events were to take a turn for the better in 1897 when he was offered a conducting post with the Moscow Private Russian Opera Company. Whilst there he learned a great deal about opera and developed a deep and lasting friendship with Feodor Chaliapin, later to become the greatest singer Russia has produced. Rachmaninov enjoyed his new job and the newspaper critics praised his work. A new phase in his career had begun.

The year 1899 brought another new experience when Rachmaninov was invited to make a concert tour of England. The main event was on 19th April when he played the C sharp minor Prelude and another item from Opus 3. He also conducted an aria from *Prince Igor* and his own Choral Fantasy, *The Rock*. Rachmaninov was not then regarded as a concert pianist; he was a composer who was invited by concert societies to play and conduct his own pieces, with one or two items from other composers sometimes included to make up the programme. Reviews in Britain were cool, but Rachmaninov was invited back to play his First Piano Concerto the following year. He assured the Philharmonic Society that he would have his second - and better - concerto to play for them by then!

Back in Russia, Rachmaninov continued his career as a conductor, directing the St. Petersburg premiere of *Aleko*, with Chaliapin in the leading role. Rachmaninov always had the greatest respect for his friend Chaliapin, who was a fine actor as well as a marvellous singer. When occasion demanded, Chaliapin had the ability to sob like a child, and bring his audience to tears with him.

In 1900 Rachmaninov suffered another of his spells of depression. A friend, trying to help, arranged for Rachmaninov to meet Tolstoy, one of his idols, at Tolstoy's house. Rachmaninov was very disappointed by the meeting; he did not like Tolstoy, and this left him even more depressed. Rachmaninov referred to him as 'a very disagreeable man'. As his condition worsened, friends persuaded him to seek medical advice, and he went to Dr Nicolai Dahl for hypnosis. The hypnosis was not a success, but Dr Dahl was interested in music, and Rachmaninov and he had many long talks about musicians which proved very beneficial, so that in time his confidence to compose returned. Rachmaninov was so grateful to his therapist that later he dedicated his Third Piano Concerto to him.

Rachmaninov must have seemed a very dour person to those around him. Not only was he himself subject to recurrent fits of depression but his whole demeanour seemed depressing. Tall, gaunt, with a craggy face and huge hands, he rarely smiled. In recent years some medical researchers have suggested that he might have suffered from Marfan's Syndrome, a genetic disorder which gives rise to, among other things, the physical characteristics that Rachmaninov possessed. Abraham Lincoln and Nicolò Paganini are also suspected by some doctors of having had the condition. Someone once described Rachmaninov as "6 feet 3 inches of gloom". But Rachmaninov had to live with the physical attributes he was born with and there is no doubt that a poetic heart beat beneath the austere exterior.

In 1901 Rachmaninov completed his Second Piano Concerto. The work was enormously popular from the start and has remained so. It appeared to many that Tchaikovsky's mantle had passed to Rachmaninov. The success of this work fully revived Rachmaninov's confidence in himself and he entered into a productive period of composition which was to last until 1917. Indeed, the majority of his 49 Opus numbers date from this period. The new century heralded changes in Rachmaninov's personal life too, for in 1902 he announced his engagement to his cousin, Natalia Satina. Everyone was surprised by this, for although the couple had known each other since childhood, a romance had not been suspected. There were difficulties in finding a priest to perform the marriage ceremony, for by Orthodox Canon Law first cousins were not allowed to marry. Also, the couple were expected to sign certificates stating that they worshipped and attended confessions regularly, and this Rachmaninov steadfastly refused to do.

Eventually a way out was found. There was apparently a greater chance of a ceremony being acceptable in an army chapel where the priests were answerable to the army authorities rather than the orthodox synod. After a large sum of money had been handed over, the military authorities saw their way clear to co-operate, and the couple were married on 12th May 1902 in the barracks of the 6th Tavricheski Regiment on the outskirts of Moscow, under the bemused gaze of the resident soldiers. After a lengthy honeymoon in Vienna, Venice and Switzerland, during which Rachmaninov completed a set of 12 songs (Op. 21) and other works, the couple moved into a flat in Moscow.

Rachmaninov was now regarded as one of the premier musicians in Russia, largely because of his compositions. But compositions, even successful ones, do not usually bring in a lot of money, and in 1902 he accepted an appointment as music teacher at St. Catherine's Ladies' College in Moscow. The duties were light, requiring his presence only once or twice a week and at examinations. In 1904 he accepted an invitation to conduct a series of operas at the Bolshoi Theatre, an invitation that was repeated in subsequent seasons, enabling him to make a name for himself as a conductor as well as a composer. However, after the massacre in the Winter Palace in 1905, Rachmaninov considered it unwise to be so closely connected with a state organisation and in 1906 he resigned the Bolshoi post.

In 1903 a daughter, Irina, was born. The child's early years were marred by recurrent illness; otherwise life was good for the Rachmaninovs. Numerous invitations to conduct many Russian orchestras were received season by season and in 1907 a new symphony (No. 2) received its first performance. In the same year another daughter, Tatiana, was born, and completed the Rachmaninov family. In 1908 Rachmaninov, now 35, performed his Second Concerto in London, Koussevitzky conducting. The critic of *The Times* wrote:

"The direct expression of the work, the extraordinary precision and exactitude of his playing, and even the strict economy of movement of arms and hands which M. Rachmaninov exercises, all contributed to the impression of completeness of performance. The slow movement was played by soloist and orchestra with deep feeling, and the brilliant effect of the finale could scarcely have been surpassed, and yet the freedom from extravagance of any kind was the most remarkable feature. We wished that all the amateur and other pianists, who delight in producing sensational effects with his Prelude in C sharp minor, could have heard the composer playing it as his second encore. His crisp, almost rigid, treatment of it would be a revelation to many."

In 1909 Rachmaninov was invited to tour the USA with the object of playing his own concertos and other works for the piano. He did not relish the prospect of going, but he wanted to buy a car and knew that he would be able to do so on the proceeds. The tour lasted from early November 1909 until the end of January 1910, the main highlight being a performance of his latest piano concerto, No. 3 in D minor, in New York on 28th November with a repeat performance in Carnegie Hall on 16th January, with Gustav Mahler conducting.

Life continued in sweet vein, marred only be the fact that the Rachmaninovs' daughters both contracted typhoid in 1913, but fortunately they recovered fully. At the time they were ill Rachmaninov was working on his largest choral work, *The Bells*, based on verses by Edgar Allan Poe. Other works of this period included his Second Piano Sonata in B flat minor. Early in 1914 he sailed for England to begin a concert tour that was to include the British premiere of *The Bells* at the Sheffield Festival in the autumn. But in August war broke out and Europe was plunged into chaos. The performance of *The Bells* was cancelled and was not given in Britain until 1921 when Sir Henry Wood presented it with the Liverpool Philharmonic Society. The Sheffield performance did not take place until 1936.

Following the outbreak of war Rachmaninov returned to Russia and once again succumbed to an attack of depression, aggravated by the death of his father in 1916. In March 1917 the Tsar abdicated and the 300 year old Romanov dynasty ceased to exist, an event which had a deep and morbid effect on Rachmaninov who was a traditionalist Russian by nature. He continued to play and to conduct in Russia as opportunity arose but after the Revolution of 1917 with its associated brutal murder of the Tsar and his family, he found himself to be part of a collective, required to attend committee meetings and to take his turn on guard duty at night. It was all foreign to Rachmaninov's nature and more than he could stand. Late in 1917 he received an invitation to take part in some concerts in Stockholm. Rachmaninov saw this as the chance he had been looking for - to escape from Russia. He went to Petrograd to apply for visas for himself and his family, and just before Christmas 1917, they all boarded a train for Scandinavia, from the same station at which Lenin had arrived a few months earlier. The train steamed though Russia into Finland. Disembarking there, Rachmaninov and his family made a cold journey through the night across Finland by sledge before boarding a train at the Swedish border to make the last leg of the journey to Stockholm. So, in this way they left Russia, and Rachmaninov never set foot in his native land again.

Sergei Rachmaninov

When Sergei Rachmaninov left Russia in 1917 he left behind nearly all his money and possessions which had been confiscated by the Communist regime but he felt it was a small price to pay for freedom. However, now that he had taken the step of starting a new life away from his native country he had to decide how to make a living to support himself and his young family. His teaching appointments and conducting contracts were behind him and there were no quick financial rewards to be gained from composition. There was only one solution; he would have to earn his living as a performer - as a concert pianist. Playing the piano in concerts and recitals was of course not new to Rachmaninov, for he had been doing it for 25 years. But essentially it had been as an exponent of his own compositions, with a handful of works by Chopin, Liszt and Tchaikovsky thrown in as makeweights. From now on, in order to make his living as a pianist, he must build up a repertoire, and do it quickly.

So, at the age of 44, Rachmaninov set to work as he had never worked before. After leaving Russia he had passed through Sweden to Denmark, and it was in Copenhagen that he rented the ground floor of a house and began to study. At his first concert on 15th February 1918 he played his own Second Piano Concerto. He then returned to Sweden to give the concerts which had been the means of his leaving Russia, and in March 1918 he played Liszt's First and Tchaikovsky's First Concertos in addition to his own Second. By September of the same year he was ready to give recitals of Beethoven, Chopin, Mozart, Schubert and Tchaikovsky.

In the summer of 1918 Rachmaninov received three separate lucrative offers from the USA, namely, to conduct the Cincinnati Symphony Orchestra for two years, to give 25 piano recitals, and to conduct 110 concerts in 30 weeks for the Boston Symphony Orchestra. Feeling he was not really used to America and its ways, Rachmaninov declined them all. Nevertheless, he decided that the United States might be the answer to his financial problems. He had no money for fares but another Russian emigré, a banker named Kamenka, loaned him the money and provided him with a guarantee against loss of earnings in the USA. Rachmaninov accepted gratefully and set sail on 1st November 1918 with his family for the start of their life in the New World. They arrived on 10th November, the day before the armistice was signed, and on Armistice Day recuperated in their hotel from the journey whilst listening to the celebrations outside.

Rachmaninov was absorbed into the American musical scene very quickly, due to the helpful efforts of Josef Hofmann and various other musicians. A concert manager, Charles Ellis, was found for him and several piano companies offered him large sums of money to play their pianos in his concerts. He declined them, accepting instead Steinway, who had not offered him any such inducement - though they did give him a piano. An American lady let him use her studio to practise, thus avoiding the problem of practising in an hotel room, and Rachmaninov gave his first concert on 8th December 1918 in Providence, Rhode Island. He then secured an engagement to play in 36 concerts through the winter, finishing in April 1919, after which he took his family to live in San Francisco before opening his next season in October 1919. He had by then extended his repertoire to include, beside his own works, numerous compositions by Beethoven, Chopin, Grieg, Liszt, Mendelssohn, Mozart, Schubert and Tchaikovsky. Later he added Debussy's *Children's Corner* Suite to the list.

At the end of 1920 Rachmaninov signed a contract with the Victor Talking Machine Company (to be taken over by RCA in 1929) which was to issue more than 100 of his recordings. This constituted the whole of his output on disc apart from some early 'hill and dale' recordings for the Edison Company. All Rachmaninov's recorded performances were eventually re-issued on long-playing records by RCA in a 5-volume series entitled 'The Complete Rachmaninov' and are now available on compact disc.

Rachmaninov also made over 30 excellent piano rolls, recorded exclusively for Ampico. When Ampico contracted Rachmaninov to make rolls, the company was very apprehensive as to whether he would be prepared to endorse the finished product, for he was known to be a perfectionist and had he been dissatisfied it could have sounded the death knell for the Ampico system. At the first recording session Rachmaninov recorded two or three master rolls, which were immediately processed and then played back. Rachmaninov sat and listened inscrutably whilst the Ampico officials watched his face apprehensively. At the conclusion of the performance there was a long pause, whilst the grim-looking Rachmaninov said nothing. Then, at last, he turned to the officials and said, "Gentlemen, I have just heard myself play!" This famous utterance, which came as a great relief to the Ampico hierarchy, gave a tremendous boost to the marketing of the Ampico system, for Rachmaninov's stamp of approval was as great a coup as they could have wished for and helped enormously in the sale of their products.

Rachmaninov was very interested in the technicalities of the roll-cutting process and used to spend many hours at the Ampico factory with Milton Suskind, their editor, checking through and editing the rolls and ensuring they were absolutely to his satisfaction. Several of the rolls were of his own compositions but other composers were also represented, including Bach, Beethoven, Bizet, Chopin, Gluck, Henselt, Kreisler, Liszt, Mendelssohn,

Mussorgsky, Paderewski, Rimsky-Korsakov, Rubinstein, Schubert and Tchaikovsky. Many of the pieces were his own arrangements. It seems likely that a musician of Rachmaninov's eminence would have been allowed to specify what he wanted to play, so the composers listed here probably represent his own choice.

In 1921 Rachmaninov applied to visit Russia, perhaps somewhat rashly in view of the circumstances of his departure, but he became ill and the visit did not take place, nor was it ever rearranged. Firmly settled in the USA, Rachmaninov made his home in New York, purchasing a 5-storey house on Riverside Drive overlooking the Hudson River. This was the centre for his tours as a concert pianist. He commanded high fees and lived in some style, employing a secretary, cook and chauffeur, all Russian. He remained Russian in outlook for the whole of his life, and made himself the centre of a small Russian community. Russia was where his roots were, and he always considered himself to be Russian even though he was permanently resident in the USA. When he was ill he even consulted Russian doctors whenever possible.

In 1922 Rachmaninov's daughter Irina married Prince Pyotr Volkonsky, but the marriage ended tragically for he died less than a year later. Irina, widowed at 22, gave birth to a baby soon afterwards; Rachmaninov's first granddaughter, Sofia. He was devoted to the child and delighted in introducing her to visitors with pride and pleasure. After the death of his son-in-law, Rachmaninov decided to form his own publishing house, to be run jointly by his two daughters. The firm was based in Paris and was called "Tair", from the names Tatiana and Irina. Its prime function was to publish the work of Russian emigré composers, and for some years Rachmaninov's own compositions were published by the firm.

In the 1922-23 season Rachmaninov tried an interesting experiment. He had grown weary of the suitcase existence of an itinerant performer when on tour and decided to hire his own personal railway carriage so that he could travel in comfort, as Paderewski had done. It was equipped with an upright piano, and obviated the need to constantly pack and unpack at hotels. However, he soon became sick of the sight of his mobile home and resumed the routine of hotel life, in spite of all its drawbacks.

From late 1923 onwards he cut down on his tours of the United States and neighbouring countries. He established a routine of remaining in America for about half the concert season (from November to March), then travelling to Europe, where he would compose in the relaxed atmosphere of various summer villas. Soon he decided he was not in the USA for enough of the year to justify the retention of an expensive residence there, and in

1925 he sold his home in Riverside Drive. When he was in the USA subsequently he rented an apartment.

It was not long after his new beginning in the USA in 1918 that Rachmaninov came to be regarded as one of the great concert pianists of the day, displaying an ability that few had suspected he possessed in the years when he had devoted himself mainly to composition and conducting. His enormous hands must have given him an advantage over most of his contemporaries in tackling music requiring a large span. But it was not just this physical attribute that made Rachmanivov a great pianist, for there is more to pianistic brilliance than the possession of large hands. Rachmaninov practised very diligently and his technique was almost flawless. Many observers considered him to be the most secure of all pianists, in the sense that he could be relied upon to perform accurately with very few wrong notes. His technical mastery was kept under the strictest control; his approach was studious, and he always strove to achieve a definitive performance. It was said of many of Rachmaninov's contemporaries that they never played the same piece twice in the same way. Rachmaninov was different; he sought to do just that, to find what to him was the 'true performance' and to stick to it. He used to say that each piece of music had a culminating point, a climax, which might be at or near the end or near the middle, depending on the music. He called it "the point". Occasionally after a recital he would walk from the stage disgusted with himself and would say, "I missed it! I missed the point!" Rachmaninov was very particular about getting his interpretations just right.

Rachmaninov's approach was always careful and intellectual. It was less spontaneous than that of, say, Josef Hofmann, and the tendency to a somewhat austere interpretation was heightened by his platform presence; rather gloomy, and lacking in any form of mannerism. Whether one prefers a Rachmaninov or a Hofmann is a matter of personal choice. But one thing is certain; Rachmaninov was regarded by his contemporary pianists as their equal and possibly their master. His rhythmic drive, accuracy and limited used of rubato was allied to an absolute clarity in the execution of complex textures, particularly in swiftly moving passages. Muffy runs were not part of Rachmaninov's style. Every note he played was clear and precise.

During Rachmaninov's vintage years as a concert pianist he composed as a relaxation but at a less prolific rate than in his years in Russia. His Fourth Piano Concerto was completed in 1926 and premiered in the March of that year. Finances were no longer a problem and in most years he would enjoy extended summer holidays in Europe, walking, driving, boating, playing tennis and chatting with friends. He was generous and gave a lot of money away. His grim features hid a personality that could in private be relaxed and amiable. In 1930 he decided to build a European home in Switzerland and bought a plot of land at Hertenstein, near Lucerne, where he had a villa built, working closely with the architect to ensure that it suited his requirements. It was called "Senar" from Sergei and Natalia.

Rachmaninov was not a politically-minded person and in the main kept out of any kind of political controversy, but in January 1931 he upset the Soviet authorities by critical remarks he made about their regime in a letter to *The New York Times*. In it he condemned the Soviet attitude towards education and various social matters. The Soviet press were not slow to respond, and for a 3 year period no-one in Russia was allowed to perform or study his work.

After a performance of his Third Piano Concerto under Sir Henry Wood in London in March 1932, Rachmaninov was presented with the Royal Philharmonic Society's Gold Medal by the Duchess of Athol in recognition of his outstanding contribution to music. Honours were beginning to flow in and later in the same year Rachmaninov celebrated the 40th anniversary of his debut as a pianist. It was an eventful year in another way, for his younger daughter, Tatiana, was married. A son, Alexander, was born in 1933.

Throughout the 1930s Rachmaninov's life followed the pattern of the 1920s. A pianist of international stature, Rachmaninov continued to compose works of importance. One of his most famous compositions, *Rhapsody on a Theme of Paganini*, appeared in 1934, and he played the piano part at the first performance of the work in Baltimore in November of that year. It received its British premiere on 7th March 1935 with the Hallé Orchestra in Manchester, when Rachmaninov was again the soloist in a performance conducted by Nicolai Malko. Soon afterwards the work was introduced to the London audience. In 1936 his Third Symphony was completed, and in the same year he travelled to Sheffield for a performance of *The Bells*, originally intended to be performed there in 1914. Isobel Baillie, the incomparable Manchester-based singer, spoke of her meeting with Rachmaninov prior to taking part in *The Bells*:

"I was first approached by Ibbs & Tillett, my agents, who asked if I would like to participate in the concert. When I readily agreed they first informed me that my vocal partners would be two long-standing friends, Parry Jones and Harold Williams, and then stipulated that I would have to travel to London in order to go through the soprano solo with the orchestra. It was with considerable exhilaration and not a little trepidation that I found myself entering the Piccadilly Hotel to meet the great man. Great man in all senses, for when I arrived at his suite he rose from a fireside chair and loomed taller and taller; it appeared as if he would never stop. Even more impressive than his slender hands was his face, the most beautiful but also the saddest I think I have ever seen. Once the pleasantries of the introduction were over he went to the piano and handed me a score. I sang the solo in its entirety to his accompaniment; what a thrill! Its long languorous lines recalling the bells of marriage and bliss, with a considerable degree of melancholy so characteristic of the composer, are a God-given gift to any lyric soprano.

> *Listen to the holy wedding bells*
> *Their melody tells of a world of happiness*
> *Like a pair of distant eyes*
> *They gaze through the quiet air of night.*

After this playthrough I took out my pencil in preparation for Rachmaninov's observations and qualifications, but to my considerable surprise he stopped me, saying: "No, that's just how I want it! I look forward so much to hearing you sing it at the Festival." That was it! It was the only time I ever sang *The Bells* but it will never be forgotten."

After more concerts in the USA, Rachmaninov was back in England in the autumn of 1938 for Sir Henry Wood's Jubilee Concert. It was originally intended that the concert should take place on St. Cecilia's Day, 22nd November, but the only time Rachmaninov was available was the first week in October because of his forthcoming winter concert tour of the United States. Consequently the concert was brought forward to 5th October. In the first part of the concert he played his Second Piano Concerto, Wood conducting, whilst after the interval he sat in the audience and thoroughly enjoyed Vaughan Williams' *Serenade to Music*, written especially for the concert, in which Isobel Baillie's beautiful voice again added distinction to the occasion. Rachmaninov gave more recitals and concerts in England in the spring of 1939, culminating in one at the Queen's Hall on 11th March which proved to be his last public performance in Britain.

Following these appearances, Rachmaninov moved on to Paris and then to his home in Switzerland. On 11th August 1939 he played Beethoven's First Piano Concerto and his own *Variations on a Theme of Paganini* at the Lucerne Festival before returning to America when war broke out. There he played in a special season arranged by the Philadelphia Orchestra to celebrate the 30th anniversary of his American debut in 1909. In the following year, 1940, his last composition, *Symphonic Dances*, was published. He was still active at 67, and in the autumn embarked on an arduous tour of the USA, not only playing but conducting as well.

Early in 1942 Rachmaninov decided to move to California. He rented a house in Beverly Hills, Los Angeles, not far from Horowitz's home, and the two eminent Russian pianists often met to play duets. Later, in June 1942, he bought a home in Elm Drive, and in July he played at the Hollywood Bowl. In October of the same year he played in Detroit. All seemed well, but in January 1943 Rachmaninov became ill, complaining of tiredness, a cough and weight loss. Pleurisy was diagnosed. But he continued to fulfil his engagements until he gave his final concert on 17th February at Knoxville, Tennessee. The highlight of the programme was one of his specialities, Chopin's B minor Sonata (The Funeral Sonata). This was a sadly appropriate work. After the concert he became very ill and was taken to the Hospital of the Good Samaritan in Beverly Hills. The rest of his concert tour was immediately cancelled. Cancer was diagnosed, in his case malignant melanoma which spread rapidly to other organs. He died on 28th March 1943, four days before his 70th birthday.

Rachmaninov must be regarded as one of the major musicians of recent times. Though 42 of his 70 years were lived in the 20th century he was at heart a 19th century musician, moulded in the classical and romantic tradition, and had little sympathy for the more modern work of his Russian contemporaries such as Prokofiev, Shostakovich and Stravinsky. His compositions are melodic. As a conductor he was regarded as a competent and capable craftsman. In the other facet of his art, that of pianist, he was one of the all-time greats, especially in the interpretation of his own compositions.

Harold Bauer

9. Harold Bauer

Let us turn back the calendar about a hundred and ten years. The scene is a room in the St. James's Hall in London. An elderly whiskered gentleman listens whilst a 10 year old boy plays the violin. When he has finished the gentleman applauds. He likes the boy's playing and predicts that he will make a great name for himself as a violinist. The man was Joseph Joachim, one of the greatest violinists of the 19th century, for whom Brahms wrote his violin concerto. The boy was Harold Bauer. Joachim was right about the boy's musicianship - but as we shall see it was not as a violinist that he was to become famous, but as a pianist.

Harold Bauer was born at New Malden, Surrey, on the southern outskirts of London, on 28th April 1873. His father, who was a good violinist, was of German birth but his mother was English. From his earliest years Harold loved music and remembered, in old age, the German bands that had been popular in his infanthood, as well as the Italian organ grinders, bagpipers, and a one-man band who used to perform near the Bauer home. Harold showed an early musical talent and on his fourth birthday he composed a polka. Nearly 40 years later he played it to the daughter of his friend and fellow musician Ossip Gabrilowitsch on her fourth birthday, much to her delight. When he was still very small his aunt gave him piano lessons and his father taught him to play the violin, using a half-sized instrument. Harold progressed rapidly with his violin playing, and as a young child started to play in public from time to time. He liked listening to music too and as soon as he was old enough he became an avid concert goer. At the St. James's Hall in South London there were Saturday afternoon and Monday evening concerts of popular classical music. He was usually taken to the afternoon ones, a six mile journey on a slow horse-drawn bus, but Harold did not mind as he was glad of the opportunity to see and hear some of the great artists of the day. The programmes reflected contemporary musical fashions, with composers such as Goetz, Raff, Rheinberger, Anton Rubinstein and Spohr well represented, and Mendelssohn still revered as a kind of court musician though he had been dead for 30 years.

When he was 10, Harold took the enterprising step of writing to Joachim, due to give a concert at the St. James's Hall the following Saturday, asking him if he would play the Bach G minor Prelude and Fugue as an encore at the forthcoming concert "because I play that piece too". Joachim wrote a very pleasant reply to the child, and invited him to play for him after the concert. The great violinist was so taken with the boy's ability that he offered to arrange a place for him at the newly-established Royal College of Music in London. For some reason the offer was not taken up, but instead he became the pupil of Adolf Politzer, who was reckoned by many to be the best violin teacher in London. Under Politzer's expert tuition Harold learned all the major violin repertoire and became his teacher's star pupil. His public appearances became regular events and Politzer used to lend Harold his fine Guarnerius violin for recitals.

All the while that his violin playing was developing the teenage Bauer continued to attend the St. James's Hall concerts and to absorb as much musical knowledge as he could. He became such a familiar figure there that the usher generally let him in free, and sometimes he would sit with the music critics, for they were always given two free tickets and generally came alone. On one occasion Bauer sat next to George Bernard Shaw, then known primarily for his music criticism. Among those appearing at the concerts regularly was Anton Rubinstein, the great Russian pianist. The pianos of those days were unequal to the demands put upon them by Rubinstein, and Bauer recalled that Rubinstein used to play two pianos alternately, playing one whilst his piano mechanic worked on the other, a procedure which continued throughout the recital. Bauer also saw and heard Clara Schumann who in those days was the Great Lady of the piano, the violinist Sarasate, and the pianist Frederic Lamond, the last and youngest pupil of Liszt. Perhaps most important of all, he was present when the youthful, golden-haired Paderewski first appeared at the St. James's Hall.

During Harold's childhood and adolescence he had no formal schooling; instead his mother taught him reading, writing and the elements of music whilst two gentlemen, one French and one German, taught him their own languages and also history and geography. But his life was not restricted, for his music took him into the outside world and he had two sisters, also good musicians, to provide as much company as he needed at home. He later described himself as a "shy and reticent boy", and claimed that he did not get much satisfaction from his solo public appearances. But he enjoyed playing with others, and at the age of 16 formed a string quartet. He was first violin, the second violin was Carl Engol (an American), viola was Emil Kreuz and cello Herbert Walem. The quartet did quite well in the London area and Harold enjoyed leading it.

By the time he was 18 years old Harold was quite a seasoned performer. He met many young artists, such as Leopold Godowsky with whom he played piano/violin duets, and it was through these friends that he learned of the life of an international musician. But he felt that he was not really making much progress, for his frequent concert appearances had all been in small halls, and there seemed to be little opportunity for a young violinist to achieve fame and fortune in Britain. He spoke about his problems to Godowsky, who immediately said, "Why don't you get out of Britain?" This set Bauer thinking, and before long he resolved to try his luck in mainland Europe as soon as he could afford to go. Fortunately his financial problem was soon solved; his ambition to take himself and his violin to the continent had become public knowledge in his neighbourhood and one day a registered envelope arrived containing the princely sum, as it was in those days, of £50 in banknotes. Enclosed was an unsigned note with the ungrammatical but welcome message that the money was "to be used to go abroad with." Harold soon discovered that the money had come from two elderly ladies who had shown kindness to him and his sisters since they were young children, and he was able to thank them.

This was just what Harold had been wanting, but first he had to fulfil a number of engagements in England and Scotland. Whilst doing so he benefited from another stroke of good fortune. He met a piano teacher, Graham Moore (soon to become Professor at the Royal College of Music in London), who was a friend of Paderewski. Moore took Harold to a Paderewski recital and afterwards to the artist's room. Then both were invited to lunch with Paderewski shortly afterwards. Moore told Paderewski all about Bauer and the great celebrity expressed interest. Next day Bauer played a few pieces for Paderewski on both the violin and the piano. It was then arranged that Bauer would become one of the artists managed by Daniel Mayer, who was Paderewski's manager and also director of the French branch of the Érard Piano Company. Paderewski told Bauer: "If you ever come to Paris I should like you to study with my friend Gorski, who is the greatest living violin teacher." He also told him that Bauer could play the piano for him sometime and that he, Paderewski, would interest himself in the young man's career. That was enough for Harold Bauer, and he left for Paris in the spring of 1893. He was then aged 20.

Once in Paris Bauer rented a cheap room, practised his violin, and the Érard firm loaned him a piano. He often visited the Gorski family, with whom Paderewski's invalid son lived whilst the great man was away on his tours. He also met and became friendly with Delius. When Paderewski returned to Paris he suggested that Bauer should get a flat near him, so that he could send his valet round to fetch Bauer when he wanted to hear Bauer play the violin. Bauer said later: "Occasionally he let me play the piano for him after he had worked on the new concertos he was studying, in which I accompanied him on a second piano." Paderewski told him he might make a unique career for himself as a performer on both instruments.

But in spite of Paderewski's interest there were few openings for violinists in Paris. Conservatory pupils got priority - it was difficult for outsiders to break into the market. Ironically, he later became one of the Conservatory's panel of judges. He scraped a living playing piano accompaniments for singers but, as in Britain, the way ahead seemed to hold no clear opportunities. Then, one day, an agent approached Bauer with an offer of a tour of Russia as piano accompanist for the singer Louise Nikita, an American whose real name was Nicholson. Her agent was her uncle. Bauer's duties were not only to accompany, but also to fill part of the programmes by playing the violin, with locally-engaged artists playing his piano accompaniment. He was engaged at a modest fee for a tour of uncertain duration, but he looked forward to it eagerly for Nikita was a great favourite in Russia. He joined the party in Berlin for rehearsals but whilst he was there Tsar Alexander III died on 1st November 1894. It was then announced from Moscow was that no public performances would be allowed during the period of court mourning of five or six weeks. Apparently the tour would have to be postponed. But Nikita's uncle was a resourceful man. He thought it might be possible to reorganise the tour using the 'Halls of the Nobility' in the smaller towns. These private halls were a great feature of Russian life in those days and the smallest towns in Russia had such buildings, which included ballrooms and restaurants. Events held in them were regarded as private functions and were therefore not subject to the national rules on public mourning. Consequently, these halls could be used for the purposes of the tour.

And so the tour went ahead, but only in the smaller towns. People came from miles around - the whole district converged on the concerts as there was little else in the way of entertainment. They were a great success - but there was a snag. In these small towns no musicians could be found who could play piano accompaniments for the violin. So Bauer had to play piano solos to make up the programmes instead of playing the violin. At the end of the period of court mourning Harold and his colleague could play where they liked and the tour moved into the larger cities where competent local musicians were available. But then the manager refused to engage an accompanist for Bauer's violin playing, on the grounds that Bauer played the piano well enough as far as he was concerned and he saw no reason for the additional expense of an accompanist. When Bauer came back to Paris he made great efforts to start playing the violin again. But his old friends there laughed because it was known that he had been playing the piano in public for several months. He was then engaged as a pianist to accompany a number of singers and instrumentalists, and finally his friends thought he had made sufficient progress for them to guarantee the expenses of a Paris recital. This recital, which was in effect an official debut as a pianist, was a great success. So Harold Bauer became a pianist in spite of himself. He had gone to Russia as a violinist who could also play the piano, and came back as a pianist who could also play the violin. Many successful piano recitals followed in the next few months and at the age of 22 he was thus established in the Parisian musical scene as a competent pianist - and all because of the death of Alexander III of Russia.

The next few years were ones of consolidation, in which his musical stature steadily increased. In the autumn of 1895 Daniel Mayer arranged a concert for him in Berlin at which he played Beethoven's *Emperor* Concerto, Saint-Saëns' G minor Concerto and Liszt's Hungarian Fantasia with the Berlin Philharmonic Orchestra. Mayer also arranged a solo recital for him in Berlin. Both these events proved to be triumphs for Bauer and led to several other concerts in Germany. Engagements started to flood in; among them Paris, Amsterdam, Madrid and a tour of Portugal. These were mainly in small halls for relatively low fees, but he was having no difficulty in making a comfortable living. Throughout these years Bauer's home continued to be in Paris, where he lived in various rented apartments. The Érard Piano Company provided him with pianos for his concerts and recitals, and the services of a tuner.

By 1900, when Bauer was 27, he had become a pianist nearing the top rank. But it was necessary in those days, as now, for a young musician to break into the American musical scene before he could be regarded as one of the leading figures of the day, and Bauer duly achieved this distinction in 1900 when he was invited to play the Brahms D minor Concerto with the Boston Symphony Orchestra. For this concert Bauer played a Mason & Hamlin piano; Steinway were not interested. The concert was a success; other recitals in Boston followed, and these led to a three month tour of the USA. His American agent, anxious to put Bauer on the American musical map, wanted to bill him rather extravagantly as "The Greatest Living Pianist". Bauer objected to this feeling, quite rightly, that he wasn't, and the agent settled for "Harold Bauer - Master Pianist", under which banner he appeared for many years. On his return to Europe he discovered that his prestige had improved considerably in his absence through complimentary news reports of his tour of the USA, and in the following few years, up to the outbreak of the 1914-1918 war, he was in great demand as a concert celebrity in Europe and in the USA. In 1908 he gave the first performance of Debussy's *Children's Corner Suite*, containing the now famous *Golliwog's Cake Walk*, by special request of the composer.

In later life Bauer asserted that in spite of his very considerable success and undoubted prestige he never got into the really "big money" class. He remained what he called "a low-priced artist". This did not worry him particularly; he had achieved as much as he wanted to, and was able to pick and choose his appearances and live the relatively modest life-style that suited him. Also, he always maintained that he did not enjoy solo appearances. Chamber music was another matter; he loved to play duets, and in trios and quartets, and had many notable musical associations with the cellist Casals, the violinists Kreisler and Ysaÿe, the pianists Ossip Gabrilowitsch and Myra Hess, and others. The famous Cortot/Casals/Thibault trio is mentioned in chapter 12 of this book; Bauer himself played frequently with Casals and Thibault, not as a stand-in for Cortot but more as an alternative, because Cortot, Casals and Thibault played together for only one month annually.

Pablo Casals, who became a life-long friend of Bauer, was an excellent observer of human nature and he gives in his writing a perceptive insight of Bauer as a young man:

"It was shortly after my debut with Lamoureux that I came to know Harold Bauer. He was then 26 and already widely known as a pianist. Actually he had started his career as a violinist. He was a handsome young man with sparkling eyes and bushy red hair; once, when he was still a youngster in England, Paderewski had told him, "You would make a fine pianist; you have such beautiful hair." When Bauer settled in Paris a few years later he did become a pianist. And what a superb one! He was an especially wonderful interpreter of Brahms, Schumann and Chopin. We took an immediate liking to one another when we met, and Bauer suggested we give some joint concerts. We arranged a number in Spain and Holland. That was in 1900. It was the beginning of a long and joyful association. In the ensuing years I would give more concerts with Bauer than with any other performer. We complemented each other wonderfully well. There was an instinctive communication between us and we shared the same views about music. From the beginning it was as if we had been playing together for years. Bauer was a delightful companion - a brilliant man, sensitive, perceptive, with a keen sense of humour and a remarkable knack for mimicry. He was an omnivorous reader - he always travelled with a dozen or so books - and when we were on a boat he would spend hours rummaging through the ship's library, making copious notes and reading late into the night. He was very fond of athletics. But he had one vexing problem; he suffered greatly from seasickness. He tried every imaginable remedy - at one time, in fact, he even wore some sort of device which was supposed to hold his stomach muscles in such a position as to prevent him from becoming ill. But nothing worked. It was a miserable affliction."

Bauer had a very close musical rapport with Casals and once described how their mutual understanding could be put to amusing use:

"Our sense of tempo was strangely identical. We invented a little parlour trick with which we mystified our friends. Standing opposite each other, one of us would announce, after a few seconds, the name of a playing card which had been privately communicated to the other by one of the spectators. We pretended this was telepathy, but it was nothing of the kind. We simply counted mentally the beats of any composition on which we had previously agreed. Four slightly different positions of the feet indicated hearts, diamonds, spades and clubs respectively, and the counting stopped at any prearranged signal, imperceptible to the audience. Try it yourself and see how you come out with the King of Spades, for instance. Possibly you may find it easy, in which case your ensemble playing will be just as good as ours was."

In the years preceding the outbreak of the First World War, Harold Bauer was spending more and more of his time touring the USA and South America, and from the time the war started he made his home in the United States, remaining there for the rest of his life when not on tour. When the war began he was 41 and had 20 years of solid achievement as a pianist to his credit. During the war he appeared in many concerts along with numerous other musicians, one of whom was Ossip Gabrilowitsch, the famous Russian pianist and son-in-law of the author Mark Twain. Their association came about because they both had the same agent, and on one occasion he booked Gabrilowitsch for a tour, thinking that Bauer was not available at the time when in fact he was. It was consequently decided that they should tour together, playing two-piano arrangements and four-handed arrangements for one piano. Their dual partnership became very well known and the two remained great friends until Gabrilowitsch's death in 1936. Another aspect of Bauer's work during the 1914-1918 war was to help raise money for distressed musicians in France, for which the French Government later awarded him the Cross of the Legion of Honour.

When hostilities ceased in 1918 Bauer founded 'The Beethoven Society of New York', a leading chamber music society to which artists gave their services free for charitable causes. Bauer's willingness to play on frequent occasions for the society is an example of his readiness to subordinate personal prestige, ambition and financial reward. The Beethoven Society continued to operate until 1938.

An important facet of Harold Bauer's career was his involvement in the player piano industry. He recorded over 130 rolls, distributed between a number of companies but mainly for the Aeolian Company's Duo-Art system. The companies he recorded rolls for and the approximate number of rolls he recorded for them were: Aeolian Company (Duo-Art) (over 100 rolls); Wilcox & White (Artrio rolls) (17); Hupfeld (at least 10); Recordo (4); Artecho (3) and Pleyela (2). In addition, Ampico issued five Bauer rolls that were adaptations from Hupfeld ones. During the 1920s Bauer continued to tour but at the same time he was under contract to the Aeolian Company to record music for their system and to edit his own recordings. As he did not command such high fees as the legendary figures of the day such as Paderewski and Godowsky, but was nevertheless a fine pianist, he was an attractive proposition to the Aeolian company. The music he recorded was probably what he was asked to record rather than what he particularly wished to, and covers a wide range. Even so it included a lot of music by the composers he particularly favoured, notably Beethoven, Brahms, Chopin, Schubert and Schumann. Amongst his many Beethoven rolls are recordings of two complete Sonatas, the *Appassionata*, Op. 57 in F minor, and the *Pathétique*, Op. 13 in C minor. Bauer also recorded some four-handed arrangements for the company with his friend Ossip Gabrilowitsch, and other four-handed arrangements with Myra Hess. His recording was done at the Aeolian Company's headquarters in New York, and apart from the many public performances Bauer gave in the company's Aeolian Hall, which seated 1200 people, he spent many hours in the offices, editing and correcting the paper rolls on which his performances had been mechanically recorded. He took infinite pains to obtain a satisfactory result.

Bauer made an interesting point concerning the adaptation of technique sometimes necessary to obtain the best results when recording for the player piano:

"I learned that it was best, in accentuating a single tone contained within a chord, to allow this tone to precede the other tones by a fraction of a second, instead of insisting that all tones be played simultaneously. This had to be done in correcting the paper rolls of the mechanical record. The illusion of simultaneity was perfect, and it sounded better that way, so I introduced this method into my technical practice."

Bauer was very important to the Aeolian Company, and his account of a special reproducing piano concert highlights the drama of those days:

"The most ambitious of the Aeolian Company's plans was to prepare records of piano concertos for performance with symphony orchestras under the leadership of their regular conductor. I believe I was the first to make such a record. It was the Saint-Saëns Concerto in G minor. Following its completion, it was performed at a special concert at the Academy of Music in Philadelphia by the Philadelphia Symphony Orchestra under the direction of Leopold Stokowski. The hall, containing invited guests only, was completely filled, and I was 'on view' in one of the prominent boxes. Although quite familiar with the practice, already adopted, of giving public performances of recorded music, I still recall with a shudder the strange feeling I experienced when, the lid of the piano having been raised and the orchestra and Stokowski having taken their places, the manager came forward and said that Mr. Harold Bauer would now play the Saint-Saëns Concerto in G minor. "You will see Mr. Bauer sitting in that box", he continued, motioning towards me. For one moment it seemed like a nightmare. But the performance was a sensational success, and it was subsequently repeated by Walter Damrosch in New York, by Alfred Hertz in San Francisco, and by a number of other organisations in various countries where the Aeolian Company had their representatives."

Bauer continued:

"Stokowski and Damrosch both told me they had never been so nervous in accompanying any soloist. In making the record, all the shorter time intervals between piano and orchestra had been allowed for by blank spaces in the revolving paper roll, but for the longer it seemed safer to arrange for the roll to be automatically stopped and started again by an electric button on the conductor's desk. If the conductor kept strict time, there was no special difficulty, but the habit of yielding to performers who required rhythmic freedom, together with an unconquerable feeling of uncertainty regarding the machine, seems to have made it sometimes impossible for the conductor to follow the performance with the necessary mechanical precision."

Bauer also made gramophone recordings but they are not as important or as numerous as the recordings he made for the reproducing piano. He recorded for HMV in Britain on a relatively small scale and the 1937-38 HMV catalogue lists a number of Bauer discs, including *Clair de Lune* by Debussy, *Novelette in D* by Schumann, and the *Appassionata* Sonata by Beethoven. A set of records was also available which reflected Bauer's lifelong interest in chamber music. This was Brahms' Quintet in F minor, Op. 34, which Bauer made with the Flonzaley Quartet. Some of these recordings continued to be listed in the HMV catalogues until the early 1950s when the issue of 78rpm recordings was gradually phased out.

In the 1920s Harold Bauer took part in the first radio link-up, connecting performers in various states throughout the USA. He was also engaged by Warner Brothers to take part in the first demonstration of moving pictures combined with sound, in which he and the violinist Efrem Zimbalist played part of Beethoven's *Kreutzer* Sonata. Bauer's busy musical life continued into the 1930s, but by then the decline of the player piano companies was so advanced that hardly any new rolls were being recorded. However, he still had as much concert work as he wanted.

Although he had a good sense of humour Bauer also had, by his own admission, a quick temper. Over the years he quarrelled with several of his musical colleagues over quite trivial matters. He could be sarcastic in a way that people often misinterpreted as vindictiveness, when he was really only intending to poke fun. Bauer used Mason & Hamlin pianos for 30 years and one of their chief tuners, 'Pop' Bacon, travelled with Bauer for many years on his tours and became a close friend. He used to advise Bauer occasionally as to his relations with other people, and was greatly concerned by Harold's habit of making occasional satirical remarks. "You ought to be careful, Mr Bauer", he used to growl amiably but apprehensively - "These people don't understand sarcasm and they don't like it. You can't tell what may happen. Suppose some big husky chap were to haul off and land you one, where would you be? You aren't in any kind of physical training, and I'm sure I don't know ... " and so his voice would trail off rather miserably.

Harold Bauer was satisfied with his lot; he had no ambitions to be hailed by the musical establishment as the world's greatest pianist, but he maintained a very high standard for his art throughout his life. He remained unpretentious and never walked from the stage feeling he had been particularly inspired or, conversely, unduly bad. Indeed, he found it difficult to assess his own performances.

Bauer could always see the funny side of life. He described one of his many amusing experiences as follows:

"I had announced a recital in San Francisco with a new program. It was a fine Sunday afternoon; I felt very well and was looking forward with pleasure to the concert. I began to play and was very disconcerted to find that one of the keys had stuck. After the first number I looked around for my tuner and then remembered with consternation that he had left for Los Angeles, where I was to play the next day. It was out of the question to get anyone else, the day being Sunday. I gritted my teeth and decided I must go through with the concert. For the rest of the programme I had but one thought - to lift up the key after I had depressed it, in order to prepare for the next stroke. All my pleasure was gone. I was in misery and wished I were dead. At long last the concert was over and I retired disconsolately to the artists' room after playing the usual encores. I found an old friend there, one of the few people on whom I could rely to tell me the truth about my playing and in whose judgment I had implicit confidence. "Well!" he said, "Whatever came over you today?" I started to explain but he interrupted me. "I want to tell you", he remarked impressively, "that I have never heard you play with the ease and freedom that you displayed today. From beginning to end you were completely absorbed in the music, and your performance was an inspired one.""

When the youthful Harold Bauer transferred his talents from the violin to the piano back in the 1890s, his professional association with the violin ceased, but he kept in practice, and remained a competent violinist throughout his life. On one occasion he and Fritz Kreisler had been appearing together at a concert, and afterwards the reception given for the artists lasted until after midnight. Bauer and Kreisler consented to do a little music making. Harold borrowed Fritz's violin, Kreisler seated himself at the piano, and together they played Beethoven's *Kreutzer* Sonata - an event widely reported in the press the next day.

In the mid 1930s Bauer was in his early sixties and decided that the time had come to cut down on his concert performances. Thereafter he limited himself to only a few concerts or recitals a year. But he did not fade away from the musical scene, for another challenging opportunity came his way. At that time Henry Ford announced that he was not going to engage any college graduates that year, on the grounds that they were "useless", knowing nothing of "real life". That set the cat among the pigeons, and the various college authorities, spurred into action, decided to employ a number of people who had made their own way in the world in various walks of life to tour the campuses, give lectures, attend lectures and seminars, and generally make themselves available to students in the hope that some of the accumulated wisdom might 'rub off'. Bauer was engaged in this capacity, and seems to have enjoyed his free-ranging duties. In addition, as a musical scholar he devoted some of his time to editing the works of Schumann and Brahms, and made arrangements and transcriptions of many works. He acquired a number of musical honours and distinctions and gave lectures at various schools of music. Bauer was active in an advisory capacity to the University of Miami until his death.

To the end of his life Harold Bauer preserved a wry sense of humour and was always ready to tell jokes intended to illustrate how, in his view, he had failed to make the 'big time' in music. He related one such story when he was in his 70s:

"I had occasion recently to telephone a large music store where there was every reason to believe I was well known. The clerk took careful note of my order and then asked my name, which I had already given him. "Mister Harold Bauer", I said carefully, thinking he had not heard me the first time. "Yes, Sir", he answered respectfully. "How is it spelled? B - O- W - .. ?" "

Harold Bauer died on 12th March 1951 in Miami, Florida, aged 77. In his lifetime he was known particularly for his interpretation of the classical composers, especially Beethoven, Brahms and Schumann, though he also helped to popularise certain French composers such as Debussy, Franck and Ravel. His art lives on through the large number of piano rolls he recorded at a time when he was at the height of his powers. Although he used to belittle his own status, he was in fact one of the best pianists of his era and was recognised as such by his musical colleagues.

Josef Lhevinne

10. Josef Lhevinne

A name to rank alongside Godowsky, Hofmann and the other great pianists of the Golden Age is that of Josef Lhevinne. Shy and unassuming by nature, he was never one to seek the limelight or court publicity. Had he been left to his own devices he might never have reached the forefront of his profession as a concert pianist. But guided by his redoubtable wife Rosina, Lhevinne came to the fore and established himself as one of the finest pianists of his generation. After his earlier very successful years his concert tours became progressively fewer in number and his recordings were sparse, the reason being that much of his time was devoted to teaching. When he did appear on the concert platform, however, he was acclaimed as a brilliant virtuoso and a poet of the piano all rolled into one. The greatest accolade that can be bestowed on him is that, like Godowsky, his skill was admired and envied by his fellow pianists. They knew that, in terms of both technique and musicality, his powers were unsurpassed.

In common with so many master pianists of his day, Josef Lhevinne hailed from Russia. His father, Arkady, was a Jewish musician, a professional trumpeter from Lodz, a city now in Poland but then in Russia. Four children were born to Arkady and his first wife; after her death he married again and seven more children were borne by his second wife, Fanny. The first four of these were girls, then came Josef who was born in Orel on 13th December 1874, and two more sons were to follow. When Josef was a year old Arkady took his family to Moscow for he had secured an appointment to play the trumpet in the orchestra of the Imperial Small Theatre there, no mean feat as Jews were usually confined to the provinces by State decree. Interestingly, none of the four daughters appears to have been musical but both Josef's brothers were later to make a living as musicians, Myron as a composer and Theodore as an orchestral member.

Josef was a quiet boy; he said later in life that he was three years old before he spoke a word. With so many children in the home, he said, there was no point in speaking as no-one would have noticed whether he spoke or not! At four he started to play the piano, an instrument the family were storing for a relative, and as might be expected from a future musical genius, he was able not only to pick out tunes but also to harmonise. Josef's father, though a fine trumpeter, was not a pianist and he arranged for a local Swedish-born musician, Nils Krysander, to give lessons to the boy. He had

---

The name was originally spelt Lhévinne but the accent fell into disuse during Josef's lifetime.

such a high regard for the child's talent that he refused any remuneration. The lessons were happy ones, and Josef, who was quite athletic, enjoyed a normal childhood. He was not, fortunately for him, subjected to a musical hothouse upbringing.

When Josef was eight years old his teacher allowed him to play publicly at various local venues, often attended by the aristocracy, and these appearances continued for three years. One such event led to his enrolment as a pupil at the Moscow Conservatory. The recital in question was a fashionable soirée at which the Grand Duke Constantine, second son of Tsar Nicholas I, happened to be present. After hearing the 11 year old Josef play Beethoven's *Moonlight* Sonata and Liszt's transcription of *Tannhäuser*, the Duke asked him if he would like to attend the Moscow Conservatory. Josef said he would. The Duke then suggested to the host, who happened to be the wealthiest person present, that *he* should pay. Put on the spot, he agreed to do so. So it was that in 1886 Josef Lhevinne was auditioned for the Conservatory by Vassily Safonoff, a former pupil of Leschetizky, who taught the more advanced students there. In later years Lhevinne described the audition:

"I played. All the time Safonoff seemed to be quietly smiling to himself as if with pleasure. Meanwhile, the Director of the Conservatory (Taneyev) had come into the room and suggested that I be placed in the preparatory class, until I had become sufficiently advanced to study with Safonoff. Safonoff would not listen to this. He insisted that other teachers would spoil me for him."

Josef was duly enrolled in Safonoff's class and soon became one of his star pupils. At 14 he and two older pupils, none other than Sergei Rachmaninov and Alexander Scriabin, were selected to play for Anton Rubinstein on one of the great man's periodic visits to the Conservatory. Josef played Beethoven's *Eroica* Variations and some of Chopin's études. At the conclusion Rubinstein wrung Josef's hand and said, "Work hard and you will be a great man!" Rubinstein was Josef's hero, and such praise from the master himself spurred him on to even greater efforts, resulting in outstanding progress.

In November 1889, when Josef was a month short of his 15th birthday, Rubinstein asked Josef if he would play as soloist in a benefit concert for widows and orphans that he was to conduct in the Hall of the Nobility in Moscow. He did so, playing Beethoven's *Emperor* Concerto, a Chopin étude, and then a Rubinstein étude as an encore. This performance, taking place as it did in a large hall under the baton of an internationally famous musician, can be regarded as his public debut as an adult pianist. Moscow's leading music critic wrote:

Josef Lhevinne

"The young pianist Josef Lhevinne's performance of Beethoven's 5th Concerto was a huge success. One can without fear predict for this youth a brilliant future. In his playing were united all the qualities necessary for a virtuoso: colossal technique, perfect tone, and a lot of musicality. In respect of the last, he expressed such maturity as one would never expect from someone of his age."

Muscovites hailed him as Rubinstein's heir apparent - an accolade also accorded occasionally to others!

Josef's studies at the Conservatory continued for two further years and in 1892 at the age of 17 he graduated with a Gold Medal. In some years no gold medals were awarded but in that particular year there was a bumper crop, for in addition to Josef Lhevinne's, gold medals were awarded to Maximov (19 years old), Rachmaninov (19) and Scriabin (20).

Josef's first professional engagement after graduation was as accompanist to Eugenio Giroldoni, an Italian baritone, work which enhanced his musical skills, for in observing his colleague he learned a lot about singing, which in turn helped him to achieve the much sought-after 'singing tone' at the piano. He then tried to establish himself as a piano soloist, and managed to secure a number of concerts in Eastern Europe for the equivalent of about £75 per concert in present-day values. All his attention was turned to the piano, for unlike Rachmaninov and Scriabin, he had no leanings towards composition.

Nevertheless, work was hard to find, but in 1895, when Josef was 20, an event occurred which gave his fledgling career a tremendous boost. Anton Rubinstein had died in November 1894 at the age of 64, but in spite of that the second International Rubinstein Piano Competition went ahead in Berlin in August 1895. Every competitor had to play a Bach prelude and fugue, the slow movement of a Mozart sonata, three works by Chopin (a ballade, mazurka and nocturne), a Liszt étude, pieces from Schumann's *Kreisleriana* or *Fantasiestücke*, one of Beethoven's last eight sonatas, and one of Rubinstein's five piano concertos. Josef chose as his Beethoven sonata Opus 106 (*Hammerklavier*). There were 30 contestants, and the 26 judges decided that Lhevinne should be the winner. This event was the world's most important piano competition and was the ideal jumping-off ground for an aspiring pianist for not only did it carry a first prize of 5000 francs but also a contract from Hermann Wolff, Europe's leading concert manager, for a tour of 40 concerts during the 1895-96 season.

The tour began with a concert in which he played Rubinstein's Fifth Concerto in Moscow's Hall of the Nobility with Josef's teacher, Safonoff, as the conductor. Josef Hofmann, then 19, played Rubinstein's Third and Fourth Concertos in other concerts of the series and these two great pianists, Lhevinne and Hofmann, were to be largely responsible for keeping

Rubinstein's music alive for the next 40 years. Later Josef played in Amsterdam with the Concertgebouw Orchestra and in Paris with the Lamoureux Orchestra. Lhevinne impressed everyone by his brilliance and delicacy, and was accepted by the critics as a front-rank pianist. Unfortunately the tour was abruptly terminated in December 1895 when he reached the age of 21, for by the law of the land he had to do a year's military service and the authorities refused permission to postpone conscription until the tour was over.

Josef Lhevinne's life and career were soon to be profoundly influenced by his marriage to Rosina, also a highly talented musician. It is therefore important to digress for a few moments from Josef's story in order to look briefly at her life and background. Rosina, also Jewish, was born in Kiev on 28th March 1880, five and a quarter years after Josef's birth. She was the younger daughter of a Dutch travelling diamond merchant named Jacques Bessie and his wife Maria. Jacques was raised in Rotterdam where the family owned a diamond business. He was groomed for the family firm and after a short spell at the University in Paris he was sent to Russia to sell their wares; it was there that he and Maria met. After their initial sojourn in Kiev following their marriage, Jacques and Maria moved to Moscow where opportunities for trade were better. Jacques was often away on business and it was Maria, a talented woman who taught French, loved literature and played the piano, who brought up Rosina and her elder sister, Sophie. The family was prosperous and employed a Swiss governess for the children, a Russian cook, and servant girls.

The family owned two grand pianos and, as was the custom in those days, Sophie was expected to learn to play. After some lessons from her mother a professional teacher was found when Sophie was 12. He was Antonin Galli, a graduate of the Moscow Conservatory. Rosina was usually present when Sophie's lessons were in progress and used to correct Sophie's mistakes from the other end of the room. It was soon evident that Rosina, then five, was the one with the musical ability. Galli suggested that the children's parents save their money for "the young one". Rosina's piano lessons began when she was six, and such was her talent that at nine she was allowed to enter the Moscow Conservatory though only three per cent of the places were allocated to Jewish students. Soon after she enrolled her teacher fell ill and Safonoff, who had become the Director, suggested she should be taught for a while by his most talented pupil, Josef Lhevinne. Josef arrived at the Bessies' home to present himself in the role of teacher. He was then 14 and, according to Rosina's later recollections, looked 18; she was nine and looked six. Recalling those early days, Rosina wrote many years later:

"The first thing he did was pat me kindly on the head. Then he put me on his knee and looked at my hands and asked what I could play on the piano. I was too shy to answer, so he asked, "Do you like music?" I nodded, and he asked if I would like him to play for me. I nodded again, and he went to the piano and played the Chopin *Barcarolle*, and that piece has had a special meaning for me ever since. The experience of him as a teacher lasted about six weeks, until Remesov became well. After that, Josef sometimes visited my parents on the informal evenings they gave for friends of the family. But he paid no more attention to me, for I was but a child, and he a great man in his teens."

This remained the extent of their relationship for some years, except for occasional social visits by the teenage Josef to Rosina's home whilst she was a student at the Conservatory. These visits were rare, until the period of Josef's conscription into the army, when he was stationed near Moscow and had a lot of time on his hands. Visits to the Bessie home then became more frequent and it was at this time, according to Josef, that they fell in love. In later years he recalled:

"I fell in love with her very suddenly. It was when she was 15 and I heard her play the Chopin E minor Concerto in Moscow with Safonoff conducting. She was so pretty and she played so beautifully."

After that they often went out together and she was invited to his parents' home for dinner.

When Josef's period of conscription ended he began to re-establish himself as a pianist. In 1898 he went to Paris to play the Third Concerto of Saint-Saëns with the Lamoureux Orchestra, and shortly afterwards he was back in Moscow as Rosina took her final examinations at the Conservatory. She excelled in them and followed in Josef's footsteps, gaining the coveted Gold Medal of the Conservatory. She was only the fifth girl ever to win the medal at the Conservatory and, at 18, the youngest.

A week after Rosina's graduation she and Josef were married, on 20th June 1898. She was 18 and he was 23. Conscious of the anti-Semitic laws in Russia, the Jewish couple decided to be baptised by a minister of the Dutch Reformed Church prior to their wedding. This was a matter of political expediency as the Jews were severely restricted by law, but it caused a temporary rift in the Lhevinne family. Josef's father disapproved of his son's baptism and refused to attend the marriage ceremony. So began the union of Russia's most talented young musical couple.

The honeymoon was spent in Pushkino, a resort town about 20 miles north of Moscow. Music did not take a back seat on the honeymoon and they discovered how their methods of learning a musical composition differed. Josef spent much more time learning a piece than Rosina; she learned it very quickly but also forgot more rapidly and perhaps did not find some of the more subtle insights that he discovered. Fine pianist as she was, she realised on their honeymoon that she would never match his ability, and there and then she made a remarkable decision; she would abandon any thoughts of a solo career and would devote herself to assisting her husband in the promotion of his musical calling. She would content herself with being Josef's wife. She hated anyone to suggest that they preferred her playing to his; she always maintained that his was far superior, and that for her to play alone would be a distraction that might hinder his career.

Following his marriage, Josef's career as a pianist gradually began to take shape. But it was not easy to get engagements, for the number of concerts and recitals that could be given in Russia was relatively small; it was opera that was most popular there. Consequently the Lhevinnes' income was low and gave cause for concern, but Rosina's parents helped them financially. As the young couple were contemplating their uncertain future their financial problems were suddenly resolved when, in 1899, Josef was offered a professorship at the Tiflis branch of the Imperial Conservatory. He accepted with alacrity and Josef and Rosina set out for Tiflis, 'The Pearl of the Caucasus', a city of 160,000 inhabitants on the River Kura between the Black and Caspian Seas.

Once settled in an apartment there with a 15 year old girl as a personal maid, the Lhevinnes began a comfortable and enjoyable existence. Josef taught with distinction at the Conservatory, they entertained visiting celebrities, and Josef was recognised by everyone in the city as a pianistic wizard. One guest who came to stay when visiting Tiflis was the young genius Josef Hofmann, who was a year younger than Josef Lhevinne. The two Josefs turned out to be kindred spirits, and so began a lifelong friendship. Josef Hofmann's remarkable memory for music is legendary, and an incident which occurred when he was staying with the Lhevinnes demonstrated his remarkable gift. Whilst in their home he picked up a copy of Liszt's arrangement of Schubert's *Die Lorelei*, music he had not seen before. After browsing through it for a few minutes, but not playing it, he put it down. At his concert that evening he concluded his scheduled programme, looked at the Lhevinnes with a twinkle in his eye, and launched into *Die Lorelei* as an encore. The Lhevinnes' hearts sank for they thought he could not possibly do justice to the piece. But he played it with brilliant assurance, glancing at the Lhevinnes from time to time as he did so. Afterwards he told Josef and Rosina how much he had enjoyed watching their alarmed faces!

Life in Tiflis was good. Josef enjoyed his work there, and had he been left to his own devices he might have stayed there to the end of his days, as he was completely unambitious and never craved for fame or fortune. But to Rosina it was obvious that Tiflis, pleasant as it was, was a musical backwater. Josef was a large fish in a very small pond, and to her it was clear he would have no opportunity there to develop his talent or further his career. She discussed the matter with him and persuaded him they would have to leave. The object of her thoughts was Berlin. It was a centre of musical excellence; there Josef would have the opportunity to stand alongside the greatest musicians of the day and to compete with them for engagements.

Josef resigned his post and he and Rosina moved to Berlin in 1902. They took an apartment and Josef looked around for opportunities. One of the first musicians they met was Busoni. He had been one of the judges at the Rubinstein Competition which Josef had won, and he invited the Lhevinnes to his home one day. There were many other guests, all pianists, and some students. After the usual cordial greetings, Busoni asked Josef to play. He did not know what was coming, so he protested he was not prepared. Busoni was not to be put off. "Play the Schumann Toccata." Lhevinne played it. "Now the Paganini-Brahms." "Now play Feux Follets", "Now Rubinstein's Octave Étude", "Now Chopin's Octave Étude", and "Now Chopin's Étude in Double Thirds". Josef played them all, with people standing around the piano. Busoni, in pensive mood, made no comment. After refreshments, Busoni bade the Lhevinnes goodbye, politely, and they left. On the way home, Josef said, "Do you think he liked my playing?" Rosina said she was sure he did, but she did not find out the real answer until about 50 years later:

"I was teaching in a master class in California and had gone to a party. A man came up and introduced himself as Mark Ginsburg. He turned to my daughter Marianna and said, "I have something to tell you that maybe your mother does not know." Then he asked, "Mrs Lhevinne, do you remember the time that Busoni invited you and your husband to come, and he played?" "Yes, Yes", I said, "I remember." "I was studying with Busoni then", said Ginsburg. "The next day we had a class, and Busoni said to us, "Yesterday I heard a young Russian pianist, and if I put you all in one pot you would not make one Lhevinne." "

Rosina was right in realising that competition would be fierce in Berlin, for d'Albert, Busoni, Carreño, Gabrilowitsch, Godowsky, Paderewski, Rosenthal and Schnabel were all active there in Lhevinne's first season. After a brief visit to Paris where he played at the Salle Érard (the critics ranking him alongside several of those named above) his Berlin debut was arranged for 22nd March 1902, with the Berlin Philharmonic Orchestra. Lhevinne played Beethoven's Fifth and Rubinstein's Fifth Concertos, along with Weber's C major Sonata, which is the sonata with the 'perpetual motion' finale. His success earned him a contract from the Hermann Wolff Company, then being managed by Louisa Wolff following the death of her husband, as well as teaching posts in Berlin. At the same time Moscow wired him the offer of a post as a Professor at the Conservatory there. Josef accepted the Moscow appointment having first ensured that he would be allowed time off to fulfil his concert engagements.

Back in Moscow, Josef and Rosina took an apartment in a 5-storey building. He was 27, with a steady income from teaching and a growing reputation as a fine pianist. Later in 1902 Rosina, then 22, was persuaded by Arthur Nikisch to play the Henselt F minor Concerto with him and the Moscow Conservatory Orchestra. It was Rosina's first solo performance since her marriage and one of the very few she ever undertook during Josef's lifetime. She was now content with the way Josef's career was progressing for already he had an international reputation as a brilliant pianist, one of the best in Europe. In 1903, playing in Vienna, Josef "took the city by storm" according to the critics and was immediately invited back to give further concerts. Well-paid engagements in Warsaw, Paris, Berlin, Vienna (again) and London followed in rapid succession, but the London concert led indirectly to his withdrawal from the concert platform for several months; he fell off his bicycle the day after his London debut and broke his leg. His activities thus curtailed, he concentrated on his teaching job at the Moscow Conservatory. He was an excellent teacher and his class grew rapidly to over 20; meanwhile, Rosina was also well established as a piano teacher, first at a finishing school for the daughters of the rich, and later, after she had discovered that the daughters of the rich were often not very interested, privately at home, where her services were soon very much in demand.

Restored to fitness in 1904, Josef Lhevinne continued to teach and resumed his concert career, the latter proving so successful that he was offered a concert tour of the USA to begin in January 1906. For financial and artistic reasons he was delighted by the offer and Rosina, knowing how her husband's career would be furthered, was totally in favour. However, she did not plan to go to the USA with her husband, partly because of her teaching commitments, but mainly because of the fact that she was pregnant. The tour was in jeopardy for a while because of a variety of adverse circumstances, but eventually the problems were resolved and Lhevinne made his American debut on 27th January 1906, with the Russian Symphony Orchestra, consisting mainly of Jewish emigrants from Russia. He played Rubinstein's Fifth Concerto, Chopin's Octave Étude (one of his specialities; he was one of the few pianists who could play it properly) and Scriabin's

Nocturne for the Left Hand. Next day the Steinway Piano Company invited him to their offices and offered him $10,000 plus expenses to make an extended concert tour of the USA during the 1906-07 season, playing exclusively Steinway pianos, and he accepted. Steinway had previously undertaken the personal management of only two pianists, Anton Rubinstein and Paderewski. As Lhevinne's short tour continued in the early months of 1906, playing with various orchestras, the critics fully endorsed Steinway's enthusiasm. Henry T. Finck likened Lhevinne to Anton Rubinstein and remarked:

"He has the great Anton's technique, his dash, his bravura, his brilliancy and a good deal of his leonine power. He can make the piano sing, too."

In March 1906 *The New York Times* printed an interview with Lhevinne, treating him as a fully-fledged celebrity. He was the musical sensation of the American season after his brief tour during which he played in New York, Chicago, Cincinnati and New Haven.

Before returning to Europe, Lhevinne resigned his Moscow Conservatory post because he had already overstayed his leave of absence and felt it would be unreasonable to ask for further lengthy periods away from Moscow.

On 21st July 1906 the Lhevinne's first child was born; a son, Constantine, named in honour of the Grand Duke who had arranged for Josef's admission to the Conservatory years earlier. He was born in Paris, for the Lhevinnes had decided that Paris would be a better starting point for Josef's forthcoming second tour of the USA than Moscow. Before leaving for the New World, Josef recorded some piano rolls for the Welte Company in Leipzig. They included Scriabin's Study for the Left Hand and Czerny's Octave Study. These rolls of 1906 are of historical importance for they pre-date by several years any other recordings made by Lhevinne (gramophone records or Ampico rolls). The Welte Company were to issue another batch of Josef Lhevinne's rolls in 1911, and he recorded for the company again during the 1920s, of which more will be said later.

In October 1906 Josef Lhevinne sailed for the USA again at Steinway's expense, this time accompanied by Rosina and their son, and also Rosina's father (her mother had died) and a maid. The first concert of the tour was with the New York Philharmonic Orchestra on 16th November 1906 and more than 100 were to follow in a season which, it was generally acknowledged, was dominated by Lhevinne and Rosenthal. During the tour Josef and Rosina made their American debut as a two-piano team in Chicago; their two-piano appearances were to be repeated occasionally throughout their lives. *The Chicago Daily Tribune* reported favourably on their recital:

"Mme Lhevinne is a dark-haired, petite young woman, who plays the piano unusually well, as far as could be judged. She and her husband thoroughly understood each other so far as musical interest was concerned and their performance deservedly found warm applause at the audience's hands."

A month later the couple played together at Carnegie Hall.

As a solo pianist in his prime, Lhevinne's playing was distinguished not only by its virtuoso quality but by an intimate understanding of the music, impeccable phrasing, and fine gradations of a singing tone. He was at his best in the works of the classical and romantic school. Music by Beethoven, Brahms, Chopin, Liszt, Schumann and Tchaikovsky (the concertos) usually formed the core of his programmes, supplemented by composers such as Rubinstein in the earlier part of his career and Debussy later. To Lhevinne, 'musicality' was everything and he hated to read reviews which referred to his "prodigious technique". He would perform even the most exhibitionist of 19th century works with a compelling musicianship. Shy and almost completely without competitive instinct, his manner was unassuming on the concert platform. A Chicago critic remarked:

"Lhevinne lacks all the qualities that the uninitiated public craves, but possesses everything that the music demands. He is authoritive, sincere, unaffected. He is a great artist, the peer of any; as a poseur he is a failure. Lhevinne is too great an artist for his own good. No showmanship, few mannerisms. Unable and unwilling to make himself a marketable commodity."

From 1906 until 1909 Lhevinne's winter seasons were spent in the USA and the summer ones in Europe, including visits to Moscow. Josef taught and made concert tours, whilst Rosina taught and enjoyed New York's cultural life when her husband was touring in America. But both felt the compelling attraction of their native Europe and they decided to make their home there. From 1909 they lived in Berlin but the tours and teaching continued as before. Josef and Rosina soon built up a large clientèle of students, more than 40 between them. They had long since learned the wisdom of insisting that every student coming to either of them should sign up for at least ten lessons; Josef had discovered years earlier that some students were not beyond taking a single lesson and then advertising themselves as "Pupil of Josef Lhevinne"!

Josef's and Rosina's temperaments were completely different; his was quiet and reserved, hers extrovert and full of vitality. Throughout their marriage they were often apart for long periods of time, and this may have contributed to the stability of their marriage, for the absences provided a respite from a clash of personalities. However, when playing together in recitals they were always 'in tune' musically. After a joint recital of the

Mozart E flat Concerto for Two Pianos a critic wrote:

"One hears [this music of Mozart] so rarely that it can be classed as a novelty. It seems to present no particular difficulties; nevertheless its interpretation cannot succeed unless the artists are endowed with a very high degree of musical sensitivity and unless they are by temperament of the highest musical taste, eschewing any tendency towards producing an effect. Madame and M. Lhevinne were truly in harmony with these demands, and the result was a purity of transmission that made a deep and profound impression. They played with that rare simplicity which shuns any attempt to draw attention to itself. Certainly the absence of the acrobatic 'tours de force' that certain contemporary virtuosos use in their playing did not detract from the interpretation of this concerto. This work demands to the highest degree the art of possessing the instruments; it demands that artists be able to give to their playing a character corresponding exactly to the character of the work itself; and it must be performed with the requisite elegance and finesse. From all these points of view, the artists had every right to the acclaim which was passionately and endlessly lavished upon them."

Early in 1914 Josef was engaged as soloist with the Moscow Philharmonic Orchestra under Sergei Rachmaninov to play Beethoven's First Concerto, the first time he had played it in public. Lhevinne and Rachmaninov had not worked together before and had never been particularly close even though they had been students together at the Conservatory. Josef said to his wife, "Rosina, do you think I ought to tell Rachmaninov I've never played the concerto in public before, and seek his advice on tempi?" Rosina agreed that he should. The Lhevinnes duly went to the Rachmaninovs for dinner and afterwards Josef nervously broached the subject. Rachmaninov and his wife burst into roars of laughter whilst Josef and Rosina sat nonplussed. Finally they stopped laughing and Rachmaninov explained that he had awakened his wife in the night and said, "You know, the Lhevinnes are coming for dinner today. Do you think I should tell him that I don't know the concerto?" This incident broke the ice between Lhevinne and Rachmaninov and they remained good friends afterwards.

In May 1914 the Lhevinnes bought a large villa at the end of the road in which they had lived in Berlin for several years, but with war imminent the purchase was ill-timed. When war came the Lhevinnes were immediately interned as aliens from a hostile country (Russia) and Jewish ones at that. As they were not seen as a threat they were allowed to continue living in their home on condition that they did not leave the area, that they report to the police regularly, obey an 8 pm curfew, and that they must not give unauthorised concerts whilst Germany and Russia were at war.

Most of the Lhevinnes' pupils, many of whom were from other countries, had left, and there was nothing to do but to sit tight and live frugally. Money was in short supply as the Lhevinnes had always banked in Moscow and their funds had been confiscated. Fortunately the house had a large garden and the family grew as much of their own produce as possible. Josef also did a little fishing, and he and Rosina collected mushrooms from the adjacent wood. One of the few remaining students, a girl, came to the Lhevinnes' assistance. Writing many years later, Rosina observed: "She took lessons from me and was the worst student of all. When her lesson was over I always had to take an aspirin and go to bed." But she looked forward to her lessons and Rosina hadn't the heart to turn her away. When war was declared the girl, Sarah, decided to stay in Berlin and her lessons continued. She shared a flat with a girl who worked at the Dutch Embassy and therefore had access to food from Holland, some of which Sarah would parcel up and take with her to the Lhevinnes when she went for her lessons. Josef, who enjoyed his food, would say to Rosina, "When will Sarah be coming for her next lesson?" and both would sit expectantly in the window waiting for her to march up the drive armed with provisions.

Because of the terms of the Lhevinnes' internment Josef made no public appearances in Berlin during the war except for two or three charity concerts. The most notable event in their personal lives during the war was the birth of their second child, Marianna, in July 1918. Interestingly, neither of the children of these talented parents turned out to be musical. This event apart, the war years were gloomy ones made even worse by the constant news of the carnage occurring daily on the battlefields. It is not surprising that memories of America assumed an idyllic air during their internment in Berlin, and once the war was over they decided to return to the USA. Josef made a brief tour of European cities in 1919 prior to their departure for New York in October of that year. Concerts were arranged as soon as they arrived and the Lhevinnes set up home in Richmond Hill Avenue, Kew Gardens, New York, in a beautiful house with spacious lawns, built on a hill top.

The Lhevinnes immediately began to take private students in their home and the trickle soon became a torrent. Both were very successful teachers in their separate ways. Josef's teaching was characterised by meticulous attention to detail; Rosina took a broader view. Said Rosina:

"Once Josef was teaching Beethoven's Sonata in E flat, Opus 31, and I was upstairs. Without exaggeration, I heard the student play the first two chords 25 times. It got so much on my nerves that I simply had to call down to him, very gently, "Josef, I cannot hear anything that he does wrong. Please tell me what you want from the boy." And he called back, "Maybe you cannot picture it from upstairs, but if you were here you would see that he holds his finger on the note too long."

Josef's concerts and recitals continued to draw praise from the critics. The veteran writer W.L. Hubbard observed:

"There come moments in the life of a concert goer when a performance is met which is so complete, so perfect, so satisfying that it becomes golden in experience and memory. From that time on his musical life is richer, his spiritual sensitivity finer, his appreciation of the beautiful truer. These are the moments really worthwhile in life, the ones that positively count."

Every year from the early 1920s onwards Josef gave a summer Master Class at the American Conservatory in Chicago and spent part of his summers at a retreat, "Bonnie Oaks" in Wisconsin, near Chicago, loaned to him by a friend. There he would indulge in his lifelong hobbies of astronomy and fishing, and would prepare his winter programmes. Lhevinne always put a lot of thought into the structure of his recitals. Whereas Schnabel would sometimes play as many as four Beethoven sonatas in one recital, Lhevinne never included more than one. He wished to entertain as well as to educate. He told one student, "A public programme should be like a good meal - not too many beefsteaks, nor too much frothy dessert."

At Bonnie Oaks, Lhevinne spent a lot of his time in 'Josef's Tower', an ex-water tower altered according to his wishes. The second (top) floor contained his observatory, complete with telescope and astronomical books, the first floor was his bedroom, with his fishing gear and a photograph of Rosina (who always stayed at home), whilst the ground floor, complete with a Steinway Grand, was where he practised and prepared his programmes for the coming season. His annual retreat to Bonnie Oaks became virtually a sacred event in his life.

In the 1920s teaching took up a high proportion of Josef Lhevinne's time and he would have made even fewer concert appearances than he did were it not for Rosina's virtual management of his career. Not only did he teach, he wrote about the subject of piano playing and in 1924 his famous book *Basic Principles of Piano Playing* was published, with a foreword by Rosina. An event which turned his career even more towards teaching was an offer in 1924 of a Professorship at the newly formed Juilliard Graduate School of Music, set up in New York as a result of a bequest of $20,000,000 in the will of Augustus D. Juilliard, a New York cotton magnate. Josef took up the appointment with enthusiasm and was such a success that he continued in the post to the end of his life, making short concert tours occasionally meanwhile. Rosina, who was also a member of the Juilliard Faculty, assisted with the teaching and gave his lessons when he was away. Initially he was paid $40 per hour and Rosina $25.

Lhevinne's long association with Steinway pianos ended in the late 1920s when he decided to play Chickering instruments instead. The reason was said to be purely technical; Steinway pianos are known to have a very strong bass register, and because of the fact that Lhevinne's left hand was his stronger one (he said it was the one he used to hit other boys with as a child!) he found it increasingly difficult, so he said, to achieve a balanced result. The flirtation with Chickering did not last long; he soon transferred to Baldwin instruments, and continued to play Baldwin pianos for the remainer of his life.

When he was not working Josef liked to indulge in his various hobbies, which included, apart from fishing and astronomy, table-tennis and bridge. Rosina, on the other hand, liked to 'talk music' with other musicians.

In the 1920s Josef made about 20 excellent piano rolls for the Ampico Company. They included complete performances of Beethoven's *Moonlight Sonata* (an incredibly popular piece in the 1920s) and Schumann's *Papillons*. He also recorded six rolls for Artecho; one each of music by Chopin, Godard, Mendelssohn, Schlözer, Schulz-Evler and Schumann. The Ampico contract led directly to a new venture for Lhevinne; broadcasting. Ampico's sales were flagging in the late 1920s, as were those of the Aeolian Company, and on New Year's Day 1928, Lhevinne broadcast in 'Ampico Hour', a programme presented by the company in an attempt to revive interest in their products. Two of Lhevinne's Ampico rolls were played in the programme and he also performed a number of pieces 'live'. Lhevinne always enjoyed playing for radio; the presence of an audience was not essential to him; indeed, he was happy in the relaxed and quiet atmosphere of the broadcasting studio.

The Ampico company was not the only one for whom Lhevinne recorded reproducing piano rolls during the 1920s. He also made a number for Welte, the company which had issued some of his recordings in 1906 and again in 1911. Altogether Welte issued a total of nearly 30 of Lhevinne's rolls. A large range of composers was represented in these recordings, namely Beethoven, Chopin, Czerny, Dohnanyi, Gluck, Godard, Liszt, Mendelssohn, Meyerbeyer, Moszkowski, Poldini, Rachmaninov, Rubinstein, Schlözer, Schubert, Schumann, Scriabin, Sgambati, J. Strauss jr., and Weber. This list shows clearly that although Lhevinne had his favourite composers, others, including some modern ones, were by no means excluded from his repertoire.

In the summer of 1928 Lhevinne began recording gramophone records for RCA, having already made some for Pathé. His recording career continued in the 1930s but he did not record as much as one might have expected considering his standing as one of the 'big four' of the Russian school of playing in the United States, the others being Hofmann, Rachmaninov and the youthful Horowitz.

Though Lhevinne's concert appearances were now fewer than before, he still delighted his audiences and the critics when he did play in public. After a performance of Chopin's études in Carnegie Hall in February 1930, William J. Henderson wrote in the American newspaper *The Sun*:

"In his youth he was a virtuoso and a magnificent stormer of the keyboard. He thundered his proclamations and sometimes stunned his hearers by sheer power and irresistable technique. This is not the Lhevinne of today. He is now a ripe and mellowed master who has found all the secrets of tone and who sheds rays of refulgent beauty through every composition he plays . . . He sees laterally across the whole breadth of every composition and perpendicularly down into its depths. He makes the plans of his readings with brains and imagination."

Always self-critical, Josef Lhevinne was never given to self praise. When he arrived home after a concert, if Rosina had not been there she would ask, "Josef, how was it?" "Rotten" was his usual reply. After a particularly fine performance the most praise he would ever permit himself was, "Well, it was all right."

Lhevinne wisely avoided Hitler's Germany during his tours of Europe in the 1930s, and in 1933 he became an American citizen at the age of 58. When the war came his tours dwindled even further and teaching took up nearly all his working time from then. He gave the occasional concert, including an annual one in the Carnegie Hall, until November 1943, and also made a number of two-piano appearances with Rosina. In the last few years of his life their joint recitals outnumbered his solo ones. Always a perfectionist, Josef Lhevinne was never satisfied until he had achieved exactly the musical effect he wanted. In one concert in which Josef was performing both before and after the interval, one of Rosina's friends called in to see him in the artists' room during the interval. "Rosina!" she told her friend when she came out, "Josef wasn't practising what he was going to play; he was practising what he had just played!"

Josef and Rosina's last performance as a two-piano team was in the Town Hall, New York, on 10th May 1944. They played a number of works together, finishing with Chopin's Rondo for Two Pianos. In August of the same year, Josef visited his daughter Marianna in Los Angeles. Whilst he was there he went for a swim in the sea one day, ventured too far out, and had difficulty getting back to the shore in the high waves that were breaking at the time. Eventually he managed to make it to the beach but the strain of the episode was thought to have damaged his heart and he was rushed to hospital. After a while he was released but his health, which had always been excellent until then, had suffered. Further work was out of the question. He insisted on going to his Kew Gardens home in New York. It was there, on 2nd December 1944, that he complained of feeling unwell, retired to bed, and within the hour died of a heart attack, 11 days before his 70th birthday.

What better tribute is there to the art of Josef Lhevinne than that of his old friend Artur Rubinstein, writing in *The New York Herald Tribune* a week after Lhevinne's death:

"With the passing away of Josef Lhevinne the musical world has lost a great artist and one of the greatest pianists of our epoch. His many friends, among whom I proudly count myself, will miss his spirited, heart-warming company; his colleagues and pupils will miss his genuine interest in their work and his ever-ready moral support. Lhevinne, in my opinion, belonged to the group one would call 'aristocrats of the keyboard'. Leopold Godowsky and Emil Sauer were 'aristocrats' but none came nearer to the ideal than Josef Lhevinne. His playing possessed what the French most love - 'éclat', clarity to the highest degree, the ability to project all the beauty and depth of a musical work with the ease of one who dominates all pianistic difficulties without ever 'showing them off'. Lhevinne had elegance, and he could also move his listeners to tears by the sheer beauty of his tone. Yes, he was the last of the great 'aristocrats'."

After Josef's death Rosina was offered her husband's teaching post at the Juilliard School, to her intense surprise as she was then 64, and was told she could continue to teach there "as long as she felt able". Over the years a galaxy of talented and prize-winning pupils passed through her hands including the American pianist Van Cliburn, and in the Juilliard's competitions over a 20-year period Rosina's pupils won 31 out of 64 contests. More remarkable still, she re-emerged in her mid seventies as a solo artist at the invitation of various concert organisers, thus coming out of a self-imposed solo retirement that had originated soon after she had married over 55 years earlier. On 25th August 1956 she played the Mozart C major Concerto in a performance whose clarity astonished and delighted her many admirers. In the 1961-62 season, when she was over 80, she played the same concerto three times and the Chopin E minor Concerto once. She also played chamber music (Dvorak's quintet) twice and made a number of benefit appearances. In January 1963 aged nearly 83 she played the Chopin E minor Concerto three times in successive days with the New York Philharmonic Orchestra under Leonard Bernstein. She also made a number of recordings, some of which are still in the catalogues. She continued teaching well into her nineties, though at the age of 96 she announced that she had decided to reduce her work load to not more than two lessons a day!

Rosina Lhevinne, who had almost died of diphtheria as a small child and was thereafter always considered 'delicate', proved the old adage that "creaking gates last the longest". Her class of students looked up to their aged teacher with awe and affection. She was still teaching long after her son had retired from his employment at the age of 67! Inevitably, comparisons were made with Clara Schumann who had survived her husband Robert by so many years. Active in mind and body almost to the end of her life, Rosina Lhevinne died at the age of 96 years and seven months on 9th November 1976, having survived her husband, the wonderfully gifted pianist Josef Lhevinne, by 32 years.

Josef Hofmann

11. Josef Hofmann

Nature has produced many musical child prodigies over the years. Some of them burst across the scene like shooting stars, only to burn out quickly. Others, when they grew up, achieved a moderate success in the world of music, but without achieving any particular distinction as their talent levelled off. A few, a very rare breed, developed and became great musicians. An example of these - one of the most remarkable prodigies of all time - was the great pianist Josef Hofmann. After an amazing childhood he went on to become one of the best pianists of his day, and some would say one of the greatest the world has known.

Josef Hofmann was fortunate in being born into a musical family and there is no doubt he inherited his parents' talent, though his achievements were soon to outstrip theirs. The family lived in Cracow, Poland, where Josef's father, Casimir, was conductor at the Cracow Opera as well as being a noted pianist and Professor at the Cracow Conservatory. Josef's mother, Matylda, was a soprano of some renown who frequently sang at the Cracow Opera and it was in Cracow that Josef Casimir Hofmann was born on 20th January 1876.

Josef clearly belonged to a home where music was all-important and by the age of three and a half he was showing exceptional talent as a pianist, having been taught by his sister who was his senior by a year and a half. He mastered his piano exercises with great facility, and his ability soon surpassed that of his sister. He was then taught by an aunt, but a year later she had taught him all she knew and the instruction was then provided by his father. At five years of age he made his public debut in a suburb of Warsaw and this was so successful that offers cascaded into the Hofmann household, inviting the child to give a series of concerts. Josef's father wisely declined most of the offers, but nevertheless permitted him to give the occasional recital, with all the proceeds going to charity, and as a result of these, word of Josef's skill gradually spread through Poland.

When he was seven, Josef played the first movement of Beethoven's First Piano Concerto, with a small orchestra, in public, and the critics were bowled over by his performance. They referred to Josef's precision, his instinctive feeling for the style of the composer, and his full, round, singing tone. About this time the great Russian pianist Anton Rubinstein heard Josef play. He was deeply impressed and informed the German impresario Hermann Wolff of the child's prowess. Influenced by the enthusiasm of the great Russian master, Wolff entreated Casimir Hofmann to allow his son to embark on concert engagements. "The world must hear him!" was the message. Eventually Casimir yielded, and the sporadic informal appearances of the young genius gave way to a series of formal concert engagements.

At the age of 10, Josef gave his first concert outside Poland. This was with the Berlin Philharmonic Orchestra in Berlin, where he played the complete First Piano Concerto of Beethoven. The concert was a sensation, acclaimed with wild applause by the audience and with fulsome praise by the critics. The triumph came as no surprise to the orchestra, who had no difficulty in recognising a born musician. At the first rehearsal they had noticed Josef pull at the coat-tails of the conductor, to tell him that the cellos were making certain small errors in one passage, a fault that few of the other instrumentalists had noticed!

After his wonderful reception in Berlin the triumphal progress of the diminutive pianist continued in Denmark, Sweden, Norway, Holland and Paris, where none other than Camille Saint-Saëns declared enthusiastically that the boy had nothing more to learn and that he was "the greatest wonder of the modern age".

America knew about the doings of young Hofmann long before his much-heralded debut in the United States. His deeds had been regularly recorded in the press and in 1887 *Harper's Young People* compared the 11 year old boy to the young Mozart, a tribute that had been bestowed a few years earlier on the youthful Busoni. The writer observed:

"For nearly four years he has been appearing before the public as a piano virtuoso. Lately he has appeared very frequently and created what the newspapers call a 'sensation'. Never was so much written about a young man by his contemporaries as has been written about this young Hofmann. Famous musicians like Rubinstein, and callous old critics like - well, most of the famous ones - have fairly gushed over him. It is a wonder that with all the attention he has received, the little fellow has not become very conceited . . . Away from music he is always a child, and his sense of humour is delightful. One day, his parents promised to pay him 25 cents for each concert, and subsequently, when he finished a concert and encores were demanded he said: "No", with a laugh, "The concert is over and I have earned my quarter." But he played encores, and upon returning to the artists' room said, "Now, in the future, you must pay me by the piece - two cents for my own compositions, and five cents for the others."

The boy who stepped onto the stage of the Metropolitan Opera House in New York on 29th November 1887 was only 11 years old but he was already a mature and experienced musician. His programme included Beethoven's First Piano Concerto, the Variations by Rameau, a Polacca by Weber (transcribed by Liszt), a set of pieces by Chopin and one of his own compositions. This was what New York had been waiting for and the atmosphere was electric as the slight figure, clad in a striped sailor shirt and knee breeches, walked onto the stage and bowed to the audience. He seated himself on the stool and with poise and assurance waited for the whispers of the audience to subside before indicating to the conductor that he was ready for the concerto to begin.

Writing in *The New York Times* the next morning, the music critic W.J. Henderson reported:

"When he concluded the concerto, a thunder of applause swept through the opera house. Many people leapt to their feet. Men shouted "Bravo!" and women waved their handkerchiefs. Pianists of repute were moved to tears - some wiped the moisture from their eyes. The child had astonished the assembly. He was a marvel ... Josef Hofmann played, not only like an artist, but like a master. The tenderness of sentiment, the poetic insight, the ability to make the music not only arouse the intelligence but more the heart of the hearer, as displayed by this child, were simply wonderful ... The feeling and intelligence shown by young Hofmann were far and away beyond his years. They showed that he was a born musician - that rare thing which the world always hungers for and greets with affectionate veneration. Suffice it to say, for the present, that Josef Hofmann, as a musical phenomenon, is worthy of the sensation which he created. More than that, he is an artist, and we can listen to his music without taking into consideration the fact that he is a child. It was not necessary to think "That is extremely good work for a child", because it would have been extremely good work for a man."

Not surprisingly, young Josef Hofmann became all the rage in America following this remarkable triumph, and his father allowed him to be booked for numerous other concerts in December 1887 and January and February 1888. In all he took part in 52 concerts in 10 weeks, sharing the programmes with other musicians. He had learned a large repertoire and could play several works with orchestra as required, for example, two Beethoven Concertos (No. 1 and No. 3), the Mozart Concerto No. 20, Mendelssohn's *Rondo Brillant* and Piano Concerto No. 1, and Weber's *Conzertstück*, Op. 79. Solo pieces included many compositions of Bach, Chopin, Gottschalk, Kalkbrenner (including the Duo for two pianos which Josef played with his father, a piece now rarely, if ever, heard), Moszkowski, Mozart, Rubinstein, Weber and himself. Not only was Josef Hofmann already a master pianist, he had an unfailingly accurate sense of pitch. Once, at the Metropolitan Opera House, he heard a tuning fork that was supposed to be tuned to 440-A. Josef said it was a shade sharp - and it was.

Josef's lengthy series of concerts soon attracted the attention of the New York Society for the Prevention of Cruelty to Children who asserted, probably with some justification, that the boy was being exploited and that his health would suffer. He was examined by a doctor on 2nd February 1888 and it was reported that he was in excellent health. But a journalist noted that "His face looked pale and there were dark rings under his eyes." Hardly surprising! The previous Wednesday he had played in New York; on Friday he was in Philadelphia; on Saturday he was giving another concert in New York before leaving for Boston where he played on Monday, and he was back in New York again for yet another concert on Wednesday. This sort of schedule was to go on for several more weeks. All this by a boy of just 12, when transport was much slower than it is now.

The 'cruelty to children' crusade was taken up by the respected pianist Ernst Perabo in a letter to the press. In it he said:

"Just because he does not make faces or turn somersaults before the piano, people think that the work is easily done. The more easily he grasps, executes and interprets, the more expensive is the fuel; excellent work exhausts the finest fibre, and the nervous system, once ruined, leaves him a wreck. We were told of the medical examination by several physicians. With all due respect to their learning, what, pray, can these persons know of the mental freight he is carrying in his memory, of intricate, abstruse, scientific difficulties, representing from eight to ten hundred pages of repertory? If his present career be continued, he will be deprived of a normal childhood."

Josef himself knew all about the controversy and warmed to the criticism. He plaintively asked a *New York Times* reporter:

"What do they want to make a little boy like me work so hard for? I am not able to do it."

Casimir Hofmann decided, at last, that enough was enough and his son should no longer be exploited, and the remaining 80 scheduled concerts of his tour were cancelled. An anonymous philanthropist (identified years later as Alfred Corning Clark of New York) gave $50,000 to the family on condition that Josef be withdrawn from the concert stage until he was 18 in order to study. When the agent who had arranged Josef's series of concerts heard about this he initiated a lawsuit for breach of contract. But another medical examination revealed that Josef, although not suffering from any organic disease, was beginning to show signs of "mental derangement". The lawsuit was withdrawn and on 28th March 1888 Josef and his family sailed for Europe.

On arrival there they went to Berlin, where Josef began a much needed and long overdue period of conventional schooling which lasted until he was nearly 16. During this time his piano studies continued, first under Casimir Hofmann and later under Moritz Moszkowski. Although Moszkowski was as enthusiastic as everyone else about Josef's ability, the lessons were not a success. "The boy knows so much", he said, "and plays so much better than I do, that I don't know how to teach him."

Early in 1892, when Josef was just 16, he became the pupil of Anton Rubinstein. It is said that he is the only private pupil ever to have been taught by Rubinstein on a regular basis. Josef had for a long time wanted to study under the great Russian pianist, but Rubinstein had always refused to accept private pupils. Then one day, at a party given in Berlin by the impresario Hermann Wolff, who had arranged Josef's tours a few years earlier, Hofmann was invited to play. He played his own Theme, Variations and Fugue, Op. 14. Rubinstein, who seems to have had a penchant for 'one liners', said, "You may not be a pianist yet, but you are certainly a musician." This seemed to be very faint praise, but Rubinstein must have been impressed because he decided there and then to accept Hofmann as his pupil. Rubinstein, generally accepted as one of the greatest pianists of the 19th century, soon grew to marvel at Josef's ability. Not usually noted for extravagant praise, Rubinstein was soon to remark of Hofmann, "He is the greatest genius of music the world has known."

Hofmann was Rubinstein's pupil for two years, until early 1894. This period of study took him to the milestone age of 18 specified in the conditions of Clark's gift. The culmination of this period of study was a concert in Hamburg on 14th March 1894, at which Hofmann played Rubinstein's own Concerto in D minor with Rubinstein conducting. This was his first concert for six years. At the end of the performance Rubinstein threw his arms round his pupil. Amid much acclaim Hofmann was thus well and truly launched on his career as an adult pianist.

In the autumn of 1894 a new tour was arranged for the 18 year old Hofmann, starting in England and continuing in Germany and Russia. Josef had bade farewell to Rubinstein in the March of that year and as fate would have it, they were never to meet again. On 19th November 1894, as Hofmann was travelling by train from London to Cheltenham for a concert engagement, a newspaper headline told him that Rubinstein had died, at the age of 64, only a few months after Hofmann's lessons with him had ended. "It seemed that I had lost not only my greatest benefactor but also the dearest person on earth", wrote Hofmann, "for not only did I admire him - I had grown to love him as well." It so happened that Hofmann was scheduled to play Chopin's B flat Sonata (the sonata with the Funeral March) in Cheltenham that evening. He played it - not only for his audience but for the great master - and he poured his soul into the music. The audience sensed the significance of what was happening and one by one they stood up as he played until all were on their feet, heads bowed, paying their own tribute to Rubinstein.

Hofmann was now a complete pianist, master of all aspects of his art, and was to remain so for over 40 years. In his heyday he was reckoned to be amongst the top few pianists of his generation along with Busoni, Godowsky, Lhevinne and one or two others. Many experts considered him to be the greatest pianist of the 20th century and some argued that he was the greatest of all time. However, these judgments are subjective and no one can justifiably rank pianists into any kind of an order of merit, though an attempt is made to do so in piano competitions. Nevertheless, he was unarguably a great pianist. Although he was a mature artist from a very early age, this maturity was even further enriched as he grew older through his intellectual appreciation of the music and the mastery of the technique of his instrument, which have rarely been matched, let alone surpassed.

What was it about Hofmann's playing that was unique, that marked him as a man apart from his fellow pianists? His contemporaries used to say that his playing combined accuracy, a wide range of tone, even passage work and faultless use of the pedals. The singing tone he managed to produce from his instrument was remarkable, and another feature of his playing was the sudden dynamic eruptions which heightened the tension and emotional content of the music he performed. With his vitality and his mastery of dynamics, rhythm and colour, Hofmann was able to produce an almost unparalleled display of the pianist's art. His playing was never dull, it never sagged; in every concert a superb and seemingly effortless performance could be virtually guaranteed.

Although Josef Hofmann learned his music in the 19th century he was essentially a transitional pianist, linking old and new styles. The sometimes exaggerated rubatos and pianistic eccentricities of Pachmann, Paderewski and those who trained under Liszt were alien to his nature. When we listen to his records or piano roll recordings today some people might think he belonged to the earlier 'romantic' school of pianists, for his playing is different from that of the modern age. But in his day he was regarded as classically accurate, taking fewer liberties in phrasing and tempo than did most other established pianists of his era. Times and perspectives change, and what was regarded as a very modern approach in the 1880s and 1890s would now be thought of as old fashioned. Nowadays the emphasis is on the strict interpretation of the composer's wishes and on a clinical and occasionally unfeeling accuracy, sometimes producing a sterile performance.

Hofmann's contemporaries of his early days would change the music and add or subtract notes if it suited them in a misplaced attempt to display their virtuosity. It was not only pianists who did it; other instrumentalists and singers were equally guilty. Hofmann never did that; he believed in textual accuracy and once wrote:

"I venture to prove to anyone who will play for me - if he be at all worth listening to - that he does not play *more* than is written (as he may think), but in fact a good deal *less* than the printed page reveals . . . The true interpretation of a piece results from a correct understanding of it, and this, in turn, depends solely upon scrupulously exact reading . . . A purposed, blatant parading of the player's self through wilful additions of nuances, shadings, effects, and what not, is tantamount to a falsification; at best it is 'playing to the galleries', charlatanism. The player should always feel convinced that he plays only what is written."

Hofmann believed that the music itself contained all that was necessary to produce a beautiful and poetic performance; it was up to the pianist to make sure it was brought out.

Not only was Hofmann's musical style modern by the standards of his day, he was also modern in his personal appearance. Not for him the extravagant manes of hair that were so popular amongst concert pianists in his early years, as adopted by Paderewski and some of the Liszt pupils. His hair was cut short (though not as short as the convict-like haircut of Rachmaninov) and he looked in every sense 'ordinary'. But as a pianist he was very far from ordinary. Though to Hofmann the music itself was more important than any showy display of skill on the part of the performer, he nevertheless recognised the important role of the artist. He once wrote :

"It is sometimes said that the too objective study of a piece may impair the 'individuality' of its rendition. Have no fear of that! If ten players study the same piece with the same degree of exactness and objectivity, depend on it: each one will still play it quite differently from the nine others, though each one may think his rendition the only correct one. For each one will express what, according to his lights, he has mentally and temperamentally absorbed. Of the distinctive feature which constitutes the difference in the ten conceptions each one will have been unconscious while it formed itself, and perhaps also afterward. But it is just this unconsciously formed feature which constitutes legitimate individuality and which alone will admit of a real fusion of the composer's and the interpreter's thought."

Hofmann made frequent tours of the United States and in 1905 he met and married an American, Marie Eustis. From then on he lived most of his life in the United States. A daughter was born but the marriage did not last long. Hofmann later married Betty Short. By this marriage there were three sons, one of whom (Anton) photographed at the age of ten looked remarkably like his father at the same age.

Hofmann achieved so much at such an early age that musical success clearly presented no problem to him. Whereas ordinary mortals would have been hard put to achieve a tenth of what Hofmann did, he took his music in his stride and still had time for other interests. His horizons were not by any means limited to music. He was well known for his interest in mechanical devices and invention, a hobby which had fascinated him since childhood. He spent endless hours in his private laboratory, translating abstract ideas into practical realities. He devised a model house which would rotate with the sun. When steam motor cars came into use, Hofmann built one for his own use. He designed the oil-burning furnace used in his home, and also invented and built air-springs and shock absorbers for use in cars. Most of these were good practical devices, well thought of in engineering circles, and more than 60 of his ideas were patented in the fields of mechanics, electricity and chemistry.

Because of the facility with which Hofmann achieved his musical success he was sometimes criticised on the grounds that deep down he lacked real feeling for the music - he just played because it all came so easily to him. His friend Artur Rubinstein wrote in old age of his first meeting with Josef Hofmann at the Hofmanns' home in Berlin when Josef was 23 and he (Artur) was only 12:

"I was to be presented to the Hofmanns, father and son; my mother had a letter of introduction to them, and I was thrilled to meet the great Josef Hofmann."

Rubinstein looked forward eagerly to the meeting, for Hofmann was already a celebrity and was hailed in Russia as heir to the still-mourned Anton Rubinstein, whilst in America Hofmann was regarded as the only serious rival to Paderewski. But when they met, Artur Rubinstein was disappointed, for it was Casimar Hofmann who listened attentively as Artur played, whilst Josef remained completely detached. According to Rubinstein, Josef appeared to be more interested in various scientific gadgets he owned, some of them said to have been given to him by Thomas Edison, the great inventor, and demonstrated these to Artur with great glee. Nevertheless, Rubinstein respected Hofmann's skill and referred to small private gatherings of musicians which took place a few years after this first meeting, at which he and Hofmann were present:

"It was on such occasions that I could appreciate Hofmann's gifts, such as his memory or his complete control of the left hand."

Interestingly, Rubinstein admitted that indirectly the presence of Hofmann made it difficult for him (Rubinstein) as a young man to get engagements in Russia. He explained the problem:

"In his early days, Hofmann held a pianistic monopoly in Russia. Having been a pupil of Anton Rubinstein, this legendary idol of the country, he was generally accepted as the rightful successor to the great man. This made other young pianists appear to be pretenders to the sacred name, which made it difficult for them in Russia."

Possibly this soured Artur Rubinstein slightly, though his relationship with Hofmann remained cordial. Writing of Hofmann when the famous pianist was at his peak, Rubinstein expressed reservations, again on the grounds of what seemed to him to be Hofmann's indifference to music. According to Rubinstein, Hofmann's main interest in the piano lay in technical matters such as possible changes in its construction, in different dispositions of the strings, in the design of the frame, in the height and width of the keys, and so on. Rubinstein recognised that Hofmann's brilliant mastery of the keyboard was inborn, but felt that his chief interest lay in dynamics, such as his habit of concluding a slowly prepared crescendo by a volcanic outburst at the climax. Yet Rubinstein conceded that Hofmann was a pianist of great stature for whenever he played a unique personality emerged.

In appearance Hofmann was short and, unusually for a pianist, he had small hands and short fingers. His remarkable technique showed beyond doubt that large hands are not an essential attribute for a great pianist. After Hofmann became famous, Steinway made a few specially-commissioned pianos for him with the keys shaved a fraction of an inch. Hofmann's interest in mechanics had prompted the thought that he might feel more comfortable on such an instrument - and so it proved - though he regularly played standard instruments as well.

It is perhaps surprising for a pianist of his brilliance that he was not a particularly good sight reader, though he could learn music quickly from the printed page when he wanted to. But Hofmann had a marvellous ear for music and could startle fellow-pianists by Liszt-like tricks in which he played back correctly music that he had heard without having ever seen it in print. Godowsky's assistant, Maurice Aronson, used to tell the story of Godowsky's *Fledermaus* transcription, a fearfully complicated and showy piece. In Berlin around the year 1900, Hofmann and Godowsky became close friends, which they were to remain, and Hofmann would call at Godowsky's home to listen whilst Godowsky was composing the piece. Hofmann's father met Godowsky by chance one day and said: "What have you done to Josef? He sits at home all day and plays Strauss waltzes." A few days later Hofmann visited his friend and played the entire transcription, note for note, never having seen the music.

Hofmann's remarkable memory for music was a very useful gift. Apart from all the other benefits, it reduced the hours necessary for practice at the keyboard. Much of Hofmann's "practice" was done lounging in an arm chair, or lying in a hammock, or even walking through the woods. He would relax mentally and consider carefully every note of a forthcoming concert programme. Shortly before the concert he would translate this mental practice into actual practice at the piano, but only when his conception of the music had been fully formed in his mind. This was not a method he recommended to other pianists who definitely needed keyboard practice, but for him it worked, due to his outstanding memory and wonderful inborn technique.

It has already been noted that Hofmann was composing music even at the age of 10 and performing it amongst the work of other composers at his concerts. He wrote several piano concertos (now seldom heard), some symphonic works including a Symphony in E major and numerous compositions for the piano. Many of these works were written under a pseudonym, 'Michel Dvorsky', which is a transliteration of the literal translation into Polish of his German name, meaning "courtyard man". For many years the identity of the real composer was kept secret. Hofmann used to deny that he had written the pieces, saying that Dvorsky was an invalid French composer. And so for years the shadowy figure of Dvorsky haunted the concert halls. Hofmann probably adopted this subterfuge so that his published music would stand on its own merits and not be carried along by his famous name as a virtuoso pianist. Finally all was revealed and in January 1924 an entire Josef Hofmann programme was presented by the Philadelphia Orchestra.

Not only was Hofmann successful as a composer and brilliantly successful as a pianist, he also became a respected teacher and theoretician during the early years of the 20th century. He published several books on piano playing including *Piano-Questions Answered* (1909) and an expanded version, *Piano-Playing, with Piano-Questions Answered* (1914). He also had many private pupils. In 1924 his work as a teacher was recognised when he was appointed Head of the Piano Section of the Curtis Institute of Music, Philadelphia, and from 1926 (the year he became a citizen of the United States) he was Head of the entire Institute, a post he held until 1938.

Hofmann's peak years as a pianist were from about 1905 to 1940 when experience and complete maturity were added to his natural talent and flair. It is fortunate that all his piano roll recordings date from this period and they provide a marvellous legacy of the output of this great artist. Altogether he recorded about 100 rolls. They were for the the Aeolian Company's Duo-Art system (about 60 rolls); Welte (over 20); Hupfeld (at least 9); and Artecho (8). In addition, two of his Hupfeld rolls were adapted and issued by Ampico.

Hofmann's Duo-Art rolls, which, as the figures indicate, comprise the bulk of his recording on roll, included eight rolls of Beethoven's music, amongst which are two complete sonatas (Op. 27, No. 2; and Op. 2, No. 3) and 19 rolls of music by Chopin. Not surprisingly, Hofmann was one of the Aeolian Company's highest paid recording artists. He was featured in a lot of the company's advertising literature for he was universally acknowledged as one of the best pianists of his day. His name was almost a household word, second only to that of the legendary Paderewski, who by the 1920s was getting past his best and who in any case was never as great a pianist as Hofmann.

Numerous advertising paragraphs attributed to Hofmann extolled the virtues of the Duo-Art system, for example:

"My Duo-Art rolls correctly reproduce my phrasing, accent, pedalling, and are endowed with my personality. They are my actual interpretation, with all that implies. One thing is certain; in the reproduction of my playing, the Duo-Art is so far superior to any other instrument of its kind there can be no real basis for comparison."

Issues of rolls used to enter and be deleted from catalogues regularly, just as compact disc recordings do nowadays, but in 1932 when the player piano industry was in rapid decline 34 of Hofmann's Duo-Art rolls were still listed in the Aeolian Company's catalogue, featuring the following composers: Beethoven (5 rolls); Chopin (10); Hofmann (1); Gluck (1); Liszt (3); Mendelssohn (3); Moszkowski (3); Rachmaninov (1); Rubinstein (3); Schumann (1); Schytte (1); Scriabin (1); and Tchaikovsky (1). Hofmann's Welte rolls included three of music by Chopin and three of Rubinstein. The others were spread amongst several composers but two complete Beethoven sonatas were included; Op. 31, No. 3; and Op. 101. The eight Artecho rolls featured six different composers.

Hofmann also made gramophone recordings but, somewhat surprisingly, not as many as would have been expected from a pianist of his stature. Also, for some reason, many of the ones he did make were not issued in his lifetime. He has the distinction of being the first professional musician ever to record, cutting cylinders as a souvenir during a visit to Edison's laboratory in New Jersey in 1887. He was then only 11. Some of the best of his recordings are said to be a series he made for HMV in the 1930s which, unaccountably, were not released. Many recordings of his actual performances in concert halls as opposed to the recording studio were discovered after his death, and the excellence of these enhances his standing as one of the major pianists of the century. A number of his 78rpm recordings were re-issued some years ago as long-playing records and many are now available on compact disc. Some of his piano roll performances have also been re-issued in record format. In the last few years of his life he made some recordings for the American company, Brunswick, but by then his powers were waning and the earlier recordings have the edge.

Throughout his period as Director of the Curtis Institute in Philadelphia Hofmann continued to tour throughout the world. He composed very little after taking up his appointment at the Institute; nearly all his 100 or so works (most of them published in some form) pre-date that period of his life. He was surrounded by many competent composers at the Institute, a large and prestigious academy, and perhaps he no longer felt the urge or need to write music himself.

In 1937 Hofmann celebrated the 50th anniversary of his debut as a concert pianist in the USA by giving a special golden-jubilee concert at the Metropolitan Opera House in New York, the scene of his triumph as a boy pianist in 1887. In this memorable anniversary performance he played his own *Chromaticon* for Piano and Orchestra, composed in 1916, and Rubinstein's D minor Concerto, as well as some of the pieces he had played at his debut concert 50 years earlier.

In 1938, at the age of 62, Hofmann decided to resign his appointment at the Curtis Institute. For the next few years, freed of his academic chores, he continued to give concert performances but on a more limited scale, and it is generally agreed by contemporary observers that he was no longer the great Hofmann of former years, though he was still a very good pianist. Artur Rubinstein attributed Hofmann's decline to over-indulgence in alcohol, but this is perhaps a somewhat unkind judgment as Hofmann was then approaching seventy and could hardly be expected to produce the fire and vitality of a 20 year old. Rubinstein himself managed to retain his powers to a great age, but few pianists are as fortunate in that respect as he was. After the war ended, Hofmann decided to 'call it a day' as far as concert work was concerned and he gave his last public performance on Wednesday, 19th January 1946, in New York. He was then one day short of his 70th birthday.

Though Hofmann's skill as a pianist had declined he had succeeded in retaining the facial features of his boyhood to a remarkable degree as he grew older; the round face and chubby cheeks, the short-cut hair, and at 70 his skin was said to be remarkably free from the lines and creases of old age. He also retained much of the spirit of his youth, and into his seventies he still enjoyed boating, hiking and table tennis which he played at home with his sons. Most concert artists in their sixties and seventies show signs of the strain of their arduous career, with its endless travel and the tension of concert appearances, but Hofmann managed to retain an aura of youthfulness.

The last few years of Hofmann's life were spent in retirement, mostly in California, where he devoted more and more time to his hobby of mechanics, and in particular to experiments on improved piano actions and recording techniques. He died in Los Angeles on 16th February 1957, aged 81.

Josef Hofmann will be remembered as one of the great pianists of the 20th century, particularly in the works of the pre-20th century composers, for he rarely played modern music. He had all the gifts of the great pianist; he could rival any virtuoso, but he always kept his talents in check. To Hofmann the music came first, and he was one of the first great pianists of the modern school. It is a pity that his gramophone recordings were not very numerous, but fortunately there is a large legacy of piano roll recordings which provide a sample of his wonderful skills.

Alfred Cortot

12. Alfred Cortot

Alfred Cortot, the concert pianist, conductor and musical scholar, was a somewhat controversial figure. For a period of about 30 years he was thought by his many admirers to be one of the greatest pianists of his day, particularly in the interpretation of Chopin and Schumann, yet others thought his playing was not particularly good. His rise to fame was meteoric, and this was followed by a long period as a top-class musician. Regrettably, Cortot's last years were marred by political controversy and physical decline. But at his best he was a wonderful pianist, the sensitivity of whose playing earned him the epithet 'The Poet of the Piano'.

Alfred Denis Cortot was born in the little Swiss town of Nyon on 26th September 1877. Alfred's mother was Swiss but his father, a works foreman, was French, and Alfred can really be regarded as of French nationality for he was to live in France for most of his life. Alfred was one of a family of six children, but paradoxically he was virtually an only child. When he was born his father was 42, his mother 40, and two of the six children had already died. His brother Oscar was then 20 and his sisters, Leah and Annette, were 14 and 12 respectively. So Alfred was very much the baby of the family. He lacked playmates, and being left so often to his own devices he became withdrawn and introverted, but at the same time his imagination developed - a valuable asset to someone of artistic temperament. It was said that when he was given a toy boat he didn't bother to sail it as other children would. His imagination was enough.

Many talented youngsters who subsequently became famous musicians did so entirely on their own initiative; the talent was there and no obstacles could hinder its development. Not so with Cortot. It is doubtful whether, as an infant, he ever harboured any particular musical thoughts. But his parents always wanted him to become a concert pianist. No doubt they spotted something special in the young child as he toyed with the keys on the neighbours' pianos. Whatever sparked off his parents' wishes for him to have a career in music, there is no doubt that by the time he was seven they, and indeed the whole family, willed him to succeed in the profession they had chosen for him. Being of an amiable disposition and obviously possessing ability, he did not object. His parents purchased a second-hand piano for him (he later described it as a 'miserable instrument') and his sisters started to teach him the elements of piano playing.

Before long his parents sought professional tuition for him. He was taken at five years of age to the Conservatory in Geneva but he did not like the place and the experiment was not a success. His parents were not to be put off and Alfred was taken to Paris for an audition at the Paris Conservatory. To the family's consternation, he failed it. But one member of the Examining Board saw talent in his playing and took him unofficially as a pupil. His sisters' amateur teaching had to be undone, for Alfred's keyboard technique needed modification.

With this successfully achieved, his skills as a pianist blossomed rapidly and at the age of 10 he was admitted into the preparatory class of the Conservatory where he studied first under Émile Descombes (one of the last of Chopin's pupils and disciples) and then Louis Diémer, a noted pianist and teacher. There followed the long months and years of unglamorous hard work familiar to all young musicians seeking to make their way in the world. In Alfred's case the effort was rewarded, for his skills steadily accumulated throughout his teenage years and in 1896, at the age of 18, he was awarded the First Prize of the Conservatory. In accordance with tradition he was granted the honour of playing at the graduation concert, and played Chopin's Ballade in A flat.

Cortot's brilliant 'premier prix' at the Conservatory virtually launched him into a career as a concert pianist, in much the same way as the winning of a televised competition does nowadays, and in the same year as his Conservatory triumph he made his debut in Paris, playing Beethoven's C minor Concerto at one of the Colonne concerts. This was received very well by the critics and the public. Other concerts followed and he soon became well known not only at the Colonne concerts but also at the Lamoureux ones as a good interpreter of Beethoven's concertos - at the early age of 20 years.

So began Alfred Cortot's professional musical career in which he appeared to be destined for the life of a concert soloist. He did indeed remain a concert pianist until old age and infirmity put a stop to the work, but from those early days he developed other musical interests in addition. When he was still only 20 he appeared with Edouard Risler, a pianist four years Cortot's senior and whom he greatly admired and respected, in concerts of two-piano arrangements of Wagner's operas.

Cortot soon fell under the spell of Wagner's music. In 1898, at 21, he was appointed first as choral coach, and then as assistant conductor, at the Opera House at Bayreuth in Bavaria. There he worked until 1901 under Mottl and Richter and studied the compositions of Wagner until he knew them off by heart, note by note, and could play arrangements of them all from memory on the piano. This was all valuable experience, and his understanding of the works was further enhanced by acting as répétiteur at the Bayreuth Festivals from 1898 until 1901.

During this period of entrancement by the music of Wagner, Cortot often acted as accompanist for the Russian soprano and Wagnerian specialist Madame Félia Litvinne, who was at that time an outstanding success at the opera in Paris, Brussels and London. She was a most accomplished singer, but because of her immense bulk she was known in Paris, rather unkindly, as the "Venus de Kilo". Though her figure was so unwieldy, she was imposing as a Wagnerian superwoman, and her physique carried her through the most exacting roles without in any way affecting the extraordinary purity of her voice. She was lucky to have the young Cortot as her accompanist, as the quality of his playing and the skill of his musicianship complemented her beautiful voice.

In 1902 Cortot returned to Paris to continue his work as a conductor. He founded the 'Société des Festivals Lyriques', and in May of that year conducted the French premiere of *Götterdämmerung* at the Théatre du Chateau d'Eau. He also conducted notable performances of other works by Wagner and began a very active campaign to promote the works of this composer. Not only did he conduct all these performances, but he was also Theatrical Director. At 24, he was thus established as a well-known figure, and Cortot's great productions of *Götterdämmerung* and *Tristan* were said to be unforgettably uplifting experiences.

Fortified by these successes, Cortot at 25 founded the 'Société des Concerts Cortot', which gave him the freedom to present the works of his choice. These included, as well as the Wagnerian epics already mentioned, the first performances in Paris of works such as Wagner's *Parsifal*, Liszt's *St. Elizabeth*, Brahms' *Requiem*, and Beethoven's *Mass in D*. He also introduced to the French repertoire a number of previously unpublished works by Magnard, Chausson and Ladmirault, side by side with well known ones by Chabrier and d'Indy. In 1904, when he was 27, the still youthful Cortot was entrusted with the direction of the concerts given by the Société Nationale, and also of the 'Concerts Populaires' at Lille, an appointment he retained until he relinquished it in 1908, and which gave to the town four seasons of great artistic activity. Cortot also conducted the second Paris performance of Wagner's *Tristan und Isolde* shortly after the famous conductor Lamoureux had directed the first.

Another important step in the rising young star's career came in 1905. In the course of his work Cortot encountered many fine musicians and in that year he began a musical collaboration with the French violinist Jacques Thibaud and the Spanish cellist Pablo Casals. The Cortot/Thibaud/Casals trio was a happy blend and was an association that lasted for thirty years. When the three started to play together as a trio Cortot was 27, Thibaud was

24 and Casals 28. The three understood each other perfectly in their music and formed a marvellously gratifying team, not only as an ensemble but also as friends. They began the custom of devoting one month each year to travelling together to give chamber music concerts and the trio soon became widely known. They also made some of the earliest recordings of classical music for the gramophone, though even earlier Casals had made some cylinder recordings around 1903. Certain of the recordings, such as the Schubert Trio in B flat, helped to dispel the earlier prejudice among musicians against the gramophone. The trio continued to record well into the 1930s when recording techniques had risen to an acceptable level, and their recordings, early and late, are cherished by collectors today. Some became classics and are still in the catalogues, having been transferred from 78s to long playing discs and later to compact disc.

One of the reasons for the great commercial success of the Cortot/Thibaud/Casals discs is the complementary musical styles of the three artists. Each was very different from the others but the efforts of the three combined to form a thrilling unity of performance. Casals was solid and secure; Cortot's playing was less controlled, more free and subtle, whilst Thibaud's playing had an inspirational, floating quality. Playing together, it is doubtful whether the combined effect has ever been bettered.

As well as conducting, directing theatrical performances and playing in the trio, Cortot somehow found time to continue his career as a concert pianist and was gradually establishing himself as one of the leading pianists of his era. In addition, he took a number of teaching posts which no doubt offered him the financial security necessary to pursue his various interests. In 1907, at the age of 29, he was appointed a Professor of Piano at his old college, the Paris Conservatory, but later resigned the post when his concert work became so pressing that he had little time to teach.

Following the outbreak of the First World War in 1914 when Cortot was 36, he did what he could to help the war effort. For a time he worked as a civil servant in Paris before it was decided by the authorities that his talents could be put to better use. The French Government decided to send their best musicians to the USA to promote their country's cause, so off went Cortot, along with Thibaud and many others. Not only did this help France, it helped Cortot himself, for it put him before the important American public and made him a celebrity in that country as well as in Europe.

In 1917 Cortot returned to the Paris Conservatory as Professor in the highest pianoforte class and he taught there with great success for a three-year period, when he again relinquished his connection with the college. In addition to these teaching appointments, Cortot was becoming a dedicated and respected musical scholar, who, during his career, was to compile several books on musical appreciation, and editions of Chopin's études, preludes and ballades in four volumes, with annotations. Cortot also wrote an authoritative work on French piano music, in two volumes. The first is devoted to the music of Debussy, Franck, Fauré, Chabrier and Dukas; the second to that of Saint-Saëns, d'Indy, Ravel and others. These works form an outstanding contribution to the literature of piano music. There were many other publications; books, booklets and articles.

When the 1914-18 war ended, Cortot resumed his full-time musical career and in 1919 he founded the 'École Normale de Musique', a premier teaching establishment. His many concert engagements made it impossible for him to devote regular uninterrupted periods to academic teaching himself, but he appointed to the staff of his École a distinguished group of teachers. However, he did do some teaching, for he made himself responsible for interpretation courses which were to become legendary. His clear mind, scholarly approach to his art and his mastery of the technique of the piano enabled him to become a fine lecturer and many of his public appearances took the form of lecture recitals. The effectiveness of these was enhanced by Cortot's deep, sonorous and expressive voice; an unusual voice for one of such slight physical frame, but having the power to hold the attention of its listeners.

Cortot seems to have been genuinely fond of teaching and is remembered with reverence and awe by a host of his former pupils, all of whom have many anecdotes concerning their lessons. In one class, scheduled to last for several hours, Cortot was upset soon after the session started by the lifeless performance of one of the pupils. Cortot closed the lid of the piano, shut the fall board over the keys, put away the music and walked round the piano gently patting it, muttering, "Poor piano! Poor piano!" He then went home! Another pupil was once invited to bring his music to Cortot's home, as for some reason it was not going to be convenient for the next lesson to take place at the teaching studio. Arriving there and expecting to find a magnificent Steinway Grand, the student was nonplussed to be confronted in Cortot's music room by a battered and lifeless old Pleyel. After an unsuccessful attempt to achieve any life or colour from the instrument, the pupil was told by Cortot, "If you can play that you're a pianist!" Then Cortot played, and he _did_ make it sound beautiful. "It's you who plays", said Cortot, "not the piano!"

There is no doubt that Cortot regarded his teaching as just as important as his playing. With his technical understanding of the instrument he knew exactly what was required from his pupils. What he aimed to do was to instil into his students the ability to project an image of the music. It was the overall view that mattered - even if this was achieved at the expense of detail. This of course reflected his own playing. By demonstration he was able to show his students how to produce tone, colour and clarity of line.

The repertoire that Cortot played at his own public recitals and concerts was drawn almost entirely from the music written in the period 1800-1914. It included the compositions of Debussy who, like himself, was concerned with projecting musical images. He became interested in contemporary music, including Prokofiev and Schoenberg, and taught it to his pupils, but he did not include it in his own recitals. The repertoire he taught was wide-ranging and not limited to any particular musical periods.

Like Godowsky, Cortot was a great student of the technique of piano playing, and discussed the subject at length in his book *Rational Principles of Pianoforte Technique*, published in 1928. This weighty tome, highly regarded by experts, goes into the technique of piano playing in a very thorough and scientific way. Numerous special exercises are presented, and the book is acknowledged to be a major contribution to the subject. Cortot does not seem to have been very interested in composition and never made a mark in that field.

In the years between the two wars Cortot missed no opportunity to further his career as a concert pianist and made numerous tours through Europe and the USA. It was during that period that he came to be regarded as one of the leading pianists of his era. There were several factors that made his playing very special. Casals referred to the 'very specific touch' that characterised his playing and said:

"He was undoubtedly one of the great pianists of our time - he had boundless élan, and astonishing power. He was also a brilliant musical scholar, whose writings on piano technique and musical appreciation gained international recognition. He interpreted Beethoven magnificently, and he had a consuming admiration for Wagner."

The 1954 edition of *Grove*, published when Cortot was still playing, said:

"He excels in the interpretation of music of the romantic and modern schools; he has amazing gifts as a pianist, and whether he is conducting or sitting at the pianoforte he uses his gifts with equal mastery. While he commands impetuosity and force, he possesses no less delicacy, accuracy, and above all a penetrating sensibility which charms and holds his hearers."

In 1975 the *International Cyclopedia's* contributor observed:

"Cortot was ranked with the leading pianists of his time. His playing was imbued with a poetic sensibility that made him an excellent interpreter of the romantic composers, in particular such as Chopin and Schumann. He was also considered outstanding in the works of the contemporary French composers, including Franck and Debussy."

More recently, Martin Cooper wrote of Cortot in these terms:

"As a pianist, he was remarkable above all for his intimate understanding of romantic music, especially Schumann, though his Chopin was prized very highly and continues, even in the comparitively primitive recordings available, to dazzle pianists by its lyrical delicacy and nobility."

Cortot belonged to the romantic era and his performances would not always accord with modern fashion. An interesting story concerns a recital Cortot gave with Wanda Landowska in the late 1920s when the two pianists played the Mozart D major Sonata for Two Pianos. In this piece there are many places where one pianist plays a passage and then the other takes up the theme. Those lucky enough to be present were fascinated by the contrast in styles. Cortot's playing was essentially of the romantic school; free, with rubato. Landowska's, compared with Cortot's, was clinical and precise. The difference befitted their specialist periods; Landowska's of the 17th and 18th centuries, Cortot's of the 19th, more expansive and eloquent. The juxtaposition of their individual contributions in solo passages, each highly individual, produced an absorbing result.

Contemporary experts from Cortot's era all agreed that he had an undoubted ability to create intensely musical performances with fine climaxes and sustained excitement. Above all, he was noted for his clarity and for the colour of his interpretations. He used to complain that nature had not given him a pianist's hands. Though his fingers were long (he had exceptionally large hands for a relatively small body) the thumb was close to the first finger which made wide stretches difficult. His looseness of wrist compensated for this. He varied his performance of the same piece from day to day perhaps more than any other contemporary pianist; astute watchers noted that he even held his hands differently on different occasions.

Though not flamboyant, Cortot in his middle years cultivated his image as a Chopin exponent by the frequent use in publicity handouts of a photograph taken when he was 38; the rather large nose, angular features and long hair bearing more than a passing resemblance to pictures of the ailing composer at the same age. There was probably a conscious attempt, when this photograph was taken, to obtain a result reminiscent of the well-known daguerreotype picture of Chopin viewed from a similar angle. Cortot was a pupil of a pupil of Chopin and it made commercial sense to use any legitimate means to identify him with the great Polish master.

Most concert pianists find it necessary to practise for several hours every day to keep their fingers in the supple condition demanded by their arduous profession. As we have seen, Cortot was a man of many parts; pianist, conductor, scholar, lecturer, writer and teacher. How then did he find time to practise enough to keep his technique up to the standard necessary to give flawless performances? The short answer is - he didn't. Of all the great pianists in the first half of the present century, Cortot was noted perhaps more than any other for playing wrong notes, sometimes cascades of them. This did not seem to worry Cortot; he had a concept of how the music should sound, and he did not mind if the actual performance fell short. It was the concept that mattered. Not only was his time for practice, which in his case was usually less than four hours per day, not adequate, there are other theories as to why he tended to play a lot of wrong notes. Some observers felt that his technique was at fault in that he held his arms too close to his body so that he was too fully stretched when playing at the extremities of the keyboard. Others noted that his adventurous approach to the music predisposed him to make mistakes. Both he and Paderewski edited editions of sheet music. Paderewski's fingering had 'safety' in mind; Cortot's was directed at producing the best dramatic effect, so that a big 'jump' would land on a strong finger. This created a marvellous effect when it worked but it was easy to go wrong. Cortot aimed at sensitivity combined with dramatic effect. To him a feeble accuracy was no good. In concert appearances some pianists, notably Godowsky, would play well within themselves to avoid mistakes. Cortot on the other hand would 'give it all he'd got' and if a few mistakes ensued, well, never mind.

Cortot's frequent mistakes and occasional memory lapses did not worry his numerous admirers, for no one doubted that his playing at its best had something special about it, a unique quality which made it different from that of any other performer. It was said that a Cortot performance could always be recognised by his touch and clarity of line. Because of this his mistakes were readily forgiven. An ardent fan once said: "I would rather have Cortot's wrong notes than my own right ones." Cortot's interpretation of Chopin was not to everyone's liking, and Artur Rubinstein referred to Cortot's treatment of the composer as suggesting "the weak tubercular artist". But no-one can please everybody, and most people regarded Cortot as a very fine player of Chopin.

Another Cortot trait that endeared him to his audiences was that he always gave them their money's worth, with long and arduous programmes. Sometimes, for example, the programme would consist of all the studies and all the preludes of Chopin. His platform manner was unpretentious. When Cortot appeared on the platform he would walk briskly to the piano, sit down and start to play almost before the applause for his entry had died down. No fuss, no fiddling with the piano stool or his coat-tails; music was produced immediately, elegantly and efficiently. At the piano he sat in a relaxed manner with his back straight. There was none of the 'head drooping over the keyboard' mannerisms so favoured by some other pianists.

Cortot was a quiet, studious, dignified individual who liked to keep his private life out of the public gaze as far as possible. His first marriage became cold and unhappy following the early death of both their children. Then, in the early 1930s, Paris society was shocked when Cortot left his wife in favour of a woman who provided him with the emotional support he needed. He was unmoved by what he regarded as bourgeois disapproval. After their eventual marriage, he and his wife (Renée Elaine) lived quietly with their son. Music was Cortot's only consuming passion, though in his younger days he enjoyed skiing and as he grew older he became interested in collecting things such as books and stamps.

Like many of the other great pianists of his generation, Cortot recorded a lot of music, not only a member of the famous Cortot/Thibaud/Casals trio, but also as a recitalist and as a soloist in concertos. As a specialist in the work of the romantic and French composers, the compositions of Chopin, Schumann and Debussy appeared often in his recorded work, though many other composers were also represented. Cortot's propensity for playing wrong notes unfortunately extended to the recording studio where not only his strengths but also his errors were encapsulated for posterity to hear. Yet at his best, when he had practised and was on top form, he was superlative.

Most of Cortot's recordings were made for HMV and he was one of their most popular artists in the classical field, having recorded a vast amount of music for the company. The 1937-38 HMV catalogue lists dozens of Cortot recordings, including various works by Albéniz, Brahms, Chopin, Debussy, Franck, Handel, Liszt and Schumann. He also recorded various 'complete sets' of groups of music of the composers in which he specialised, for example Debussy's preludes, all the preludes and ballades and many of the études and waltzes of Chopin, the *Kinderszenen* of Schumann and groups of works by other composers. In addition, he recorded much chamber music, not only as a member of the Cortot/Thibaud/Casals trio, but also in duets, mainly with Casals (cello) or with Thibaud (violin) but occasionally with others.

Cortot was always ready to experiment in his performances, even in his recordings. In one session, whilst recording some music by Ravel with the famous soprano Maggie Teyte, he felt that what the composer intended was a drum-like effect from the bass strings. With the permission of the singer, he suspended a piece of paper between the hammers and the strings of the piano in the lower register, producing an interesting timpani-like effect. It is doubtful whether many present-day musicians would dare to do such a thing. Having listened to the recording, we feel that Cortot may well have been right in his objective, and we applaud him for having the courage of his convictions.

Cortot also recorded about 50 rolls for the reproducing piano. Most of his rolls (27 of them) were for the Aeolian Company's Duo-Art system, but he also recorded for Philipps (about 10 rolls), Hupfeld (11) and Pleyela (2). Two of his Hupfeld rolls (Liszt's Hungarian Rhapsody No. 2 and Mendelssohn's *Variations Sérieuses*) were adapted and issued by Ampico. Ten of his Duo-Art rolls were of Chopin's music. By 1932 when the player piano companies were in decline, 16 of his Duo-Art rolls were still listed in the Aeolian Company's catalogue, the composers concerned being Bach (1 roll), Chabrier (2), Chopin (6), Fauré (1), Liszt (2), Saint-Saëns (1), Schubert (2) and Scriabin (1). Surprisingly, Cortot made no Duo-Art piano rolls of Schumann's music though he was a notable Schumann interpreter. Perhaps the Aeolian Company considered Schumann to be well represented already in their lists. The only Schumann roll he recorded was part of Carnaval, Op. 14, for Pleyela. No doubt the music as he initially recorded it for the player piano was marred by wrong notes, but here the piano roll system scored over its gramophone record counterpart, in that such errors could be easily corrected during editing, and certainly were. This enabled some fine rolls to be marketed in Cortot's name. A particular favourite, owned by many collectors, is the Cortot Duo-Art roll of Chopin's Andante Spianato and Grande Polonaise in E flat, Op. 22; a memorable performance.

As well as making rolls for the Aeolian Company, Cortot also assisted the firm in their advertising campaigns to promote the Duo-Art system in various interesting ways as the companies fought tooth and nail to out-do each other in trying to show the superiority of their particular system. At one London concert a performance of a Liszt Hungarian Rhapsody was shared between Cortot playing the piano, and a music roll previously recorded by Cortot. The effect was so satisfactory that Ernest Newman, the leading British music critic of the day, said, "With one's eyes closed it was impossible to tell which was which."

In 1934 Cortot, then 57, was created a Commandeur de la Légion d'Honneur for his services to music and was told in the citation speech, "Cortot, you are a living miracle!" From then until the outbreak of the Second World War he was universally regarded as the leading figure of the day in French music. Those years really marked the apex of his career, and he was still at the height of his powers in 1939 when the Second World War began.

But soon afterwards events were to occur that dimmed the lustre of his long and distinguished career. During the 1930s Cortot had boycotted Germany and Italy because of their totalitarian governments, but when war came he remained active in French music during the German occupation. Not only did he conduct and play at concerts in France, but he also gave them in Germany, though only on condition that he was also allowed to play to French prisoners of war. He also rose to an influential position in the Ministry of Education. Perhaps his love of German culture, exemplified by his admiration of Wagner, predisposed him towards the German occupation. Maybe he found it difficult to say "No" to the German demands and took the easy way out by doing what they asked. Or possibly he was just naïve. Whatever his motives, there is little doubt he collaborated with the Germans. According to his old friend and colleague Pablo Casals, Cortot turned up sheepishly on Casals' doorstep after the war. Casals recalled:

"Cortot had greatly aged and at first made a half-hearted attempt to excuse what he had done. Then he blurted out: "It's true, Pablo. What they say is true. I was a collaborator. I worked with the Germans. I am ashamed, dreadfully ashamed. I have come to ask your forgiveness."

Casals told him:

"I am glad that you tell the truth. Because of that I forgive you. I give you my hand."

It is easy to blame Cortot for his sins, but Dame Myra Hess, rightly regarded as a great patriot on account of her National Gallery concerts which continued throughout the London blitz, always refused after the war to join in the condemnation of Cortot. She maintained that, had the Germans reached London, it would not have been easy to decide whether or not to continue the National Gallery concerts. Would it have been in the best interests of the British people for her and other musicians to refuse to give them any more music? It would have been a difficult dilemma.

Because of Cortot's collaboration with the Nazis he was arrested by the French authorities late in 1944. He was soon released, but feelings against him ran high and for some time after the war it is hardly surprising that he was persona non grata in France and several other countries including Britain. This cast a cloud over his final years, and he lost many friends as a result. Introverted and opinionated as he was, he was not an easy man to get to know. An acquaintance of 50 years' standing said she knew the 'real' Cortot no better at the end than at the beginning. Inevitably for one having such definite views on music and everything else, he made some enemies. One fellow musician who had settled in the USA after the Second World War remarked that he looked in the obituary column of his newspaper every morning to see whether either Cortot or another famous musician he disliked might be in it, and preferably both!

It was against the background of his collaboration with the Germans that Cortot tried to pick up the threads of his career after the war. He was nearly 70 when musical life started to return to normal and it might have been best for him to have retired, but he had no such thoughts. Once the antagonism towards him as a collaborator had begun to subside he resumed his travels and continued to tour as a concert pianist for several more years. But he was not the Cortot of old. The magic had gone, and though he could still give a creditable performance, his powers of memory were clearly failing.

Even in his prime Cortot was apt to suffer the occasional memory lapse during performances, but as he grew older they became more frequent. On one sad occasion in London, Cortot was playing the F minor Concerto of Chopin, a piece he had played hundreds of times before, when he lost the thread. An impasse was reached, and all that the ageing pianist could do was to indicate with magnanimous gestures that he was to blame, it was not the accompanying orchestra that had broken down, but himself. In this period of his life Cortot was no longer a great pianist. But he was a living legend and was still in demand. The older generation wanted to see and hear their hero of years past, whilst the younger people, who knew Cortot only by reputation, were curious to hear him play. Consequently by 1952, his popularity had reached a post-war peak, with 135 performances in the year. In that year, which also marked his 75th birthday, he made an extensive tour of South America. It proved to be his last major tour.

After this 'Indian summer' Cortot, feeling his age, appeared in public only on rare occasions, though he continued to record and to teach. His final public recital was given on 10th July 1958 when Cortot, then 80, together with the 81 year old Pablo Casals, gave a stirring performance of the Beethoven A major Sonata for Cello and Piano, plus the Variations on a Theme from *The Magic Flute*. The applause seemed endless. Backstage, Cortot said, "We ought to have played all five Beethoven Sonatas. Pablo goes around playing them with any old pianist!" He was referring to Casals' recent association with the distinguished pianists Rudolph Serkin and Wilhelm Kempff!

Cortot had by then played in more than 6,000 concerts and recitals during his career and had been at the top of his profession as an internationally-known figure for 60 years. What more could anyone ask? His final years were spent in retirement in Lausanne, Switzerland, about twenty miles from his birthplace, thus giving his life a neat symmetry. He died there, aged 84, on 15th June 1962.

Alfred Cortot

For many years Cortot had been an avid and systematic collector, and he cherished and catalogued a large library of musical autographs, books, first and early editions, portraits, letters, coins and stamps. After his death the collection was dispersed. Some of the printed music, much of it of great rarity, went to the British Museum and some to various universities and other foundations in the United States.

In retrospect, Cortot is remembered as one of the foremost pianists of a bygone age. Along with Busoni, Godowsky, Hofmann and others in this book, he represented the best of his era. He did not have the charisma of Paderewski but he had his faithful followers and at his best his playing had a magical, poetic quality quite different from that of any other pianist.

Ossip Gabrilowitsch

13. Ossip Gabrilowitsch

Ossip Gabrilowitsch never liked the name 'Ossip', still less his middle name of Salomonovitch. But 'Ossip' he was to one and all, and few musicians have been more popular than he, not only with audiences, but also amongst fellow artists. A familiar figure in his characteristic high collar which became almost a trademark, he excelled in the dual role of pianist and conductor. As a person he was respected for his integrity and his friendly, unselfish nature. Always ready to help others, he was quick to jump to the defence of any musician who in his opinion was being unjustly vilified and he was the enemy of anyone who degraded his profession. A fine musician and a gentle and unassuming man, his life was cut short when he was still at the height of his powers.

The Gabrilowitsch family were citizens of St. Petersburg, Russia. Solomon Gabrilowitsch, Ossip's father, had set up in business as the owner of a bookshop soon after his marriage to Rosa Segal. The enterprise was not a commercial success, for Solomon was more interested in reading the books in his stock than selling them. Taking his wife and their young son George to Paris, he studied law at the Sorbonne for two years before completing his studies in Heidelberg. Back in St. Petersburg he had to pass further examinations in Russian law before he could practise in Russia. This he did brilliantly at St. Petersburg University and, aided by his integrity and a sharp mind, he soon rose to a prominent position, which in turn led to the acquisition of considerable wealth.

Solomon's wife, Rosa, came from a small town near the Russian-German border and spoke German fluently. Indeed, she often conversed in the German language with her children, George, Ossip Salomonovitch (born in St. Petersburg on 7th February 1878), Polya and Artur. French was taught to the children by a French governess, so the children were soon proficient in Russian, French and German. Artur, the youngest of the family, eventually followed his father into the legal profession whilst George became a newspaper editor and owner.

Ossip was clearly the musical member of the family. Described by his sister as "a tiny little fellow with light brown curls, bright eyes and round cheeks", Ossip's talents at three years of age were often shown off to friends; he could sing the songs his nurse taught him in a clear voice with impeccable precision. Though the family was Jewish by ancestry they had never formally accepted the Jewish or any other religious faith, and when the children were small they were often taken by their nurse to the local Greek

Orthodox Church. They enjoyed its impressive ritual and Ossip, at six and seven years old, delighted in the whole service, especially the musical content, to the extent that he played 'priests' at home and swung imitation incense. He was a clever child, good at drawing as well as music.

George, Ossip's brother and his senior by 11 years, gave Ossip his first piano lessons when he was five, and soon afterwards a professional teacher, Mme Olga Theodorwitsch, was engaged. Ossip's brilliant command of the instrument was enough to persuade his father that Ossip should become a musician, but his mother was against the idea, believing that his prospects might be limited to becoming a piano teacher. She wanted him to be a professional artist. At last, through influential contacts, the opinion of Anton Rubinstein was sought. Ossip, then ten years old, was ushered into the great man's presence and underwent his examination. "Of course he must become a musician", proclaimed Rubinstein, "for he will be great among the great. He must enter the Conservatory at once!"

The Master's decision was of course final, so Ossip entered the Conservatory in St. Petersburg (a musical conservatory and a high school combined) and studied there for six years as a day pupil. Besides his work at the Conservatory he spent a few hours daily in further study of languages, mathematics and history with his tutors at home. He liked all his subjects except mathematics.

Ossip was an immediate success at the Conservatory, impressing his teachers so much that he was allowed to play in public concerts almost from the start, a privilege allowed only in the case of exceptionally talented pupils, and he often appeared as a soloist or in programmes of chamber music. The great violinist Leopold Auer, head of the violin department and teacher of Heifetz, Elman and Zimbalist, appointed little Ossip to play his piano accompaniments, not only in the Conservatory concerts but in professional appearances as well. After three or four years the rare quality of his ability was recognised throughout St. Petersburg, so that as a lad of 13 and 14 he was invited to play to exclusive gatherings in the homes of distinguished musicians, intellectuals and socialites.

Ossip's piano teacher at the Conservatory was Professor Tolstoff, who was very proud of his pupil. He also studied composition with Rubinstein and Glazunov. Ossip had a pleasant personality; success as a pianist never went to his head and he was a favourite with everyone. In his mid teens his skill was being recognised not only by his teachers but by musicians of the stature of Rimsky-Korsakoff and Cui. At the end of his six years of study Ossip graduated with honours and was awarded the top prize - a grand piano.

With his formal studies at the Conservatory completed, Ossip embarked on the final stage of his preparation for the concert platform. This came about through the good offices of Mme Essipoff, the former wife of Theodor Leschetizky. She was living in St. Petersburg at the time. A brilliant concert pianist in her own right and assistant to Leschetizky before their recent divorce, she had often heard Ossip play in St. Petersburg and took a kindly interest in his artistic development, though he was not her pupil. She suggested that although he was receiving excellent instruction from Professor Tolstoff, he ought to take a series of lessons from her former husband as a final preparation for a professional career.

In due course Mme Essipoff wrote to Leschetizky and informed him that a youth of true genius would shortly arrive in Vienna to study with him before making his debut as a concert pianist. The plans pleased Ossip's parents, and aided by some preliminary instruction in 'The Leschetizky Method' from Mme Essipoff, the 16 year old Ossip went to Vienna in the autumn of 1894 accompanied by his mother and sister. They remained with him for the first season but the following year he was left to continue his studies with Leschetizky alone.

Leschetizky believed that a young man should touch life in all its phases, good and bad. He thought Ossip was too sensitive for his own good and too sheltered in his upbringing. He therefore plunged him into days and nights of a hardening existence. Most of the nights were spent conversing with 'The Professor' and his friends or playing billiards with them. But as far as Ossip's piano technique was concerned, Leschetizky was satisfied. It was all there.

After two years' study with Leschetizky, Gabrilowitsch made his official public debut in Berlin in October 1896 in a recital of pieces by various composers. It was a sensational success, inducing comments such as, "a new star has arisen on the musical horizon." Ossip was advised by the impresario Hermann Wolff to give a second recital at once, on the principle "strike while the iron's hot", and juggled with the dates of the engagements of other artists to fit him in. A third recital then followed, after which he was engaged to play a Beethoven concerto at the Gewandhaus in Leipzig under the celebrated Hungarian conductor Arthur Nikisch. A fourth recital, again in Berlin, completed his initial triumph.

Ossip Gabrilowitsch, sensitive young man that he was, tended to be put off by the presence of eminent pianists at his early recitals. Artur Rubinstein told the story of an early Gabrilowitsch recital in Berlin. As Gabrilowitsch was about to begin to play he noticed Busoni at the back of the hall; Ossip felt intimidated by Busoni's steely glare which seemed to be on him, and remained with him, for each piece he played. His performance suffered and he felt dejected as the concert finished. At the end, people in the audience moved forward, including Busoni. As he neared the platform Ossip saw - it wasn't Busoni at all! All his apprehension had been for nothing.

A few months later, in 1897, Ossip was engaged to play under Hans Richter in London during the June and July concert season. But he strained his left arm during practice and the performance had to be cancelled. He never recovered entirely from the strained muscle and the injury left a permanent weakness. Nevertheless, in the years that followed his debut he steadily made a name for himself as an excellent pianist, enjoying successful tours of Germany, Austria, Russia, France and England. In 1900 he made his first visit to the USA in a tour arranged by Mr. A. M. Wright of the Everett Piano Company (later Ossip changed to Mason & Hamlin pianos) and made his debut there on 11th November in Carnegie Hall, with a Tchaikovsky concerto conducted by Walter Damrosch. The tour was such a success that further tours of the USA were made in 1901, 1906, 1909 and 1914.

Ossip had another reason to be grateful to Leschetizky, apart from the fact he had put him on the road to success. When Ossip and his friend Mark Hambourg made a social visit to their former teacher in Vienna, they were introduced to Clara Clemens. She was the daughter of Samuel L. Clemens, better known as Mark Twain, and she had been given the opportunity to have piano lessons with Leschetizky in Vienna whilst her parents were staying at the Hotel Metropole nearby. Though her talents as a pianist were modest by Leschetizky's standards she was a good musician and later achieved a prominent position in the musical world as a singer. Leschetizky had given Clara a piece by Mendelssohn to learn. At the weekly gathering of Leschetizky's students and former students, over 50 people in all, Clara was terrified when it was her turn to play. Her small hands could not cope very well with the necessary stretches. At the conclusion of her recital she fled the room in tears. Most of the class were highly amused, but Ossip followed her and consoled her. He persuaded her to remain for the rest of the evening and literally provided a shoulder to cry on. They were friends from then on.

At an early point in their friendship, Ossip, serious and possessed of the highest integrity, told Clara, "I wish you to know something about me that you may not have heard." She wondered what on earth was coming. Ossip went on, "You and I are not of the same race. I descend from the Jewish people." Clara, brought up to believe in the crass stupidity of racial prejudice, was of course not bothered in the slightest but liked Ossip all the more for his frankness and honesty. She later wrote:

"It was characteristic of his disposition to regulate with meticulous precision all his associations, whether with people, or with affairs of art and business. He would not run the risk of being ignorant of anything connected with himself which, if I knew it, could possibly cause a shadow in my thoughts. This quality was more developed in him than in anyone I have ever seen. Letting things take care of themselves was not in his nature."

The friendship of Ossip and Clara soon turned into a romance but it was not of the lightning variety. He was frequently touring, so they met only rarely though they corresponded (in German) frequently. When he was in the USA in 1902 he visited the Clemens family in New York, then the couple met again in Paris later in the same year when Clara had gone to the city for singing lessons. They announced their engagement in 1902 but it was later broken off because Clara soon decided she did not want marriage; she wanted her own career as a singer.

Clara's mother died in 1904 as a consequence of a heart attack suffered in Europe in 1902. Meanwhile, the correspondence between Ossip and Clara was maintained regularly until 1909, which turned out to be an eventful year. Clara, who was at her parents' home at the time, knew that Ossip was touring the USA, playing at concerts all over the country, and she knew that he had recently had a minor operation. One day a lady came to the Clemens household from a neighbouring town on a purely social visit. During the conversation she spoke of having spent the last few days in a New York hospital where one of her children had been undergoing an operation. "We had the same surgeon that operated on the Russian pianist, Gabrilowitsch. What a shame he is dying! Such a fine fellow, they say!" "Who is dying?" asked Clara, shocked and bewildered. "The pianist. It is only a question of hours!"

Clara rushed to the hospital in a state of shock. At the hospital she asked, fearfully, "Is he still living?" "Yes", replied the nurse in charge. "But he is dying, and the doctors have left strict instructions to admit no-one." "But if he is dying, what harm can it do for me to see him?" pleaded Clara. Faced with such logic, medical ethics finally capitulated and she was allowed in. "There he lay", said Clara later, "white, still. No light in his eyes. No movement or recognition." She lay her hand on his head and spoke to him. His eyes flickered and he spoke a few words. Next day he gave a faint smile. Said Clara, "I knew then that God would work a miracle." The fever that had burned for days gradually subsided. It was clear to Clara that love had won where medical science had failed.

A few days later, Ossip, worn out and depressed, said it would have been better to have let him die. "Why resuscitate me and then leave me?" he asked. She hinted at another possibility. "Do you mean it?" he asked. "Yes, I mean it!" said Clara. When he was strong enough to leave hospital Ossip convalesced at the Clemens' country home. It appeared that his illness had started off as a cold which had turned into a serious form of mastoiditis; the operation had seemed at the time to have been successful but complications set in and but for Clara's timely arrival on the scene Ossip would probably have died.

The wedding took place in October 1909 at the Clemens' Redding home in the presence of only a few guests. Samuel Clemens was dressed in his blue and red Oxford cap and gown, and the couple were married by the same old clergyman, Joseph Twitchell, who had married Samuel and his wife many years earlier. The couple honeymooned in Atlantic City, but Ossip, never the strongest of mortals physically, developed appendicitis and had to return to New York for another operation. After he had recovered the couple decided to set up home in Germany.

Their departure to Europe marked the end of an era for Clara. Her famous father was suffering from heart disease and in 1910 he died. Mark Twain had once said: "I came in with Halley's Comet and I shall be most disappointed if I don't go out with it." He got his wish. Soon afterwards the family home caught fire and was burned to the ground, a dramatic end to 'Stormfield' as Mark Twain had called it.

Clara had of course made a number of visits to Europe with her parents but it was Ossip who was the real European, by birth and by the nature of his profession, and most of his concerts and recitals between the years 1898 and 1910 had taken place there. He had also added another talent to his repertoire, having studied conducting with Arthur Nikisch in 1905 and 1906. This led to several conducting engagements, including one in Manchester.

When they arrived in Europe after their marriage, Ossip and Clara settled in Munich, living initially in the Palast Hotel in that city. It was in Munich that the couple's only child, Nina, was born in 1910. Sadly, Samuel Clemens never saw his granddaughter. Not long afterwards a little tragedy occurred when the family's dog, Fix, was run over by a car and killed, an event which upset Ossip very much. Always kind to animals, there is a story concerning a kitten that does him credit. Once, in Nuremberg, he failed to turn up at the station to meet his sister Polya who was visiting him. Knowing the whereabouts of his hotel which was not far away she walked towards it and found Ossip in the street surrounded by an amused crowd. He was feeding a kitten. It appears that on his way to the station to meet Polya he had found the kitten, thin and starving. Realising its desperate situation he had carried it to a nearby café and bought food for it.

Ossip found plenty of engagements in Germany and in 1911 he and Clara moved into their first real home, in Nymphenburg, five miles from the centre of Munich. There they began a life of peace and contentment that was to last three years. By now Ossip spoke perfect English; Clara tried to learn Russian but soon gave up! The couple intended to spend their lives in Munich and might have done so had not fate intervened. Munich had a fine Opera House and Company which was conducted by Felix Mottl when the Gabrilowitsches first moved to the district. After Mottl's death in 1911 Bruno Walter was brought in from Vienna to fill the vacancy. Ossip had met and worked with him years earlier and a rich friendship began between the Gabrilowitsch and Walter families. Life was pleasant in those 'peace before the storm' years. Summers were spent in a rented house in Kreuth, near Tegernsee and Bruno and Elsa Walter took a house nearby. The families met daily for walks. Leopold Stokowski and his wife, the pianist Olga Samaroff, stayed at a nearby inn. Other visitors were the distinguished American music critic Henry T. Finck and a shy young man named Wilhelm Furtwängler, just starting out on what was to be a distinguished conducting career.

Ossip and Clara's idyllic life was abruptly shattered in August 1914 when war broke out. Ossip had assumed that as a musician, well known and respected in the Munich district, war, if it came, would pass him by. But he was wrong. He was a Jew, and a Russian Jew at that - the worst possible combination in the eyes of the ruling authority. Moreover, the fate of people such as he depended on the part of Germany in which they lived. Whereas Josef and Rosina Lhevinne who were living in Berlin were tolerated by the local authorities and were subject only to restrictions in their movements, the area to the south of Munich was in the hands of a trigger-happy set of military personnel who dragged off hapless individuals to a camp at nearby Miesbach where many were summarily shot for no greater crime than the fact that they were Jews or Russians, or even worse, both.

When soldiers came hammering on the Gabrilowitsch door at their summer home near Tegernsee and dragged Ossip away with them it was clear he was in mortal danger. There was hysteria in the streets and no Russian was safe. As Ossip was led away he called to his wife, "Greet Bruno for me", which she correctly interpreted as his coded way of saying, in the presence of the soldiers, "Get Bruno Walter's help if you can!" The telephone had been cut off and the house was surrounded, but Clara was able to sneak out of the large garden by a secret route, pass an urgent message to Bruno Walter via a mutual friend, and then get back into the house again, all undetected.

Walter knew the Russian Ambassador to Bavaria, Herr Treutner, and persuaded him to give orders that Gabrilowitsch was not to be taken to Miesbach, which was little better than an execution centre, but was instead to be taken from the Tegernsee Prison to Munich. He was detained there overnight and then told that he and Clara must get out of Germany immediately and with as little fuss as possible if they valued their lives. Leaving their possessions behind, Ossip, Clara, Nina and Nina's nurse caught the almost-empty Munich to Bolzano train, which took them out of Germany; thence, by a circuitous route, they made their way into Switzerland. After spending a few weeks at an hotel in Zurich they left for Naples, hoping to sail for the USA, Clara's home country. Initially there were problems in getting permission to leave because of the fact that Nina's nurse was German, but in September 1914 the party set sail for the USA on the Cunard cargo-liner *Carpathia*. This ship, which was destined to be sunk by a German U-boat in 1918 whilst en route to New York, had hit the headlines in 1912 when she picked up survivors from the *Titanic*.

After they arrived in the United States, Ossip suffered from melancholia for a while. The war sickened him, but his spirits revived after a holiday in St. Albans, Vermont, taken at the suggestion of the Stokowskis who were spending the summer there. His enthusiasm for life took a further uplift when concert engagements were secured and it was not long before he was touring in the United States as actively as he had been in Europe. He renewed his friendship with many other musicians including Friedberg, Godowsky, Hofmann, Kreisler, Schelling, Frank and Walter Damrosch, and Harold Bauer. Gabrilowitsch struck up a particular friendship with Bauer which was to prove lifelong. They established a close musical rapport, appearing together in joint recitals in the USA in 1914 soon after the start of the war. During the next 20 years they made many concert appearances together.

Gabrilowitsch's honesty in opposing what appeared to him to be humbug is illustrated by a letter he sent to a newspaper following a violent campaign against German music:

"Dear Sir,

I have your letter requesting me to express my views on Mrs. X's recent article concerning German music. Inasmuch as the works of German classics have been retained in concert programmes in France and England, it seems to me to be perfectly safe to adopt the same policy in America, I cannot share Mrs. X's apprehension that the patriotism of any loyal American might be endangered by hearing the compositions of Bach, Beethoven, Wagner or any other German

composers who have been dead for thirty, fifty or a hundred years. If any person's loyalty is as unstable as that, such a person should properly be interned.
Sincerely yours,
Ossip Gabrilowitsch.

Ossip had already taken steps to become an American citizen but in the face of irrational criticism and Clara's known pacifist views, the couple had to make public statements saying they loved America more than any other country before his application was accepted.

In the 1917-18 season Gabrilowitsch conducted three orchestral concerts in New York City for the benefit of Russian refugees. These were received so enthusiastically by the press that speculation arose as to the likelihood of his being offered the permanent conductorship of a major orchestra. This duly occurred; he was invited to become conductor of the Boston Symphony Orchestra - a very prestigious appointment, but turned it down on the grounds that he wished to continue his career as a concert pianist, and because of the large number of concerts the orchestra gave it would be impossible for him to do that. True to his unselfish nature he wrote to the manager of the orchestra recommending Rachmaninov for the post, saying that Rachmaninov (then still in Russia) was in great financial distress, that he would make a better conductor than himself (Gabrilowitsch), and "To get Rachmaninov would be a splendid thing for Boston."

The Boston authorities acted on Gabrilowitsch's advice; Rachmaninov was offered the Boston post but he declined. Gabrilowitsch soon received other offers and decided to accept an invitation to become conductor of the Detroit Symphony Orchestra. He chose Detroit mainly because the orchestra gave fewer concerts than most, which would allow him to combine his career as pianist and conductor. Every other week he could take part in engagements as a pianist out of town since he was to have an assistant conductor who would do preliminary work in connection with the concerts.

The prospect of becoming conductor of the Detroit Symphony Orchestra presented a challenge for it was small, run down, and needed to be built up. There were few first-rate instrumentalists in the orchestra when Gabrilowitsch took it over, so he had to embark on a widespread hunt for musicians. There were many difficulties. Musicians could not be poached from other orchestras and he had to fight with the unions before he could import musicians from other cities; the unions wanted all the orchestral members to be from Detroit. Gabrilowitsch instigated a comprehensive programme of auditioning and in one day heard 27 oboes, 64 flutes and 87 horns.

In the face of union intransigence in demanding the employment of only Detroit musicians, Gabrilowitsch decided it was impossible to form a first-rate orchestra, and on 19th June 1918 he tendered his resignation. However, the unions realised it would be unwise to kill the goose that laid the golden egg; eventually the disputes were resolved and the resignation withdrawn.

Gabrilowitsch also benefited from a musical windfall. The Boston Symphony Orchestra had sacked its German conductor, Dr Carl Muck, on political grounds. It was the vacancy thus caused that had led to Gabrilowitsch being offered the Boston job. The reason for the sacking was that Dr Muck had made no secret of the fact that his wartime sympathies lay with Germany and once the United States entered the war this did not do much for his popularity. After his dismissal he was interned for the duration. A number of excellent members of his orchestra resigned in protest at the sacking and several were snapped up by Gabrilowitsch for his Detroit Orchestra. By the autumn of 1919 he had an orchestra of 90 musicians and over the next few years, by the process of replacing musicians who resigned or retired by better ones, he built up an ensemble of formidable quality.

In his first Detroit season things went well, and the orchestra toured middle-west cities. He was good at getting the best from his musicians and was very popular with all of them. One orchestral member said:

"When we sit under his baton he makes us into artists. He transforms us into something greater than we know ourselves to be. He actually draws the music from us. We _must_ play it as he wants it."

Gabrilowitsch never allowed himself more than a one-year contract with the Detroit Symphony Orchestra, feeling always that he did not want to be tied down to a permanent conductorship. But 17 annual contracts succeeded the first one, and he attracted sufficient funds in the form of donations in his first year of tenure to have a new $1,000,000 permanent hall, called Orchestra Hall, built for the orchestra in 1919.

Gabrilowitsch was completely unaffected by fame and would talk to anyone. Once, whilst passing a house where a young woman was singing as she worked, he stopped to listen. Unaware that she had an audience she emerged from the house and he complimented her on her voice. Blushingly she thanked him, not knowing who he was. "Do you like music too?" she asked. Gabrilowitsch said, "I just play the piano a little." Some months later the young woman told a friend, "When finally I attended a symphony concert and saw my acquaintance standing on the rostrum my thoughts went wild. So it was Gabrilowitsch, the great Gabrilowitsch, who had said, "I just play the piano a little." I could hardly take it in, such bewildering modesty."

Ossip Gabrilowitsch

Gabrilowitsch could always take a joke against himself. One day he agreed to audition a young piano student in his hotel room. The boy struggled; it was awful. After the boy left Gabrilowitsch's room by a side door, Gabrilowitsch went out by the main door to get some fresh air. He was greeted outside his room enthusiastically by a small group of hotel workers; the lift man, chambermaids and so on. "Mr. Gabrilowitsch", explained the spokesman, "we couldn't resist the temptation of listening at your door. Gosh, it was marvellous!" "So glad you enjoyed it!" was Ossip's ironic reply.

A feature of Gabrilowitsch's career was a series of concerts he gave first in Europe before the 1914-18 war, and then repeated many times in later years in the USA. They were entitled: "The development of the piano concerto from the days of the clavichord to the present time." A lot of work went into these concerts, six in number, in which he spanned the time scale from Bach to the 20th century. In the series he played sixteen concertos, by Bach, Mozart, Beethoven, Mendelssohn, Schumann, Chopin, Liszt, Rubinstein, Tchaikovsky, Brahms, Saint-Saëns, Grieg and Rachmaninov, as well as two works for piano and orchestra by Franck and Weber which were of somewhat similar form to concertos. The programme notes were written by the famous critic James Huneker and each concerto was preceded by an interesting and amusing talk by Gabrilowitsch. The object of the series was to combine education of the public with artistic enjoyment. The success of the series ensured constant demands for its repetition.

Over the years many amusing incidents occurred when Gabrilowitsch was on tour. Responsibility for packing his clothes was left to his maid and on two occasions she forgot to pack the trousers he wore at concerts. Each time the omission was not discovered until just before the concert was due to begin. The first time he borrowed the percussion player's trousers, and the audience was left muttering to one another as the orchestra came in, "Why is old - - - (the percussion player) wearing striped trousers?" On the second occasion Gabrilowitsch was due to share a recital with the pianist Ernest Hutcheson, the two pianists playing alternate pieces. When Hutcheson arrived he was startled to be greeted by Gabrilowitsch saying, "Your trousers! I must have your trousers!" Few people knew the reason for the slightly longer than usual delays between their successive appearances.

Gabrilowitsch confined himself professionally to playing the piano, conducting and to the very considerable administrative chores of running a large orchestra, a task he attended to meticulously. In spite of many appeals he never had the time nor the inclination to give lessons, and he composed only the occasional short piece of music. He was often asked to edit musical publications, collections of favourite works, books on the technique of piano playing or the art of interpreting the classics, but always declined with the reply, "No time!" But he never stinted himself in helping unemployed musicians, writers and painters, and he took part in and helped to organise (with Harold Bauer and Ernest Schelling) the famous 1924 concert for the benefit of Moritz Moszkowski who had fallen upon hard times. Appearing with the conductor Walter Damrosch were Harold Bauer, Ignaz Friedman, Rudolph Ganz, Leopold Godowsky, Percy Grainger, Ernest Hutcheson, Alexander Lambert, Josef Lhevinne, Yolanda Mero, Ernest Schelling, Germaine Schnitzer, Sigismond Stojowski, Fannie Bloomfield Zeisler and Ossip Gabrilowitsch himself. In 1925 he appeared in another Gala Concert at Carnegie Hall marking the 80th birthday of his old associate, the violinist Leopold Auer. Also appearing with Gabrilowitsch were Jascha Heifetz, Efrem Zimbalist, Josef Hofmann and Sergei Rachmaninov.

Gabrilowitsch never allowed his work as a conductor to detract from his skill as a pianist and he remained a top class pianist for the whole of his career. He enjoyed playing the piano and this was as important to him as his conducting; he practised diligently and never allowed his skill to lapse. As a pianist he was noted for his clear, poetic interpretations. His playing was reflective rather than dramatic, but when the occasion or the music demanded he could display a fiery temperament, and would astonish his listeners by the surging power of his playing, as well as dazzling them by its brilliance or charming by its beauty.

During the 1920s Gabrilowitsch conducted for several seasons at the Hollywood Bowl, often playing a concerto as well as conducting. As a conductor, Gabrilowitsch had to play balanced programmes but he was not in sympathy with ultra-modern music. He accepted Debussy and he played music by Bloch, Ravel, Reger, Schoenberg, Stravinsky and others. But the opera *Wozzeck*, a musical drama in three acts and 15 scenes by Berg angered him. He once listened to Prokofiev playing his own piano music. "He plays mighty well", whispered Ossip to Clara, "but if that is good music it is time for me to die." Another time, when he was giving one of his own modern music recitals, he played five pieces by Schoenberg. Afterwards a lady who was a stranger to him exclaimed effusively, "Mr. Gabrilowitsch, now that I have heard you play Schoenberg I know what he means at last!" "Well, madam", replied Gabrilowitsch, "If you understand what he means you must explain it to me, for I don't know what it is all about!" Of the modern American composers of that time, Ossip conducted works by Felix Borowski, John Carpenter, Rubin Goldmark, Josef Hofmann, Edgar Stillman Kelley, John Powell and Ernest Schelling. He particularly liked Daniel

Gregory Mason's compositions and thought him a better composer than Edward MacDowell.

Gabrilowitsch was a non-smoker but he had two dangerous habits, overwork and overworry. He tended to be pessimistic by nature, but when he was not worrying he could be witty and jovial. For many years he used to carry around a little toy device which would make a noise like a cow in pain. He would actuate it during unduly lengthy, pompous and tedious gatherings, causing everyone to rush to the window looking for the distressed animal. At home he was quiet and relaxed, far removed from the image of the great conductor. Someone once asked his daughter Nina, when she was a young child, how she occupied her time. "I play the piano." "What does your mother do?" "She sings." "And your father?" "Oh, he listens."

Gabrilowitsch recorded for Victrola but his output amounted to only a dozen or so discs, including some in conjunction with his old friend Harold Bauer, and others with the Flonzalay Quartet. More important than his gramophone recordings are his player piano rolls, of which he made well over 80. Interestingly, he probably recorded for more different companies, eight of them, than any other recording artist. In descending order of the number of rolls known to have been issued, the companies were Hupfeld (16 rolls), Aeolian (Duo-Art) (16), Philipps (14), Artrio (11), Recordo (11), Welte (9), Ampico (6) and Artecho (4). There may have been more. Many different composers are represented including major ones like Brahms, Chopin and Schumann but there are also rolls of music by lesser composers such as Glazunov, Grainger, Henselt, Moszkowski, Raff and Cyril Scott. Particularly notable amongst the list of Gabrilowitsch's rolls is a 3-roll set for Ampico of Schumann's Fantasie in C. Some of his Duo-Art rolls were 4-handed arrangements recorded jointly with Harold Bauer. When he was recording for the player piano Gabrilowitsch used to help in the editing process in order to ensure a good result, and the recordings do him credit.

During the 1920s when the player piano was at the peak of its popularity, Gabrilowitsch used to take part sometimes in a joke of a kind that was very popular at the time. A grand piano would be placed in the corner of a room at a social gathering with its keyboard facing away from the audience. Gabrilowitsch would be invited to play, and part way through the performance he would get up and walk away whilst the piano (a Duo-Art instrument) continued to play to the startled and unsuspecting audience. The Aeolian Company naturally seized on this sort of event and gratefully used it in their advertisements.

In addition to the usual orchestral repertoire, Ossip introduced Oratorio to Detroit. With the Detroit Symphony Chorus his orchestra performed

Elijah, *Messiah* and Verdi's *Requiem*. These were so well received that in 1926 they performed Bach's *St. Matthew Passion* with two orchestras, two main choirs, a boys' choir and five soloists; 400 performers in all. This was repeated in the next two seasons, then in 1928 by popular demand it was taken to New York with two performances in Carnegie Hall on 5th and 7th April 1928. Ossip requested that as these were religious performances there should be no applause. The critics said the *St. Matthew Passion* performances were unforgettable - "an unrelenting drama in sound".

In 1927 Gabrilowitsch resigned from the Advisory Board of the Schubert Centenary Committee on artistic grounds. The committee, some time after putting forward its initial proposals, had come up with a late idea which at the time was unknown to Gabrilowitsch; it was to offer a prize for the best attempt to complete Schubert's 'Unfinished' Symphony. There were aspirants in 26 countries. Gabrilowitsch wrote a letter in which he stated that the scheme was "like adding arms to the Venus de Milo" and continued:

"Such an undertaking is undignified and inartistic. Moreover it is entirely superfluous. I regret I cannot be associated with a musical escapade of this sort. I request that my name be eliminated from your Advisory Committee."

He sent copies to the leading New York papers and a commotion was created in the musical world. The project was abandoned.

In the early 1930s Gabrilowitsch continued on an annual basis as conductor of the Detroit Symphony Orchestra though he was beset by many financial problems in the prevailing depression, and, at one period shortly after the Wall Street Crash, the orchestra was kept in existence only by the timely intervention of rich benefactors. It was always Gabrilowitsch's philosophy that his concerts should give the utmost pleasure to his audiences, a fact which led to an interesting example of the difference between his views and those of Leopold Stokowski. Stokowski was at the time the permanent conductor of the Philadelphia Orchestra and Ossip was engaged as a guest conductor to give a few concerts every year. Stokowski had requested that there should be no applause at the end of any performance he conducted, feeling that it spoilt the artistic mood. For Ossip's next concert the audience did not know whether to applaud or not. So Ossip told them he liked the audience to participate and if they wanted to respond to be warm and spontaneous - in Europe, he told them, they called 'Bravo!' and so on. Prolonged applause and cheers greeted this announcement! This resulted in the publication of a cartoon in *Musical America*, depicting a small group of seated individuals, bound, gagged and glum, labelled "Stokowski-esque", whilst next to them was another group, jumping up and down, happy and applauding wildly, labelled "Gabrilowitsch-esque".

Gabrilowitsch, a well liked and universally respected figure in the musical scene, received honorary doctorates from Yale (1924), Michigan (1928) and Wayne (Detroit) in 1935. No one expected in 1935 that his distinguished career was almost at an end, but so it was to prove. On 14th March 1935 he closed the symphonic season with a piano concerto (Chopin's Concerto in E minor, Op. 11), Beethoven's *Egmont* Overture, Op. 84 and Tchaikovsky's 6th Symphony (*The Pathétique*). The whole audience stood to applaud him and they cheered him from the platform. What they did not know was that it was the last time he would play or conduct in the orchestra's hall. On 23rd March he gave the final concert of his current historical concert series though he was far from well. He had suffered an internal haemorrhage the previous night and should not have appeared but, selfless as usual, he did not want to disappoint the audience. At the conclusion he made a short speech in which he courteously thanked all those who had worked to make the concerts a success, and with that he gracefully bowed out of public life.

On 25th March, two days after this concert, he was taken to the Henry Ford Hospital, supposedly for two or three days of medical tests, but he remained there for six months. The initial diagnosis had confirmed the presence of cancer and an operation was performed. In the autumn he was allowed home but it was a melancholy time, for in spite of occasional remissions his condition never really improved. Gabrilowitsch spent the last year of his life at home; occasionally he played the piano for as long as he was able, and he learned a few new pieces. One day, near the end of his life when he was in great pain, Clara wanted to send their chauffeur to fetch the nurse to give him an urgent pain-killing injection. It was typical of Gabrilowitsch that he insisted on the chauffeur finishing his supper first. Gabrilowitsch died peacefully on 14th September 1936, with rain, thunder and lightning adding to the desolation of the event. He was 58 years old. A funeral service was held in Orchestra Hall on 16th September with 1500 mourners present.

It is sad that the final 18 months of Ossip Gabrilowitsch's life were clouded by pain and misery, but the world of music can count itself fortunate that he was able to give so much pleasure for more than 40 years not only as a fine conductor but also as one of the world's best pianists. He is a musician to be remembered with respect and affection.

Great Pianists of the Golden Age

Mark Hambourg

14. Mark Hambourg

There must have been something rather special about Eastern Europe, particularly Poland and Russia, in the latter part of the nineteenth century. Perhaps it was the general environment; alternatively it could have been just the innate ability of the population. Whatever the reason, the fact is that the area produced a seemingly endless stream of brilliant musicians, the majority of whom left their native shores at the earliest opportunity for the greater freedom of the USA. A few remained in their home countries or other parts of Europe and a small number settled in Britain, where they soon became stalwarts of the musical scene. One of this latter group was Mark Hambourg, a powerful virtuoso pianist with a style reminiscent of Anton Rubinstein, his fellow countryman of an earlier generation. Not only did he play like the great Russian pianist, he also looked like him. Hambourg was based in Britain for most of his long life, and from his early youth was one of the most popular and respected pianists on the international concert circuit.

The Hambourg family lived in Voronesch (spelt Voronezh on modern maps), a town in South Russia. But they often spent their holidays in the village of Bogutchar, two or three days' journey away, at the home of an uncle who was the local doctor. It was in Bogutchar that Mark Hambourg was born on 31st May 1879. He was the first born of the family but three brothers were to follow; Jan, Boris and Clement, as well as three sisters, Galia, Luba and Munia. Mark had the unusual distinction at that time of being born in a bath. Most country houses in those days possessed an outhouse with a steam bath in it; a kind of Turkish bath. These baths were very popular and it was there that Mark made his entry into the world, amid steam and soapsuds.

Mark's father, Michael Hambourg, was a restless man of many talents. Trained for the church, he had turned to music and studied under Nicholas Rubinstein, brother of Anton. Michael earned his living by teaching music and ancient Hebrew, but he was also of a practical disposition and was adept at mending watches. Not only did Mark have a musical father but his mother, Catherine, was a professional singer. It is therefore hardly surprising that Mark rapidly absorbed the folk songs sung to him by his nurse and family.

At the time of Mark's birth his father was Head of the Conservatory of Voronesch, and Mark's days were divided between Voronesch and the country house at Bogutchar. Teaching arrangements at the Conservatory were informal; Michael used to take his young son to work with him, and at the age of three Mark used to stand beside his father and 'conduct' with him in the singing classes. This was no mere juvenile mimicry, as Mark was 'en rapport' with the music to a remarkable degree for someone so young. He received no formal piano instruction in those early years but when he was nearly five an aunt taught him a Czerny study, the plan being that on his fifth birthday he would play it to his father as a surprise. His father really *was* surprised when he heard it; in fact he was astonished at the child's fluency and from then onwards he taught the boy himself.

Learning the piano held no terrors for Mark; it came to him quite naturally, but his father wisely limited his practice to one hour daily. A matter of more serious concern was the disease rife at the time and Mark survived severe attacks of rheumatic fever and typhoid as a child. The typhoid nearly killed him but he managed to survive and fortunately retained a strong constitution which was to be an asset in his career.

At six years of age Mark learned the G minor Sonata of Beethoven, Op. 49, No. 2. Shortly afterwards his father moved to Moscow where he became a Professor of Pianoforte at the Moscow Conservatory. The move was made with Mark in mind; Michael recognised his son's outstanding talent and felt he would fare better musically in Moscow than in Voronesch. Mark was duly enrolled at the Conservatory where he was taught the piano, nominally at least, by a man named Schostakowsky, but in reality most of what he learned came from his father. Progress continued apace and at seven he learned and could play the 48 Preludes and Fugues of Bach.

Though the Conservatory was really a musical institution, lip service was paid to the provision of a general education. This was something of a problem for Mark as he had never really had any formal tuition other than music. How could he pass the general examinations? Fortunately the examiners were most anxious for him to succeed as they were well aware of his great musical gifts, and were determined that he must pass at any price. Mark's family told the story of what took place:

Examiner: "How do you spell so-and-so?"
Mark: "Er - er - er!"
Examiner: "Do you spell it this way, my boy?" (indicating the correct spelling).
Mark (greatly relieved): "Yes, sir, certainly."
Examiner: "Mark Hambourg is efficient in spelling, he passes the examination."

And so on; through all the subjects the examiner prompted the answers, and at the end Mark was pronounced successful.

In Moscow Mark was exposed to the wider world of music and he attended many recitals given by famous musicians. At eight, he himself gave a concert at the Hall of the Great Nobles in Moscow, with the Moscow Philharmonic Society, playing Handel's *Harmonious Blacksmith* Variations and Mozart's Piano Concerto in D minor, K. 466. At another concert soon afterwards he played Field's Concerto in E flat, again with an orchestra. On this occasion the Grand Duke Constantine was present and spoke to Mark after the performance. After talking about music for a while he asked Mark what he would most like to possess in the world. "A really big toy engine", Mark replied shyly. "Well, we must see about this!" said the Grand Duke. The next day there appeared at Mark's home a large parcel containing a marvellous toy engine. From then on Mark began to feel that "concertising" was a wonderful profession, and looked forward eagerly to the future!

Life in Moscow in those days was very unsettled, for it was a time of great political unrest. Police were everywhere, people were arrested by the score for trivial or imagined offences, and there was fighting in the streets. Naturally Michael Hambourg was concerned for the safety of his family and for Mark's musical development. At the suggestion of a well known singer, Mme Eugénie Papritz who regularly sang in London, Michael decided to take Mark to England.

Michael and his son set sail for Britain, arriving in London in the spring of 1889 when Mark was nearly 10. Neither knew a word of English, but lodgings had already been arranged, and through the good offices of other Russians in London they were put in touch with Daniel Mayer, the concert agent. Mayer at that time was enjoying great success for he had recently introduced Paderewski to the London public in appearances that had been greeted with tumultuous acclaim. Mayer took Mark to play for Paderewski who was very complimentary about the boy's talent. With Paderewski's 'stamp of approval', Mayer looked for an early opportunity to place the child pianist before the London public.

The chance was not long in coming. One of Mayer's artists was the pianist Mme Nathalie Janotha, a well-known and highly respected Polish musician who had studied under Clara Schumann and Brahms. Her concerts always had an extra element of interest - the presence of a magnificent black cat, without which, she declared, she could not play a note, and which always sat smugly on the piano in front of her. Mayer craftily used one of her recitals to introduce Mark Hambourg. As she took her final bow at the close, Mayer rushed Mark onto the stage and settled him at the piano before the audience had time to leave. Their curiosity thus roused, they were virtually forced to listen. This clever act on Mayer's part succeeded, because the audience marvelled at the skills of the diminutive figure. He was soon asked to play at a few afternoon engagements.

Meanwhile another British concert agent, Nathaniel Vert, was so impressed by Mark's ability that he offered him a three-year contract. Vert was a shrewd agent who had managed Josef Hofmann, another child prodigy, in Britain the previous year. Hofmann's earlier tours as a child pianist in America under the management of Henry Abbey had occasioned much criticism on the grounds that Hofmann had been exploited. In the aftermath of these charges managers had to be rather wary when presenting child artists, so the contract Vert arranged for Mark stipulated that no more than 25 concerts per year would be given. Under Vert's aegis Mark gave a debut recital at the Old Prince's Hall, London on 12th July 1890 when he was just 11 and another on 21st July. His ability can be gauged by the fact that his performance included such works as Bach's Chromatic Fantasie and Fugue, and Beethoven's *Funeral March* Sonata in A flat, Op. 26.

In the autumn of 1890 Mark played in Manchester, Birmingham, Hull and also in Scotland. The concerts were financially successful and on the proceeds Michael Hambourg was able to bring his wife and other children from Moscow to London. Mark's mother was anxious to give their children English-sounding names, and for a while Mark was known as Max, it being thought, for some reason, that Max sounded more English than Mark. Mark's father, who had by now acquired a working knowledge of English, as had Mark, was earning his living as a piano teacher and benefited from introductions provided by Paderewski. Mark continued to give some public recitals and many at private functions. He also played at some of the concerts of the impresario Percy Harrison.

One of the private venues at which Mark often played was the studio of Felix Moscheles, the painter, who was the godson of Felix Mendelssohn. He was the son of Ignaz Moscheles, who had been a pupil of Beethoven. Mark had been introduced to Moscheles by a Russian political refugee, Sergei Stepniak who in 1895 had the misfortune to be run over and killed by a train at the only level crossing left in London. Moscheles' studio was a meeting place for many of the people in the world of art, music and politics, and over the years Mark met there such people as Frederick Delius, Keir Hardie, Bernard Shaw, Ellen Terry, James Ramsey MacDonald, Oscar Wilde, Senator Lafontaine and Vladimir Lenin. His acquaintance with famous people such as these helped him in securing further engagements.

Mark Hambourg admired Paderewski, then the lion of the London musical scene, "as a god" (his own words) and there is little doubt that he modelled some of his technique on that of the great man. Meanwhile Mark's brothers Jan (violin) and Boris (cello) were also showing exceptional musical ability and both were destined to become well-known professional musicians. Clement, Mark's other brother and their sister Galia were both gifted pianists.

Early in 1891, Moscheles and some of his friends asked Hans Richter, the famous conductor, for advice on how Mark's musical career could best be furthered. Richter suggested that Mark be withdrawn from the concert platform for a period and be sent to study under a leading teacher. Leschetizky's name was suggested and, assisted by a donation generously made by Paderewski, Mark and his father left for Vienna in the summer of 1891, arriving there in the November of the same year when Mark was twelve and a half. Leschetizky was away at the time but as an audition he played Bach's Chromatic Fantasie and Fugue to Mme Essipoff who was Leschetizky's assistant and was also the current Mrs Leschetizky, though they were to be divorced soon afterwards. He was promptly enrolled and put into lodgings.

On Leschetizky's return Mark began studies with 'The Professor' as he was known, learning a new piece every week to play at the weekly class lesson. There he met Ossip Gabrilowitsch, a fellow student of Leschetizky's, and liked him. Later Artur Schnabel also joined the class. It was not long before Mark became Leschetizky's star pupil and in April 1894, when he was 14, he was allowed to take his first professional engagement in Vienna, at a private party given by Prince Pallavicini. He was paid in gold pieces, which he gave to his mother. She was so proud of this success that she had them set into a broach. He learned many concertos under Leschetizky, including the then new C minor Concerto of Saint-Saëns and was awarded the Liszt Scholarship, the value of which was 500 marks.

On Sunday, 3rd March 1895 the 15 year old pianist made his official debut as an adult when he played the Chopin E minor Concerto in Vienna with Hans Richter conducting. Amongst those present in the audience were Leschetizky and Eduard Hanslick, the famous critic. Other engagements soon followed, including a notable one in which he was soloist with the Berlin Philharmonic Orchestra on 3rd April in Berlin as stand-in for Mme Sophie Menter who was ill. On this occasion he was woken early on the morning of the concert and asked whether he could play Liszt's Hungarian Fantasia (Fantasia on Hungarian folk tunes) that evening. He could! Felix Weingartner was the conductor and Busoni was in the audience and enjoyed the performance.

After these successes, Mark's studies with Leschetizky were deemed to be completed and he was considered to be well and truly launched on his career as a concert pianist, a career which was to last for another sixty years. Before Mark left Leschetizky in 1894, the old teacher made a charming and generous gesture. Before Mark bade him farewell, Leschetizky said, "I have a little present for you", and handed him a purse containing all the money he had paid for his lessons during his three years of study with him. "You will need the money more than I do", he said, "and I have kept it for you all this time, to prove my affection and interest, and my regard for your future career." Mark was deeply touched by this.

The first tour he was offered was of Australia. Mark accepted with alacrity. His function was to act as the pianist in a professional party which included two singers whom he was to accompany, as well as to play as a soloist. When the scheduled concerts were finished the singers went home but Mark was invited to give further concerts with an improved contract in which he took 50% of the gross profits. This enabled him to acquire the sort of experience necessary to survive as a concert pianist, enduring lengthy and tiring travel and playing a variety of pianos in many different types of hall, often under primitive conditions. At last the tour ended and in November 1895 he went home to London via the Seychelles and Madagascar, arriving back in England a vastly more mature pianist than the boy who had gone to Vienna four years earlier, though he was still only 16.

On his return engagements flooded in. He appeared with the veteran violinist Joachim (64) and the even older cellist Piatti (73) at the 'Monday Pops'. 'Bicycling' as it was then called was a craze that had recently come into vogue, and one day when Mark was whizzing past St. James's Hall in London on his cycle he nearly achieved the unwanted distinction of knocking over the aged Piatti as he was crossing the road. "Boy, Boy!" cried the old musician; "Learn to ride your bicycle more slowly and to play your scales more rapidly!"

A particular highlight came one day when Hambourg played the Rubinstein Concerto in D minor at a concert with the London Philharmonic Society, deputising for Paderewski who was ill. In 1896 he played in Brussels and also made his Paris debut. In the same year he toured Germany in a series of concerts arranged by the impresario Hermann Wolff, and whilst there he met members of the Mendelssohn family. In 1897 Mark was off to Australia again, this time taking with him his brother Jan, then 15, making his professional debut as a violinist. Back in England in 1898, Mark played at a major concert in London with the Colonne Orchestra of Paris before embarking on another hectic tour of the provinces with Daniel Mayer as his agent. In 1898 Mark travelled to Vienna, and spent the summer with Leschetizky at his holiday home in Bad Ischl. Although this was primarily a social occasion, Mark sought advice from his old teacher concerning his technique, as should any good professional.

In October of the same year Mark began his first tour of the United States, playing in concerts in New York with the Boston Symphony Orchestra and the New York Philharmonic Orchestra, Naturally the preparation for these concerts involved a great deal of practice and this led directly to a rather entertaining dispute. Hambourg had hired a piano to practise in his hotel room. A lady in a nearby room objected to his early start, much to Hambourg's amusement, as she was given to holding noisy parties late into the night. For a while cold war prevailed, neither party giving an inch. But then the lady took the advantage. She hired a pianola and persisted in playing a roll of whatever piece Hambourg happened to be practising. He was so driven to distraction by this that negotiations were re-opened and eventually a truce was called.

After his New York concerts Hambourg toured the USA, playing in many different states including California. He was sponsored on this tour by the Knabe Piano Company. In Los Angeles there had been a flood; the streets were awash and hardly anyone turned up for Hambourg's recital. Stoically he gave it just the same, to only three people, an event recorded prominently in the local press. The local populace admired his professionalism in fulfilling his engagement so much that when he offered to repeat the recital once conditions were back to normal a day or two later, he played to a full house. On a subsequent tour, in 1902, he was presented to President Theodore Roosevelt.

From the time of Mark Hambourg's arrival in Britain in 1899 he had regarded himself as a British citizen and he was naturalised officially as a 17 year old in 1896. Throughout his subsequent travellings, and there were many, he was therefore a British subject, a pillar of the British musical establishment, and a great ambassador for Britain. Blessed with a strong constitution, he was able to sustain his technique whilst playing in an enormous number of concerts which involved a vast amount of travelling. Tours followed each other in rapid succession and it is unnecessary to catalogue them all, but his concert activities easily outnumbered those of any of his contemporaries.

In August 1901 Hambourg was asked to stand in for Busoni, who was ill, in a series of joint recitals at the Glasgow Exhibition with Ysaÿe, the famous Belgian violinist. They then gave some recitals in England, and Hambourg said that Ysaÿe had influenced him musically more than any other musician since Leschetizky. Busoni, who following his recovery replaced Mark in Glasgow, told Henry Wood that in his opinion Hambourg possessed the greatest talent in the piano world at that time. Hambourg played his 1000th concert on 16th June 1906 when he was still only 27 years old.

It is not difficult to appreciate why Mark Hambourg was such a popular and successful pianist. He had immense natural ability and flair, a powerful technique, and a wide-ranging repertoire. Internationally he was known mainly as an exponent of the romantic tradition. All the virtuoso works of Chopin, Liszt and Schumann were amongst his specialities. But he did not limit himself to the fiery and physically-demanding compositions to which his technique was so well fitted. He also excelled in the quieter, more reflective repertoire. Indeed, Beethoven's *Moonlight* Sonata became a theme tune for Hambourg; it found a place in most of the thousands of recitals he gave up and down the country and throughout the world.

Hambourg's repertoire was not restricted to long-established works. During his career he was to give a number of first performances of works of modern composers. He gave the first London performance of Busoni's Piano Concerto (with choral ending), Op. 39, with the composer conducting. Other first performances he gave included a Debussy Suite and his *Prélude à l'Après Midi d'un Faune* (in an arrangement for piano by Leonard Borwick), Ravel's *Jeux d'Eau* and *Gaspard de la Nuit*, and various works by Albéniz, de Falla, Granados and Malipiero.

Hambourg was short in stature but strongly built, with a large, lion-like head surmounted by a mass of hair. Not only did he resemble Anton Rubinstein, but there was also a passing likeness to the Beethoven of popular imagination - a useful attribute for a concert pianist. Though he was undoubtedly a brilliant pianist he was unpretentious and was always happy to tell stories against himself. His platform manner was genial and uncomplicated, enabling him to maintain an easy rapport with his audiences. In short, his combination of musical skills and personal attributes endeared him to the general public.

In 1907 Mark Hambourg married Dorothea, daughter of Sir Kenneth Muir-Mackenzie. Sir Kenneth was an eminent lawyer, a barrister of Lincoln's Inn and a holder of many important offices. Later he was created a Baron and became a whip in the House of Lords in the 1923 Labour Government. Subsequently he was made Lord-in-Waiting at Buckingham Palace and a Privy Councillor. Mark had first met Dorothea whilst she was studying the violin with Ysaÿe at his summer school in the Ardennes. Students came from all over the world to attend his classes, amongst them not only Dorothea but also Mark's younger brother, Jan. It was whilst visiting Jan that Mark met Dorothea. When Mark went to see his future father-in-law before the wedding, Sir Kenneth said, "I am delighted my daughter is bringing a musician into the family, but at the same time I must tell you that you must not expect my friends to be your friends."

Muir-Mackenzie was a true Victorian in an era when "mere musicians" were expected to know their place. However, things did not turn out as Mark's father-in-law had supposed, for the two of them became the best of friends and Muir-Mackenzie's friends became Mark's as well. Thus Mark's circle widened to include bishops, cabinet ministers, Lord Chancellors, diplomats and generals. Even Winston Churchill was one of his friends. Mark Hambourg knew them all and thus, through his marriage, he became a member of a circle that acquainted him with the social and political life of Britain.

Mark Hambourg's marriage was to be long and happy and was to be blest with four daughters, one of whom, Michal, followed in her father's footsteps by becoming a professional concert pianist. The couple's first daughter was born the year after the marriage and soon afterwards Mark embarked on another strenuous tour of Australia, this time accompanied by his wife, baby and 42 large bottles of sterilised milk! Hambourg's life continued to be a whirl of frantic activity as he played in concerts and recitals throughout the world. He also began a series of chamber music recitals with his younger brothers Jan (violin) and Boris (cello).

In his music-making career, Mark soon learned the art of tact, and came to understand that the conduct of a concert is not always governed by musical considerations alone. In one concert in Cardiff, he played Liszt's *Hungarian Fantasia* with an amateur orchestra. During the rehearsal the flute player kept coming in at the wrong time, and when Hambourg complained to the highly able conductor he explained anxiously, "For God's sake, Mr Hambourg, don't interfere with the flute player as he is our principal subscriber and supporter, and if he is not allowed to play just whenever it suits him he will withdraw his money!" Hambourg was mollified by this unassailable explanation and felt relieved every time he heard the strange improvisations on the flute, feeling that every note might represent another guinea in the coffers of the orchestra.

A career as a travelling virtuoso can lead to many interesting experiences, as Hambourg discovered in full measure. Once, in Australia, a cloud of large red flying ants descended on the auditorium, so that he had to endeavour to pour his soul into the music whilst surrounded by swarms of these insects. On another occasion, this time in India, two notes of the piano jammed during the performance and Hambourg decided to stop and ask a piano technician to investigate the problem so that the recital could continue. The technician discovered two enormous cockroaches jammed in the mechanism; he withdrew them with tweezers and proudly held them aloft for the audience to see!

Odd events were not confined to overseas tours. In a concert on Brighton pier, Hambourg was in the middle of playing the Liszt Concerto in E flat when the hind leg of the piano gradually gave way and, much to his consternation, the keyboard slowly reared up in front of him. Luckily an old packing case was found to shore up the defective instrument and normal service was soon resumed. Another time Hambourg and the members of the orchestra were nonplussed by the antics of a trumpet player who was the worse for liquor. He kept coming in at the wrong moment and, unmindful of the admonishments of the conductor, kept up a series of random blasts on his instrument until he sank down in an exhausted stupor and had to be carried out of the hall. Such were the trials of a concert pianist!

In 1910 Mark's father decided, at the age of 60, to pull up his roots once again. This time he emigrated to Canada. Mark had recently toured there and had brought back favourable reports of Canada as a land of opportunity. He was soon joined by his sons Jan and Boris. Mark, however, chose to stay in England and in the following year he and his wife bought a house in Cumberland Terrace, Regent's Park, London. It was to remain their home for the next 28 years.

In 1913 Hambourg once again met his old teacher, Theodor Leschetizky. The location was Berlin where Leschetizky, now 83 years old and nearly blind, was awaiting operations for cataracts. In spite of the old man's age and infirmity his mind was as nimble as ever and Mark played for him on several occasions. "You play more like Anton Rubinstein than anyone I have ever heard!" said Leschetizky.

Whilst in Berlin Mark had sensed an increase in political tension and had noticed regular movements of troops. When the war started in 1914, organised musical activity ceased abruptly, and Mark was at a loss to know what to do. He was then 35. He had rented a seaside cottage in Deal and spent some of his time there, playing a lot of golf, a game he had taken up some years earlier. The well-known antagonism towards anything or anyone German during the First World War extended to some misplaced insults being directed at Hambourg, presumably because his name resembled that of the German city, a fact sufficient to lead some simple-minded souls to the conclusion that he must be a German. He suffered further innuendo from *The London Mail* to the effect that "Mark Hambourg passes himself off as a Russian when his real nationality is well known", an assertion which ignored the fact that his Russian birth and early life were well documented and that he had been a naturalised British subject for nearly 20 years. He took the newspaper to court and won substantial damages, benefiting by the attendant publicity which confirmed his true nationality.

In November 1914 Hambourg left for another tour of America, unexpectedly meeting Pablo Casals, also bound for the USA, at Euston station. They travelled in adjacent cabins on the *Adriatic* and enjoyed numerous games of cards together en route. They arrived at the end of November and Hambourg was soon in action, playing at a party given by G. Schirmer Inc., the music publishers, for all the distinguished musicians who were in New York at the time. There were 26 pianists of international reputation present, as were 125 composers, according to contemporary reports. Six pianists took part in improvisations on six pianos; one was Hambourg, and the others were Bauer, Busoni, Friedberg, Gabrilowitsch and Hofmann. Hambourg met many well-known musicians whilst in the United States and saw a lot of Godowsky, Hofmann and Kreisler in particular.

After a tour of Canada with the singers Maggie Teyte and Edmund Burke, Hambourg was keen to return to Britain to see his family. He had intended sailing with many of his friends on the *Lusitania* but was persuaded to travel a week earlier on the *St. Louis* by Mr M.P. Grace of the shipping and banking firm of Grace Brothers. "You must travel with me", he said, "You will be quiet and will have the best accommodation, and we can keep each other company." Hambourg accepted the invitation and they set sail on the American liner on 17th April 1915. It is fortunate that they did. Mark probably owed his life to Mr Grace for most of his friends drowned on the final tragic voyage of the *Lusitania*, torpedoed off Ireland by a U-boat a few days afterwards.

Disembarking in Liverpool, Hambourg soon launched himself into the charitable and fund-raising opportunities that were beginning to open up. For the rest of the war, along with many other musicians, he pursued this work with his usual great vigour, playing in hospitals, prisons, at gatherings of troops, and wherever the chance arose to be of assistance. One of the most requested pieces in those days was Rachmaninov's C sharp minor Prelude; another was Beethoven's *Moonlight* Sonata, especially the first movement. He gave a series of recitals in the Aeolian Hall, London, featuring the works of early English composers such as Arne, Blow, Bull, Byrd, Gibbons and Purcell, and travelled around the country playing in charity concerts. Sometimes he played at the London Coliseum, which was not a normal concert venue. His programmes on the tour included a lot of Bach, Beethoven, Chopin, Schubert and Schumann. He had a special programme printed listing 100 standard classics from his repertoire, any of which he would play on request.

Mark played at the London Coliseum during an air raid, and was caught in a number of other air raids which, though not on the scale of those of the

1939-45 war, nevertheless inflicted many casualties and did considerable damage. Some of his concerts were held in strange surroundings. In an open-air concert in aid of the War Savings Committee the piano was placed on a plinth in Trafalgar Square next to the paws of one of the lions. On another occasion, he played in Waring & Gillow's store in Oxford Street, and on yet another he gave a concert in the City Temple in Holborn, assisted by the redoubtable Miss Carrie Tubb who sang from the pulpit. Hambourg's wife, Dorothea, also helped the war effort by her voluntary work, becoming an active member of the Volunteer Aid Detachment.

When Armistice Day came in 1918, Hambourg was booked to play in Leeds and very nearly failed to arrive, for the trains were overcrowded with jubilant passengers. The concert was held in an unreal atmosphere of euphoria; no-one really wanted to listen to music - everyone was excited and just wanted to go out to shout and celebrate, as did Mark himself.

After the war Hambourg's international career as a concert pianist and recitalist continued but it was now a changed world. Gone were the leisurely days of the Victorian and Edwardian eras. It was a new world of hustle and bustle. Cars had hitherto been a rarity; now they were commonplace. Travel was becoming faster and more reliable and people were even beginning to travel by commercial aeroplane. This was the world in which Hambourg proceeded serenely in the occupation in which he was a supreme exponent. And all the time he made gramophone records. His recording career had begun in 1909 when he was taken by Lionel Powell to the small, dark offices in City Road, London, where The Gramophone Co. Ltd. (about to become HMV) had a studio. According to Hambourg's later recollection, he played *The Bee's Wedding* (known alternatively as *The Spinning Song*) by Mendelssohn, or something of a similar nature, as his first essay into recording. This and other early recordings were successful and Hambourg was to become a prolific recording artist.

In the early days of Hambourg's recording career the techniques were primitive and it was impossible to introduce any real dynamic range into the finished product. This problem was of course shared by all recording pianists at that time. The piano tone always sounded thin on the record, like the plucked strings of a banjo or guitar. HMV used an old tinny piano, which apparently suited the microphone, for whenever a better instrument was tried the results were worse. Loud pieces reproduced better when played quickly, soft passages were less satisfactory, and slow, legato movements were unobtainable. Nor could anything be recorded on one side of a disc that took longer than four minutes. Thus, for the longer pieces, the pianist had the undesirable options of playing faster, making cuts in the music, or stopping abruptly at an inappropriate point and continuing on the next side.

After the mid-1920s Hambourg found the recordings more satisfactory, for the electric process removed some of the objections that had prevailed before. Not only was the quality of reproduction improved but 35 to 40 seconds could be added to the length of each side of a record. Even so, only about five minutes per side maximum could be achieved, and longer pieces such as sonatas or concertos had to be issued on several records. Hambourg featured in an enormous number of recordings for HMV, playing music by composers of widely differing styles, but including a lot of pieces by Chopin, Liszt and Schumann. By 1937 the HMV catalogue contained no fewer than 45 of his records (all double-sided, 78rpm) of which 19 were 10 inch discs and 26 were 12 inch. These included Beethoven's Piano Concerto No. 3 with Dr (later Sir) Malcolm Sargent conducting, and Beethoven's *Moonlight* and *Pathétique* Sonatas. In addition there were five other records (two 10 inch and three 12 inch) in which Mark Hambourg and his daughter Michal played music for two pianos. Hambourg was undoubtedly a stalwart of the recording scene so far as HMV was concerned.

Mark Hambourg also recorded rolls for the reproducing piano but he was much less prolific in that area than many of the pianists in this book. His main output on roll was for Hupfeld, for whom he recorded at least 17 rolls, including three of Anton Rubinstein's music and three of Schumann. For the Aeolian Company's Duo-Art system he recorded six rolls, the composers represented being Hambourg himself (*Volkslied*), Henselt, Leschetizky, Anton Rubinstein (2 rolls) and Tchaikovsky. Seven rolls were recorded for Welte; compositions by Bach, Beethoven, Chopin (2), Liszt and Rubinstein (2). He recorded two rolls for Ampico; the Chopin *Black Key* Étude and a Liszt *Étude de Concert*. Finally, one roll, a piece by Rubinstein, appeared on the Artecho label. Thus the total number of Hambourg's rolls was only about 33. Hambourg expressed misgivings about the player piano on the grounds of what he called "its precision, its unerring correctness".

In his long and distinguished career there were few major concert venues in Britain at which Mark Hambourg did not appear. Once he was appearing at the Winter Gardens, Blackpool and on the same bill was a famous lady singer. She, fishing for compliments, asked the manager of the Winter Gardens who could be relied upon to pull in the biggest crowds. "Rain, madam!" said the hard-headed Lancastrian. She never forgave him!

Apart from his professional work, Hambourg's main pastimes were golf (in his younger days), membership of the Savage Club in London where he and the friends of his generation spent many a long hour playing cards, and collecting. He was an avid collector and his interest began early. "From the age of five I showed all the promise of becoming the proprietor of a junk shop", he said. His taste was wide-ranging, embracing stamps, coins, books, old glass (especially English of the period 1780-1830), antique clothing, walking sticks, snuff boxes, Persian vases, small Egyptian mummies, watches, clocks, ladies' lorgnettes, precious stones, primitive pictures, furniture, silver and china. Taking pride of place were items of musical interest, especially two Chopin manuscripts, bequeathed by Felix Moscheles, who in turn had inherited them from his father, Ignaz, of two Études (D minor and F minor); a fragment of a Liszt manuscript (ten bars of his *Consolation* in G flat); and even a fragment of a Beethoven manuscript (unreadable), believed to be 32 bars for the beginning of a Tenth Symphony. He also possessed Liszt's red leather cigar case (again bequeathed by Felix Moscheles) and a lock of Anton Rubinstein's hair!

Between the two wars, Mark Hambourg remained one of the major concert pianists of the world. Just before the start of the Second World War, when Mark was 60, he and his family moved to a house in St. John's Wood, London. It was there that they were based during the war, which Hambourg spent, as he had the first, playing in concerts throughout the length and breadth of Britain to assist the war effort in whatever way he could. He was playing at a concert in Bournemouth in 1941 when Paderewski's death was announced just before the start of his programme. At the end of the scheduled items Mark played Chopin's Funeral March in honour of the great pianist, to whom he owed so much.

In London Mark Hambourg had many adventures during the blitz, as did everyone who lived there. Sometimes recitals had to be abandoned when the air raid sirens went; at other times he broadcast from the basement of the Paris Cinema in Lower Regent Street as bombs fell nearby. He and his family often slept in their two Morrison shelters, one for Mark and his wife, the other for one of their daughters, whilst Mark's baby grandson lay under Mark's Blüthner grand piano. Fortunately Mark's family, their home and even his collection of antique glass survived the war almost unscathed.

Whenever Mark Hambourg played outside London the German bombers seemed to follow. His arrival in whichever town he was visiting appeared to be the signal for the air raid sirens to sound. Even when he stayed with his brother-in-law Sir Robert Clive in Ashdown Forest, Sussex, in what he had expected would be a peaceful retreat, he discoved he was on 'Bomb Alley' where the flying bombs came over day and night.

Hambourg's career as a concert pianist was a busy one but he had found time in 1922 to write a book, *How to Play the Piano*, and he wrote two volumes of autobiography, published in 1931 and 1951. In his younger days he composed a few short items of music for the piano which were probably intended primarily for use as encores. Amongst them were Variations on a Theme of Paganini; Volkslied; Espièglerie; Romance; and Impromptu Minuet. He also played the piano in a number of films, the most important of which was *The Common Touch*, which was released in 1941. In this he had to be dressed up as a broken-down old street musician, playing the first section of Tchaikovsky's Concerto in B flat minor, apparently on an old upright piano. The sound track was superb, for in reality he had recorded the piece beforehand on a first-class concert grand, and the technicians synchronised the film to the music.

Inevitably as Hambourg grew older, his technique as a pianist began to suffer, but he was an old campaigner and was willing to go on playing as long as he felt able, provided the public still wanted to hear him. In his seventies, troubled by arthritis and gout, he would hobble onto the concert stage, hook his stick over the piano, and give a performance which belied his years. In 1950 he played music by Beethoven and Chopin at the Covent Garden Opera House to celebrate the Diamond Jubilee of his London debut in 1890. His last public performance was on 2nd March 1955 for a Henry Wood birthday memorial concert at the Royal Albert Hall, when he performed the Tchaikovsky Concerto in B flat minor. He was then nearly 76. After that he enjoyed an honourable retirement until his death five years later in Cambridge, on 26th August 1960, at the age of 81.

By modern standards Hambourg's style of playing is regarded as outdated, for he was the last of a line of virtuoso pianists who were concerned with an individual and personal artistic conception rather than a literal, scholarly treatment of the music. For this reason it has been fashionable in recent years to belittle him. But in his day, when artistic standpoints were different, he was second to none. Moreover, as a dynamic and popular personality, he won the respect and admiration of the musical general public.

Wanda Landowska

15. Wanda Landowska

At the present time the music of the baroque period and earlier is extremely popular. J.S. Bach and Handel are rightly regarded as giants of their art, whilst the keyboard compositions of Couperin, Rameau, Scarlatti and their contemporaries are held in the highest esteem. It was not always so. A hundred years ago some of the most notable of these musicians were virtually forgotten names, whose volumes of compositions were banished to the darkest cobweb-ridden recesses of music collections. It is to a small band of enthusiasts that we owe the revival that took place early in the 20th century in the fortunes of these composers. One of the leaders of this movement was the great keyboard performer Wanda Landowska. Trained as a pianist, she devoted most of her life to the resurrection of the harpsichord as an instrument worthy of serious consideration. She is now remembered as the musician who put the harpsichord back 'on the map' and as one of the greatest practioners of the art of harpsichord playing.

It was in Warsaw, the capital of Poland, that Wanda Landowska was born. There is some doubt about the year but the present consensus of opinion is that she was born in 1879, the year quoted on her passport. The date, 5th July, is not in dispute. The Landowski family were professional people of ample means, Jewish by ancestry but Roman Catholic by conversion. Wanda's father was a lawyer and her mother a talented linguist; both loved music and were good amateur musicians. The Landowskis' musical gatherings were highly regarded in Warsaw and were attended by many important and influential people.

This, then, was the environment in which Wanda spent her earliest years and she soon showed an interest in music. She started to learn to play the piano at the age of four, and progressed rapidly. Whilst still a child she was taught by two eminent musicians, Jan Kleczynski, who had written a learned and lengthy treatise on Chopin, and the concert pianist Alexander Michalowski, who at the time was a noted interpreter of Chopin's ballades and études. Wanda liked and respected Michalowski and later wrote:

"He was a marvellous master. He played constantly for his pupils, thus adding greatly to his teaching. I often had the feeling that he was playing especially for me because he felt my musicality. I understood him."

Being a Polish girl and exposed to the influence of these two Chopin experts, Wanda might have been expected to become another Polish pianist specialising in the compositions of the great national composer. But it was not to be, for from her early childhood, when she had been fascinated by

Rameau's *Tambourin* played by a visitor to her home, Wanda had inclined not towards Chopin or any of his contemporaries but to the earlier music of Rameau, Bach, Haydn and Mozart. Wisely, Wanda's teachers left her to her own inclinations, and over the years her fascination for the works of the pre-19th century composers steadily grew.

In 1895, when she was 16 years old, Wanda moved to Berlin to study composition with Heinrich Urban who, 13 years earlier, had taught Paderewski. A young student who had recently left Berlin was Josef Hofmann, her fellow countryman, who was three years older than Wanda. He had already achieved fame as a child prodigy and was soon to become one of the world's great pianists. Whilst she was still a student Wanda began to give public performances and these were immediately hailed as a great success. Contemporary reports referred to her as a 'born pianist'.

In 1900 Wanda eloped to Paris with Henri Lew, who was a journalist, actor and an authority on Hebrew folklore. She was still only 21 but now had the technical expertise at her fingertips to make her living as a pianist in Paris, which was one of the great centres of European musical activity. Her marriage provided some degree of security as well as a shared interest in certain types of music. She next embarked on what she had longed to do since childhood; studying the lives, times and music of Bach, Haydn and the other musicians of their period and earlier.

Wanda Landowska was entranced by the baroque period. The more she studied it, the more deeply immersed she became in that era, and she decided to devote her life to the revival of 17th and 18th century music, and to its interpretation. As she became increasingly engrossed in her studies it became apparent to her that the piano was an unsatisfactory instrument for the performance of early keyboard music. Many of the compositions of that period had been written for the harpsichord, the piano not yet being invented, and to Wanda it seemed obvious that the music could therefore only be truly interpreted on that instrument.

The lack of a suitable harpsichord presented a problem, for at the turn of the century harpsichords had long been obsolete and ignored. Consequently very few working harpsichords survived and those that did exist were feeble, tinny instruments, little more than curiosities. However, she obtained one from the Pleyel Piano Company and experimented with it. This was a specimen of a small batch that the company had produced in 1889, a wooden-framed instrument loosely based on 18th century models. From the days of her earliest public performances as a pianist Wanda had included pieces by Bach, Rameau and Haydn in her recitals, and with the aid of this newly-acquired instrument she started, in 1903, to interpolate music played on the harpsichord into her piano recitals; first of all just one piece, and then more, until it occupied an entire programme. Nowadays no-one would raise an eyebrow at this, but at that time such a thing was unheard of.

These recitals proved successful. The public liked what they heard and Landowska was able to bring to the notice of the musical public many compositions of Bach, Couperin, Rameau and Scarlatti that were largely unknown at the time. She gave regular recitals, and in between recitals she studied. Day after day, year after year, her time was spent in libraries whilst she immersed herself in the life and culture of the 17th and 18th centuries. She was aided in this task by her husband who was well versed in the skills of obtaining relevant information from libraries. Unaided by the modern benefits of photocopiers and microfilm, Wanda and Henri must have copied thousands of sheets of music and other documents by hand. She also visited museums and studied collections of ancient instruments.

Gradually Wanda put all her work together and, aided by her husband, her years of research finally came to fruition with the publication in 1909 of her book, *Musique Ancienne*. Written in French, it shed new light on the work of the great musicians of the 17th and 18th centuries. Its tone was stridently in defence of the work of the baroque composers, an approach that might seem unnecessary now but at that time, when their work was often summarily dismissed, was very necessary. Many long-forgotten or long-lost manuscripts had been found by Landowska during her researches and appeared or were referred to in the book. It was a monumental work and it established Landowska as a noted musicologist as well as a pianist and harpsichordist of ever-increasing fame and popularity. The book was translated into English and republished in 1924 as *Music of the Past*.

It was during these first few years of the present century that Landowska's pioneer work in championing the harpsichord started to bear fruit. She began to be noticed by influential people in the world of music as well as by leading figures in other branches of art, including Auguste Rodin and Leo Tolstoy. She stayed at Tolstoy's estate twice, in 1907 and 1909, and on each occasion she had her harpsichord transported there with her. But her efforts to restore the harpsichord to its former important place in the world of music did not win universal approval. Many musicians, whilst supporting her laudable attempts to re-popularise early music, nevertheless thought that the re-introduction of the harpsichord would jeopardise the revival of the music. They felt, as do many people now, that early music sounds better on modern instruments, and that the early composers used harpsichords for the simple reason that nothing better was available at the time.

There is no definite answer to these criticisms. At the present time there is a strong movement to play early music on "period instruments". Some people like it; some do not. The "anti period instrument" camp believes that the early composers would have jumped at the chance of using 20th century instruments, with their stronger tone, had they been available in their day. Would Scarlatti have been horrified to hear his sonatas played on a modern Steinway Grand or would he have been delighted that his music could achieve such a marvellous fullness of tone? No-one knows. People will continue to incline towards whichever view appeals to them irrespective of whatever those having the opposite view may say. Landowska was of course aware of all these arguments ninety and a hundred years ago but she stuck to her guns and was undaunted by adverse criticism regarding her use of the harpsichord.

Not only did Landowska move increasingly to the harpsichord, playing less and less on the piano, but she had a series of bigger and better harpsichords built to her specification. For years she had dreamed of having an 'ideal' harpsichord, and the practical-minded Landowska therefore had talks with Gustave Lyon, the Head of the Pleyel Piano Company. Along with her husband and Pleyel's Chief Engineer she visited a number of museums, especially the Musikhistorischen Museum in Cologne. Many plans were drawn up by the Pleyel engineers and submitted to Landowska until a design was produced that was exactly what she wanted.

The construction took several years but in 1912 the new 2-manual harpsichord was ready. It was the first of her special custom-built instruments. In accordance with Landowska's specific requirement it had a 16-foot register in addition to its 8-foot and 4-foot registers.* Most early harpsichords of the original harpsichord era had only 8-foot and 4-foot registers. Moreover, the new instrument differed from the original ones in other respects. Its changes in register were controlled by pedal rather than by hand-operated levers as in the authentic instruments; the size, general appearance and dip of its keys more closely resembled those of a piano than those of the early harpsichords, and it had a stouter soundboard giving a more full-bodied tone. Furthermore, its plectra were of leather rather than of quill as in original harpsichords. The instrument was also equipped with a coupler and a lute stop. Later, Landowska had harpsichords built which had iron frames instead of the wooden ones always found in the authentic period instruments.

---

*An 8-foot register sounds at the pitch indicated by the music; 4-foot sounds an octave higher than that indicated and 16-foot sounds an octave lower than indicated.

Because of all these technical refinements, Landowska was open to further criticism from those who wished to undermine her attempts to play 17th and 18th century music on period instruments. Her instruments were not, her critics said, "genuine". They were of modern design and therefore could not be considered truly authentic. Consequently, Landowska had managed to introduce a new factor into the "period instruments versus modern instruments" controversy. There was now a third possibility; instruments of a type associated with an earlier period but with an updated design and construction. It all gave the musicologists something to argue about!

Whatever the pros and cons of the arguments, Landowska's instruments, for all their refinements, were very definitely harpsichords. Landowska felt that, had the development of the harpsichord progressed in the 17th century, harpsichords such as the ones whose design and construction she initiated would have been the ultimate versions of the instrument. In addition, the technical refinements which had been built into her instruments at her specification, in particular the use of pedals instead of hand levers for changes in register, enabled her to play with a dash and brilliance previously unheard. Using her new harpsichords, Landowska was able to breathe fresh life into old and long-forgotten music. She had re-kindled interest in a rich musical heritage which had lain dormant for a century and she felt that her instruments accorded with the spirit of the baroque era.

By 1913 Wanda Landowska was the undisputed queen of the art of playing the harpsichord and it was largely through her efforts that the instrument was once again considered respectable. She now occupied a unique position in music, for though there were many notable pianists there was only one top-class harpsichordist - Wanda Landowska.

In 1913 Landowska started a harpsichord class at the Hochschule für Musik in Berlin at the invitation of Hermann Kretzschmar, the Director, but the project had hardly got into its stride when war came in August 1914. Wanda and her husband were officially enemy aliens in German eyes, being Polish by birth, and their passports were confiscated. Though they were not allowed to leave Berlin they were not viewed by the German regime as a threat. Landowska and her husband were regarded as civil prisoners on parole, as were the Lhevinnes who also lived in Berlin, and she was allowed to continue teaching. The couple's married life appears to have been rather unconventional. According to Harvey Sachs, Landowska's biographer, Lew's mistress shared their home with them.

Following the signing of the Armistice in November 1918, Wanda Landowska and her husband decided to return to France. However, at that point fate took a hand, for Lew was killed in a car accident in Berlin. After this tragedy Wanda Landowska went to Switzerland and then back to Paris, alone. There she settled, and resumed her tours and instructional classes.

In 1923, aged 44, Wanda made her first tour of Europe, Asia and North and South America. Her first appearance in the United States was on 20th November 1923 as soloist with the Philadelphia Orchestra under Leopold Stokowski. She also gave courses and held public lectures in many major cities and and was now acknowledged as the world's leading harpsichordist.

This was the period of her life when Landowska's gramophone recording career began, and over the next thirty years or so she was to make many records that have now become collectors' items, for her interpretations are regarded by many people as definitive. She had in fact made recordings of a different kind earlier, for she had cut 11 piano rolls for the Welte Company as early as 1905, playing compositions by Bach, Berlioz-Liszt, Chopin, Dandrieu, Daquin, Durante (a 17th century Italian composer), Scarlatti, Schubert and Schumann, though the piano roll production process at that time was less satisfactory than it was to become later. But after those early piano rolls her recording work was set aside for several years. When she resumed gramophone recording, she worked for HMV initially and later for RCA Victor, her output consisting mainly but not entirely of the baroque period. Naturally enough, most of her releases featured composers such as Bach, Cato, Chambionnières, Couperin, Handel, Lully, Mozart, Oginski, Pachelbel, Purcell, Rameau, Scarlatti and Vivaldi. The majority of her 78rpm recordings were made in France and are regarded as particularly fine and well balanced.

The Welte piano rolls of 1905 referred to above were not the only rolls she recorded. She made others, at a later date, for Hupfeld (at least 10 rolls), Duo-Art (7), Artecho (1) and Pleyela (1). Perhaps the most important item on her list of piano rolls was her recording on three rolls of Mozart's Sonata in D, K. 576. She recorded this sonata for Duo-Art and also for Hupfeld. The Hupfeld rolls of the sonata were adapted and issued by Ampico; consequently the sonata appeared in the lists of three different companies. The Duo-Art rolls, which were issued during the years 1924 to 1928, included, apart from the 3-roll set of the Mozart sonata, Beethoven's *Andante Favori* and Landowska's own transcription of *Valses Viennoisses* based on music by Lanner, the early 19th century Austrian composer. The Artecho roll was a Schumann waltz and the Pleyela one was a Scarlatti sonata. Though Landowska's piano rolls were few in number (totalling only about 30, excluding the Ampico adaptations from Hupfeld) the playing is of a fine quality and they are highly regarded by player piano enthusiasts.

Landowska soon found that concert tours were a highly profitable business, and between 1923 and 1926 she made four trips to the USA, taking her harpsichords with her. "I arrived there like a lion tamer", she wrote later, "dragging along four large Pleyel harpsichords." It was during this period that she persuaded the Pleyel Company to use iron frames in her harpsichords to make them more resistant to changes in climatic conditions. On the proceeds of her first tour she bought a new home in 1925 in Saint-Leu-la-Forêt, just north of Paris. It was more than just a home, for there she set up her vast library and her collection of antique and modern instruments. The house had an enormous garden and in it she arranged for a small concert hall to be built. There, in 1927, she inaugurated her Sunday afternoon recitals, which were always something of an occasion. They were given to selected audiences of musicians, writers, painters, sculptors and lovers of music, who converged there from all over the world.

The recitals consisted in the main of more demanding and less 'popular' music than she would play in her recitals on tour. She also founded her 'École de Musique' at her home and taught many talented students there, including Clifford Curzon and also Ralph Kirkpatrick who subsequently achieved fame as an authority on the music of Dominico Scarlatti. In 1933 she presented the first public keyboard performance in modern times of Bach's *Goldberg Variations*. Her later recording of this set of pieces frequently appears in record catalogues today as a re-issue.

Landowska's interpretation of baroque music was not to everyone's taste. Brought up at the height of the romantic period as she was, many experts felt that she took liberties with the wishes of the composers - that her interpretations of the earlier composers were in fact too romantic. Landowska countered these arguments by pointing out that a rigidly strict adherence to the markings on the music could lead to a lifeless, sterile, arid performance. These are of course matters over which musical experts can argue indefinitely and there is no right or wrong answer. One thing is certain; her interpretations are more strictly controlled, more precise and less free, than those of most of her contemporary pianists who learned their music in the late romantic era. To many people, then and now, Landowska was a fine performer and her interpretations are brilliant and well-balanced.

Above all, Landowska had spent a lifetime studying the music she played, and it took a brave person to assert that she was not interpreting it correctly. As she herself would say in her concert performances of the 1930s when introducing a composition to the audience: "I'm now going to play such-and-such a piece. I've been practising this piece for 45 years." Few could quibble when faced with Landowska's undoubted scholarship and her dedication to her instrument. What is more, she was never reticent about airing her views on the interpretation of Bach and his contemporaries. A famous Landowska story concerns a heated argument she once had with another Bach specialist, a woman, over the way certain ornaments in the music should be played. Neither would give an inch. Eventually Landowska haughtily terminated the conversation by remarking, "Very well, my dear, you continue to play Bach your way and I'll continue to play him *his* way!"

Though Landowska was regarded primarily as the harpsichord's supreme and undisputed exponent, she was almost as well known for her writings on 17th and 18th century music. Apart from her classic book *Musique Ancienne* she contributed numerous articles to music journals for the whole of her working life, on subjects such as the work of various individual composers and on many aspects of music and its interpretation, thereby enhancing her worldwide reputation as a musical scholar. She also wrote extensive notes for all her concert programmes. In addition, she composed a number of small pieces, constructed in the classical style, and sometimes included them in her recitals.

Throughout the 1930s Landowska continued to give recitals and master classes at her home, to record, and occasionally to tour. Her work had re-established the harpsichord and her recordings sold well. The 1937-38 HMV catalogue lists Landowska recordings of works by Bach, Byrd, Daquin, Handel, Mozart and Rameau. Not all her recordings were of the harpsichord; for instance, her performance of the Mozart Concerto in D major, No. 26 (*The Coronation*) was for piano and orchestra, as it should have been, but all her solo work involved the harpsichord. She never gave up playing the piano completely. She was regarded as an authority on the interpretation of Mozart's concertos on the piano and wrote cadenzas for them. Her playing of these concertos as a pianist remained a standard part of her repertoire though she was known primarily as a harpsichordist.

Landowska's recitals were almost as remarkable for the showmanship she displayed as for her playing. She was a great believer in 'atmosphere' - in setting the scene. The stage would be arranged as though it were a living room - a lamp to the left of the keyboard - the stage nearly darkened. Landowska required her audiences to be present several minutes before the performance began and to wait quietly, thus heightening the tension. At the appointed time Landowska would glide onto the stage, hands clasped in an attitude of prayer and head turned upwards, apparently in communion with the long-departed great masters. In appearance she was gaunt, frail-looking and scraggy. She had a large nose, of which she must have been proud, for most of her publicity photographs were taken in profile. However, once she seated herself at the harpsichord and began to play her seeming frailty was soon forgotten. Whilst some critics thought, as already noted, that she over-romanticised the baroque composers, most felt that she maintained a correct balance between classical precision and freedom from rigidity, particularly regarding her treatment of ornamentation. The sparkling vitality of her playing on her custom-built harpsichords was a revelation to many who had been brought up to believe that music of the pre-romantic era was dull and lifeless.

Landowska's success and popularity were maintained throughout the 1930s and her work in restoring the harpsichord to its former glory was appreciated by many modern composers, some of whom, notably de Falla and Poulenc, wrote new harpsichord works especially for her. She continued to record as the war clouds once again gathered over Europe, she lectured at the Sorbonne, and gave classes at the École Normale in Paris. In France she was a national institution.

When war came in 1939, Landowska was 60 years old and still living and working in Saint-Leu. She stayed there and continued working for a while, but when the German army approached Paris in the spring of 1940 it was clear she would have to abandon her home. This she did, leaving behind almost all her musical possessions including her collection of instruments and her library of some 10,000 volumes. She fled to the south of France with her student and companion Denise Restout, but soon found life under the Vichy Republic unpalatable. Late in 1941 she embarked with Restout for the USA and arrived there on 7th December 1941, the day that Japan attacked Pearl Harbor. Landowska had lost nearly all her possessions, for the Germans had looted her Saint-Leu home and her belongings had mostly disappeared or been stolen.

Nevertheless, Landowska at 62 bravely began working again. She performed, taught, and embarked on a new series of recordings using whatever harpsichords were available. In fact this phase of her recording career was to last for the rest of her life, for she recorded a vast quantity of music in the United States (for RCA Victor) at an age when most people would have retired. These late American recordings differ in sound quality from the pre-war French ones, for whereas the earlier ones made the listeners feel that they were sitting listening to the instrument in a concert hall, the American ones gave the impression that the microphone was placed inside the harpsichord. Given the twangy and strident nature of the instrument's sound this can lead to a somewhat overpowering effect in large doses. Even so, the recordings enable us to hear Landowska's definitive interpretations of many works she had not recorded previously.

Landowska's first public performance following her arrival in the United States in 1941 was at the Town Hall in New York in February 1942, when she played the *Goldberg Variations* - her first recital in the United States for 14 years. She was to reside in New York until 1947 and was a very active figure in the musical scene of the city during that period.

When the war ended, Landowska thought of going back to her home in Saint-Leu but the Paris of 1945 was very different from that of 1939 and she knew that to return to her looted home would evoke many bitter memories. The clock could not be turned back. Also, she was now 66, and there would be many practical difficulties in moving to Paris. Above all, she had carved out a new career for herself in the United States and was well settled. She therefore decided to stay. But she opted for a more rural setting than New York and in 1947 she rented a house in Lakeville, Connecticut.

In Lakeville the pattern of her life continued in much the same way as before; she studied, she wrote and she recorded. Occasionally she gave a public performance. In the early 1950s she recorded the complete *Well Tempered Clavier* of Bach. She referred to this monumental recording as her "last will and testament". Every few weeks a recording crew from RCA would arrive in Lakeville and would set up their equipment in her home. They would stay for two or three days whilst she recorded some of the '48', after which they would depart, returning on another occasion when Landowska was ready to record the next batch. When the process was eventually completed and all the recordings were 'in the can' Landowska was 75 years old. Even this did not mark the end of her recording career, for the technicians returned in later years, up to 1959, for Landowska to record various works by a number of composers of the baroque period.

Landowska's last public performance was given in 1954 at the Frick Museum in New York. After that, though her recording work continued, she confined her other work to studying, writing and teaching. In July 1959 she celebrated her 80th birthday but died a few weeks later on 16th August 1959, full of years and honours. Five years later, in 1964, Denise Restout and Robert Hawkins published a compilation of a selection of Landowska's writings entitled *Landowska on Music*.

Though she was not the only musician who dedicated herself to reviving interest in 17th and 18th century music, Landowska was certainly in the forefront of the movement. Moreover, she was without doubt the musician to whom we are most indebted for reviving an interest in the harpsichord after more than a century of oblivion. That in itself was enough to secure Landowska's place in music's hall of fame. Before she came on the scene the work of the earlier composers was usually interpreted in the form of transcriptions, such as those of Bach's music by Busoni, Liszt and Tausig. Once Landowska had started to play these works on the harpsichord, having studied the composers' intentions carefully, the transcriptions which had once been popular no longer sounded 'right'. Landowska had founded a new era. It would, we feel, be wrong to bar Landowska from a book devoted to great pianists on the pedantic grounds that she was primarily a harpsichordist. As a great exponent of the keyboard, not only on the harpsichord but also the piano, she deserves her place.

Artur Schnabel

16. Artur Schnabel

Most great performers are specialists to some extent. Rarely does a pianist devote equal attention to all types of music. A specialist *par excellence* was the pianist Artur Schnabel, who seldom played the 'virtuoso' compositions of Liszt, Chopin and others, nor the music of the late romantic or modern schools. Schnabel limited himself, in his mature years, to composers of the great classical period; Mozart, Beethoven and Schubert, together with a few later composers such as Schumann and Brahms. Most of all, his name will be for ever associated with the piano music of Beethoven.

The Schnabel family was resident in Lipnik, a small village in a sector of northern Austria which is now part of Poland. Isidor Schnabel was an Austrian-Jewish textile merchant and although he was not rich he and his wife, Ernestine, lived in reasonable comfort. They had three children; two girls, and Artur, who was born at the family home in Lipnik on 17th April 1882. There is another, much larger, Lipnik in Carinthia, southern Austria. In later life it often amused Artur Schnabel to see himself described in concert programme notes as "the Carinthian pianist". Artur's sisters were older than he, Clara by six years and Frieda by one, so he received plenty of sisterly attention. When Clara was 10 years old she started to take piano lessons, and the four year old Artur copied what she was doing. Before very long he was far surpassing her achievements and his exceptional talent was quickly recognised. Lessons were hurriedly arranged, progress was made at a breakneck pace, and Artur was soon amazing the local people with his astonishing prowess.

Interestingly, Artur's musical genius was not accompanied by any corresponding knowledge of the mechanics of the piano. His only foray into an understanding of its mechanism came one day when his parents were out. He and one of his sisters dismantled part of the piano to try to find how it worked and an expensive repair was required. The experiment was not repeated! Artur never showed much interest in piano mechanisms after that, unlike some other famous pianists such as Grainger and Hofmann, both of whom understood and made various modifications to the mechanism of their pianos.

After Artur had been taught by his sister's piano teacher for a while it was clear that more advanced tuition was urgently needed. The family had meanwhile moved to Vienna, and Artur was taken at the age of seven to the Conservatory of the Society of the Friends of Music for a talent test which, needless to say, he passed easily. He was too young to attend the Conservatory but Hans Schmidt, a Professor there, took him as a private pupil, while his general education was provided by a private tutor. Schmidt was a capable but not particularly inspiring teacher. Schnabel later recalled him as "an old man with a long white beard" (he was actually about 55) but as Schnabel admitted, nearly *all* the men in Vienna in those days seemed to be old men with long white beards!

From the time of Artur's audition it was recognised that he had a musical talent and potential far above the ordinary; indeed, that he had all the qualities necessary to become a first-rate professional musician. Thus, as he later pointed out, he was considered to be a professional musician by the decision of his parents and patrons, and no other career was ever contemplated for him other than that of a pianist. "They made me a pianist", said Schnabel in his autobiography. "I had no choice." He said that otherwise he might have become a composer, for composing was, and remained, his first love.

Whilst he was studying in Vienna, Artur and his family were supported financially by three wealthy families who had taken an interest in him. Indeed, they supported him for eight years, but remained in the background themselves and never asked or expected to hear him play. This of course eased matters for the Schnabel family and enabled Artur to concentrate on music.

At eight years of age Artur gave a very successful semi-private concert in a local music shop, playing Mozart's Concerto No. 20 in D minor, K. 466. Fortunately, although his parents were ambitious for him, they were not greedy and he was not thrust into the limelight as a prodigy, unlike some other children in Vienna at the time who were exhibited as musical geniuses, only to fizzle out as they grew up. No publicity was sought for or by Artur; all his life he shunned it, believing that he should be judged on artistic considerations alone and that being so, it should not be necessary to 'blow one's own trumpet'.

After two years of study under Professor Schmidt, Artur was again ready for a new teacher. Only the very best could add anything to what he had learned under the estimable Schmidt, and that meant Leschetizky, doyen of the world's piano teachers. Artur was taken to the great man and played for him. Leschetizky then asked him to sight-read the score of *Cavalleria Rusticana* which had appeared only one week previously. He evidently passed this test to the old Professor's satisfaction for he was immediately enrolled as a pupil, at the age of ten. Leschetizky employed a number of assistants who helped with the teaching, and in addition some pupils were taught by Mme Essipoff, herself a brilliant concert pianist, who was Leschetizky's wife at the time but about to be divorced. She taught Artur for a year, during which period Leschetizky rarely heard him, but after that he was taught by another assistant, Mme Brée, and by Leschetizky himself.

It was at Leschetizky's studios that Schnabel came into contact with the 'international crowd', the brilliant and aspiring young pianists who had flocked to the great teacher from all over the world. Fellow-students there included Ignaz Friedman, Ossip Gabrilowitsch, Katharine Goodson and Mark Hambourg. Most of them lived in lodgings but Artur lived at home with his family, though his father was frequently away on business.

Soon after the start of his studies with Leschetizky it was decided that Artur should have lessons in composition, and Anton Bruckner who lived in Vienna was suggested as a teacher. His mother took him to Bruckner's house and they climbed a flight of steps to the front door. After they had knocked they heard the sound of slippered feet approaching on the other side of the door; it opened just wide enough for a bald-headed man to peep out. Artur noticed a hallway stacked with piles of music. "What do you want?" the man asked. Artur's mother briefly explained. "I don't teach children!" growled the man, and pushed them out. That, according to Schnabel, was the extent of his musical association with Bruckner!

Fortunately another teacher was found and his beneficial influence fully complemented Artur's studies with Leschetizky; Artur became a pupil, for musical theory, of Dr Eusabius Mandyczewski who was Brahms' amanuensis. He was an excellent teacher and Artur studied with him for several years. Mandyczewski's official appointment was as archivist at the Society for the Friends of Music. As he had to be at work by 9.15 each morning Artur used to arrive for his lessons at 8 o'clock. But after the lessons Mandyczewski often used to take his pupil with him to the Society's library, where Artur was allowed to browse amongst the unique and priceless manuscripts, absorbing a great deal of musical heritage in doing so. This was a highly rewarding phase of his musical education and his association with Mandyczewski also brought him into personal contact with Brahms, Hugo Wolf and other leading musicians of the day.

When Artur was 11 years old his family moved to Bielitz, and from then on he lived in lodgings in Vienna. Meanwhile, his skill as a pianist was continuing to develop and by the age of 14 he was regarded by Leschetizky virtually as an adult, complete musician. At the same age he was allowed to appear in a public performance, his first official appearance for six years. By this stage, criticism of his playing had virtually ceased and Leschetizky used to send many of his pupils to Artur for advice on interpretation.

Schnabel said that his only real rival in Leschetizky's formidable array of talented pupils at the time was Mark Hambourg, three years his senior. But their styles were completely different and Leschetizky, wise teacher that he was, always channelled each pupil's skills into the type of music that suited him or her best. Hambourg was the dashing virtuoso, able to play the most fiendishly difficult music with consummate ease. According to Schnabel, Hambourg had "elemental qualities". Artur was a more thoughtful breed; though technically brilliant, it was as an interpreter of the music that his class showed. Leschetizky used to say to Schnabel: "Artur, you will never be a pianist - you are a musician!" In Schnabel's view, he could have said of Hambourg, "You will never be a musician - you are a pianist!"

Whilst in Vienna, Artur made many friends, including Ossip Gabrilowitsch and Ignaz Friedman, and the three of them sometimes used to visit Samuel Clemens (Mark Twain) and his daughters at the Hotel Metropole. One of the daughters, Clara, later married Ossip Gabrilowitsch. Throughout all these years Artur composed music, most of it now long forgotten, but important to him at the time. His music came easily to him but by his own admission he was lazy and lacked discipline. Nevertheless he achieved all he needed to do, and the discipline developed later.

After four years of study with Leschetizky there was little more that the Professor could teach him and lessons gradually tailed off. He was still too young to go out into the world on his own, but in 1898, when Schnabel was 16, Leschetizky decided that his pupil was now ready to make his own living. He felt that Artur had exhausted what Vienna had to offer, and that Berlin was the best place for him to seek a new beginning. The young pianist took with him to Berlin letters of recommendation from Leschetizky and others and he soon began to make his mark on the musical life of the city. He settled himself in lodgings and in a few months time a debut recital was arranged for him in a small hall, under the management of Hermann Wolff, the famous Berlin impresario who handled the affairs of many of the leading European pianists. In his recital he played a Schubert sonata, a daring thing to do as they were rarely performed at the time. As he later explained, he included it in the programme because he liked it - not to be different. This characteristic remained with Schnabel throughout his life; to play the music he enjoyed playing, rather than to build up a repertoire of what the public was thought to want. Perhaps that is partly why he became such a satisfying pianist.

In Berlin the youthful pianist lived a free and easy lifestyle; the music came to him effortlessly, and there was plenty of time left for leisure and enjoyment, including playing cards and billiards late into the night. There were also many girl friends, including a 'special' one. Looking back later at those early years, the mature Schnabel did not very much like what he saw, for the young Schnabel was lacking in the qualities of discipline and responsibility that were later to characterise his life and music. But the musicianship was already there and Wolff soon procured other engagements for him, including 15 concerts in Norway. On the journey there he saw the sea for the first time. Most of his Norwegian engagements were as accompanist to a violinist, but he did have the opportunity on one occasion to play Beethoven's Fourth Piano Concerto with an orchestra.

Artur became officially resident in Berlin in 1900 and the city was to remain his home and base of operations until 1933 when Hitler came to power. Concerts were arranged at major halls in Munich and Leipzig and these proved very successful. He played works by Brahms and Schubert in both these cities and was amused to find that the Leipzig critics liked his Brahms but not his Schubert - and the Munich critics vice versa! After that Schnabel never lost much sleep over what the critics said.

By the age of 20 Artur Schnabel had become a well-known pianist in Germany, his career having progressed steadily and rapidly since its beginning four years earlier. He used Bechstein pianos and the firm allowed him the use of one of their grand pianos on permanent loan at his lodgings. Schnabel always liked Bechsteins, and used them almost exclusively in Europe for the rest of his life. At 20 he was engaged as soloist with the Berlin Philharmonic Orchestra in Berlin and Hamburg under Arthur Nikisch, proof if any were required, that he had at last 'arrived'.

Meanwhile Schnabel was still finding time to compose, and his own piano concerto was performed with the Berlin Philharmonic Orchestra before an invited audience. Schnabel was the soloist and his friends helped with the expenses, for such a work could not be expected to be a viable financial concert proposition.

His repertoire was reasonably wide-ranging at this stage of his career and he gave the first performance in Berlin of Paderewski's only piano concerto. But as his fame in Germany and Europe spread, he gradually narrowed his range of music almost exclusively to the 'classical' composers. That is not to say that the volume of his repertoire was reduced; it was probably increased, for as time went on he extended it to include virtually all the piano music of Beethoven, Brahms, Schubert, Schumann and, eventually, Mozart.

Schnabel mixed with the rich and famous. He often performed with the veteran violinist Joachim. With success came money. But he was generous by nature and gave some of it away. In the same way that others had helped him, Schnabel even as a very young man helped many other musicians, amongst whom were numbered two aspiring young conductors, Wilhelm Furtwängler and Otto Klemperer.

Schnabel's rise to fame during the early years of this century was achieved largely through his brilliance as a solo concert pianist, but he had another musical love, apart from composing. This was chamber music, and during his career he was to appear regularly in a number of notable long-standing chamber music ensembles. He gave many joint recitals with the violinist Carl Flesch and later formed a trio with Alfred Wittenberg (violin) and Anton Hekking (cello). Other famous musicians with whom he regularly appeared in ensembles at various stages of his career included Hugo Becker, Pierre Fournier, Paul Hindemith and Pablo Casals.

In 1905, when Artur was 23, he married Therese Behr, a contralto singer, who was then 29. Their relationship had begun five years earlier when it was arranged that Artur, then only 18, together with a young Belgian violinist should go on a concert tour of East Prussia. Their main function was to accompany the singer, Therese Behr, whom they had not met. She was the 'star' and they were subsidiary artists, though her career had begun only about three years before theirs. Prior to the concert the three of them went off on a sleigh ride and it soon became evident that Therese and Artur got on very well together. Between the later concerts she and Artur used to go out for further excursions and a romance soon developed. A year later they were secretly engaged and their marriage took place four years afterwards. The marriage was to be a long and happy one and there is no doubt that Therese, an expert in the singing of Schubert's and Brahms' lieder, influenced his artistic development in a beneficial way. Two boys were born; Karl Ulrich in August 1909, and Stefan in February 1912.

Throughout the years 1900 to 1914 Schnabel's musical stature steadily increased and by the outbreak of war he was universally regarded as one of the best pianists in Europe. Most of his concert successes had been achieved in Germany, but he had also performed in most of the leading centres of Europe, including London, where in 1904 he played the B flat Concerto of Brahms with the Royal Philharmonic Society, Hans Richter conducting. Schnabel returned to London in 1905 and on both occasions was very well received. It is interesting that he knew no English at the time. His first lesson in English did not come until 1920 when he was 38.

When war broke out in 1914 Schnabel, at 32, was eligible for German military service as a holder of an Austrian passport resident in Berlin, but he was rejected on medical grounds. In truth these were somewhat contrived, involving a slightly defective toe, and the real reason he was not called up was that the authorities thought he would be more useful to them by continuing his profession as a pianist. During the war he played a lot in Germany where, surprisingly, concert performances continued much as before, and he also gave concerts in other countries which were not at war with Germany, including Holland, Switzerland and the Scandinavian countries.

In 1917 Germany's attitude to Austria and its citizens hardened, as it was felt the Austrians were not pursuing hostilities with as much zeal as they might. Consequently Schnabel was deemed fit for military service, but strings were pulled behind the scenes and he was never actually called up. When the Kaiser abdicated in November 1918 and the Armistice was declared, a phase of Schnabel's musical life ended, for everyone recognised that Europe would never be the same again. A new era was about to begin and it was in the next few years that Schnabel was transformed, in the opinion of the musical public, from a very good pianist to a great one.

The years 1919-24 were musically the happiest and most stimulating Schnabel had so far experienced. His personal life was happy too; his marriage to Therese provided much-needed stability and was ideal in all respects, whilst his two small sons were well, full of life and already showing talent. But in 1921 there occurred a bolt from the blue that might have shaken a weaker marriage. One day a young woman of 22 arrived unexpectedly at the Schnabel household and announced that she was Artur Schnabel's daughter and that her mother was a well-known violinist. Artur did not dispute the claim, nor indeed could he have done, for in facial features she strongly resembled her father. Her name was Elisabeth (nicknamed Ellie) and she had been brought up by an industrialist in Vienna. She was a talented pianist, as the family soon realised when she played for them, and also composed music of various types under her professional name of Elizabeth Rostra. Therese Schnabel might well have been forgiven for having mixed feelings about this unexpected arrival but the young lady had a delightful personality, the Schnabel boys liked her, and she was soon accepted as one of the family circle. Ellie was already married and had a young son so the 39 year old Artur Schnabel discovered he was already a grandfather of two years' standing. To his credit he never tried to hide the fact of his youthful indiscretion as a 16 year old in Berlin.

In 1921 Schnabel made his first visit to the USA and performed in an extensive concert tour. He was not impressed by the circumstances of his first public appearance there when he was "dragged off", as he put it, shortly after disembarking to play in a charity concert (as were several of the other pianists in this book) for the benefit of Moritz Moszkowski, reportedly ill and destitute in Paris. Fifteen well-known pianists appeared on the Carnegie Hall stage playing on 15 pianos of five different makes, playing singly, two by two, and all together while Walter Damrosch conducted. They then performed the several movements of Schumann's *Carnaval* in rotation, whilst the *Preamble* and *Finale* were played by all together. Apart from Schnabel, the pianists included Wilhelm Backhaus, Harold Bauer, Ignaz Friedman, Ossip Gabrilowitsch, Josef Lhevinne and Elly Ney. A vast sum of money was collected.

After this rather 'showbiz' introduction to the USA, Schnabel launched himself into the formal business of music making, starting with a Christmas Day concert played before a small audience. As was his usual custom, Schnabel played no encores and his programme was what the Americans called "severely classical". Managers found it difficult to 'place' Schnabel in the smaller halls across the USA, for the American public was not used to listening to a whole programme of sonatas. Nevertheless, he made no concessions to the box office, and played only the music *he* liked, which was ideal for the classical connoisseur. Schnabel was contracted to play only the Knabe piano (a make associated with the American Piano Company) in the USA, and this caused a certain amount of friction between Schnabel and his managers, for he did not like the company's instruments.

Because of this problem, together with the difficulties associated with his choice of programmes, Schnabel made little impact on the USA initially. The Americans regarded him very much as a pianist whose heart was in Europe rather than with them. As part of his contract he was called upon to make a number of piano roll recordings for Ampico (the piano roll wing of the American Piano Company) eight of which were issued. The composers represented were Bach (*Italian Concerto*, on 3 rolls); Beethoven (Minuet in G, and Rondo, Op. 51, No. 2 in G major); Brahms (Rhapsody, Op. 79, No. 2 in G minor); Schubert (Scherzo, No. 1 in B flat); and Weber (*Invitation to the Dance*, Op. 65). Schnabel had by then learned a smattering of the English language and, always fond of making puns, said, "These recordings seemed to be the only way I could play a rôle in America."

These eight Ampico rolls comprised only a small fraction of his recordings for the player piano. In all he recorded over 60 rolls, for five companies including Ampico. The largest batch was for Philipps, for whom Schnabel recorded about 22 rolls. As might be expected, Beethoven is well represented with four rolls and Brahms with eight. More surprisingly there are four rolls of the music of Erich Korngold who went on to make a career in writing music for films. For Welte he recorded about 13 rolls, including two of Bach, four of Chopin, for whose playing he was not noted, and two of

Schubert. Schnabel recorded at least 15 rolls for Hupfeld including four of Chopin, two Beethoven and three Schubert. To complete the list, Schnabel recorded three rolls for Artecho; one each of music by Lanner, Schubert and Weber. He did not record for Duo-Art. It is not surprising that most of his piano roll work was for the three big European companies, Hupfeld, Philipps and Welte. He had recorded his rolls for these companies in Europe before ever visiting the USA where his Ampico rolls were recorded.

In spite of Schnabel's misgivings about his first visit to the USA and especially about the Knabe piano, he was back again the following year for another tour, again playing only the Knabe. Presumably the financial rewards were very compelling. He had wanted to play Steinways but the Steinway Company, arch rivals of Bechstein, would not let him use their pianos unless he contracted to play no other make of piano in concert appearances in the USA or Europe. This he was not prepared to do. Consequently he was compelled to continue with Knabe which he still disliked. He was particularly exasperated when, in one concert, the Knabe piano broke down and had to be removed. Another had to be found before the performance could continue. Disillusioned by Knabe, Schnabel made no more tours of the USA until 1930. In that year Steinway were still adamant about their exclusivity rules. Consequently their pianos could not be used, but Bechstein sent two concert grands to the USA for Schnabel's use, plus technicians to service them, in order to promote the Bechstein company in the USA. In 1933 Steinway relented and agreed to supply their pianos and servicing facilites to Schnabel in America, whilst allowing him to continue using Bechsteins in Europe.

In 1925 Schnabel returned to England in a tour arranged by the Bechstein Company and from then on he came back to the British Isles every year until 1939, including in his itineries concerts in Scotland and Ireland. One of his favourite venues was the Free Trade Hall in Manchester (a building blitzed during the 1939-45 war) which he described as "one of the few heated concert halls in England". In this country he often stayed with Mr and Mrs Sam Courtauld (Mr Courtauld was head of the textile firm and a notable musical benefactor) and often appeared in the Courtauld/Sargent concerts. Young Malcolm Sargent was a rapidly rising conductor and ideally fitted to present these concerts, aimed at making good music available at a low entrance charge.

As early as 1911, Schnabel had played an all-Beethoven programme of sonatas in Hamburg, but it was after he had edited the 32 Beethoven Sonatas and the *Diabelli Variations* for the Ullstein Publishing Company in 1924 that he became deeply, and for a time almost totally, immersed in the piano music of Beethoven. In the January and February of 1927, a year which marked the centenary of Beethoven's death, he played the 32 Beethoven sonatas in a series of matinée concerts in Berlin on seven successive Sundays. Between 1932 and 1934 he played them all again, first in Berlin, and then in London. These concerts marked the climax of his career and set him apart as the supreme Beethoven interpreter. According to Grove:

"It was his articulation of scale passages, accompaniments, and figurations of every kind, as well as his power of individualising every strand of the texture that helped to make his playing unique. It was not the melody that suffered, but the other elements that took on an unheard of vitality."

What attracted Schnabel to the classical composers, and to Beethoven in particular, was that their music presented a challenge of interpretation. He was not interested in the 'fireworks' of Liszt and others. He cared only for music which, as he used to say, "was better than it could be performed". Without that, he would not have devoted himself to a lifetime of piano playing. Perhaps that was the real meaning of Leschetizky's famous remark, "You will never be a pianist - you are a musician." For Schnabel, the piano was only a medium through which the music came alive. He once said: "The notes I handle no better than many pianists. But the pauses between the notes - Ah! That is where the art resides!"

Schnabel had always been fond of teaching, from the days when Leschetizky had referred his fellow pupils to him, and teaching remained one of his important occupations throughout his professional life. He never taught piano playing technique, even to highly gifted students. His lessons were really in the form of 'Master Classes', where established pianists came to him for advice and help with interpretation. Such a pianist was Clifford Curzon and there were several others who subsequently became world famous. In 1925 his teaching entered another phase when he was invited to take the piano class at the State Academy in Berlin, a post he occupied with distinction for five years. His teaching was wide-ranging and embraced modern compositions as well as classical. He never restricted his tuition to the type of music which comprised his own repertoire.

Schnabel's composition complemented his teaching. His work included the piano concerto referred to earlier (written when he was 19), three symphonies, a rhapsody for orchestra, three string quartets, other chamber music, piano pieces and many songs, mostly written in the modern 'atonal' idiom. This might seem odd for a 'classical' specialist, but others have also composed in a style different from that in which as pianists they have made their name. No doubt the contrast between ancient and modern provided a stimulating relaxation. Schnabel always claimed that composition was his first musical love but, ironically, his output in that field has virtually disappeared into oblivion. On the other hand, he is still revered as one of the master pianists of the century.

In the early 1930s, when Schnabel was at the height of his powers, he was invited by Fred Gaisberg to make a series of recordings for HMV at their Abbey Road studios in London. He was reluctant at first, saying that no single performance can be good enough for all time. But once he had agreed to record he warmed to the task and during the next few years he recorded a vast amount of music, mostly at Abbey Road, including all Beethoven's piano sonatas and much of the master's other piano music. He used to stay at the home of a friend in St. John's Wood and walk down to the studio ("the torture chamber" as he called it) to record. Nearly all these recordings, featuring mainly Beethoven but also including other classical composers, were made in the years 1932-1939. The vast majority of Schnabel's recordings were of himself alone or of piano concertos with himself as soloist. But he also recorded some chamber music with the *Pro Arte* string quartet, and a few compositions for two pianos with his son Karl Ulrich, notably Mozart's Concerto in E flat for Two Pianos, K. 365, and Bach's Concerto in C major for Two Pianos. There were also one or two discs of Schnabel as accompanist to his wife, Therese Schnabel (contralto).

Schnabel's recordings of the piano music of Beethoven soon came to be regarded as definitive performances and set him apart as the greatest Beethoven interpreter of his generation. In his recordings, as in his concert appearances, it was the interpretation of the music that was all-important, rather than the merely technical business of playing the notes correctly. In the days when Schnabel made his recordings there was no 'splicing in' of corrections; up to five minutes of a composition had to be recorded in one 'take' and the best of a number of takes was issued after the performer had listened to and commented on the playbacks. It was commonplace for Schnabel to select a take that had more wrong notes than some of the others. It was the musicality that mattered. If a recording manager might venture to suggest that a different take had less mistakes than the one Schnabel had selected, he would reply in his thick Austrian accent, "Ah, yes - but it don't sound so gut!"

After Hitler came to power in Germany some of Schnabel's contracts there were cancelled because he was Jewish. He decided to leave Germany and, accompanied by his family, he spent his summers in Italy and his winters in Britain for several years. It was in 1933, the year that he left Germany, that he was offered, and accepted, the Honorary Degree of Doctor of Music at Manchester University. Normally about six honorary degrees are conferred on eminent people in various fields of activity at the same ceremony. Schnabel knew he would not be available to attend on the appointed day, so asked if the degree could be conferred on some other occasion. The University said it would arrange a special ceremony for Schnabel alone, but requested that he might play something or give a lecture so that the proceedings would not be unduly brief. Schnabel responded by saying he did not want to play, but would give a lecture, which he did. His *Reflections On Music,* which the University later published, is an interesting and wide-ranging exposition of his views on various aspects of musical thought.

Schnabel and his wife and sons decided to move to the USA when war again appeared to be imminent, and after many administrative problems with visas, caused by the fact that he was still officially an Austrian citizen, they arrived there in 1939. Schnabel spent the war there, occupying himself with composing, teaching, lecturing (often to university students) and performing. He was nearly 60 when America entered the war in 1941 and his days as a touring pianist were nearing their end. In 1940-41 he appeared in only two concerts; these were at the Carnegie Hall and featured all-Mozart programmes. Mozart was a composer to whom he became closer as he grew older. In 1942-43 there was a temporary increase in his concert appearances. In that season he played at recitals in the larger American cities from coast to coast and, probably for the first time in his life, repeated the same programme in all of them. In 1943 he severed his connection with his concert managers. He felt they were an unnecessary intrusion into his art, for they always wanted a say in the composition of his programmes. Schnabel's view was that he would play what he wanted; if the public wished to come, they would. If they didn't want to, they wouldn't. They did! Thereafter he confined himself in the USA to an occasional concert here and there; his status was such that he could choose. His many series of lectures to students at various universities, with lengthy question and answer sessions, served to enhance his rapport with the young.

In appearance Schnabel was short (about 5 feet 4 inches) and thickset. His physical stature was in marked contrast to that of his wife, who was slim and nearly 6 feet tall. Some people regarded his manner on the concert platform as unnecessarily cold and austere, especially in his later years, for he had no mannerisms and on occasions he would seem aloof. When he walked onto the stage he would face the audience, bow formally and sit down at the piano. The stocky figure, the grey moustache and stiff grey hair looked somewhat forbidding. He did not throw himself about or move his arms much except to get from one part of the keyboard to another. Nor did he droop his head over the keys. He sat relaxed, on a high-backed chair, often leaning slightly back. Thunderous cadences could be produced when required with no apparent physical effort. His playing in soft passages was superb. When the music ended he would bow curtly again and leave the platform. There were never any encores. Though some thought his manner too formal, to Schnabel the personality of the performer was of no consequence. It was the interpretation of the music that mattered.

When the war ended in 1945 Schnabel was 63; he resumed his concerts abroad but on a reduced scale. He had been shattered to discover that his 84 year old mother had fallen a victim to the Nazi atrocities, but sought solace in his music. In the early post-war years he appeared in a number of concerts at the Royal Albert Hall in London, holding 7,000 and filled to capacity. Whilst he was in London he made a few more recordings at Abbey Road and he also played at the Edinburgh Festival in 1947 and 1948.

Schnabel had always enjoyed excellent health and until his mid sixties he had never missed a concert engagement through illness, so it was believed. The cigar-smoking Schnabel seemed to be one of nature's survivors. But in the post-war years his health started to deteriorate. First he was troubled by cataracts, which were unfortunately of a type that could not be operated on satisfactorily. This meant that the keyboard appeared to him only as a blur. Then, in the spring of 1948, whilst on a short concert tour of the Pacific coast of the United States, he began to get warning signs of heart trouble. He recovered, returned to England to broadcast on the Third Programme, and gradually resumed his normal work.

But on 11th December 1948 Schnabel suffered a coronary thrombosis. Again he recovered, and was fit enough to play in a few concerts the following year. He continued to make occasional recordings and sporadic concert appearances until early 1951, when he gave what proved to be his last major public performance, at the Hunter College Auditorium in New York. After that his health problems began to multiply. He and Therese flew to Switzerland for a holiday but the flight aggravated his difficulties. His heart trouble became worse, other complications followed, and he became seriously ill. Arrangements were made for him to be taken to a sanitorium in Sonnenberg. But before that happened another medical crisis occurred and on 15th August 1951 he died at the hotel where he and Therese were staying. He was 69 years old. His wife, though six years older than he, was to survive him by eight years.

So ended the life of a remarkable musician, a pianist of the highest order, and the one largely responsible for placing the piano music of Beethoven in the position of high esteem in which it is held today.

Great Pianists of the Golden Age

Percy Grainger

17. Percy Grainger

The world of music has, over the years, produced quite a crop of strange characters, but perhaps none has been odder than Percy Grainger. A self-confessed masochist with strong racialist views, he despised the Jews and extolled the 'blue-eyed' races. Yet, from his earliest youth his talent for music was never in dispute. A child prodigy, he had achieved fame as a pianist by the age of 25 and from then on he was never out of the limelight. His views on musical terminology were highly original and many of his musical ideas were regarded as too advanced for their day. Grainger was well-known not only as a pianist but also as a composer. He was one of a small number of musicians who used traditional folk song themes as a basis for compositions of quality and distinction.

George Percy Grainger (he was always called Percy) was born in Melbourne, Australia, on 8th July 1882. His father, John, who was a well-known architect and engineer, was born in London and had moved to Australia only five years previously. His mother, Rose (née Aldridge) was born in Adelaide of British parents who emigrated to Australia in 1847. Percy's mother adopted a possessive attitude from his birth and exercised a formidable influence on his life. John and Rose Grainger were an incompatible couple. There was little domestic bliss in the Grainger household and John left home when Percy was eight, never to return. Thereafter Percy saw his father only on rare occasions.

Percy received practically no formal schooling and was educated at home by his mother in a rather 'hothouse' atmosphere. She was an excellent musician and taught him to play the piano. His talent soon became apparent and from the age of 10 he was taught by the German musician Louis Pabst, a former pupil of Anton Rubinstein who, after a successful tour of Australia as a concert pianist in 1885, had set up an Academy of Music in Melbourne. Percy's progress was rapid and he gave many recitals in Melbourne and other cities in Australia when he was between the ages of 10 and 12. These were a brilliant success. One critic, reporting on a recital given in the Melbourne Exhibition Building (capacity 20,000) when Percy was 12 referred to "The flaxen-haired phenomenon who plays like a master."

Shortly afterwards it was decided that Percy's musical education would best be advanced by a period of study in Europe, and the Hoch Conservatory in Frankfurt was selected as the appropriate establishment. Money was obviously required to enable him to go, so Percy's friends and well-wishers arranged a special benefit concert on his behalf. This took place at the

Melbourne Town Hall on 14th May 1895, two months before his 13th birthday, and the hall was packed with people who had come to wish the boy well and contribute to his future education. He played a selection of pieces by Bach, the Pastorale by Scarlatti, the Allegro and Andante from Beethoven's Sonata in G major, Op. 14, and Pabst's arrangement of the Minuet from Handel's *Samson*. His performance drew wild applause and much praise. The following week he gave a recital at a small hall in Adelaide, after which he and his mother packed their belongings in readiness for their new life on the other side of the world.

It was on 29th May 1895 that Percy and Rose Grainger sailed from Adelaide for Europe with £50 between them raised by the benefit concert in Melbourne Town Hall. On their arrival in Frankfurt, Percy soon learned the German language. His stay in Frankfurt was to last six years and it was there that he developed from a child pianist into an adult performer under his teachers James Kwast (piano) and Iwan Knorr (theory and composition). Percy became somewhat disillusioned with the piano tuition he received from Kwast and in 1896 Rose Grainger wrote to her old friend Nellie Melba, the famous singer, to ask what should be done. She advised that Percy should be sent to study under Leschetizky in Vienna, but for unknown reasons Rose did not take up Melba's suggestion; instead Percy soldiered on in Frankfurt.

Apart from his formal studies at the Conservatory, Percy also learned a lot about composition from Karl Klimsch, an amateur musician not connected with the Conservatory, and he benefited enormously from his contacts with a talented group of musicians from England who were also studying at the Conservatory, amongst them Roger Quilter, Henry Balfour Gardiner, Cyril Scott and Norman O'Neill. These four, along with Grainger, became known as 'The Frankfurt Five' or 'The Frankfurt Gang'. An important arrival in 1898-99 was Ethel Liggins, 12 years old, who later, as Ethel Leginska, was to become arguably the world's foremost woman pianist. Another facet of Percy's musical education in Frankfurt was the opportunity to hear the piano playing of distinguished visitors, including d'Albert, Lamond and Gabrilowitsch.

By 1901 Grainger had mastered a large number of items for solo piano and also several concertos, including those of Grieg, Schumann and Haydn, and some of those of Beethoven, Brahms, Mozart, Saint-Saëns and Tchaikovsky. He had enough material in his repertoire to launch out on his own as a pianist and in May 1901 Percy and Rose Grainger arrived in London. He soon became well-known there as a society pianist - his good looks, charm and talent ensuring ample invitations from well-to-do hostesses. During the course of these engagements he appeared on the same programmes as artists such as Hamilton Harty, Maggie Teyte, Pablo Casals and even Harry Lauder.

As Grainger's fame grew he was soon in demand as a concert artist and by 1902 was a frequent performer at provincial concerts. In 1903 he was introduced to the great Italian pianist, Ferruccio Busoni, in London and was allowed to play to him. Percy made such an impact that the Master took the youthful pianist under his wing for a while and taught him free of charge in Berlin. Busoni was impressed not only by Percy's playing but also by his compositions and by his charm, so that the relationship was at first very cordial. Busoni gave Percy a large photograph of himself and wrote on it: "To my dear Percy Grainger (as dear as he will surely be great). Very affectionately, Ferruccio Busoni."

But the relationship with Busoni soon soured. Busoni, great pianist that he was, liked to fill his house with adoring disciples. The highly individual Grainger failed to conform to that pattern. Furthermore, Percy liked to compose and play music that interested him, rather than to practise the studies that Busoni set. This irritated Busoni and he became very sarcastic towards the young Australian. Busoni would call in all his students when Grainger arrived for a lesson. "We will now listen to Mr Percy Grainger, who does not like to practise, play some octave runs", Busoni would announce then, nodding to Grainger, would call, "So! Lay on!" "My runs were, and still are, quite awful", Grainger recalled. "Busoni would laugh till the tears ran down his cheeks. I laughed too. We all enjoyed it thoroughly."

Grainger's ragged octaves were, however, often followed by an encore, very different in mood. Sometimes Percy would play a piece by Bach or Mozart, playing it, as an eye-witness recalled,

"With that wonderful feeling that is certainly the essence of his genius, and Busoni's students would spontaneously burst into applause. They used to call Percy 'The Kreisler of the Piano'. It made Busoni furious. He was a terribly jealous man."

In spite of the clash of personalities, Grainger's period of study with Busoni was a great help to him. He learned a lot about technique, and the contact with other musicians in Berlin widened his horizons. Grainger's love of the music of Bach originated from his studies with Busoni, and he became a brilliant exponent of the Bach-Busoni transcriptions. Although Busoni scorned Grainger's lack of application, he nevertheless took a great interest in his compositions and encouraged him to compose.

Percy Grainger's lessons with Busoni only lasted a few months and in 1903-1904 he went on a concert tour of Australia, New Zealand and South

Africa. He returned to Britain after these tours and soon became fully established as a mature artist, playing at major London concerts under conductors such as Charles Villiers Stanford and Henry Wood. He also played in many concerts outside London, for example with Hans Richter and the Hallé Orchestra in Manchester.

In 1906 Grainger met the Norwegian composer Edvard Grieg in London and this event was to give a tremendous boost to Percy's career. Grieg, who knew some of Percy's compositions, asked to see him and to hear him play. He took an immediate liking to the young pianist and moreover was very enthusiastic about Grainger's talent. In March 1907 Grieg gave an interview with a Danish newspaper, in which he said:

"I have written Norwegian Peasant Dances that none of my countrymen can play, and here comes this Australian who plays them as they ought to be played! He is a genius that we Scandinavians cannot do other than love!"

These widely reported remarks did more than anything else to promote Grainger's name as a pianist in Britain, and he became famous virtually overnight. Not that Grieg was entirely unqualified in his praise. A year after their first meeting he told Grainger: "Mind you! You don't play the folksongs according to _my_ intentions! But don't alter a thing. I love individuality!"

So ardent was Grieg in his admiration for Grainger that he chose him to play the solo part in his piano concerto to be played at the Leeds Festival in October 1907, which Grieg himself was to conduct. In the summer of 1907 Grainger stayed with the Griegs at Troldhaugen to enable the work to be prepared. This gave Grainger an invaluable insight into Grieg's musical thinking. Grainger returned to England on 4th August 1907 and was the last visitor to Troldhaugen before Grieg's death which took place unexpectedly on 4th September. The Leeds concert went ahead, taking on the character of a memorial to Grieg, with Grainger as soloist in the Grieg Concerto. Grainger's performance of this concerto and Grieg's other works for the piano were so highly regarded that he became the definitive interpreter of Grieg. All this helped immensely in establishing Grainger's position as one of the leading pianists of the day. In the 1907-08 season he played in 80 towns and cities throughout the British Isles.

Percy and Rose Grainger were based in London from 1901 to 1914, apart from the short spell he spent in Berlin with Busoni, and it was in those years that Percy established a reputation as a composer. Grainger always put his composing before his piano playing and said that he only played the piano to enable him to make enough money to compose. As a youth Percy was interested in the folk music of various lands and this led him into the field of collecting folk tunes and arranging them into compositions worthy of the concert platform. He joined the English Folk Song Society in 1905. Some tunes were sent to him by friends who knew of his interest but he also used to go out collecting, particularly in Gloucestershire, Lincolnshire and Worcestershire, taking down songs that old men and women sang to him. After the first few collecting forays he armed himself with an Edison recording phonograph to record the songs instead of the note pad he had used previously, and was one of the first people to use the method. The compositions that Percy created from these songs made him as famous a composer as he was a pianist, and it is through these pieces that he is best remembered as a composer today.

One of the high spots of Grainger's role as a collector of folk songs came in 1905 when he made a number of visits to Lincolnshire during and after the North Lincolnshire Musical Competition Festival held at Brigg. One of the old Lincolnshire songs was sung by Joseph Taylor, a 72 year old, and its melody so haunted Grainger that he arranged it into the composition we now know as *Brigg Fair*. Later, Grainger's friend Frederick Delius asked Grainger if he could use the material to make his own arrangement and he readily agreed. It is Delius's version (which was dedicated to Grainger) that is now better remembered than Grainger's own, which in a sense is unfortunate as Delius did no more than develop a stage further the work that Grainger presented to him. Nevertheless Grainger appears to have been happy with the arrangement. Joseph Taylor, the old man who first sang the song to Grainger, was an honoured guest, along with Grainger and Delius, when in March 1908 Beecham conducted a programme of Delius's music at the Queen's Hall in London which included the first performance of Delius's English Rhapsody, *Brigg Fair*. The Gramophone Company (soon to become HMV) followed up Grainger's pioneering work by re-recording John Taylor singing his songs and issued them as commercial recordings.

Grainger's most active period as a recorder and collector of folk songs was in the years 1905 to 1908. Between 1905 and 1918 he made arrangements of many of these folk songs and dances, including *Country Gardens*, *Molly On the Shore* and *Shepherd's Hey*. Grainger asserted that the theme of *Country Gardens*, a composition which brought him more money in royalties than any other, was a variant of *The Vicar of Bray* and that *Shepherd's Hey* was a variant of *The Keel Row*. He also collected sea shanties and London street cries. Grainger said that he never altered the tune of the folk songs and maintained that he was "the servant of the tune".

As a collector of folk songs Grainger was something of a lone figure. Although he was a member of the English Folk Song Society he was never really part of the official folk song establishment which existed then, and still exists today, nor did his views on what was legitimate in the arrangement of folk song material often coincide with the official view. The differences grew and from about 1908 and 1909 Grainger faded out of the folk song collecting fraternity. Nevertheless his contribution in this field is a major one which is sometimes unjustifiably ignored by music historians.

At the same time as he was making his folk song arrangements, Grainger wrote a few popular tunes such as *Handel in the Strand* and *Mock Morris* as well as a lot of more 'serious' works. Some of these latter pieces were well ahead of their time musically and were to a large extent unplayed in public, partly because they were considered unplayable. He experimented with unusual rhythms and inclined towards 'beatless' music where there is no standard pulse. As early as 1901 he wrote a passage of music which contained 42 time signature changes in 44 bars. It is hardly surprising that few pianists were inclined to play it!

Grainger composed music throughout his life and the pieces he wrote covered the whole musical spectrum from simple to very complex. He achieved moderate success, especially in the USA, with some of his choral, orchestral and military band music and with his settings of some of Kipling's poems. A few of his pieces, for instance *Lullaby - Tribute To Foster*, are regarded by some musicians as being in the traditions of Chopin and Liszt. He could when necessary compose a good tune of his own - he did not rely exclusively on folk themes - and his music is full of vitality.

It is interesting to note that although Grainger was a brilliant and famous pianist, few of his compositions were originally written for the piano. He wrote mainly for small groups of players, or small orchestras, or voices, and would later transcribe the music for the piano as and when necessary. He disliked writing for a large orchestra, believing that it suppressed the individuality of the separate players. In recitals given by Grainger his audiences always expected to hear at least one of his short popular pieces, so he usually obliged by playing one or more of them as encores. No doubt he became as tired of them as did Paderewski of his famous Minuet, or Rachmaninov of the C sharp minor Prelude. In later years Grainger often appeared on concert platforms as pianist, composer and conductor, all in the same programme. He took his composition very seriously and would sometimes waive his fee as pianist provided the management allowed some of his compositions to appear on the programme.

Grainger transcribed his own compositions (or "dished them up" as he put it) in many forms; for one piano, in easy and difficult versions; two pianos; wind instruments; orchestra; and so on. All of these he did himself, and the many different settings in which his music was available helped to supply him with a steady income from royalties. For instance, *Country Gardens* was available to pianists as Piano Solo; Piano Solo (easy version); Piano Solo (especially easy version); One Piano (four hands); Two Pianos (four hands); and Two Pianos (eight hands). These were in addition to the instrumental and orchestral versions. *Harvest Hymn* was published in eight versions. These examples are by no means untypical. He also transcribed ("dished up"!) orchestral music by many other composers.

On 4th August 1914 the First World War began and Percy and Rose Grainger made the hasty decision to leave Britain and go to the United States. Percy's reason was selfish but honest and logical. He felt that his destiny was to be Australia's first notable composer and if he were to be killed this laudable objective would be unattainable. At the end of August mother and son sailed from Liverpool for the USA on Cunard's *Laconia*, arriving in Boston on 8th September. From there they made their way to New York, where they set up residence. Percy soon made contact with the music publishing company of G. Schirmer Inc., who thereafter published most of his music. It was that company which arranged for his musical engagements to be managed in the USA by Antonia Sawyer, whose office was in the Aeolian Building in West 43rd Street. The partnership worked well and a series of concerts was soon arranged.

Grainger's official debut in the United States came on 23rd January 1915 in a Saturday afternoon concert at the Aeolian Hall with the Symphony Society of New York, conducted by Walter Damrosch. The orchestra performed *Molly On the Shore*, *Irish Tune from County Derry* and *Shepherd's Hey*, with Grainger playing the piano part in the latter piece. Grainger was appearing as a member of the orchestra rather than as an official soloist and therefore received little publicity, but word of the concert spread and his next engagement on 11th February, again at Aeolian Hall, was a sell-out. This time the music critics of all the major New York newspapers were present. Grainger appeared as soloist on this occasion, playing the Bach-Busoni Organ Prelude and Fugue in D major; Brahms' *Handel Variations*; three pieces from Grieg's Op. 66 and Op. 72; his own *Colonial Song* and *Mock Morris*; the Nouvelle Étude No. 2 in A major by Chopin; Ravel's *Ondine*; and *Triana* by Albéniz. Grainger was received with rapturous praise and his reputation in the USA was instantly established. The following day Henry T. Finck, drawing heavily on Schumann's immortal pronouncement on Chopin, wrote in the *Evening Post*, "Hats Off! A Genius!" Grainger was 32 at the time. From that day he was a truly international figure on the concert stage and as a composer and remained so for the rest of his life. Over the years he did much to popularise the music of Albéniz, Debussy, Delius, Granados and Ravel by often including their compositions in his programmes.

Grainger's sudden departure from England to the United States within a month of the outbreak of war did not pass unnoticed and provoked much adverse comment and criticism in Britain. But hostility towards him thawed somewhat after he enlisted in the United States Army as a bandsman when America entered the war in 1917. He became an American citizen in June 1918, was demobilised in February 1919, and except for frequent concert tour absences, lived in the same house in White Plains, near New York City, from 1921 until his death.

Although Grainger was such a fine musician he was prone to the occasional memory lapse. In 1903, as a young man of 21, he was practising in the Pier Concert Hall in Bexhill-on-Sea for a recital due to include his friend Cyril Scott's First Piano Sonata. He had difficulty remembering the music and later wrote:

"As I sat and practised I could not memorise the sonata. As I heard the waves lapping under the pier and thought of my love of the sea and hatred of the concert platform and my love for my friend's composition and my unableness to play it, I felt such a strong urge to drown myself in the sea."

Even as a mature pianist, acknowledged as one of the world's best, the occasional difficulty in remembering the music was never far away. He once had to improvise his way through the last movement of the Schumann Concerto, an event he often remembered with horror. Sometimes he was full of self-doubt. He sometimes said that as he stood in the wings awaiting his entry he felt faced with the simple choice of shooting himself or quickly preparing a speech apologising for the mess his audience was about to hear. Needless to say his fears were almost always groundless.

Percy Grainger's attempts to belittle his own abilities as a pianist should not be taken too seriously, for despite his own and Busoni's reservations about his technique he was without doubt a very fine pianist. His tone was superb, his style free and his technique innate. The dash and fire of his playing reflected the style of his compositions; lively, hearty, flamboyant, restless, yet warm and well-rounded. To these qualities he added poetry, grace and strength. Rarely did a Grainger performance leave a feeling of disappointment, whether the music was his own, or that of Grieg, in the interpretation of which he was masterly, or of the great classical and romantic composers.

Grainger's first gramophone recordings were made in 1908 for The Gramophone Company and comprised three single-sided discs, the records consisting of the cadenza from the first movement of Grieg's Piano

Concerto, Liszt's Hungarian Rhapsody No. 12 (abridged) and Stanford's *Irish March Jig* arranged by Grainger. These early discs were the first of what was to be a prolific output, for his recording career was to extend almost 50 years, to 1957. The quality of reproduction of the earlier records is obviously very poor by modern standards and in the late ones he was past his prime as a pianist. But his recordings from the 1920s and 1930s portray Grainger at his best. Only his early recordings (the 1908 ones referred to above and some made in 1914) were for HMV; in the USA he recorded a vast amount of music for Columbia then, late in his career, there followed a few recordings for RCA-Victor (issued in Britain under the HMV label) and Decca. He recorded well over 150 tracks altogether, of music by 20 composers, namely: Bach, Brahms, Chopin, Debussy, Dett, Gluck, Grainger, Grieg, Guion, Handel, Horn, Liszt, MacDowell, Scharwenka, Schumann, Scott, Sinding, Stanford, Strauss (Richard) and Tchaikovsky. Not surprisingly Grainger himself heads the list of composers in terms of the number of tracks of their music recorded, followed by, in descending order of the number of tracks, Chopin, Brahms, Schumann, Bach, Grieg and Liszt. Two commercial recordings exist of Grainger as soloist in the Grieg Piano Concerto, in the interpretation of which he was particularly noted. Both are live broadcasts and can be categorised as "late Grainger". One was recorded at the Hollywood Bowl in 1945 with the Hollywood Bowl Symphony Orchestra under Leopold Stokowski; the other dates from October 1956 and was recorded with the Southeast Iowa Symphony Orchestra with Richard A. Morse conducting.

Grainger also recorded about 65 piano rolls under contract to the Aeolian Company for the Duo-Art reproducing piano. These date from the years 1915 to 1932 when he was at the peak of his powers as a pianist, and when the recording process and the mechanism of reproducing pianos had reached a high level of technical perfection. Especially prominent in his Duo-Art list are compositions by himself and Grieg. Grainger understood the mechanics of the Duo-Art system and was fascinated by them. At the height of his career he often gave recitals using a Duo-Art Steinway Grand in which the compositions were played alternately by himself and the reproducing mechanism, using Grainger rolls. He saw the potential of the player piano as an instrument of composition, for rolls could be cut involving rhythms which would be difficult or impossible to play manually. Amongst Percy Grainger's Duo-Art recordings were several 4-handed arrangements recorded with other pianists, namely Ralph Leopold (6 rolls); Lotta Mills Hough (2 rolls); Cyril Scott (2 rolls); and his mother, Rose Grainger (1 roll). Grainger recorded piano rolls only for the Aeolian Company.

Grainger was a musician of international stature as a pianist, composer, and occasionally as a conductor. He also did a certain amount of teaching; he gave Master Classes in Chicago in the 1920s and he taught at New York University for a year from the summer of 1932. But what of Grainger as a man? Physically he was good-looking and athletic. As a youth he could perform tricks on a bicycle; stand still on it, cycle backwards, and so on. In the earliest years of his career as a concert pianist he did a lot of running and before a recital he would often 'jog' into the foyer of the concert hall in his running shorts, to the amazement of the formally-dressed assembling audience. In his late 50s he would entertain friends' children by turning cartwheels for them, and at the age of 67 he would jump five feet down from the orchestra platform at the end of a rehearsal.

Grainger always enjoyed outdoor life and loved long-distance walking. At the age of 21 he once walked 65 miles between midnight, after a Friday evening concert, and 6 pm the next day before the Saturday evening concert, believing that the best mode of transportation between the two towns was by foot. A health and fresh air fiend, he became a vegetarian in 1924 and remained so, though he did not particularly like vegetables. He had a good sense of humour. When he had to play a piece containing a glissando (for instance, *Shepherd's Hey*) he would sometimes protect his fingers by means of a handkerchief, and at informal recitals he would attach the handkerchief by elastic to the inside of his top pocket to ensure its rapid return at the completion of a run - an effect which always amused his audience.

In spite of these engaging aspects to his personality, Grainger was a very odd man indeed, a highly eccentric and strange character of truly Freudian complexity. He lived with his mother, to whom he was devoted, until he was 40, when she died in tragic circumstances following a period of illness and mental instability. She fell or jumped (there was no conclusive evidence) from the window of the agent Antonia Sawyer's office in the 18th storey of the Aeolian Building in New York when Antonia was temporarily absent, having gone to fetch some medicine for Rose. Percy was in Los Angeles at the time, playing to a full house. Rose Grainger had organised Percy's life, chosen his friends and arranged his personal affairs and he had always been content to let her do so. She had dominated his life, but that is what Percy had wanted. He respected her tremendously, to the extent that on his musical scores he always used the name Percy Aldridge Grainger, adopting his mother's maiden name. Her death came as a shattering blow to him and even after her death Rose's influence stayed with him for the rest of his life.

A remarkable feature of Percy Grainger's weird personality is that he was a masochist who enjoyed self-flagellation. He used to take whips with him on his tours and took photographs of injuries he had inflicted on himself. However, he was kind, gentle and generous to other people and frequently gave large sums of money to 'hangers-on'. He had a talent for art and was a brilliant linguist, fluent in several languages.

Grainger was bigoted, anti-Semitic (yet numbered Jews amongst his friends) and believed the Nordic 'blue-eyed' races to be superior. He believed that all the best composers had blue eyes. These fantasies probably date from his childhood when his mother taught him Nordic folk lore. She was as attracted to the Nordic physical features as he was and she used to peroxide Percy's hair to ensure a continuation of his fair-haired appearance as he grew older. After Rose's death he continued the same practice himself. Grainger developed his own strange method of phraseology and spelling, and adopted what he called 'blue-eyed English', preferring to use no Greek or Latin words. He disliked the Italian words used by most composers for stating tempo and dynamics and used English words and phrases of his own making instead, e.g. 'louden lots', 'slow off', 'hold back slightly', play 'bumpingly', 'thumpingly', etc.

Percy Grainger never bothered much about his personal appearance, which was so unconventional that he was arrested several times by zealous American policemen who suspected him of being a criminal. These episodes usually ended amicably with the officer concerned being given a complimentary ticket for Grainger's next concert. He did not mind what people thought about his house; he never had it painted and the grass around it was cut only once in the 40 years he lived there. Grainger's eccentricities extended to the concert platform. If he was playing at an informal concert he was known to produce a railway timetable and look up the time of his train home during a few bars' rest in a concerto.

On 9th August 1928 the 46 year old Percy Grainger married Ella Viola Ström, a Swedish poet and painter, in a spectacular ceremony at the Hollywood Bowl, and afterwards conducted an orchestral composition he had written especially for his bride. She was somewhat taken aback to discover some of her husband's eccentricities but the marriage survived and she probably acted as a steadying influence on him.

In the mid 1930s Grainger set up a Percy Grainger Museum in his native Melbourne. His life after marriage followed the same pattern as before but as he grew older he started to cut down on the big concerts and preferred to play in smaller halls, and only when he needed the money. This continued through the 1940s and 1950s. In 1952 he reached the age of 70. In his 70s Grainger said that one of the joys of old age was that no-one expected you to play the correct notes any more; provided you managed to complete the performance and didn't actually die of a stroke on the stage, the audience would go home happy and satisfied.

In old age, between his sporadic concert appearances, Percy Grainger entertained himself at home with the design of what he called "free music machines"; strange, Heath Robinson contraptions producing music of Stockhausen type but by mechanical means. Some of the machines he used involved pianolas with strings attached to the keys, actuating mechanical and electronic devices. He produced detailed and complicated drawings of these remarkable machines.

About the time of his 70th birthday Grainger developed cancer of the prostrate. An operation was performed, followed by another some years later, which enabled him to continue the lifestyle of his old age - leisure interspersed with concerts and short tours - for several more years. In 1957 he and Ella went to Denmark where he performed the Grieg Concerto with the Aarhus Symphony Orchestra conducted by Per Dreier. The performance was recorded but no discs were issued. By then Grainger was 75 years old and very ill indeed; it is therefore not surprising that his playing was liberally scattered with wrong notes. Even so it reached the heart of the music. Benjamin Britten heard the recording and described the performance as the noblest ever committed to record.

After the visit to Denmark, Grainger and Ella came to Britain in the spring of 1957. In the May of that year he rehearsed two military bands in the playing of some of his own band compositions. He also appeared on television (his only television appearance), in a programme from the BBC's Birmingham studios, in which he played his own *Handel in the Strand* and Grieg's *To the Spring*. At the end of May he and Ella went home to the United States. Though constantly battling against cancer he was well enough in the winter of 1957-58 to play in twelve concerts in the United States; in Michigan, North Carolina, Texas, Cincinnati, Wisconsin and California. Over the next couple of years he continued to appear in public occasionally. His last public performance was on 29th April 1960 at Dartmouth College in Hanover, New Hampshire, when he gave an illustrated talk in the morning and conducted his own composition *The Power of Rome and the Christian Heart* in the afternoon, as part of the annual Festival of Music.

After that his health declined steadily and he died at the age of 78 on 20th February 1961 in White Plains Hospital, New York. Percy Grainger remained eccentric to the last. In his will, made several years earlier, he had requested that after his death the flesh be removed from his bones and his skeleton should if possible be displayed in the Grainger Museum in

Melbourne. The request was not granted. His body was flown to Australia and was interred in the Aldridge family vault in Adelaide.

Towards the end of Grainger's life the popularity of his compositions was on the wane, with the notable exception of *Country Gardens* and one or two other light pieces in similar vein. This decline continued after his death and during most of the 1960s little was heard of Grainger's music. But fashions change; it often happens that the work of a half-forgotten composer begins to take on a new lease of life and that is precisely what happened in the case of Grainger. In the 1970s his music began to be played once again; a new biography by John Bird was published, and in the late 1970s a gramophone record of his piano music, played by Daniel Adni exactly according to Grainger's instructions, was released. In 1982, to celebrate the centenary of Grainger's birth, a new edition of his piano music was issued. Grainger is now once again acknowledged as a composer worthy of serious appraisal. Whilst not to be compared with the great composers, his work is nevertheless original and valuable. And as a pianist, there were few in the first half of the 20th century who were more skilful and talented than he. The vitality of his compositions and the enduring quality of his gramophone and piano roll recordings are a fitting memorial to an unusual man and a fine musician.

Wilhelm Backhaus

18. Wilhelm Backhaus

Many great concert pianists have lived long lives and been blessed with the ability to retain their skills to an advanced age and even to improve with the years like good wine. Artur Rubinstein was a classic example and Wilhelm Backhaus was another. Born when Liszt was still alive and 17 years before Queen Victoria died, he was still making gramophone recordings and travelling the world as a concert pianist late in the 1960s, long after Rock and Roll had come and gone, and when even the Beatles were past their first flush of fame. A truly great pianist, he was at the top of his profession for nearly 70 years and left a huge legacy of recordings on disc and piano roll.

Wilhelm Backhaus was born in Leipzig, Germany on 26th March 1884, the son of Guido Backhaus and his wife Clara, née Schonberg. Like most of the pianists whose lives are recalled in this book, his musical skills showed themselves very early and at four years of age he was able to play the piano very competently. When he was eight he made his public debut and at 10 his studies started in earnest when he was enrolled as a pupil at the Leipzig Conservatory where his piano teacher was Alois Reckendorf. In the years that followed his talent blossomed and word of his extraordinary abilities spread. In 1895, when he was only 11, he was taken to one of Eugen d'Albert's concerts and after the concert met Brahms, who gave young Wilhelm a confectionery bar, which the child so revered that he kept it for years, refusing to eat it.

In 1899, when Wilhelm was 15, the Conservatory staff decided they had taught him all they could, and he went to study with Eugen d'Albert in Frankfurt-am-Main where the famous virtuoso (nicknamed 'The Little Giant') was based. Wilhelm stayed with him for only a year and was then taught for a brief period by Alexander Siloti, a Russian pianist who later settled in the United States where he enjoyed a successful career. In 1900 Backhaus embarked on a major tour of Europe in which he gave piano recitals and concerts. During the tour he made his first public appearance in Britain when he played at the St. James's Hall in Piccadilly. It was said that already, at 16, he had mastered and memorised about 300 compositions including a dozen concertos.

In the following year Backhaus played in two of Henry Wood's Promenade Concerts, which had then been running for only six years. Wood was always on the lookout for young musicians of exceptional promise for not only were his concerts graced by the leading musicians of the day, but he also liked to include a sprinkling of new talent. Musicians like Backhaus were just what he was looking for. Recalling their first meeting, Wood wrote:

"This remarkable young pianist was first brought to me by Otto Kling, at that time manager of the London branch of Breitkopf and Härtel. I remember him bringing this fair-headed, shy boy to my home in Langham Place. As it happened, I was not able to offer him an engagement at once, as all our arrangements were made for some time ahead, but I promised Kling I would do all I could for him at the earliest opportunity. I had noted the purity of his tone and that his technique was of a high order, and I foretold that he would become a virtuoso. I remember him playing Strauss's *Burlesque* and the delightfully picturesque and rarely-played *Sortilegi* by Pick-Mangiagalli, both for piano and orchestra."

In the first of the two Promenade Concerts in which Backhaus appeared in 1901 (Wood had evidently found it possible to fit him in) he played Mendelssohn's Piano Concerto No. 1 in G minor, and on his second appearance he played the Paganini-Brahms Variations. In the same season of concerts another young pianist, Mark Hambourg (22) also made his Promenade debut, playing Liszt's E flat Piano Concerto.

Backhaus's British connections were not limited to his appearances on the concert platform in London. He had friends at St. Annes-on-Sea in Lancashire; they were Germans who had opened a school of music there, and he visited them often. He frequently played in the north of England, including Manchester, where he also had German friends.

Backhaus appeared with the Hallé Orchestra under Hans Richter in the Manchester concert seasons of 1901-2 and 1902-3 when he was still a teenager. On the first of these occasions he performed at two days' notice in place of his former teacher, Alexander Siloti, who had been taken ill, and played the Beethoven G major Concerto. He continued to appear regularly with the Hallé until 1910. Many years later Backhaus spoke with affection of his association with Richter in Manchester:

"It was Richter who first asked me to study the Brahms B flat Concerto. He had conducted it the first time it was played in Vienna, and Brahms had played the piano. I don't think that was the first performance, I think that was earlier in Budapest, but it was wonderful for me to play it with Richter, who had played it with the composer."

In addition to the Hallé concerts, a series of concerts and recitals called the Schiller-Anstalt concerts was also held in Manchester at that time under the direction of Carl Fuchs, a cellist. So it is hardly surprising that this group of German expatriates invited Backhaus, an eminent visitor from their country, to perform in their concerts. Others who appeared with the group in the 1904-05 season were Richard Strauss, the Russian violinist Adolph

Brodsky and the French pianist Édouard Risler, all top-class musical practitioners in their own fields. The hall used for the concerts was on a site now occupied by the Manchester Royal Eye Hospital on Oxford Road.

Through his brilliant playing Backhaus had become as well-known in the north of England as in London and his path to fame was smoothed by the generosity of a Lancashire family of music lovers who financed his ventures during the early years of his career when he was still establishing himself.

In 1904 the Royal Manchester College of Music was looking for someone to fill the post of Professor of Piano vacated by Arthur Friedheim, who had resigned after only one year and returned to America. Wilhelm Backhaus, still only 20, was appointed to the post with effect from 1st January 1905. Backhaus was now known internationally and it was agreed that he be allowed to pursue his concert engagements whilst occupying his teaching post. In 1905, whilst holding this appointment, he won the prestigious Rubinstein Prize, worth 5,000 francs, in Paris, which put the official seal on his status as a pianist of international standing. In the same year he was hailed in Britain as a genius for his playing of two "newly discovered" Hungarian Rhapsodies by Liszt.

The Royal Manchester College of Music in those days had very high academic standards but it was not a rich organisation and the pennies had to be watched as carefully as the pounds. In 1904 a "low pressure heating apparatus" was installed at a cost of £227 in order to take some of the chill out of the Manchester air, and the Registrar, who had been allowed a telephone in 1903, was "empowered to purchase a type-writing machine" according to the College's annual report.

Backhaus, like his predecessor Friedheim, soon found that his concert work and the frequent absences from the College necessitated by it left little time for teaching, and after only one year in the post he resigned.* However, relationships between himself and the College were, and remained, amicable, culminating in the College granting him Honorary Membership 60 years later when he was 80. After Backhaus resigned he was succeeded by another distinguished pianist, Egon Petri, who was a friend and former pupil of Busoni.

The severence of his formal links with the Royal Manchester College of

---

* Several dictionaries of music state that Backhaus was on the staff of the College for several years (some say 1905-11) but this is not true. The authors' enquiries at the Royal Northern College of Music, into which the RMCM was incorporated when the RNCM was founded and which inherited all the RMCM files, indicate that Backhaus held an appointment at the College for one year only. This is confirmed in Michael Kennedy's book *The History of the Royal Manchester College of Music*.

Music allowed Backhaus to devote his energies to concert tours, and in the next few years he became a seasoned performer throughout Europe. The Philadelphia-based music magazine *The Étude* wrote of him:

"His public appearances in Europe revealed intellectual and emotional power of the loftiest order accompanied by one of the most astonishing technical equipments ever possessed by a pianist."

As a sort of "holiday", Backhaus spent the summers of 1907 and 1908 in the German town of Sondershausen, 65 miles west of Leipzig, where he was engaged to give Master Classes to young pianists. But these were only brief interludes in his busy concert career.

Life on the concert circuit for Backhaus, the rising young star, was not all serious and earnest. There were many amusing incidents. On one occasion, after playing at the Royal Albert Hall, he left to catch the night boat to the Continent where he was due to play at the Cologne Festival next day. Unfortunately a huge procession of 10,000 suffragettes happened to be passing by and he was delayed so long he had to abandon his cab and with it his luggage. With the help of a policeman he managed to cross the militant throng to the other side of the road where he got another cab, raced to the station and jumped on the train just as it was about to leave. Next morning he arrived in Cologne at 11 o'clock with the concert scheduled for 12 noon. He didn't even have a toothbrush with him and certainly no evening dress, which was the customary wear in Germany even for morning concerts. A noble member of the committee volunteered to undress himself and did so. Although the trousers were satisfactory, the dress coat which he had kindly offered swamped the then slim and youthful pianist. So the conductor, Fritz Steinbach, requested that the members of the orchestra slowly file past the pianist who tried on their coats in turn, as in the story of Cinderella and the glass slipper. As might be expected, it was the last that fitted best.

In 1909 Backhaus made his first gramophone recording, a Prelude in C sharp by Bach, to be followed over the years by many more. He sailed to the USA in 1911 to make his concert debut in the New World where, in spite of what *The Étude* had reported earlier, he was still almost unknown. His debut in the United States took place on 5th January 1912 when he was soloist in a performance of Beethoven's *Emperor* Concerto with Walter Damrosch conducting. Backhaus's tour of the United States continued until 1914 and was a triumph.

Meanwhile Backhaus's list of gramophone recordings steadily grew. HMV's catalogues of discs available during the war years of 1914-18 list several of his recordings including a disc comprising two of Schubert's compositions, *Moment Musical* (the catalogue does not specify which one) and *Hark! Hark! The Lark!* on a violet-label 12-inch record costing seven shillings, and another of similar type and cost comprising Chopin's Étude, Op. 10, No. 7 and a Waltz in D flat which must have been either Op. 64, No. 1 or Op. 70, No. 3. Seven shillings was of course a considerable sum in those days; a week's wage for many people. Slightly cheaper at six shillings each were his 12-inch black-label records of Smetena's Bohemian Dance and Chopin's Waltz in A flat, Op. 42, both "played on a Chappell Concert Grand Piano". In those days, worn-out or broken HMV records could be redeemed at the rate of 9d each for 12-inch records and 6d each for 10-inch records on condition that a new HMV record was purchased for each old one returned. It is interesting and slightly surprising that Backhaus's recordings were included in the HMV catalogue at all during the First World War, bearing in mind the bitter feelings against anything or anyone German at that time.

Recording for the gramophone was to be an important facet of Backhaus's career. To some of the earlier pianists in this book recordings were little more than a curiosity, but for others, especially some of the later ones, they were important and Backhaus falls very definitely into this group. He recorded mainly for HMV and Decca and was one of the pianists whose recording career spanned the period from the early days of the acoustic era to the days of stereo recordings.

As a young man Backhaus was engaged by the Hupfeld Company of Leipzig to record piano rolls. His association with the company was hardly surprising, for he was born and bred in Leipzig and studied at the Conservatory there. The Hupfeld Company was 'just along the road' from his home so he and Hupfeld knew about each other from the days of his early youth. The precise dates when he made his recordings are not known but many of them, and probably most, were made before the First World War when the pianist was still in his twenties.

At least 155 of Backhaus's rolls were issued by Hupfeld and he may possibly have recorded others. Of these 155 rolls, it is interesting to look at the distribution of numbers of rolls amongst the 40 composers represented in his recordings. At the time Backhaus recorded his Hupfeld rolls he was still a relatively junior pianist in international terms, so it can be assumed that the rolls he recorded were, in the main, those that Hupfeld wanted, rather than those he particularly wished to record. Consequently, as he recorded such a large number of rolls for the company, a glance through the list gives an idea of the relative popularity of various composers at that time.

The numbers in the following list are the numbers of Hupfeld piano rolls recorded by Backhaus for each composer. In the case of little-known composers a Christian name has been included.

d'Albert	3	Grieg	13	Saint-Saëns	1
Bach	1	Haydn	2	Sauer	2
Beethoven	21	Klindworth, Karl	1	Schubert	6
Benedict, Julius	1	Liszt	12	Schumann	5
Bennett	3	MacDowell	3	Schütt	2
Berlioz	1	Mendelssohn	11	Seeling, Hans	2
Bizet	1	Moscheles	1	Singer, Otto	1
Brahms	2	Moszkowski	8	Strauss, J.	2
Busoni	1	Mozart	4	Strauss, R.	6
Chopin	10	Paderewski	2	Tausig	1
Debussy	1	Reckendorf		Tchaikovsky	7
Glazunov	1	(Backhaus's teacher)	1	Wagner	1
Godard	1	Reinecke, Carl	3	Weber	3
Gounod	2	Rubinstein	6		

The total of this list is 155, i.e. the number of Hupfeld rolls Backhaus is known to have recorded. It will be noted that the list contains a number of works by composers who at the time were contemporary or modern, some of them, for example Benedict (1804-85), Klindworth (1830-1916) and Seeling (b.1863; date of death unknown), have disappeared without trace and their works are now rarely, if ever, performed. It must have been thought at the time that those composers' rolls would sell, otherwise they would not have been included in the catalogues. The list shows that Backhaus recorded a lot of Beethoven rolls. He came to be recognised, as the years went by, as a superb interpreter of Beethoven's music. Perhaps the Hupfeld Company was aware of his exceptional skills in the interpretation of Beethoven even in those early days.

It would be difficult to summarise briefly the type of music represented in *all* these Hupfeld recordings as there are so many of them, but a brief review will be given here of the four composers of whose music Backhaus recorded more than ten rolls. Amongst Backhaus's Hupfeld recordings of Beethoven's music were two Piano Concertos (No. 3, Op. 37 and No. 5, Op. 73) transcribed for piano alone; and six Piano Sonatas, namely, Op. 2, No. 2; Op. 10, Nos, 1, 2 and 3; Op. 106 and Op. 111. He also recorded the first movement of another sonata, Op. 13. The Chopin rolls were what might be termed a representative selection of Chopin, including a Ballade, Op. 47; three études; Fantasie Impromptu, Op. 66; four preludes; a Scherzo, Op. 31; and a Waltz, Op. 34, No. 1. The Grieg rolls include the Piano Concerto in A, Op. 16, transcribed for piano alone; and a piano arrangement of the

Holberg Suite, Op. 40. Amongst the Liszt rolls are two *Études d'Execution Transcendante* (Nos. 4 and 7); Polonaises Nos. 1 and 2; and the Hungarian Rhapsody, No. 8. Backhaus's Mendelssohn rolls include transcriptions for piano alone of the two Piano Concertos, No. 1 in G minor, Op. 25 and No. 2 in D minor, Op. 40.

Soon after Backhaus's first concert tour of the United States in 1912-14, three of his Hupfeld rolls were adapted by the American Piano Company, under licence from Hupfeld, and issued as Ampico reproducing rolls. They were: *Du Bist die Ruh (Thou Art Repose)* by Schubert (transcribed by Liszt); Valse Caprice by Rubinstein; and Valse Brilliant, Op. 34, No. 1 in A flat by Chopin. These three rolls are the sum total of Backhaus's rolls issued by Ampico.

Backhaus recorded four rolls for the German reproducing piano company, Welte. They were recorded in Freiburg, home of the Welte Company, and date from about 1919-1920. The titles he recorded for Welte were Schubert's Marche Militaire in E flat, Op. 51, No. 3 transcribed for solo piano by Backhaus; Schubert's *Wanderer* Fantasia, Op. 15 (on two rolls); and the second movement (Larghetto) of Chopin's Piano Concerto No. 1 in E flat transcribed for piano alone by Backhaus. He did not record for the other big German piano roll producing company, Philipps of Frankfurt.

The First World War put a stop to Backhaus's travels from Germany but as soon as it was over he resumed his career. In 1923 and 1926 he made further concert tours of the USA, but after those tours he did not visit the United States again until after the Second World War. He came to Britain many times in the 1920s, playing in London and other major cities and he also toured throughout South America, Australasia and the Far East.

During a tour of Australia in 1926 Backhaus was invited to visit the religious community of Loreto in Perth to play for the nuns. The main purpose of his visit was to enable him to listen to the playing of a young Tasmanian girl who was being cared for by the sisters. Her name was Eileen Joyce. He was so impressed by her talents that he informed Australia's leading newspapers of his discovery. A committee was set up under the State Premier to decide her future and raise funds. Percy Grainger was summoned and he requested that she should not be sent to Europe but should study under the best available Australian teachers, either in her home country or in the United States, to preserve the 'Australian' qualities in her playing. He suggested that she should go to study with the Australian pianist and teacher Ernest Hutcheson, then Dean of the Juilliard School of Music, and also offered her a free Scholarship for his own classes currently being held in Chicago. Backhaus, hearing of this, disagreed and recommended that she should be trained in Germany. The committee adopted Backhaus's suggestion rather than Grainger's, and she was sent to Leipzig for her musical studies. Later she became an internationally-acclaimed pianist.

Backhaus's gramophone recording career continued in the 1920s and between 1923 and 1926 (during his tours of the United States) he also recorded 18 piano rolls for the Aeolian Company's Duo-Art system. Thirteen composers were represented: Beethoven (1 roll); Brahms (2); Chopin (1); Delibes (1); Kreisler (1); Liszt (1); Mendelssohn (4); Mozart (1); Pick-Mangiagalli (1); Schumann (1); Smetena (1); R. Strauss (1); and Wagner (2). Three of the Mendelssohn rolls consist of a transcription for piano alone of his G minor Concerto, Op. 25.

During the 1920s it became fashionable for pianists to play 'All Beethoven' programmes or 'All Chopin', and so on. Backhaus, along with most other pianists, joined in the fashion, and once even gave an 'All C sharp minor' programme!

Backhaus's association with Manchester which had begun in the early years of the century extended into the 1920s and early 1930s when Hamilton Harty (knighted in 1925) was conductor of the Hallé Orchestra. Backhaus was only one of many famous soloists to appear with the Hallé under Harty. The violinists included Heifetz, Huberman, Thibaud, Elman and Ysaÿe; Casals (cello) also appeared; and the pianists, apart from Backhaus, included Busoni, Gieseking, Haskil, Myra Hess, Hofmann, Horowitz, Rachmaninov, Rosenthal, Artur Rubinstein and Siloti. A roll of honour indeed! Backhaus enjoyed playing with the Hallé and once said he wished he could afford to engage Harty and the Hallé to accompany him at all his concerts.

The Hallé Orchestra under Harty had a very high reputation. Once, when Schnabel was playing the Brahms B flat Concerto with them, he had a slight memory lapse in the finale and missed out two bars. Harty and the orchestra quick-wittedly covered the lapse and few people noticed. Afterwards Schnabel did not refer to the incident but told Harty he thought the Hallé was almost as good as the Berlin Philharmonic. "They're better", said Harty, "they play two more bars of the concerto!"

By the 1920s Backhaus was recognised as one of the great pianists of his time. His technique was always safe and reliable; he knew exactly what he wanted to do and had the ability to do it. As a youngster he was able to astonish by the sheer brilliance of his virtuosity. When he grew older he lost none of his technique but he became, as one observer remarked, "a devotedly unselfish mouthpiece" for the music he played. From his middle years onwards he was particularly esteemed as an interpreter of the composers of the late 18th and the 19th centuries; Mozart, Beethoven,

Schubert, Chopin, Schumann, Mendelssohn, Liszt and Brahms. Neville Cardus was always moved by Backhaus's playing and wrote in *The Manchester Guardian*:

"His Chopin had no rubato indulgences; he was one of the first pianists to concentrate on the strong harmonic core of Chopin; his performances of the Études had as much of fine thinking as technical and romantic urgency. He brought out the nobility of Schumann."

Of Backhaus's performance of Schubert's *Wanderer* Fantasia Cardus wrote:

". . . . of its breadth of energy and eloquent yet well-reined melody, touched with the grandeur always implicit in certain moods of Schubert."

Backhaus's performance of Brahms' Second Piano Concerto with Harty and the Hallé made such an impression on Cardus that he recalled it clearly over 30 years later, regarding it as "a critic's touchstone, a high standard for subsequent comparison."

In 1930 Backhaus bought a large house in Lugano, Switzerland, and when he was not touring he lived there with his wife Alma (formerly Herzberg) who was Brazilian. They had no children. He used to teach a few pupils there, when he was not on tour, until the end of his life. Eventually Backhaus took Swiss nationality.

During the 1920s and 1930s Backhaus's list of gramophone recordings steadily grew. He recorded all the Chopin études and his 1930s recording of Schumann's Fantasie in C on 78rpm discs is cherished by collectors. The 1937-38 HMV catalogue contains nearly a page of Backhaus records, all 78s of course. Not only are Bach, Mozart, Beethoven, Schubert, Schumann and Liszt well represented but also Albéniz and Delibes, composers not usually associated with Backhaus. Some of Backhaus's recordings of the music of Beethoven, Brahms and Chopin are singled out for special mention in *The Record Guide* by Edward Sackville-West and Desmond Shawe-Taylor, published in 1951.

When the Second World War started in 1939 Backhaus was 55 and obviously his career as a travelling virtuoso was curtailed for the duration of hostilities. No doubt he was glad of his move from Germany to Switzerland. When the war ended in 1945 he was 61 and in the light of his 6-year enforced absence from his touring life one wonders whether any thoughts of retirement might have crossed his mind. Evidently not, or if they did they were soon banished, for as soon as normal travel was re-established Backhaus took up his itinerant career where he had left off in 1939 and in fact it was to continue for nearly a quarter of a century more. In the immediate post-war years there was a certain amount of animosity towards

Backhaus because of the fact that he had accepted a German musical post under the Nazi regime in 1933. Cortot and Gieseking encountered similar problems, with more justification on their cases. But in his many visits to Britain during the immediate post-war years he quickly restored himself to favour in the hearts of music lovers and any reservations about his conduct were soon forgotten.

In 1954 Backhaus once again visited the United States for a concert tour. He gave a recital on 30th March of that year, four days after his 70th birthday. It was his first concert in the USA for 28 years. Olin Downes, reviewing the concert for *The New York Times*, alluded to this lengthy gap when he referred to the performance as "One of the greatest interpretations of Beethoven's music heard here in as long a time."

Backhaus's career as a concert pianist and recording artist continued unchanged through the 1950s and into the 1960s. His appearance was almost unrecognisable from the youthful, vigorous pianist who had taken Britain by storm in the early 1900s. He was now an old man and looked it; dignified, erect, solidly built, but his face was lined and craggy. Most people in his audiences were not born when his career began. No doubt he benefited from the veneration accorded to antiquity. His listeners wanted to hear this great pianist from a former era. But they did not need to make allowances for his age. He was still a great pianist.

Backhaus's demeanour at the piano was dignified, in keeping with his general appearance. He never indulged in show. His gestures were sparse and his attitude one of intense concentration. In conversation he was warm and witty though he tended to be laconic. After his early forays into teaching in Manchester and Sonderhausen and a short spell at the Curtis Institute in Philadelphia, he had taught only to a small select band of pupils at home in Lugano. But he was always anxious, even as an old man, to work on and improve his own playing. When he was once asked if he taught, he replied with a straight face, "Yes, me." He did not take up conducting as many pianists do, nor does he seem to have been interested in composition. The piano was his life.

In 1960 *The Times* interviewed Backhaus and an edited version of the conversation was published in an article on 11th April 1960 under the heading "Travelling Virtuoso". At 76, Backhaus was re-visiting England after a four year absence. The interviews on which the article was based took place during breaks in rehearsals with the London Symphony Orchestra at the Royal Festival Hall. The interviewer referred to Backhaus as "a pianist of commanding authority and ripe wisdom", qualities which he said appeared in Backhaus's conversation as well as in his playing.

In the introduction to the article the writer commented:

"He turns a shrewd thoughtfulness upon the questions he is asked and is likely to spring clean them in the interests of logic and clarity so that his answers at times go deeper than the questioner might anticipate. What he says is re-inforced, one feels, not only by richness of musical experience but also by an observant, speculative outlook; furthermore, in spite of his avowed dislike of interviews, it is enlivened by quiet, ready humour."

The interviewer reported that although the years sat lightly on Backhaus, he was planning to work less in the future. Said Backhaus:

"I should like to give 20 or 30 concerts a year now. The sort of life I lead is a gypsy life, one loses a lot of things people have who live at home. I have a home in Lugano but when can I be there? The greatest difficulty now is how to make a choice of what to do. You tell people your plans and they agree the plans are wise but then they say to you, "You must come to us next year of course." "

Backhaus went on to explain that the international virtuoso is compelled to narrow his repertoire by the demands of his audiences. They expected him to play Beethoven so he had to. He pointed out that if he lived and played only in one town he would have to choose from a wider repertoire. A travelling virtuoso has great travelling expenses and no retirement pension so that he has to ask high fees and take notice of what people demand. Backhaus added:

"Beethoven wrote 32 sonatas so there isn't time to play so many modern things; if he had written only 16 I should play more of other composers."

The interviewer remarked to Backhaus that he tended to be described as "a representative of the great classical tradition", but the description left the pianist unmoved. He felt it came only from the user's subjective attitude:

"We all use the word tradition but what do we mean by it? What is the classical tradition? I don't know. I grew up in Leipzig, at the Conservatory; that may have coloured me, but if it did I was unconscious of it. I try to play Beethoven as I feel it, as I try to imagine the man, not what story he is telling me, but what he is feeling. Somebody might play Beethoven quite differently but I should not want to say that he is wrong. I don't want to lay down the law. Critics are more likely to do that. Criticism is a great thing, a wonderful art, a necessary part of our musical life. But I give much time and thought and what little talent I have to playing and along comes Mr. Thingummytite and says, "All Wrong!" It is the critics who have put me in a certain river without my knowing it. If Beethoven came back, what would he say of us? Who would he say was right? We don't know.

"Sometimes when people talk about classical pianists they mean boring, as opposed to romantic. I want to make Beethoven alive, whether it is romantic or not. It is modern, I want people to understand that. Beethoven is 'The Book With the Seven Seals' to me; to play the G major Concerto perfectly, you need God's grace to help you."

In response to a question from *The Times'* interviewer about pianists of the past, Backhaus had a telling point to make:

"When people say today that we play better than Liszt or [Anton] Rubinstein, it's all nonsense. It is not a fair question to ask how Liszt would rank among modern pianists. He was a towering personality and he would tower above the pianists of today because rank in that sense is a matter of personality."

Backhaus was true to his promise of giving 20 or 30 concerts a year even as he entered his 80s. In 1965, reporting on two "All Beethoven" recitals, *The New York Times'* critic, Harold C. Schonberg, said that the audience "seemed to include at least one pianist every square yard, so deeply was Mr Backhaus admired amongst those who knew the instrument."

In view of Backhaus's indefatigable mode of life it is difficult to see how he ever had much time for anything other than his concert tours, but in successive editions of *Who's Who* he gave his recreations as walking, motoring and bridge.

During his career Wilhelm Backhaus had made an enormous number of records, starting with his acoustic disc of the Bach Prelude in 1909. Some compositions had been re-recorded two or three times through the years as technical standards of recording and reproduction improved, first with the invention of electric recording in the mid-1920s, then with the introduction of the long playing record in the 1940s and finally with stereo in the 1960s. He had recorded almost the whole of Beethoven's music for the piano, a great deal of Mozart and Brahms including both Brahms' concertos, the concertos of Schumann and Grieg and many works by Liszt and Chopin including all the Chopin études. He also recorded, with Pierre Fournier, the Brahms cello sonatas and with the International Quartet and Charles Hobday Schubert's *Trout Quintet*.

In 1964, at the age of 80, Backhaus embarked on yet another recording project, this time for London Records, a subsidiary of Decca. It was to re-record all the 32 Beethoven sonatas in stereo. He had recorded them all at least twice before but these previous recordings of the works were in mono. The plan was for Backhaus to record them over a period of years as his timetable of engagements permitted, and for the company to issue them one by one as they were completed. When the first record was released, Howard Klein, reviewing it in *The New York Times*, called the results "astonishing for their youthfulness and vigour".

In the same year that Backhaus started this series of recordings, the Royal Manchester College of Music conferred its highest honour on him, that of Honorary Membership of the College, at a ceremony held on 20th May 1965. It had been hoped that Sir John Barbirolli would be present to receive his own Honorary Membership of the College (bestowed some years earlier but never officially conferred) in person and then confer Backhaus's, but illness prevented Barbirolli's attendance. Instead it was conferred by Lucy Pierce, a recently-retired long-serving member of the college staff, who had been a pupil of Backhaus when he was a Professor at the College 60 years earlier.

Wilhelm Backhaus's 85th birthday came and went in March 1969 and there appeared to be little diminution in his ability to cope with the rigours of a travelling virtuoso's life. But at the end of June that year he had a heart attack whilst giving a concert in southern Austria. He was taken to hospital at Villach and died there a week later, on 7th July 1969. So ended a professional career of almost 70 years. During the preceding five years he had worked in the Decca recording studios on the Beethoven sonatas when time permitted, and at the time of his death all the sonatas had been recorded except *The Hammerklavier*, Op. 106. This major recording project was testimony to his long-lasting vitality. Some Backhaus recordings are still in the catalogues today, more than 25 years after his death.

Backhaus's contribution to music was that he was one of the greatest pianists on the concert circuit for well over half a century and, through his recordings, his skill and talents are still with us. What more could anyone ask?

Ethel Leginska

19. Ethel Leginska

The name Ethel Leginska perhaps conjures up in our minds an image of a rather formidable lady from Eastern Europe, of similar background to the famous Polish pianists of the nineteenth century. Nothing could be further from the truth, for she was English in ancestry, birth and upbringing; a Yorkshire girl, and her Polish-sounding name was taken solely for the purpose of promoting her career. In her long life she achieved fame in four different spheres of music - as pianist, composer, conductor and teacher - and became one of the leading musical personalities of her time.

The Yorkshire town of Kingston-upon-Hull of a hundred and ten years ago was one of the major seaports in Britain. Industry and commerce were thriving as merchants traded with Europe and outposts of the Empire. Iron steamers with their tall, narrow funnels competed for berths with sea-going sailing ships and barges. The result was a thicket of masts, funnels, smoke and hurried activity; all the ingredients, in fact, of a prosperous centre of trade. Not half a mile from this bustling scene a baby girl was born on 13th April 1886. Her name was Ethel Annie Liggins.

The Liggins family were not directly concerned with the seafaring trade, though they profited from it by the town's general prosperity. Ethel's father, Thomas Edward Liggins, was a builder who had studied architecture. He had followed in the tradition of his father, also called Thomas, who was a well-known builder and architect in Hull, and a partner in the local building firm of Hockney and Liggins. When the younger Tom Liggins was 24 years old he married Anne Peck of Hull, and they bought a house at 22, Pemberton Street, just off Holderness Road. Ethel was born the following year at the family home; she was to be the couple's only child. The family business was a successful one and the Liggins family was sufficiently well off to employ a succession of maids, one at a time, in keeping with the custom of business families of the period.

It was soon apparent that Ethel was good at music and piano lessons were arranged for her as soon as she was old enough to sit comfortably on a stool in front of the piano keyboard. One of the household maids later recalled that Ethel could play at sight the music that was purchased for her and immediately afterwards could play it again from memory. She also had an acute sense of pitch. Where Ethel's musical talent came from remains a mystery for there were no musicians in the family. Her formal schooling was provided by her mother, a bright, forward-looking woman who encouraged her daughter's great talent for music and instilled into her a knowledge and love of English literature which remained with her throughout her life.

Ethel's musical ability was obvious for all to see and soon attracted attention outside the family circle. At the age of about six she was 'taken up', i.e. assisted financially and in other ways, by Mary Wilson, wife of Arthur Wilson, the head of the famous Hull shipping line of Thomas Wilson Sons & Co. For part of the year Ethel stayed at Tranby Croft (now a Girls' Public School), the home at that time of the Wilson family, which was situated about four miles west of the centre of Hull. Many distinguished guests stayed there from time to time and Ethel used to be brought down from the nursery wing to entertain them in the music salon.

The Prince of Wales (later King Edward VII) often visited Yorkshire during the racing season and Ethel played for him at Tranby Croft when she was still a small child. It was whilst the Prince of Wales was staying at Tranby Croft in 1890 for the Doncaster races that the famous 'baccarat affair' took place. It involved an allegation of cheating at cards against Sir Edward Gordon Cumming, a well-known society figure, and was followed by a widely reported court case in which the Prince was called as a witness.

Ethel was not in any way exploited by the Wilsons - their intention was only to provide her with the necessary advice, funds and facilities that would enable her to realise her talents and which her family, though by no means poor, were not rich enough to provide. Later in life Ethel composed a suite of pieces dedicated to the Wilson family. They were impressionist compositions, one of which represented the funeral procession of the late Arthur Wilson in 1909. On that occasion the coffin was carried on a horse-drawn cart and the music suggested the rumbling of the cart as it was drawn over muddy, rutted ground.

When Ethel was nearly seven she began lessons with a new piano teacher, Mrs Russell Starr, who as Annie Jane Martin had trained at the Royal Academy of Music in London. The association prospered and Ethel was allowed to make limited public appearances almost immediately, the first when she was still only six. Mrs Russell Starr was a fine teacher who remained active in her profession until shortly before her death in 1933 at the age of about 80. Under her wise tutelage Ethel's talents were skilfully guided and her London debut took place on 19th June 1896, at the Queen's Hall, when she had reached the age of 10 years and two months. It had been scheduled to occur several weeks earlier, but had to be postponed when she fell victim to an attack of measles.

The programme of this recital was an ambitious one of 18 pieces, and the event was rapturously received by the public and critics. *The Sunday Times'* report (21st June 1896) is typical:

"The little Yorkshire musical wonder, Miss Ethel Liggins, is undoubtedly entitled to a place in the ever-growing list of piano prodigies. She is only a child of ten, and already possesses a remarkable execution, in addition to a memory that was good enough to enable her to play some 18 pieces without music at Queen's Hall on Friday. She has been carefully taught, and in the course of time should develop her exceptional talent to good purpose."

Ethel's later career was to fully justify these prophetic words. A few months after the London recital, Ethel repeated her successful programme, with minor changes, at a recital given at the Assembly Rooms in Jarrett Street, Hull. The programme showed a photograph of the little 10 year old girl with dark, wavy hair, dressed in an 'Alice-in-Wonderland' type of frock. The programme of music that Ethel played is quoted here in full:

Prelude and Fugue in B flat	*Bach*
Gigue in A minor	*Bach*
Italian Concerto (Finale)	*Bach*
Sonata in A	*Scarlatti*
Sonata in D (all three movements)	*Mozart*
Adagio Grazioso from Sonata, Op. 31, No. 1	*Beethoven*
Songs Without Words, Nos. 30, 34 and 47	*Mendelssohn*
Moment Musical	*Schubert*
Impromptu in E flat	*Schubert*
Waltz in G flat	*Chopin*
Impromptu	*Chopin*
Waltz in E flat	*Chopin*
Waltz in A flat	*Chopin*
Nocturne in B flat	*Field*
La Fileuse	*Raff*
Polka	*Raff*

These details are taken from the official programme of the Hull recital and in some cases the precise works cannot be specified (e.g. *Moment Musical*) as no further information is given. But irrespective of the exact details, the programme was clearly a formidable one for a 10 year old.

During these childhood years Ethel continued to share her time between Tranby Croft and her parents' home. Though the Liggins family lived in Hull, they also owned a substantial terraced house at Hornsea, on the Yorkshire coast a few miles north of Hull, and used to spend their summer months there. The house was near the railway station which enabled Tom Liggins to travel by train to Hull to work.

Ethel continued to study with Mrs Russell Starr for another two years following her London debut, but at the end of that time she was clearly ready for the next stage in her musical education. In 1898, at the age of 12, Ethel won a scholarship to study at the Hoch Conservatory in Frankfurt, and left Britain for the first time. A number of other talented musicians, all several years older than Ethel, were already studying there, including Percy Grainger and Roger Quilter. Henry Balfour Gardiner had recently left but still came back for vacation study. The stimulating atmosphere engendered by such fine young musicians as these must have benefited Ethel's progress tremendously. In turn, she impressed them. Percy Grainger later recalled:

"When Ethel Liggins (later Ethel Leginska) turned up from Hull around 1898/9 she eclipsed us all with her girlishly winsome Mozart playing. She was about 12 or 13 years old."

Ethel stayed at the Hoch Conservatory in Frankfurt for four years, until 1902.

For ten years or so Ethel had been meeting all sorts of influential people, first when she played for them at the Wilsons' houseparties at Tranby Croft, and later at musical evenings at the home of Lady Henrietta de Grey in London. Lady de Grey was a prominent figure in the London musical scene who took a lot of young artists under her wing. Another contact who was to have a significant impact on Ethel's career was Lady Maud Warrender. It was she who, around 1902, suggested to Ethel that she should change her name from Liggins to Leginska, on the grounds that a Polish-sounding name would help her artistic career, for in those days most of the best-known pianists were Polish or Russian.

Lady Maud Warrender, daughter of the Earl of Shaftsbury and wife of the one-time captain of the Royal Yacht, was a singer of considerable ability, and by virtue of her social position she was able to move in exalted musical circles. One of her books is full of statements such as "One day when Paderewski was lunching with me . . ." Her suggestion was valuable and not to be ignored. Moreover it appealed to Ethel who was very ambitious and keen to further her prospects by all reasonable means. So from the age of about 16, Ethel Liggins became Ethel Leginska, and was to remain so for the rest of her life. She used the name even when writing to her friends in Yorkshire; its use was not restricted to professional purposes.

During the Frankfurt period, opportunities to give recitals had become a normal part of Ethel's routine and by 1902, when she was 16, she was a very accomplished pianist. Word of her abilities had spread on the musical grapevine and in the same year she was invited to make her London debut as an adult pianist. This took place at the Royal Albert Hall.

As the period of study in Frankfurt drew to its close, Ethel's ambitions turned towards Vienna where the great Theodor Leschetizky lived and taught. He had been Paderewski's teacher, as well as the teacher of many other famous pianists, and Paderewski's brilliant successes on the concert platform had benefited his former teacher by the reflected glory, so that almost everyone who had pretentions to success as a pianist wanted to be taught by Leschetizky. Ethel was no exception; she was a very determined young woman and duly achieved her ambition. Owing to his advancing years (he was 72 at the time) Leschetizky had not wanted to take any more pupils but after Ethel had played for him for two hours he not only agreed to accept her as a pupil but also told her he would teach her free of charge and, if necessary, would pay her living expenses in Vienna. She studied with him from 1902 until 1905 when she was 19 and ready for a career as a concert pianist. In 1906 she made her orchestral debut in a Promenade Concert when she played the Concerto in F minor of Henselt at the Queen's Hall, London, under the baton of Henry Wood, a performance that was highly praised by the famous conductor.

A sad event occurred during Ethel's years as a student in Europe, when her mother died of smallpox during an epidemic of the disease in Hull. This cast a long shadow over what was otherwise a happy and triumphant period of learning and achievement. Her mother had always given her every possible encouragement and had been her mentor, teacher and friend. From her Ethel had inherited, or acquired, forthright views on how things should be done. Her death must have deepened Ethel's resolve to succeed in her chosen profession.

After the Promenade Concert there followed other London appearances including one at the Royal Albert Hall, and Ethel was soon in regular demand as a recitalist and concert pianist, not only in Britain but also in Europe. She was clearly not quiet or shy, but a girl of spirit, determination and ambition, and was not without an eye to publicity. In 1906, when she was 20, she met and was soon entranced by Karl Germain, the famous American magician, who at the time was appearing in Britain. According to Cramer, Germain's biographer, there followed in rapid succession tête-à-têtes, private dinners, romantic motoring through Kensington Gardens, and even punting on the upper reaches of the Thames. The affair reached whirlwind proportions and during this period Ethel even helped Germain on occasion in his stage act. A photograph exists of Ethel, taken on the stage of St. George's Hall in London, posing in one of Germain's cabinets.

But the romance came to nothing and in 1907 Ethel married Emerson Whithorne, an American musician from Cleveland, Ohio, who was two years older than herself. He too had studied with Leschetizky at the same time as Ethel and later he studied with Schnabel. Ethel was a better pianist than he was, and from 1907 to 1909 he acted as her agent whilst she toured Germany giving concerts. In 1908 a son, Cedric Villiers, was born and for a while all seemed well. But the marriage soon ran into difficulties, whether due to a clash of personalities, different career interests, or some other cause, is unknown. The couple were separated by 1912 and in 1915 the American newspapers were full of their sensational divorce suit, complete with a custody battle over six year old Cedric. Ethel claimed that Whithorne had deserted her and insisted that she could earn enough to support the child. But later she lost custody of her son to her ex-husband's parents. After the divorce Emerson earned his living as a music critic and composer, producing a long list of published works. Later he married again; he died in 1958.

Throughout the period of Ethel Leginska's unsatisfactory marriage her career continued to prosper. Late in 1912, following the separation from her husband, Ethel went to America and on 13th January 1913 she made her official United States debut in a recital at the Aeolian Hall, New York. The programme she selected for this important event was:

Rondo à Capriccio, Op. 129	*Beethoven*
Andante Favori in F, Op. 53	*Beethoven*
Variations on a Theme of Paganini, Op. 35	*Brahms*
Sonata No. 3 in F minor, Op. 5	*Brahms*
A group of pieces	*Chopin*
Mazeppa Étude	*Liszt*

This debut recital in the USA, given when she was 26, was the making of Leginska as an international concert pianist. Richard Aldrich's review in *The New York Times*, headed "Mlle Leginska's Recital: Young English Pianist Plays with Brilliancy and Poetic Feeling", was fulsome in its praise. The report referred to "gifts of inestimable value . . . full of high lights and deep shadows, and yet not lacking in artistic tenderness". Continuing in similar vein, the review drew attention to Leginska's "great brilliancy and feeling, strength of arm and finger, and endurance". Referring to Leginska's interpretation of the Brahms F minor Sonata, the writer commented:

"There were moments of exquisite beauty in her interpretation of the andante and its echo, the intermezzo, a beauty that was expressed in the delicacy of the haunting melody and in many subtle shadings of the total colour."

These opinions were echoed in the other leading New York papers. Her debut recital had been a triumph; a success from which she never looked back.

Between 1913 and 1919 Leginska appeared in every New York season and travelled the length and breadth of the United States, playing to full houses. Aldrich said she showed great delicacy of interpretation, was marvellous in Beethoven's *Waldstein* Sonata, and also played Bach, Mozart and Schubert very well. She was also known for her 'all Chopin' recitals. Her concerts were well received by the public and the critics from the start, so much so that from the date of her American debut she based herself in New York for several years, and was destined to reside in the United States for most of the rest of her life, though she made frequent visits and tours to Britain and the continent.

Leginska extended her travels to Canada and other parts of the North American continent, appearing with the leading orchestras and conductors of the day. In those years she established herself indisputably as one of the foremost women pianists of her time, and after the death of Teresa Carreño in 1917 she was generally regarded as the world's leading woman pianist. She made no concessions to the supposed weaker physique of women compared with men. Anything men played, she played.

Leginska' success was based on her great skill and musicality. She was second to none in terms of technical ability and interpretation. But added to that was her personality. Audiences were fascinated by the tiny, charismatic figure, looking for all the world like a heroine in a silent movie. But her fragile appearance belied her abilities. All who heard Leginska were agreed that she was able to hold her audience by the power of her personal magnetism. The effect of a Leginska performance was almost hypnotic. And it was not only the audiences who were 'hooked' by Leginska's unique gifts. The critics too continued to be unanimous in their praise. The crowning moment came in 1917 when Paul Morris of *The New York Herald* bestowed on Leginska the title "The Paderewski of Women Pianists". The name stuck and remained with Leginska throughout her life. To be compared with Paderewski, the world's greatest pianist so far as the man in the street was concerned, was the ultimate accolade.

Not only was Ethel Leginska a notable and colourful pianist, she added to the charisma of her image by the events of her private life and her readiness to give interviews to newspapers and periodicals. Her name was never out of the news for long. For example, in the February of 1909 when she was only 22, Ethel was to have played at a concert in London but after leaving Maida Vale in the morning she disappeared, and no trace of her was found that day. Her husband, when interviewed by the newspapers, said she was "impulsive and erratic" by nature, but said he could not understand her disappearance. Friends discounted suggestions that the disappearance was staged for publicity purposes. Next day Ethel turned up in Birmingham, and Emerson made a special journey there to fetch her. He said she was suffering from "nerves and stage fright". Such events were guaranteed to keep Ethel in the public eye.

In one of her numerous interviews in the United States during the First World War she asserted that the only way a woman could succeed as a concert pianist was to emulate a man in dress and hairstyle. Stating that the conventional bare-shouldered evening dress of women artists was a terrible handicap in concert halls which were often unheated, she devised her own costume, consisting of a black silk skirt and black velvet jacket over a white brocade vest and and silk shirt with a man's-style collar and cuffs. She also adopted a hair style resembling that of Paderewski and Liszt, which was much copied by other young women. Not only in her unconventional dress, which aroused both interest and much publicity, did she show a definite knack for self-promotion. When she caught her finger in a door in 1916, she promptly sent an X-ray photograph of the bruised digit to the magazine *Musical America* which published it. She also played a long, difficult programme without interval breaks at the Carnegie Hall in 1916, another feat that hit the headlines.

In 1919, after seven highly successful seasons of constant touring throughout the United States, Ethel Leginska announced that she intended to withdraw from performing for a season in order to devote herself to composition and teaching. As a preparation, Ethel had been studying composition since the summer of 1918 under the guidance of Ernest Bloch in New York. During the next few years a number of Leginska's published compositions appeared; orchestral works as well as music for the piano. One of the first of these was *Four Poems for String Quartet*, the first performance of which was given by the London String Quartet at the Aeolian Hall, London, on 14th June 1921. In the same year another composition, *Beyond the Fields We Know* (a symphonic poem) was given its first performance. Afterwards the compositions followed in rapid succession, including *Two Short Poems* (1922), first performed in February 1924 with Pierre Monteux conducting; *Quatre Sujets Barbares* (1923), (a four-movement suite); and *Six Nursery Rhymes* for soprano and small orchestra (1923), performed by the Boston Philharmonic Orchestra in 1926. These were by no means the only ones, for there were numerous other songs and piano works written in the early 1920s.

Now established in her late thirties as a brilliant pianist and a minor composer, Ethel Leginska turned her attention to conducting. In October 1924 she conducted the Paris Conservatory Orchestra and in the following month she conducted the London Symphony Orchestra. Several other orchestras invited Leginska to conduct them, including the Munich Konzertverein Orchestra and the Berlin Philharmonic. She claimed to be the first woman to conduct all of these orchestras, though her assertion that she was the first to conduct the Berlin Philharmonic was disputed by Antonia Brico, who said she held that distinction. All these appearances took place in Europe, but in January 1925 Ethel was back in the United States to conduct the New York Symphony Orchestra in Beethoven's 7th Symphony at the Carnegie Hall; the first appearance of a woman on the Carnegie Hall podium. She conducted the People's Symphony Orchestra in April and the Los Angeles Symphony in August.

Whilst Ethel Leginska was using her new-found skills as a conductor she continued to give recitals as a solo pianist and in 1925 there occurred a curious episode similar to the one that had taken place 16 years previously in London, when she failed to turn up for a recital. This time, in January 1925, she was due to give a recital at the Carnegie Hall, but disappeared. The affair hit the headlines in *The New York Times* and in the other American papers. *The New York Times* speculated that she "fled because her hands were not in good shape". Four days later the same newspaper reported: "Leginska is found, her mind a blank: reported in Boston." Leginska and her friends kept all details secret, but insisted that she did not disappear for the sake of publicity. A statement from the Bureau of Missing Persons attributed the disappearance to "a nervous breakdown due to overwork". This incident, coupled with the similar one earlier, was sufficient for some people to tag Leginska 'The Disappearing Pianist', a nickname which stuck harder than it deserved.

During the 1920s, when Leginska was at the summit of her career as a pianist, she recorded several works on disc, firstly a number of acoustic recordings for Pathé and later some electric recordings for Columbia which went on sale in Britain and the United States. Particularly notable in the latter group are a set of Schubert discs which Columbia issued in 1928 to commemorate the centenary of his death. She also made a total of about 75 recordings for the reproducing piano, shared between Duo-Art (25 rolls, plus six special rolls); Artrio (34 rolls); Recordo (7 rolls); and Ampico (3 rolls). They were available during the 1920s and 1930s.

Leginska's Duo-Art rolls cover the whole gamut of music from Bach, Beethoven, Chopin, Schubert, Schumann and others to Rimsky-Korsakov. She also recorded one of her own compositions, *Cradle Song*, for Duo-Art. The special Duo-Art rolls include two Beethoven 'biographical rolls' recorded jointly with Josef Hofmann, Harold Bauer and Albert Stoessel, and a 3-roll set of a transcription of Mozart's Sonata in D for Two Pianos, K. 448, in which Leginska plays the second piano part only. Rolls of this type were marketed to assist good pianists in their practice of the other piano part.

Leginska's Artrio rolls cover a musical range as wide as that of the Duo-Art ones and include a set of six *Souvenirs d'Italie* composed by her teacher, Leschetizky; the only complete set of these pieces recorded on piano roll. The seven Recordo rolls were each of music of a different composer: Chaminade, Chopin, Leschetizky, MacDowell, Moszkowski, Nevin and Sieveking. Leginska's three Ampico rolls include Daquin's *Le Coucou,* the only roll of this composition available on Ampico.

In 1926 Ethel Leginska founded the 100-man Boston Philharmonic Orchestra (all men except the harpist and pianist) which was intended to make good music available to the masses by charging low prices for admission to concerts. During the next few years she was to make hundreds of appearances as a conductor and director of her own orchestras. But her career as a concert pianist was not neglected and she often appeared as a pianist only, or conducting from the piano when a piano concerto formed part of the programme.

The new orchestra gave its first performance on 24th October 1926 with a programme consisting of overtures by Weber and Wagner, Beethoven's 5th Symphony, the premiere of Rudolph Peterka's *The Triumph of Life*, and Liszt's Hungarian Fantasia with Leginska as soloist. The concert attracted excellent reviews. *The Boston Herald* referred to the event as an 'Auspicious Beginning', whilst *The Boston Globe* reported:

"Yesterday she won her first great triumph. She and the Boston Philharmonic Orchestra gave 5,000 people a brilliant and enjoyable concert. If ever a wreath of laurel publicly bestowed was deserved, Leginska deserved the one she got yesterday."

Six concerts were given during the 1926-27 season, mostly in Boston's huge Mechanics Institute Hall, and they attracted a total attendance of 18,000 people. For the final concert of the season on 10th April 1927 there was a different venue, the Boston Opera House. The programme included Beethoven's Piano Concerto No. 3 in C minor, Op. 37, but it was an unconventional performance. The piano part of the first movement (*Allegro con brio*) was played by a Duo-Art reproducing piano using a music roll previously recorded by Leginska. During the performance of this movement Leginska sat in a prominent position among the audience. The second movement (*Largo*) and third (*Rondo*) were played by Leginska herself in the normal way. Such performances, sponsored by the leading manufacturers of reproducing pianos, were common in those days and provided valuable advertising material for the manufacturing companies, especially when backed by a statement from the pianist extolling the virtues of the instrument and confirming the veracity of its performance, as happened in this case.

Although Leginska's orchestra had been successful in artistic terms, the cost of running it proved too high and it was disbanded after only one season. But Leginska was in great demand as a guest conductor and soloist. In one such concert held on 19th April 1927 with the Chicago Women's Symphony Orchestra she conducted a concert which included Mozart's Piano Concerto No. 23 in A, K. 488, in the last concert of the orchestra's 1926-27 season, Leginska conducting from the piano as usual. Reviews referred to the concert as "The climax of the season."

Undaunted by the financial problems of the Boston Philharmonic Orchestra, Leginska formed the Boston Women's Symphony Orchestra. It gave its first real concert (following a semi-public trial) on 12th December 1927, to mixed reviews. The orchestra consisted of about 64 performers, all women, all of whom had been selected and trained by Leginska herself. Works by women composers were often played, and Leginska included at least one new or unknown work by a composer of either sex in every programme, as she had done with the Boston Philharmonic Orchestra. The second concert on 12th April 1928 featured, among other works, Leginska's own Fantasie for Piano and Orchestra which, according to *The Boston Herald*, "was not old-fashioned" . . . for it had "fascinating discords and modern rhythms." Several other concerts followed to complete the season.

In its second season in 1928-29, Leginska took the Boston Women's Symphony Orchestra on tour, presenting 52 programmes in 38 cities in 43 days. In what was described as its "Triumphal Return from the Grand Tour" the orchestra played in Boston on 17th February 1929, the programme including Mendelssohn's Piano Concerto in G minor, Op. 25, with Leginska as soloist. Of this concerto *The Boston Transcript* wrote enthusiastically, referring to Leginska's "high-powered performance" and her "galvanising personality". The final performance of the season was on 15th April 1929. It was reported that less than 100 seats were unsold. A month later, on 11th May 1929, the versatile Leginska conducted a performance in English of Bizet's *Carmen* at Boston's Jordan Hall.

When the third season of the Boston Women's Symphony Orchestra ended in 1930 the orchestra had played more than 200 symphonic concerts in 21 states during its three years of existence, always with Leginska as conductor and often also as soloist in the performance of many piano concertos. Unfortunately for Leginska she could not have formed her orchestra at a worse time, though no-one could have foreseen events. The height of her efforts coincided with the Wall Street Crash of 1929, after which very few people could spare any money to go to orchestral concerts, especially those given by newly-established orchestras. The difficulties were so great that a concert given on 29th January 1930 turned out to be the orchestra's last, its financial position proving untenable.

But Leginska did not give up. In 1932 she founded and conducted another orchestra, this time called the National Women's Symphony Orchestra, and based in New York City. The opening performance on 12th March 1932 consisted of Glinka's Overture *Russlan and Ludmilla*; Schumann's Spring Symphony in B flat; Mozart's Piano Concerto in A, K. 488, with Leginska as soloist; Rimsky-Korsakov's *Russian Easter*; Debussy's *Cortège et Air de Danse* from the Cantata *L'Enfant Prodigue*; and Wagner's Overture *Rienzi*. It was well received but the United States was by then in deep depression and the orchestra was disbanded soon afterwards.

There is no doubt that Leginska had to overcome a lot of prejudice in her attempts to be taken seriously as a conductor, but she stuck to her ideals with commendable fortitude. The male critics' reviews varied from good to downright patronising. For example, on 10th January 1925 *The New York Herald Tribune* remarked:

"It is to her credit that nothing serious occurred to mar the performance."

In even worse vein, a sneering critic of *The Boston Post* opined on 14th October 1929 :

"Granted that women performers are not likely to attain masculine proficiencies with such unfeminine instruments as the double bass, French horns, trombones, and tuba, the players of these instruments in Miss Leginska's present orchestra are at least adequate to any ordinary demands that may be placed upon them. The band as a whole plays with a gratifying, even a surprising, effectiveness."

Between 1930 and 1932 Leginska found time amidst her conducting engagements to compose her first opera, *The Rose and the Ring*, based on a satire by Thackeray, but it lay unperformed until 1957 when Leginska herself, then 71, conducted the premiere in Los Angeles. Her next opera, *Gale (The Haunting)*, written between 1934 and 1935, fared better, for it was presented at the Chicago Opera House on 23rd November 1935, with Leginska conducting. This event made history, for she was the first woman to write an opera and conduct its performance in a major opera house.

Although she had been based in the United States since 1912, Ethel Leginska made frequent visits to Britain and Europe and kept in touch with her family and a few friends. Her father, Tom Liggins, had died in 1924, having lived long enough to see his daughter acclaimed internationally as a musician. In the 1930s Leginska used to come to Britain when she wanted to work in peaceful surroundings, sometimes renting a cottage in a rural location in Suffolk. *The Rose and the Ring* was completed there.

When the Second World War broke out in 1939 Ethel Leginska was 53 years old, with many achievements to her name as pianist, composer and conductor. She knew that concert tours would be impossible for the forseeable future and decided at that point in her life to give up the world of the performer and to concentrate instead on teaching the art of piano playing to gifted students. She made her home and set up a studio at 254, South Hobart, Los Angeles. She lived there alone but her friend, Miss Lucille Oliver who lived elsewhere, was her constant companion and helper. Miss Oliver, who was a good musician herself, was nearly always present when lessons were in progress. She cooked, answered correspondence and did some teaching, helping with Ethel's junior students, as well as teaching some of her own pupils.

Ethel Leginska, always known to her students as Madame Leginska, had two 5ft or 6ft Steinway grand pianos in her studio. Her fame as a pianist and her teaching ability were such that she attracted many talented students, some of them very young. The decision to quit the ranks of travelling concert pianists was probably a wise one for she had no more worlds to conquer in the profession that she had followed since making her debut as a fully-fledged pianist under Henry Wood. There is much to be said in favour of retiring at the top.

For Leginska the move to full-time teaching was not a shot in the dark, as she had taken pupils and enjoyed teaching for the whole of her adult career as concert pianist and conductor. She had all the attributes required of a good teacher. One former pupil, Joan Meggett, wrote:

"She was a knowledgeable and exciting teacher as well as a fine pianist, illustrating points herself from her remarkable memory."

Another former student, the concert pianist Marilyn Neeley, studied under Ethel Leginska for several years and wrote to the authors as follows:

"I have a powerful overall impression of a very strong-willed woman, with positive, unequivocal ideas, a drive for technical perfection and a regimen for achieving this . . . Mme Leginska stressed perfection in all matters, musical and technical. Needless to say this created great tension when playing for her. Nearly every lesson proceeded with the student playing one beat - on rare occasions a complete measure or two - and Mme Leginska shouting "No!" She demonstrated constantly, and we would copy until the correct effect was achieved. Her culminating remark was always "You must always try to play something better than anyone has ever played it . . ."

Marilyn Neeley continued:

"Another advantage Mme Leginska provided was the monthly recital. Many teachers do have occasional studio recitals throughout the year, but few that I know make it the kind of 'professional event' that Mme Leginska did. Although they were held in her living room with cookies and punch in the back yard afterwards, we were expected to behave and play as if we were in the Carnegie Hall. To add to the tension, Mme Leginska sat several feet away and shouted, "Go on! Go on!" if a student stumbled. Many people wince when I relate this and say that that takes the 'fun' out of learning and performing. That may well be true, but Mme Leginska was not teaching the average music-lover to have fun and 'relax with music'. She was preparing professionals, in every sense of the word, who must, indeed, "Go on!" no matter what happens on stage. She has, in fact, been criticised for frightening so many students out of music, but I think she felt her mission was to train potential artists; the rest could always find teachers who would encourage them to enjoy themselves at the piano.

"In addition to the monthly recitals, her unflagging energy and dedication provided two more experiences for us: (1) Orchestral (concerto) performances, and (2) The 'all the works of one composer' series. She loved conducting; she would, at least once a year, hire and conduct an orchestra for accompaniments to student concerto performances (from Mozart to Tchaikovsky) in a large public hall. If no orchestra was available, Mme Leginska herself played the orchestral accompaniments of the concertos, reduced for the piano, while her students played the solo parts. Also, nearly every year she would have a series featuring the works of a given composer, played by her students. In fact, my first major public appearance was at age five, playing the E flat major Prelude and Fugue of the second volume of the *Well Tempered Clavier* in her series covering all the keyboard works of Bach. The chance to hear all these works was an enormous heritage in itself . . . I am aware of the tremendous debt I owe to Ethel Leginska in truly preparing me for every aspect of the musical and pianistic art."

From these recollections we see a picture of a talented, energetic and dedicated teacher. Physically Ethel Leginska was short in stature, but in personality she was a giant, a dynamic character. She was very demanding in all matters, musical and otherwise, and never hesitated to give an opinion. If the occasion was right she enjoyed a joke - but with her pupils the humour had to come from her; it was *not* appropriate for her pupils to joke with her! She spoke very little about her past to her students, especially about her life in England, but she always retained some of her English accent, which became more noticeable when she was angry and she was very fond of quoting English poetry. Her English origin and upbringing remained entrenched in her memory even though most of her life had been spent in the United States. But the only aspect of her past life that she spoke of to her pupils was her period of study with Leschetizky, whom she frequently quoted and whose teaching methods she followed. When it came to motivating her students prior to their giving a public recital she was superb; no football coach knew more about how to get the best from his protégés on a big occasion than Leginska.

Through the 1940s and 1950s Ethel Leginska continued to teach, and she also composed. Occasionally she gave private recitals at which she introduced some of her own compositions. In 1960 there was another highlight in Leginska's long career which combined all four of her talents - as pianist, composer, conductor and teacher. A programme of her compositions was presented on 12th May at the Wilshire Ebell Theatre in Los Angeles by a number of soloists and a small chamber orchestra. Some of Leginska's students took part and Leginska accompanied the singers on the piano in the vocal pieces, as well as conducting the orchestra. She was then 74 and age does not appear to have wearied her unduly. Rachel Morton wrote in the *Long Beach Press Telegram:*

"At one time Ethel Leginska was one of the most famous of women pianists. Coming from England she took this country by storm. I can see her with her shock of curly dark hair and magnetic personality thrilling Carnegie Hall audiences. There is still the heavy shock of curly hair, now graying, and the same vital personality, though time has frailed the lithe figure."

In the early 1960s, when Leginska was in her mid seventies, she underwent an operation for breast cancer, but recovered well and continued teaching. In 1969 her opera *Joan of Arc* (libretto by Mark Twain) was presented at the Wilshire Ebell Theatre with Anne Marie Biggs in the title role. Leginska was then 83 years old, not in good health, and unable to conduct the performance herself. Nevertheless, she was still teaching full-time and, energetic to the end, she taught until days before her death. This came about as the result of a stroke suffered as she was playing the piano. She collapsed and was taken to hospital but died three days later, on 26th February 1970, aged 83. Her lifetime's work is poignantly summed up by the terse entries on her death certificate:

Kind of industry or business: Music
Number of years in this occupation: 75

When Ethel Leginska was born, horse transport was the order of the day in our towns. Before she died, men had walked on the moon and daily life had changed almost beyond recognition. Between these two eras she had packed almost 80 years of outstanding musical activity and had achieved many notable 'firsts', particularly with regard to the place of women in the world of music. Little Ethel Liggins, the girl who had skipped along the pavements of Hull's Pemberton Street, had crossed many bridges on her way to becoming Madame Leginska, the famous musician. She is now hardly remembered at all by the musical establishment. But this forgotten genius was one of the most colourful and compelling figures of her generation and her achievements are a tribute to her unique personality and talent.

Artur Rubinstein

20. Artur Rubinstein

Artur Rubinstein was the archetypal concert pianist; suave, confident, polished, assured. There were few realms of the piano repertoire he did not explore; no type of music to which he was incapable of doing justice. During the last 40 years of his life many regarded him as the greatest living concert pianist and by virtue of his personality and his Polish birth he established a particular reputation as an interpreter of Chopin's music. His career was phenomenally long, spanning nearly 80 years, but he moved with the times so that his interpretations were never regarded as old-fashioned. It is remarkable to realise that a pianist who was at the top of his profession until the mid 1970s lived, as a young man, in the era of giants such as his namesake Anton Rubinstein who belonged to what now seems a distant age.

Rubinstein's career can be split into two phases. In his youth everything came to him perhaps too easily; he was so talented that he could give a good account of himself in recitals with a minimum of preparation or study. He spent the first 30 years of the present century enjoying the good things in life and an assured place amongst the better concert pianists of the day. But for the first half of his life he was not a truly great pianist. In the mid 1930s he found fresh resolve and impetus. He worked at his technique as he had never worked before and transformed himself into a supreme pianist, acknowledged as second to none in his profession. He retained this status for the next 40 years and it is this second Rubinstein whose life and career deserve to be remembered.

It was in Lodz, situated in a part of Poland then under Russian rule, that Artur Rubinstein was born on 28th January 1887 into a well-to-do Jewish family; his father was the owner of a handloom factory. The youngest of seven children, there were no talented parents, brothers or sisters to guide him musically, for he was the only one in the family to possess any aptitude in that direction. His earliest musical experiences came not from lessons or visits to concerts but from street sounds; the sing-song of Jewish pedlars, the ice-cream sellers, the calls of peasant women and the Lodz factory sirens. All this registered in his mind. He taught himself to play the piano at two, and at three years of age he was able to play a variety of tunes. After early studies with a local teacher called Adolph Prechner in Lodz his family arranged for the talented child to have lessons in Warsaw with an eminent teacher, Alexander Rozycki, and by the age of seven he had progressed so well that on 14th December 1894 he played pieces by Mozart, Schubert and Mendelssohn at a charity concert in Warsaw.

Artur's ability was clearly quite exceptional and his uncle Nathan made arrangements for him to be assessed by a top-class musician, none other than the great violinist and conductor Joseph Joachim. It so happened that Artur's sister was travelling to Berlin in preparation for her marriage, so she took Artur, who was eight at the time, along with her to meet the great man. Artur displayed his talents, which made such an impression on Joachim that he immediately offered to take the boy under his wing. Joachim had many wealthy and influential friends and persuaded three of them to finance Artur so that he could stay in Berlin and receive the best possible instruction.

So it came about that Artur took up residence there to be taught piano by Heinrich Barth, a former pupil of Liszt, von Bülow and Tausig, whilst his studies in harmony and counterpoint were placed in the hands of Robert Kahn of the Berlin Hochschule, and composition with Max Bruch, the eminent German composer. All this was under the general supervision of Joachim himself, who took overall responsibility for the boy's future, a task he undertook from Artur's arrival in Berlin at eight years of age until he was 15. It is interesting to note that in 1979 when a sale of some of Joachim's personal effects was held, Uncle Nathan's letter to Joachim, in which he asked Joachim to hear Artur play, was amongst them and was purchased by Rubinstein.

Artur's rich talent enabled him to derive maximum benefit from his studies. Though he hated practising he possessed tremendous natural musical dexterity, the ability to sight-read complex music and to memorise rapidly. This ensured a continuation of his rapid progress. At the age of 11 he played Mozart's A major Concerto, K. 488 in Potsdam and in December 1900, at the age of 13, he made his Berlin debut, playing the same concerto under the baton of his mentor, Joachim. In this concert, which took place at the Berlin Hochschule, he also played the Saint-Saëns G minor Concerto and a group of solo pieces by Chopin and Schumann. Soon afterwards he gave recitals in Dresden and Hamburg, performances which marked the end of his years as a child prodigy.

In 1902, when Artur was 15, he appeared as soloist with the Warsaw Symphony Orchestra conducted by Emil Mlynarski, who was later to become his father-in-law, though no-one could have suspected it at the time for Mlynarski's daughter, Aniela, was not yet born. Soon afterwards he was invited by Serge Koussevitzky to accompany him and his orchestra on a lengthy tour of Russia. The next step in his musical education was in 1903 when he went for a few lessons with Paderewski. The famous pianist, then exalted in concert halls all over the world, so took to his 16 year old pupil that Artur was invited to stay at Paderewski's home in Switzerland for three months, a period that must have been beneficial to him. By the time his study with Paderewski was completed Artur felt sufficiently self-confident to make his own way in the musical world and in 1905, with Joachim's approval, he went to Paris. There he gave six recitals and also played with the Lamoureux Orchestra, so impressing Saint-Saëns with his performance of the Saint-Saëns G minor Concerto that the old French composer commented: "He is one of the greatest pianists I know", and predicted a rosy future for the youngster. Rubinstein met many other leading musicians whilst in Paris, including Dukas, Ravel and Thibaud.

The success of the youthful pianist can be gauged from the fact that at 18 he secured a contract to tour the USA. His American debut came at the very beginning of 1906 when he played the Chopin E minor Concerto in Philadelphia. A few days later, on 8th January, he played the Saint-Saëns G minor Concerto at the Carnegie Hall with the Philadelphia Orchestra and followed this up the next week with a recital at the Old Casino Theatre in New York. A lengthy tour had been arranged for him, some 75 concerts and recitals in three months, and this was duly completed with moderate success. But he failed to achieve the ecstatic acclaim that he would have liked. Years later he summed up his reaction philosophically:

"I was not a prodigy any more, and [at 19] I was not a mature artist. The critics were severe, much too severe. I thought I had lost America for ever."

Returning to Europe, Artur virtually dropped out of public sight for three or four years. To his great credit he decided to withdraw from public performances for a while in order to work hard and to study, far from the limelight, with a view to surmounting (as he himself put it) "the greatest hurdle in the path of a prodigy, that of shedding immaturity." When he reappeared in Berlin in 1910 some of his friends enquired where he had been. "Oh, I have been dead for a few years!" said Rubinstein. Those missing years had been spent in Paris, and without doubt he benefited from his lengthy period of study.

Back on the concert platform again, things went better for the re-vitalised young pianist than they had in America. Though still not the master pianist he was to become (he once said he used to miss out as many as 30 per cent of the notes in those early days) his performances were good enough to satisfy all but the most knowledgeable and critical of concert-goers. He toured Austria, Italy and Russia and made his British debut in 1912, accompanying the cellist Pablo Casals in a recital at the Queen's Hall in London, and then appearing in a solo recital at the Bechstein Hall. By 1914 he was a well-known pianist throughout Europe and his easy personal charm ensured an open door to social gatherings wherever he went.

When the Great War broke out in 1914 Rubinstein was in London, where his knowledge of languages was put to good use when he enrolled as an interpreter at Allied Headquarters. Though not grammatically accurate in all his languages he could converse fluently in Polish, Russian, German, French and English and later mastered Italian, Spanish and Portuguese. In future years when he was often the centre of attention at international social events he would switch from one language to another as appropriate when he moved around from guest to guest. During the war he was so distressed by the way some German soldiers treated civilians that he said he would never play in Germany again - a vow he kept to the end of his life. But he gave many concerts in Britain during the war, including a series of 30 as accompanist to the Belgian violinist Eugène Ysaÿe, all of them benefit performances to help the Allied cause. In 1915 he appeared in a Royal Philharmonic Orchestra concert under Sir Thomas Beecham, playing the Saint-Saëns G minor Concerto, one of his specialities.

In 1916 Rubinstein was invited to give four concerts in Spain. He quickly developed a flair for Spanish and Latin-American music and soon established a rapport with the Spanish people. His concerts were so successful that he stayed on to give 120 in all. A great success there socially as well as musically, Rubinstein was entertained in style by the Spanish Royal Family and was fêted wherever he went. His interpretations of the piano music of Albéniz and de Falla were regarded as absolutely true to their Spanish origins. From Spain Rubinstein went on to South America where he became as great a favourite as he had been in Spain. The Brazilian composer Villa-Lobos later dedicated his *Rudepôema*, generally regarded as one of the most difficult piano pieces ever written, to Rubinstein, who was capable of dashing it off with the utmost ease.

When the tour of South America ended Rubinstein decided to try his luck in the United States once more. By then (1919) he had tasted fame and fortune to an extent he had not dreamed of in his earlier years. Still only just over 30 years of age, he was to remain a rich man for the rest of his life. His 1919 tour of the USA began with a recital in Carnegie Hall on 20th February of that year. This time his reception by the critics was better than in those far-off days of 1906. The veteran critic James Huneker, who had seen all the great pianists of his time, reported:

"Rubinstein's finger velocity, staccato, brilliant, incisive, with a splendid left hand, are all undeniable qualities, coupled with a sweet, singing touch and a musical temperament - in all, traits sufficient to equip a half-dozen artists."

With words like these ringing in his ears, Rubinstein could hardly fail to succeed as he continued his tour across America.

In financial terms, and also artistically, if the words of Huneker and other critics of the day are anything to go by, Rubinstein was a success. And yet, he still did not capture the hearts and imagination of the American musical public as he was to do later. Perhaps the reason was that his technique was still somewhat erratic, as he freely admitted in later life, so that he failed to maintain a uniformly high standard of performance from day to day. He was lazy and still hated practising. Because of his enormous natural gifts he was able to play moderately well on a limited amount of practice. The same applied when Rubinstein made other tours of the United States between 1919 and 1927; so far as the American people were concerned he was a very good pianist, but he was not a great one. And there were a lot of very good pianists around.

During the 1920s Rubinstein regularly toured Europe as well as America and he appeared at the Queen's Hall in London in concerts conducted by Sir Henry Wood and others. It was also at this time that he recorded piano rolls for the Aeolian Company and 18 of his Duo-Art rolls were issued. The composers represented in this musical offering were Albéniz (3 rolls); Brahms (3); Chopin (5); Debussy (3); de Falla (1); Prokofiev (1); Rimsky-Korsakov (1) and Schumann (1). He also recorded nine rolls for the rival Ampico system, of music by Albéniz (2 rolls); Chopin (2); Debussy (1); Liszt (1); Anton Rubinstein (1) and Schumann (2). Those days (1920-1930) marked the heyday of the player piano industry and his piano rolls helped almost as much as did his concert appearances to keep his name in the public eye.

Rubinstein never made any secret of his zest for life and his romances and exploits are fully documented in two large volumes of autobiography, *My Young Years* (published in 1973) and *My Many Years* (1980). He once said that Wine, Women and Song as applied to him was "80 per cent women and only 20 per cent wine and song." In the 1920s he had admired and been friendly with Aniela Mlynarska who, as mentioned earlier, was the daughter of the Polish conductor Emil Mlynarski. However, she married the Polish pianist Mieczyslaw Munz who in 1925 had made a name for himself when he stood in at short notice for Ethel Leginska when she failed to appear for a Carnegie Hall recital. He later became Professor of Piano at the Curtis Institute of Music and came to be regarded as one of the leading piano teachers in America. However, the marriage was unhappy and ended in divorce, after which Rubinstein and Aniela resumed their relationship. On 27th July 1932 Artur, then 45 years old, and Anelia (Nela), 22 years his junior, were married at Caxton Hall in London. The marriage provided Artur with the stability he had long needed.

After his marriage Rubinstein became a different man. He knew he had long been regarded as one of the better pianists of the day, a status he had achieved with a minimum of effort, but he was also well aware that he was still not thought of as a great pianist. He decided that if ever he was to move into the top bracket, now was the time. He knew he had the ability to achieve this goal, and he felt he owed it to his wife and himself to do it. Moreover he was painfully aware of the brilliant success his young rival, Vladimir Horowitz, was enjoying. He did not want Horowitz to receive all the glory whilst he remained an also-ran. Rubinstein summed up his change in outlook like this: "Suddenly I became conscious of every wrong note. Was it to be said of me that I *could* have been a great pianist? Was this the kind of legacy to leave to my wife and children?" He was almost in despair over Horowitz's success in Paris. "He tore it [Paris] from my hands. I saw in him another Liszt, capable of dominating his time. I wanted to throw everything aside . . . Before I died, I wanted to show what I could do."

So Rubinstein's marriage and the musical presence of Horowitz were the catalysts that triggered his re-birth as an artist, and the emergence of Rubinstein the great pianist. He and Nela took a chalet in the Alps and he worked methodically on his technique on an upright piano in a garage, week after week, month after month. He was not taking revenge on Horowitz but on himself, for all the years when he had made do with 'adequate' performances, falling short of the very best. For three or four years he worked and when he was ready, in 1937, a new tour of the United States was arranged. His New York debut (he always called it his 'real' debut, ignoring all his earlier tours) was on 21st November 1937. This time he took the United States by storm and from then on he never looked back. After his period of contemplation and technical consolidation his technique was faultless, his musical understanding brilliant. A pianist who had moved with the times, his interpretations were free of the distortions and sentimental excesses commonplace amongst many of the pianists of his youth. The warmth, accuracy and eloquence of his playing has ensured his place as one of the great pianists of the twentieth century.

Rubinstein and his family spent the Second World War in the United States and he became a United States citizen in 1946. But he was cosmopolitan by nature and for years maintained apartments in New York, Beverly Hills (Los Angeles), Paris and Geneva. Always on the move, never in one place for long, he once said that his Beverly Hills home was his 32nd 'permanent' home. His travels are reflected in the country of birth of his four children. Eva was born in Buenos Aires in 1933, Paul in Warsaw (1935), and Alina (1945) and John Arthur (1946) in Hollywood.

Towards the end of his period of technical reappraisal in the 1930s Rubinstein's recording career began in earnest and was to continue almost to the end of his life. He recorded for RCA-Victor and his output was enormous. Many of the piano works of Chopin were included, as were three versions of the Beethoven concertos, along with a vast cross-section of the general musical repertoire. A large number of his recordings are available now on cassette and compact disc, including most of his Chopin, so there is still plenty of opportunity to enjoy his stylish playing.

After the war Rubinstein founded the Frederic Chopin fund to help needy European musicians to buy instruments and scores. He also discovered that a lot of easy money was to be made from films and he played the piano music for the sound tracks of *I've Always Loved You* (1946), *Song of Love* (1947) and *Night Song* (also 1947). The recording work for one of these films took him three days for which he was paid $85,000. He also appeared in a couple of films as himself, namely *Carnegie Hall* (1947) and *Of Men and Music* (1951).

Meanwhile Rubinstein indefatigably continued his tours, which were to go on for nearly 30 years more. In 1958 when he was over 70 he gave a concert in Warsaw, his first in Poland for 20 years and was received as a kind of second Paderewski. He was asked to play in Lodz, his birthplace, but refused. He felt the occasion would be too sad, for the cemetery where his parents were buried had been destroyed and the streets where he had lived and known everyone had all gone. However, the following year he returned to Poland and, after a personal appeal from the mayor of Lodz, he did go there, and played in the hall where he had played as a boy 63 years earlier. He received the Honorary Citizenship of Lodz at a special ceremony.

In 1962, in 40 days between 30th October and 10th December, he gave 10 concerts all with different programmes at the Carnegie Hall in New York to celebrate the 25th anniversary of his 'real' debut in the United States in 1937, and also to commemorate his association with the impresario Sol Hurok over a similar period. It was Hurok who had brought Rubinstein back to the USA in 1937 and the association had been a happy and profitable one. Most of the proceeds of these Carnegie Hall concerts were given to charities. Rubinstein toured Russia in 1964, his first visit there for 30 years, and played in Moscow, Leningrad and Kiev. His performances there were treated with tremendous emotional acclaim.

Rubinstein continued as he grew older to enjoy his opulent lifestyle, his Havana cigars, good food and wine. A witty raconteur, his favourite topic of conversation was himself and his exploits. He liked to be the centre of attention wherever he went. His musical memories went back so far that there were few top-class musicians of the 20th or late 19th centuries whom he had not known personally. Possessed of the ability to recall instantly a vast number of events from his store of musical knowledge, he was always in demand for interviews. In them he was never at a loss for words. But few musicians were close friends:

"On the whole", said Rubinstein, "my contacts with musical colleagues never resulted in close friendships. They constantly talked shop, managers, fees, travel expenses and gossip, but hardly ever a serious word about music. I preferred the company of writers ... Singers have no limit to their conceit. The same goes for most conductors."

Amongst the writers with whom he was on cordial terms at various stages of his life were Arnold Bennett, Aldous Huxley and Ernest Hemmingway. Pablo Picasso was a close friend, as were some other famous painters. As a resident of Beverly Hills in the immediate post-war period and 'star' of some films in his own right he also knew most of the leading Hollywood film actors and actresses of the day.

Rubinstein was not a modest man. He enjoyed a lifetime of adulation and could be forgiven for believing he was an exceptionally gifted person, for indeed he was. But unlike some possessed of equal fame he always retained an interest in other people, especially musicians and others of Polish birth.

An important aspect of the last 30 years of Rubinstein's life was his passionate support for Israel. Recalling the setting up of the State in 1948, he said, "My heart swelled with joy - my throat was full of tears." In the years following the founding of the new State he was to visit Israel many times and played in numerous concerts with the Israel Philharmonic Orchestra in Jerusalem and Tel Aviv. Rubinstein played Beethoven's *Emperor* Concerto in Tel Aviv in 1960 at the opening of a new concert hall with Leonard Bernstein conducting. Also appearing in the gala celebrations were Isaac Stern (violin) and Paul Tortelier (cello), the latter standing in for Gregor Piatigorsky who was unable to attend. The Prime Minister, David Ben-Gurion, gave a long inaugural speech in Hebrew which neither Rubinstein, Stern or Bernstein could understand. It was translated for them by Tortelier, the one Christian of the quartet! He had lived for a year with his family in a kibbutz and had learned the Hebrew language.

Many more visits to Israel were to follow and Rubinstein helped the musical development of the State by donating the proceeds of concerts to worthy causes. In recognition of his work for Israel, an International Piano Competition bearing his name was instituted in Jerusalem in 1974. He was reluctant at first to allow this to happen, for he felt himself unworthy of the honour, but finally accepted after a personal request from the then Prime Minister, Mrs Golda Meir.

The Artur Rubinstein Piano competition proved to be a great success. A jury of fine musicians assessed the contestants and one of the judges, Arturo Michelangeli, gave a concert, the proceeds of which contributed to the expenses of the competition. Prizes went to the young pianists Emanuel Ax, Eugen Indjic, Janina Fialkowska and Seta Tanyel. Later one of these pianists, Janina Fialkowska, a young Canadian, became a close personal friend of the Rubinsteins and stayed at their home. Artur helped her to secure concert engagements, as indeed he did for various other young pianists who impressed him, notably François Dubois. He used to achieve this by promising to take part in a concert provided that his protégé would be offered a concert in the same city in the following season.

As Rubinstein grew older there was little noticeable diminution in his energies or skills. At 70 he was still giving 100 concerts a year. In his 70s and 80s he would play both Brahms concertos or three by Beethoven in a single evening. He still seemed to possess the powers of a young man. After a lifetime as a concert pianist honours were being collected at a rapid rate. He was a member of the French Académie des Beaux Arts and was awarded membership of the French Légion d'Honneur and the Order of Polonia Restituta of Poland. He received the Gold Medal of the Royal Philharmonic Society of London in 1961 and held many honorary doctorates from American universities. In 1976 he was presented with the United States Medal of Freedom by President Ford.

Rubinstein must have been one of the few men who were unconditionally happy with their lot. "I am the happiest man alive", he once said. Blest with tremendous vitality, his zest for life translated itself into his music. Perhaps that was one of the secrets of his extraordinary success. He had no need to depend on the mannerisms that are the hallmark of many a lesser pianist. His personality expressed itself in music; the happier he was, the better his music. Rubinstein found happiness in all sorts of situations. He relished the company of taxi drivers, business men, politicians or artists. He liked them all and could regale any gathering for hours with his fund of stories. When he travelled around the world he was not just a tourist but a student of the life in which he found himself. Nor was he the temperamental virtuoso. Whether on the concert platform or in the recording studio, music was his work, his vocation, his business. When he turned up at the film studio for the first time to make *I Will Always Love You* there was trepidation amongst the staff, many of whom had plenty of experience of temperamental musicians. They need not have worried. He took off his coat, rolled up his sleeves, and said: "Let's make some music." His views about his life and work were uncomplicated. He did not compose or conduct, nor did he teach. The one thing he was able to do, and do supremely well, was play the piano. When he was not doing that, or preparing for it, he was enjoying himself. But he was a cultured man who enjoyed travelling and collecting books and works of art.

Rubinstein was primarily a soloist, but like many of the other great pianists whose lives are glimpsed in this book he also enjoyed playing in chamber groups, particularly in his later years. On many occasions he partnered Jascha Heifetz, Emanuel Feuermann and Henryk Szeryng in the Guarneri Quartet in live performances and recordings. Another famous partnership which also made many excellent recordings was the trio of Rubinstein, Jascha Heifetz (violin) and Gregor Piatigorsky (cello).

Rubinstein never sought the limelight when playing with other musicians; he considered they all deserved equal credit for their contribution, but he was a stickler for tradition. This once led to a light-hearted quarrel with Heifetz, when the violinist complained that the publicity literature and posters for the trio always bore the names Rubinstein/Heifetz/Piatigorsky in the same order. Heifetz suggested the order should be changed for different appearances so that all three musicians were named first, in rotation. Rubinstein argued that the names of all performers in trios are traditionally published in the order piano/violin/cello. Heifetz still thought that the order should be changed, whereupon Rubinstein told him, "If God played the violin, it would still be printed Rubinstein, God and Piatigorsky!" Heifetz gave up the struggle.

When Rubinstein was in his early 80s a film documentary was made, for French television, featuring Rubinstein's life and work. In it he talked about his life, his music, his family - anything he could think of - and he also played the piano in various outstanding locations, such as Persopolis, in front of the magnificent ruins of Darius and Xerxes. The man who invited Rubinstein to embark on the project was Bernard Gavoty, critic of *Le Figaro*. Although intended for television the film was edited for the cinema and had a gala opening at a cinema on the Champs Elysées. It proved so successful that it was adapted for the American market. For this purpose Rubinstein re-recorded the text in English instead of the original French. The film was then sent to Hollywood to compete for an Oscar, which it duly won. Rubinstein was unable to attend the presentation as he was playing at a concert in New York on the day in question, but the award was presented to Nela on Artur's behalf by Fred Astaire. A special 'Oscar' statuette was made for Artur personally; it was later brought to his home by Gregory Peck.

In the early 1970s, when he was in his mid 80s, Rubinstein set out on a series of tours which were to be his last. Typical of the recitals was the one he gave in Manchester on 17th April 1973, in which the programme was as follows:

Sonata in B flat major, D. 960	*Schubert*
Nocturne in F sharp major, Op. 15, No. 2	*Chopin*
Scherzo in C sharp minor, Op. 39	*Chopin*
Fantasiestücke, Op. 12	*Schumann*
Hungarian Rhapsody No. 12 in C minor	*Liszt*

Rubinstein concluded the evening by playing four encores which he announced himself; a waltz by Chabrier; a Chopin étude; Mendelssohn's *Spinning Song*; and a piece by Villa-Lobos. Michael Kennedy wrote in *The Daily Telegraph* the next day:

"Artur Rubinstein's recital in the Free Trade Hall last night was the great artistic experience for which one had hoped but had not presumed to expect. If it proves to be his last in Manchester, as has been threatened, then the vast audience will keep a memory of him in full figure and at the height of his powers. His programme, which was lengthened by four superb encores, would have tested a pianist half this octogenarian's age, but he ended even fresher than he began, or so it sounded."

After describing Rubinstein's unique qualities in the earlier movements of the Schubert performance Michael Kennedy continued:

"To convey the intimate tranquillity of the slow movement in this big hall in itself demands rare artistry, but it was a feat he repeated several times; most notably in a sublimely poetic performance of Schumann's *Fantasiestücke*, where all the tenderness of the young love that inspired the music flowed from his fingers. The sheer joy of his playing *Fabel* will remain a treasured memory. So will the astonishing performance of Chopin's C sharp minor Scherzo. He began as if impatient with fingers, keys and even Chopin for not letting the music go as fast as he felt it should. Then his playing blossomed forth into the most magical and jubilant sounds."

"Finally there was Liszt's 12th Hungarian Rhapsody played not ostentatiously but with supremely aristocratic and elegant virtuosity. It brought the audience to their feet in acclamation, and as if this were not enough his last encore was a Villa-Lobos item almost insolent in the strength and agility of the playing, as if to say: "Follow that!" Wisely even he did not make the attempt."

"So he left us on the crest. It was an evening imbued with musical integrity and dignity which are rare in any generation. There are and will be other great pianists; there will never be another Rubinstein."

Rubinstein in his 80s had demonstrated that he was still a great pianist; there was no need to make concessions for his advanced age, and he was still a favourite with young people. But eventually failing eyesight dictated that he could not be far from the end of the road as a performer. The trouble was diagnosed as retinitis pigmentosa which gradually causes increasing blindness, starting with the loss of peripheral vision. There is no cure for the condition; in his case it was a by-product of old age. In the years that followed, Rubinstein made a few more recordings but his concert appearances were very much curtailed and were soon to end. On 15th March 1976 Rubinstein commemorated the 70th anniversary of his Carnegie Hall debut with a recital in the same hall. At 89 he was still, as Harold Schonberg wrote in *The New York Times*:

"A great pianist on anybody's terms; the old lion can still tear apart the piano when he desires."

It was at about this time, in London, that Rubinstein made his last recordings, Schumann's *Fantasiestücke* and Beethoven's E flat Sonata, Op. 31, No. 3. The final performance of his career was given on 30th April 1976 at the Wigmore Hall, London, a recital given for the benefit of the hall which was threatened by demolition. It was in this hall, then known as Bechstein Hall, that he had given his first London recital. After playing there in his 90th year in the last public performance of his life, Rubinstein said:

"It made me think of my whole career in the form of a sonata. The first movement represented the struggles of my youth, the following andante for the beginning of a more serious aspect of my talent, a scherzo represented well the unexpected great success, and the finale turned out to be a wonderful moving end."

Eighty-two years had passed since he had given his first public concert in Warsaw as a seven year old and more than 60 years since his first appearance in Britain as a professional pianist. Furthermore he had been generally reckoned to be one of the present century's great pianists for the last 40 years of his incredibly long professional life. After his Wigmore Hall performance he slipped quietly into retirement.

Rubinstein's last few years were spent in Paris, which he loved, and in London or Geneva. He gave interviews from time to time and in 1977 appeared in a film documentary, *Rubinstein at 90*. In one of his interviews he explained how, in his later years, he had come to be particularly identified with the music of Chopin. His Polish birth helped in that respect, but more than that it was the manner in which his personality was attuned to that of Chopin. Rubinstein noticed that different countries responded in different ways to the composers in his repertoire:

"The Italians have always been a little hard on Mozart, the Latins can't bear Brahms. But one composer, Chopin, is adored everywhere. His music speaks to me; he speaks my language. It is as if I composed it myself. Chopin loved Italian opera and some of the melodies are to me like arias. After many years I finally found a way to *sing* his music. Not with my mouth, but with the whole of me; my hands, my head, my heart."

In addition to Chopin, Rubinstein was renowned for his performances of Bach, Beethoven, Brahms, Debussy, Schubert, Schumann and a host of other composers. His technique was marvellous, his tone warm and rich, and his phrasing lyrical. A fellow musician described his playing as "distilled poetry". It is therefore not surprising that he was held in high regard by many modern composers who considered him to be their ideal interpreter. Several of them dedicated compositions to him, including Stravinsky, Prokofiev, Szymanowski, Tansman, Villa-Lobos, Milhaud, Poulenc, Ponce and Carpenter.

Rubinstein had many affairs during his long marriage but whilst he was still playing he exercised discretion to ensure that his private life looked respectable. Once he retired it seemed he no longer cared and at the age of 89, amid much family trauma, he left his 68 year old wife to live with Annabelle Whitestone, an Englishwoman of 31 whom his publisher had assigned to him to help with the second volume of his autobiography. She had been living with the Rubinsteins for some time before the final break. Rubinstein ardently declared his love for her in a widely published interview he gave at the age of 95.

When he was 93 Rubinstein developed prostate cancer. His health then steadily failed and he died at his Geneva apartment on 20th December 1982, just over a month before his 96th birthday. He had expressed a wish to be buried in Israel but in fact he was cremated in Switzerland and his ashes were then flown to Jerusalem to be interred. They were placed in a section of the cemetery separate from the main part, for Jewish law forbids cremation.

So ended quietly the life of one of the major concert pianists of the present century. A man of talent, flair, style and immense musicality, his life enriched the musical world for three quarters of a century. His counsellor as a child had been Joachim, a man born in 1831 who had known Mendelssohn and Schumann. But in spite of these links with the distant past his career extended into the age of digital recording and his musical interpretations ensure that he is remembered as a thoroughly modern musician.

Great Pianists of the Golden Age

Benno Moiseiwitsch

21. Benno Moiseiwitsch

Though Benno Moiseiwitsch was born and bred in Russia, he came to be regarded as a British musician, for it was in this country that he made his home and, in the fullness of time, he earned the respect and affection of the British people. In a long and successful career he achieved fame as one of the finest concert pianists of his day. He was also a notable recording artist, not only for the gramophone but also for the player piano. Active until relatively recent times, he was one of the last of the great masters of the keyboard which Eastern Europe produced so prolifically during the reign of Queen Victoria.

It was in the beautiful Black Sea town of Odessa that Benno Moiseiwitsch was born on 22nd February 1890. He was not the first famous pianist to be born there, for the equally celebrated, though markedly different, Vladimir de Pachmann also hailed from the same town. But Pachmann was 41 years old when Benno was born and had long since left Odessa. Benno's real name was Benjuma (pronounced Ben-you-mah). His parents called him by this name but it was as Benno that he was known outside his family for most of his life. He was one of a large family and in order of birth he came somewhere near the middle.

Benno's family were all talented, in a variety of ways, but he was the only musician among them. His sister Sonia was to play an important part in the development of his career through her husband Sasha Konievsky, a business executive. His brother John was a first-rate mathematician and inventor; another brother, Boris, went to the USA to become a manufacturer of precision instruments, whilst yet another, Vladimir, became an engineer and eventually settled in England. Benno's father, David, was a horse breeder and an expert on pedigree stock, a very strong man physically, whilst his mother, Esther, was of artistic disposition. Benno inherited the physical strength and fitness of his father and the artistic sensitivity of his mother, both essential qualities for a future itinerant virtuoso.

Odessa was home to Benno; that was where he was born and grew up. Not only was it a centre of culture, it was a focal point of travel and adventure, and as a boy he used to sit on the sea-front watching the comings and goings of the steam ships and sailing vessels. Even as a child he was convinced that one day he would become a concert pianist. That was his ambition; all that he ever wanted to do. The departures of the ships to faraway and romantic places symbolised in his youthful mind the possibilities of the years ahead.

At about six or seven years old Benno was taken to the Odessa Opera House and was enthralled by the performance. Even then he was showing unusual musical promise; his mother realised he had real talent and for a while she gave him piano lessons. He did not just play the music, he was able to interpret it, unlike most young children, and would announce, "this is laughing music", or whatever the mood of the music happened to be, and would improvise accordingly. Later a professional piano teacher was employed. Benno did not like him very much and as soon as he had gone after a lesson Benno would accurately mimic on the piano the cadences of the man's voice which, though bringing gentle reproof from his parents, also caused much amusement.

Benno was a lively and mischievous child, liked by everyone, but he hated routine practice. "If only John could have invented a pianola for me" he once said later, referring to his brother. Nevertheless he worked dutifully through his well-thumbed copy of Czerny's Studies until he knew them off by heart, and by seven or eight years of age he had developed a formidable technique. He was never content to play in a routine way, without understanding the music. Once when he was learning a piece by Mozart he spent days picking through the sections of the composition slowly, bit by bit, without playing the whole piece. "Why don't you play the piece properly, Benjuma?" asked his mother. "You can do better than that." "I'm trying to understand it", said Benno. Then one day, in the early hours of the morning when the family were all sleeping, they suddenly awoke to the strains of the Mozart piece being played with fluency and sparkle on the piano downstairs. "I kept waking up", explained Benno, "hearing parts of the music in my mind. Then suddenly I woke up and heard it streaming through my head, just as it should sound. It was lovely. I had to come down and play it."

After this incident his mother realised that his talent and musical understanding were well above the ordinary and she took him for an audition at the Imperial School of Music in Odessa. "Why do you think you should have a place at this special school of music?" he was asked. "Let me play the piano for you", answered Benno. He played - and was awarded a place on the spot. So began Benno's full-time musical studies, but he did not always see eye to eye with his tutors. After a while he brought home his first report:

"Moiseiwitsch, Benjuma. Inattentive, mischievous. Does not like to practise his special exercises."

Naturally his parents asked Benno to explain. He did:

"Some of the teachers are so stiff, and they play badly. They play the right notes, but I don't like the way they play so I don't listen properly. Chopin is sad and beautiful, like Autumn, and Old Safranov plays it thump, thump, thump, like this:"

Benno clumped up and down the room.

"It sounds as though he plays with his mittens on."

The fact that Benno had strong ideas of his own inevitably led to a few conflicts at the school, but his tutors were perhaps not as musically insensitive as Benno thought, for they clearly recognised his outstanding ability. He did exceptionally well in his musical studies and was also proficient in the general curriculum of mathematics, history, etc. In those days the Imperial School offered an award, the Rubinstein Prize, to the most able pupil. One day at breakfast Benno's mother said to him: "I hear the Rubinstein Prize contest was held yesterday. Have you any idea who won it?" "Yes", said Benno. "I did." At this the rest of the family nearly choked on their breakfast, for Benno had not mentioned the matter and had won the prize, at 9 years old, in competition with 17 and 18 year olds. Benno had played a long and difficult piece by Schumann and the citation spoke of his "brilliant and individual playing." When asked by the press for his ideas about the music he played he said it "reminded me of a man standing at the helm of a ship, sailing it through a storm, with lots of strong sea." By all accounts he had played the piece with remarkable passion, beautiful timing and some unconventional use of the *crescendo*. When one of his professors asked him about the use of these crescendos, Benno explained that he had had to achieve the result he wanted by means of reverberation because he could not reach the pedals properly.

After this triumph, Benno was of course a boy wonder. There were full accounts of his success in all the newspapers and his parents were approached by an impresario offering Benno a concert tour of Russia and parts of Europe, to be accompanied on the journeys by his mother. But Benno's parents wisely resisted the temptation. The impresario had not heard Benno play; all he knew of him was through the press reports, and Benno's parents concluded that he was not interested in Benno as a person or as a musician, but only in the money he could make from him as a child prodigy. And so Benno continued at the Imperial School where he enjoyed his music, his games, and the friendship of his contemporaries. He remained there until he was 15.

Russia in those days (1905) was in a state of acute political unrest, and for some time the Moiseiwitsch family had been contemplating the uncertain future of their country. Several of Benno's brothers had talked of leaving Russia and making their homes elsewhere and after several family councils it was decided who would go and who would stay. Boris was to go to the

USA, where gold was thought to abound on the pavements, and John and Benno would go to England.

John hoped to get a job in an engineering firm, whilst Benno, it was expected, would be enrolled at the Royal Academy of Music in London. The Moiseiwitsch family had acquaintances in England and letters had been sent to smooth the way for both the Moiseiwitsch boys. After a tiring journey through Germany and France, Benno and his elder brother John disembarked at Dover and from there travelled to London. Accommodation had been found for them and after a few days, when the brothers had acclimatised themselves, Benno turned up for his appointment at the Royal Academy, armed with a letter from the Imperial School in Odessa. He played well at his audition, after which the grave-faced elderly men who had been listening to his performance jabbered away between themselves in what to Benno was a foreign language. At length the verdict was transmitted to Benno, via an interpreter. "We can't teach you anything. You'll have to find another country."

More family conferences followed, this time by letter. As a result of these Sonia, Benno's eldest sister who was married to the wealthy Sasha Konievsky and living in Switzerland, arranged for Benno to go to Vienna to try his luck with the great Leschetizky, teacher of the world's best pianists. And so Benno's journeys began again, overland to Switzerland and thence to Vienna, accompanied by Sasha, his brother-in-law. Sasha arranged for Benno to practise for a small private recital which he could play for Leschetizky and for this purpose Benno prepared Chopin's *Revolutionary Study*.

Three years previously Leschetizky had told Ethel Leginska he was too old to take any new students and it was only after listening to her bewitching playing for two hours that he finally relented, accepted her, and told her he would teach her without charge. Now, three years older at 75, it was obvious that the old professor would be very reluctant to accept Benno. On the appointed day Benno, having prepared a programme of music, arrived at Leschetizky's studios armed with his references. The great teacher listened as he played the programme he had practised and then announced: "I could play it better with my left foot. Practise control for two months and come back." Benno felt rebuffed by this reaction initially but he soon cheered up as his brother-in-law pointed out that Leschetizky had not rejected him out of hand; Sasha encouraged him to do exactly as Leschetizky had instructed. Leschetizky was a wise old man. He had obviously recognised talent in the youthful pianist, otherwise he would have told him to go away and not come back, for he was a teacher only of the very best students. His remark to Benno was made to test his dedication, to find whether he 'had what it takes'.

Benno spent the next few weeks in careful study and then played for Leschetizky again, whereupon he was enrolled immediately, at the age of 15, as a special pupil. "You're beginning to hear yourself seriously", said Leschetizky. Benno knew exactly what he meant by this remark, and always remembered it. Throughout his career he sought perfection in his own playing by listening to it carefully and then amending it if necessary. On many occasions he would receive tumultuous applause after a concert or recital but if he himself felt he had not played as well as he might have done he would go back to his home or hotel and work through the problem passages afterwards.

Moiseiwitsch's period of study in Vienna was a happy one; the old man and the young one got on very well together and enjoyed an excellent musical rapport. One of Leschetizky's private jokes with his pupils was to sit at the other end of the room from the piano with his back turned towards it and ask someone to play; he would then try to identify the student. After a year's study with Leschetizky, when Benno was still only 16, the old teacher could identify his playing without fail.

During the Vienna years Sasha kept an eye on Benno, who was getting plenty of attention. He was good-looking and confident, and life outside Leschetizky's studios became a social whirl; society, girls, music, arts. It was a happy time which he enjoyed. After three years' study, Leschetizky told Benno there was no more he could teach him. Benno thanked him, as Leschetizky had thanked his own teacher, Czerny, 60 years earlier. "The Old Man says I'm ready to make my debut as a concert pianist", explained Benno to his brother John when he returned to England.

Benno's first public appearance in Britain was at a recital given in the Reading Town Hall in 1908, which was well received by the audience. He was then ready for his London debut, and John and his friends undertook to prepare the ground. John was a clever and thoughtful man; he decided it would be useless for Benno to appear in a small hall with few journalists present; only a big occasion would do for Benno's debut. But if a large hall was hired for an unknown artist, no-one would come. John thought this problem out, and decided that the answer was a joint programme. Benno would appear in conjunction with an established artist - a non-pianist. But who? John had pondered this problem too. The answer - Melba! The great Nellie Melba, then at the summit of her career. But surely she wouldn't consent to appearing with an unknown 19 year old? But again John paved the way carefully. Many letters of recommendation were collected before an approach was made to the great singer. Fortunately she agreed to audition Benno. He played Beethoven's *Hammerklavier* Sonata for her, and she was captivated not only by the musical ability but also the charm of the good-looking and personable young man.

Their joint programme was arranged and the concert took place at the Queen's Hall, London, in 1909. It was a great success; Benno was called upon to play several encores and took numerous curtain calls. Moreover the press reports the next day were very good. From that day on he was an established success. Many more concerts and recitals were arranged and on each occasion careful attention was paid to advance publicity. These early appearances were a triumph. With success came money. At 19 Benno was well-off. He could stay at first class hotels, dine at the best restaurants, entertain socially on a lavish scale, and he was to be in this happy situation for most of the rest of his life. Even when playing in a remote venue he received more money for one concert than most people earned in a month, and he could play 20 such concerts in four weeks. There was also no problem in getting engagements abroad, for music has no language barrier.

Thus, the young man of 19 was suddenly a celebrity and was the possessor of money, leisure when he wanted it, and the opportunity to travel. The golden years had begun and were to last for half a century. Benno realised he was to be one of the favoured. But he was intelligent and shrewd. He knew that he must maintain his skill if the good things were to continue. Consequently he maintained a regime of several hours' practice a day for most of his career, using a dummy keyboard when he was staying in hotels. He made his home in London, where the cost of living in those pre First World War days was low and income tax was 1/6d in the £. He rented high-class furnished rooms in the West End and employed a resident housekeeper. Many well-known people used to meet there. Benno liked England and planned that other members of the family, including his parents and brother Vladimir should come to England too, which they eventually did. For this purpose he systematically put money aside to pay for their emigration from Russia.

During the next few years Benno Moiseiwitsch emerged as a pianist of the highest class. His interpretations were fiery, effortlessly brilliant and powerful, with a singing tone, firmly controlled yet subtle rhythm, and a strong poetic expression. 'Moiseiwitsch double octaves', thumbs louder than fifth fingers, became a household phrase among pianists. He liked to keep the music fresh by varying his interpretations and it used to be said that Moiseiwitsch never played a piece twice in the same way. His repertoire in those early years was large and varied, and in one season he played as many as 20 different concertos. Brilliant pianist as he was, his career was assisted by his platform presence, a factor so important in the life of an artist. He had a force and stylishness bordering on the aristocratic, which compelled attention. Even in his youth he had the ability to look distinguished on the concert platform, an attribute which became even more marked as he grew older.

When he was not performing or practising Moiseiwitsch's lifestyle soon developed a regular pattern. He enjoyed going to the races and liked to have a flutter; he joined two London clubs and enjoyed the evenings spent in their smoke-filled rooms in the company of his friends, and he was an excellent player of bridge and poker, sometimes playing for high stakes in the latter game, in which he was a great student of 'systems'.

Once when he was walking home late at night he helped someone who had been robbed in the street. When the police asked him whether he had seen the thieves he gave the sort of reply one might expect from a musician:

"In that light, no. But I did hear them. One of them babbled in a Greek accent - the other is a Latin, and when excited his voice ascends to E flat."

In 1914 Benno married Daisy Kennedy, a very talented professional violinist from Australia. She was said to be "a beautiful girl, with a lovely complexion, offset by her striking auburn hair." She and Benno met at a party given by friends who had decided to bring them together. "We must invite Benno when Daisy comes", they said, "they're bound to hit it off". And hit it off they did, for the two were married after a short courtship. Benno was then 24 and Daisy 21. But the outbreak of war later that year put a stop to the smooth course of both their careers.

When the war started Benno suffered various emotional conflicts. Should he go back to Russia, which was also at war with Germany, or what? He still did not regard himself as English, never having been naturalised, and used to get very depressed about the situation. His solution was to play in numerous concerts, for the troops, hospital patients, and so on, often under primitive conditions, and this period proved to be one of the busiest in his life. Many people felt that his playing became even better than it had been before as a result of these experiences and acquired a depth of feeling which gave a new dimension to his music.

The Russian revolution of 1917 saddened him greatly, as it did many Russian musicians, and for a while he became obsessed with the Russian master musicians of the past; Tchaikovsky and also Rachmaninov who, although a contemporary, wrote music of 19th century style. It was as though Moiseiwitsch was saying "I am a product of the Old Russia." Indeed, for the rest of his life he rarely played music by the more modern

Russian composers such as Prokofiev, Shostakovich and Stravinsky. He became a great friend of Rachmaninov and Moiseiwitsch's interpretation of the Rachmaninov Second Concerto came to be regarded as the definitive performance of the work after that of Rachmaninov himself. Rachmaninov regarded Moiseiwitsch as his heir apparent as a performer of his works and often complained with feigned envy that Moiseiwitsch played his compositions better than he did. Whilst seated at the piano, Moiseiwitsch's features were often marked by a semblance of utter impassivity, possibly modelled on Rachmaninov, his friend and musical idol.

Benno began recording for HMV early in his career and even during the 1914-18 war when he was still in his mid-twenties there were eight of his records in the HMV catalogue. All were violet-label records; one 10-inch costing five shillings and the rest were 12-inch at seven shillings each. The 10-inch disc was of Daquin's *Le Coucou* and the 12-inch discs were of music by Brahms, Chopin, Debussy, Ravel and Scriabin.

After the 1914-18 war it gradually became clear that Russia would never be the same again as the Communist hold grew stronger with the passing years. Benno's politics were governed by his heart, and he never liked to be drawn on the subject. Any thought of a return to Russia was out of the question - his home was now in England. He and Daisy lived in a large house in London with seven servants, and by the 1920s there were two children, Tanya and Sandra. But life was not all it might be at the Moiseiwitsch home. Though Benno was only 24 when he married he had already lived a bachelor life too long to fall easily into a life of domesticity and most of his evenings, through to the early hours of the mornings, continued to be spent at his clubs.

Daisy had readily set her violin aside when the children arrived but she had not travelled 12,000 miles to Britain in order to succumb to permanent retirement from her profession. She felt she was being taken for granted, so she started to move in her own social circle independently of Benno. There she met John Drinkwater, a distinguished-looking author and playwright, and after a while she told Benno (according to his biographer, Maurice Moiseiwitsch) that she had fallen in love with her new acquaintance. Benno was shocked and dismayed. He felt bitter and his pride was hurt. In 1924, after 10 years of marriage, he divorced Daisy and she married John Drinkwater. They had a daughter, but thirteen years after the marriage, in 1937, Drinkwater died and Daisy then had to try to resume her long-interrupted career as a violinist. She took custody of the two Moiseiwitsch daughters but Benno saw them often. One of them, Tanya, became a successful stage designer.

After the breakdown of his marriage Benno became something of a recluse for a while, but his tours to all parts of the world continued, as well as his tours of Britain. Numerous interesting and sometimes amusing episodes occurred during these tours. Once when he was in the USA he was playing in a hall that was supposed to be soundproofed from the outside world, but it was not equipped to cope with the din of thunderstorms. It was a hot, sultry day and Benno was about to play some of the quieter, more delicate compositions of Chopin when a storm broke with violent and noisy intensity. He looked at the audience, shrugged, seated himself at the piano, and played Liszt's *Grand Galop Chromatique*, which is a well-known rival to most thunderstorms when played by someone with the fire of Moiseiwitsch. The storm enhanced the effect of the work, as Benno knew it would, and he was wildly applauded. So popular was this brilliant effort that for weeks afterwards he was called upon to include the same showy piece in his programmes wherever he played.

On another occasion, also in the States, Benno noticed as he walked onto the platform to begin his recital that a block of seats at the front of the hall was empty. As he settled himself to start he was annoyed to see that the management allowed a party of latecomers to march forward noisily to occupy these places. They were ugly-looking customers and some of them pulled out newspapers and comics to read as they sat down. Later the party left just before the end of the recital. Afterwards Benno asked the manager of the hall why they had been allowed to disturb the start and finish of the performance and why people who had paid high prices for front-row seats should bring newspapers and comics to read. The manager explained:

"There was nothing we could do. Al Capone is a music lover, but his bodyguards aren't at all interested. They all have to come in and leave alone because Capone could be bumped off if he mingled with a crowd."

There is a postscript to this event. The next morning a man with an enormous basket of fruit and flowers called to see Benno at his hotel. He was one of Capone's acolytes. With the flowers there was a card which said:

"If the boys bother you let me know. Do you know the Rossini piano stuff by Liszt?" (He was referring to Liszt's piano transcriptions of the Rossini operas.) "Play it next time, maybe. With best wishes from a Friend and Music Lover."

Benno was told later that he should have kept the card because in some towns in the States there were professional claques who tried to blackmail artists by threatening to spoil their performances. These were the 'boys' against whom 'Friend and Music Lover' offered his protection. During his career Benno made over 20 tours of the United States and there were few parts of the world in which he never played.

Meanwhile Benno had made more gramophone records for HMV and he continued to record for them for the rest of his working life. In 1937 five Moisewitsch records (all of them 78s) were on offer, featuring works by Brahms, Chopin, Ravel, Scarlatti and Schumann, and in 1965 nine long-playing records were available, the composers being Beethoven, Chopin, Grieg, Mussorgsky, Rachmaninov and Schumann. Not until the late 1970s did the number of Moiseiwitsch recordings in the catalogue dwindle and finally disappear so, although he was never a prolific recording artist, his discs were in the catalogues continuously for over 50 years. Some of his records have now been re-issued on compact disc.

Benno also recorded for the reproducing piano. He was almost a "one company" man, for just one roll of his was issued by the Aeolian Company for their Duo-Art system; the rest of his rolls, about 30 of them, were recorded for Ampico. Moiseiwitsch's Ampico piano rolls all date from the period between the end of the 1914-18 war and 1930. The Moisewitsch of the piano roll recordings was therefore the young Moiseiwitsch, full of fire and vigour, not the mellowed artist of his more mature years. The thirty rolls include multiple-roll sets of individual compositions, for example Schumann's *Carnaval* was issued on four rolls, as opposed to two on Duo-Art issues of the same piece recorded by other artists. As in his gramophone recordings, a wide spectrum of music is represented and the Ampico rolls present music by Brahms, Chopin, Debussy, Delibes, Granados, Ibert, Leschetizky, Palmgren, Ravel, Schubert, Schumann, Scriabin, Tchaikovsky and Wagner (transcribed by Liszt). The solitary Duo-Art roll was a title that also appeared in his list of Ampico rolls (*Passepied* from the Incidental Music to *Le Roi S'Amuse* by Delibes). It was a late Duo-Art roll and as the Aeolian Company and Ampico amalgamated during the 1930s it may well have been an adaptation from the Ampico roll. Moiseiwitsch was one of the small band of pianists who were interested in the roll-making process and liked to help out with the editing in any possible way to ensure the best result.

The dynamic, good-looking young man was an excellent box-office draw and was one of Ampico's most valuable assets, not only because of the quality of his piano roll recording but also because of his usefulness in furthering the company's promotional efforts. For example, an Ampico advertisement in the 1926 issue of *The Purchaser's Guide to the Music Industries* reported that:

"On 3rd February 1920, there was given in Carnegie Hall, New York, a remarkable concert in which five of the world's greatest pianists, Godowsky, Levitzki, Moiseiwitsch, Ornstein and Rubinstein appeared in a joint recital, in which their playing was heard in direct comparison with the Ampico. This most exacting test resulted in a complete triumph for the Ampico."

During the late 1920s, after his divorce, Moiseiwitsch gradually resumed his bachelor habits, but his friends noticed a somewhat cynical aspect to his personality that had previously been absent. He owned a large Packard car, lived a life of luxury, enjoyed romantic attachments to various women, and revelled in the adulation of his audiences, particularly young ones. He was a good conversationalist and raconteur and was addicted to golf. These pastimes, along with his love of card games, comprised his leisure.

On his travels in Britain and abroad he met nearly everyone of note. After one concert in the United States someone pushed a rather shy, grey-haired little man into his dressing room. "He didn't want to come in because he thought you would be too busy to have a word with him", Benno was told. The face seemed very familiar and Benno racked his brain to try to remember who he was. "I'm obviously expected to recognise him", Benno thought. "With his shock of grey hair - is it Harpo Marx? It can't be, surely." The man said something about being jealous of Benno, as he himself was an amateur on the violin. "Surely, Harpo Marx plays the harp", Benno mused. Benno began to ramble on about the spinet and harpsichord, looking for some response that might give a clue to the visitor's identity, but the little man remained bashful and stared solemnly, meeting all overtures in silence. Then he said suddenly, "Tell me, Moiseiwitsch, do you think it is possible to discover a mathematical formula for the melodic line in music? I have often wondered . . . and it seems to me a marvellously exciting field for research." At that point in the conversation Benno realised that the man was Albert Einstein. Later Benno begged Einstein - "For heaven's sake, don't try to formulate melodic lines. Let there be one department in life which is free from science!" Einstein smiled, and promised to abandon the idea.

In 1929 Benno went on a tour of the Far East and whilst he was in Shanghai he met a beautiful and rich society woman. There was a whirlwind romance and he and Anita were married in the same year. He was then nearly 40. The couple came back to England and bought a handsome house in Maidenhead, with a pied-à-terre in London. The two were very happy together and a son, Boris, was born, who as a young man 20 years later was said to look remarkably like Rudolph Valentino. During the 1930s Benno's life settled into a happy routine. He was content, he was playing better than ever, and was acknowledged as one of the world's finest pianists. Moreover he was now completely absorbed into the British musical scene and in 1937 he became a British subject. But soon afterwards, totally unexpectedly, his life was shattered when Anita died as a result of complications following an attack of pneumonia. She was in her early 40s. Naturally Benno was grief-stricken and became more self-absorbed than before. His friends noticed that from then onwards he lacked a lot of the sparkle, humour and gaiety of former days.

With the outbreak of the Second World War in 1939, Benno was once again thrust into a whirl of hectic activity. He welcomed the opportunity to do something to help the war effort, and the constant travel and work helped to prevent him brooding. He played at hundreds of concerts during the war, including a hundred for Mrs Clementine Churchill's 'Aid to Russia' fund, and many observers felt that the flowering of Benno's career achieved its full bloom in this period. Sometimes he would play three concertos in the same concert. His most favoured composers at this period of his life were Beethoven, Chopin and Rachmaninov.

Benno's nephew and biographer Maurice Moiseiwitsch described a typical concert. Whilst walking through London one day during the period of the blitz he happened to notice a poster advertising one of Moiseiwitsch's recitals. Feeling that if Benno was prepared to risk his neck by playing in the blitz he deserved support, Maurice went along. The scene was as one would expect at the time; the hall was full of soldiers, sailors, airmen, WAAFs, WRENs and nurses, all in uniform. Maurice perched himself beside a huge soldier wearing a beret and built like a tank. Benno, wearing a lounge suit, came onto the platform and was accorded a tremendous ovation. He launched into his programme, a typical Moiseiwitsch one with music by Beethoven, Chopin and Schumann, each piece receiving rapturous applause at its conclusion. Benno then played the *Revolutionary Study* of Chopin, a wonderful work full of challenge, heartbreak, defiance, turbulence and drama. The performance was superb and part way through Maurice became conscious of a curious sighing and coughing sound beside him. He turned a little impatiently - and noticed that his neighbour, the huge man, trained to kill, was weeping. This massive soldier continued to sit there, tears streaming down his face, as Benno's emotional performance unfurled. To Maurice Moiseiwitsch it was the most poignant of all experiences.

Over the years Moiseiwitsch had lost none of his skill as a pianist. Indeed, it was generally agreed that as his playing matured it had become even better than ever. As well as his dedication to the music of his old friend, Rachmaninov, and his skilful performances of it, he was also a master of the interpretation of Tchaikovsky's music and the works of Chopin and Schumann. In addition, he excelled in the music of Beethoven, Liszt and in the early French and Italian repertoire, such as the compositions of Rameau and Scarlatti. In short, his range was wide. At his best he was a supreme colourist, giving more contrasts of light and shade than almost any other pianist, combining this with a mastery of tone and dramatic flair unsurpassed even by Cortot.

In the course of his career Moiseiwitsch's interpretations changed, which is not surprising, for old age and youth view things differently. Late in life he took part in a radio programme during which one of his piano rolls dating from 1922 was played as the pianist listened. At the end of the piece the interviewer cast doubt on the accuracy of piano roll recordings, stating that he had heard Moiseiwitsch play the same piece many times in the last few years, and it had never sounded as it did in the performance they had just heard. Moiseiwitsch thought for a moment, and said, "I *used* to play it *exactly* like that when I was young."

Benno idolised the Churchills. He was a frequent visitor to Chequers and during and after the war he often soothed the weary statesman with his music. It was widely thought that he would be knighted for his fund-raising efforts and his part in raising national morale during the war, but in the event he was awarded a C.B.E.

During the 1950s Benno continued to tour but in a more leisurely way. He enjoyed a comfortable prosperity and lived in a large house in St. John's Wood, London, though he was to be found in the Savage or Devonshire Club most evenings of the week. Now in his sixties, he was still a fine pianist. A dignified, silver-haired, rather sad-looking figure, he was still able to stir the emotions of his audiences through his memorable playing.

By the early 1960s Benno's career was near its end. His popularity with the musical public was as great as ever, but his zest for life had gone. When he appeared on television in John Freeman's *Face To Face* programme he seemed to be a tired and dejected old man, smoking throughout the interview and answering the questions rather wearily and without any enthusiasm. He may have been unwell at the time for soon afterwards, in 1962, he was stricken with heart disease and was taken to the London Clinic. He made a partial recovery but it was followed by a relapse and he died in London on 9th April 1963, aged 73.

Benno Moiseiwitsch was a musician who limited himself to playing the piano, which was the one thing he was supremely good at. He never conducted, nor did he teach, and he hardly composed a note of music in his life. But as a pianist he was one of the world's best, a man who will live long in the memories of those who saw and heard him. For those who did not, his records and piano rolls provide a hint of his exceptional talents.

Great Pianists of the Golden Age

Myra Hess

A recital at the National Gallery, 10th April 1943

22. Myra Hess

The famous Viennese piano teacher, Theodor Leschetizky, once asserted in one of his more flippant moods that three ingredients go into the making of a virtuoso pianist; Jewish birth, Slavic ancestry and manifestations of a prodigious musical talent in early childhood. Myra Hess came from a Jewish family but that was the only one of Leschetizky's three requirements she possessed. She was of German, not Slavic extraction, but was as British as roast beef and Yorkshire pudding; indeed, she was thought of as one of the most British of all musicians. Finally, though she was a good musician as a girl, she was never a prodigy. As a teenager and young adult her rise to fame was slow, but once she reached the top she never looked back. She remained at the summit of her profession as a pianist for 50 years and was one of the most respected figures in British music.

The family name of Hess is thought to have originated from the German district of Hessen, from whence Myra's ancestors came. Her grandfather, Samuel Hess, had left his native country in the 1840s in order to found a textile business in London, and in about 1847 he married and bought a house in Islington. Three sons and four daughters were born. Frederick Hess was the fifth child and was born in 1855; he eventually joined his father's textile business and he married in 1884. His bride, Lizzie Jacobs (Lizzie was her real name, not an abbreviation), was one of the five daughters of John Jacobs, a well-known shopkeeper from Paddington. She was a good pianist and had a pleasant singing voice. Four children were born; the eldest, a girl, in 1884, then came two boys, and the youngest, Julia Myra, on 25th February 1890, three days after the birth of Benno Moiseiwitsch in faraway Odessa. The name Julia was after a paternal aunt but it was soon dropped by the family and the little girl was always known as Myra; later in life she regretted this, for she preferred the name Julia to Myra. The family lived an orthodox Jewish life in Kilburn, though not as strictly orthodox as the previous generation, and Myra was brought up in a staid Victorian atmosphere.

Myra began piano lessons at the age of five and soon became a competent pianist but not an outstanding one for her age. Her hands were small, which presented problems, but she enjoyed playing and did not object to long hours of practice which gradually developed her hand and arm muscles. At seven her piano playing had developed to such an extent that her family decided to take her to the Trinity College of Music so that her ability could be assessed by experts. Their opinion was that she was a very capable pianist and they conferred on her the Trinity College Certificate; she was the youngest to receive the award. At eight she made her first public appearance in a charity concert. In March 1901, at the age of 11, she played one of Liszt's Hungarian Rhapsodies in public.

Myra by this time was obviously a very good pianist but not a brilliant prodigy as, for example, was Busoni at the same age. Following a period of study under Julian Pascal and Orlando Morgan at the Guildhall School of Music she won the Steinway Medal and Scholarship in 1902. In the same year she was featured in an article in *The Sketch* which hailed her as "a particularly promising young pianist." Myra was probably the only Jewish girl of her years to enjoy the distinction of seeing her portrait in one of London's leading illustrated weeklies. Photographs of her at this age show her as small, of pleasant appearance, with long black hair.

Myra's musical talent continued to develop - it was a case of steady growth rather than instinctive brilliance. In 1902 she enrolled as a student at the Royal Academy of Music in London where she made friends with Harriet Cohen and Irene Scharrer, both of whom were to become well-known pianists, and it was Irene, a year older than Myra, who persuaded Myra in the autumn of 1903 to join the piano class of her own teacher, Tobias Matthay, at the Academy.

Matthay, who was nicknamed 'The English Leschetizky', was one of the most famous piano teachers Great Britain has produced and possessed impeccable musical credentials, having as a young man won a scholarship to the Royal Academy where he studied under such eminent Victorian musicians as Sir William Sterndale Bennett, Sir Arthur Sullivan and Ebenezer Prout. Apart from Irene and Myra, Matthay's pupils included Arnold Bax and Eric Coates. Bax described Irene and Myra as "two small and eternally giggling girls". Irene at an early age had a remarkable technique. Once, after she had played the Chopin *Black Key* Étude for her professors, one of them said: "Now play it on the white keys." After a moment's pause she did, brilliantly. Myra at the same age did not have that sort of ability, but Irene's skill acted as a spur to her and accelerated her development.

Myra and Irene remained lifelong friends and often played together in later years. Both girls got on famously with Tobias Matthay ("Uncle Tobs") who soon discovered that Myra was an 'undisciplined' pianist, and he reshaped her playing onto a firm technical footing. He also helped her to conquer an inherent nervousness when playing in public and always urged her to "Enjoy yourself - enjoy the music." With the College's permission, Myra in her teens was giving an increasing number of public performances and by 1905, at 15, she had played in most of London's smaller concert halls.

Throughout her years at the Royal Academy Myra's skills steadily developed, and before leaving in 1906 she had carried off all the Academy honours, including a prize for composition in 1905 for the best English ballad and the prestigious Gold Medal for Pianoforte. Tobias Matthay was the only piano teacher Myra ever had, apart from her childhood ones. She trusted his musical judgments implicitly and after she became an established artist she used to visit him at his country home in Surrey before each concert season so that he could preview her programmes and offer advice. This continued until Matthay died in 1945. During Myra's long and distinguished career her admiring public found it difficult to believe, especially those in the United States, that her musicianship was the result of study with a single teacher, and an Englishman at that.

In 1907, when she was 17, Myra made her official debut in a major London concert hall. She hired the Queen's Hall, and also the young Mr Thomas Beecham and his New Symphony Orchestra, in a concert that cost her £87 to stage and brought in £80. The loss was of little importance - the purpose of the concert was to put herself 'on the map' in a big concert where the national critics were present. She played the Beethoven G major Concerto, the Saint-Saëns C minor Concerto and a group of solos including pieces by Chopin and Brahms. Myra was given an ovation by the audience and good notices in the press, but the success of the concert did not lead to immediate engagements. Long-term success had to be earned the hard way. In this concert Myra played a Steinway piano although until the start of the First World War she usually played a Bechstein. During the war the Bechstein Company, being German, was forced to close its showrooms and concert hall, Bechstein Hall in Wigmore Street. The hall re-opened under new management after the war as Wigmore Hall, which it has remained. After 1920 Myra played only Steinway pianos.

On 25th January 1908 Myra gave a solo recital at London's Aeolian Hall - again well received - and two months later at the same hall she appeared in an all-Beethoven recital, a daring choice of programme in those days. Myra's Promenade Concert debut took place on 2nd September 1908 when she played Liszt's E flat Concerto under Henry Wood for a three guinea fee. This was the first of 92 concerts in which she appeared with the famous conductor. Sir Henry said 30 years later, referring to Myra's debut:

"Myra Hess has never lost the fascination she exerted over her audience then. Her musicianship has matured - whose does not in 30 years? - but she was the great artist, even then."

But financial success was slow in coming and the years from 1908 to 1914 were lean ones in which she supported herself financially mainly by teaching. Many years later, in the 1930s, she was asked by an interviewer if her reputation was assured after her Queen's Hall debut in 1907. She replied:

"No. It took me years before I was established. People think because I have a good time now, it all came easily. For years I had to make my living by teaching. I had a very slow success. My reputation in England was built by giving a recital every season, and it took every penny I could save to pay for it."

In 1907 Myra was introduced to Aldo Antionetti, a rising young violin virtuoso who had already appeared with leading orchestras on the continent. They often appeared on the concert platform together over the next couple of years and by 1910 the couple were in love. In 1910 Myra went to Holland at the invitation of friends and made a short concert tour with Aldo, playing in the smaller halls. He wanted to marry her but she refused him because he wanted her to give up her career after marriage, which she was not prepared to do. After the breakdown of their romance he soon married someone else and disappeared from her life. Myra never did marry and the Antionetti relationship seems to have been her only real romance. Later in life she received other proposals of marriage but rejected them. She was happily settled in the routine of her career by then.

Myra always loved her music. She once spent a summer holiday with friends and they decided to hire an upright piano so that she could practise. On the day it was due to arrive she insisted on going to meet it. It was on a carrier's open cart, but undeterred she climbed aboard, found a crate to use as a piano stool and, much to the amusement of onlookers, she played from this precarious perch as the cart and contents trundled their way on a three-mile journey along an unmade road to her friends' home.

In 1912 Myra made her first appearance at an important Dutch concert when she stood in for someone who was ill and played the Schumann Concerto at the Concertgebouw. Shortly afterwards she stood in for Carl Friedberg at another concert in Holland. Both these concerts were a brilliant success and through them Myra became as well-known in Holland as in London. They were followed by a tour of England in 1914. It was only then that she was becoming nationally known in her own land.

From about 1910 Myra's relationship with her father was increasingly strained and eventually they became estranged. He had been brought up in a strict Victorian, Jewish environment and believed it was the duty of unmarried daughters to forego their ambitions and devote themselves to the whims and needs of their parents. Myra could not accept that view and moreover she rebelled at the Jewish orthodoxy whose practices seemed to her to be archaic and stuffy. Myra's father's business was doing badly and he eventually went bankrupt. Myra was not earning much in those days as her concert appearances were few and far between. Only her teaching enabled her to eke out a meagre income.

The breaking point in Myra's uneasy relationship with her father came when he urged her to play in the music halls in order to earn some money. She regarded this as an insult to her artistic integrity; the final straw in a series of differences. This happened in 1914 and she decided there was no alternative but to leave home; commonplace enough now but unusual then. She went to live with friends and at the same time turned her back on Jewish orthodoxy. Her mother was not part of these disputes. Indeed, after Myra's estrangement from her father, who died in 1916, Myra became closer to her mother than before. Her mother lived until 1930, dying at the age of 67. She was buried alongside her husband in the Jewish Cemetery at Golders Green.

In 1916 Myra bought a house in North London, the first of three London homes. She had always lived in London and was to live there for the rest of her life. During the 1914-18 war her opportunites to give conventional public concerts were limited but she helped to maintain the nation's morale, as did several of the pianists in this book, by playing to entertain servicemen, hospital patients, etc. Like other musicians she had to be careful what she played during the war because of anti-German feeling. Even Schumann's *Warum?* had to be billed as *Pourquoi?*

When the war ended Myra, at 28, was able to resume her concert career. She was now finding it much easier to secure concert engagements. In the years 1918 to 1920 she appeared 54 times with orchestras in London and the provinces and by 1920 she was in such demand that she played in nearly a hundred concerts during the year. In 1921 she gave three sold-out recitals in a month and was able to command a fee of 20 or 25 guineas for each appearance - a substantial sum in those days.

A big breakthrough followed in 1922 in the form of an invitation to tour the USA. Myra's New York debut was on 17th January 1922 at the Aeolian Hall. The Aeolian Company's buildings housed an auditorium with a seating capacity of 1200. For many years it was the home of the New York Symphony Orchestra founded by Leopold Damrosch and conducted by his son Walter. Just 66 people attended Myra's New York debut - about usual, so it was said, for an unknown artist. But the 66 included well-known critics; they gave her wonderful reports, and her reputation was made. The *Tribune* critic remarked:

"She played her way into the hearts and minds of the American audience".

This was a prophetic statement, for Myra was always a big favourite in

America. She was to continue to delight her audiences there for the next 40 years. Later in her debut tour of the USA another critic wrote:

"This young woman has captured the American public. Her entrance is greeted with a storm of applause which many pianists fail to receive at the end of a recital".

Myra's technical skill won much praise. A critic observed:

"She is a pianist of the new school, whose playing has clarity, textual accuracy, delicate color and classical proportion."

Not only was Myra Hess a brilliant pianist, but her pleasant looks and serene stage presence undoubtedly also contributed to her success. Her 'presence' seems to have been a key to her popularity. Though not beautiful, she appeared so on stage and somehow seemed to captivate her audience.

After that first tour Myra toured the USA and Canada nearly every year up to the outbreak of the Second World War. Her North American tours would begin in December or January and on their completion she would work mainly in Britain or Holland, where she had an enormous following, for the rest of the year, with a month or two in Britain during the summer as a working holiday. Sometimes she toured other European countries. Her agent in the USA (except in Boston where she had a different agent) was Annie Friedberg, sister of the pianist Carl Friedberg. Annie took a 20 per cent fee but as far as Myra was concerned it was money well spent for Annie was an excellent agent who was very adept at securing remunerative contracts for her client. Moreover, Myra liked her, and they remained personal friends until Annie's death in 1953. From the late 1920s onwards Myra was one of the big box-office attractions in the USA, comparable in popularity with Paderewski and Hofmann.

Myra's famous transcription for piano of Bach's Cantata No. 147, *Jesu, Joy of Man's Desiring* was made early in the 1920s. She had long been interested in the Cantata, having heard it in a chapel service around the year 1916, and after she heard it again at the London Bach Festival in April 1920 she decided to arrange it for the piano. She did so, and played it at recitals (America first heard it in 1925) and privately on a number of occasions for friends and colleagues. One of them was Hubert Foss, head of the music section of the Oxford University Press, and he persuaded her to let his company publish it. The first edition appeared in 1926 and it soon became a best seller. It was published in several versions; for piano; piano (4 hands); two pianos; and so on.

Just as Percy Grainger's *Country Gardens* made more money for him in royalties than any one of his other compositions, so Myra's *Jesu, Joy of Man's Desiring* made more money for her in royalties than she ever made from her 'unadulterated' Bach playing. Everywhere she went she was expected to play the piece and it became indelibly associated with her name. Myra's favourite story about the piece concerned a British soldier heard whistling it on a train during the Second World War. "Do you like Bach?" someone asked. "That's not Bach, that's Myra Hess!" was the indignant reply. *Jesu, Joy* was not the only one of Bach's pieces she transcribed for the piano; there were several others including the *Adagio* from the Organ Toccata in C major, No. 1 and *Sleepers, Wake* from Cantata No. 140. She also made piano arrangements of music by other baroque composers. But *Jesu, Joy* remained the best known of her transcriptions.

A mark of Myra's concert successes in the USA was the presentation to her of a Steinway grand piano by the makers in 1925, and afterwards the Steinway Company allowed her two grands for her exclusive use on tours. Earlier she had had to make do with whatever instrument the particular hall contained. The years 1922 to 1939 were marvellous ones for Myra. In 1932 she played in 38 cities in the USA and during the tour played Bach's Triple Concerto with Harold Bauer and Ernest Schelling. She always travelled with a companion who was also a friend. In her earlier years it was Miss Hare, her companion and secretary, until her death in 1930. After that it was Anita Gunn, a local friend who also acted as her secretary. She went with Myra on her 1931 tour of the United States and continued to go with her on her travels for the next 30 years, except during the Second World War when Myra had to find another secretary and companion because Anita was working as an ambulance driver in London.

An important aspect of Myra's career was her teaching. As a young woman she had been forced to teach to make a living, but she soon discovered she was good at it and enjoyed it. Consequently she continued to teach throughout her life in the limited periods when she was not on tour, and many talented musicians passed through her hands.

In 1939 Myra completed her 15th tour of the USA. Apart from her brilliant and consistent successes on the concert platform in North America, Britain, Holland and other European countries including Eastern Europe, she also became a regular radio performer. Her first broadcast was from Savoy Hill on 22nd July 1927 and in the 1930s she was one of the BBC's most popular artists. She was awarded the C.B.E. in the New Year's Honours List of 1936 whilst recovering from an operation for appendicitis. Her health at that time had not been too good; two years previously she had had to have a radical mastectomy operation following cystic mastitis. However, she recovered completely from this and was soon touring as energetically as ever.

In Myra's early days as a concert pianist her repertoire was wide-ranging and included many compositions by contemporary composers such as Bax, Bridge, Debussy, Delius, de Falla, Granados, Ravel and Scriabin. As she became successful and famous she concentrated more on the earlier composers whose music she preferred and the others almost disappeared from her programmes. When an interviewer asked her later in her career for her opinion of the modern French composers she told him:

"Their works are the shrimp cocktails of music. Every now and again I, too, like shrimp cocktails, but for a steady diet I prefer roast beef."

For Myra that meant Bach, Beethoven, Brahms, Mozart and Schumann. In the interpretation of the music of composers such as these she was superb. Her playing had classical precision combined with warmth, poetic imagination, thoughtfulness and humour. A performance by Myra Hess was always marked by her wonderful feel for the music.

When war was declared in 1939 Myra, then 49, immediately cancelled her forthcoming tour of the USA at great financial loss to herself and, unlike some of her fellow musicians, announced that she would stay in England for the duration of the war. At first she worked for the Womens' Voluntary Service (WVS) but soon turned her attention to the problem of what she could do to lift the spirits of the people. All entertainments had shut down and there was an atmosphere of gloom, despondency and cultural blackout. Even the BBC seemed to be offering very little music except Sandy Macpherson's theatre organ which seemed to play all day long.

Myra believed that the morale of the British public would be raised if music of high quality could be presented regularly, preferably daily, in the centre of London. The National Gallery in Trafalgar Square was then standing empty, bereft of its paintings which had been taken away for safety, though the empty frames still hung on the walls, and it seemed an ideal location. Myra and some of her friends approached the Gallery's director, Sir Kenneth Clark (who later wrote and presented the television series *Civilisation*), and he and the Gallery's trustees readily agreed to Myra's proposal to institute daily chamber music concerts there. Myra relinquished a lot of lucrative work to become organiser and regular performer, a task she continued throughout the war, to the benefit of public and artists alike. All artists were paid a fee of five guineas, except Myra herself who took no fee, whether they were famous or up-and-coming. The admission charge was one shilling and proceeds went to the Musicians' Benevolent Fund.

The establishment of the National Gallery Concerts was a great act of faith on Myra's part. That they proved to be such a remarkable success was due largely to her effervescent drive and enthusiasm. The first concert was held on Tuesday, 10th October 1939; no one knew with any certainty how many people to expect, but about 500 chairs were set out. In the event 1,000 turned up and the recital was a triumph. Myra played two sonatas by Scarlatti, Beethoven's *Appassionata* Sonata, two Bach preludes and fugues, some Schubert dances, a waltz and a nocturne by Chopin, three intermezzi by Brahms, and her own arrangement of *Jesu, Joy of Man's Desiring*. Sir Kenneth Clark wrote later:

"The people had come with anxious, hungry faces, but as they listened to the music and looked at Myra's rapt expression they lost the thought of their private worries. I have never seen faces so transformed, and said to myself, "This is how men and women must have looked at the great preachers who gave them back their courage and faith." "

The concerts were to last six and a half years and took place at midday, Monday to Friday. They were quite informal; there was no advanced booking and there were no seat reservations. In those days most people had an important job to do, but they came to the concerts in their lunch breaks and were free to come and go between movements. At a later date a canteen was opened.

Myra played once a week or once every two weeks on average and gave 146 recitals in all; she attended most of the others. From September 1940 to June 1941 they were held in the National Gallery's downstairs shelter because of the blitz. Myra once expressed her thanks to two artists for playing on as bombs could be heard exploding nearby. One of them said: "But we were playing Beethoven. What better way to die than playing Beethoven?" The concerts won for Myra a special place in the affection of the British people. She could so easily have gone to the USA as some other musicians had done, especially as she was so popular there, but she chose to stay on in her own home city in spite of the bombs. Members of the Royal Family, in particular Queen Elizabeth (now the Queen Mother) attended the concerts on a number of occasions and many of them were broadcast. Myra was created a Dame Commander of the British Empire in the Birthday Honours of June 1941 and she played at the 1,000th concert held on 23rd July 1943. After the huge blitzes in London in the early 1940s there was a period of relative calm and it was then that the concerts reverted to the main hall in the National Gallery. Later in the war flying bombs began to rain down on London with little or no warning and once again the concerts were held in an atmosphere of danger and tension.

The National Gallery Concerts were such a great success that when the war ended Myra and many other people wanted them to continue, believing that music should have a permanent place in the National Gallery building.

But the Gallery's trustees were against the idea, arguing that music was not part of the building's heritage or tradition and that it must therefore revert in due course to its intended purpose. And so the paintings gradually started to return. A year's extension of the agreement with the concert organisers was granted so that music could continue over a transitional period but, much to Myra's disappointment, the concerts finally had to stop and the 1,698th and last of the midday concerts was given on Wednesday, 10th April 1946. Myra did not play on that occasion, but made a speech in which she spoke with great feeling, thanking all those who had helped in making the concerts such a success. Her own final appearance in the concerts had taken place five days earlier, on 5th April, before a capacity auduence of 1,036 people, when she had played two Beethoven sonatas, Op. 110 and 111. She had told the audience then that she would be unable to perform at the final concert because the emotion would be too great.

During the years when Myra was organising and playing in these concerts she often played elsewhere, including the wartime Promenade Concerts, and she used also to make short concert tours to various parts of the British Isles. Towards the end of the war she flew to Holland to play before that country was fully liberated.

The war years and the National Gallery Concerts marked the peak of Myra's career, but after the war she still continued to enjoy tremendous popularity, appearing as a solo pianist and also with many notable musicians including Pablo Casals in 1945-46 and Wilhelm Furtwängler and the Berlin Philharmonic Orchestra in 1948. Her regular tours to the USA resumed and were to continue up to her 69th year. The 1950s were in fact vintage years for her, just as the 1930s had been. At her first post-war concert in New York Myra made her entrance in the same old black dress that she had worn pre-war and was given a thunderous ovation lasting for minutes; from this occasion until her last tour she was always greeted with tremendous affection. In these post-war tours she often used to have her sheet music in front of her as she played, and though this surprised the critics at first they soon got used to the idea. Myra in her later years rarely played 'fireworks' music such as that of Liszt in public, but she gave fine interpretations of the classical music in which she specialised. Someone once said:

"So often we go to a concert to hear so-and-so; with Dame Myra we go to hear the music."

Myra Hess's gramophone recording career spanned 31 years and embraced the eras of the 78rpm record (from 1928 when she made her first recording to 1950) and the long-playing disc (from the early 1950s). Her first commercial recordings of 1928 were made for the Columbia Company in the USA. In that year she made over 20 recordings of works by many composers ranging from Bach to de Falla and Ravel. More recordings followed, this time in Britain for Columbia (U.K.) in 1931, 1936 and 1937. Between 1937 and 1950 she recorded for The Gramophone Company (HMV) in London. Most of her post-1931 recordings were of the music of classical composers, but by no means all, for composers such as Matthay (her teacher) and her friend Howard Ferguson featured in her lists. In 1952 she made the first of her long-playing discs for Columbia (USA) - the Mozart Concerto in E flat, K. 271, with the Perpignan Festival Orchestra conducted by Pablo Casals, and followed this up with more records, again for Columbia (USA) in 1953, of music by Brahms, Schubert and Schumann. In 1954 and 1959 she made some long-playing records for HMV in London, the music consisting of compositions by Bach-Hess (*Jesu, Joy of Man's Desiring*), Beethoven, Brahms, Granados, Mendelssohn Scarlatti and Schumann.

Myra's records always sold well and are of excellent musical quality. Many a music lover brought up in the 1930s will remember her famous 78rpm recording of *Jesu, Joy*, coupled with Scarlatti's Sonata in G major (Longo 387), surely one of the best and most popular classical 78s of all time. In recent years many of Myra's records have been re-issued, first in long-playing form and now on compact disc, as have the records of many other great pianists of the past. Many non-commercially issued recordings of Myra Hess's playing exist in addition to the records mentioned above, in the form of recordings of live concerts and studio performances made by the BBC and several other organisations. Some of her wartime recitals at the National Gallery were recorded on film.

Pre-dating all these gramophone records were 15 Duo-Art piano roll recordings, two of them 4-handed arrangements with Harold Bauer, which Myra made for the Aeolian Company (the only manufacturer for whom she recorded piano rolls) in the period 1922 to 1929. Most were recorded in New York but a few were made in London. These rolls were made at a fairly early stage in her career (she was then in her thirties) when she played music by a wide range of composers. The rolls included several compositions by composers who were then modern, such as Debussy and Szymanowski and little-known composers such as Burgmein (a pen-name of Giulio Ricordi), Paradies and Pierné. The great composers were nevertheless well represented by Bach, Beethoven, Brahms and Scarlatti. The Scarlatti roll is of the G major Sonata and must be one of the most delightful piano rolls ever made. Perhaps its early commercial success was the reason she recorded the piece on disc for Columbia in 1928.

Myra had a good sense of humour. A favourite party trick was to entertain friends by playing a fiery Chopin study - at the end she would toss to the admiring audience an orange she had been holding in her palm during the performance. She could do a good imitation of Queen Victoria (or at any rate the popular perception of Queen Victoria) and in her younger days was something of a practical joker. She had a warm and generous nature and helped many young musicians.

In the post-war years Myra Hess was acknowledged as one of the most respected figures in British music. The regard in which she was held can be gauged by the fact that seven British universities conferred honorary degrees on her. They were Cambridge, Durham, Leeds, London, Manchester, Reading and St. Andrews.

Myra was still at her peak as she entered the 1960s and her own 70s. On 13th February 1960, 12 days before her 70th birthday, she played Beethoven's last three sonatas at the Carnegie Hall, followed by several encores. Later in the year she played in some concerts at the Royal Festival Hall. It seemed that she would go on performing for years more. But it was not to be and her final years were sad ones. In September 1960 she suffered a mild heart attack but recovered well enough to continue her normal engagements a few weeks later. She began another tour of America in January 1961. She was not feeling well from the start and after giving only two concerts in which she was not at her best, she suffered a stroke at her New York hotel in February. The rest of the tour was cancelled and she was brought home to London in April, which was the earliest she was allowed to travel.

Myra fought her illness, which had left some paralysis of the left arm, very bravely, so much so that she was able to appear on 8th September 1961 at the Royal Albert Hall with Sir Adrian Boult, and at the Royal Festival Hall on 28th September, when she played two Mozart concertos. But she was struggling not only against the effects of the stroke but also increasing rheumatism and arthritis in her hands, which in addition were getting cracked and sore. On 31st October 1961 she played the Mozart A major Concerto, K. 488, again with Sir Adrian Boult, at a concert commemorating the 21st anniversary of the Battle of Britain. This turned out to be Myra's last public performance, though she made a live broadcast recital in December of the same year and a recorded one in January 1962, neither of which was said to be up to her usual standard. By then her infirmities were taking their toll. In hope, a number of future engagements were 'pencilled in', but no-one except perhaps Myra herself thought there was much hope of her fulfilling them.

When Myra at last accepted the fact that her career as a concert pianist was over, a period of deep depression set in. Playing the piano was the only life she had ever wanted. To alleviate her depression she extended her teaching, a notable pupil being Stephen Bishop-Kovacevich, who made his Promenade Concert debut in August 1962 at a concert Myra was to have given. But Myra, who had always had such a tremendous rapport with her audiences, missed her 50 happy years of concert life very badly, and because of her arthritic hands even the joy of being able to play informally to her friends in retirement was denied her. Her condition was not helped by unsuccessful surgery in 1964, and after a prolonged period of poor health she died at her North London home on 25th November 1965, aged 75. It was an unhappy end to an outstanding life.

In 1972 many of Myra's musical effects were bequeathed to the British Museum, including the original manuscript of *Jesu, Joy of Man's Desiring*, her collected concert programmes, 1907-62, and the files and indexes of the National Gallery Concerts, 1939-46.

Myra Hess will be remembered as one of the most notable pianists Great Britain has produced, and a brilliant interpreter of the classical composers. Over and above that, she was a much-loved figure, respected and admired for her work in the dark days of the war when she stayed in London and made a magnificent contribution to national morale by playing through the blitz. It was her finest hour, and her actions embodied the spirit of the British people.

Great Pianists of the Golden Age

Walter Gieseking

23. Walter Gieseking

Walter Gieseking was an interesting pianist and in some ways a paradoxical figure. A physically large man, one might have expected him to be renowned for his fire and power, but instead he was famous for his delicacy of touch and tone. He was born of German parents and lived most of his life in Germany, but it was not the German composers who were his forte. On the contrary, he was world-famous for his interpretation of the music of the French impressionists. Undoubtedly he was one of the world's major pianists for 30 years from the early 1920s. He made a number of piano rolls and recorded a vast amount of music for the gramophone. Many of his records were considered to be classics in their day.

It was in Lyons, in the south of France, that Walter Wilhelm Gieseking was born on 5th November 1895 - bonfire night in Britain but just another day in France. Both his parents were German. His father, Wilhelm, was a distinguished physician and entomologist then living in France. His mother's name was Martha (née Bethke). Dr Gieseking was a keen amateur musician who played the flute and piano, and he ensured that his young son was brought up in an educated and musical environment.

When Walter was only four, Dr Gieseking took up a post in Italy and it was on the French and Italian Rivieras that Walter spent most of his boyhood, though the family's travels took them through much of the south of France and Italy. Walter claimed that he had little formal musical tuition in his early years, as he explained many years later:

"I was, from a tiny chap, very fond of music, and picked up my piano playing somehow by myself. I read and played everything I could lay hands on."

His piano playing had in fact begun at the age of four. His father insisted that he should learn two instruments, so for a time he practised the violin as well as the piano. He did not reach a very advanced stage in his violin playing but fifty years later he said:

"Even now I can still extract wondrous sounds from a violin, rendering faithfully the screeches of an angry cat."

In his early piano lessons Walter was probably instructed in correct fingering by his father, for he appears not to have had any other teacher at that stage. Nor did he go to school; the family was well-off and he was educated privately at home. Like all future concert pianists, Walter was a bright little child who took to music like a duck to water. He also had a great aptitude for languages and at quite an early age became fluent in French, German and Italian. So, whilst his father attended to his medical duties and collected butterflies, Walter developed his various skills, musical and otherwise.

In 1911 the family moved to Hanover. Walter, at 16, had by then become a proficient pianist and was admitted to the Hanover Conservatory where he joined the class of Professor Karl Leimer. It seems that Leimer's method of teaching was similar in many ways to that of Leschetizky, perhaps the greatest of all piano teachers. He believed in 'relaxation'. Leimer's teaching philosophy was:

"Achieve absolute and immediate repose between one effort and the next, so as to avoid any contraction of the fingers or hardening of touch. All the rest will be added to you."

Leimer's methods suited Walter, who was to follow his teacher's advice for the whole of his career. Leimer was in fact the only professional piano teacher Gieseking ever had. In 1912, a year after joining Leimer's class, Walter was allowed to make his first public appearance. When war broke out in August 1914 Walter, who was then 18, was allowed to defer his call-up in order to continue his studies at the Conservatory. He was such an accomplished pianist that in 1915, when he was 19, he appeared in a series of six recitals in Hanover, in the course of which he played the complete set of Beethoven's 32 piano sonatas. In 1916, at the age of 20, he graduated from the Conservatory.

As soon as he graduated Gieseking was conscripted for military service and spent the rest of the war (1916-18) as a regimental bandsman in the German army. In this capacity he played as a jazz pianist or tympanist in his battalion symphony orchestra. It was fortunate indeed for him that his superiors delegated him to that particular duty, in view of the slaughter that was occurring daily on the European battlefields.

Soon after the end of the war in 1918 he was demobilised. Like most graduate students, Gieseking, now 23, had virtually no funds and had to set about earning himself some money. However, he had plenty of determination and knew how to teach. He soon established a small clientèle of pupils, and at the same time he began to earn additional money as an accompanist, chamber music player and opera coach. He also secured engagements as a solo pianist. His early recital programmes included a lot of new or unfamiliar music, and he became a champion of composers such as Busoni, Schoenberg, Szymanowski and Hindemith. His rapidly growing reputation ensured that he was becoming known outside Germany and he was also meeting many established musicians. In 1923 he gave the first performance of Pfitzner's Piano Concerto with Fritz Busch as conductor, a highly successful event that led to many more engagements in Germany and elsewhere. So at last he was making his mark, though his rise had been far from meteoric.

One of the reasons that led to Gieseking's increasing success, apart from his excellent technique, was his ability to learn new pieces very quickly. In 1926 he told the music journalist Harriette Brower:

"To commit to memory is a very simple matter to me, unless the composition happens to be very difficult. A great deal can be accomplished by reading the music through away from the piano. As I read it the eye takes in the characters on the printed page while the ear hears them mentally. After a few times reading through, I often know the piece, can go to the piano and play it from memory."

Nearly thirty years later he said virtually the same thing in an interview with Bernard Gavoty of *Le Figaro*:

"When I began to play in public I had no time at all for learning new works on the piano. It then occurred to me that it is better to study the music with the eyes than with the fingers, since visual memory is less fallible than muscular, especially in the case of really complicated music, such as the atonalities of Stravinsky, Hindemith and Schoenberg. This I can learn much more thoroughly by simply reading it. I work in the train; the music is burned into my brain and, once fixed there, cannot be dislodged. I need only turn over the score to assure myself that not one note has been forgotten. Apart from that, I trust to my fingers, so thoroughly drilled in the past. They go where they should."

These were no idle words; Gieseking's ability to learn quickly without recourse to a piano was well recognised, and there are many examples of his having learned long and complicated compositions in a day or two.

Gieseking's gift for rapidly memorising a musical score was also possessed by one of the 20th century's greatest pianists, Josef Hofmann. Hofmann's method of learning new pieces and of playing them through in his mind, identical to Gieseking's, was often puzzling to his friends. They would come into a room where he was sitting in an easy chair with his eyes closed or, sometimes, gazing into space. When asked what he was doing he would say "Practising." For both of them the preparation in the mind was all-important; having decided what needed to be done and exactly how a piece should be played, they knew their fingers had the ability to accomplish it. To them the actual execution was a minor matter.

In 1923 Gieseking gave his first London recital. It was well received by the public and by the critics, who commented favourably on his remarkable command of delicate shades of tone. From that time onwards he was a regular visitor to Britain. In 1925, already regarded at the age of 29 as one of the leading young concert pianists in Europe, he was married in Germany to Annie Haake of Hanover. In 1928 he made his Paris debut. Contemporary reports say that he "enraptured Paris".

It is a generally accepted fact that a pianist cannot be regarded as a truly international figure until a successful tour of the United States has been achieved. In Gieseking's case this occurred in 1926. His American debut was at the Aeolian Hall, New York on 22nd February of that year when he played the Hindemith Concerto with the New York Symphony Orchestra. It was the first performance of the work in America. Reporting on his debut appearance, the eminent critic W.J. Henderson remarked:

"Yet a young man, his recital repertoire is one of the four largest amongst present day pianists . . . Not a pianist of bold, thundering type, but one of genuine musicianship, dignity of purpose and distinguished accomplishment."

In similar vein, Olin Downes said in *The New York Times*:

"He has the touch and the technical proficiency of the true artist."

Gieseking made a number of piano roll recordings for the Welte Company of Freiburg when he was still in his twenties. His first rolls date from about 1923 when he was 27. About 28 Welte rolls were issued. The earlier ones were recorded in Freiburg and the later ones at Welte's American headquarters in New York during Gieseking's first tour of the United States. The music featured in these recordings was by Bach (3 rolls), Beethoven (2), Brahms (1), Debussy (11), Grieg (1), Liszt (1), Niemann (3), Ravel (1), Anton Rubinstein (1), Schoenberg (1), Schubert (1) and Richard Strauss (2). Years later (after Gieseking's death) some of them were re-issued on long-playing gramophone discs. The fact that no less than 11 Debussy rolls are included is a measure of Gieseking's reputation, even then, as an interpreter of Debussy's music. Also included amongst the Welte rolls is an excellent 2-roll set of Bach's Italian Concerto in F.

The Welte Company must have had a high regard for Gieseking, as they featured the young pianist prominently in their advertisements alongside such established masters as Pachmann and Paderewski. Moreover they saw fit to use his name in the list of those testifying to the efficacy of the Welte system. A statement attributed to Gieseking appeared in the Welte advertisements in the 1920s:

"The reproduction of my piano-playing in the Welte-Mignon is by far the most finished and faithful that I have ever heard and exceeds greatly my highest expectations. I am full of sincerest unstinted admiration."

About the same time as he recorded the first of his Welte rolls, Gieseking was contracted by the Hupfeld Company of Leipzig, which was only about 120 miles from his home in Hanover, to record for them, and 39 of his piano rolls were issued by the company. The composers represented were Bach (7 rolls), Brahms (4), Chopin (1), Debussy (7), Liszt (1), Mussorgsky (4), Niemann (6), Ravel (2), Schoenberg (1), Schubert (1), Schumann (3) and

Szymanowski (2). There are some interesting compositions amongst them. The Bach rolls include a 4-roll set of his English Suite No. 6; the Brahms rolls are all intermezzi (from Op. 116, 117, 118 and 119); the Mussorgsky rolls are a 4-roll set of *Pictures at an Exhibition*; and the Schumann rolls are a 3-roll set of his Fantasia, Op. 17. Hupfeld rolls were licensed for distribution in Britain through Blüthner of London and were available as 'Triphonola' reproducing-piano rolls or 'Animatic hand-played artist rolls'. 'Hand-played' rolls recorded faithfully the pianist's performance except that, unlike true 'reproducing' rolls, the dynamics were not reproduced automatically by the roll; they had to be provided by the person playing the roll, with guidance from information printed on the roll itself. One of the 'Animatic' rolls was reviewed in the October 1925 issue of *The Musical Times*. William Delasaire, the reviewer, reported:

"The Animatic rolls include a specially distinguished performance of Debussy's *Reflets dans L'Eau* by Walter Gieseking. I fancy that we have been privileged to hear him twice in this country, when his playing was universally praised, its most remarkable feature being, I thought, his wonderful control of the softer tone-colours. In this roll, of course, we are left to emulate these to the best of our ability, but all the beauty of his tempi and nuance are represented, supplying a powerful stimulus to the imagination."

Some of the Hupfeld rolls that Gieseking made in Germany were technically adapted under licence by the Ampico Company in America and four of them were issued by that company in 1926 as Ampico reproducing rolls. They were:

La Damoiselle Élue (Prelude in C major)	*Debussy*	Issued April 1926
Singende Fontane (Singing Fountain) (Nocturne, Op. 30 in D major)	*Niemann*	Issued April 1926
Ballade, Op. 38, No. 2 in F major	*Chopin*	Issued May 1926
Hommage à Rameau (Images, Series 1, No. 2)	*Debussy*	Issued August 1926

Again Debussy's music features strongly, which shows that Gieseking was accepted as a leading interpreter of Debussy's music even in the mid 1920s. Nor is it surprising that he recorded a piece by Walter Niemann (1876-1953), a minor German composer who wrote over 150 piano pieces, for Niemann was the type of musician whose work Gieseking liked to promote. (He had recorded the same piece for Welte as well as Hupfeld.) What is more surprising is that one of the rolls was of a Chopin ballade, for Gieseking never felt much affinity with Chopin's music and rarely played any of his compositions in public. Perhaps the Hupfeld Company had asked him to record it in order to fill a gap in their catalogued list of Chopin's works.

It is clear from William Delasaire's remarks in *The Musical Times* and the remarks of other critics quoted earlier that the 30 year old pianist was already celebrated for his control of the more delicate shades of the instrument. This was to remain his hallmark throughout his career. Even then, as a relatively young man, he was acclaimed as a musician of outstanding skill and sensitivity. Moreover, his readiness to tackle contemporary music stood him in good stead as not many musicians were prepared to do so.

One of the reasons for Gieseking's wonderful skill in the interpretation of the compositions of Debussy and Ravel is simply that he liked their music. He once wrote:

"It is interesting to see that the American concert audiences are, generally speaking, much more familiar with Debussy's music than the listeners in several European countries, where Debussy is still considered as a dangerous revolutionary. In America Debussy (and also Ravel) is not a "modern composer" but one of the greatest creative geniuses of music.

I am proud and happy that my name is so often associated with Debussy's music, this marvellous music that seems to me so perfectly natural - and naturally perfect, so absolutely sincere - and beautiful!"

On the subject of Ravel's music, Gieseking wrote:

"I feel boundless admiration and affection for the works of Maurice Ravel, for not only are they wondrously beautiful, but they also contain the most pianistic music yet written and employ the resources of the modern piano in the most perfect and universal manner.

Maurice Ravel will for ever be among the great and glorious names of music, not merely French, but European."

In the 1930s Gieseking's life followed a regular pattern. Much of the year was of course spent in touring to give concerts and recitals. About two months of each year were spent at home (he had moved to Wiesbaden) with his wife and their two young daughters, Jutta and Freya. One of his hobbies was mountain climbing and he was also interested in entomology. In the latter respect he followed in the footsteps of his father and from his travels he used to bring back quantities of butterflies that he had collected. Gieseking lived a placid, homely life and his physical appearance did not call to mind the popular image of a concert pianist. On tour he could easily have been taken for a family doctor or business man. Huge, bald, and with grey-blue eyes, he looked rather like a much enlarged version of the former Soviet President, Mikhail Gorbachev.

Gieseking was fortunate in that he did not need to practise very much to maintain his skills. In 1926 he told Harriette Brower:

"I really need very little practise, as I do not forget what I have learned; my fingers don't forget either. In the summer I take a couple of months off for rest and recreation, and often I do not touch a piano or even see one, in all that time. But this seems to make no difference to my playing. After the vacation I can return and at once give a recital or play with orchestra without the least difficulty. All of which proves I do not need much visible practise. During my concert season, of course, I have little time for practise, but I can study new works, on trains, as I travel about."

Thirty years later Gieseking was still telling interviewers much the same thing. His standards of playing had been maintained throughout this period, which proves that his claim was indeed true.

The delicacy of tone produced by a man of Gieseking's large size was remarkable. He was 6ft 3 inches tall and burly to match, but caressed the keys like Pachmann. Bernard Gavoty, describing a typical Gieseking performance (albeit in flowery terms) tells us:

" . . . he possesses an athletic body and powerful great arms. Beside him the piano is a mere toy. To reduce himself to its proportions he slumps forward on the leather-covered stool, bending his great height almost double. The massive dome of his head, framed in silver, is bowed almost to the keyboard. He raises his hands; just as he is about to strike the notes he checks them; you would think they weighed a hundredweight apiece for his face turns crimson with the strain. Suddenly they drop and there follows, not the crash we are expecting, but the most etherial of pianissimi. We hold our breath so as not to break the spell. If we shut our eyes the illusion is complete. This is no onslaught but a caress; not hammer blows but the flutter of moths' wings. At Gieseking's touch the piano is transformed from a percussion instrument into a magic chest from which his charmed fingers draw the slumbering harmonies. We open our eyes and all is changed. Can the enchanter really be this giant in agony, frenziedly twisting his head like a man in a steel trap? Can Gieseking really be this maniac who is desperately tearing the heart out of the piano? Unseen, his hands glide over the keyboard; seen, they almost smash it to pieces. It is like a sledge-hammer gently cracking a nut. Infinite power is being used for the most delicate operation."

Similar sentiments were later expressed, rather more tersely, by another critic writing in *The Times*:

"His physical height and bulk served to re-inforce the impression of delicacy in his playing. He would sit hunched, but still towering over the keyboard and from his fingers would pour ripples of Scarlatti, diamond-like Mozart, and multi-hued washes of exquisite tone in Debussy. But he was more than a miniaturist and could command breadth and intellectual grasp, though compared with his elder contemporary, Schnabel, he was a romantic who did not rely on Beethoven and Brahms for his recital programmes so much as on composers with whom sensibility was the predominant consideration."

Gieseking's contemporaries were united in their view that his playing of Debussy was unsurpassed; many thought no other pianist could even equal him in the playing of his music. Much the same could be said of his playing of Ravel. In his interpretations of the music of these two composers, contemporary critics referred to various qualities that made his playing special, including transparency and delicacy of tone, supreme refinements of nuance and colour, and dexterity of technique.

Whether it was Gieseking's cosmopolitan upbringing in France and Italy that enabled him to identify with the music of Debussy and Ravel, or just that he liked their music, no one can tell. Cortot was a great French pianist but did not concentrate his talents on French music. But although Gieseking excelled in Debussy, Ravel and a few modern composers of lesser standing, some of the great German and Austrian composers also figured in his repertoire. In particular, Gieseking was a noted exponent of Mozart's music. He also played all the Beethoven sonatas often, and had done so since playing them all in six recitals at the age of 19. He played the Beethoven concertos regularly and Schumann's piano works were included in his repertoire, as were the keyboard compositions of Bach and Scarlatti. Only Chopin, of the great composers, failed to figure regularly in his recitals.

When the Second World War began in 1939 Gieseking was still only 43 years old and was at the peak of his powers. He spent the war in Germany and, like Cortot, left himself open to allegations of collaboration with the Nazi regime by playing in public under the approving eye of the Nazi hierarchy. But whereas Cortot played in France under an occupying force, Gieseking had been domiciled in Germany for nearly 30 years so it is somewhat difficult to see how else he could have conducted himself. Whatever the rights and wrongs of Gieseking's conduct, the Americans took exception. He became the centre of a political controversy when he arrived in the United States early in 1949 for a concert tour. He was accused of wartime cultural collaboration with the Nazis and public protests forced the cancellation of his scheduled performances at Carnegie Hall. He was later cleared by an Allied court in Germany and appeared again before a packed house at a Carnegie Hall recital on 22nd April 1953.

At this stage of his career Gieseking was still travelling widely as a pianist. In the previous year (1952, when he was 56) he had flown 75,000 miles. In one of his tours of Japan in the early 1950s he gave a long series of recitals over a period of seventeen days in the enormous Hyba Hall in Tokyo which had a capacity of 3,500. It was filled at every performance. It was said that before the last recital he gave in the Carnegie Hall in New York the box offices were overwhelmed by people wanting tickets and the hall was sold out in two hours.

Like most pianists, Gieseking composed a few musical items. The main ones among them were:

Quintet for piano, oboe, clarinet, French horn and bassoon (date unknown)

Sonatina for flute and piano   1937

Variations for flute or violin and piano on a theme by Grieg   1938

Serenade for string quartet   1939

He also wrote a number of piano pieces and made several piano transcriptions of songs by Richard Strauss. None of these pieces is regarded as of any great consequence and they are now rarely, if ever, heard.

Following Gieseking's piano roll recordings of the 1920s he went on in the 1930s to make a large number of gramophone records for Columbia. The 1950-51 Columbia catalogue contained more than a page of Gieseking's records, 31 of them in fact, though it has to be remembered that they were all 78rpm discs (this date was just pre-LP) so that several records were required to make up a long piece such as a concerto. Included amongst the recordings were some of Debussy's music and two Beethoven sonatas (Op. 53 in C major, the *Waldstein*, and Op. 26 in A flat major). The composers represented in the list of Gieseking records available at that time, apart from Beethoven and Debussy, were Bach, César Franck, Grieg and Liszt. Surprisingly, there was no Mozart, though a lot of Gieseking's recordings of his music were soon to be available.

The orchestral recordings were made in collaboration with various eminent conductors and orchestras and included Beethoven's Concerto No. 1 in C major, Op. 15 with the Berlin State Opera House Orchestra under Hans Rosbaud; Beethoven's Concerto No. 5 in E flat (*The Emperor*) with the Vienna Philharmonic Orchestra under Bruno Walter; the Grieg Concerto in A minor, Op. 16 with the Berlin State Opera House Orchestra conducted by Hans Rosbaud; and the Liszt Concerto No. 1 in E flat with the London Philharmonic Orchestra under Sir Henry Wood. Also included in the orchestral recordings were the César Franck *Symphonic Variations*, again with the London Philharmonic Orchestra conducted by Sir Henry Wood. Several of Gieseking's discs were strongly recommended in the well-known book *The Record Guide* by Edward Sackville-West and Desmond Shawe-Taylor which was published in 1951.

With the introduction of the long-playing record around the year 1950, Gieseking was called upon to spend lengthy periods of time in the recording studios re-recording his repertoire for the new type of disc. By 1955 a large number of Gieseking's long-playing discs were on the market including three of Beethoven's concertos and several of his best known sonatas, the Grieg concerto, concertos by Mozart, and all Mozart's solo piano compositions (on 11 records), plus works by Brahms and Schumann. Perhaps the most valuable of all his recordings are those of Debussy and Ravel. He recorded the complete series of the piano music of these composers and it is generally acknowledged that in doing so he set standards which have yet to be surpassed.

When making his recordings Gieseking was prepared to put in sustained periods of work. In recording the complete solo piano works of Mozart, for example, it was said that he spent a whole month (August 1953) in EMI's recording studios. (Columbia had long since been part of the EMI Empire.) Bearing in mind the 'homework' that must have been done beforehand in preparing for this mammoth task, these recordings are quite an achievement. Gieseking's records have stood the test of time and some are still available at the time of writing. Inevitably though, fashions change, and modern pianists do not always play pieces in the way that Gieseking did.

Leschetizky always used to impress on his pupils the need to listen to their own playing. Gieseking was not a Leschetizky pupil but he knew the importance of that particular piece of advice. Throughout his career he never ceased to listen carefully to his own performances, to every sound made by his fingers, and to be alertly aware of every detail of his pedalling, to ensure that his interpretations would never become incorrect or stereotyped but would always retain their freshness. Perhaps that is one of the great secrets of his success.

Gieseking acquired many honours. France conferred upon him the Grand Prix for Recording, and made him a Chevalier of the Legion of Honour. He still found time to do a little teaching and was a Professor at the Saarbrüchen Conservatory.

In December 1955 Gieseking suffered a severe personal tragedy when his wife, Annie, was killed in a road accident near Stuttgart. Gieseking himself received severe head injuries in the accident, as a result of which he was kept in hospital for six weeks. However, after a period of convalescence he gradually resumed his career. But misfortune soon struck again. On 19th October 1956 he travelled from Germany to England to undertake a formidable task - the recording of all Beethoven's piano sonatas - to complement his recordings of Mozart's entire compositions for solo piano made three years earlier. No sooner had he begun than he was struck down by illness and was rushed into hospital in London on 24th October. The problem was diagnosed as acute pancreatitis. This is a disease we all have to hope we do not get, for even if the best available treatment is promptly initiated the condition often proves rapidly fatal. Unhappily this is what happened in Walter Gieseking's case and he died on 26th October 1956, aged 60, two days after his admission to hospital and only a week after his arrival in Britain. He was survived by his two daughters. His autobiography, *So Wurde Ich Pianist*, assembled from his notes, was published in 1963, seven years after his death.

Gieseking's sudden death at a relatively early age was mourned in the world of music. But in the course of a career lasting over 30 years nearly all that he was capable of achieving had been achieved and most of his repertoire had been recorded on piano roll or gramophone disc. It is through these recordings that he is now best remembered.

Vladimir Horowitz

24. Vladimir Horowitz

Vladimir Horowitz was a marvel - the pianistic wonder of the twentieth century. From the moment he burst upon the musical scene like a tornado, his position was unique. No other pianist had a technique quite like Horowitz; no other pianist had a style so different from the other master pianists of his era. In a way he was a throwback to an earlier generation, for at heart he was a romantic, prepared to disobey the composer's instructions if it suited him, yet at the same time he was deeply conscious of the composer's overall intentions. His amazing fingerwork astounded his audiences for over 60 years; even when he was in his eighties there was no need to make concessions for his age, for he retained his skill to the end of his days although he was prepared to display it in public only rarely. It would have been foolish for any young pianist to have tried to copy him for he was inimitable. His way of playing was entirely his own. Horowitz was Horowitz; a man apart.

Horowitz was yet another product of what used to be known as the Eastern Bloc, fertile breeding ground of a seemingly endless stream of brilliant musicians including pianists. It was in Kiev in the Ukraine that Vladimir Horowitz was born on 1st October 1904. His family was Jewish, quite well-to-do, and musical. His father, Samuel, was an electrical engineer, successful in his profession, who represented the interests in Kiev of the American company Westinghouse and the German company Allgemeine Elektrische Gesellschaft. One of his pastimes was playing the cello. Vladimir's mother, Sophie, was an excellent amateur pianist; an elder brother became a violin teacher at the Moscow Conservatory and a younger sister established herself as a concert pianist in Russia. Thus music was in the Horowitz blood and it is appropriate that the house where Vladimir was born was in a road called by the Russian equivalent of 'Musical Lane'.

Vladimir's first piano instruction was provided by his mother who taught him from the age of six until he was nine. His special talents were not slow to show themselves and at nine he entered the Kiev Conservatory where his piano lessons were provided at first by Sergei Tarnowsky, then by Vladimir Puchalsky who had taught Vladimir Horowitz's mother years earlier. Later, at the age of 15, he was taught by Felix Blumenfeld who had been a pupil of Anton Rubinstein. Though he was destined to become an outstanding pianist, Vladimir's main interest in those early years was his composition. No doubt his intense study in that area stood him in good stead in later years in his preparation for concerts and recitals.

Vladimir Horowitz studied at the Kiev Conservatory for seven years, graduating at the age of sixteen with the highest honours in the summer of 1921. By then the Russian revolution had taken place, an event which had been disastrous for the Horowitz family as Vladimir's father lost all his savings in 24 hours. Mindful of the impoverished condition of his parents, brothers and sisters, and knowing that composition would be unlikely to bring rapid financial rewards, the youthful musician decided to concentrate on his piano playing.

Horowitz had already made a semi-public debut as a 15 year old on 30th May 1920, but the real beginning of his remarkable career dates from a concert given in 1922, the year after his graduation. This appearance was arranged for him by his uncle, a music critic, and took place in Kharkov. It was an immediate and sensational success, and for some time afterwards the musical talk in Kharkov was all about the 18 year old pianist's brilliant virtuosity. One successful concert was followed by another, and in all he gave 13 in the city. Virtually unknown outside Kharkov, he was glad to play for whatever fee he could get, and in fact his efforts were rewarded for the most part not in money, which in those post-revolution days was scarce, but in clothing, food and household appliances.

Those Kharkov appearances 'made' Horowitz. Word of the brilliant youngster spread round Russia like wildfire and in the next couple of years he was engaged for 70 appearances in Russia of which 23 were in Leningrad. Others were in Kharkov, Moscow and his home town of Kiev. Possessing an insatiable musical appetite, he soon built up an enormous repertoire. As a result he was able to play a different programme in all of his 70 concerts, more than 200 compositions altogether.

It was not long before Horowitz was invited to play outside Russia, and as his tour of Russia drew to its close a small number of engagements in Germany were arranged. For Horowitz to leave Russia he required an exit visa but it was readily obtained, for in those days the Communist regime encouraged visits abroad for study purposes. So in 1925 the 20 year old pianist obtained his visa under the pretext of wanting to take lessons from Artur Schnabel. Following a relatively quiet start to his tour at a small concert in Hamburg he came back to his hotel one late afternoon after a walk to find the hotel manager waiting for him. It appeared that a lady pianist who was due to play Tchaikovsky's First Concerto that evening had been taken ill; could he play it instead? Horowitz drank a glass of milk, got himself ready, and went to the concert hall.

He arrived just as the symphony which preceded the concerto was finishing. The conductor, Eugen Papst, went to the artists' room when the symphony ended not knowing whether or not there was going to be a pianist to play the concerto. He found young Horowitz waiting. He told him what tempo he would be using and said: "Just watch my baton and everything will be all right." Papst need not have worried. After the first few bars he was amazed and at the end he rushed to congratulate Horowitz. The concert was a phenomenal success and the critics observed that Hamburg had not seen such a triumph since Caruso's debut there. Another concert was arranged immediately and within two hours of its announcement 3,000 tickets had been sold. These events paved the way for a successful tour of Germany which included Horowitz's Berlin debut on 2nd January 1926.

In the next two years Horowitz played in all the major musical centres of Europe including London and Paris where he was received rapturously. He appeared with the most important orchestras of several countries under all the famous conductors of the day and gave performances before kings and queens. He had truly arrived. Still in his early twenties he was already one of the most brilliantly successful pianists of the day; fiery, a second Liszt, able to dash off the most horrendously difficult pieces with an innocent nonchalance. This ability, coupled with his impish smile at the conclusion of his performances, made him the darling of his audiences.

After the American impresario Arthur Judson heard Horowitz play in Paris, he immediately signed him up for a tour of the United States. Horowitz left for the USA and after a number of appearances in Chicago and other cities, his official New York debut took place on 12th January 1928 in a concert which lived in the memory of all who were present. He was engaged as soloist with the New York Philharmonic Orchestra to play the Tchaikovsky B flat minor Concerto under the baton of none other than Sir Thomas Beecham, who was making his American debut.

Sir Thomas was a strong-willed and forceful character. Horowitz, in his quiet way, was another. The two of them could not agree in rehearsals about tempo, Sir Thomas insisting on a much slower pace than the dynamic Horowitz wanted. On the night of the concert, Horowitz restrained himself to the sedate pace set by Sir Thomas for two movements but was not happy about the result. In the last movement he decided, as Schonberg in his book *The Great Pianists* put it, "to go down with all guns firing." He set off at a cracking pace in the final movement, leaving Beecham behind, and the orchestra never caught up, ending the concerto a whole bar behind Horowitz. Beecham was distinctly not amused and the incident provoked one of his waspish impromptu diatribes from the rostrum. Yet, although the two had not been in accord musically, each having a totally different conception of how the music should be played, the performance had been lively and memorable and did neither any harm. Paradoxically, the concert established for ever Horowitz's fame in the United States.

Later in the same year Horowitz had a few 'lessons' with Schnabel, as had been intended when he applied for his Russian exit visa, but they were more in the nature of advisory sessions than lessons in the true sense. It is difficult to think of two musicians possessing more contrasting styles than Horowitz, the dynamic and impetuous young virtuoso and Schnabel, the severe, possibly austere, classicist. Indeed, there were many people in the late twenties and early thirties who regarded Horowitz as a dynamic refuge from Schnabel's rigidly classical style.

In 1927 Horowitz recorded 12 piano rolls for the Welte Company of Freiburg at their New York headquarters. The composers represented were Bach (2 rolls), Bizet (1), Chopin (3), Horowitz (1), Liszt (1), Mozart (1), Rachmaninov (2) and Schubert (1). There are some interesting rolls among them. The Bizet roll was Horowitz's own transcription for piano of Variations on *Carmen*. Two of the Bach rolls were transcriptions of organ music by Busoni; the other was a prelude from the *Well Tempered Clavier*. One of the Chopin rolls was of two études, Op. 10, No. 8 in F and No. 5 in G flat (*Black Key*), and the other two Chopin rolls were of three mazurkas, Op. 30, No. 4 in C sharp minor on one roll and Op. 63, No. 2 in F minor and No. 3 in C sharp minor on the other. The Horowitz composition was his *Moment Exotique*. Both the Rachmaninov rolls were of preludes; one roll was Op. 23, No. 5 in G minor and there were two on the other roll, Op. 32, No. 5 in G and No. 12 in G sharp minor.

Shortly after recording these rolls for Welte, Horowitz recorded seven piano rolls for the Aeolian Company's Duo-Art system. Again they were recorded in New York, this time at the Aeolian Company's headquarters, and were issued between 1928 and 1932. Included amongst them were one of his own compositions, Valse in F minor. The other pieces (each roll featured a different composer) were Bizet's *Carmen* Variations (Horowitz's own arrangement); *Danse Macabre* by Saint-Saëns (transcribed by Liszt); *Doumka*, Op. 59 by Tchaikovsky; *Love's Message* by Schubert (transcribed by Liszt); Two études of Chopin, Op. 10, No. 6 in E flat minor, and Op. 25, No. 12 in C minor (*Arpeggios*); and two Rachmaninov preludes, Op. 32, No. 10 in B minor and Op. 32, No. 8 in A minor.

The last Horowitz roll to be issued was his Duo-Art recording of the two Rachmaninov preludes. It was released in April 1932, which is a very late date for the issue of new piano rolls. The player piano industry was in terminal decline by then and very few new rolls were being produced. These 19 rolls, 12 for Welte and seven for Duo-Art, comprise Horowitz's entire output of piano roll recordings. In the 1980s Horowitz was one of the few pianists who had made piano roll recordings still to be professionally active. Shura Cherkassky was another, and has died only recently.

Horowitz had left Russia 'temporarily' in 1925 to undertake his tour of Europe; he had then gone straight to the USA for his tour. When he left Russia it had been his intention to return. But following his American debut and his subsequent further concerts there, he found life in the USA so much to his liking that he decided to stay. He based himself in New York and toured throughout the USA, appearing with all the big orchestras, and though he was still well under thirty years of age his name became synonymous with pianistic success. In 1931 he played at the White House at the invitation of President Hoover. At that time he had very little knowledge of the English language and was worried about how he should converse with the distinguished guests at the reception afterwards. He was advised by the Steinway representatives simply to repeat, "I am delighted" when people greeted him. As the 75 diplomats filed past he was heard to say, amiably, "I am delighted. I am delightful."

Having made his home in the USA, and enjoying every minute of his new life there, Russia seemed like a distant dream. He felt no immediate urge to go back, and as time went by any lingering desire there was dwindled even further. It was in fact to be sixty years from leaving his native land before he set foot there again in what was to be a triumphal 'return of the native'. His success in the USA in those early days could be gauged by the yardstick of the fees he received for his appearances. In 1928 it was $500 a recital; in 1929 $1,000 and in 1930 $1,500. By 1930 he was fulfilling 100 engagements a year in the USA alone.

After Horowitz had established himself in the United States in the late 1920s his stature as a major artist never waned. When the ageing Ignace Paderewski heard him in 1930 in Chicago he wrote of the young pianist's performance in glowing terms:

"I must admit that I liked him very much; I liked both his playing and his general bearing . . . He was self-disciplined, and, above all, he has rhythm and tone. I only heard him play the D minor Concerto by Rachmaninov, but it was very fine indeed. Of course, I cannot tell how he tackles the great classical composers, what he does with Bach, Beethoven, Chopin or Schumann. If he does not get spoiled, and if he can keep up his great power, he ought to go very far. Without any doubt he is the most convincing among the younger pianists."

These complimentary words were penned by the great pianist when Horowitz was only 25. Horowitz did keep up the power that Paderewski referred to; indeed he retained it to the end of his life.

In 1932 Horowitz was engaged to play at the last concert of Arturo Toscanini's season with the New York Philharmonic Orchestra. The chosen piece was Beethoven's *Emperor* Concerto and in preparation Horowitz took part in a number of conferences at Toscanini's suite at the Hotel Astor. The old and young musicians quickly became friends and in the following summer Horowitz was invited to Toscanini's home overlooking Lake Maggiore in Northern Italy. A friendship developed between Horowitz and Toscanini's daughter, Wanda, and later in the same year (1933) Vladimir and Wanda were married. In 1934 the couple's only child was born, a daughter, Sonia. She became a good pianist and had a special talent for painting.

Horowitz was always a very highly-strung pianist. Though he was tremendously successful in the early 1930s he lived on his nerves. Introvert by nature, he enjoyed playing the piano at home to an intimate circle of friends but in spite of his genius the confrontation with audiences in public concerts was apt to become an ordeal. Matters came to a head in the mid 1930s when he felt he could no longer continue his career, at any rate for the time being. From 1936 to 1939 he retired from the concert platform. He was reticent about the reasons for this lengthy absence and it has remained something of a mystery. There were rumours that he had had a nervous breakdown, that he was receiving treatment for a medical condition or that he had had a serious operation. Horowitz never offered a convincing explanation, though he hinted that he needed a period of prolonged rest and study. He finally reappeared before an audience at the Lucerne Festival in 1939, playing Brahms' Second Piano Concerto under Toscanini. From then on his career continued as it had before its interruption, at any rate for a further 14 years.

Horowitz had lived in the USA for over 10 years when war came in Europe in 1939. In 1944, three years after the United States entered the war, he became a citizen of that country at the age of 40. In the early 1940s he lived in Los Angeles and became very friendly with Rachmaninov, his idol. The two of them often played two-piano arrangements at Rachmaninov's home. Later he moved back to New York. The years 1939 to 1953 mark the high plateau of Horowitz's career and in that period he gave numerous concerts and recitals. With Horowitz in middle age, at the peak of his career, it is instructive to look at the reasons for his outstanding success.

Horowitz in his young days was a phenomenon, quite unlike any other pianist, and in a long life he changed little. His style was, and remained, highly individual. He was never regarded as the greatest of interpreters, but as a virtuoso he has never been equalled in the opinion of many musicians, particularly in the works of composers such as Liszt, whom he greatly admired. Indeed, whilst Liszt was perhaps the greatest pianist of the 19th century, many regard Horowitz as the nearest approach to Liszt in the twentieth. Possessed of a clear, metallic, somewhat brittle tone, achieved from immensely strong fingers capable of astonishingly rapid movement, he was able to play with tremendous speed, force and control. Every note was played crisply and clearly; there were no slurs, no muffy notes, and he made the piano 'sing'. Even when he was in his 80s, Horowitz retained the ability to sound different from any other pianist so that his interpretations were usually instantly recognisable.

Horowitz's style was particularly suited to the grand virtuoso examples of the piano repertoire, such as the concertos and other piano works of Liszt, Rachmaninov and Tchaikovsky. Yet paradoxically he also excelled in simple miniatures; the sonatas of Clementi, Mozart and Scarlatti and even the works of composers such as Moszkowski. Horowitz's playing of Mozart had an exquisite simplicity. All his great powers were kept in reserve as the music unfurled in beautiful, almost childlike, serenity.

As to Horowitz's interpretations, opinions of music critics were divided. Labelled as 'one of the last of the romantics', Horowitz was on occasions torn apart in critics' reports for tinkering with the composer's instructions. He was not above playing the music according to the Horowitz conception rather than to the composer's, and he was sometimes accused of editing the notes. Much ink was spilled by vitriolic critics in condemning such sins. After one of Horowitz's recitals the American critic Virgil Thomson called Horowitz "a master of exaggeration and misinterpretation", and continued in the following vein:

"One should not gather from this that Horowitz's interpretations are absolutely wrong and indefensible; some are, some are not. But anyone who has never heard the works which Horowitz played last night might easily come to think that Bach was a musician of the Leopold Stokowski type, Brahms a sort of frivolous Gershwin employed by a first-class night club, and Chopin but a gypsy violinist."

Such comments, surely an overstatement, caused Horowitz's career to be clouded in controversy so far as the musical purists were concerned. Even the *New Grove Dictionary of Music and Musicians* published in 1980, a set of volumes not usually noted for outspoken comment, qualifies its praise by a final stinging remark:

"In music that has characteristics perfectly complemented by his playing, Moszkowski, Liszt, Prokofiev, for example, he is brilliantly effective, and he has illuminated some interesting music like Schumann's *Kreisleriana* and much of Scriabin. Horowitz illustrates that an astounding instrumental gift carries no guarantee about musical understanding."

Many of Horowitz's interpretations, particularly, for example, in the works of the classical composers such as Beethoven, were always regarded as suspect in that they were highly individual and even idiosyncratic. But then, Horowitz was a highly individual pianist. It would be a dull world if all pianists were the same, if a committee of learned musicians were to lay down a framework for a definitive performance of every piece of music that has ever been composed. Whilst there is freedom there will always be an individual genius who fails to fit into the accepted pattern, and Horowitz was one of them. The concert-going public cared little about the critics' opinions of Horowitz. The public saw him as a man apart, a supreme genius, a wayward but brilliant virtuoso who was incapable of giving a dull, lifeless performance. From his earliest days in the USA he was no stranger to controversy, but a Horowitz recital was always guaranteed to fill a concert hall, an ability that remained with him into old age. The concert-going public loved him.

Interestingly for one who was noted as a great virtuoso, Horowitz did not find it necessary to throw himself around in front of the piano as he played. He had a quiet, dignified bearing at the instrument and his arm movement was kept to a minimum. His great power was achieved almost entirely from his immensely strong fingers trained by meticulous exercise to respond to his requirements. When asked about his 'phenomenal technique' (an overworked expression but Horowitz had it if anyone had) he put it all down to practice. But many good professional pianists spend hours a day in practice without developing the skills of Horowitz. So his practice must be regarded as subsidiary to his innate genius.

Horowitz's gramophone recording career began when he was still in his twenties and continued until relatively recent times. The companies he recorded for were CBS, HMV and RCA-Victor. He enjoyed recording, for it can be done in a congenial atmosphere (some of the recordings were made in his own home) free from the stress that, to him, an audience induced. His recordings were numerous and will therefore be reviewed only briefly. He recorded all kinds of music, from Scarlatti to Debussy, with a concentration on the type of music best suited to his style, for example, the concertos of Rachmaninov and Tchaikovsky. The miniature pieces which he played so cleanly and well are represented, as are some of the pianistic 'tours de force' which evoked the rage of his critics, such as his own arrangements of Sousa's *Stars and Stripes for Ever* and Bizet's *Carmen*. Whether or not one likes his recordings depends on the same arguments that apply for and against his concert performances. They might not always please the musical purist but invariably they are 'different' and moreover, technically brilliant.

Vladimir Horowitz

Even after Horowitz resumed his career in 1939 following his three-year lay-off he remained a highly-strung and unwilling performer. Fussy about his food and something of a hypochondriac, he often cancelled concert appearances because of a variety of maladies, real or imagined. Oscar Levant, the American pianist who was also a hypochondriac, once suggested that he and Horowitz should form a duo piano team so that they could cancel concerts together. From time to time Horowitz would take a few private students; one of them once went to see Horowitz when he was ill and said:

"His bedroom looked like a chemist's shop. I never saw such medication. Bottles everywhere. Black drapes and black shades drawn in the middle of the afternoon in July. Horowitz was lying on his back with his eyes covered with plastic eye shades and he was wearing ear plugs. He always complained to me about his stomach problems."

When Horowitz went to concerts given by other pianists his thoughts were not always on a high musical or intellectual plane. On one occasion his pupil Ivan Davis drove Horowitz to a Carnegie Hall concert given by Rudolph and Peter Serkin. Afterwards, backstage amongst the autograph hunters, Horowitz kept looking at his watch. Davis thought that Horowitz, who was always something of a loner, was worried about all the people surrounding him. But the problem was different. When they got into the car, Horowitz said: "Got to get home because the Emmy Awards are on television and I've got to see if *Naked City* wins." It was his favourite programme.

In 1953 Horowitz once again retired from the concert platform, the nervous strain of concert appearances having taken its toll. His retirement was not complete because he continued to make recordings from time to time. His renewed absence from public performances was to last twelve years. He had no intention at the outset of being away so long; it was his idea originally only to take a year off. In an interview some years later he said:

"When I used to tour, I took the train. I didn't sleep well, I didn't eat well. I didn't even like the train. Four concerts a week and travelling on the train were just too much. I suddenly felt very tired and decided to take a year off. Then, you see, I enjoyed the peaceful life so much, I kept taking a year off."

Asked whether he had received hospital treatment during that period Horowitz made no direct reply:

"I guess human nature is prone to respond more to bad news than good news. Anyhow, in those twelve years I made seven recordings, so I guess I couldn't have been mad if I did that."

After those twelve fallow years which took Horowitz from the age of 48 to 60 it was finally announced in 1965 that he would be returning to

Carnegie Hall for a recital. He had decided that time was slipping by and if ever he was to make a comeback it must be done straight away. The excitement generated was terrific. Wanda Horowitz told *The New York Times*, "Horowitz is like a fifth Beatle!" On 9th May 1965 the recital took place and was a resounding success financially and artistically. Horowitz was evidently satisfied with the experiment and thereafter resumed his concert career, though on his own terms. These included afternoon recitals only (he felt he was at his best in the afternoon), high fees, and no long distance travel from New York.

Asked in an interview whether his playing had mellowed since his early years, Horowitz replied:

"I've mellowed a bit. Perhaps in these later years there has also been a change in some of my attitudes. Before, I was always aware there was a public in the hall, and I played to please the public. You know, pleasing the public is not always an easy task. In the thirties, I played so many concerts, and often my manager would tell me that I played too serious a programme. For example, he asked me to take out the Chopin G minor Ballade because it was too difficult for the public at that time. Then at times he told me I was playing "too dry". How do they expect me to play? Wet? Consequently I tried playing for the public, and I selected music that I thought would be pleasing to them. Times are different now. Today I play the music I want and I just try to do my best.

"Another change has been that I now do exactly what I want to do, and when I choose to do it. If I feel like it, I can play three concerts a year or I can play twenty. Before I was always entangled with management, fulfilling obligations, discussing business affairs, and things like that. Now that's all over with, and that's what I'm happy about. If I want to play in New York I do; if I want to play five times I play five times. I make the decision. I've also simplified business arrangements by making all concerts I play a single admission. They're not part of a series. I also continue to insist on afternoon concerts because that's when I'm freshest and I believe it is also the best time for the audience."

In his recitals and concerts Horowitz used his own Steinway piano which was transported to every city where he played. The art of Horowitz, as indeed of any pianist, depends on the piano manufacturer's skill, so it is instructive to hear what Horowitz had to say about pianos:

"I like to use my own piano for concerts. All pianos are more or less good but they need constant care and don't often receive it. At least every month or two they should be tuned and voiced. If this isn't done, within a year's time the piano will run down like a human being who neglects his health. Pianos change their timbre and tone with the weather, the atmospheric conditions or movement. When they come from the factory they are like a new car. You can't drive them at top speed. There's a difference in pianos from different areas. For instance, the German Steinway differs from the American Steinway. The German wood cannot tolerate much change in the climate, so it starts losing its voicing. European felt is different too. A piano has some 11,000 parts and if one of those goes awry then the piano doesn't function right. A piano is very vulnerable. I have my piano tuned once a month when I'm at home, whether I play it or not."

When Horowitz resumed his concert career in 1965, albeit on a reduced scale and on his own terms, he soon demonstrated that little if any of his skill and bravura had been lost. But, nervous as always, and ever a reluctant performer, he continued to cancel concerts on many occasions and from 1969 to 1974 he performed in public only rarely. He made a number of new recordings, however, and in the mid 1970s many of his old ones were reissued. On the subject of recording, Horowitz told an interviewer:

"I never listen to my own recordings because I don't want to influence myself. Each time I play it is different. The great danger in listening to records is imitation. When Chopin taught and his pupils tried to imitate him, he sent them home and told them to bring something of their own.

"So many times people who are studying piano study with recordings, and they are so used to hearing note-perfect performances on record that they want to duplicate the same note-perfect performance in the concert hall. They are not concerned about projecting the spirit of the music because they are concentrating so much on the notes; it becomes an obsession with them. If they make a smudge or something they think it is a bad performance. A few wrong notes are not a crime.

"An artist isn't the same day after day so there can never be a 'final' interpretation. It will be changing always. If I made four recordings of the same piece within a month, each would be different. I am not an assembly-line pianist. With recordings today, it is mechanically possible to do what I sweated so many years to develop. So I do not allow the tone quality in my recordings to be altered or changed. If I make a mistake I will do it over, but nothing can be touched. Recordings are like photographs; sometimes you recognise the person and sometimes you don't. That's what happens very often in recordings."

When he was asked in the same interview for his opinion on modern (20th century) music, Horowitz replied:

"Much of it has a percussive sound, and I am against using the piano in that way. Even some of the music of Bartók and Stravinsky is too percussive for me. It may be beautiful music, but I really don't care to play it. I can listen to it and enjoy it, though. I also find it difficult to comprehend how some pianists are able to cover the gamut of repertoire from Bach to ultracontemporary in such a short time. Surely it must be difficult to make this transition because a certain amount of Bartók may become mixed up with Chopin, and of course it doesn't belong there at all. So much contemporary music is often played with very little expression. You have to maintain its rhythm and life, and it is very difficult to go from that to a Chopin waltz. It is a real aesthetic change of gears. Nevertheless, some pianists seem able to capitalise on playing modern music without playing Chopin, and Schumann too. It's a question of personality. No one forces a pianist into a certain repertoire. That one must decide for himself."

In 1972 Horowitz, then 68, was awarded the Gold Medal of the Royal Philharmonic Society as a mark of the esteem in which he was held in Britain. But as he moved into his seventies the number of his public appearances was curtailed still further; indeed, he confined himself to the occasional major concert, but he appeared more often following the untimely death of his daughter, Sonia, in 1975. On 8th January 1978 he performed Rachmaninov's Third Piano Concerto with Eugene Ormandy and the New York Philharmonic Orchestra and on 26th February of the same year he played at the White House, at the invitation of President Carter, to celebrate the 50th anniversary of his American debut. On 22nd May 1982, at the request of the Prince of Wales, he gave a recital at the Royal Festival Hall in London. This was his first appearance in London for 31 years. He had established a large following in Japan through his recordings and in June 1983 he gave a series of concerts in Tokyo and other Japanese cities.

Horowitz in his late seventies had become a pillar of the musical establishment though his interpretations remained as individual, some said wayward, as ever. His triumphal reappearances were not yet over, for in 1986 at the age of 81, he was involved in one of the most remarkable recitals that the world of music had known for years. Musicians and others had on many occasions urged him to re-visit Russia but he had always declined, feeling that all associations with his homeland were 'water under the bridge' and best left undisturbed.

However, Horowitz was finally persuaded to go and in the spring of 1986, after the details had been worked out to his satisfaction, he finally returned to his native land. The visit was facilitated by the newly-proclaimed Gorbachev-Reagan détente, one aspect of which was the encouragement of cultural exchanges. The conditions Horowitz imposed were stringent and included the requirements that he must have a supply of his own food flown in fresh, and he must play his own Steinway. All this was duly arranged and eventually the day came, 20th April 1986, when the 81 year old virtuoso once more played in the country of his birth. There was great competition for seats (and standing places) for Horowitz's recital, which was held in the Great Hall of the Moscow Conservatory and was relayed on television to all parts of the world. He played music by Mozart, Scarlatti, Chopin, Rachmaninov and others. To the Russians, especially the younger generation who knew Horowitz only from his recordings, it was a revelation. To Horowitz it was a glorious homecoming.

After that triumph there were no more worlds for Horowitz to conquer and he slipped into retirement. He died on 5th November 1989 at his Manhattan home following a heart attack. He was 85.

As a musician of such recent memory, it is difficult to put Horowitz's skills into any sort of historical perspective, especially as his performances have always been surrounded by an element of controversy. Fortunately he made lots of recordings which were always popular with the public and earned him 18 Grammy awards. Many of his records are now available on compact disc so people who enjoyed Horowitz's style of playing still have ample opportunity to enjoy it.

Much of the criticism of Horowitz's playing has been unfair, for although he was quite capable of unleashing the most astonishing display of pianistic pyrotechnics, as in his arrangement of Sousa's *The Stars and Stripes for Ever*, he generally left such excesses to the end of his programmes when he played them as encores. For the most part his playing of the classical compositions was kept under severe control though his interpretations were often regarded as unusual. It has been said that people went to Schnabel's recitals because they wanted to hear Beethoven; when they went to Horowitz's performances they most definitely went to hear Horowitz. Always ready to take risks, to stretch his technique to the utmost, his audience was generally kept on tenterhooks, wondering whether he could possibly pass the severe pianistic tests he set himself. He usually did, and the audience went away exhilarated. A Horowitz recital was a contest - it provided excitement to a degree that few other pianists have ever achieved.

Great Pianists of the Golden Age

Dinu Lipatti

25. Dinu Lipatti

In his short life Dinu Lipatti achieved greatness. Had he been born a few years earlier he would have been much sought after to record for the big player piano companies. Had he lived longer he might still be delighting us with his playing, for he would now be in his late seventies, an age at which several of the pianists in this book were still professionally active. But fate decreed otherwise. Lipatti's brief career on the concert platform was dogged by illness which curtailed the number of his performances and prevented tours to distant countries. He died at the tragically early age of 33, an age when most master pianists are settling into their stride and looking forward to forty more years of travelling the world. But his reputation is based not on the quantity of what he achieved but on the quality.

Brief though Lipatti's life was, he deserves a place in this book as one of the great pianists of his time. Mercifully for posterity, the last few years of his life coincided with a big improvement in gramophone recording techniques. That, coupled with the fact that Lipatti was a perfectionist who would not allow his discs to be released unless they satisfied his stringent artistic standards, enables us still to enjoy his playing through his recordings. Some of his interpretations have come to be regarded as classics, unsurpassed by any of the work of pianists of more recent times.

Dinu Lipatti came from a cultured Rumanian family with a long established musical heritage. His grandfather, Constantin Lipatti, was a music lover who played the guitar and flute very well. He often organised private concerts with his daughter, Sofia, who was a fine pianist and graduate of the Vienna Conservatory. Dinu's father, Theodor, was also an accomplished musician who had studied the violin with Carl Flesch and later, in Paris, with Pablo Sarasate. However, a career in music was not for him; he decided to become a diplomat and achieved considerable success in his chosen profession. But music remained an important part of his life and he continued to play the violin for his own circle of friends and at charity concerts. He also became a collector of good quality violins and numbered a Stradivarius and an Amati amongst his specimens. Theodor married Ann, née Racoviceanu, who was a good pianist, and she used to accompany the violin playing of her husband. It was in Bucharest that their son, Dinu Lipatti, was born on 19th March 1917. The name 'Dinu' is a diminutive of his baptismal name of Constantin. The importance of music to the family is illustrated by the fact that George Enescu, the celebrated Rumanian musician, was a godfather at Dinu's baptism.

The children of talented musicians do not always show great musical ability themselves, but Dinu was one who did. He started to play the piano by ear remarkably well at a very early age without any formal training and he also learned to play the violin. Recognising his unique natural gifts, his parents were divided as to which way his talents should be directed, for as a young child he seemed to be equally talented at both instruments. Theodor, whose violin studies had not taken him beyond the amateur stage, wanted Dinu to become a violinist whereas his mother, a pianist, wanted him to concentrate on the piano.

Before long the issue more or less settled itself, for Dinu showed such an astonishing ability at the piano it was obvious which way he should go. When he was still very young he could reproduce correctly at the piano any tune he heard, even before he knew any musical notation. In some ways this lack of formal knowledge may have helped his development, for he was able to represent in sound the images of what he saw and heard, unrestricted by any confines of musical convention. Like Schumann and Elgar, he could accurately portray in music the personalities of people around him.

Though at this stage Dinu was receiving no formal instruction, his father spent an hour or two with him each day in 'conferences' at which the pair would improvise on the piano and violin. Dinu's improvisations could really be regarded as original compositions and at the request of his father they were transcribed by a composer friend, Joseph Paschill, into a book with the title *Dinu Lipatti's Compositions* inscribed prominently on the cover.

For five years Dinu's family were his sole teachers and their skill and enthusiasm roused in him a passionate interest in music. At six, as a birthday celebration, he performed in public for the first time, and included one of his own compositions in his recital along with the works of others. For a few months longer Dinu's parents continued to teach him, but it was becoming obvious to them that the time had come when an outside teacher had to be found, and at seven he was placed in the hands of an excellent teacher and founder of a music school, Mihail Jora, who later recalled his first meeting with Dinu:

"One gloomy autumn day a small, delicate child was brought to me by his father who asked me to be his son's tutor. When I asked him what he knew, he said, "Nothing. He does not even know the names of the notes but he plays the piano by ear and composes." I had seen children of this kind before in my room, so I was none too hopeful. Rather bored, I asked the child to sit down at the piano. This time, however, the joke was on me. Little Lipatti, as I was to call him for many years, possessed an intuition and a musical gift which were altogether unusual."

Over the next four years Jora gave his small pupil a thorough musical education as well as instructing him in playing the piano. At 11 Dinu was well up to the standard required to enter the Bucharest Conservatory and there he was entrusted to a lady teacher, the aptly named Florica Musicescu, who was a stickler for perfection. Recalling Dinu's studies with her she wrote:

"What impressed me about Dinu already when he was a child was - in addition to the extraordinary capacity for assimilation and work - his surprising skill. He could reproduce with remarkable accuracy any musical idea that passed through his mind or that he had heard, from the very first moment without the slightest hesitation and in its entire harmonic element - an ability which, as a rule, needs lengthy studies to develop."

The Conservatory staff were well aware of Dinu's outstanding ability and potential but they wisely kept him on a tight rein. Whereas his parents were in favour of putting him before the public as soon as possible, the Conservatory maintained a regime of the most strict musical discipline. Though they encouraged him in every way in the acquisition of musical knowledge they forbad him to perform in public until, in their opinion, he was ready. Dinu accepted this without question. This regime averted any possibility of his becoming 'swollen headed' had he been of that disposition. Moreover, the severely disciplined nature of his studies promoted a healthy attitude of self-criticism in everything he did, one that remained with him to the end of his life. He knew his own ability and had the confidence to improve continually on his inborn gifts. But he was modest and his personality was such that he gained maximum benefit from his musical studies.

Dinu's progress at the Bucharest Conservatory was remarkable. Florica Musicescu was just the sort of teacher he needed, a fact he recognised clearly when he later said:

"It is to Miss Musicescu that I owe all I know about the craft of playing the piano."

At 15, after four years of study, it was deemed that the Conservatory could teach him nothing more and that he was ready to stand on his own feet. After graduation his first major engagement, on 10th February 1933 when he was still only 15, was with the Bucharest Philharmonic Orchestra conducted by Alfred Alessandrescu, when he played Liszt's E major Concerto. Success was instantaneous and complete; press notices were excellent and it was clear to everyone that a new star had arisen in the world of music. Soon he was invited back to play with the orchestra again. This time the work was Chopin's E minor Concerto and the conductor was George Georgescu, a man with whom he was to collaborate in numerous concerts during the next few years, not only in Rumania but also in other parts of Europe.

In 1934 Dinu entered for the Vienna International Piano Competition, a very prestigious event. He was one of the youngest in the competition, for competitors had to be at least 16 years old as a condition of entry, but his performances were good enough to earn him second place in a field of 250 entrants. One of the judges was Alfred Cortot, the distinguished French pianist and conductor. Cortot, shrewd and sensitive musician that he was, knew an outstanding pianist when he heard one, and was outraged by the result. He resigned in protest, declaring publicly that Lipatti should have won by a big margin. Dinu, modest and always factual and critical, was satisfied with the result and magnanimous in defeat, if defeat is the right word for coming in second among so many. In a letter to a friend he wrote:

"I've managed to carry off the second prize. The first prize was awarded to a Pole who possesses great experience, much sureness and calm."

This comment illustrates Dinu's lack of envy and his characteristic fairness in pointing out the merits of his fellow competitor. Whether Dinu's place was first or second made little difference to his career prospects; he had demonstrated his skills as a pianist and his other musical abilities. For someone of such relative inexperience to carry off a major prize, albeit second, at the age of 16 was a triumph.

Cortot, who had returned to Paris in high dudgeon, offered Lipatti the chance to study and work with him should he so wish. Dinu was glad to avail himself of this offer from such an eminent pianist and departed for Paris. Never one to feel that he had no more to learn, he enrolled at Cortot's École Normale de Musique. There he continued his studies in composition, this time with Paul Dukas, Nadia Boulanger and Igor Stravinsky whilst taking lessons in conducting from Diran Alexanian and Charles Münch and in piano from Cortot himself. All of these eminent musicians recognised that he was no ordinary student but was already a mature, top-class musician who needed only experience and guidance to develop into one of the world's great pianists. After one term Dukas said of Lipatti:

"Exceptionally gifted, he only requires to work to achieve through his own experience a perfect mastery of his talent. This young Rumanian is my best student and at the same time a virtuoso at the piano. I think he will become a second Enescu."

Cortot was very proud of his recruit. After Dinu had played in front of other students in his master class for the first time, Cortot asked his audience, "Have you any criticisms to make? I haven't any. It's perfect!"

Later, Dinu played the Sonata in F sharp minor of his godfather and friend, George Enescu, at the first performance of the sonata in Paris. The composer, who was present, said: "You have expressed precisely my intention." Later he remarked: "Lipatti plays the sonata better than I do."

Dinu gave his first full recital in Paris on 20th May 1935, at the École Normale de Musique when he was 18. All the critics spoke highly of his performance. *La Revue Musicale* reported:

"One does not often meet first-rate musical gifts and genuine musical qualities in the same performer. This is, however, the case with Dinu Lipatti, a young Rumanian pianist, who played for the first time in Paris. An unusually serious programme commanded the admiration of the most competent musicians. Lipatti possesses the gift of an exceptional sonority - never superficial, even in the most subtle pianissimi - completely devoid of harshness in his fortes, but of a continuous, well-apportioned fullness. This very young and already great pianist has in him all the possibilities of a brilliant future."

From the date of this recital Lipatti was regarded as a top-class pianist, able to turn his talent to any type of music from baroque to contemporary. He often played in concerts of Rumanian music, thereby helping to promote and popularise the compositions of his countrymen. He had been composing music for years, and many of his own compositions were included in these concerts, notably his Sonatina for Piano and Violin, Suite for Two Pianos and Sinfonia Concertante for Two Pianos and String Orchestra in which his fellow pianist was often Clara Haskil who was also Rumanian.

In the following few years, Dinu Lipatti's musical stature steadily grew and his reputation was soon assured. His studies in Paris alternated with visits to Rumania where he gave concerts with the Bucharest Philharmonic Orchestra and he appeared in chamber music recitals with Enescu and others. In March 1939, aged nearly 22, he played at the Salle Pleyel in Paris, scene of many notable recitals by famous pianists of the past, and achieved an especial triumph. The press were unanimous in their praise. *Le Journal des Débats* wrote:

"The perfect instrumentalist in him shows from the very first that, without losing any of his brilliant skill, he can give himself up completely to the outbursts of a disciplined, at times burning, enthusiasm."

Le Ménestrel reported:

"What is most fascinating about him is this visible effort to think and to do uprightly. There is not the least concern to assert himself but only the desire to give as true as possible a rendering of the music."

Though Lipatti is remembered as a pianist he had always been a prolific composer and there is little doubt that his deep understanding of the process of musical composition helped him, as a pianist, in the interpretation of music by other composers. Several of his compositions, including some of those mentioned earlier, were entered for competitions and won prizes, for example his Symphonic Suite *The Gipsies* which won the George Enescu First Prize in 1934 and the Silver Medal of the French Republic in 1937, and Sinfonia Concertante for Two Pianos and String Orchestra for which he was awarded the Young Composers' Prize in 1940.

Always a student at heart, Dinu never felt that he 'knew it all' and as a mature pianist of the first rank and a composer of growing reputation he still wrote many letters to his former teachers seeking their advice and help. The correspondence took the form of lessons; manuscripts went to and fro in the post so that Lipatti could seek advice on how compositions that he had performed successfully could be improved even further. Mihail Jora, Mme Musicescu and George Enescu were consulted often, as were the eminent musicians at the École Normale de Musique. It was not that he was unsure of himself musically; rather that he was a perfectionist and welcomed the views of all the knowledgeable musicians he felt could help him. His artistic development in Paris was further aided by coming into contact with other well-known musicians; Backhaus, Fischer, Hindemith, Honegger, Kempff and Schnabel were some of them, and there were many more.

Throughout the years 1935 to 1939 Dinu was based in Paris where his life centred around the group of brilliant musicians at the École Normale de Musique. In 1939, his formal studies there completed, he decided to go back to Rumania. During the next four years he gave concerts there, but his work as a concert pianist at that time was obviously severely curtailed because of the war. Nevertheless he performed often in German-occupied Rumania and travelled abroad to Austria, Bulgaria, Czechoslovakia, Germany and Italy, playing in recitals and as a soloist with the Bucharest Philharmonic Orchestra and he appeared as soloist with such famous conductors as Willem Mengelberg. He also made a concert tour to Finland and Sweden. On the Scandinavian tour he was accompanied by his future wife, Madeleine Cantacuzene, a concert pianist and teacher, and at the end of the tour the two musicians decided not to go straight back to Rumania. Instead they went to Switzerland, a neutral country, and appeared in two-piano recitals there towards the end of 1943. Shortly afterwards they were married and decided to settle in Switzerland. They made their home in Geneva.

It was about then that the first major symptoms of the illness that was to cut short Dinu Lipatti's life a few years later began to appear. Never the most robust of individuals, it was at first thought that he had tuberculosis. At that time the best treatment for this disease was rest in a cold and elevated environment, and for that reason he counted himself fortunate to be living in Switzerland. But the disease was unresponsive to the country's beneficial climate; periods of remission alternated with attacks of illness. When this illness, which turned out not to be tuberculosis but an even more serious condition, relented, as it periodically did, he made concert tours.

It is instructive to consider Lipatti's art as a pianist, to discover what it was that made his playing so special. It might be tempting to think that he was not one of the all-time greats, that it was only the fact of his early death that turned him into a cult figure. Nothing could be further from the truth, for he was recognised as a great pianist long before his death; in fact before he even became ill. His frequent illnesses during the last few years of his life might lead one to suppose that he was a kind of ailing, sickly genius, a sort of wax image of the kind of musician that Chopin is often wrongly supposed to have been. But Lipatti was not at all like that. His skill was innate but his musicianship was built on a careful study of the life and work of all the composers whose music he played. He had the greatest respect for the written musical text, and once wrote, "Not for a single moment must we fail to observe the text as though we had to answer for it every day to a merciless judge." But he was not a pedant, a mere mechanical reproducer of the notes and written instructions, for within the constraints of the text he excelled as an interpreter.

Lipatti was not only a brilliant virtuoso but also a musician of the rarest sensibility and delicacy. His command of tone and phrasing was superb, the crispness of his fingerwork was a revelation. He varied his fingerwork and touch according to the type of music he was playing perhaps more than any pianist of his day, so that whatever the period of the music he was playing, his interpretation combined all that was best in the music with the finest facets of the pianist's art.

Composing and playing the piano were not the only strings to Lipatti's bow, so to speak, for he also established something of a reputation as a music critic and as a teacher. As a critic he did not just 'criticise' in a formal way but was ready at all times to learn from what he had heard whilst as a teacher, he learned from his pupils just as they learned from him. He had taught from a relatively early age but teaching played a much larger role in his life from 1944 when he was appointed 'Professeur de Virtuosité' at the Geneva Conservatory where, 20 years earlier, the Spanish pianist José Iturbi had been Head of the Piano Department. Lipatti was to remain in this post and serve with distinction for nearly all the remainder of his life. On his appointment the Bulletin of the Conservatory, dated April 1944, referred in lyrical terms to their newest recruit:

"Though almost all our teachers are Swiss, it is but natural that in exceptional cases we should make room for a foreigner of great talent. This is precisely what our canton and federal authorities meant when, after lengthy and exacting investigation, they granted the right to be a teacher to Dinu Lipatti . . . Today Dinu Lipatti takes his place in the brilliant succession that made the glory of the Geneva Conservatoire . . . We wish him a brilliant career in our institution!"

His teaching took the form of Master Classes in which, far from being prescriptive as to the way a piece should be played, there was always a two-way exchange of views. Needless to say, the members of his class thought the world of their brilliant teacher. Madeleine Lipatti once said, "He has no students - only disciples."

When the war ended in 1945 he was of course free to travel where he wanted, but the ever-increasing inroads of his disease restricted his opportunities and he consequently had to turn down lucrative offers to tour the USA, South America and Australia. Nevertheless he travelled widely in Europe, visiting Britain four times in the immediate post-war years. These were Lipatti's years of triumph as the brightest young star in the pianistic sky. His concert appearances in Britain and elsewhere represented a considerable triumph of will over illness and suffering, for his playing was accomplished against an increasing background of pain. Because of his indomitable spirit the suffering did not show in his brilliant performances. But towards the end of the 1940s his health was so poor that some of his performances had to be cancelled, including one he had been booked to give with the Hallé Orchestra in Manchester in November 1948, when he was to have played the Mozart C major Concerto, K. 467.

Understandably, Lipatti gradually came to prefer the recording medium to the concert platform, mainly due to the more relaxed environment which was also beneficial from the point of view of coping with his illness, but also because of his extreme perfectionism. In a concert or recital there is only one opportunity to achieve the desired result, but in the recording studio passages could be repeated until Lipatti, his own severest critic, was satisfied.

Lipatti's recordings were made mainly for Columbia. After making a test recording in 1936 his first commercial disc appeared in 1937 when he was 20; in it he played four-handed (on two pianos) with Nadia Boulanger in Brahms' Waltzes, Op. 39. Over the next 13 years a small but steady trickle of recordings was made, which included some of the major works of the concert repertoire: the piano concertos of Grieg and Schumann; a concerto of Mozart, No. 21 in C, K. 467; and works by Bach, Brahms, Chopin, Enescu, Liszt, Ravel, Scarlatti, Schubert and Lipatti himself. Some of the

Bach performances are regarded as particularly memorable and in the opinion of many judges have had no superior either before or since. But perhaps taking pride of place in his recorded work are the Chopin recordings, where the composer is portrayed not as frail, gentle, docile and wistful, as might be expected from a recording made by an ailing pianist playing the work of a consumptive composer. On the contrary, Lipatti's playing of Chopin's music is vibrant and vivacious.

Dinu Lipatti did not record any piano rolls and is the only pianist in this book not to have done so. His first commercial disc recording had appeared when he was 20; by then (1937) the player piano companies were virtually dead, having been finished off by the much-improved quality of gramophone recordings and the rise during the late 1920s and early 1930s of broadcasting. A few rolls of earlier vintage continued to be sold up to the outbreak of the Second World War, after which the industry virtually ceased to exist.

Lipatti's features were pale and tranquil, but it was said of him that he "radiated extraordinary purity since he had preserved intact the gaiety and gravity of childhood." In spite of his illness he was not given to self-pity nor was he a man in need of constant support and protection. He did not have the appearance of the dreamy musician that the public usually expects. He was tidy, skilful and active and his interests were wide, including such practical ones as gardening and experimenting with mechanical devices. Shy by nature, he could nevertheless be energetic and authoritative. He was optimistic and free of the romantic melancholy with which those who die young are often posthumously surrounded.

During the post-war years when Lipatti was at the height of his powers as a pianist he still found time to compose music. Over the years, from 1922 when little Dinu Lipatti's compositions were compiled into a book by Joseph Paschill, an impressive list of works was produced and published, of which the most notable are a Piano Sonata (1932); Violin Sonatina (1933); Symphonic Poem, *Satravii* (1933); Symphonic Suite, *Gipsies* (1934); Concertino in the Classic Style for Piano and String Orchestra (1936); Fantasy for Piano Trio (1936); Nocturne for Piano (1937); Suite for Two Pianos (1938); Sinfonia Concertante for Two Pianos and Orchestra (1938); Improvisation for Piano Trio (1939); Three Nocturnes for Piano (1939); Fantasy for Piano (1940); Piano Sonatina for the Left Hand (1941); Three Rumanian Dances for Two Pianos (1943); an arrangement of the same piece for Piano and Orchestra (1945); and *Aubade* for Wind Quartet (1949). In addition he composed the music for a number of songs and wrote cadenzas for a piano concerto by Haydn and four by Mozart. He also transcribed a number of Scarlatti's sonatas for wind quintet and some of J.S. Bach's organ works for piano.

But in spite of Dinu Lipatti's skills as a composer, teacher and music critic it is as a brilliant pianist that he is best remembered. His contemporaries held him in the highest esteem and the 'old guard' of professional pianists accepted him as probably the most talented of the younger generation. Once, after he had sought advice from his friend and former teacher Alfred Cortot, the old musician wrote:

"Dear Dinu, You have often done me the honour of asking my opinion on the purity of your interpretations which you blended with a care for the greatest perfection. I had nothing to teach you. As a matter of fact, there was a lot to learn from you. As the teacher of Schubert's wonderful childhood said of him, "You have grasped the entire essence of music." "

As the 1940s ended and 1950 dawned, Dinu Lipatti's illness, which had eventually been diagnosed as lymphogranulomatosis, a rare form of leukaemia, was increasingly taking its toll so that his public appearances and even his recording sessions diminished to the stage when they were few and far between. Walter Legge, head of Columbia's recording operations, had hoped that Lipatti would eventually be able to record most of Chopin's piano music; the waltzes and several other pieces had already been recorded. To make things easier for the seriously ill pianist, Legge brought a mobile recording studio to Lipatti's garden in Geneva in July 1950 and set up microphones in his home so that he could record there. In fact he was so ill that he was able to record only a few more pieces.

The 1950-51 Columbia catalogue contained half a page of Lipatti's recordings. Included amongst them are Grieg's Concerto in A minor, Op. 16, with the Philharmonia Orchestra conducted by Alceo Galliera and the Schumann Concerto in A minor, Op. 54, again with the Philharmonia Orchestra, this time conducted by Herbert von Karajan. Also included amongst the list of recordings available at that time were a number of solo compositions by Chopin, Liszt and Ravel. In the following year's catalogue, 1951-52, some of Lipatti's recordings of Bach's works had been added, including Myra Hess's arrangement of *Jesu, Joy of Man's Desiring*, and a Mozart Sonata, No. 8 in A minor, K.310. Most of these were still listed in the 1965 catalogue and more besides, including the Mozart Piano Concerto No. 21 in C, K.467 and some of Schubert's impromptus. Several of Lipatti's recordings have been re-issued in recent years and are currently available on compact disc.

Though Lipatti's recordings are not numerous by the standards of present-day pianists, their quality is enough to give the present younger generation some idea of his brilliant skills and powers of interpretation. The legacy of his recordings is priceless even though they represent only a small fraction of what he would have achieved had he enjoyed good health.

By August 1950 Lipatti was very ill indeed; much too ill to give his Master Classes at the Geneva Conservatory and his wife, Madeleine, was engaged to give them in his place. Her musical ideas were the same as Dinu's. Further public performances seemed to be out of the question. But he had made a promise some time earlier to appear at the Besançon Festival in September of that year and his name had been pencilled in. Unwilling to disappoint his many ardent admirers he made one great final effort. His friends tried to persuade him to abandon the recital but he refused saying, "I promised. I will play." Some said it was a sacrifice to the altar of music. This final recital took place on 16th September 1950 and was recorded. Though so gravely ill and weak that he had to be taken to the concert hall in an ambulance, he gave his performance and the recording shows that his technical correctness, perfectionism and idealism stayed with him to the end. The recording of the recital is now available on compact disc. It is the final tangible testimony to the skills of this great pianist.

Eleven weeks later, on 2nd December 1950, Dinu Lipatti died, aged 33. His early and tragic death was mourned in musical circles the world over. A few days later George Enescu wrote:

"The fact that Lipatti has left us is, for his friends, a sorrow of the heart, for music a loss which will take a long time to retrieve. He was indeed one of the great performers of his time. For a time I thought he would be a violinist. Finally he became the wonderful pianist we know."

Lipatti's spirit lives on in memory and some of his remarkable skills can still be enjoyed through his recordings. It was said of Lipatti in his lifetime that his performances were compelling; they created in the listener a desire to listen to and savour every note. Perhaps it was this quality more than any other that raised his playing above that of most other pianists, that made him rather special.

Bibliography

References are listed in reverse chronological order (latest first).

List A. Musical Encyclopaedias, Dictionaries etc. with References to the Musicians in this Book.

The New Grove Dictionary of Women Composers. Edited by Julie Anne Sadie & Rhian Samuel. Macmillan, London, 1994.
The Concise Baker's Biographical Dictionary of Composers and Musicians. Edited by Nicolas Slonimsky. Simon Schuster, London, 1990.
Baker's Biographical Dictionary of Musicians. 7th Edn. Edited by Nicolas Slonimsky. Oxford University Press/Schirmer, New York, 1984 (and earlier editions of 'Baker').
The New Grove Dictionary of Music and Musicians. Edited by Stanley Sadie. Macmillan, London, 1980.
Das Grosse Lexikon der Musik. Herder, Freiberg, Basel, Vienna, 1976.
International Cyclopedia of Music and Musicians. 10th Edn. Edited by Oscar Thompson. Dent, London, 1975 (and earlier editions).
Musik Lexikon. Edited by Williblad Garlitt, H. Riemann. B. Schott's Söhne, Mainz, 1972-75.
Index to Biographies of Contemporary Composers. S. Bull. Scarecrow Press, Metuchen, New Jersey, 1974.
Biographical Dictionary of American Music. C. E. Claghem. Parker, New York, 1973.
Who's Who in Music. 5th Edn. Burke's Peerage, London, 1969 (and earlier editions).
Die Musik in Geschichte und Gegenwart. Barenreiter Kassel, Basel, Paris, London, New York, 1966.
Who's Who of American Women. 3rd Edn. Marquis Who's Who Inc., Chicago, 1964.
Enciclopedia della Musica. Ricordi, Milan, 1963.
Encyclopédie de la Musique. Fasquelle, Paris, 1961.
Muzicka Enciklopedija. Edited by J. Andreas. Leksikografskog Zovoda Fnrj., Zagreb, 1958.
The Concise Encyclopaedia of Music and Musicians. Edited by M. Cooper. Hutchinson, London, 1958.
Lexikon der Neuen Musik. F. K. Prieberg. Alber, Munich, 1958.
Encyclopedie van de Muziek. Elsevier, Amsterdam, 1956-57.
A Critical Dictionary of Composers and Their Music. Dobson, London, 1954.
The International Who Is Who in Music. 5th Edn. (mid-century). Edited by J.T.H. Mize. Lee Stern Press, Chicago, 1951.
Everyman's Dictionary of Music. Edited by Eric Blom. Dent, London, 1946.
The New Encyclopaedia of Music and Musicians. Edited by W.S. Pratt. Macmillan, New York, 1943.
The Macmillan Encyclopaedia of Music and Musicians. Compiled by A.E. Weir. Macmillan, London, 1938.
Dizionario Universale dei Musicisti. Edited by Carlo Schmidl. Sonzogno, Milan, 1926-37.
Geillustredd Muzicklexicon. Edited by G. Keller & P. Kruseman. Kruseman, Gravenhage, 1932.

Bibliography

Dictionary of Modern Musicians. Edited by A. Eaglefield-Hull. Dent, London, 1924.
International Who's Who in Music and Musical Gazetteer. Edited by César Saerchinger. Current Literature Publishing Co., New York, 1918.
Pitman's Encyclopaedia of Music and Musicians. Pitman, London, 1913.
Who's Who and *Who Was Who.* Various years. Adam & Charles Black, London.

List B. General Books, Articles, etc. with References to the Pianists in this Book.

Never Sing Louder than Lovely. Isobel Baillie. Hutchinson, London, 1982.
Virtuoso. Harvey Sachs. Thomas & Hudson, London, 1981.
Notable American Women: The Modern Period. Harvard University Press, Cambridge (Mass.) and London, 1980.
Unsung: A History of Women in American Music. Christine Amner. Greenwood Press, Westport, C.T., 1980.
Women in American Music: A Bibliography of Music and Literature. Adrienne Block and Carol Neuls-Bates. Greenwood Press, Westport, C.T., 1979.
Musicians Since 1900. David Ewen. H.W. Wilson, New York, 1976.
Contemporary American Composers. Compiled by Ruth E. Anderson. G.K. Hall, Boston (Mass.), 1976.
Famous Pianists and Their Technique. R.C. Gerig. David & Charles, Newton Abbot, 1976.
The Distaff'd Composers. D. Burns. *Music Journal,* London, March 1974.
Great Pianists of Our Time. Joachim Kaiser. George Allen & Unwin Ltd., London, 1971.
Joys and Sorrows. Pablo Casals. Macdonald, London, 1970.
The Great Pianists. Harold C. Schonberg. Gollancz, London, 1964 (revised 1970).
Modern Masters of the Keyboard. Harriette Brower. Books for Libraries Press, Freeport, New York, 1969. (Reprint of a book first published in 1926.)
Player Piano Treasury. 3rd Edn. Harvey Roehl. Vestal Press, New York, 1964.
French Piano Music. Norman Demuth. Museum Press Ltd., London, 1959.
Duet for Three Hands. Cyril Smith. Angus & Robertson, London, 1958.
Speaking of Pianists. A. Chasins. Alfred A. Knopf, New York, 1957.
Music Makers. R. Gelatt. Alfred A. Knopf, New York, 1953.
The Eighth Octave. Mark Hambourg. Williams & Norgate, London, 1951.
Music Criticisms, 1846-99. Eduard Hanslick. Penguin Books, London, 1950.
Men and Women Who Make Music. David Ewen. Merlin Press Inc., New York, 1949.
Queen's Hall, 1893-1941. Robert Elkin. Rider & Co., London, 1944.
'Étude' Historical Music Portrait Series. *Étude.* January 1932 to October 1940.
My Life of Music. Henry J. Wood. Gollancz, London, 1938.
American Women in Creative Music. E.N.C. Barnes. Musical Education Publishers, Washington, D.C., 1936.
Women's Work in Music. A. Elson and E. Truette. Page, Boston (Mass.), 1931.
From Piano To Forté. Mark Hambourg. Cassell & Co. Ltd., London, 1931.
Noted Names in Music. (Selected composers to 1927). W.J. Baltzell. O. Ditson, Boston (Mass.), 1927.
Modern Musicians. J. Cuthbert Hadden. T.N. Foulis, London, 1914.

List C. Selective List of Biographies and Autobiographies of the Pianists in this Book and Treatises which they themselves wrote.

Note that many of them contain information and anecdotes about other pianists apart from the subject of the particular book.

1. Camille Saint-Saëns
Saint-Saëns and His Circle. James Harding. Chapman & Hall, London, 1965.
Saint-Saëns. Arthur Harvey. John Lane, The Bodley Head, London, 1921.

2. Vladimir de Pachmann
Pachmann and Chopin. K.S. Sorabjii. *Around Music,* London, 1932.
Music Portfolios. The Strand Magazine, London, 1921.

3. Teresa Carreño
Teresa Carreño, 1853-1917. Israel Peño. Caracas, 1953.
Esbozo Biografico de Teresa Carreño. A. Marquez Rodriguez. Caracas, 1953.
Teresa Carreño - By the Grace of God. Marta Milinowska. Yale University Press, New Haven, 1940. Reprinted by Da Capo Press, New York, 1977.

4. Ignace Paderewski
The Paderewski Paradox. Ronald Stevensen. Klavar Music Foundation of Great Britain, Lincoln, 1992.
Paderewski. Adam Zamoyski. Collins, London & New York, 1982.
Paderewski As I Knew Him. From the diary of Aniela Strakacz. Rutgers University Press, New Brunswick, 1949.
The Paderewski Memoirs. (Paderewski's reminiscences). Mary Lawton. Collins, London, 1939. Mary Lawton wrote up her conversations with Paderewski which had taken place at the Carlton Hotel, London. These memoirs cover Paderewski's life up to 1914 and a few later events are referred to. A second volume covering his life after 1914 was planned but Paderewski died before the further conversations took place.
Paderewski: Musician and Statesman. R. Landau. T.Y. Crowell, New York, 1933.
Note: This is a selection of the best references. There are many books on Paderewski.

5. Moriz Rosenthal
Rosenthal. (With a discography by H.L. Anderson and P. Saul.) *Recorded Sound,* vii (1962).

6. Ferruccio Busoni
Busoni, the Composer. Antony Beaumont. Faber & Faber, London, 1985.
Ferruccio Busoni. H.H. Stuckenschmidt. Calder & Boyars, London, 1970.
Ferruccio Busoni: Letters To His Wife. Translated by Rosamond Ley. Edward Arnold, London, 1938.
Ferruccio Busoni. E.J. Dent. Oxford University Press, 1933.

7. Leopold Godowsky
The Published Music of Leopold Godowsky. Leonard S. Saxe. *Notes,* March, 1957. (Contains an annotated list of original works, arrangements and editions.)
Leopold Godowsky as Creative Transcriber. K.S. Sorabjii. *Mi Contra Fa,* London, 1947.
Key to the Miniatures of Leopold Godowsky. M. Aronson, New York, 1935.

Bibliography

8. Sergei Rachmaninov
A Catalogue of the Compositions of Sergei Rachmaninov. R. Threlfall and C. Norris. Scolar Pub. Co., London, 1982.
Rakhmaninov. Geoffrey Norris. J.M. Dent & Sons, London, 1976.
Sergei Rachmaninov and His Music. R. Threlfall, London, 1973.
Sergei Rachmaninov. J. Culshaw. Dennis Dobson, London, 1949.
Rachmaninov: A Biographical Sketch. Watson Lyle. W. Reeves, London, 1939.
Rachmaninov's Recollections. Oskar von Riesemann. Books for Libraries Press, New York, 1934. (Reprinted 1970).
A comprehensive bibliography on Rachmaninov is given at the end of Geoffrey Norris's book.

9. Harold Bauer
Joys and Sorrows. Pablo Casals. Macdonald, London, 1970.
Harold Bauer - His Book. (Autobiography). W.W. Norton & Co. Inc., New York, 1948.
Self-Portrait of the Artist as a Young Man. (Autobiographical article). *Musical Quarterly*, October, 1947.

10. Josef Lhevinne
A Century of Music Making: The Lives of Josef and Rosina Lhevinne. Robert K. Wallace. Indiana University Press, Bloomington & London, 1976.
Josef Lhevinne. G. Sherman. *Recorded Sound*, xliv, p. 784, 1971 (with Discography by H.L. Anderson).
Basic Principles of Piano Playing. Josef Lhevinne. Theodore Presser Co., Philadelphia, 1924. Reprinted in paperback by Dover Publications, New York, 1972, with a Foreword by Rosina Lhevinne.

11. Josef Hofmann
Josef Hofmann Discography. International Piano Library Bulletin,
    (i), 1967, No. 2, p. 9; Nos. 3 to 4, p. 11.
    (ii), 1968, No. 1, p. 3; No. 3, p. 3.
Piano Questions Answered. Josef Hofmann. Theodore Presser Co., Philadelphia, 1909. (Reprinted 1976).
Piano Playing. Josef Hofmann. Theodore Presser Co., Philadelphia, 1908. (Reprinted 1976).

12. Alfred Cortot
Cortot Discography. F.F. Clough and G.J. Cuming. *Gramophone Record Review*, New Series, No. 50, p. 135, 1957.
Alfred Cortot. Conversations with Bernard Gavoty. René Kister, Geneva, 1955.
Aspects de Chopin. Alfred Cortot. Paris, 1949. (English translation 1951.)
La Musique Française de Piano. Alfred Cortot. Paris, 1938.
Principes Rationnels de la Technique Pianistique. Alfred Cortot. Paris, 1928. English translation, *Rational Principles of Piano Playing*, Oliver Ditson Co., Boston, Mass., 1930.

13. Ossip Gabrilowitsch
My Husband Gabrilowitsch. Clara Clemens. Harper Bros., New York, 1938.

14. Mark Hambourg
Dictionary of National Biography. Volume covering 1951-60. Edited by E.T. Wilkins and Helen M. Palmer. Oxford University Press, 1971.
The Eighth Octave. Mark Hambourg. Williams & Norgate, London, 1951.
From Piano To Forté. Mark Hambourg. Cassell & Co. Ltd., London, 1931.

15. Wanda Landowska
Landowska On Music. Edited by Denise Restout and R. Hawkins. Secker & Warburg, London, 1965. Published six years after Landowska's death, this is a selection of her writings, with photographs and discography.
Wanda Landowska. Conversations with Bernard Gavoty. René Kister, Geneva, 1957.
Music Makers. Ronald Gelatt. Alfred A. Knopf, New York, 1953.
Wanda Landowska et le Retour aux Humanités. A. Schaeffner. *Revue Musicale,* Paris, June, 1927.

16. Artur Schnabel
The Teaching of Artur Schnabel. A collection of his writings, compiled by Konrad Wolff. Faber & Faber, London, 1972.
My Life and Music. Artur Schnabel. Colin Smythe, Gerrards Cross, 1970.
Artur Schnabel: A Biography. César Saerchinger. Cassell & Co. Ltd., London, 1957.
Music and the Line of Most Resistance. Artur Schnabel. Princeton University Press, 1942.
Reflections On Music. (*Betrachtungen über Musik*). A lecture delivered at the University of Manchester on 9th May 1933 on the occasion of the conferment of Schnabel's Honorary Degree. Manchester University Press, 1933.

17. Percy Grainger
Percy Grainger. John Bird. Elek Books, London, 1977. A paperback edition, with additions, was published by Faber & Faber, London, in 1982.
Percy Grainger: A Catalogue of the Music. Edited by D. Tall, London, 1982.
The Percy Grainger Companion. L. Foreman. Thames Publishing Co., London, 1981.
A Complete Catalogue of the Works of Percy Grainger. Edited by Teresa Balough, Perth, 1975.
Percy Grainger, the Inveterate Innovator. T.C. Slattery, Evanston, 1974.
The Running Pianist. R.L. Taylor. Doubleday, New York, 1950.
Percy Grainger, A Cosmopolitan Composer. Music Quarterly, April, 1937.
Percy Aldridge Grainger - A Study. D.C. Parker. G. Schirmer, New York and Boston, 1918.
Percy Grainger, The Music and the Man. Cyril Scott. *Music Quarterly,* July, 1916.

18. Wilhelm Backhaus
The Hallé, 1858-1983. Michael Kennedy. Manchester University Press, 1982.
The Henry Wood Proms. David Cox. British Broadcasting Corporation, London, 1980.
The History of the Royal Manchester College of Music, 1893-1972. Michael Kennedy. Manchester University Press, 1971.
Obituaries of Backhaus in *The Times, The Guardian, The Daily Telegraph,* and *The New York Times* (all in the editions of 7th July 1969) and *The Observer* (13th July 1969).
Travelling Virtuoso. Article in *The Times,* 11th April 1960.
My Life of Music. Henry J. Wood. Gollancz, London, 1938.

Bibliography

19. Ethel Leginska
No books on Ethel Leginska have yet been published but a biography by the authors of this book, *Leginska - Forgotten Genius of Music*, is completed and will be published shortly by The North West Player Piano Association. Most of the information for the 'Leginska' chapter in the present book has been compiled through the authors' researches from original sources in Britain (Hull in particular) and the USA.

20. Artur Rubinstein
Arthur Rubinstein. Harvey Sachs. Weidenfeld & Nicolson, London, 1996.
My Many Years. Artur Rubinstein. Jonathan Cape, London and Alfred A Knopf, New York, 1980.
My Young Years. Artur Rubinstein. Same publishers as *My Many Years*, 1973.
Artur Rubinstein. Bernard Gavoty. René Kister, Geneva, 1955.

21. Benno Moiseiwitsch
Benno Moiseiwitsch. Maurice Moiseiwitsch. Frederick Muller Ltd., London, 1965.

22. Myra Hess
Myra Hess: A Portrait. Marian McKenna. Hamish Hamilton, London, 1976.
Myra Hess, By Her Friends. (16 contributors). Edited by D. Lassimonde and H. Ferguson. Hamish Hamilton, London, 1966.
Myra Hess Discography. F.F. Clough and G.J. Cuming. *Recorded Sound*, No. 24, p. 104, 1966.
Myra Hess. Howard Ferguson. *Recorded Sound*, 1966.
Tobias Matthay. Myra Hess. *Recorded Sound*, No. 24, p. 98, 1966. (Transcribed from a broadcast talk of 1949).

23. Walter Gieseking
Walter Gieseking: A Critical Discography. Emmet M. Ford. *AMICA Journal*, Vol. 18, No. 4, May 1981.
Modern Masters of the Keyboard. Harriette Brower. Books for Libraries Press, Freeport, New York, 1969. (Reprint of a book first published in 1926).
The Times, 27th October 1956. Obituary of Walter Gieseking.
Walter Gieseking. Bernard Gavoty. René Kister, Geneva, 1955.

24. Vladimir Horowitz
Horowitz: A Biography. Glenn Plaskin. Macdonald & Co., New York, 1983.

25. Dinu Lipatti
Lipatti. Dragos Tanasescu and Grigore Bargauanu. Translated from Rumanian by C. Grindea. Kahn & Averill, London, 1988.
Lipatti. Dragos Tanasescu. Meridiane, Bucharest, 1965.
Dinu Lipatti. B. Siki. *Recorded Sound*, No. 15, p. 232, 1964.
La Vie du Pianiste Dinu Lipatti Écrite Par Sa Mère. (The Life of Dinu Lipatti Written By His Mother). A. Lipatti. Paris, 1954.
Hommage à Dinu Lipatti. M. Lipatti. Geneva, 1952.
Dinu Lipatti. Walter Legge. *Gramophone*, xxviii (1951). Reprinted in *The Gramophone Jubilee Book*, p. 202ff, London, 1973.

List D. References to Recorded Music
a) Gramophone
Catalogue of Recordings of Classical Pianists born to 1872. J. Methuen-Campbell. Disco Epsom Ltd., Chipping Norton, 1984.
The Guinness Book of Recorded Sound. Robert and Celia Dearling, with Brian Rust. Guinness Books, Enfield, 1984.
The Incredible Music Machine. J. Lowe, R. Miller and R. Roar. Quartet Books, London, 1982.
The Record Guide. E. Sackville-West and D. Shawe-Taylor. Collins, London, 1951.
Gramophone Records of the First World War. An undated compilation of the HMV catalogues of 1914-18. David & Charles, Newton Abbot.

In addition to the above, many present and old record catalogues have been consulted including those issued by Columbia, Decca, Deutsche Grammophon, HMV, Nimbus, Parlophone, Pathé, Pavilion, Phillips and RCA-Victor.

b) Player Piano
Duo-Art:
Catalogue of Duo-Art Piano Rolls. Compiled by Charles D. Smith. The Player Shop, Monrovia, California, 1987.
The Complete Duo-Art Classical Catalogue. Compiled by Albert M. Petrak. Klavier Records, Hollywood, California, 1975. (Revised and reprinted from a list prepared in 1961).
Music for the Pianola and Duo-Art. The Aeolian Company, New York, 1932.
Duo-Art Piano Music. A complete classified and illustrated catalogue, to 1927. The Aeolian Company, New York, 1927. A supplement was issued in 1932.

Ampico:
Ampico was The American Piano Company, also known as The Ampico Corporation.
The Complete Catalogue of Ampico Reproducing Piano Rolls. Compiled by Elaine Obenchain. W.H. Edgerton, Darien, Connecticut, 1977.
A Catalogue of Music for the Ampico. A complete classified and illustrated catalogue to 1925. The Ampico Corporation, New York, 1925.

Welte:
The Welte-Mignon: Its Music and Musicians. Compiled by C.D. Smith and R.J. Howe. Vestal Press, New York, 1994.

General:
The Classical Reproducing Piano Roll. A catalogue index. Compiled by Larry Sitsky. Greenwood Press, Westport, Connecticut. 1990.

In addition to the above, various company catalogues dating from the earlier years of the century have been consulted for the following roll-producing companies: Aeolian, Ampico, Hupfeld, Philipps, Welte and Wilcox & White.

Appendix 1. Recordings: Gramophone Records (Discography)

Most of the records of the pianists whose lives form the subject of this book are of the 78rpm pre-LP variety which have long since ceased to be offered commercially in their original form. Some of the pianists recorded prolifically, for example Paderewski, Rubinstein and Schnabel; others such as Busoni and Carreño not at all or only rarely. Many records of the more recent pianists including Rubinstein and Horowitz are readily available. There are four main sources of acquiring recordings of the earlier pianists of the Golden Age:

1) Brand new re-issues on compact disc of their old recordings. They are produced regularly but often soon disappear from the catalogues. It is wise to snap them up when possible, if interested.
2) Re-issues as in (1) from the recent past but which are no longer available in the current lists. They can often be found as 'deletions' in the 'historic' section of displays at record retailers and in second-hand record shops.
3) Original old (second-hand) 78rpm recordings. There are specialist record shops which deal in these, e.g. *The Record Exchange* of Lower Hillgate, Stockport which stocks thousands of them.
4) Record fairs, jumble sales, car boot sales, charity shops, general second-hand shops, and the like. All sorts of gems can be found in such places.

It would be pointless to list hundreds of 78rpm records that have long since ceased to be readily available. Several years ago we prepared an extensive discography of the recordings of the pianists in this book (LP, Cassette and CD) that were or had recently been available, and we updated it from time to time. However, the record market has suffered a dramatic change in recent years. LPs are now almost unobtainable except in specialist shops and the number of cassettes on the market is rapidly decreasing.

It has been decided, in view of the demise of the long-playing record and cassette, not to include a list of old records that are no longer generally available but to present instead a discography consisting entirely of compact discs that are known to be available at the time of writing (January 1996). The discography does not give all discs that are currently available but nearly all are listed. In general the only recordings omitted are for pianists who have a lot of recordings to their name, in which case discs have been omitted in which they are only one contributor to the disc amongst many others. In the case of pianists for whom few recordings are available all their currently-available discs are listed. Even a single CD, or one or two tracks from a CD in some cases, is enough to give an impression of the playing of the various pianists. Many of the CDs quoted here are issued by the smaller companies which specialise in historic re-issues and have acquired the right to re-issue recordings originally made for the larger companies such as HMV and Columbia. However, the larger companies themselves also issue various series of historic recordings from time to time. Moreover, the recordings of pianists such as Gieseking, Horowitz and Rubinstein are not yet regarded as historic and still figure in the standard lists of the large companies.

Note: i) The companies listed alongside the pianists' names are the ones for whom they recorded. 'G &T' is an abbreviation for The Gramophone and Typewriter Company, the forerunner of The Gramophone Company and HMV.

ii) 'exc' in brackets means excerpts from the composition(s) named.

1. Camille Saint-Saëns   G & T/HMV
Archiphon:
ARC 106 Piano roll recordings of Saint-Saëns, Reinecke and Leschetizky. Several short pieces are played, shared between the three pianists.
Condon Collection:
690.07.004 Piano roll recordings of six pianists including Saint-Saëns.

None of Saint-Saëns' disc recordings is currently available on CD but some of his HMV recordings of 1919 (78s) may still be obtainable from specialist second-hand dealers.

2. Vladimir de Pachmann   G & T/Gramophone Co./Victor/Columbia/HMV
Pavilion Records:
OPAL CD 9840 Music by Chopin, Schumann, Raff and Verdi/Liszt.

3. Teresa Carreño
Carreño made no disc recordings and none of her piano roll recordings is currently available on disc though some are soon to be issued by Nimbus Records.

4. Ignace Paderewski   Gramophone Co./Victor/HMV
Pavilion Records:
GEMM 9323 Chopin I: A selection.
GEMM 9397 Chopin II: A further selection.
GEMM 9499 The Art of Paderewski I. Haydn, Mozart, Beethoven, Schubert and some of Paderewski's own compositions.
GEMM 9943 The Art of Paderewski II. Couperin, Liszt, Stojowski, Schelling and Wagner.
GEMM 9109 The Art of Paderewski III. Schumann, Mendelssohn, Debussy, Rubinstein and Brahms.
OPAL 9839 Pupils of Leschetizky. Paderewski plays two compositions of Chopin. The disc also features Bauer, Gabrilowitsch, Hambourg, Leginska, Moiseiwitsch and others.
RCA:
1 CD:MP GD 60923 Paderewski plays Beethoven, Chopin, Liszt, Schumann and Wagner-Schelling.
Nimbus:
NI8801 The Grand Piano Era. Paderewski plays one track; his own *Caprice*, Op. 14, No. 3 (from Duo-Art piano rolls).
NI8802 The Polish Virtuoso. Paderewski plays six of the tracks, all of which are his own compositions, including the famous *Minuet* and *Caprice* (from Duo-Art piano rolls).

5. Moriz Rosenthal   Parlophone/Edison/Victor/HMV
Pavilion Records:
GEMM 9339 Moriz Rosenthal I. Mainly Chopin but also includes Strauss's Op. 314 and *Vienna Carnival*.
GEMM 9963 Moriz Rosenthal II. Chopin, and works by Liszt, Albéniz, Debussy, Liadov and Rosenthal himself.
APR:
APR 7002 The Complete HMV Recordings, 1934-37. Works by Chopin, Liszt, Rosenthal and Schubert.
APR 7013 Romantic Piano Rarities. Rosenthal is one of several contributors including

Discography

Rachmaninov, Godowsky, Lhevinne and Hofmann. Works by several composers. Rosenthal plays his own *Papillons* and *Blue Danube* Paraphrase.
Video Artists International:
VAIA 1019 J. Strauss -Virtuoso Piano Transcriptions. Several pianists contribute. Rosenthal plays his *Blue Danube* Paraphrase.

6. Ferruccio Busoni Columbia (a few acoustic recordings only)
Pavilion Records:
GEMM CD 9347 Busoni/Petri. Complete recordings of Busoni, and Petri plays works by Busoni.
GEMM CD 9014 Busoni and His Circle I.   Mainly performances by Busoni's pupils.
GEMM CD 9156 Busoni and His Circle II.   More performances by Busoni's pupils.
Symposium:
SYMCD 1145 Music by Alkan, Bach, Beethoven, Chopin and Liszt, played by Busoni, Grainger and Petri.
Condon Collection:
690.07.014 Piano Roll Rarities, Vol.I. Piano roll performances of various pianists including Busoni.
Nimbus:
NI 8801 The Grand Piano Era. Busoni features on one track in which he plays his own transcription of Bach's Suite for Solo Violin in D (from Duo-Art piano rolls).

7. Leopold Godowsky Columbia/Brunswick
APR:
APR 7010 Godowsky: UK Columbia Records, 1928-30. Beethoven: Piano Sonata No. 26; Grieg: Ballade, Op. 24; Schumann: *Carnaval*; Chopin: Nocturnes (exc.) and Piano Sonata No. 2.
APR 7011 Godowsky: American Recordings, 1913-26. Music by many different composers.
APR 7013 Romantic Piano Rarities, Vol. I. Contributions from Godowsky and others.

8. Sergei Rachmaninov Victor/Edison
Pavilion Records:
GEMM CD 9414 Rachmaninov Conducts His Own Compositions. 3rd Symphony, *Vocalise* and *The Isle of the Dead*. These are said to be his only works recorded as a conductor.
GEMM CD 9457 Rachmaninov Plays. Bach, Beethoven, Chopin, Debussy, Handel, Liszt, Mendelssohn, Mussorgsky, Schubert, Strauss and Tchaikovsky.
Decca:
CD 425 964-2 Ampico piano roll recordings of his own compositions. Prelude in C sharp minor, *Élegie*, *Barcarolle*, *Humoresque*, etc.
CD 440 066-2 Rachmaninov's Ampico piano roll recordings of the music of other composers including Bach, Beethoven, Chopin, Paderewski, Schubert and Tchaikovsky.
RCA:
10 CD:MP 09026-61265-2 (10 CD set) The Complete RCA Recordings.
1 CD:MP GD 87766 Rachmaninov plays Rachmaninov. Solo works and transcriptions of music by Bach, Mendelssohn and Mussorgsky.
1 CD:MP 09026-62533-2 Rachmaninov plays Chopin. Includes a Sonata, Ballade, Grand Valse Brillante, Valse Brillante, Waltz, Scherzo, Mazurkas and Nocturnes.
3 CD:MP 09026-61879-2 (3 CD set) Music by Grieg performed by Rachmaninov and various other artists.
1 CD RD 85997 Rachmaninov plays his Piano Concertos Nos. 2 and 3 (Philadelphia Orch./ Ormandy).
2 CD:MP 09026-61658-2 (2 CD set) Rachmaninov plays Rachmaninov. 1st, 2nd, 3rd and 4th

Piano Concertos and *Rhapsody on a Theme of Paganini* (Philadelphia Orch./Ormandy & Stokowski).
1 CD:MP 07863-56659-2   Concertos 1 and 4 and *Rhapsody on a Theme of Paganini* (Philadelphia Orch./Ormandy & Stokowski.)

9. Harold Bauer   HMV/ Victor/ Schirmer
Biddulph:
LAB 072/3 Flonzaley Quartet Play Romantic Masterworks. Chamber music by Schubert, Schumann and Brahms.
LHW 007 Harold Bauer, 1924-28 Victor Recordings. Works by Bach, Bauer, Beethoven, Chopin, Durand, Kozeluch, Liszt, Rubinstein, Saint-Saëns, Schubert, Schumann and Schütt.
LHW 009 Harold Bauer, Victor and Schirmer Records. Works by Bach, Brahms, Chopin, Couperin, Debussy, Handel, Grieg, Mendelssohn, Scarlatti, Schubert and Schumann.
Condon Collection:
690.07.008 Piano rolls of music by various composers played by Wandowska, Hess and Bauer.
Simax:
PSC 1809-2 Grieg - Historical Piano Recordings. Contributions from many pianists including Bauer.
Pavilion Records:
OPAL CD 9839 Pupils of Leschetizky. Bauer was not a Leschitizky pupil but Gabrilowitsch was and the disc includes Bauer and Gabrilowitsch playing 4-handed arrangements of Arensky's Suite for Two Pianos (Waltz), Op. 15 and Schütt's *Impromptu Rococo*, Op. 58, No. 2. The disc also features Gabrilowitsch, Hambourg, Leginska, Moiseiwitsch, Paderewski and others.
Nimbus Records:
NI 8801 Bauer plays one track, Schumann's Toccata, Op. 7 (from a Duo-Art piano roll).

10. Josef Lhevinne   Victor/Pathé/Marconi
Dante:
HPC 008 Josef Lhevinne. Lhevinne plays music by Beethoven, Chopin, Debussy, Liszt, Mozart, Rachmaninov, Schulz-Evler and Tchaikovsky. Also, Josef and Rosina Lhevinne play Mozart's Sonata for Two Pianos, K. 488.
APR:
APR 7013 Romantic Piano Rarities, Vol. I. Music by various composers. Lhevinne is one of several contributors.
Condon Collection:
690.07. 014 Piano Roll Rarities, Vol. I. Music by various composers. Lhevinne is one of several contributors.
Video Artists International:
VAIA 1019 J. Strauss, Virtuoso Piano Transcriptions. Lhevinne is one of several contributors. In the recent past L'Oiseau Lyre have issued a number of recordings of Lhevinne's Ampico piano rolls but they are not in their catalogue at the present time. A recently deleted disc of Rosina Lhevinne playing Mozart's Concerto No. 21 with the Juilliard Orchestra (CBS CD 44845) may still be obtainable.

11. Josef Hofmann   Columbia/HMV/Brunswick
Video Artists International:
VAIA 1020 The Complete Josef Hofmann, Vol. II. Hofmann plays music by Beethoven, Brahms, Chopin, Hofmann, Mendelssohn, Moszkowski and Rachmaninov.
VAIA 1036 The Complete Josef Hofmann, Vol. III. Hofmann plays music by Beethoven, Chopin, Dillon, Gluck, Grieg, Hofmann, Liszt, Mendelssohn, Moszkowski, Paderewski, Parker, Rachmaninov, Rubinstein, Schubert, Schumann and Sternberg.

Discography

VAIA 1047 The Complete Josef Hofmann, Vol. IV. Hofmann plays music by Beethoven, Chopin, Gluck, Hofmann, Liszt, Rachmaninov, Rubinstein, Scarlatti and Wagner.
APR:
APR 7013 Romantic Piano Rarities. Hofmann and other artists play music by various composers.
Simax:
PSC 1809(1) Grieg: Historical Piano Recordings. Contributions from various pianists including Hofmann.
Nimbus Records (from Duo-Art piano rolls):
NI 8803 Josef Hofmann plays Chopin. A selection of 12 Chopin items.
NI 8802 The Polish Virtuoso. Six of the tracks are Hofmann recordings; music by Hofmann himself (2 tracks) and Moszkowski (4).
NI 8801 The Grand Piano Era. Hofmann plays three of the tracks; Chopin: Nocturne, Op. 27, No. 2 and Scherzo in C sharp minor; and Moszkowski: *Étincelles*, Op. 36.
NI 7811 Ernestine Schumann-Heinck: Opera and Song Recital. Hofmann contributes to some of the tracks.

12. Alfred Cortot HMV

Pavilion Records:
GEMM 9134 Cortot/Teyte. Songs Maggie Teyte recorded with Cortot as accompanist in 1936.
GEMM 9491 Cortot: French Concertos. Chopin: Concerto No. 2; Saint-Saëns: Concerto No. 4; and Ravel's Concerto for the Left Hand.
GEMM 9396 Cortot plays Liszt: A number of works recorded between 1919 and 1937.
GEMM 9931 Cortot plays Schumann: I and GEMM 9332 Cortot plays Schumann: II. Included in these two discs are *Carnaval, Kinderszenen, Études Symphoniques, Davidsbundlertänze, Papillons, Kreisleriana* and extracts from *Fantasiestücke*, Op. 12.
HMV:
CDH 7 61050 1 Chopin: Various works including Preludes, Impromptus, Barcarolle, Op. 60 and Berceuse, Op. 57.
CDZ 767359 2 (6 CD set) Chopin: Piano Works.
CHS 7 64057 2 (3 CD set) Piano Trios, with Pablo Casals and Jacques Thibaud. Beethoven, Haydn, Mendelssohn, Schubert, Schumann and Brahms' Double Concerto.
Suite:
CDS 1 6003 Chopin: 24 Preludes, Op. 28; Sonata No. 2, Op. 5 (recorded 1955).
Biddulph:
LHW 001 Cortot plays Chopin.
LHW 002 Cortot plays Weber and Mendelssohn.
LHW 003 Cortot plays Schumann, Vol. I.
LHW 004 Cortot plays Schumann, Vol. II.
LHW 005 Cortot plays Schumann, Vol. III.
LHW 006 Cortot plays Debussy and Ravel.
Dante:
HPC 003 Cortot plays Chopin.
HPC 004/5 Cortot plays Schumann.
Music and Arts:
MACD-317 Cortot plays Chopin.
MACD-615 Cortot - Rare 78s.
MACD-662 Cortot plays Weber and Liszt.
MACD-858 Cortot plays Schumann.

13. Ossip Gabrilowitsch   RCA Victor

Pavilion Records:
OPAL CD 9839 Pupils of Leschetizky. On this disc Gabrilowitsch plays two 4-handed arrangements with Harold Bauer: Arensky's Suite for Two Pianos, Op. 15 (Waltz); and Schütt's *Impromptu Rococo*, Op. 58, No. 2. The disc also features Bauer, Hambourg, Leginska, Moiseiwitsch, Paderewski and others.

Biddulph:
LAB 072/3 Flonzaley Quartet play Romantic Masterworks. Gabrilowitsch and Bauer contribute in chamber music by Brahms, Mendelssohn, Schubert and Schumann.

14. Mark Hambourg   HMV

Pavilion Records:
GEMM CD 9147 Beethoven: Piano Concerto No. 3; Liszt: *Concerto Pathetique* (with his daughter Michal Hambourg) and music by Bach, Dvorak, Falla, Mendelssohn and Moszkowski.
OPAL CD 9839 Pupils of Leschetizky. On this disc Hambourg plays music by Scarlatti: *The Cat's Fugue*; Gluck/Sgambati: Melodie from *Orfeo;* Beethoven: Finale to Sonata, Op. 2 No. 3; and Strauss/ Tausig: *The Kiss Waltz*. The disc also features Bauer, Gabrilowitsch, Leginska, Moiseiwitsch, Paderewski and others.

15. Wanda Landowska   HMV/RCA Victor

Pavilion Records:
GEMM 9489 Landowska - Bach: Includes some of the *English Suites*, *French Suites*, *Little Preludes*, a Partita, a Fantasia, Prelude and Fugue in C minor, and Toccata in D.
GEMM 9490 Landowska - Handel: Includes Concerto in B flat and six sonatas.
GEMM 9019 Landowska - Musique Ancienne I: Works by Byrd, Couperin, Pachelbel, Purcell, Rameau and Scarlatti.
GEMM 9096 Landowska - Musique Ancienne II: Mainly Couperin but also includes Preludes and Fugues from Book 1 of Bach's *The Well-Tempered Clavier*.

RCA:
2 CD:MP GD 60919 Bach: *Goldberg Variations*, Partita No. 2, 2-Part and 3-Part Inventions, etc.
2 CD:MP GD 86217 (2 CD set). Bach: *The Well-Tempered Clavier*, Part 1.
3 CD:MP GD 87825 (3 CD set). Bach: *The Well-Tempered Clavier*, Part II.

Biddulph:
LHW 016 Landowska - The Early Recordings, 1923-30. Landowska plays music by Bach, Byrd, Couperin, Daquin, Handel, Landowska, Mozart, Rameau and Scarlatti.
LHW 013 Landowska plays Mozart.   Piano Concerto No. 26 (Landowska Orch./Goehr); Fantasia, K. 397; Piano Sonatas, K. 332 and K. 576.

Music Memoria:
MM 30444 Wanda Landowska Harpsichord Recital.   Landowska plays music by Chambonnières, Couperin, Daquin, Landowska and Lully.
MM 3045 Wanda Landowska Plays Handel. Various Keyboard Suites and Organ Concertos (Landowska Orch./Bigot).

16. Artur Schnabel   HMV

Pavilion Records:
GEMM 9063 Beethoven Concertos: Concerto No. 4 (1933 and 1947 recordings) and other works by Beethoven; Bagatelle, Op. 126, No. 6 (*Für Elise*); Rondo in C, Op. 51, No. 1.
GEMM 9083 Beethoven I: Sonatas Nos. 1 - 6, 19 & 20; Rondo in A; Rondo à Capriccio in G.
GEMM 9099 Beethoven II: Sonatas Nos. 7 - 13 and Minuet in E flat.
GEMM 9123 Beethoven III: Sonatas Nos. 14 - 18; Six Variations, Op. 33.

Discography

GEMM 9139 Beethoven IV: Sonatas Nos. 28, 29 (*Hammerklavier*), 30, 31, 32; *Diabelli Variations*; Bagatelles, Op. 126.
GEMM 9142 Beethoven V: Sonatas Nos. 21, 23 (*Appassionata*), 24, 25, 26 (*Les Adieux*), 27; *Eroica Variations*; Fantasie in G minor; *Für Elise*.
GEMM 9026 Szigeti (violin)/Schnabel: Sonatas: Mozart, K.481; Beethoven: No. 5 in F, Op. 24 and No. 10 in G, Op. 96.
GEMM 9378 Beethoven: *Diabelli Variations*.
GEMM 9399 Bach & Brahms I: Bach: Concerto for Two Claviers; Brahms: Piano Concerto No. 2 (LSO & BBC SO/Boult).
GEMM 9376 Bach & Brahms II: Bach: Toccatas BWV 911 & 912; Brahms: Piano Concerto No. 1 (LPO/Szell).
HMV:
CHS 7 63765 2 (8 CD set) Beethoven: Piano Sonatas.
CHS 7 63703 2 (3 CD set) Mozart: Piano Concertos Nos. 10, 19 - 21, 24 and 27; Concerto for Two Pianos, K. 365 (with Karl Ulrich Schnabel); Piano Sonatas K. 332 and 570; Rondo, K. 511.
CDH 7 61021 2 Schubert: Impromptus, D. 899 and 935; Allegretto, D. 915.
CHS 7 64259 2 (2 CD set) Schubert: Piano Sonatas Nos. 17, 20 and 21; *Moments Musicaux*, D. 780; March, D. 606.
RCA:
1CD:MP 09026-61393-2 Beethoven: Piano Concertos Nos. 4 and 5 (Chicago SO/Stock).
Music and Arts:
MACD - 750 Schnabel plays Mozart. Piano Concerto No. 20 (NYPO/Szell); Piano Concerto No. 17 (exc.) (New Friends of Music Orch./Stiedry); Piano Sonata, K. 533.

17. Percy Grainger   HMV/Columbia
Pavilion Records:
GEMM 9957 Grainger I: Grainger plays music by Bach/Grainger, Bach/Liszt, Bach/Busoni, Chopin, Debussy, Grainger, Grieg and Schumann.
GEMM 9013 Grainger II: Grainger plays Chopin: Sonatas Nos. 2 and 3; Schumann: *Symphonic Études*; Byrd: Variations.
Biddulph:
LHW 008 Percy Grainger - Grainger plays Schumann and Brahms. Schumann: Piano Sonata No. 2; Romance, Op. 28 (exc.); *Fantasiestücke*, Op. 12 (exc.); Symphonic Studies; Brahms: Waltzes, Op. 39 (exc.); Piano Sonata No. 3.
LHW 010 Grainger plays Bach and Chopin. Bach: Prelude and Fugue, BWV 543; Toccata and Fugue, BWV 565; Fantasia and Fugue, BWV 542; Chopin: Piano Sonatas Nos. 2 and 3; Études (exc.).
Simax:
PSC 1809(1) Grieg - Historical Piano Recordings. Contributions from Grainger and many others.
Nimbus Records:
NI 8801 The Grand Piano Era. Grainger plays Stanford's *Maguire's Kick* (arr. Grainger) from *Four Irish Dances*, Op. 79 (from a Duo-Art piano roll).

18. Wilhelm Backhaus   HMV/Decca
Pavilion Records:
GEMM 9385 Backhaus plays Brahms: Ballades, Intermezzi, Rhapsodies and other shorter pieces. Recorded in the mid 1930s.
GEMM 9902 Backhaus plays Chopin: The 24 Études; Berceuse; Grande Valse Brillante; Valse in D flat, Fantasie Impromptu in C; also Liszt's *Waldesrauschen*.

Decca:
CD 433 901-2 Bach: *English Suite* No. 6; *French Suite* No. 5; Haydn: Piano Sonata No. 34.
CDs 433 882-2 (8 CD set) Beethoven: Piano Sonatas Nos. 1 - 32.
CDs 433 891-2 (3 CD set) Beethoven: Piano Concertos Nos. 1 - 5; *Diabelli Variations* (Wiener Philharmoniker/Schmidt-Isserstedt).
CD 425 066-2 Beethoven: Piano Concertos Nos. 4 and 5 (Wiener Philharmoniker/Krauss).
CD 425 973-2 Brahms: Cello Sonatas (with Pierre Fournier).
CD 433 895-2 (2 CD set) Brahms: Piano Concertos Nos. 1 and 2 (Wiener Phil./Böhm).
CD 433 900-2 Mozart: Piano Sonatas, K. 282, 283, 330 and 332.
CD 433 898-2 Mozart: Piano Concerto No. 27, K. 595 (Wiener Philharmoniker/Böhm); Piano Sonatas K. 331 and 457; Rondo, K. 511.
CD 433 902-2 Schubert: *Six Moments Musicaux*, D. 780; Two Impromptus.
CD 433 899-2 Schumann: Piano Concerto (Wiener Phil./Wand); *Waldszenen*, Op. 82.
CD 433 903-2 (10 CD set) Beethoven: Piano Concertos; Brahms: Piano Concertos; Various compositions by Bach, Haydn, Mozart, Schubert, Schumann and others.
Suite:
CDS 1 6008 Beethoven: Piano Concerto No. 5 (Orch. Filarmonica di Berlino/Knappertbusch); Sonata No. 21, Op. 53.
Biddulph:
LHW 017 Backhaus plays Brahms - Vol. I. Piano Concerto No. 1 (BBC SO/Boult); Scherzo, Op. 4 (exc.); Waltzes, Op. 39 (exc.); *Hungarian Dances* (exc.).
LHW 019 Backhaus plays Brahms - Vol. II. Waltzes, Op. 39 (exc.); Piano Pieces, Op. 76 (exc.); Rhapsodies, Op. 79; Piano Pieces, Op. 116, 117, 118, 119 (exc.).
Memoria: (not to be confused with Music Memoria)
99 1009 Backhaus plays Mozart. Fantasia, K. 475; Piano Sonatas, K. 457, 330 and 331; Rondo, K. 511.
Condon Collection:
690.07.013 Backhaus Piano Rolls. A selection of Backhaus's piano rolls.

19. Ethel Leginska Pathé/Columbia
Pavilion Records:
OPAL CD 9839 Pupils of Leschetizky. Leginska plays two items: Schubert: Impromptu in A flat, Op. 142, No. 2 (rec. 1928); and Liszt: *Hungarian Rhapsody* No. 8 (abridged) (rec. 1926). Disc also features Bauer, Gabrilowitsch, Hambourg, Moiseiwitsch, Paderewski and others.

20. Artur Rubinstein RCA Victor/Decca
Pavilion Records:
GEMM 9464 Chopin: 4 Scherzi; 2 Mazurkas; Berceuse; Barcarolle; plus pieces by Brahms, Debussy, Albéniz and Granados. (Recorded 1927 to 1933).
HMV:
CHS 7 64491 2 (2 CD set) Chopin: Piano Concertos Nos. 1 and 2 (LSO/Barbirolli); 19 Nocturnes; Valse, Op. 64, No. 2.
CHS 7 64933 2 (5 CD set) Chopin: Piano Concertos Nos. 1 and 2 (LSO/Barbirolli); Nocturnes; Mazurkas; Scherzi; Polonaises; Andante Spianato and Grande Polonaise, Op. 32; Berceuse, Op. 57; Barcarolle, Op. 60; 2 Valses.
CHS 7 64697 2 (3 CD set) Chopin: Mazurkas; Polonaises; Scherzi; Andante Spianato and Grand Polonaise; Barcarolle, Op. 60; Berceuse, Op. 57; Valse, Op. 34, No. 1.
RCA:
Rubinstein recorded prolifically for RCA. A large number of issues are still available on compact disc; many of these are multi-CD sets (e.g. much of Chopin's piano music on 11CDs) amounting to a total of well over 70 CDs. Rubinstein recorded most of the major piano works

Discography

of the great composers and several minor ones and many of his recordings are still available. All codes start with a number, 1CD, 3CD, etc. indicating the number of CDs in the set.

1 CD:MP 09026-62590-2 Bach: Chaconne (trans. Busoni): Franck: Prelude, Chorale & Fugue; Liszt: Sonata in B minor.
3 CD:MP 09026-61260-2 Beethoven: The Five Concertos (Symphony of the Air/Krips) and Sonata, Op. 31, No. 3.
1 CD: RD 85675 Beethoven: Piano Concertos Nos. 2 and 3 (Boston SO/Leinsdorf).
1 CD: RD 85676 Beethoven: Piano Concertos Nos. 4 and 5. (Boston SO/Leinsdorf).
1 CD: RD 89389 Beethoven: Piano Concerto No. 5. (London PO/Barenboim).
1 CD:MP GD 60261 Beethoven: Piano Concerto No. 3 (NBC SO/Toscanini).
1 CD:MP 09026-61760-2 Beethoven and Schubert: Chamber music (with Heifetz and Feuermann).
1 CD:MP 09026-61443-2 Beethoven: Piano Sonatas Nos. 8, 14, 23 and 26.
1 CD:MP 09026-61263-2 Brahms: Piano Concerto No. 1 (Chicago SO/Reiner) and other items.
1 CD:MP 09026-61442-2 Brahms: Piano Concerto No. 2 (RCA Vict. SO/Krips) and other items.
1 CD: RD 85669 Brahms & Schumann: Piano Quintets (with the Guarneri Quartet).
1 CD:MP GD 85677 Brahms: Piano Quartets Nos. 1 and 3 (with the Guarneri Quartet).
1 CD: RD 86260 Brahms: Trios Nos. 1 and 2 (with Szeryng and Fournier).
1 CD:MP 09026-61763-2 Brahms: Trio No. 1, Op. 8 (with Heifetz and Feuermann);
1 CD:MP GD 86264 Brahms: Sonatas Nos. 1 & 3; Beethoven: Op. 30, No. 3 (with H. Szeryng).
1 CD:MP 09026-62592-2 Brahms: Cello Sonatas (with G. Piatigorsky) and 5 Intermezzi.
1 CD:MP 09026-61862-2 Brahms: Piano Sonata No. 3; Ballades, Op. 10 and other items.
1 CD: RD 85612 Chopin: Piano Concertos No. 1 (New SO of London/Skrowaczewski) and No. 2 (Symphony of the Air/Wallenstein).
1 CD:MP GD 60404 Chopin: Piano Concerto No. 2 (Philadelphia Orch./Ormandy); *Fantasia on Polish Airs;* and Andante Spianato and Grand Polonaise.
11 CD:MP GD60822 (RCA's 11 CD set) The Chopin Collection: Ballades, Barcarolle, Berceuse, Concertos, Fantasie, Impromptus, Mazurkas, Nocturnes, Polonaises, Preludes, Scherzos, Sonatas, Waltzes et al.
1 CD:MP GD 87725 The Chopin Collection: Highlights.
1 CD: RD 89651 Chopin: Ballades 1 to 4; Scherzos 1 to 4.
2 CD: RD 85171 Chopin: 51 Mazurkas.
2 CD: RD 89563 Chopin: 19 Nocturnes.
1 CD: RD 89911 Chopin: Grande Polonaise; 4 Impromptus; Barcarolle; 3 Nouvelles Études; Bolero; Berceuse; Tarantelle; Andante Spianato and Grande Polonaise.
1 CD: RD 89814 Chopin: Polonaises, Nos. 1 to 7.
1 CD:MP GD 60047 Chopin: Preludes, Op. 28; Sonata No. 2 and other items.
1 CD: RD 89812 Chopin: Sonatas Nos. 2 and 3; Fantasie, Op. 49.
1 CD: RD 89564 Chopin: Waltzes, Nos. 1 to 14.
1 CD: RD 86263 Dvorak: Quintet, Op. 81; Quartet, Op. 96 (with the Guarneri Quartet).
1 CD:MP 09026-61863-2 de Falla: Various items; Franck: Symphonic Variations (Symphony of the Air/Wallenstein); Saint-Saëns: Piano Concerto No. 2 (Philadelphia Orchestra/Ormandy).
1 CD:MP GD 60046 de Falla: Various items; Liszt: Piano Concerto No. 1 (Dallas SO/Dorati) and Szymanowski: *Symphonie Concertante*, Op. 60.
1 CD:MP 09026-61496-2 Franck: Symphonic Variations (Symphony of the Air/Wallenstein); Liszt: Piano Concerto. No. 1 (RCA Victor Orch./Wallenstein) and Saint-Saëns: Piano Concerto No. 2 (Symphony of the Air/Wallenstein).
1 CD:MP 09026-61262-2 Grieg: Piano Concerto (Un-named Orchestra/Wallenstein).
1 CD:MP 09026-61883-2 Grieg: Piano Concerto (Philadelphia Orch./Ormandy) and other items.
3 CD:MP 09026-61879-2 Grieg: Historic Recordings. Various artists including Rubinstein.

1 CD:MP GD 87967 Mozart: Piano Concertos Nos. 20 and 21 (Symphony of the Air/ Wallenstein); Haydn: Andante and Variations.
1 CD:MP 09026-61860-2 Liszt: Various items including Hungarian Rhapsodies Nos. 10 & 12.
1 CD:MP 09026-61767-2 Mendelssohn: Trio for Violin and Cello, Op. 49; Tchaikovsky: Trio for Violin and Cello, Op. 50 (with Jascha Heifetz and Gregor Piatigorsky).
1 CD:MP 09026-61859-2 Mozart: Piano Concertos, No. 17 (RCA Victor SO/Wallenstein) and No. 23 (Saint Louis SO/Golschmann).
1 CD:MP GD 87968 Mozart: Piano Concertos, No. 23 (RCA Victor SO/Wallenstein) and No. 24 (RCA Victor SO/Krips) and Rondo, K. 511.
1 CD:MP GD 60406 Mozart: Quartets, K. 478 and 493 (with the Guarneri Quartet).
1 CD: RD 84934 Rachmaninov: Concerto No. 2 and *Rhapsody on a Theme of Paganini* (Chicago SO/Reiner).
1 CD:MP GD 86262 Schubert: Trio, D. 898, Op. 99; Schumann: Trio, Op. 63 (with Szeryng and Fournier).
1 CD:MP 09026-61444-2 Schumann: Piano Concerto (RCA Victor SO/Krips) and other items.
1 CD: RD 85667 Schumann: *Carnaval, Fantasiestücke, Prophet Bird, Romance*.
1 CD:MP 09026-61264-2 Schumann: *Kreisleriana*, Op. 16; Fantasia, Op. 17.
1 CD:MP 09026-61775-2 Debussy: Sonata No. 3; Martinu: Duo for Violin and Cello; Ravel: Minuet and Trio in A minor; Respighi: Sonata in B minor (with Heifetz, Bay and Piatigorsky).
1 CD:MP GD 60211 Highlights from the Rubinstein Collection.
1 CD:MP 09026-61445-2 Rubinstein: Carnegie Hall Highlights.
1 CD: 09026-61160-2 Rubinstein: The Last Recital for Israel.
1 CD:MP 09026-61446-2 Music of France: Ravel, Poulenc, Chabrier, Debussy, etc.
1 CD:MP 09026-61261-2 Music of Spain: Albéniz, Granados, Mompou, etc.
There are several other RCA compact discs in which Rubinstein is one of many contributors.
Condon Collection:
690.07.007 Piano roll performances of the music of various composers. Contributions from Rubinstein, Bauer, Hess, Landowska and others.
Decca videotape recordings:
The company has issued two videotape recordings of Rubinstein concerts:
VHS 071 109-3 Beethoven: Piano Concerto No. 3 and Brahms: Piano Concerto No. 1. Both with the Concertgebouw Orchestra/Heitink.
VHS 071 100-3 Rubinstein in Concert. Grieg: Piano Concerto; Chopin: Piano Concerto No. 2; Saint-Saëns: Piano Concerto No. 2. Both with the LSO/Previn.
RCA videotape recording:
1 VHS 74321-10488-3 Rubinstein: The Last Recital for Israel. Beethoven: Piano Sonata No. 23 (*Appassionata*); Schumann: *Fantasiestücke*; Debussy and Chopin (several items of each).

21. Benno Moiseiwitsch HMV

Pavilion Records:
GEMM 9135 Moiseiwitsch I. Brahms: *Handel Variations*; Mendelssohn: Concerto No. 1 and works by Schumann, Liszt, Stravinsky, Debussy and Ravel.
GEMM 9192 (2 CD set) Moiseiwitsch in Recital. Schumann: *Études Symphoniques*; *Kreisleriana*; *Carnaval*; Chopin: *Études*, Fantasie Impromptu and Sonata in B minor; Mussorgsky: *Pictures at an Exhibition*; Palgrem: *West Finnish Dance*; Beethoven: *Andante Favori*.
OPAL 9839 Pupils of Leschetizky. Moiseiwitsch plays Weber's *Perpetuum Mobile* and Leschetizky's Arabesque in A flat. The disc also features Bauer, Gabrilowitsch, Hambourg, Leginska, Paderewski and others.
RCA:
2 CD:MP 09026-61739-2 Chamber music (selections) with Jascha Heifetz and others.

Discography

APR:
APR 5505 Moiseiwitsch - Rachmaninov Recordings, 1937-43. Piano Concerto No. 2 (LPO/Goehr); *Rhapsody on a Theme of Paganini* (LPO/Cameron); Preludes (exc.); *Moments Musicaux*, Op. 161 (exc.). Also includes Mendelssohn: *A Midsummer Night's Dream* (exc.).
APR 7005 Benno Moiseiwitsch - Solo Recordings, 1938-50. Music by Beethoven, Chopin, Debussy, Liszt, Mendelssohn, Mussorgsky, Ravel, Schumann and Weber.
Koch International Classics:
37035-2 Benno Moiseiwitsch - A Centenary Celebration. Beethoven: Piano Concerto No. 5 (LPO/Szell); Liszt: *Hungarian Fantasie* (LPO/Lambert); Medtner: *Fairy Tales*, Op. 34 (exc.); Prokofiev: *Pieces*, Op. 4; Godowsky: *Fledermaus Potpourri*.
Testament:
SBT 1023 Moiseiwitsch plays Schumann and Brahms. Brahms: *Handel Variations*; Schumann: Fantasie; *Fantasiestücke*, Op. 12.

22. Myra Hess Columbia/HMV
Pavilion Records:
GEMM 9114 Hess - A Cameo. Includes her own *Jesu, Joy of Man's Desiring* and Mozart's Piano Concerto No. 9 in E flat, K.271.
GEMM 9462 Hess I. Schubert: Sonata No. 20 in A, D. 959; Beethoven: Sonata No. 28 in A, Op. 101; Bach/Hess *Jesu, Joy of Man's Desiring* and other items.
GEMM 9463 Hess II. Schumann: *Carnaval* (1937 recording) and Piano Concerto (un-named orchestra cond. Goehr); Griffe: *The White Peacock*; MacDowell: *AD 1620*.
Biddulph:
LHW 024 Myra Hess - The Complete Solo American Columbia Recordings. Music by Bach, Beethoven, Brahms, Debussy, Falla, Griffes, Mendelssohn, Palgrem, Ravel, Schubert, Schumann and Scarlatti.
Dutton Laboratories:
CDLX 7005 Dame Myra Hess. Schumann: Piano Concerto (Un-named SO/Goehr); *Carnaval*; Franck: *Symphonic Variations* (CBO/Cameron); Bach-Hess: *Jesu, Joy of Man's Desiring*.
Condon Collection:
690.07.008 Piano Roll Performances. Various composers. Contributions from Myra Hess and Wanda Landowska.

23. Walter Gieseking Columbia/EMI
Pavilion Records:
GEMM 9449 Gieseking. Ravel: *Gaspard* and *Miroirs*, Nos. 4 & 5; Debussy: Preludes, Book 1; *Estampes*; *L'Isle Joyeuse* (Records dating from 1938).
GEMM 9930 Gieseking I - A Cross-section of his Work. Music by Bach, Beethoven, Brahms, Mendelssohn, Debussy, Poulenc, Fauré and Scriabin.
GEMM 9011 Gieseking II - A 'Baroque to Modern' Programme. Bach: *Italian Concerto*; Beethoven: Sonata No. 17; Chopin: Mazurka in A minor and Berceuse; Falla: *Nights in the Gardens of Spain*; Liszt: Hungarian Rhapsody No. 12; Scriabin: Sonata No. 5.
HMV:
CDZ 7 62857 2 Beethoven: Piano Sonatas, No. 8 (*Pathétique*), 9, 10, 13 and 14 (*Moonlight*).
CDH 7 61004 2 2 Debussy: Preludes, Books 1 and 2.
CHS 7 63688 2 (8 CD set) Mozart: Complete Solo Piano Works.
Deutsche Grammophon:
429 929 2 (3 CD set): Bach: *The Well-Tempered Clavier* (complete).
Video Artists International:
VAIA 1008 Gieseking Plays Beethoven. Piano Sonatas Nos. 17, 21, 23 and 28; Bagatelles (exc.).

APR:
APR 5511 Gieseking - First Concerto Recordings, Vol. I. Mozart: Piano Concerto No. 9; Piano Sonata K. 570; Beethoven: Piano Concerto No. 1 (Berlin State Opera Orch./Rosbaud).
APR 5512 Gieseking - First Concerto Recordings, Vol. II. Beethoven: Piano Concerto Nos. 4 (Saxon State. Orch./Böhm) and 5 (Vienna PO/Walter); Bach: Partitas, 825-30 (exc.).
Music and Arts:
MACD-612 Walter Gieseking - Historical Broadcasts, 1944-5. Music by Bach, Beethoven, Debussy, Mozart, Ravel and Scarlatti.
Condon Collection:
690.07.01 Music by Debussy (piano roll recordings). Contributions from Gieseking and others.

24. Vladimir Horowitz   HMV/RCA Victor

Deutsche Grammophon:
423 287-2 Horowitz plays Mozart. Piano Concerto No. 23, K. 488 (Orch. del Teatro alla Scala/Giulini); Piano Sonata, K. 333.
419 045-2 Mozart: Piano Sonata, K. 330; and works by Bach, Chopin, Liszt, Moszkowski, Rachmaninov, Schubert, Schumann and Scriabin.
445 517-2 Mozart: Piano Sonatas, K. 281, 330, 333; Rondo, K. 485; Adagio, K. 540.
427 772-2 Horowitz at Home. Mozart: Piano Sonata, K. 281, Rondo, K. 485 and Adagio, K. 540; Schubert: *Moment Musical*, D. 780, No. 3; Liszt-Schubert: *Ständchen*, Valses-Caprices Nos. 6 and 7.
435 025-2 Horowitz the Poet. Schubert: Piano Sonata, D. 960; Schumann: *Kinderszenen*.
419 045-2 The Last Romantic. Schumann: *Novellette*, Op. 21, No. 1, and works by Bach-Busoni, Chopin, Liszt, Moszkowski, Mozart, Rachmaninov, Schubert and Scriabin.
419 217-2 Schumann: Studio Recordings, 1985 (New York). Works by Liszt, Scarlatti, Schubert, Schumann and Scriabin.
419 499-2 Horowitz in Moscow (April 1986). Works by Scarlatti, Mozart, Rachmaninov, Scriabin, Schubert-Liszt, Liszt, Chopin, Schumann and Moszkowski.
RCA:
Like Rubinstein, Horowitz recorded a lot of music for RCA, though not quite the vast amount that Rubinstein recorded. Notable amongst the collection is the 22 CD set of the complete Horowitz RCA recordings.
1 CD:MP GD 60377 Barber, Kabalevsky and Prokofiev: Piano Sonatas, etc.
1 CD:MP GD 87992 Beethoven: Piano Concerto No. 5 (RCA Victor Orchestra/Reiner); Tchaikovsky: Piano Concerto No. 1 (NBC SO/Toscanini).
1 CD:MP 09026-60986-2 Beethoven: Sonata No. 7; Scarlatti Sonatas and Chopin items.
1 CD:MP GD 60375 Beethoven: Sonatas Nos. 14 (*Moonlight*), 21 (*Waldstein*) and 23 (*Appassionata*).
1 CD:MP GD 60523 Brahms: Piano Concerto No. 2 (NBC SO/Toscanini); Liszt: Sonata No. 104 and Hungarian Rhapsody No. 2; Schubert: Impromptu, D. 899, No. 3.
1 CD:MP GD 60319 Brahms: Piano Concerto No. 2; Tchaikovsky: Piano Concerto No. 1 (NBC SO/Toscanini).
1 CD:MP GD 87752 Chopin: Vol. I. Ballades, Barcarolle, Études; various other items.
1 CD:MP GD 60376 Chopin: Vol. II. Piano Sonatas, Nocturnes, Mazurkas etc.
1 CD:MP 09026-60987-2 Chopin: Vol. 3. Ballade No. 4, Scherzos, Nocturnes, etc.
1 CD:MP GD 87753 Clementi: Piano Sonatas.
1 CD: 09026-61415-2 Liszt: Piano Sonata; Ballade No. 2; *Mephisto Waltz* etc.
1 CD:MP GD 60321 Mussorgsky: *Pictures at an Exhibition;* Tchaikovsky: Piano Concerto No. 1 (NBC SO/Toscanini).
1 CD:MP GD60449 Mussorgsky and Tchaikovsky: As previous disc but includes other items.
1 CD:MP GD 60526 Mussorgsky: *Pictures at an Exhibition* and other items.

Discography

1 CD: 09026-61564-2 Rachmaninov: Piano Concerto No. 3 (New York PO/Ormandy).
1 CD:MP GD 87754 Rachmaninov: Piano Concerto No. 3 (RCA Victor SO/Reiner) and other items.
1 CD:MP GD 60463 Schumann: *Kinderszenen, Variations on a Theme of Clara Wieck*, etc.
1 CD:MP GD 86680 Schumann: Piano Sonata, *Fantasiestücke*, Grand Sonata No. 3, etc.
1 CD:MP GD 86215 Scriabin: Sonatas, *Präludien*, Études, etc.
22 CD:MP 09026-61655-2 (22 CD set) The Vladimir Horowitz Edition, complete.
1 CD:MP 09026-61414-2 Horowitz in London: Chopin, Schumann, Scriabin, etc.
1 CD:MP 09026-61416-2 Horowitz at the Met: Scarlatti, Chopin, Liszt, Rachmaninov.
1 CD: 09026-62643-2 Horowitz: The Private Collection, Vol. 1. Bach, Chopin, Clementi, Liszt, Mendelssohn, Rachmaninov.
1 CD: 09026-62644-2 Horowitz: The Private Collection, Vol. II. Barber, Debussy, Kabalevsky, Poulenc, Prokofiev.
1 CD:MP GD 60461 Beethoven: Sonata No. 14, Op. 27, No. 2 (*Moonlight*); Haydn: Sonata Hob. XVI:52; Schumann: *Traumerei*; Scarlatti: K. 380; Bach (tr. Busoni): *Come, Redeemer*; Brahms: Sonata No. 3 for Violin and Piano (with Nathan Milstein).
1 CD:MP GD 60451 Music by Czerny, Rode, Mozart, Mendelssohn and Schubert.
1 CD:MP GD 87755 Horowitz Encores. Horowitz's Variations on Bizet's *Carmen* and Sousa's *The Stars and Stripes Forever*; Debussy, Mozart, Saint-Saëns/Liszt/Horowitz, etc.
Sony Classical:
13 CDs SX 13K 53456 (13 CD set) Horowitz: The Complete Masterwork Recordings.
The set is available as separate components as follows:
Vol. I.   2CDs S2K 53457 (2 CD set) The Studio Recordings, 1962-63. Chopin, Schubert, Schumann, Liszt and Beethoven.
Vol II.   CD SK 53460   The Celebrated Scarlatti Recordings. Sonatas, L. 9, 21, 22, 118, 129, 147, 164, 187, 188, 203, 241, 267, 349, 391, 424, 465, 481, 528.
Vol. III.   3CDs S3K 53461 (3 CD set) The Historic Return. Bach-Busoni, Schumann, Scriabin, Mozart, Haydn, Chopin, Liszt.
Vol. IV.   CD SK 53465   The Legendary 1968 TV Concert. Chopin, Scarlatti, Schumann, Scriabin, Bizet-Horowitz (*Carmen* Variations).
Vol. V.   CD SK 53466   A Baroque and Classical Recital. Clementi, Bach-Busoni, Scarlatti, Beethoven.
Vol. VI.   CD SK 53467   Beethoven. Sonatas No. 14, Op. 27, No. 2 (*Moonlight*); No. 21, Op. 53 (*Waldstein*); No. 23, Op. 57 (*Appassionata*).
Vol. VII. 2 CDs S2K 53468 (2 CD set) Early Romantics. Chopin: Études, Preludes, Polonaises, Mazurkas, Waltzes, etc; Schumann: *Variations on a Theme by Clara Wieck*; *Kreisleriana*, Op. 16.
Vol. VIII. CD SK 53471   The Romantic and Impressionist Era. Schubert: Two Impromptus; Liszt: *Consolation* No. 2, Scherzo and March; Debussy: Étude, No. 11; Mendelssohn: Étude, Op. 104b, No. 3.
Vol. IX.   CD SK 53472   Late Russian Romantics. A large number of works by Scriabin, Medtner and Rachmaninov.
CD SK 45818   Horowitz: The Last Recording. A number of works by Haydn, Liszt and Wagner-Liszt.
CD SK 48093   Horowitz: Discovered Treasures. Previously unreleased studio recordings of works by Scarlatti, Bach-Busoni, Clementi, Chopin, Medtner, Scriabin and Liszt.
Music and Arts:
MACD 666   Vladimir Horowitz in Recital. Music by Clementi, Chopin, Horowitz (*Carmen* Variations), Liszt, Moszkowski, Rachmaninov, Scarlatti and Schumann.

Condon Collection:
690.07.009 Piano roll recordings of Horowitz and Prokofiev.
Deutsche Grammophon videotape recordings:
VHS: PAL 072 115-3 Horowitz Plays Mozart. Piano Concerto No. 23 (Orchestra del Teatro alla Scala/Giulini).
VHS: PAL 073 118-3 Rachmaninov: Piano Concerto No. 3 (New York PO/Mehta).
VHS: PAL 073 107-3 Live Recording of a Recital in Vienna. Horowitz plays Mozart, Liszt-Schubert, Schumann, Moszkowski and Chopin.
VHS: PAL 072 121-3 Live Recording of a Recital in Vienna. Horowitz plays music including Schumann's *Kinderszenen*; Mozart's Sonata K. 333 and items by Schubert, Chopin, Liszt-Schubert, Liszt and Moszkowski.
Sony videotape recordings:
VHS SHV 53478 Vladimir Horowitz: A Reminiscence. Music by Beethoven, Chopin, Clementi, Liszt, Moszkowski, Mozart, Rachmaninov, Scarlatti, Schumann, Scriabin, Tchaikovsky and Youmans.
VHS SHV 64545 Horowitz in Moscow (April 1986 recital). Music by Scarlatti, Mozart, Rachmaninov, Scriabin, Schubert, Schubert-Liszt, Liszt, Chopin and Moszkowski.

25. Dinu Lipatti Columbia

Pavilion Records:
GEMM 9994 Mainly music played by Nadia Boulanger but she is joined in Brahms' *Lieberslieder Waltzer* by her then youthful pupil Dinu Lipatti.
HMV:
CDH 7 63497 2 Chopin: Piano Concerto No. 1 (Zürich Tonhalle Orch./Ackermann); Grieg: Piano Concerto (Philharmonia Orch./Gallieri).
CDH 7 69802 2 Chopin: Waltzes, Nos. 1-14; Barcarolle, Op. 60; Nocturne, Op. 27, No. 2; Mazurka, Op. 50, No. 3.
CDH 7 69792 2 Mozart: Piano Concerto No. 21 (Orch. du Festival de Lucerne/Karajan); Schumann: Piano Concerto (Philharmonia Orch./Karajan).
CZS 7 67163 2 (5 CD set) The Legacy of Dinu Lipatti. Lipatti plays music by Bach, Scarlatti, Mozart, Schubert, Schumann, Grieg, Chopin, Liszt, Ravel, Brahms, Enescu.
CDH 5 65116 2 Dinu Lipatti - Last Recital. Bach, Mozart, Schubert, Chopin. (Recorded at Besançon, 16th September 1950).
CDH 7 63038 2 Chopin: Sonata No. 3; Liszt: *Sonetto del Petrarca*, No. 104; Ravel: *Alborada del Gracioso*; Brahms: Waltzes, Op. 39; Enescu: Sonata No. 3.
CDH 7 69800 2 Bach: Partita, BWV 825; Mozart: Sonata, K. 310; Scarlatti: 2 Sonatas; Schubert: 2 Impromptus.
Jecklin:
JD 541-2 Bach and Chopin Piano Works. Bach: Harpsichord Concerto BWV 1052 (Concertgebouw Orch./van Beinum) (1947 recording); Chopin: Piano Concerto No. 1 (Zürich Tonhalle Orch./Ackermann) (1950 recording); Nocturnes (exc.); Études (exc.).

Note: In October 1995 Nimbus Records launched a new label, *Grand Piano*, devoted to the issue of a series of 40 to 50 compact discs, presenting the Duo-Art piano rolls of many pianists of the past. They will be issued over a five-year period. The piano rolls are from the collection of Gerald C. Stonehill of London and are played on a modern Steinway Grand. Pianists in this book who have been or will be featured are: Backhaus, Bauer, Busoni, Carreño, Cortot, Gabrilowitsch, Godowsky, Grainger, Hambourg, Hess, Hofmann, Horowitz, Landowska, Leginska, Pachmann, Paderewski, Rubinstein and Saint-Saëns. The only ones from the book to have appeared so far under this label at the time of writing are Bauer, Busoni, Grainger, Hofmann and Paderewski. Their entries are included in the above discography.

Appendix 2. Piano Roll Recordings (Rollography)

The "reproducing piano", which uses specially recorded perforated paper rolls, is able to reproduce in accurate detail the exact performance of the pianist who made the recording, within the technical limitations of the instrument. Because of the poor quality of reproduction of gramophone recordings in the early part of the present century, and especially prior to the introduction of electric recording in 1925, the reproducing player piano usually provides a more authentic account of a pianist's performances than the gramophone disc for pianists of that era. It is obviously necessary to have a reproducing piano to play the rolls, but fortunately many hundreds of such pianos in good working order still exist in Britain, the United States and elsewhere, lovingly cared for by devoted enthusiasts who are always happy to demonstrate their instruments to anyone who is interested. There are several Player Piano Associations and the major ones are listed in Appendix 3. By joining one of these, one has the opportunity to attend meetings in the homes of members to hear and enjoy the performances of famous pianists of the past.

It is interesting to observe the type of 'classical' music (using 'classical' in its wide sense, as opposed to 'popular') that was in demand in the period when the rolls were made, i.e. the middle of the Golden Age. A perusal of the lists of rolls produced by the major companies is enlightening in this regard. Most of the great composers were of course popular then, as now, though Mozart was not played a lot. But composers such as Henselt, MacDowell, Moszkowski and Rubinstein whose music was often played then have all but disappeared from modern programmes.

The three reproducing piano systems most frequently encountered now are the Duo-Art (manufactured by the Aeolian Company), the Ampico (made by the American Piano Company, which became the Ampico Corporation) and the Welte-Mignon, produced by the Welte Company of Freiburg which later set up an additional factory in New York. (The word "Mignon" (small) was introduced to distinguish the company's player pianos from the huge orchestrions (mechanical organs) for which the firm was noted). The products of the three companies are placed in the order Duo-Art, Ampico and Welte in this Appendix as this represents the order of survival rate of the instruments. There are still quite a lot of Duo-Art instruments about in good working order, rather less Ampicos, and even fewer Weltes. But chronologically Welte came first; their reproducing system was introduced around 1904 whereas Duo-Art and Ampico were not launched until about 1913. The fact that Welte is the earliest system makes it of historical importance in that the company was able to issue reproducing piano rolls of musicians of the period of Grieg, for example, who died as long ago as 1907.

All three companies issued rolls in large numbers but after a peak in 1925-26 there was a rapid decline in player piano sales which was attributable to the rise of radio and the introduction of electric gramophone recording with a consequent improvement in quality. Business slumped dramatically and roll production was thereafter concentrated on the popular music of the day such as songs from the shows. Few new classical rolls were issued after about 1928. Before the end of the 1920s Welte went into receivership. The Aeolian Company and Ampico struggled on into the 1930s but following a fire at the Aeolian Company's New York factory in 1935 the two companies merged. From then on Duo-Art and Ampico rolls were manufactured in small numbers under the same roof. A few late Ampico issues (e.g. some of Paderewski's in 1939) were adaptations of much earlier Duo-Art recordings.

All the normal type of Duo-Art, Ampico and Welte rolls recorded by the pianists in this book are listed in this Appendix, provided they were issued commercially. Non-standard rolls are not listed, e.g. 'accompaniment' rolls which provided instrumentalists (such as violinists) or singers with an accompaniment. Unissued rolls are not listed.

Several other companies also issued reproducing piano rolls, notably Hupfeld of Leipzig which produced vast numbers of rolls and boasted a huge catalogue, the Philipps Company which produced Ducartist rolls, the Wilcox & White Company which manufactured Artrio, and smaller companies which produced makes such as Artecho, Recordo and Virtuola. Also, many rolls were produced which resulted from "hand-played" recordings but lacking the expression dynamics in the roll; thus the "expression" had to be put in by the "pianolist" playing the roll, but the notes were played by the pianist who recorded the roll. None of this latter group of companies, even Hupfeld, competed in the long-term with the "Big Three" (Aeolian, Ampico and Welte) and the number of instruments using their systems which still exist in working condition today is very small indeed. It would be pointless to list hundreds of reproducing-piano rolls which can only rarely be played. For this reason only a brief summary is given of the rolls that the pianists in this book made for this group of companies, whereas their Duo-Art, Ampico and Welte rolls are listed in full.

A great many of the rolls listed below were also issued in other forms, with different serial numbers, e.g. "Audiographic" or "Annotated" versions with explanatory notes or pictures which unfurled as the rolls played. They were sold mainly for educational purposes. The serial numbers of these alternative versions are known but they are not listed here as the perforated music roll itself is identical with that of the rolls listed below. There were also annotated 'biographical' rolls comprising a collection of appropriate musical examples of the work of a particular composer.

In the case of Duo-Art rolls with 5-digit numbers the last digit (sometimes preceded by a hyphen) is generally a price code and was omitted from many official Duo-Art lists.

In the case of Ampico rolls the following points apply:
(i) The words "for Hupfeld" in the following lists indicates that the original recordings were made by the Hupfeld Company but were later adapted for issue by Ampico.
(ii) Identical Ampico recordings were often re-issued with different serial numbers. In these circumstances the most commonly used numbers are quoted.
(iii) When compositions had foreign titles Ampico often used either the English or foreign form with no apparent pattern. Sometimes the catalogue gave an English title whilst the label on the roll itself gave a foreign one, or vice versa; sometimes the containing box gave an English title and the roll inside a foreign one.

Abbreviations: tr. = transcribed by;   arr. = arranged by.

Information on the rolls is listed in the order:

Roll Number	Composer	Composition	Date of Issue
			(not date of recording)

The month and year are given when known; otherwise just the year. Where there is

Rollography

some doubt about the date of issue this is indicated by a question mark. When the date of issue is unknown but the roll was first mentioned in, say, the September 1923 compilation, this is indicated in the date column as 'by 9/23'.

1. Camille Saint-Saëns
Duo-Art:

5907	Chopin	Impromptu No. 2, Op. 36 in F sharp	7/17
5945	Saint-Saëns	Mazurka No. 1, Op. 21 in G minor	11/17
5674	Saint-Saëns	Mazurka No. 3, Op. 66 in B minor	9/15
5696	Saint-Saëns	*Samson et Delila*, Improvation on *Dance of the Priestesses of Dagon* and *Spring Voices are Singing*	11/15
5673	Saint-Saëns	Valse Mignonne, Op. 104 in E flat	7/15
5831	Saint-Saëns	Valse Nonchalante, Op. 110 in D flat	11/16

Ampico (for Hupfeld):

54686	Saint-Saëns	*Samson et Delila*. Finale, Act. 1	by 7/20
57234	Saint-Saëns	Valse Langoureuse, Op. 120	by 7/20

Welte:

804	Beethoven	Sonata, Op. 31, No. 1 in G. 2nd Mvt: Adagio grazioso	1905
808	Chopin	Étude, Op. 10, No. 3 in E	1905
807	Chopin	Nocturne, Op. 15, No 2 in F sharp	12/05
802	Saint-Saëns	Gavotte, Op. 90 in F	12/05
798	Saint-Saëns	*Le Rouet d'Omphale*, Op. 31	1905
799	Saint-Saëns	Mazurka No. 3, Op. 66 in B minor	1905
801	Saint-Saëns	*Reverie à Blidah*, Op. 60, No. 3 in A	12/05
800	Saint-Saëns	*Rhapsody d'Auvergne*, Op. 73 in C	12/05
797	Saint-Saëns	*Samson et Delila*. Finale to Act 1	12/05
795	Saint-Saëns	Symphony, No. 2 in A, Op. 55. Adagio (transcription)	1905
803	Saint-Saëns	Valse Mignonne, Op. 104 in E flat	1905
796	Saint-Saëns	Valse Nonchalante, Op. 110 in D flat	12/05
806	Schumann	*Waldszenen*, Op. 82, No. 9: *Abschied* (*Farewell*)	1905

Other manufacturers:
Saint-Saëns recorded at least 15 rolls for Hupfeld, eight for Philipps and one for Artecho. All these recordings were of his own music.

2. Vladimir de Pachmann
Duo-Art:

025	Chopin	Ballade, No. 3 in A flat, Op. 47	by 9/23
056	Chopin	Étude in E minor, Op. 25, No. 5	by 9/23
044	Chopin	Impromptu in A flat, Op. 29	by 9/23
021	Chopin	Mazurka in B minor, Op. 33, No. 4	by 9/23
013	Chopin	Nocturne in F sharp, Op. 15, No. 2	by 9/23
6795	Chopin	Nocturne in C sharp minor, Op. 27, No. 1	10/24
047	Chopin	Nocturne in D flat, Op. 27, No. 2	by 9/23
016	Chopin	Nocturne in E minor, Op. 72, No.1 (also on 6675)	by 9/23 & 10/23
045	Chopin	Polonaise in C sharp minor, Op. 26, No. 1	by 9/23
015	Chopin	Prelude in D flat, Op. 28, No. 15 (*Raindrop*)	by 9/23
018	Chopin	Valse in C sharp minor, Op. 64, No. 2	by 9/23
057	Mendelssohn	Song Without Words, No 46 in G minor, Op. 102, No. 4	by 9/23

Pachmann also contributed, with Bauer, Fryer, Godowsky, Hofmann, Hughes and Paderewski, to a Biographical Roll of Chopin (D-429). 11/27

375

Ampico:	None.		
Welte:			
7244	Bach	Italian Concerto, 1st Mvt: Allegro animato	1/26
7245	Bach	Ditto, 2nd Mvt: Andante molto espressivo	1/26
7246	Bach	Ditto, 3rd Mvt: Presto giocoso	1/26
7227	Chopin	Ballade, Op. 47	12/25
1215	Chopin	Étude, Op. 25, No. 2 in F minor	?1906
7204	Chopin	Impromptu, Op. 36 in F sharp	11/25
1221	Chopin	Mazurka, Op. 56, No. 2 in C	?1906
1222	Chopin	Mazurka, Op. 67, No. 4 in A minor	?1906
7247	Chopin	Ditto, new recording	11/25
7229	Chopin	Mazurkas, Op. 24, No. 4 in B flat minor; Op. 67, No.1 in G	12/25
7206	Chopin	Mazurkas, Op. 50, No. 2 in A flat; Op. 56, No. 2 in C	11/25
1218	Chopin	Nocturne, Op. 27, No. 2 in D flat	?1906
7263	Chopin	Nocturne, Op. 32, No. 1 in B	2/26
7203	Chopin	Nocturne, Op. 55, No. 1 in F minor	11/25
7202	Chopin	Nocturne, Op. 72, No. 1 in E minor (Posthumous)	11/25
1212	Chopin	Prelude, Op. 28, No. 16 in B flat minor	2/06
1213	Chopin	Prelude, Op. 28, No. 20 in C minor	2/06
1214	Chopin	Prelude, Op. 28, No. 23 in F	2/06
1219	Chopin	Waltz, Op. 34, No. 1 in A flat	2/06
7228	Chopin	Waltz, Op. 34, No. 3 in F	12/25
1220	Chopin	Waltz, Op. 64, No. 1 in D flat (*Minute Waltz*)	2/06
7205	Chopin	Ditto, new recording	11/25
7209	Chopin	Waltz, Op. 64, No. 2 in C sharp minor	11/25
7207	Godowsky	*Waltzermasken*, No. 14 (*Französisch*)	11/25
7208	Henselt	Étude, Op. 13, No. 2 (*La Gondola*) (tr. Pachmann)	11/25
1216	Liszt	Grand Étude de Concert, Op. 25, No. 2 in F minor	2/06
1210	Mendelssohn	Song Without Words, No. 21, Op. 53, No. 3 in G minor	?1906
1209	Mendelssohn	Song Without Words, No. 25, Op. 62, No. 1 in G	2/06
1204	Mozart	Sonata, K. 331 in A. 1st Mvt: Andante grazioso	2/06
1205	Mozart	Ditto, 2nd Mvt: Menuett and trio	2/06
1206	Mozart	Ditto, 3rd Mvt: Rondo à la Turka	2/06
1227	Pachmann	Improvisation in the form of a Gondola Song	?1906
1226	Pachmann	Improvisation on Chopin's *The Maiden's Prayer*	1906
1228	Pachmann	Sabouroff (Polka)	2/06
1223	Raff	*La Fileuse* (*The Spinning Girl*), Op. 157, No. 2 (tr. Henselt)	2/06
1211	Schubert	*Moment Musical*, Op. 94, No. 3 in F minor	2/06
1207	Schumann	Romance, Op. 32, No. 3 in D minor	6/26
1208	Schumann	*Waldszenen*, Op. 82, No. 7 (*The Prophet Bird*)	1906
7201	Verdi	*Rigoletto* - Paraphrase (tr. Liszt)	11/25

Other manufacturers:
Pachmann recorded seven rolls for Artecho; music by Chopin (3 rolls), Liszt, Mendelssohn, Schubert and Schumann (one each).

3. Teresa Carreño
Duo-Art:

5602	Beethoven	Sonata No. 14 in C sharp minor, Op. 27, No. 2 (*Moonlight*). 1st Mvt: Adagio sostenuto	?12/14
5603	Beethoven	2nd Mvt: Allegretto and 3rd Mvt: Presto agitato	?12/14

5707	Carreño	*Mi Teresita* (Petite Valse)	12/15
5601	Chopin	Polonaise in A flat, Op. 53 (*Heroic*)	?12/14
6020	Handel	*The Harmonious Blacksmith* (Air and Variations) (Suite No. 5 in E)	5/18
5615	MacDowell	Étude de Concert in F sharp minor, Op. 36	2/15
5609	MacDowell	*Hexentanz* (*Witches' Dance*), Op. 17, No. 2	1/15
5645	Rubinstein	Barcarolle (4th) in G minor, Op. 50, No. 3	5/15

Ampico (for Hupfeld):

50832	Carreño	Spanish Dance	by 7/20
53045	Chopin	Berceuse in D flat, Op. 57	by 7/20
50015	Schubert	Impromptu in G flat, Op. 90, No. 3	by 7/20
54754	Tchaikovsky	Nocturne in F, Op. 10, No. 1	by 7/20

Welte:

372	Beethoven	Sonata, Op. 53 in C (*Waldstein*). 1st Mvt: Allegro con brio	4/05
373	Beethoven	Ditto, 2nd mvt: Introduzione (adagio molto) and 3rd Mvt: (Allegretto moderato)	4/05
371	Carreño	*Little Waltz* in D	4/05
367	Chopin	Ballade, Op. 23 in G minor	4/05
369	Chopin	Ballade, Op. 47 in A flat	4/05
364	Chopin	Nocturne, Op. 37, No. 2 in G	4/05
366	Chopin	Nocturne, Op. 48, No. 1 in C minor	4/05
368	Liszt	*Années de Pelerinage*, 2nd year, No. 4 in D flat	4/05
365	Liszt	Hungarian Rhapsody, No. 6 in D flat	4/05
360	Schubert	*Soirées de Vienne*, No. 6 in A minor (tr. Liszt)	4/05
361	Schumann	Fantasia, Op. 17 in C 1st Mvt: Il tutto fantastico appassionata	4/05
362, 362a	Schumann	Ditto, 2nd Mvt: Moderato con energico (Parts I and II)	4/05
363	Schumann	Ditto, 3rd Mvt: Lento sustenato	4/05
370	Smetena	*Am Seegestade*, Op. 17	4/05

Other manufacturers:

Carreño recorded about a dozen rolls for Hupfeld. They included three of Anton Rubinstein's pieces, two of Chopin, two Schubert and two Tchaikovsky. For Philipps she recorded at least 27 rolls including six Beethoven, eight Chopin and six Liszt. She made three rolls for Artecho, including her own *Little Waltz*, and two for Recordo, which again included *Little Waltz*.

4. Ignace Paderewski

Duo-Art:

6929	Beethoven	Sonata No. 14 in C sharp minor, Op. 27, No. 2 (*Moonlight*). 1st Mvt: Adagio sostenuto and 2nd Mvt: Allegretto	11/27
6930	Beethoven	Ditto, 3rd Mvt: Presto agitato	11/25
6832	Chopin	Ballade (3rd) in A flat, Op. 47	1/25
8088	Chopin	Ballade (1st) in G minor, Op. 23	?
8022	Chopin	Étude in G flat, Op. 10, No. 5 (*Black Key*)	?
6097	Chopin	Étude in G flat, Op. 25, No. 9 (*Butterfly*)	by 4/19
6809	Chopin	Mazurka in A minor, Op. 17, No. 4	11/24
6566	Chopin	Mazurka in B flat minor, Op. 24, No. 4	11/22
6847	Chopin	Nocturne in G, Op. 37, No. 2	2/25
6140	Chopin	Polonaise in A, Op. 40, No. 1 (*Military*)	12/19

7160	Chopin	Scherzo (3rd) in C sharp minor, Op. 39	10/27
6551	Chopin	Valse in A flat, Op. 34, No. 1	9/22
6618	Chopin	Valse in A flat, Op. 42	4/23
6567	Chopin/Liszt	Chant Polonaise, Op. 74, No. 5 (*My Joy*)	1/22
6594	Chopin/Liszt	*The Maiden's Wish*, Op. 74, No. 1	1/23
7186	Debussy	*Reflets dans L'Eau. Images*, No. 1	12/27
75098	Liszt	*La Campanella*, from the *Paganini Études*, No. 3 in G sharp minor	?11/36
6670	Liszt	Hungarian Rhapsody, No. 2 in C sharp minor	10/23
6568	Liszt	Hungarian Rhapsody, No. 10 in E	11/22
6569	Mendelssohn	Song Without Words, No. 34, Op. 67, No. 4 in C (*Spinning Song*)	11/22
6558	Paderewski	Caprice in G (Genre Scarlatti), Op. 14, No. 3	10/22
7285	Paderewski	*Légende*, Op. 16, No. 1	10/28
6681	Paderewski	Mélodie, Op. 8, No. 3	11/23
6100	Paderewski	Minuet in G, Op. 14, No. 1	by 4/19
6562	Paderewski	Nocturne in B flat, Op. 16, No. 4	11/22
7446-4	Paderewski	*Cracovienne Fantastique*, Op. 14, No. 6 (from *Humoresques de Concert*)	3/32
7215	Schelling	Nocturne (*Ragusa*)	3/28
6794	Schubert	Impromptu in A flat, Op. 142, No. 2	10/24
7348	Schubert	Impromptu in B flat, Op. 142, No. 3 (*Rosamunde*)	10/29
6694	Schubert/Liszt	*Hark! Hark! The Lark!*	12/23
7435	Schubert/Liszt	Valse Caprice (from *Soirées de Vienne*)	10/31
7262	Schumann	*Nachtstück*, Op. 23, No. 4 in F	10/28
8020	Schumann	*Prophet Bird*, Op. 82, No. 7, from *Waldszenen*	?
75088	Wagner/Liszt	*Isolde's Love Death (from Tristan and Isolde)*	10/36

    Paderewski also contributed, with Bauer, Fryer, Godowsky, Hofmann, Hughes and Pachmann, to a Biographical Roll of Chopin (D-429).   11/27

    He also contributed, with Bauer, Cortot, Friedman and Gabrilowitsch to a Biographical Roll of Schubert (D-717).   11/28

Ampico:
Paderewski's Ampico rolls are early 1939 adaptations of earlier Duo-Art recordings.

71773	Beethoven	Sonata No. 14 in C sharp minor, Op. 27, No. 2 (*Moonlight*) 1st Mvt: Adagio sostenuto and 2nd Mvt: Allegretto	
71783	Beethoven	Ditto, 3rd Mvt: Presto agitato	
71793	Chopin	Nocturne in G, Op. 37, No. 2	
71813	Liszt	Hungarian Rhapsody, No. 2 in C sharp minor	
71801	Paderewski	Minuet in G, Op. 14, No. 1	

Welte:

1246	Beethoven	Sonata, Op. 27, No. 2 in C sharp minor (*Moonlight*) 1st Mvt: Adagio sostenuto and 2nd Mvt: Allegretto	2/06
1247	Beethoven	Ditto, 3rd Mvt: Presto agitato	2/06
1249	Chopin	Ballade, Op. 47 in A flat	2/06
1254	Chopin	Étude, Op. 10, No. 3 in E	2/06
1253	Chopin	Étude, Op. 25, No. 9 in G flat (*Butterfly*)	2/06
1251	Chopin	Mazurka, Op. 24, No. 4 in B flat minor	2/06
1255	Chopin	Nocturne, Op. 37, No. 2 in G	2/06
1256	Chopin	Polonaise, Op. 53 in A flat (*Heroic*)	2/06
1257	Chopin	Waltz, Op. 64, No. 2 in C sharp minor	2/06

1259	Liszt	Hungarian Rhapsody, No. 10 in E	2/06
1263	Paderewski	Minuet, Op. 14, No. 1 in F	2/06
1262	Paderewski	Nocturne, Op. 16, No. 4	2/06
1260	Schubert	*Der Erlkönig (The Erlking)* (tr. Liszt)	2/06
1261	Schubert	*Hark! Hark! The Lark!* (tr. Liszt)	2/06
1248	Schubert	Impromptu, Op. 142, No. 3 in B flat (*Rosamunde*)	2/06

Other manufacturers:

Paderewski recorded at least eight rolls for Artecho; Beethoven (1), Chopin (4), Paderewski (Minuet, Op. 14, No. 1 and Nocturne, Op. 16, No. 4) and Schubert's Impromptu, Op. 142, No. 3 (the *Rosamunde* Impromptu), which he also recorded for Duo-Art and Welte.

5. Moriz Rosenthal
Ampico:
(Rosenthal recorded only for Ampico).

69701	Albéniz	*Orientale*, from *Chants d'Espagne (Songs of Spain)*, Op. 232, No. 2	3/29
67133	Bortkiewicz	Étude in D flat, Op. 15, No. 8	2/27
62961	Chopin	Étude in G sharp minor, Op. 25, No. 6	4/24
64123	Chopin	Waltz in A flat, Op. 42	3/25
66603	Chopin	Chant Polonaise, Op. 74, No. 5 (*Mes Joies*)	10/26
71673	Handel	*Harmonious Blacksmith Variations* (Suite No. 5 in E)	Spring '37
67771	Mendelssohn	Song Without Words, No.1, Op. 19 (*Fond Memories*)	7/27
67431	Mendelssohn	Song Without Words, No. 30, Op. 62, No. 6 (*Spring Song*)	4/27
63831	Rosenthal	*Papillons (Butterflies)*	12/24
64451	Rosenthal	Prelude in F sharp minor	5/25
70553	Rubinstein	Valse Caprice in E flat	3/30
65313	Strauss/Rosenthal	*Carnaval de Vienne;* Humoresque on Themes of J. Strauss	12/25

6. Ferruccio Busoni
Duo-Art:

6928	Bach	Chaconne (tr. Busoni) from Sonata in D minor for solo violin	11/25
	Chopin	24 Preludes, Op. 28, complete, as below:	

One per roll:
023		No. 3 in G	by 9/23
035		No. 16 in B flat minor	by 9/23
039		No. 23 in F (Duplicated on 0249 below)	by 9/23
040		No. 24 in D minor (Duplicated on 0249 below)	by 9/23

Two per roll:
024		No. 1 in C; No. 2 in A minor; by 9/23. (Also on 66690; 10/23)	
027		No. 7 in A; No. 8 in F sharp minor	by 9/23
031		No. 12 in G sharp minor; No. 13 in F sharp	by 9/23
033		No. 14 in E flat minor; No. 15 in D flat (*Raindrop*)	by 9/23
036		No. 17 in A flat; No. 18 in F minor	by 9/23
037		No. 19 in E flat; No. 20 in C minor	by 9/23
038		No. 21 in B flat; No. 22 in G minor	by 9/23
0249		No. 23 in F; No. 24 in D minor	3/27

Three per roll:
014		No. 4 in E minor; No. 5 in D; No. 6 in B minor	by 9/23
017		No. 9 in E; No. 10 in C sharp minor; No. 11 in B	by 9/23

5698	Liszt	*La Campanella*, from the *Paganini Études*, No. 3	11/15
5686	Liszt	*Étude d'Execution Transcendante*, No. 5	
		(*Feux Follets* - *Will o' the Wisp*)	10/15
5671	Liszt	*La Chasse*, from the *Paganini Études*, No. 5 in E	7/15
5675	Liszt	Polonaise, No. 2 in E (arr. Busoni)	9/15

Ampico (for Hupfeld):

50047	Chopin	Ballade (1st) in G minor, Op. 23	by 7/20
51364	Liszt	Étude de Concert, No. 2 in F minor (*Dance of the Gnomes*)	by 7/20
62633	Liszt	Nocturne, *Soirées Musicales de Rossini*, No. 10	12/23
50676	Verdi/Liszt	*Rigoletto* - Paraphrase	by 7/20

Welte:

All Busoni's Welte rolls are believed to have been recorded in two sessions, in 1905 and 1907.

439	Bach	*Choralvorspiel, Nun Freut Euch, Lieben Christen* (tr. Busoni)	2/05
463	Bach	*Wachet Auf, Ruft Uns die Stimme* (tr. Busoni)	Either '05 or '07
443	Beethoven	*Adelaide*, Op. 46 (tr. Liszt)	Probably '05
1322	Beethoven	*Ruins of Athens* (Fantasia) (tr. Liszt)	3/07
1321	Bellini	*Norma* (Fantasia) (tr. Liszt)	3/07
441	Chopin	Nocturne, Op. 15, No. 2 in F sharp	6/05
440	Chopin	Polonaise, Op. 53 in A flat (*Heroic*)	6/05
1319	Chopin	Prelude, Op. 28, No. 15 in D flat (*Raindrop*)	3/07
442	Donizetti	Valse Caprice on Themes from *Lucia* and *Parisina* (tr. Liszt)	11/05
444	Liszt	*Paganini Étude* No. 3 (*La Campanella*)	11/05
1320	Liszt	Polonaise, No. 2 in E	Probably '07
1323	Mozart	*Don Giovanni* - *Reminiscences* (tr. Liszt)	Probably '07
446	Schubert	Hungarian March in C minor (tr. Liszt)	6/05
445	Verdi	*Rigoletto* - Paraphrase (tr. Liszt)	9/05

Other manufacturers:

Busoni recorded about 14 rolls for Hupfeld. They include five of Liszt's music, four of Chopin and one Bach-Busoni. He recorded about 16 solo rolls for Philipps; included are three Beethoven, three Liszt, three Bach-Busoni and two Beethoven-Busoni. Busoni also made eight 4-handed recordings for the Philipps Company with Michael Zadora, which include two pieces by Schubert and three by Schumann. In addition, he recorded six rolls for Artecho; three of music by Chopin and three of Liszt.

7. Leopold Godowsky

Duo-Art:

5793	Chopin	Ballade (1st) in G minor, Op. 23	6/16
5741	Chopin	Écossaises, Op. 72	3/16
5771	Chopin	Nocturne in E flat, Op. 9, No. 2	5/16
5740	Henselt	Berceuse in G flat	3/16
5840	Henselt	*La Gondola*, Op. 13, No. 2	12/16
5872	Moszkowski	Polonaise in E flat, Op. 17, No. 1	3/17
5752	Rubinstein	Serenade in D minor	4/16
5855	Schumann	*Träumerei*, from *Kinderszenen*, Op. 15, No. 7	1/17

Godowsky also contributed, with Bauer, Fryer, Hofmann, Hughes, Pachmann and Paderewski, to a Biographical Roll of Chopin (D-429). 11/27

Ampico:

60023	Bishop	*Home Sweet Home*	9/21
59911	Bohm	*Calm as the Night* (*Still wie die Nacht*) (tr. Godowsky)	8/21
56084	Chopin	Andante Spianato and Grande Polonaise, Op. 22	by 7/20

51126	Chopin	Ballade (3rd) in A flat, Op. 47	by 7/20
50214	Chopin	Berceuse in D flat, Op. 57	by 7/20
56834	Chopin	Nocturne in G, Op. 37, No. 2	by 7/20
56336	Chopin	Polonaise in A flat, Op. 53 (*Heroic*)	by 7/20
51116	Chopin	Scherzo in C sharp minor, Op. 39	by 7/20
54944	Chopin	Waltz in E minor (Posthumous)	by 7/20
51554	Chopin	Waltz in A flat, Op. 42	by 7/20
54954	Chopin	Waltz in C sharp minor, Op. 64, No. 2	by 7/20
50482	Chopin	Waltz in G flat, Op. 70, No. 1	by 7/20
64051	Chopin/Liszt	Chant Polonaise in G flat, Op. 74, No. 5 (*Mes Joies*)	2/25
58233	Godowsky	Humoresque, from *The Miniatures*	9/20
5285K	Liszt	*La Campanella* (*Paganini Étude*, No. 3)	pre-1920
51164	Liszt	Étude de Concert, No.2 in F minor (*Dance of the Gnomes*)	by 7/20
62711	MacDowell	*March Wind*, Op. 46, No. 10 in E flat	1/24
56142	Schubert	*Moment Musical* in F minor, Op. 94, No. 3	by 7/20
58365	Schumann	*Nachtstück* in F, Op. 23, No. 4	10/20
50453	Schumann	*The Prophet Bird*, Op. 82, No. 7	by 7/20
59883	Straus (Oscar)	*The Last Waltz*	7/21

Welte:
None.

Other manufacturers:

Godowsky recorded over 40 rolls for Hupfeld, nearly half of which are of Chopin's music. For Artrio he recorded at least 24 rolls, including five of Chopin, and four pieces from his own *Triakontameron*. He made at least 24 rolls for Recordo; Chopin (4), Godowsky himself (4), Rachmaninov (2) and one each of the music of 14 other composers. In addition he recorded nine rolls for Artecho including five of the music of Chopin.

8. Sergei Rachmaninov

Ampico:

(Rachmaninov recorded only for Ampico).

66483	Bach	Sarabande in D (Partita No. 4)	9/26
68771	Beethoven	Turkish March from *The Ruins of Athens* (arr. Rubinstein)	4/28
61601	Bizet	Minuet from *L'Arlésienne* (tr. Rachmaninov)	1/23
67673	Chopin	Nocturne in F, Op. 15, No. 1	6/27
71173	Chopin	Scherzo in B flat minor, Op. 31	10/33
59743	Chopin	Waltz in E flat, Op. 18	6/21
63311	Chopin	Waltz Brillant in F, Op. 34, No. 3	7/24
62803	Chopin/Liszt	Chant Polonaise, Op. 74, No. 1 (*Maiden's Wish*)	2/24
64921	Gluck/Sgambati	Mélodie in D minor	9/25
62971	Henselt	*Were I a Bird* (*Si Oiseau J'Étais*), Op. 2, No. 6	4/24
66143	Kreisler	*Liebesfreud* (*Love's Joy*) (tr. Rachmaninov)	6/26
62103	Kreisler	*Liebeslied* (*Love's Sorrow*) (tr. Rachmaninov)	6/23

The above two pieces are from *Alt Wienertanzweisen* (*Old Viennese Dance Melodies*)

59661	Mendelssohn	Song Without Words No. 34, Op. 67, No. 4 (*Spinning Song*)	5/21
60641	Mussorgsky	*Hopak* (tr. Rachmaninov)	4/22
68283	Paderewski	Minuet in G, Op. 14, No. 1	11/27
57604	Rachmaninov	Barcarolle in G minor, Op. 10, No. 3	4/20
69253	Rachmaninov	Élegie in E flat minor, Op. 3, No. 1	10/28
69593	Rachmaninov	*Étude Tableaux* (*Picture Study*) in B minor, Op. 39, No. 4	2/29
60891	Rachmaninov	*Étude Tableaux* in A minor, Op. 39, No. 6	7/22

57965	Rachmaninov	Humoresque in G, Op. 10, No. 5	by 7/20
61761	Rachmaninov	*Lilacs* (Transcription)	3/23
57545	Rachmaninov	Mélodie in E, Op. 3, No. 5	by 7/20
57905	Rachmaninov	*Polichinelle* in F sharp minor, Op. 3, No. 4	by 7/20
57275	Rachmaninov	Polka de W.R.	by 1920
57504	Rachmaninov	Prelude in C sharp minor, Op. 3, No. 2	10/19
57525	Rachmaninov	Prelude in G minor, Op. 23, No. 5	4/20
62441	Rachmaninov	Serenade in B flat minor, Op. 3, No. 5	10/23
70301	Rimsky-Korsakov	*Flight of the Bumble Bee*	11/29
69893	Rubinstein	Barcarolle in A minor	6/29
69373	Schubert	Impromptu in A flat, Op. 90, No. 4	11/28
64561	Schubert	*Das Wandern*, in B flat (tr. Liszt)	6/25
65771	Schubert	*The Brooklet*, in G (tr. Rachmaninov)	3/26
71511	Smith (John S.)	*The Star-Spangled Banner* (words by Francis Scott Key). A re-release of an earlier recording (57282)	6/36
57914	Tchaikovsky	*Troika* in E, Op. 37A, No. 11	by 7/20
62531	Tchaikovsky	Valse in A flat, Op. 40, No. 8	11/23

9. Harold Bauer

Duo-Art:

6446	Alkan	*The Wind (Le Vent)*, Op. 15, No. 2	6/21
5849	Arensky	Valse, Op. 15 (arr. 4 hands; with Ossip Gabrilowitsch)	12/16
7371	Bach	Chorale, from Cantata 147 (tr. Bauer)	12/29
7316	Bach	Chromatic Fantasia and Fugue in D minor, Part I, Fantasia	4/29
7317	Bach	Ditto, Part II, Fugue	4/29
5650	Bach	Prelude and Fugue No 5 in D from *The Well-Tempered Clavier*	5/15
6392	Bach	Two-part Inventions, Nos. 1, 6 and 8	2/21
6820	Bauer	*Barberini's Minuet*	12/24

The following are three 18th century traditional tunes, arranged by Bauer:

70390		*Dolce Far Niente (Sweet Idleness)* (Gondolier's Song of Old Venice, No. 5)	7/26
6873		*Motley*, No. 3; *Flourish*, No. 4	5/25
6837		*Ye Sweet Retreat*	2/23
5060	Beethoven	Allegro from String Quartet, Op. 18, No. 4 in C minor (arr. Bauer)	3/23
7106	Beethoven	Andante and Variations from String Quartet, Op. 18, No. 5 in A. 3rd Mvt. (arr. Bauer)	4/27
6380	Beethoven	Gavotte in F, attributed to Beethoven (edited by Bauer)	1/21
72130	Beethoven	Sonata, Op. 6 in D for Two Pianos (Primo part only)	2/28
71750	Beethoven	Sonata, Op. 7 in E flat. 1st Mvt: Allegro	11/27
71760	Beethoven	Ditto, 2nd Mvt: Largo. (Some sources add 3rd Mvt.)	11/27
71770	Beethoven	Ditto, 3rd Mvt: Rondo. (Some sources list this as 4th Mvt.)	11/27
5691	Beethoven	Sonata (*Pathétique*), Op. 13 in C minor. 1st Mvt: Grave; Molto allegro d'molto con brio	10/15
5703	Beethoven	Ditto: 2nd Mvt: Adagio cantabile	11/15
5711	Beethoven	Ditto: 3rd Mvt: Rondo (Allegro)	12/15
6065	Beethoven	Sonata (*Appassionata*), Op. 57 in F minor 1st Mvt: Allegro assai	11/18

Rollography

6080	Beethoven	2nd Mvt: Andante con moto;	
		3rd Mvt: Allegro ma non troppo	12/18
5837	Beethoven	*Turkish March* fr. *Ruins of Athens*, Op. 113 (tr. Rubinstein)	12/16
6098	Bizet	*Chanson d'Avril* (*Song of April*). (tr. Buonamici)	2/19
5889	Boccherini	Famous Minuet in A	5/17
74039	Brahms	Capriccio, Op. 76, No. 5 in C sharp minor	7/30
5814	Brahms	*Hungarian Dance*, No. 5 in C sharp minor	9/16
5947	Brahms	Ditto, No. 6 in D	11/17
5668	Brahms	Ditto, No. 8 in A minor	7/15
A-80	Brahms	Intermezzo, Op. 117, No. 1 in E flat	8/28
6559	Brahms	Ditto, No. 2 in B flat minor	10/22
74220	Brahms	Intermezzo, Op. 119, No. 2 in E minor	12/30
7069	Burgmein	*Pierrot and Pierrette's Story* (*Pierrot's Serenade, Love Duet,*	
		Marriage Ball, Wedding March) (Duet with Myra Hess)	10/26
69550	Chaminade	*Pierrette*, Op. 41 from *Airs de Ballet*	1/26
5627	Chopin	Étude, Op. 10, No. 2 (*Revolutionary*)	3/15
7120	Chopin	Étude, Op. 25, No. 7 in C sharp minor	5/27
74518	Chopin	Études (Posthumous), No. 1 in F minor and No. 3 in D,	
		from *Trois Nouvelles Études*	4/32
6266	Chopin	Fantasie, Op. 49 in F minor	4/20
6058	Chopin	Fantasie Impromptu, Op. 66, in C sharp minor	10/18
6482	Chopin	Mazurka, Op. 33, No. 2 in D	11/21
6308	Chopin	Nocturne, Op. 15, No. 2 in F sharp	7/20
5728	Chopin	Nocturne, Op. 48, No. 1 in C minor	2/16
6796	Chopin	Polonaise, Op. 26, No. 1 in C sharp minor	10/24
6990	Chopin	Polonaise, Op. 26, No. 2 in E flat minor (*Revolt/Siberian*)	4/26
7148	Chopin	Polonaise, Op. 40, No, 2 in C minor	9/27
6506	Chopin	Scherzo (3rd), Op. 39 in C sharp minor	2/22
5854	Chopin	Sonata, Op. 58 in B minor. 1st Mvt: Allegro maestoso	1/17
5862	Chopin	Ditto, 2nd Mvt: Scherzo (Molto vivace)	2/17
5874	Chopin	Ditto, 3rd Mvt: Largo	3/17
5877	Chopin	Ditto, 4th Mvt: Presto, non tanto	4/17
8019	Chopin	Valse Brillante, Op. 34, No. 3 in F	?
5635	Chopin	Valse, Op. 42 in A flat (Grande)	4/15
6328	Chopin	Valse, Op. 64, No. 1 in D flat (*Minute*)	9/20
6599	Debussy	*La Soirée dans Grenade*, from *Estampes*, No. 2	2/23
6932	Durand	Valse, Op. 83 in E flat	11/25
6468	Handel	Air and Variations in E, from *The Harmonious Blacksmith*	9/21
6373	Handel	Largo in G, from *Xerxes*	12/20
514-4	Haydn	Adagio from String Quartet, Op. 76, No. 3,	
		2nd Mvt.(arr. Bauer)	11/24
7254	Haydn	*Gypsy Rondo* from Trio No. 5 in G (arr. Bauer)	9/28
6005	Liszt	Étude No. 2 in E flat (Andante capriccioso) from	
		Grandes Études de Paganini	4/18
74010	Liszt	*Églogue* from *Years of Pilgrimage*, 1st year, No. 7	6/30
72610	MacDowell	*From the Depths*, Op. 55, No. 6, from *Sea Pieces*	10/28
7350	Mattei	*Non e Ver* (*'Tis Not True*), Op. 171, No. 25 (tr. Lange)	10/29
510-4	Mendelssohn	Canzonetta, fr. String Quartet, Op. 12 in E flat (arr. Bauer)	11/23
66140	Mendelssohn	Étude, Op. 104 (Book 2) in B flat	4/23
6094	Moszkowski	Polonaise, Op. 11, No. 1 in E flat	1/19

71620	Moszkowski	Romance, Op. 42, No. 1	10/27
7073	Mozart	Fantasia, No. 4 in C minor (Adagio)	11/26
74110	Mozart	Minuet, from Divertimento (Sextet) (tr. Bauer)	10/30
6463	Paderewski	Polonaise, Op. 9, No. 6	8/21
7239	Pierné	March of the Little Leaden Soldiers, Op. 14, No. 6 (arr. 4 hands; with Myra Hess)	6/28
6186	Rameau	Musette	10/19
6057	Rubinstein	Kamennoi-Ostrow (Rocky Isle), Op. 10, Portrait, No. 22 in F sharp	9/18
5953	Saint-Saëns	Concerto (2nd), Op. 22 in G minor, 1st Mvt: Andante sostenuto. (Orch. Accomp. adapted and added by Bauer)	12/17
5963	Saint-Saëns	Ditto, 2nd Mvt: Allegro scherzando	1/18
5973	Saint-Saëns	Ditto, 3rd Mvt: Presto	2/18
6416	Scharwenka	Polish Dance, Op. 3, No. 1	5/21
67690	Schubert	Scherzo, from String Quartet, No. 6 in D minor. 3rd Mvt. (arr. Bauer)	6/24
6487	Schubert	Marche Militaire, Op. 51, No. 1 (for 4 hands. With Ossip Gabrilowitsch)	12/21
6671	Schubert	Serenade, from Swan Songs, No. 4. (tr. Liszt)	10/23
6212	Schubert	Minuet in D minor, from Second Fantasie	12/19
6986	Schuett	A La Bien Aimée. Concert Waltz, Op. 59, No. 2 in D	3/26
6251	Schumann	Album for the Young, Op. 68. The Merry Farmer, Poor Orphan, The Hunting Song, Knight Rupert	3/20
7224	Schumann	Kinderszenen (Scenes from Childhood), Op. 15. Nos. 1, 2, 3, 4, 5, 6, 8, 9, 12.	4/28
5682	Schumann	Novelette, Op. 21, No. 1 in F	9/15
6921	Schumann	Novelette, Op. 21, No. 2 in D	10/25
5749	Schumann	Sonata, Op. 11, No. 1 in F sharp minor, Introduction, Un poco adagio	4/16
5750	Schumann	Ditto, 1st Mvt: Un poco adagio, allegro vivace	4/16
5769	Schumann	Ditto, 2nd Mvt: Andante cantabile (Aria)	5/16
5787	Schumann	Ditto, 3rd Mvt: Scherzo e intermezzo	6/16
5800	Schumann	Ditto, 4th Mvt: Finale (allegro un poco maestoso)	7/16
6498	Schumann	Toccata, Op. 7 in C	1/22
73460	Schumann	Träumerie	9/29
5960	Sibelius	Valse Triste Op. 44 in G minor	3/18
6717	Tchaikovsky	Andante Cantabile, from String Quartet, Op. 11, No. 1 in D (arr. Bauer)	2/24
6345	Weber	Rondo Brillante (La Gaieté), Op. 62	10/20

Bauer also contributed, with Hofmann, Leginska and Stoessel, to two Biographical Rolls of Beethoven (Roll 1: D-333; Roll 2: D-335; both 10/26); with Fryer, Godowsky, Hofmann, Hughes, Pachmann and Paderewski to a Biographical Roll of Chopin (D-429; 11/27); and with Cortot, Friedman, Gabrilowitsch and Paderewski to a Biographical Roll of Schubert (D-717; 11/28).

Ampico (for Hupfeld):

50405	Beethoven	Sonata No. 14 in C sharp minor, Op. 27, No. 2 (Moonlight) 1st Mvt: Adagio sostenuto	by 7/20
50337	Beethoven	Ditto, 2nd Mvt: Allegretto and 3rd Mvt: Presto agitato	by 7/20
54814	Liszt	Waldesrauschen (Murmuring Woods)	by 7/20
51517	Schubert	Impromptu, Op. 90, No. 4 in A flat	by 7/20
66371	Schumann	Novelette, Op. 21, No. 7 in E	8/26

Rollography

Welte: None.
Other manufacturers:
Bauer recorded at least 10 rolls for Hupfeld; music by Beethoven, Brahms, Chopin, Liszt, Mendelssohn, Schubert, Schumann and Wagner. For Artrio he recorded about 17 rolls featuring the music of 11 different composers. He recorded two rolls for Pleyela (Bach and Emmanuel Moor); three for Artecho (Brassin, Liszt and Wagner) and four for Recordo (Chopin, Grainger, Liszt and Mendelssohn).

10. Josef Lhevinne
Duo-Art: None.
Ampico:

66713	Albéniz	*Córdoba, Chants d'Espagne* (Songs of Spain), Op. 232, No. 4	11/26
68473	Albéniz	*Sevilla, Suite Espagnole* (*Spanish Suite*), No. 3	1/28
66613	Beethoven	Sonata No. 14 in C sharp minor (*Moonlight*)	
		1st Mvt: Adagio sostenuto	10/26
67283	Beethoven	2nd Mvt: Allegretto; 3rd Mvt: Presto agitato	3/27
68001	Chopin	Études, Op. 10, No. 11 in E flat; Op. 25, No. 9 in G flat	9/27
62883	Chopin	Nocturne in B, Op. 9, No. 3	3/24
69833	Chopin	Polonaise in A flat, Op. 53 (*Heroic*)	5/29
64273	Cui	*Causerie* (*Conversation*), Étude in F, Op. 40, No. 6	4/25
69693	Liszt	*Gondoliera. Années de Pelèrinage* (2me année)	
		Venezia e Napoli, No. 1	3/29
68653	Liszt	*Liebestraum* (*Love's Dream*). Nocturne, No. 3 in A flat	3/28
62523	Liszt	*Die Lorelei*	11/23
63903	Liszt/Busoni	*La Campanella* (*Paganini Étude*, No. 3)	1/25
63513	Mendelssohn	*Auf Flügeln des Gesanges* (*On Wings of Song*) (tr. Liszt)	9/24
64933	Rubinstein	*Kammenoi-Ostrow* (*Rocky Isle*), Op. 10, No. 22	
		in F sharp (*Rêve Angélique*) (*Angelic Dream*)	9/25
65213	Schubert/Liszt	*Valse Caprice, Soirées de Vienne* (*Evenings in Vienna*), No. 6	11/25
70963	Schubert/Tausig	*Marche Militaire*	3/32
70783	Schumann	*Papillons* (*Butterflies*), Op. 2. Part I: Nos. 1 - 9	11/30
70793	Schumann	Ditto, Part II: Nos. 10 - 12. (Complete on No. 100605)	11/30
68113	Schütt	*À La Bien Aimée* (*To the Well-Beloved*), Op. 59, No. 2	10/27
70441	Sinding	*Frühlingsrauschen* (*Rustle of Spring*), Op. 32, No. 3	1/30
67563	Strauss	*An den Schönen Blauen Donau*. Concert Arabesque on	
		The Blue Danube Waltz (Arr. Schulz-Evler)	5/27
63243	Tausig	*Ungarische Zigeunerweisen* (*Hungarian Gypsy Dances*)	6/24

Welte:

2434	Beethoven	*Ruins of Athens - Chorus of Dervishes* (tr. Saint-Saëns)	?1911
4056	Beethoven	*Écosaisses* (*Scottish Dances*) in E flat (tr. Busoni)	?1920
1297	Chopin	Étude, Op. 25, No. 10 in B minor (Study in Octaves)	10/06
2440	Chopin	Étude, Op. 25, No. 12 in C minor	1911
2438	Chopin	Mazurka, Op. 33, No. 2 in D	1911
2430	Czerny	Octave Study, Op. 740, No. 5	7/11
4062	Dohnanyi	Étude Caprice, Op. 28, No. 6 in F minor	?1920
1303	Gluck	*Iphigenie in Aulis*. Gavotte (tr. Brahms)	10/06
1298	Godard	*En Route*, Op. 107, No. 12 in B flat (Scherzo)	10/06
1302	Liszt	*Die Lorelei*	10/06
1299	Mendelssohn	*Charakterstücke*, Op. 7, No. 7 in E	10/06
2441	Meyerbeer	*Robert le Diable* (tr. Liszt)	1911

2435	Moszkowski	Minuet, Op. 17, No. 2 in G	1911
4058	Poldini	*Marche Mignonne*, Op. 15, No. 2	?1920
4059	Rachmaninov	Prelude, Op. 23, No. 2 in B flat	?1920
2436	Rubinstein	Barcarolle No. 6, Op. 104, No. 4 in C minor	1911
2431	Rubinstein	*Kamennoi-Ostrow*, Op. 10, No. 22 in F sharp	1911
1304	Rubinstein	*Le Bal* (*The Ball*), Op. 14, No. 6	10/06
2437	Rubinstein	Prelude, Op. 75, No. 9 in F	1911
1296	Schlözer, Paul de	*Étude de Concert*, Op. 1, No. 1 in E flat	10/06
4057	Schubert	*Der Lindenbaum*, Op. 89, No. 5, (tr. Liszt)	?1920
4060, 4061	Schumann	Études Symphoniques, Op. 13 (on 2 rolls)	?1920
1301	Schumann	Toccata, Op. 7 in C	1906
1300	Scriabin	Nocturne for Left Hand Alone, Op. 9, No. 2 in D flat	10/06
2433	Sgambati	*Vecchio Minuetto*, Op. 18, No. 2	7/11
1305	Strauss	*An den Schönen Blauen Donau* (Arabesque)(tr.Schulz-Evler)	10/06
2439	Weber	Sonata No. 1, Op. 24 in C. 4th Mvt: Rondo	1911

Other manufacturers:
 Lhevinne made six rolls for Artecho; one each of music by Chopin, Godard, Mendelssohn, Schlözer, Schulz-Evler and Schumann.

11. Josef Hofmann
Duo-Art:

6610	Beethoven	Rondo à Capriccio in G, Op. 129 (*Rage over a Lost Penny*)	3/23
6327	Beethoven	Turkish March from *The Ruins of Athens* (tr. Rubinstein)	9/20
6101	Beethoven	Sonata No. 14 in C sharp minor, Op. 27, No. 2 (*Moonlight*)	
		1st Mvt: Adagio sostenuto	6/19
6102	Beethoven	Ditto, 2nd Mvt: Allegretto	7/19
6103	Beethoven	Ditto, 3rd Mvt: Presto agitato	9/19
7305	Beethoven	Sonata No. 3 in C, Op. 2, No. 3	
		1st Mvt: Allegro con brio	2/29
7306	Beethoven	Ditto, 2nd Mvt: Adagio and 3rd Mvt: Scherzo allegro	2/29
7307	Beethoven	Ditto, 4th Mvt: Allegro assai	2/29
6239	Chopin	Sonata No. 2 in B flat minor, Op. 35	
		1st Mvt: Grave, doppio movimento	2/20
6258	Chopin	Ditto, 2nd Mvt: Scherzo	3/20
6272	Chopin	Ditto, 3rd Mvt: Marche Funèbre; 4th Mvt: Presto	4/20
7066	Chopin	Berceuse in D flat, Op. 57	10/26
6915-6	Chopin	Piano Concerto in E minor, Op. 11 (arr. Hofmann)	
		1st Mvt: Allegro maestoso, Pt. I	10/25
69168	Chopin	Ditto, 1st Mvt: Allegro maestoso, Pt. II	10/25
6917-4	Chopin	Ditto, 2nd Mvt: Romanza (Lhargetto)	10/25
6918	Chopin	Ditto, 3rd Mvt: Rondo (Vivace)	10/25
6573	Chopin	Nocturne in D flat, Op. 27, No. 2	11/22
7318	Chopin	Nocturne in F sharp minor, Op. 48, No. 2	4/29
7108	Chopin	Nocturne in F minor, Op. 55, No. 1	3/27
6720	Chopin	Polonaise in A, Op. 40, No. 1 (*Military*)	2/24
6550	Chopin	Polonaise in A flat, Op. 53 (*Heroic*)	9/22
6992	Chopin	Scherzo (1st) in B minor, Op. 20	4/26
6118	Chopin	Scherzo (2nd) in B flat minor, Op. 31	6/19
8007	Chopin	Scherzo (3rd) in C sharp minor, Op. 39	?
7085	Chopin	Valse Brillante in A flat, Op. 34, No. 1	12/26

Rollography

6401	Chopin	Valse in A flat, Op. 42	3/21
6073	Chopin	Valse in C sharp minor, Op. 64, No. 2	4/19
6513	Dvorsky (Hofmann)	*The Sanctuary*	3/22
6389	Gluck	Mélodie in G minor fr. *Orpheus and Euridice* (tr. Sgambati)	2/21
6821	Hofmann	Berceuse	12/24
6753	Hofmann	Étude for the Left Hand	5/24
6845	Hofmann	*Kaleidoscope*, Op. 40, No. 4	2/25
6696	Hofmann	Nocturne (*Complaint*) from *Mignonettes*	12/23
6139	Liszt	Hungarian Rhapsody, No 12 in C sharp minor	12/19
7369	Liszt	*Liebestraum* (Nocturne No. 3)	12/29
6375	Liszt	Tarantella, from *Years of Pilgrimage*, No. 3	12/20
7349	Liszt	Valse Impromptu in A minor	10/29
6708	Liszt	*Waldersrauschen (Murmuring Woods)* (Concert Études, No.1)	1/24
6119	Mendelssohn	Andante and Rondo Capriccioso in E, Op. 14	4/19
7273	Mendelssohn	Songs Without Words, No. 25, Op. 62, No. 1; No. 34, Op. 67, No. 4 in C (*Spinning Song*)	11/28
68740	Mendelssohn	Song Without Words, No. 30, Op. 62, No. 6 (*Spring Song*)	5/25
6953	Moszkowsky	Caprice Espagñole in A, Op. 37	1/26
6598	Moszkowski	*Étincelles* (*Sparks*), Op. 36, No. 6	2/23
6615	Moszkowski	*Guitarre*, Op. 45, No. 2	4/23
6074	Moszkowski	*The Juggleress*, Op. 52, No. 4	4/19
6525	Rachmaninov	Prelude in C sharp minor, Op. 3, No. 2	4/22
6229	Rachmaninov	Prelude in G minor, Op. 23, No. 5	1/20
6682	Rubinstein	Barcarolle (2nd) in A minor, Op. 30	11/23
6099	Rubinstein	Melody in F, Op. 3, No. 1	10/19
6561	Rubinstein	Valse Caprice in E flat	10/22
8005	Scarlatti	Pastorale and Capriccio	?
7227	Schuett	*Valse Bluette*, Op. 25	4/28
7072	Schumann	*El Contrabandista* (*The Smuggler*) (tr. Tausig)	11/26
6665	Schumann	*Aufschwung* (*Soaring*) from *Fantasiestücke*, Op.12, No. 2	10/23
7163	Schytte	*Forest Elves*, Op. 70, No. 5	10/27
6583	Scriabin	*Poème*, Op. 32, No. 1	1/21
6507	Sternberg	Étude de Concert, Op. 103, No. 3	2/22
7115	Tchaikovsky	Humoresque in E minor, Op. 10, No. 2	4/27
7286	Weber	*Perpetual Motion* (Rondo from Sonata, Op. 24 in C)	12/18
6812	Woods (Edna)	Valse Phantastique	11/24

Hofmann also contributed, with Bauer, Leginska and Stoessel, to two Biographical Rolls of Beethoven (Roll 1: D-333; Roll 2: D-335; both 10/26); with Bauer, Fryer, Godowsky, Hughes, Pachmann and Paderewski to a Biographical Roll of Chopin (D-429; 11/27); and with Backhaus, Kovacz and Rubinstein to a Biographical Roll of Mendelssohn (D-743; 1/29).

Ampico (for Hupfeld):

60371	Mendelssohn	Scherzo (Capriccio) in E minor, Op. 16, No. 2	2/22
50557	Wagner	Overture to *Tannhäuser*	by 7/20

Welte:

The rolls not dated 1905 are thought to have been recorded in 1913 and are dated as such in the following list.

3026	Beethoven	Sonata, Op. 101 in A. 1st Mvt: Allegretto, ma non troppo; 2nd Mvt: Vivace alla marcia	1913
3027	Beethoven	Ditto: 3rd Mvt: Allegro risoluto	1913

3024	Beethoven	Sonata, Op. 31, No. 3 in E flat. 1st Mvt: Allegro, and 2nd Mvt: Scherzo; allegretto vivace	1913
3025	Beethoven	Ditto, 3rd Mvt: Menuett and trio, moderato e grazioso, and 4th Mvt: Presto con fuoco	1913
668	Chopin	Nocturne, Op. 27, No. 2 in D flat	10/05
3028	Chopin	Polonaise Fantasie in A flat, Op. 61	1913
669	Chopin	Polonaise, Op. 44 in F sharp minor	10/05
3029	Handel	Variations in D minor	1913
3030	Hofmann	Barcarolle, Op. 22, No. 1 in F sharp minor	1913
3031	Mendelssohn	Andante and Rondo Capriccioso in E, Op. 14	1913
666	Moszkowski	Caprice Espagñole, Op. 37 in A minor	10/05
667	Moszkowski	*La Jongleuse (The Juggleress)*, Op. 52, No. 4 in E flat	10/05
3032	Paderewski	*Légende*, Op. 16, No. 1 in A flat	1913
3034	Rachmaninov	Polka de W.R.	1913
3033	Rachmaninov	Prelude, Op. 23, No. 3 in D minor	1913
661	Rubinstein	Album of National Dances; German Dance, Op. 82, No. 5 in F	10/05
660	Rubinstein	Melody, Op. 3, No. 1 in F	10/05
3035	Rubinstein	Scherzo, Op. 75, No. 5 in F	1913
665	Schubert	*Der Erlkönig (The Erlking)* (tr. Liszt)	10/05
664	Schumann	*Der Contrabandist (The Smuggler)* - Romance (tr. Tausig)	10/05
3036	Sgambati	*Nenia*, Op. 18, No. 3	1913
663	Wagner	*Die Walküre, Magic Fire Music* (tr. Brassin)	10/05
662	Wagner	*Tannhäuser* Overture (tr. Liszt)	10/05

Other manufacturers:

Hofmann recorded at least nine rolls for Hupfeld, featuring music by Brassin, Chopin, Hofmann, Leschetizky, Liszt, Mendelssohn, Schumann, Scriabin and Wagner. He also recorded eight rolls for Artecho; Chopin (1), Moszkowski (2), Rachmaninov (1), Rubinstein (2), Schumann (1) and Sgambati (1).

12. Alfred Cortot
Duo-Art:

71020	Albéniz	*Under the Palms* (Spanish Dance), Op. 232, No. 3	2/27
6330	Bach/Cortot	Adagio, tr. from the F minor Violin Concerto	4/21
8006	Beethoven	Sonata No. 29 in B flat, Op. 106 (*Hammerklavier*) Second movement only: Scherzo	?
7109	Beethoven	Sonata No. 30 in E, Op. 109. 1st Mvt: Adagio espressivo, and 2nd Mvt: Prestissimo	3/27
7110	Beethoven	Ditto, 3rd Mvt: Andante and variations	3/27
69690	Chabrier	*Album Leaf*	2/26
69100	Chabrier	*Idylle, Pièce Pittoresque*, No. 6	9/25
6365	Chopin	Andante Spianato and Grande Polonaise, Op. 22	11/20
6606	Chopin	Étude in A minor, Op. 25, No. 11 (*Winter Wind*)	3/23
67409	Chopin	Étude in D flat, Op. 25, No. 8	4/24
7088	Chopin	Étude in C minor, Op. 25, No. 12 (*Arpeggios*)	1/27
6524	Chopin	Étude in E, Op. 10, No. 3	4/22
6593	Chopin	Études, Op. 25, No.9 (*Butterfly*); Op. 10, No.5 (*Black Key*)	1/23
7327	Chopin	Impromptu in G flat, Op. 51	5/29
7397	Chopin	Nocturne, Op. 55, No. 2 in E flat	5/30
6773	Chopin	Prelude in D flat, Op. 28, No. 15 (*Raindrop*)	8/24

6478	Chopin/Liszt	The Maiden's Wish, Op. 74, No. 1	10/21
6241	Fauré	Berceuse from *The Dolly Suite*	2/20
6664	Liszt	At the Spring, from *Years of Pilgrimage*; 1st year, No. 4	10/23
3099	Liszt	Hungarian Rhapsody, No. 2 in C sharp minor	?
6135	Liszt	Hungarian Rhapsody, No. 11 in A minor	4/19
7240	Purcell	Minuets (17th century), from Suites 1 and 8 (arr. Cortot)	6/28
6372	Saint-Saëns	Étude en Forme de Valse, in D flat, Op. 52, No. 6	12/20
6441	Schubert	Impromptu, Op. 142, No. 3 in B flat (*Rosamunde*)	7/21
6126	Schubert	*Litany for all Souls' Day* (tr. Cortot)	3/19
6623	Scriabin	Étude (*Pathetic*) in D sharp minor, Op. 8, No. 12	5/23

Cortot also contributed, with Bauer, Friedman, Gabrilowitsch and Paderewski, to a Biographical Roll of Schubert (D-717). 11/28

Ampico (for Hupfeld):
| 59263 | Liszt | Hungarian Rhapsody, No. 2 in C sharp minor | 3/21 |
| 66033 | Mendelssohn | *Variations Sérieuses*, in D minor, Op. 54 | 5/26 |

Welte: None.
Other manufacturers:

Cortot recorded at least eleven rolls for Hupfeld, two of which were of Chopin's Sonata, Op. 58 in B minor. The other nine were of music by Chabrier, Chevillard, Chopin (Ballade, Op. 38), Daquin, Fauré, Franck, Liszt, Mendelsson and Schubert. For Philipps he recorded about 10 rolls, including three of Liszt and five of music by French composers (Chabrier (2), Godard, Fauré and Saint-Saëns). Two recordings (of Chopin and Schumann) were issued by the French piano company Pleyel on the Pleyela label.

13. Ossip Gabrilowitsch
Duo-Art:
5849	Arensky	Valse, from Suite Op. 15 (arr. 4 hands; with Harold Bauer)	12/16
6414	Chopin	Étude in F, Op. 10, No. 8	5/21
6349	Chopin	Étude in F minor, Op. 25, No. 2	11/20
7074	Chopin	Fantasie Impromptu in C sharp minor, Op. 66	11/26
6273	Chopin	Valse (Posth.) in E minor	4/20
5659	Fauré	Songs Without Words, Op. 17, No. 3 (*Romance*)	6/15
6926	Gabrilowitsch	Mélodie in E minor, Op. 8, No. 1	11/25
538	Haydn	Symphony No. 100 in G (*Military*) (Transcription) 3rd Mvt: Minuet in G	12/27
5670	Leschetizky	Intermezzo in Octaves, Op. 44, No. 4	7/15
66730	Mendelssohn	Song Without Words, No. 34, Op. 67, No. 4 in C (*Spinning Song*)	10/23
5804	Rachmaninov	Prelude in C sharp minor, Op. 3, No. 2	9/16
6211	Sapellnikov	Danse des Elfes, Op. 3	12/19
6487	Schubert	Marche Militaire, Op. 51, No. 1 (arr. 4 hands; with H.Bauer)	12/21
5841	Schubert	Moment Musical in F minor, Op. 94, No. 3	12/16
7284	Schumann	Novellete in B minor, Op. 99, No. 9	12/28

Gabrilowitsch also contributed, with Bauer, Cortot, Friedman and Paderewski, to a Biographical Roll of Schubert (D-717). 11/28

Ampico:
50383	Bach	Bourrée (Gavotte)	by 7/20
50624	Glazunov	Gavotte, Op. 49, No. 3	by 7/20
66633	Schumann	Fantasie in C, Op.17 1st Mvt: Part I: Allegro, molto, appassionato	10/26

66641	Schumann	Ditto, 1st Mvt: Part II: Allegro, molto, appassionato	10/26
66843	Schumann	Ditto, 2nd Mvt: Maestoso	10/26
65881	Tchaikovsky	Nocturne in C sharp minor, Op. 19, No. 4	4/26

Welte:

293	Brahms	Intermezzo, Op. 119, No. 2 in E minor	4/05
294	Brahms	Rhapsody, Op. 119, No. 4 in E flat	4/05
298	Chopin	Mazurka, Op. 33, No. 4 in B minor	1905
301	Chopin	Nocturne, Op. 15, No. 1 in F	4/05
297	Gabrilowitsch	Caprice Burlesque, Op. 3, No. 1 in G flat	3/05
302	Gabrilowitsch	Gavotte, Op. 2, No. 3 in D minor	1905
296	Raff	Suite, Op. 204, No. 3 in D (*Rigaudon*)	4/05
300	Schumann	*Nachtstück*, Op. 23, No. 4 in F	4/05
295	Tchaikovsky	*The Seasons*, Op. 37A, No. 10 (*October*)	4/05

Other manufacturers:

Gabrilowitsch recorded for five companies in addition to the three quoted above. He recorded at least 16 rolls for Hupfeld, including two of Bach, two Schubert and three Schumann. For Artrio he recorded about 11 rolls involving ten different composers. He made at least 14 rolls for Philipps including four of Schubert, three of Glazunov and two of Moszkowski. A Gabrilowitsch composition (Mélodie, Op. 8, No. 1) was also included. He recorded four rolls for Artecho (each of a different composer) and 11 for Recordo featuring nine different composers. Thus, Gabrilowitsch recorded for eight roll-producing companies in all.

14. Mark Hambourg
Duo-Art:

5652	Hambourg	*Volkslied* (*Chant Populaire*)	5/15
5908	Henselt	*Ave Maria* (Étude), Op. 5, No. 4 (from Twelve Études)	7/17
5699	Leschetizky	*La Source* (*The Spring*). Étude, Op. 36, No. 4	11/15
5654	Rubinstein	Nocturne in G, Op. 75, No. 8	6/15
6014	Rubinstein	*Polka Bohème* in G, Op. 82, No. 7	5/18
5957	Tchaikovsky	*Chanson Triste*, Op. 40, No. 2	12/17

Ampico:

55502	Chopin	Étude in G flat, Op. 10, No. 5 (*Black Key*)	by 7/20
55574	Liszt	Étude de Concert, No. 3 in D flat	by 7/20

Welte:

928	Bach	Organ Prelude and Fugue in D major (tr. d'Albert)	11/05
929	Beethoven	Sonata, Op. 2, No. 3. 4th Mvt: Rondo	11/05
932	Chopin	Étude, Op. 10, No. 5 in G flat	1905
931	Chopin	Mazurka, Op. 17, No. 4 in A minor (Posth.)	1905
936	Liszt	Polonaise, No. 2 in E	6/05
934	Rubinstein	*Le Bal* (*The Ball*), Op. 14, No. 4 in A flat	1905
933	Rubinstein	Nocturne, Op. 75, No. 8 in G	1905

Other manufacturers:

Hambourg recorded at least 17 rolls for Hupfeld, including three of Rubinstein's music and three of Schumann. The other rolls were the music of ten different composers. One Hambourg roll was issued by Artecho - a piece by Rubinstein.

15. Wanda Landowska
Duo-Art:

71350	Beethoven	Andante in F, Op. 35 (*Andanti Favori*)	7/27
9260	Beethoven	Sonata No. 12 in A flat, Op. 26. 1st Mvt: Andante con variazioni, and 2nd Mvt: Scherzo: Allegro molto	12/18

9270	Beethoven	Ditto: 3rd Mvt: Marcia funebre sulla morte d'un éroe, and 4th Mvt: Rondo: Allegro	12/28
6828	Lanner/Landowska	*Valses Viennoises*	12/24
67560	Mozart	Sonata No. 17 in D, K. 576. 1st Mvt: Allegro	5/24
67760	Mozart	Ditto: 2nd Mvt: Adagio	8/24
67850	Mozart:	Ditto: 3rd Mvt: Allegretto	9/24

Ampico (for Hupfeld):

66333	Mozart	Sonata No. 17 in D, K. 576. 1st Mvt: Allegro	7/26
66743	Mozart	Ditto, 2nd Mvt: Adagio, and 3rd Mvt: Allegretto	11/26

Welte:

955	Bach	English Suite, No. 5 in E minor. *Passepied*	1905
954	Bach	Partita, No. 1 in B. Minuet and Gigue	1905
965	Berlioz	*La Damnation de Faust. Danse de Sylphes* (tr. Liszt)	1905
963	Chopin	Waltz, Op. 64, No. 1 in D flat (*Minute Waltz*)	1905
964	Chopin	Waltz, Op. 69, No. 2 in B minor	1905
956	Dandrieu	*Les Cascades*	1905
960	Daquin	*L'Hirondelle* (*The Swallow*)	1905
957	Durante	Divertimento in G minor	1905
958	Scarlatti	Pastorale in E minor (arr. Tausig)	1905
962	Schubert	Walzerkette from *Die Schöne Müllerin* (tr. Landowska)	1905
961	Schumann	Waltz in A minor	1905

Other manufacturers:

Landowska recorded at least 10 rolls for Hupfeld including the same Mozart sonata as above (see Duo-Art and Ampico lists) and extracts from Bach's English Suites. Other composers represented were Berlioz, Dandrieu, Daquin, Haydn, Pasquino, Scarlatti and Wagner. She recorded one roll for Pleyela (a Scarlatti sonata) and one for Artecho - a waltz by Schumann.

16. Artur Schnabel

Duo-Art: None.

Ampico:

62721	Bach	Italian Concerto. 1st Mvt: Allegro	1/24
62733	Bach	Ditto, 2nd Mvt: Andante	1/24
62741	Bach	Ditto, 3rd Mvt: Presto	1/24
62291	Beethoven	Minuet in G	8/23
60613	Beethoven	Rondo in G, Op. 51, No. 2	8/22
62353	Brahms	Rhapsody in G minor, Op. 79, No. 2	9/23
62011	Schubert	Scherzo, No. 1 in B flat (Posth.)	5/23
60603	Weber	*Invitation to the Dance*, Op. 65	5/22

Welte:

389	Bach	English Suite, No. 5 in E minor (Gigue)	1905
396	Bach	Toccata in G	1905
386	Brahms	Intermezzo, Op. 119, No. 3 in C	1905
390	Chopin	Étude, Op. 10, No. 5 in G flat (*Black Key*)	5/05
387	Chopin	Étude, Op. 25, No. 2 in F minor	1905
393	Chopin	Nocturne, Op. 15, No. 3 in G minor	1905
394	Chopin	Prelude, Op. 28, No. 23 in F	1905
384	Lanner	*Old Vienna* Waltzes	5/05
385	Schnabel	*Valse Noble*, Op. 77 in C	1905
383	Schubert	Impromptu, Op. 90, No. 4 in A flat	5/05

395	Schubert	Nachgelassene Klavierstücke	1905
382	Strauss, Josef	Dorf Schwalbenaus Österreich (Village Swallows), Op. 164	5/05
388	Weber	Invitation to the Dance, Op. 65	5/05

Other manufacturers:

Schnabel recorded at least 15 rolls for Hupfeld, including three of Chopin, two Beethoven and two Schubert. For Philipps he recorded about 22 rolls including four of Beethoven and eight of Brahms. Surprisingly, there are four rolls of the music of Erich Korngold. Schnabel also recorded three rolls for Artecho; one each of music by Lanner, Schubert and Weber.

17. Percy Grainger
Duo-Art:
(Grainger recorded only for Duo-Art.)

7161-4	Bach	Organ Fantasia and Fugue in G minor (arr. Liszt) Part I: Fantasia	10/27
71740	Bach	Ditto: Part II: Fugue	11/27
524	Bizet	L'Arlésienne Suite. 4-handed arrangement with Grainger playing both parts. Part I: Prelude and minuetto	9/26
525	Bizet	Ditto, Part II: Adagietto and carillon	10/26
6718	Brahms	Cradle Song, Op. 49, No. 4	2/24
6548	Chopin	Étude (Posth.), No. 2 in A flat, from Trois Nouvelles Études	9/22
6409	Debussy	Toccata in C sharp from Pour Le Piano - Suite	4/21
71900	Delius	North Country Sketches, arr. for Two Pianos; 1. Autumn: The Wind Soughs in the Trees	12/27
71910	Delius	Ditto, 2. Winter Landscape; 3: Dance	12/27
71920	Delius	Ditto, 4. The March of Spring; Woodlands, Meadows and Silent Moors (all recorded with Ralph Leopold)	12/27
74439	Delius	Brigg Fair, arr. Juhl (arr. 4 hands; with Ralph Leopold)	1/32
6339	Dett	Juba Dance	10/20
6931	Fauré	Nell, Op. 18, No. 1 (tr. Grainger)	11/25
6415	Gardiner	Humoresque	5/21
6368	Grainger	Children's March: Over the Hills and Far Away (for two pianos; with Lotta Mills Hough)	12/20
5666	Grainger	Colonial Song	7/15
6194	Grainger	Country Gardens (No. 22 of British Folk Song Settings) (replaced earlier recording of 5/19)	5/29
6997	Grainger	Eastern Intermezzo	5/26
6072	Grainger	Gay But Wistful (from In a Nutshell Suite)	11/18
6059	Grainger	Gum Suckers' March (from In a Nutshell Suite)	10/18
5679	Grainger	Irish Tune from County Derry (Londonderry Air) (No. 6 of British Folk Song Settings)	9/15
7274	Grainger	Jutish Melody (No. 8 of Danish Folk Song Settings)	11/28
5821	Grainger	Lullaby from Tribute to Foster	10/16
5688	Grainger	Mock Morris	10/15
6284	Grainger	Molly on the Shore (Irish Reel) (No. 8 of British Folk Song Settings)	5/20
6030	Grainger	One More Day, My John (No. 1 of Sea Chanty Settings)	6/18
7083	Grainger	Sheep and Goat "Walkin' to the Pasture" (arr. Guion) (from Cowboys and Old Fiddlers' Breakdown)	12/26
5661	Grainger	Shepherds' Hey (No. 4 of British Folk Song Settings)	6/15
66170	Grainger	Spoon River (No. 1 of American Folk Song Settings)	4/23

5712	Grainger	*Sussex Mummers' Christmas Carol* (No. 2 of British Folk Song Settings)	12/15
6444	Grainger	*Turkey in the Straw* (Arr. Guion) from *Cowboys and Old Fiddlers' Breakdown*	6/21
6760	Grainger	Two Musical Relics of My Mother: *Hermund the Evil* and *As Sally Sat A-Weeping*. Played by Percy Grainger and his mother, Rose Grainger	6/24
5735	Grainger	*Walking Tune*, from *Music Room Tit-Bits*, No. 3	3/16
6824	Grainger	Zanzibar Boat Song	12/24
7437	Grieg	Ballade in G minor, Op. 24	11/31
6475	Grieg	Piano Concerto in A minor (arr. Grainger) 1st Mvt: Allegro molto moderato	10/21
6479	Grieg	2nd Mvt: Adagio	11/21
6485	Grieg	3rd Mvt: Allegro moderato e marcato	12/21
6693	Grieg	*Erotikon*, Op. 43, No. 5	12/23
7377	Grieg	Norwegian Folk Songs, Op. 66. Nos. 1, 2, 14, 10, 19, 16, 18	1/30
6522	Grieg	*Peer Gynt*, from Suite No. 1, Op. 46 1. *Morning*; 3. *Anitra's Dance*	4/22
6530	Grieg	Ditto, 2. *Asa's Death*; 4. *In the Hall of the Mountain King*	5/22
6206	Grieg	*To the Spring*, Op. 43, No. 6	12/19
7370	Grieg	*Wedding Day at Troldhaugen*, Op. 65, No. 6	12/29
6754	Handel	Hornpipe from *The Water Music Suite* (tr. Grainger)	4/24
6497	Liszt	Hungarian Rhapsody, No. 12 in C sharp minor	1/22
6668	Liszt	Polonaise, No. 2 in E	10/23
6384	Schumann	Romance, Op. 28, No. 2 in F sharp	1/21
73610	Schumann	Sonata No. 2 in G minor, Op. 22. 1st Mvt: Presto	11/29
73620	Schumann	Ditto, 2nd Mvt: Andantino	11/29
73630	Schumann	Ditto, 3rd Mvt: Scherzo and 4th Mvt: Rondo (Finale)	11/29
6859	Schumann	Symphonic Studies, Op. 13. Part I: Nos. 1 - 7	3/25
6868	Schumann	Ditto, Part II: Nos. 8 - 12	4/25
7252	Scott	Lento (No. 1 from *Two Pierrot Pieces*, Op. 35)	9/28
7217	Scott	*Lotus Land*, Op. 47, No. 1	3/28
6514	Scott/Grainger	Symphonic Dance, No. 1 (arr. 4 hands; with Cyril Scott)	3/22
6572	Stanford/Grainger	*Leprechaun's Dance* (No. 3 of Four Irish Dances)	11/22
5838	Stanford/Grainger	*Macguire's Kick* (No. 1 of Four Irish Dances)	12/16
6117	Stanford/Grainger	*Reel* (No. 4 of Four Irish Dances)	4/19
7400	Strauss (R)	*Till Eulenspiegel's Merry Pranks* (arr. 4 hands; with R. Leopold)	6/30
7300	Strauss/Grainger	*Ramble* on the Love Duet from *The Rose Bearer*	3/29
6798	Tchaikovsky	*Nutcracker Suite*, Op. 71A. Concert Paraphrase by Grainger Part I: March; *Dance of the Sugar-plum Fairy*; Russian Dance; *Trepak*	10/24
6810	Tchaikovsky	Ditto, Part II: *Arab Dance*, *Chinese Dance*, *Dance of the Reed Flutes*	11/24
6085	Tchaikovsky	Ditto, Part III: *Waltz of the Flowers*	12/18
7351	Tchaikovsky	*Romeo and Juliet*: Fantasy-Overture, arranged for four hands. Played by Percy Grainger and Ralph Leopold	10/29

18. Wilhelm Backhaus
Duo-Art:

70650	Beethoven	Sonata (*Pathétique*), Op. 13 in C minor 1st Mvt: Grave; Allegro di molto e con brio	10/26

6813-4 (2 rolls)	Brahms	Variations on a Theme of Paganini, arr. from Paganini's Caprice, Op. 1, No. 24 by Brahms in his Op. 35. Book 1: Nos. 1, 3, 7, 12, 13; Book 2: Nos. 3, 4, 5, 6, 7, 8, 10, 11, 14.	1/24
6848	Chopin	Romance (Larghetto from Concerto, Op. 11 in E minor) (tr. Backhaus)	2/25
6698	Delibes	Waltz from *Naila, the Fairy of the Spring* Ballet (tr. Dohnanyi)	12/23
7058	Kreisler	*Liebeslied* (*Love's Sorrow*), from *Old Viennese Dance Tunes*, No. 2 (tr. Rachmaninov)	9/26
72710	Liszt	Étude (*Leggierezza*) No. 2 in F minor, from *Grand Concert Études*	1/28
6967	Mendelssohn	Concerto, Op. 25 in G minor (arr. Backhaus) 1st Mvt: Allegro con fuoco	2/26
6968	Mendelssohn	Ditto, 2nd Mvt: Andante in E	2/26
6981	Mendelssohn	Ditto, 3rd Mvt: Presto, molto allegro e vivace	3/26
7010	Mendelssohn	*Elfin Chorus* from *A Midsummer Night's Dream*, Op. 21 (tr. Liszt)	6/26
68250	Mozart	Serenade from *Don Juan* (*Don Giovanni*) (tr. Backhaus)	12/24
6667	Pick-Mangiagalli	*La Danse d'Olaf*, Op. 33, No. 2	10/23
6958	Schumann	*Dedication* (*Widmung*), Op. 25, No. 1 (tr. Liszt)	1/26
67610	Smetena	Bohemian Dance (Caprice Bohemien) in F	6/24
6684	Strauss	Serenade, Op. 17, No. 2 (tr. Backhaus)	11/23
7391	Wagner	March from *Tannhäuser*, Act 2, Scene 4	4/30
7301	Wagner	Prelude (Symphonic Introduction) from *The Meistersingers of Nuremberg* (tr. Hutcheson)	3/29

Backhaus also contributed, with Bourne, Fischer and Nikisch, to a Biographical Roll of Brahms (D-45).   10/26

He also contributed, with Hofmann, Kovacz and Rubinstein to a Biographical Roll of Mendelssohn (D-743).   1/29

Ampico (for Hupfeld):

52645	Chopin	Waltz Brillant, Op. 34, No. 1 in A flat	by 7/20
56965	Rubinstein	*Valse Caprice*	by 7/20
50614	Schubert/Liszt	*Du Bist Die Ruh* (*Thou Art Repose*)	by 7/20

Welte:

3310	Chopin	Concerto No. 1, Op. 11 in E minor 2nd Mvt: Romance - Larghetto (tr. Backhaus)	?1919
3309	Schubert	Marche Militaire, Op. 51, No. 3 in E flat (tr. Backhaus)	?1919
3312	Schubert	*Wanderer* Fantasia, Op. 15. 1st Mvt: Allegro con fuoco, and 2nd Mvt: Adagio	?1919
3313	Schubert	3rd Mvt: Presto, and 4th Mvt: Allegro	?1919

Other manufacturers:

Backhaus recorded an enormous number of rolls for the Hupfeld Company - over 150 of them. All the major composers are well represented, as are many minor ones.

19. Ethel Leginska
Duo-Art:

6885	Bach	Prelude and Fugue from *The Well-Tempered Clavier*, No. 3 in C	6/25
6743	Beethoven	Minuet, No. 2 in G	4/24
6957	Beethoven	Eight Variations on the theme *Tändeln und Scherzen*	1/26

5644	Chopin	Ballade (1st) in G minor, Op. 23	5/15
7075	Chopin	Nocturne in E flat, Op. 9, No. 2	11/26
6707	Chopin	Valse in E minor (Posthumous)	1/24
6822	Leginska	*Cradle Song*	12/24
6388	Leschetizky	Arabesque en Forme d'Étude, Op. 45, No. 1	2/21
6539	Leschetizky	*The Two Larks* (Impromptu), Op. 2, No. 1	6/22
6731	Liadov	*The Music Box* (*Une Tabatière à Musique*), Op. 32	3/24
7396	Liszt	Hungarian Rhapsody, No. 8 in F sharp minor (Capriccio)	5/30
5585	Mendelssohn	Songs Without Words, No. 30, Op.62, No. 6 (*Spring Song*)	?11/14
7137	Mendelssohn	Songs Without Words, No. 44, Op. 102, No. 2 and No. 10, Op. 30, No. 4	7/27
6159	Moszkowski	Valse in A flat, Op. 34, No. 1	6/19
6217	Rameau	Gavotte and Variations (tr. Leschetizky)	12/19
6549	Rimsky-Korsakov	*Hymn to the Sun* from *The Golden Cockerel*	9/22
5587	Rubinstein	Valse Caprice in E flat	?11/14
5583	Rubinstein	Melody in F, Op. 3, No. 1	?11/14
5582	Schubert/Liszt	*Hark! Hark! The Lark!*	?11/14
5584	Schubert	Marche Militaire, Op. 51, No. 1 (arr. Tausig)	?11/14
5586	Schumann	*Träumerei,* from *Kinderszenen*, Op. 15, No. 7	?11/14
6592	Strauss	Concert Arabesques on Motives from the Waltz *By the Beautiful Blue Danube* (tr. Schulz-Evler)	1/23
7352	Tchaikovsky	*Autumn Song*, Op. 37A, from *The Seasons* (No. 10 - October)	10/29
7359	Tchaikovsky	*Festival Overture "1812"*, Op. 49	11/29
6999	Weber	*Oberon* Overture	5/26

Leginska also contributed, with Bauer, Hofmann and Stoessel, to two Biographical Rolls of Beethoven (Roll 1: D-333; Roll 2: D-335). both 10/26

Ampico:

52553	Daquin	*Le Coucou*	by 7/20
55396	Liszt	Hungarian Rhapsody, No. 8 in F sharp minor (Capriccio)	by 7/20
53927	Strauss	*Blue Danube* - Concert Arabesque. (tr. Schulz-Evler; arr. Leginska)	by 7/20

Welte: None.
Other manufacturers:

Leginska recorded 34 rolls for Artrio, the composers ranging from Beethoven to Nevin. Included amongst them are seven compositions by her teacher, Leschetizky, including a six-roll set of his *Souvenirs d'Italie*, the only complete recording of this composition made for the reproducing piano. She also made seven rolls for Recordo, one each of music by Chaminade, Chopin, Leschetizky, MacDowell, Moszkowski, Nevin and Sieveking.

20. Artur Rubinstein
Duo-Art:

6204	Albéniz	*El Albaicin* (*Iberia*). Suite for Piano	12/19
6378	Albéniz	*Evocation* (*Iberia*)	12/20
6298	Albéniz	*Sevillanas*, No. 3 from *Suite Espagñole*, Op. 47, No. 3	6/20
6596	Brahms	Capriccio in B minor, Op. 76, No. 2	2/23
6971	Brahms	Intermezzo in A, Op. 118, No. 2	2/26
6744	Brahms	Rhapsody in B minor, Op. 79, No. 1	4/21
6252	Chopin	Ballade (3rd) in A flat, Op. 47	3/20
6542	Chopin	Barcarolle in F sharp, Op. 60	7/22

6162	Chopin	Nocturne in F sharp, Op. 15, No. 2	7/19
6505	Chopin	Polonaise in F sharp minor, Op. 44	2/22
6811	Chopin	Preludes, Op. 28, Nos. 1, 4, 10, 21, 24	11/24
6354	Debussy	Danse	11/20
6834	Debussy	*L'Isle Joyeuse*	1/25
6182	Debussy	*La Plus Que Lente* (Valse)	10/19
6755	de Falla	*Ritual Fire Dance*, from *El Amor Brujo* (tr. Rubinstein)	5/24
6922	Prokofiev	*Suggestion Diabolique*, Op. 4, No. 4	10/25
6857	Rimsky-Korsakov	*Le Coq d'Or* - Selections	3/25
6560	Schumann	*Papillons*, Op. 2	10/22
		Also on rolls 0328 (Part I) and 0329 (Part II)	

Rubinstein also contributed, with Backhaus, Hofmann and Kovacz, to a Biographical Roll of Mendelssohn (D-743). 1/29

Ampico:

57446	Albéniz	*Cordoba, Chants d'Espagne* (*Songs of Spain*), Op. 232, No. 4	by 7/20
57556	Albéniz	*Iberia, Triana*	by 7/20
57775	Chopin	Étude in E, Op. 10, No. 3	4/20
57296	Chopin	Polonaise in A, Op. 40, No. 1 (*Military*)	by 7/20
57667	Debussy	*La Cathédrale Engloutie* (*The Submerged Cathedral*)	by 7/20
58087	Liszt	Hungarian Rhapsody, No. 12 in C sharp minor	by 7/20
57516	Rubinstein (Anton)	Barcarolle in A minor	10/19
57304	Schumann	*Des Abends* (*In the Evening*) from *Fantasiestücke*, Op. 12, No. 1	by 7/20
57384	Schumann	*In the Night*, from *Fantasiestücke*, Op. 12, No. 5	by 7/20

Welte: None.

Other manufacturers:
None. He recorded only for Duo-Art and Ampico.

21. Benno Moiseiwitsch

Duo-Art:
One roll only:

75176	Delibes	*Passepied*, from the incidental music to *Le Roi S'Amuse*	?10/37

Ampico:

59084	Brahms	Capriccio in B minor, Op. 76, No. 2	2/21
68553	Brahms	Intermezzo in E flat minor, Op. 118, No. 6	2/28
66153	Brahms	Waltzes, Op. 39, Nos. 1, 2, 14, 16, 13	6/26
61313	Brahms	Waltzes, Op. 39, Nos. 5, 6, 15	12/22
69053	Chopin	Impromptu in F sharp, Op. 36	7/28
67143	Chopin	Nocturne in E minor, Op. 72, No. 1	2/27
61843	Chopin	Sonata in B minor, Op. 58. 1st Mvt: Allegro maestoso	4/23
65181	Chopin	Ditto, 2nd Mvt: Scherzo	11/25
65193	Chopin	Ditto, 3rd Mvt: Largo	11/25
65203	Chopin	Ditto, 4th Mvt: Presto non tanto	11/25
68871	Chopin	Waltz in E minor (Posthumous)	5/28
67761	Debussy	Prélude: *La Fille aux Cheveux de Lin* (*The Girl with the Flaxen Hair*). Vol. I, No. 8	7/27
57973	Debussy	Prélude: *Minstrels*. Vol. I, No. 12	by 7/20
71741	Delibes	*Passepied*	9/37

Rollography

68023	Granados	*Danzas Españolas (Spanish Dances)*, Op. 37, No. 6 in D	9/27
70161	Ibert	*Le Petit Âne Blanc (The Little White Donkey)*	9/29
62791	Leschetizky	*Arabesque en Forme d'Étude*, Op. 45, No. 1	2/24
59671	Palgrem	*Refrain de Berceuse (Cradle Song)*	5/21
69441	Palgrem	*Rococo*	12/28
57836	Ravel	*Jeux d'Eaux (The Fountain)*	by 7/20
59731	Schubert/Liszt	*Hark! Hark! The Lark!*	6/21
65733	)		
65743	) Schumann	*Carnaval*, Op. 9 (on four rolls)	3/26
65753	)		
65763	)		
57936	Scriabin	*Nocturne for the Left Hand Alone*	by 7/20
68301	Tchaikovsky	*Humoresque in E minor*, Op. 10, No. 2	11/27
70423, 70433	Wagner/Liszt	*Tannhäuser Overture* - Concert Paraphrase (on two rolls)	1/30
70593	Wagner/Liszt	*Liebestod* - Tristan und Isolde	4/30

Welte: None.
Other manufacturers: None.

22. Myra Hess
Duo-Art:
(Myra Hess recorded <u>only</u> for Duo Art).

0210	Bach	Chorale Prelude *Whitsuntide (Komm Gott Schöpfer, Heilliger Geist* (arr. Busoni)	1/29
7236	Bach	Toccata in G	5/28
0276	Beethoven	Sonata, No. 25 in G, Op. 79. 1st Mvt: Presto alla tedesca	4/29
0277	Beethoven	2nd Mvt: Mignon - andante espressivo	4/29
0278	Beethoven	3rd Mvt: Vivace	4/29
6911	Brahms	Intermezzo in C, Op. 119, No. 3	9/25
6705	Brahms	Rhapsody in E flat, Op. 119, No. 4	1/24
7069	Burgmein	*Pierrot and Pierrette's Story (Pierrot's Serenade, Love Duet, Marriage Ball, Wedding March)* (Duet with Harold Bauer)	10/26
6927	Debussy	*The Engulfed Cathedral*, from Préludes, Book 1, No. 10	11/25
062	Debussy	*Voiles (Sails)* from Préludes, Book 1, No. 2	by 9/23
6658	Paradies	Toccata in A	9/23
7239	Pierné	*March of the Little Leaden Soldiers*, Op. 14, No. 6. (Duet with Harold Bauer)	6/28
8011	Rachmaninov	Prelude in C sharp minor, Op. 3, No. 2	?
7059	Scarlatti	Sonata in G, Vol. 1, No. 14 (revised Dukas)	9/26
0208	Szymanowski	Étude in B flat minor, Op. 4, No. 3	3/27

23. Walter Gieseking
Duo-Art: None.
Ampico (for Hupfeld):

66023	Chopin	Ballade (2nd), Op. 38 in F	5/26
65853	Debussy	*La Demoiselle Élue (The Chosen Maiden)* (Prélude in C)	4/26
66363	Debussy	*Hommage à Rameau*. *Images*, Series 1, No. 2	4/26
65863	Niemann	*Singende Fontane (Singing Fountain)* (Nocturne, Op. 30 in D)	4/26

Welte:
Some of Gieseking's Welte rolls were recorded in 1923-24 and the remainder in 1926-27.

3820	Bach	Italian Concerto, 1st Mvt: Allegro animato	1923-24
3821	Bach	Ditto, 2nd Mvt: Andante molto espressivo	1923-24
3822	Bach	Partita, No. 1 in B. Allemande, Courante, Sarabande	1923-24
3823	Beethoven	Violin Sonata, Op. 47 in A minor (*Kreutzer*) arr. for piano 1st Mvt: Adagio sostenuto, presto	1923-24
3824	Beethoven	Ditto, 2nd Mvt: Andante with variations	1923-24
3825	Brahms	Intermezzo, Op. 117, No. 3 in C sharp minor	1923-24
3827	Debussy	*Images*, Series I, No. 2 - *Hommage à Rameau*	1923-24
3828	Debussy	*Images*, Series II, No. 3 - *Poissons d'Or*	1923-24
7576	Debussy	*Le Coin des Enfants*, No. 1 (*Dr Gradus and Parnassum*) and No. 2 (*Jimbo's Lullaby*)	1/27
7577	Debussy	Ditto, No. 3 (*Serenade of the Doll*)	1/27
7578	Debussy	Ditto, No. 4 (*The Snow is Dancing*); No. 5 (*The Little Shepherd*); and No. 6 (*Golliwog's Cake Walk*)	1/27
3826	Debussy	*Masques*	1923-24
7606	Debussy	Préludes, Book I, No. 1 - *Danseuses de Delphes*	3/27
7328	Debussy	Ditto, No. 10 - *La Cathédrale Engloutie*	4/26
7329	Debussy	Ditto, Nos. 11 (*Le Danse de Puck*) and 12 (*Minstrels*)	4/26
7607	Debussy	Ditto, Nos. 2 (*Voiles*) and 3 (*Le Vent dans la Plaine*)	3/27
7637	Debussy	Ditto, Nos. 4 (*Le Sons et les Parfums Tournent dans l'Air du Soir*) and 5 (*Les Collines d'Anacapri*)	4/27
7300	Grieg	*Lyrische Stücke*, Op. 68, No. 5 (*French Serenade*) and Op. 62, No. 3 (*Cradle Song*)	3/26
3829	Liszt	Hungarian Rhapsody, No. 14 in F minor	1923-24
7363	Niemann	*Das Magische Buch*, Op. 92, No. 1 (*Kolibri*)	5/26
7364	Niemann	Ditto, No. 6 (*The Silver Cascade*)	5/26
3830	Niemann	*Das Singende Fontane*, Op. 30	1923-24
3831	Ravel	*Gaspard de la Nuit*, No. 1 (*Ondine*)	1923-24
7465	Rubinstein	*Kamennoi-Ostrow*, Op. 10, No. 22 in F sharp	9/26
3832	Schoenberg	Sechs Kleine Klavierstücke, Op. 19	1923-24
7301	Schubert	*Du Bist die Ruh* (tr. Liszt)	3/26
7601	Strauss, R	*Allerseelen* (*All Souls' Day*), Op. 10, No. 8 (tr. Reger)	2/27
7299	Strauss, R	*Traum Durch die Dämmerung* (from 3 Songs, Op.29; tr. Reger)	3/26

Other manufacturers:

Gieseking recorded at least 39 rolls for Hupfeld, including seven of Bach, seven of Debussy and six of Niemann.

24. Vladimir Horowitz
Duo-Art:

7250	Bizet	*Carmen* Variations (arr. Horowitz)	10/28
7287	Chopin	Études, Op. 10, No. 6 in E flat minor and Op. 25, No. 12 in C minor	12/28
7360	Horowitz	Valse in F minor	11/29
7450	Rachmaninov	Preludes, Op. 32, No. 10 in B minor and Op. 32, No. 8 in A minor	4/32
7447	Saint-Saëns	*Danse Macabre* in G minor, Op. 40, from *Four Symphonic Poems* (tr. Liszt)	3/32

7282	Schubert	*Love's Message*, from *Swan Songs* (tr. Liszt)	2/29
7281	Tchaikovsky	*Dumka*, Op. 59	1/29

Ampico: None.
Welte:

4124	Bach	Organ Toccata, Adagio and Fugue in C (tr. Busoni)	4/27
4127	Bach	*Well-Tempered Clavier*. Prelude and Fugue in D, Book 1, No. 5 (tr. Busoni)	5/27
4120	Bizet	*Carmen* - Variations (tr. Horowitz)	3/27
4130	Chopin	Études, Op. 10, Nos. 8 in F; 5 in G flat (*Black Key*)	2/27
4125	Chopin	Mazurka, Op. 30, No. 4 in C sharp minor	3/27
4126	Chopin	Mazurkas, Op. 63. Nos. 2 in F minor; 3 in C sharp minor	2/27
4119	Horowitz	*Moment Exotique*	2/27
4122	Liszt	*Valse Oubliée*	1/27
4128	Mozart	*Figaro* Fantasie (tr. Liszt; amended by Busoni)	4/27
4188	Rachmaninov	Prelude, Op. 23, No. 5 in G minor	3/27
4123	Rachmaninov	Preludes, Op. 32, Nos. 5 in G and 12 in G sharp minor	3/27
4121	Schubert	*Liebesbotschaft* (*Swan Song*, No. 10). (tr. Liszt)	1/27

Other manufacturers: None.

25. Dinu Lipatti
Lipatti did not record any piano rolls.

An additional Duo-Art roll (a curiosity).

In 1877 a number of well-known composers collaborated in writing a set of 24 Variations and a Finale on the piece generally known as *Chopsticks*. The paraphrases were published in 1879. They came to the attention of Liszt, who wrote an Andante. In 1925 or thereabouts the Aeolian Company decided to have ten of their prominent recording artists make a roll of ten of the paraphrases including the one by Liszt. Only one copy of the roll was produced. All the artists autographed the roll and it was packaged in a fancy box. It was then auctioned at a benefit concert at the Metropolitan Opera House and was bought, it is believed, by Cornelius Bliss for $8,000.

In the 1960s the original master roll was discovered and it has since been duplicated. It is interesting to note here the titles of the ten variations and the pianists who played them. Four of the pianists are featured in this book. The following list identifies the ten paraphrases by composer and performer:

1.	Valse by Cui	-	Rudolph Ganz
2.	Polka by Borodin	-	Josef Hofmann
3.	Tarantella by Rimsky-Korsakov	-	Harold Bauer
4.	Valse by Liadov	-	Ernest Hutcheson
5.	Andante by Liszt	-	Yolando Mero
6.	Grotesque Fugue by Rimsky-Korsakov	-	Alexander Siloti
7.	Polka by Borodin	-	Ernest Schelling
8.	Gallop by Liadov	-	Ethel Leginska
9.	Gigue by Liadov	-	Myra Hess
10.	Mazurka by Borodin	-	Guiomar Novaes

Appendix 3. Player Piano Associations

Great Britain:

The Player Piano Group (PPG)

Founded in London in 1959. Has about 300 members throughout Britain but mainly in the south, and some overseas members. Holds regular meetings.

    Secretary: Mr. A.C. Austin
                93, Evelyn Avenue
                Ruislip
                Middlesex HA4 8AH

The North West Player Piano Association (NWPPA)

Founded in Manchester in 1972. Has about 200 members throughout Britain but mainly in the north, and some overseas members. Holds regular meetings.

    Secretary: Mr. E. Whittle
                47, Raikes Road
                Preston
                Lancs PR1 5EQ

The above Associations are not rivals and many members belong to both. The existence of two Associations is for geographical convenience, so that members do not have to travel too far to meetings.

USA:

Automatic Musical Instruments Collectors' Association (AMICA)

    Founded in San Francisco in 1963. Has members in the USA, Britain and elsewhere.

    Secretary: Mr. R. Pratt
                515, Scott Street
                Sandusky
                Ohio 48870-3736

Netherlands:

Nederlanse Pianola Vereniging (NPV)

    Secretary: Mr. M.R. Graus
                Korte Dijk 10
                2871 CB Schoonhoven

Germany:

Gesellschaft für Selbstspielende Musikinstruments e.V.

    Secretary: Mr. J. Hocker
                Heiligenstock 46
                51465, Bergisch Gladbach 2

Index

Composers' names are included in this index in cases where the reference in the text is an important part of the story; for example, when a pianist is known as a good interpreter of the composer's music. They are not included when the reference in the text is only to one of their compositions (as in lists of recordings) unless it is considered to be important.

Abbey, Henry, 190
Adni, Daniel, 241
Albéniz, Isaac, 64, 194, 236, 276
d'Albert, Eugen, 34, 35, 36, 59, 76, 131, 230, 243
d'Albert, Eugenia (daughter of d'Albert and Carreño), 35
d'Albert, Hertha (daughter of d'Albert and Carreño), 35
d'Albert, Wolfgang (Eugen d'Albert's son), 35
Aldrich, Richard, 50, 262
Aldridge, Rose; see Grainger, Rose
Alessandrescu, Alfred, 343
Alexander III, Tsar, 116, 117
Alexanian, Diran, 344
Antionetti, Aldo, 304
Arensky, Anton, 99
Arne, Thomas, 197
Aronson, Maurice, 151
Ashkenazy, Vladimir, xiii
Astaire, Fred, 282
Athol, Duchess of, 109
Auber, Daniel, 2, 29
Auer, Leopold, 172, 182
Ax, Emanuel, 281

Bach, Johann Sebastian, 16, 74, 78, 79, 80, 83, 127, 178, 181, 197, 203, 204, 205, 210, 212, 213, 231, 262, 270, 285, 306-307, 308, 322, 331, 333, 337, 348, 349
Backhaus, Alma (née Herzberg) (Wilhelm's wife), 251
Backhaus, Clara (née Schonberg) (Wilhelm's mother), 243
Backhaus, Guido (Wilhelm's father), 243

Backhaus, Wilhelm, 222, 243-255, 346
Bacon, 'Pop', 122
Baillie, Dame Isobel, 109, 110
Balzac, Honoré de, 1
Barbirolli, Sir John, 255
Barenboim, Daniel, xiii
Barth, Heinrich, 274
Bartók, Béla, 337
Bauer, Harold, 56, 79, 113-123, 178, 182, 183, 197, 222, 265, 307, 311
Bax, Sir Arnold, 302, 308
Bazin, Emmanuel, 29
Beatles, The, 243, 336
Becker, Hugo, 220
Beecham, Sir Thomas, 9, 233, 276, 303, 329
Beethoven, Ludwig van, 1, 5, 11, 15, 18, 29, 34, 59, 63, 64, 75, 80, 83, 105, 106, 119, 120, 123, 127, 134, 137, 158, 162, 178, 181, 190, 194, 197, 200, 201, 215, 219, 223, 224, 225, 227, 248, 250, 253, 254, 279, 285, 298, 308, 309, 316, 321, 322, 324, 331, 334, 339
Behr, Therese; see Schnabel, Therese
Ben-Gurion, David, 280
Bennett, Arnold, 280
Bennett, Sir William Sterndale, 302
Berg, Alban, 182
Berlioz, Hector, 2, 3, 29
Bernstein, Leonard, 140, 280
Bessie, Jacques, 128, 130, 133
Bessie, Maria, 128, 130, 133
Bessie, Rosina; see Lhevinne, Rosina
Bessie, Sophie, 128
Bethke, Martha; see Gieseking, Martha
Biggs, Anne Marie, 271

Bird, John, 241
Bischoff, Mrs, 31, 37
Bishop-Kovacevich, Stephen, 313
Bizet, Georges, 3, 334
Bloch, Ernest, 182, 264
Bloomfield Zeisler, Fannie; see Zeisler, Fannie Bloomfield
Blow, John, 197
Blumenfeld, Fannie; see Zeisler, Fannie Bloomfield
Blumenfeld, Felix, 327
Bock, Hugo, 43
Borowski, Felix, 182
Borwick, Leonard, 194
Boulanger, Nadia, 344, 348
Boult, Sir Adrian, 312
Brahms, Johannes, 15, 45, 61, 74, 76, 113, 118, 120, 123, 134, 181, 189, 215, 217, 219, 220, 243, 244, 250, 251, 254, 284, 285, 308, 322, 333, 348
Brailowsky, Alexander, 79
Brée, Malwine, 217
Brico, Antonia, 265
Bridge, Frank, 308
Britten, Benjamin, 240
Brodsky, Adolph, 245
Brower, Harriette, 64, 65, 317, 321
Bruch, Max, 6, 36, 274
Bruckner, Anton, 217
Bull, John, 197
Bülow, Hans von, 31, 274
Burke, Edmund, 197
Busch, Fritz, 316
Busoni, Anna (née Weiss) (Ferruccio's mother), 73, 74, 76, 77
Busoni, Benvenuto (Ferruccio's son), 77, 79, 80
Busoni, Ferdinando (Ferruccio's father), 73, 74, 75, 76, 77
Busoni, Ferruccio, ix, xii, xiii, 14, 67, 73-83, 85, 87, 95, 131, 144, 148, 169, 173, 174, 191, 193, 194, 197, 213, 231, 232, 236, 245, 250, 302, 316
Busoni, Gerda (née Sjöstrand) (Ferruccio's wife), 77, 78, 79, 82
Busoni, Raffaello (Ferruccio's son), 77, 79
Bussine, Romain, 4
Butakov, Pyotr, 97
Byrd, William, 197

Cantacuzene, Madeleine; see Lipatti, Madeleine
Capone, Al, 295
Cardus, Neville, 251
Carpenter, John, 182, 285
Carreño, Clorinda (Teresa's mother), 23, 24, 25, 27, 29
Carreño, Emilia (Teresa's sister), 24, 25
Carreño, Manuel (Teresa's father), 23, 24, 25, 26, 27, 28, 29, 30, 31
Carreño, Teresa, 23-39, 59, 78, 87, 131, 263
Carter, President Jimmy, 338
Caruso, Enrico, 329
Casals, Pablo, 118, 119, 159, 160, 162, 165, 167, 168, 197, 220, 231, 250, 275, 310, 311
Cavaillé-Coll, Aristide, 3
Chabrier, Emmanuel, 161
Chaliapin, Feodor, 101, 102
Chaplin, Charles, 94
Chasins, Abram, 88
Cherkassky, Shura, 331
Cherubini, Luigi, 2
Chopin, Frederick, 1, 12, 14, 15, 16, 17, 18, 19, 20, 25, 29, 47, 56, 59, 63, 64, 65, 70, 78, 83, 89, 90, 92, 94, 105, 106, 118, 120, 127, 134, 157, 158, 161, 162, 163, 164, 165, 181, 194, 197, 199, 200, 201, 203, 204, 215, 234, 235, 250, 251, 254, 263, 273, 279, 284, 285, 288, 298, 312, 319, 320, 322, 331, 333, 336, 337, 338, 347, 348, 349
Churchill, Clementine, 298, 299
Churchill, Sir Winston, 195, 299
Clark, Alfred Corning, 146, 147
Clark, Sir Kenneth, 308, 309
Clemenceau, Georges, 53
Clemens, Clara; see Gabrilowitsch, Clara
Clemens, Samuel L ('Mark Twain'), 119, 174, 176, 218, 271
Clementi, Muzio, 19, 65, 333
Cliburn, Van, 140
Clive, Sir Robert, 200
Coates, Eric, 302
Cohen, Harriet, 302
Colonne, Édouard, 46, 158, 192
Constantine, Grand Duke, 126, 133, 189
Cooper, Martin, 163

Index

Cortot, Alfred, xi, 118, 157-169, 252, 299, 322, 344, 350
Cortot, Annette (Alfred's sister), 157
Cortot, Leah (Alfred's sister), 157
Cortot, Oscar (Alfred's brother), 157
Cortot, Renée-Elaine (Alfred's second wife), 165
Couperin, François, 203, 205
Courtauld, Samuel, 223
Courtauld, Mrs Samuel, 223
Cross, Gustav, 98
Cui, César, 172
Cumming, Sir Edward Gordon, 258
Curzon, Clifford, 209, 224
Czerny, Carl, 65, 288, 291

Dachs, Joseph, 11
Dahl, Nicolai, 102
Damrosch, Frank, 178
Damrosch, Leopold, 305
Damrosch, Walter, 39, 62, 121, 174, 178, 182, 222, 235, 246, 305
Davis, Ivan, 335
Debussy, Claude, 7, 64, 106, 117, 123, 134, 161, 162, 163, 165, 182, 194, 236, 285, 308, 318, 319, 320, 321, 322, 324, 334
Delasaire, William, 319, 320
Delibes, Léo, 3
Delius, Frederick, 76, 115, 190, 233, 236, 308
Demyansky, Vladimir, 98
Dent, Edward, 83
Descombes, Émile, 158
Devries, Herman, 70
Diémer, Louis, 158
Downes, Olin, 252, 318
Dreier, Per, 240
Dreyfus, Captain Alfred, 12
Drinkwater, John, 294
Dubassov, Mr, 77
Dubois, Mme Camille, 47
Dubois, François, 281
Dukas, Paul, 161, 275, 344
Dvorsky, Michel (pseudonym of Josef Hofmann), 152

Edison, Thomas, 150, 153, 233
Einstein, Albert, 297

Elgar, Sir Edward, 342
Elizabeth, HM The Queen (now the Queen Mother), 309
Elkin, Robert, 18
Ellis, Charles, 105
Elman, Mischa, 39, 172, 250
Enescu, George, 341, 344, 345, 346, 348, 351
Engol, Carl, 114
Érard, Mme, 28
Essipoff, Mme Annette, 46, 47, 173, 191, 217
Eustis, Marie; see Hofmann, Marie

Falla, Manuel de, 194, 211, 276, 308
Fauré, Gabriel, 3, 6, 161
Feinberg, Herr, 85
Ferguson, Howard, 311
Feuermann, Emanuel, 282
Fialkowska, Janina, 281
Field, John, 97
Finck, Henry T, 133, 177, 235
Fischer, Edwin, 50, 346
Flesch, Carl, 220, 341
Ford, President Gerald, 281
Ford, Henry, 123
Foss, Hubert, 306
Foster, Stephen, 234
Fournier, Pierre, 220, 254
Franchomme, Auguste, 47
Franck, César, 3, 123, 161, 163, 181
Franz Josef I, Emperor of Austria, 62
Freeman, John, 299
Friedberg, Annie, 306
Friedberg, Carl, 79, 178, 197, 304, 306
Friedheim, Arthur, 245
Friedman, Ignaz, 87, 182, 217, 218, 222
Fuchs, Carl, 244
Furtwängler, Wilhelm, 177, 220, 310

Gabrilowitsch, Artur (Ossip's brother), 171
Gabrilowitsch, Clara (née Clemens) (Ossip's wife), 174, 175, 176, 177, 178, 179, 182, 183, 185, 218
Gabrilowitsch, George (Ossip's brother), 171, 172
Gabrilowitsch, Nina (Ossip's daughter), 113, 176, 178, 183

403

Gabrilowitsch, Ossip, 113, 118, 119, 120, 131, 171-185, 191, 197, 217, 218, 222, 230
Gabrilowitsch, Polya (Ossip's sister), 171, 173, 176
Gabrilowitsch, Rosa (née Segal) (Ossip's mother), 171, 172, 173
Gabrilowitsch, Solomon (Ossip's father), 171, 172
Gaisberg, Fred, 56, 225
Galamian, Ivan, ix
Galli, Antonin, 128
Galliera, Alceo, 350
Ganz, Rudolph, 79, 182
Ganz, Wilhelm, 11, 12
Gardiner, Henry Balfour, 230, 260
Gavoty, Bernard, 282, 317, 321
Georgescu, George, 343
Gerig, R.C., ix
Germain, Karl, 261
Gershwin, Frances, 94
Gershwin, George, 94, 333
Gershwin, Ira, 94
Gibbons, Orlando, 197
Gieseking, Annie (née Haake) (Walter's wife), 317, 320, 324
Gieseking, Freya (Walter's daughter), 320, 325
Gieseking, Jutta (Walter's daughter), 320, 325
Gieseking, Martha (née Bethke) (Walter's mother), 315
Gieseking, Walter, 250, 252, 315-325
Gieseking, Wilhelm (Walter's father), 315, 320
Gigli, Benjamino, viii
Ginsburg, Mark, 131
Giroldoni, Eugenio, 127
Glazunov, Alexander, 101, 172
Godowsky, Anna (Leopold's mother), 85
Godowsky, Dagmar (Leopold's daughter), 94
Godowsky, Frieda (née Saxe) (Leopold's wife), 86, 87, 94
Godowsky, Gutram (Leopold's son), 94
Godowsky, Leopold, ix, 14, 68, 85-95, 114, 115, 120, 125, 131, 140, 148, 151, 162, 164, 169, 178, 182, 197, 296
Godowsky, Leopold jr. (Leopold's son), 94

Godowsky, Mathew (Leopold's father), 85
Godowsky, Vaneta (Leopold's daughter), 94
Goetz, Hermann, 113
Golath, Mr, 59
Goldmark, Rubin, 182
Goodson, Katharine, 217
Gorbachev, President Mikhail, 320, 338
Gorska, Helena; see Paderewska, Helena
Gorski, Wladyslaw, 115
Gottschalk, Louis Moreau, 23, 26, 27, 28, 29, 35
Gounod, Charles, 2, 3, 29
Grace, M. P., 197
Grainger, Ella (née Ström) (Percy's wife), 239, 240
Grainger, John (Percy's father), 229
Grainger, Percy, 79, 81, 182, 215, 229-241, 249, 250, 260, 306
Grainger, Rose (Percy's mother), 229, 230, 232, 235, 237, 238, 239
Granados, Enrique, 236, 308
de Grey, Lady Henrietta, 260
Grieg, Edvard, 6, 76, 106, 181, 232, 236, 237, 254
Grock (stage name of Wettach, Adrien), 18
Gunn, Anita, 307
Gutheil, Karl, 100

Haake, Annie; see Gieseking, Annie
Hadden, J. Cuthbert, 15
Hallé, Sir Charles, 30, 47
Hambourg, Boris (Mark's brother), 187, 190, 195, 196
Hambourg, Catherine (Mark's mother), 187, 191
Hambourg, Clement (Mark's brother), 187, 191
Hambourg, Dorothea, (née Muir-MacKenzie) (Mark's wife), 194, 195, 196, 198, 200
Hambourg, Galia (Mark's sister), 187, 191
Hambourg, Jan (Mark's brother), 187, 190, 192, 194, 195, 196
Hambourg, Luba, (Mark's sister), 187
Hambourg, Mark, 50, 66, 67, 79, 87, 94, 174, 187-201, 217, 218, 244
Hambourg, Michael (Mark's father), 187, 188, 189, 190, 191, 196

Index

Hambourg, Michal (Mark's daughter), 195, 199
Hambourg, Munia (Mark's sister), 187
Handel, George Frideric, 203
Hanslick, Eduard, 61, 64, 191
Hardie, Keir, 190
Hare, Miss, 307
Harrison, L. F., 26
Harrison, Percy, 190
Harty, Sir Hamilton, 231, 250, 251
Haskil, Clara, 250, 345
Hawkins, Robert, 212
Haydn, Josef, 204, 349
Héglon, Meyriane, 8
Heifetz, Jascha, 172, 182, 250, 282
Heine, Heinrich, 60
Hekking, Anton, 220
Hemmingway, Ernest, 280
Henderson, William J., 139, 145, 318
Hengel (music publisher), 29
Henselt, Adolf von, 16
Hertz, Alfred, 121
Herzberg, Alma; see Backhaus, Alma
Hess, Frederick (Myra's father), 301, 304, 305
Hess, Lizzie (née Jacobs) (Myra's mother), 301, 305
Hess, Dame Myra, 118, 120, 167, 250, 301-313
Hess, Samuel (Myra's grandfather), 301
Hindemith, Paul, 220, 316, 317, 346
Hitler, Adolf, 70, 139, 219, 225
Hobbs, Sir Jack, viii
Hobday, Charles, 254
Hockney & Liggins, builders, 257
Hofmann, Anton (Josef's son), 149
Hofmann, Betty (née Short) (Josef's second wife), 149
Hofmann, Casimir (Josef's father), 143, 144, 145, 146, 150, 151
Hofmann, Josef, 36, 62, 79, 87, 88, 105, 108, 125, 127, 130, 139, 143-155, 169, 178, 182, 190, 197, 204, 215, 250, 265, 306, 317
Hofmann, Marie (née Eustis) (Josef's first wife), 149
Hofmann, Matylda (Josef's mother), 143
Hohenus, Julius, 25
Honegger, Arthur, 346

Hoover, President Herbert, 331
Horowitz, Samuel (Vladimir's father), 327, 328
Horowitz, Sonia (Vladimir's daughter), 332, 338
Horowitz, Sophie (Vladimir's mother), 327, 328
Horowitz, Vladimir, 110, 139, 250, 278, 327-339
Horowitz, Wanda (née Toscanini) (Vladimir's wife), 332, 336
Hough, Lotta Mills, 237
Hubbard, W. L., 137
Huberman, Bronislaw, 250
Huneker, James, 16, 32, 181, 276, 277
Hurok, Sol, 279
Hutcheson, Ernest, 39, 181, 182, 249
Hutton, Sir Leonard, viii
Huxley, Aldous, 280

Indjic, Eugen, 281
d'Indy, Vincent, 161
Iturbi, José, 347

Jacobs, John (Myra Hess's maternal grandfather), 301
Jacobs, Lizzie; see Hess, Lizzie
Jaell, Alfred, 28
Janotha, Mme Nathalie, 189
Jarnach, Philipp, 80
Joachim, Joseph, ix, 30, 43, 85, 113, 192, 219, 274, 275, 285
Johnson, James P., 90
Jones, Parry, 109
Jora, Mihail, 342, 343, 346
Joseffy, Rafael, 32, 59, 60, 79
Joyce, Eileen, 249, 250
Judson, Arthur, 329
Juilliard, Augustus D., 137, 140

Kahn, Robert, 274
Kamenka, Mr, 105
Kanner, Hedwig (née Loewy); see Rosenthal, Hedwig
Kanner, Oscar, 71
Karajan, Herbert von, 350
Kelley, Edgar Stillman, 182
Kellogg, Clara Louise, 85
Kempff, Wilhelm, 168, 346

Kennedy, Daisy; see Moiseiwitsch, Daisy
Kennedy, Michael, 245, 283
Kiel, Friedrich, 43
Kipling, Rudyard, 234
Kirkpatrick, Ralph, 209
Kleczynski, Jan, 203
Klein, Howard, 254
Klemperer, Otto, 220
Klimsch, Karl, 230
Kling, Otto, 244
Knorr, Iwan, 230
Kogel, Gustav, 34
Konievsky, Sasha, 287, 290, 291
Korngold, Erich, 222
Korsak, Antonina; see Paderewska, Antonina
Koussevitzky, Serge, 103, 274
Kreisler, Fritz, 62, 118, 122, 123, 178, 197, 231
Kretzschmar, Hermann, 207
Kreuz, Emil, 114
Krysander, Nils, 125
Kwast, James, 230

Labori, Fernand, 12
Lafontaine, Senator, 190
Lalo, Édouard, 3
Lambert, Alexander, 182
Lamond, Frederic, 114, 230
Lamoureux, Charles, 46, 118, 128, 129, 158, 159, 275
Landowska, Wanda, 163, 203-213
Lauder, Sir Harry, 231
Legge, Walter, 350
Leginska, Ethel (née Liggins), 230, 257-271, 277, 290
Leimer, Karl, 316
Lenin, Vladimir, 104, 190
Leopold, Ralph, 237
Leschetizky, Theodor, x, 44, 45, 46, 47, 62, 65, 126, 173, 174, 191, 192, 193, 196, 216, 217, 218, 224, 230, 260, 261, 266, 270, 290, 291, 301, 302, 316, 324
Levant, Oscar, 335
Levitzky, Mischa, 296
Lew, Henri (Wanda Landowska's husband), 204, 205, 207, 208
Lhevinne, Arkady (Josef's father), 125, 129

Lhevinne, Constantine (Josef's son), 133, 141
Lhevinne, Fanny (Josef's mother), 125
Lhevinne, Josef, 125-141, 148, 177, 182, 207, 222
Lhevinne, Marianna (Josef's daughter), 131, 136, 139
Lhevinne, Myron (Josef's brother), 125
Lhevinne, Rosina (née Bessie) (Josef's wife), 125, 128-141, 177, 207
Lhevinne, Theodore (Josef's brother), 125
Liberace, Walter (Valentino, Wladzin), 15
Liggins, Anne (née Peck) (Ethel Leginska's mother), 257, 261
Liggins, Ethel; see Leginska, Ethel
Liggins, Thomas Edward (Ethel Leginska's father), 257, 259, 268
Liggins, Thomas (Ethel Leginska's grandfather), 257
Lill, John, 41
Lincoln, President Abraham, 27, 39, 102
Lipatti, Ann (née Racoviceanu) (Dinu's mother), 341, 342
Lipatti, Constantin (Dinu's grandfather), 341
Lipatti, Dinu, 341-351
Lipatti, Madeleine (née Cantacuzene) (Dinu's wife), 346, 348, 351
Lipatti, Sofia (Dinu's aunt), 341
Lipatti, Theodor (Dinu's father), 341, 342
Liszt, Franz, x, 1, 2, 3, 4, 14, 16, 28, 47, 48, 59, 60, 61, 65, 66, 67, 71, 73, 75, 78, 79, 81, 83, 89, 98, 105, 106, 114, 127, 134, 148, 149, 151, 166, 181, 191, 194, 199, 200, 213, 215, 224, 234, 243, 245, 251, 254, 264, 274, 278, 298, 310, 329, 332, 333, 348
Litvinne, Mme Félia, 159
Loewy, Hedwig; see Rosenthal, Hedwig
Lucca, Pauline, 46
Lyon, Gustave, 206

MacDonald, James Ramsey, 190
MacDowell, Edward, 32, 35, 183
Macpherson, Sandy, 308
Mahler, Gustav, 76, 104
Malipiero, Francesco, 194
Malko, Nicolai, 109
Mandyczewski, Eusebius, 217

Index

Mapleston, Colonel, 30
Martin, Annie Jane; see Russell Starr, Mrs
Marx, Harpo, 297
Mason, Daniel G., 182-183
Massenet, Jules, 3, 5, 6
Matthay, Tobias, 302, 303, 311
Matthias, Georges, 29
Maximov, Leonid, 127
Mayer, Daniel, 47, 115, 117, 189, 192
Meggett, Joan, 269
Meir, Golda, 281
Melba, Dame Nellie, viii, 230, 291, 292
Mendelssohn, Felix, 1, 16, 25, 29, 99, 106, 113, 181, 190, 251, 285
Mengelberg, Willem, 346
Menter, Sophie, 191
Mero, Yolanda, 182
Messager, André, 3
Michalowski, Alexander, 203
Michelangeli, Arturo, 281
Mikuli, Karol, 59
Milhaud, Darius, 285
Mlynarska, Aniela; see Rubinstein, Aniela
Mlynarski, Emil, 274, 277
Modrzejewska, Helena, 44
Moiseiwitsch, Anita (Benno's second wife), 297, 298
Moiseiwitsch, Benno, 287-299, 301
Moiseiwitsch, Boris (Benno's brother), 287, 289
Moiseiwitsch, Boris (Benno's son), 297
Moiseiwitsch, Daisy (née Kennedy) (Benno's first wife), 293, 294
Moiseiwitsch, David (Benno's father), 287, 289, 292
Moiseiwitsch, Esther (Benno's mother), 287, 288, 289, 292
Moiseiwitsch, John (Benno's brother), 287, 288, 290, 291
Moiseiwitsch, Maurice (Benno's nephew and biographer), 294, 298
Moiseiwitsch, Sandra (Benno's daughter), 294
Moiseiwitsch, Sonia (Benno's sister), 287, 290
Moiseiwitsch, Tanya (Benno's daughter), 294

Moiseiwitsch, Vladimir (Benno's brother), 287, 292
Monteux, Pierre, 264
Moore, Graham, 115
Morgan, Orlando, 302
Morris, Paul, 263
Morse, Richard A., 237
Morton, Rachel, 271
Moscheles, Felix, 190, 191, 200
Moscheles, Ignaz, 65, 190, 200
Moszkowski, Moritz, 44, 146 - 147, 182, 221, 333
Mottl, Felix, 158, 177
Mozart, Wolfgang Amadeus, 2, 5, 45, 46, 75, 78, 105, 106, 127, 144, 204, 215, 219, 226, 250, 254, 260, 262, 270, 284, 288, 308, 321, 322, 324, 333, 338, 349
Muck, Carl, 180
Muir-Mackenzie, Dorothea; see Hambourg, Dorothea
Muir-Mackenzie, Sir Kenneth, 194, 195
Münch, Charles, 344
Munz, Mieczyslaw, 277
Musicescu, Florica, 343, 346
Musin, Ovide, 86

Neeley, Marilyn, 269-270
Newman, Ernest, 100, 166
Newman, Robert, 49
Ney, Elly, 222
Nicholas I, Tsar, 126
Nicholas II, Tsar, 104
Niemann, Walter, 319
Nikisch, Arthur, 77, 132, 173, 176, 219
Nikita, Louise (Nicholson, Louise), 116
Nossig, Alfred, 51

Oakey, Marguerite; see de Pachmann, Marguerite
Oliver, Lucille, 269
O'Neill, Norman, 230
Ornatskaya, Anna, 97
Ornstein, Leo, 296

Pabst, Louis, 229, 230
Pachmann, Marguerite de (née Oakey) (Vladimir's first wife), 12
Pachmann, Vladimir de, x, xii, xiii, 11-21, 49, 64, 87, 90, 148, 287, 318, 321

Paderewska, Antonina (Ignace's sister), 41, 42
Paderewska, Antonina (née Korsak) (Ignace's first wife), 42, 51
Paderewska, Helena (née Gorska) (Ignace's second wife), 51, 53, 55
Paderewski, Alfred (Ignace's son), 42, 43, 51, 55, 115
Paderewski, Ignace, x, xi, xii, xiii, 14, 39, 41-57, 59, 85, 87, 88, 95, 100, 107, 114, 115, 116, 118, 120, 131, 133, 148, 149, 150, 153, 164, 169, 189, 190, 191, 192, 200, 204, 219, 234, 260, 261, 263, 264, 274, 275, 279, 306, 318, 331
Paderewski, Jan (Ignace's father), 41
Paganini, Nicolò, 102
Pallavicini, Prince, 191
Papritz, Mme Eugénie, 189
Papst, Eugen, 328, 329
Pascal, Julian, 302
Paschill, Joseph, 342, 349
Patti, Adelina, 29, 30
Peck, Anne; see Liggins, Anne
Peck, Gregory, 282
Perabo, Ernst, 146
Petri, Egon, 79, 245
Pfitzner, Hans, 316
Piatigorsky, Gregor, 280, 282
Piatti, Alfredo, 192
Picasso, Pablo, 280
Pierce, Lucy, 255
Planté, François, 28
Poe, Edgar Allan, 104
Politzer, Adolf, 114
Ponce, Manuel, 285
Portman, Eric, 56
Poulenc, Francis, 211, 285
Powell, John, 182
Powell, Lionel, 198
Prechner, Adolph, 273
Prokofiev, Serge, 111, 162, 182, 285, 294, 333
Prout, Ebenezer, 302
Puchalsky, Vladimir, 327
Purcell, Henry, 197
Pushkin, Alexander, 100

Quilter, Roger, 230, 260

Rachmaninov, Alexander (Sergei's grandson), 109
Rachmaninov, Arkady (Sergei's grandfather), 97
Rachmaninov, Arkady (Sergei's brother), 97
Rachmaninov, Elena (Sergei's sister), 97, 98
Rachmaninov, Irina (Sergei's daughter), 103, 104, 107
Rachmaninov, Lyubov (Sergei's mother), 97, 98
Rachmaninov, Natalia (née Satina) (Sergei's wife), 102, 109, 135
Rachmaninov, Sergei, x, xii, 95, 97-111, 126, 127, 135, 139, 149, 179, 181, 182, 234, 250, 293, 294, 298, 332, 333, 334, 338
Rachmaninov, Sofia (Sergei's sister), 97, 98
Rachmaninov, Sofia (Sergei's granddaughter), 107
Rachmaninov, Tatiana (Sergei's daughter), 103, 104, 107, 109
Rachmaninov, Varvara (Sergei's sister), 97
Rachmaninov, Vasily (Sergei's father), 97, 98, 100, 104
Rachmaninov, Vladimir (Sergei's brother), 97, 98
Racoviceanu, Ann; see Lipatti, Ann
Raff, Joachim, 113
Rameau, Jean Philippe, 203, 205, 298
Ravel, Maurice, 7, 123, 161, 165, 182, 236, 275, 308, 320, 322, 324, 348
Reagan, President Ronald, 338
Reckendorf, Alois, 243
Reger, Max, 182
Remesov, S. M., 129
Restout, Denise, 211, 212
Rheinberger, Josef, 113
Richter, Hans, 30, 63, 76, 158, 174, 191, 220, 232, 244
Rimsky-Korsakov, Nikolay, 172
Risler, Édouard, 158, 245
Robinson, William Heath, 240
Rodin, Auguste, 205
Roosevelt, President Franklin D., 56
Roosevelt, President Theodore, 193

Index

Rosbaud, Hans, 323
Rosen, Baroness de; see Paderewska, Helena
Rosenthal, Auguste (Moriz's mother), 59
Rosenthal, Hedwig (née Loewy) (Moriz's wife), 65, 70, 71
Rosenthal, Moriz, 14, 49, 59-71, 87, 131, 133, 250
Rossini, Gioacchino, 3, 28, 29, 79
Rostra, Elizabeth (Professional name of Artur Schnabel's daughter Elisabeth; known to the Schnabel family as Ellie), 221
Rozycki, Alexander, 273
Rubets, Alexander, 98
Rubinstein, Alina (Artur's daughter), 278
Rubinstein, Aniela (née Mlynarska) (Artur's wife), 274, 277, 278, 282, 285
Rubinstein, Anton, 3, 4, 29, 30, 32, 34, 35, 44, 48, 63, 66, 67, 74, 76, 77, 99, 100, 113, 114, 126, 127, 128, 131, 133, 134, 143, 144, 147, 148, 150, 172, 181, 187, 194, 196, 200, 229, 245, 254, 273, 289, 327
Rubinstein, Artur, ix, 19, 94, 140, 150, 151, 154, 164, 173, 243, 250, 273-285, 296
Rubinstein, Eva (Artur's daughter), 278
Rubinstein, John (Artur's son), 278
Rubinstein, Nicholas (Anton's brother), 187
Rubinstein, Paul (Artur's son), 278
Rutherford, Sir Ernest, viii

Sachs, Harvey, 207
Sackville-West, Edward, 251, 323
Safonoff, Vassily, 77, 126, 127, 128, 129
Safranov, Mr, 289
Saint-Saëns, André (Camille's son), 4, 5
Saint-Saëns, Camille, 1-9, 28, 47, 50, 65, 86, 144, 161, 181, 275
Saint-Saëns, Jean (Camille's son), 4, 5
Saint-Saëns, Marie (née Truffot) (Camille's wife), 4, 5
Samaroff, Olga, 177, 178
Saperton, David, 94
Sarasate, Pablo de, 43, 114, 341
Sargent, Sir Malcolm, 199, 223
Satina, Natalia; see Rachmaninov, Natalia

Sauer, Emil, 48, 140
Sauret, Émile, 30, 31, 32
Sauret, Émilita (Teresa Carreño's daughter), 31, 37
Sawyer, Antonia, 235, 238
Saxe, Frieda; see Godowsky, Frieda
Scarlatti, Dominico, 16, 19, 203, 205, 206, 209, 299, 311, 321, 322, 333, 334, 338, 348, 350
Scharrer, Irene, 302
Scharwenka, Xaver, 64, 65
Schelling, Ernest, 51, 178, 182, 307
Schmidt, Hans, 216
Schnabel, Artur, 66, 131, 137, 191, 215-227, 250, 261, 321, 328, 330, 339, 346
Schnabel, Clara (Artur's sister), 215
Schnabel, Ernestine (Artur's mother), 215, 217, 227
Schnabel, Frieda (Artur's sister), 215
Schnabel, Isidor (Artur's father), 215, 217
Schnabel, Karl Ulrich (Artur's son), 220, 221, 225, 226
Schnabel, Stefan (Artur's son), 220, 221, 226
Schnabel, Therese (née Behr) (Artur's wife; appeared professionally as Therese Behr-Schnabel), 220, 221, 225, 226, 227
Schnitzer, Germaine, 182
Schoenberg, Arnold, 1, 162, 182, 316, 317
Schonberg, Clara; see Backhaus, Clara
Schonberg, Harold C., 254, 284, 329
Schostakowsky, Mr, 188
Schubert, Franz, 1, 64, 105, 106, 120, 184, 197, 215, 219, 220, 251, 263, 265, 285, 348, 350
Schumann, Clara, 30, 34, 39, 114, 141, 189
Schumann, Robert, 1, 15, 29, 78, 118, 120, 123, 127, 134, 141, 157, 162, 163, 165, 166, 181, 194, 197, 199, 215, 219, 235, 236, 251, 254, 265, 285, 289, 298, 308, 322, 331, 333, 338, 342
Schytte, Ludvig, 68
Scott, Cyril, 230, 236, 237
Scriabin, Alexander, 64, 126, 127, 308, 333
Segal, Rosa; see Gabrilowitsch, Rosa
Seghers, François, 2, 4

Serkin, Peter, 335
Serkin, Rudolph, 168, 335
Shaftsbury, Earl of, 260
Shattuck, Arthur, 66
Shaw, George Bernard, 13, 88, 114, 190
Shawe-Taylor, Desmond, 251, 323
Short, Betty; see Hofmann, Betty
Shostakovich, Dmitri, 111, 294
Sibelius, Jean, 77
Sidonius, Sanctus, 1
Siloti, Alexander, 98, 99, 100, 243, 244, 250
Sjöstrand, Gerda; see Busoni, Gerda
Sousa, John Philip, 334, 339
Sowinski, Peter, 41
Spohr, Louis, 113
Stanford, Sir Charles Villiers, 232
Starr, Mrs Russell, 258, 259
Stavenhagen, Bernhard, 66
Steinbach, Fritz, 246
Steinway, Charles, 39
Stepniak, Sergei, 190
Stern, Isaac, 280
Stockhausen, Karlheinz, 1, 240
Stoessel, Albert, 265
Stojowski, Sigismond, 182
Stokowski, Leopold, 120, 121, 177, 178, 184, 208, 237, 333
Strauss, Johann II, 68, 69, 70, 151
Strauss, Richard, 43, 244, 323
Stravinsky, Igor, 1, 111, 182, 285, 294, 317, 337, 344
Ström, Ella; see Grainger, Ella
Sullivan, Sir Arthur, 30, 302
Suskind, Milton, 106
Szeryng, Henryk, 282
Szymanowski, Karol, 285, 316

Tagliapietra, Arturo (Teresa Carreño's fourth husband), 36, 37, 38
Tagliapietra, Giovanni (Teresa Carreño's second husband), 32, 33, 36
Tagliapietri, Giovanni (Teresa Carreño's son), 32, 37
Tagliapietra, Lulu (Teresa Carreño's daughter), 32
Tagliapietra, Teresita (Teresa Carreño's daughter), 32, 37, 38
Taneyev, Sergius, 126

Tansman, Alexander, 285
Tanyel, Seta, 281
Tarnowsky, Sergei, 327
Tausig, Carl, 59, 60, 61, 213, 274
Taylor, Joseph, 233
Tchaikovsky, Peter, 4, 6, 46, 99, 101, 102, 105, 106, 134, 181, 270, 293, 298, 333, 334
Tempest, Marie, 56
Terry, Ellen, 190
Teyte, Maggie, 165, 197, 231
Thackeray, William M., 268
Thalberg, Sigismond, 23, 27
Theodorwitsch, Olga, 172
Thibaud, Jacques, 118, 159, 160, 165, 250, 275
Thomas, Ambroise, 29
Thomson, Virgil, 333
Thursby, Emma, 86
Tietjens, Thérèse, 30
Tolstoff, Professor, 172, 173
Tolstoy, Leo, 102, 205
Toro, Clorinda Garcia Sena y; see Carreño, Clorinda
Tortelier, Paul, 280
Toscanini, Arturo, 332
Toscanini, Wanda; see Horowitz, Wanda
Treutner, Herr, 178
Truffot, Marie; see Saint-Saëns, Marie
Tua, Maria (known as Teresina), 101
Tubb, Carrie, 198
Twain, Mark; see Clemens, Samuel L
Twitchell, Joseph, 176

Urban, Heinrich, 44, 204

Valentino, Rudolph, 94, 297
Vaughan Williams, Ralph, 110
Verdi, Giuseppe, 78
Vert, Nathaniel, 190
Victoria, HM The Queen, 6, 47, 243, 287, 312
Villa-Lobos, Heitor, 276, 285
Vivier, Eugène, 28
Vogrich, Max, 35
Volkonsky, Prince Pyotr, 107

Wagner, Richard, 3, 7, 158, 159, 162, 167, 178

Index

Walem, Herbert, 114
Wales, HRH The Prince of (later King Edward VII), 258
Wales, HRH The Prince of (Prince Charles), 338
Waller, Thomas 'Fats', 90
Walter, Bruno, 177, 178, 323
Walter, Elsa, 177
Warrender, Lady Maud, 260
Weber, Carl Maria von, 11, 181
Weingartner, Felix, 191
Weiss, Anna; see Busoni, Anna
Weiss, Josef, 87
Whitestone, Annabelle, 285
Whithorne, Cedric Villiers (Ethel Leginska's son), 262
Whithorne, Roy Emerson (Ethel Leginska's husband), 261, 262, 263
Whittern, Roy Emerson; later name taken by Whithorne, Roy Emerson
Wilde, Oscar, 190
Wilhelm II of Germany, Kaiser, 63, 221
Willaume, Gabriel, 8
Williams, Harold, 109

Wilson, Arthur, 258
Wilson, Mary Emma, 258
Wilson, President Woodrow, 39
Wittenberg, Alfred, 220
Wolf, Hugo, 217
Wolff, Hermann, 33, 34, 127, 132, 143, 147, 173, 192, 218, 219
Wolff, Louisa, 132
Wood, H. J. (Sir Henry Wood's father), 50
Wood, Sir Henry J., 7, 9, 36, 39, 49, 50, 63, 67, 68, 81, 104, 109, 110, 193, 201, 232, 243, 244, 261, 269, 277, 303, 323
Wright, A. M., 174

Ysaÿe, Eugène, 118, 193, 194, 250, 276

Zadora, Michael, 82
Zeisler, Fannie Bloomfield, 62, 182
Zeisler, Sigmund, 62
Zimbalist, Efrem, 121, 172, 182
Zverev, Anna, 99
Zverev, Nikolai, 98, 99, 100

Great Pianists of the Golden Age

List of the Pianists in this Book and their Lifespans

Pianist	Lifespan
Camille Saint-Saëns	1835-1921
Vladimir de Pachmann	1848-1933
Teresa Carreño	1853-1917
Ignace Paderewski	1860-1941
Moriz Rosenthal	1862-1946
Ferruccio Busoni	1866-1924
Leopold Godowsky	1870-1938
Sergei Rachmaninov	1873-1943
Harold Bauer	1873-1951
Josef Lhevinne	1874-1944
Josef Hofmann	1876-1957
Alfred Cortot	1877-1962
Ossip Gabrilowitsch	1878-1936
Mark Hambourg	1879-1960
Wanda Landowska	1879-1959
Artur Schnabel	1882-1951
Percy Grainger	1882-1961
Wilhelm Backhaus	1884-1969
Ethel Leginska	1886-1970
Artur Rubinstein	1887-1982
Benno Moiseiwitsch	1890-1963
Myra Hess	1890-1965
Walter Gieseking	1895-1956
Vladimir Horowitz	1904-1989
Dinu Lipatti	1917-1950

1840　1860　1880　1900　1920　1940　1960　1980